Scott Foresman - Addison Wesley
MIDDLE SCHOOL MATH
Course 3

Randall I. Charles   John A. Dossey   Steven J. Leinwand
Cathy L. Seeley   Charles B. Vonder Embse

L. Carey Bolster • Janet H. Caldwell • Dwight A. Cooley • Warren D. Crown
Linda Proudfit • Alma B. Ramírez • Jeanne F. Ramos • Freddie Lee Renfro
David Robitaille • Jane Swafford

Scott Foresman
Addison Wesley

Editorial Offices: Menlo Park, California • Glenview, Illinois
Sales Offices: Reading, Massachusetts • Atlanta, Georgia • Glenview, Illinois
Carrollton, Texas • Menlo Park, California

http://www.sf.aw.com

Cover artist: Robert Silvers, 28, started taking photographs and playing with computers at the same time, about 19 years ago. He always thought of computer programming as a way to express himself much as he does with photography. Silvers has melded his interests to produce the image on this cover.

Printed in the United States of America

ISBN 0-201-36415-8

3 4 5 6 7 8 9 10 – VH – 02 01 00 99

FROM THE AUTHORS

Dear Student,

     We have designed a unique mathematics program that answers the question students your age have been asking for years about their math lessons: "When am I ever going to use this?"

     In *Scott Foresman - Addison Wesley Middle School Math,* you'll learn about math in your own world and develop problem-solving techniques that will work for you in everyday life. The chapters have two or three sections, each with a useful math topic and an interesting theme. For example, you'll relate ratios to special effects, linear equations to pets, and rational numbers to water.

     Each section begins with an opportunity to explore new topics and make your own conjectures. Lessons are presented clearly with examples and chances to try the math yourself. Then, real kids like you and your friends say what they think about each concept and show how they understand it. And every section contains links to the World Wide Web, making your math book a dynamic link to an ever-expanding universe of knowledge.

     You will soon realize how mathematics is not only useful, but also connected to you and your life as you continue to experience the real world. We trust that each of you will gain the knowledge necessary to be successful and to be everything you want to be.

Randall I. Charles   *John A. Dossey*   *Steven J. Leinwand*

Cathy L. Seeley   *Charles B. Vonder Embse*

L. Carey Bolster   *Janet H. Caldwell*   *Dwight A. Cooley*   *Warren D. Crown*   *Linda Proudfit*

Alma B. Ramírez   *Jeanne F. Ramos*   *Freddie Lee Renfro*   *David Robitaille*   *Jane Swafford*

Authors

L. Carey Bolster
Public Broadcasting System
Alexandria, Virginia

Randall I. Charles
San Jose State University
San Jose, California

Warren D. Crown
Rutgers, the State University of New Jersey
New Brunswick, New Jersey

Steven J. Leinwand
Connecticut Department of Education
Hartford, Connecticut

Alma B. Ramírez
Oakland Charter Academy
Oakland, California

Freddie Lee Renfro
Fort Bend Independent School District
Sugarland, Texas

Cathy L. Seeley
Texas SSI in Math and Science
Austin, Texas

Charles B. Vonder Embse
Central Michigan University
Mount Pleasant, Michigan

Janet H. Caldwell
Rowan College of New Jersey
Glassboro, New Jersey

Dwight A. Cooley
M. L. Phillips Elementary School
Fort Worth, Texas

John A. Dossey
Illinois State University
Normal, Illinois

Linda Proudfit
Governors State University
University Park, Illinois

Jeanne F. Ramos
Nobel Middle School
Los Angeles, California

David Robitaille
University of British Columbia
Vancouver, British Columbia, Canada

Jane Swafford
Illinois State University
Normal, Illinois

Problem Solving in Chapter 1

Use real-world data to solve problems involving money and surveys.

TECHNOLOGY

- Spreadsheet
- Calculator
- World Wide Web
- Interactive CD-ROM

Algebra

Make and use scatterplots to look for trends by plotting the data points.

CHAPTER

| 1 | 2 | 3 | 4 | 5 | 6 | 7 | 8 | 9 | 10 | 11 | 12 |

DATA ANALYSIS...2

SECTION 1A
Data Presentations

SECTION 1B
Using Data to Answer Questions

Problem Solving in Chapter 2

Use positive and negative numbers to solve problems about currency and our changing earth.

TECHNOLOGY

• Scientific Calculator
• Spreadsheet
• World Wide Web
• Interactive CD-ROM

Algebra

Solve equations with positive and negative numbers using your knowledge of operations.

CHAPTER

| 1 | **2** | 3 | 4 | 5 | 6 | 7 | 8 | 9 | 10 | 11 | 12 |

INTEGERS...58

SECTION 2A

Operations Using Integers

SECTION 2B

Extending Integers

Problem Solving
in Chapter 3

TECHNOLOGY

x **Algebra**

Use formulas and algebra to solve problems about flight, energy, and electricity.

• Graphing Utility
• Spreadsheet
• World Wide Web
• Interactive CD-ROM

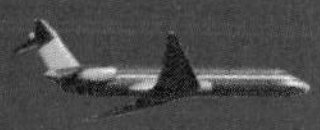

Learn methods for solving algebraic expressions and equations involving variables.

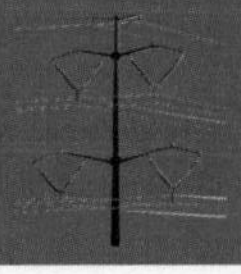

CHAPTER

| 1 | 2 | **3** | 4 | 5 | 6 | 7 | 8 | 9 | 10 | 11 | 12 |

THE LANGUAGE OF ALGEBRA: VARIABLES, EXPRESSIONS, AND EQUATIONS...118

Problem Solving in Chapter 4

Use algebra to solve problems about pets and outdoor recreation.

TECHNOLOGY

- Graphing Utility
- Spreadsheet
- World Wide Web
- Interactive CD-ROM

x Algebra

Solve and graph two-variable equations and inequalities.

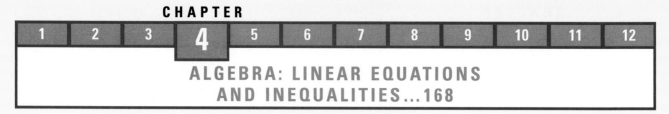

CHAPTER

| 1 | 2 | 3 | **4** | 5 | 6 | 7 | 8 | 9 | 10 | 11 | 12 |

ALGEBRA: LINEAR EQUATIONS AND INEQUALITIES...168

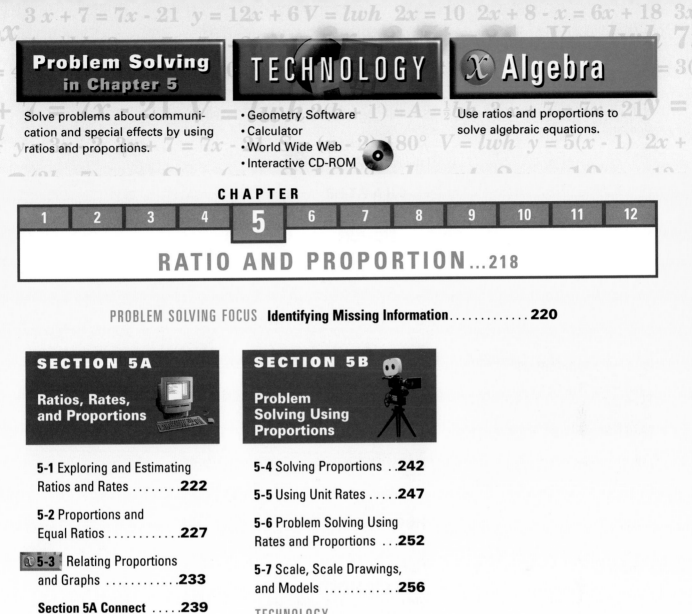

Problem Solving in Chapter 5

Solve problems about communication and special effects by using ratios and proportions.

TECHNOLOGY
- Geometry Software
- Calculator
- World Wide Web
- Interactive CD-ROM

𝓍 Algebra

Use ratios and proportions to solve algebraic equations.

CHAPTER

| 1 | 2 | 3 | 4 | **5** | 6 | 7 | 8 | 9 | 10 | 11 | 12 |

RATIO AND PROPORTION...218

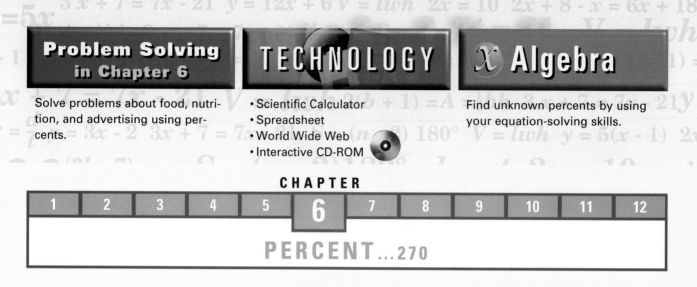

Problem Solving in Chapter 6

Solve problems about food, nutrition, and advertising using percents.

TECHNOLOGY

- Scientific Calculator
- Spreadsheet
- World Wide Web
- Interactive CD-ROM

𝑥 Algebra

Find unknown percents by using your equation-solving skills.

CHAPTER

| 1 | 2 | 3 | 4 | 5 | **6** | 7 | 8 | 9 | 10 | 11 | 12 |

PERCENT...270

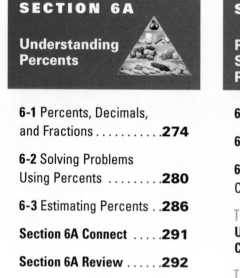

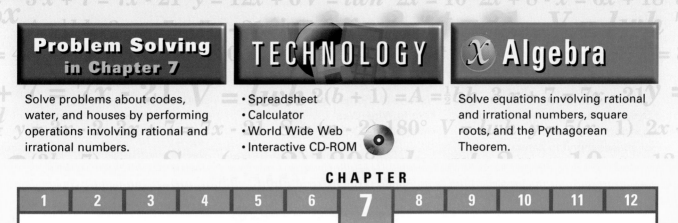

Problem Solving
in Chapter 7

Solve problems about codes, water, and houses by performing operations involving rational and irrational numbers.

TECHNOLOGY

- Spreadsheet
- Calculator
- World Wide Web
- Interactive CD-ROM

𝑥 Algebra

Solve equations involving rational and irrational numbers, square roots, and the Pythagorean Theorem.

CHAPTER

| 1 | 2 | 3 | 4 | 5 | 6 | **7** | 8 | 9 | 10 | 11 | 12 |

NUMBER SENSE, RATIONAL NUMBERS, AND IRRATIONAL NUMBERS...320

Problem Solving in Chapter 8

Learn how the Global Positioning System uses measurement and position. Investigate the geometry of shapes found in nature.

TECHNOLOGY

• Geometry Software
• World Wide Web
• Interactive CD-ROM

ⓧ Algebra

Use formulas to find areas and perimeters of geometric shapes.

CHAPTER

| 1 | 2 | 3 | 4 | 5 | 6 | 7 | **8** | 9 | 10 | 11 | 12 |

GEOMETRY AND MEASUREMENT...386

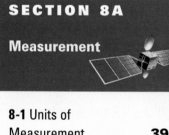

Problem Solving in Chapter 9

Solve problems about perimeter, area, and volume in the theater and package delivery.

TECHNOLOGY
• Geometry Software
• Spreadsheet
• World Wide Web
• Interactive CD-ROM

𝒳 Algebra

Find the area and volume of three-dimensional shapes by using geometric formulas.

CHAPTER

| 1 | 2 | 3 | 4 | 5 | 6 | 7 | 8 | **9** | 10 | 11 | 12 |

AREA AND VOLUME...440

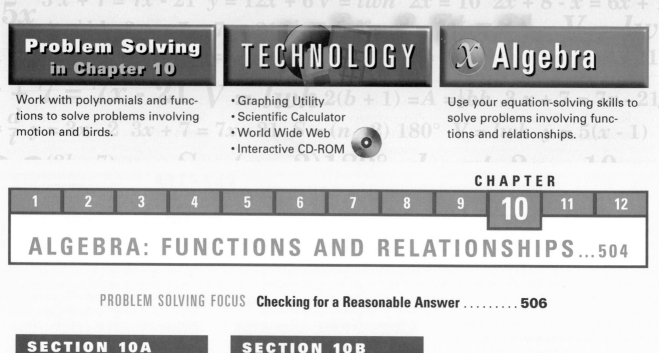

Problem Solving in Chapter 10

Work with polynomials and functions to solve problems involving motion and birds.

TECHNOLOGY

- Graphing Utility
- Scientific Calculator
- World Wide Web
- Interactive CD-ROM

x Algebra

Use your equation-solving skills to solve problems involving functions and relationships.

CHAPTER

| 1 | 2 | 3 | 4 | 5 | 6 | 7 | 8 | 9 | **10** | 11 | 12 |

ALGEBRA: FUNCTIONS AND RELATIONSHIPS...504

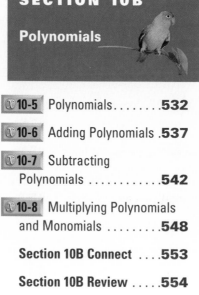

Problem Solving in Chapter 11

Identify similar and congruent figures in bridges and investigate the use of transformations in Native American arts and crafts.

TECHNOLOGY

- Geometry Software
- World Wide Web
- Interactive CD-ROM

x Algebra

Solve for unknown values to determine if figures are similar or congruent.

CHAPTER

| 1 | 2 | 3 | 4 | 5 | 6 | 7 | 8 | 9 | 10 | **11** | 12 |

SIMILARITY, CONGRUENCE, AND TRANSFORMATIONS...560

SECTION 11A

Similarity and Congruence

SECTION 11B

Transformations

Problem Solving in Chapter 12

The Olympics and birthdays provide situations where counting and probability are used.

TECHNOLOGY

- Graphing Utility
- Scientific Calculator
- World Wide Web
- Interactive CD-ROM

ⓧ Algebra

Solve algebraic equations to determine probability.

| 1 | 2 | 3 | 4 | 5 | 6 | 7 | 8 | 9 | 10 | 11 | **CHAPTER 12** |

COUNTING AND PROBABILITY...622

Internet Connections

The world of math is connected to the world around you in so many interesting ways. We'd like to invite you to explore these connections on the World Wide Web.

To begin your journey, you will need a web browser. Use your browser to visit the home page for *Mathsurf* by typing in *http://www.mathsurf.com.*

You'll find more web addresses at the top of each chapter opener and section opener that send you directly to pages that relate to your chapter or section.

SEARCH

Cultural Link
www.mathsurf.com/8/ch7/p

Social Studies Link
www.mathsurf.com/8/ch7/social

www.mathsurf.com/8/ch7/water

umber Sens

People of the

Babatunde Olatunji, a mas
drummer originally from Niger
refers to repeating decimals
when describing recurring
patterns in drum rhythms.

...c., Pythagoras
...ed that musical tones
...t combine to give pleasing
...harmonies have small arithmetic
...ratios to one
...another, such as
...1:1, 2:1, 3:2,
...and 4:3.

Arts & Literature

Within the beauty of poetry,
stanzas of poems often fit a
framework of numbers of
syllables and lines. The
Japanese Haiku consists of
17 syllables in a 5 - 7 - 5 pattern.
Kono michi ya
Yuku hito nashi ni
Aki no kure

320

and Irrational Numbers

Social Studies

In 1917, the British Secret
Service deciphered a
nume...
the Ge...
minis...
Zimm...
his m...
It con...
if the...
war, t...
Germ...
New ...
now ...
the Zi...

SECTION **Rational Numbers**
7B ▶ Geography Link ▶ Consum...

"Water, water
everywhere,
and all the boards
did shrink.
Water, water
everywhere,
nor any drop
to drink."
—Samuel Taylor Coleridge,
The Rime of the Ancient Mariner
(1772–1834)

When the poet wrote these lines,
he was talking about sailors
adrift in a sea of salt water.

Although about ⅔ of Earth's surface is
water, only about 3% of all Earth's water is
fresh water. Approximately ⅔ of all Earth's
fresh water is locked in glacial ice. Of the
remaining fresh water, only about 5% is
available as surface water in streams and
lakes. Most fresh water is underground.

As the human population increases,
more fresh water is needed to grow food
and for people to drink. Like the sailors in
Coleridge's poem, we may be surrounded
by water but lacking in fresh water to drink.

Will There Drop To Drink?

What is meant by "surface water"?

What do you think most of the
surface fresh water is used for?

Do you think there was more
freshwater in the poet Coleridge's
lifetime? Explain.

343

Problem Solving and Applications

Math is all around you. Having good math skills can help you solve problems every day. What types of problems can you solve using mathematics?

Problem Solving
Understand
Plan
Solve
Look Back

Problem Solving STRATEGIES

Problem Solving TIP

WHAT DO YOU THINK?

Food & Nutirition

Cheese Pizza Composition

- 1%
- 13% 8%
- 32%
- 46%

Water
Carbohydrates
Protein
Fat
Minerals

page 275

How do you read a graph to find the percent of a cheese pizza that is not water?

Bridges

876 ft
30

page 583

How does the total length of a bridge depend upon its height?

Theater

6 ft
9 ft

page 451

How do the area and perimeter of a stage compare to its scale model?

Outdoor Recreation

2 ft.
10 ft.

page 193

How do you use vertical and horizontal distances to find slope?

Motion

=1
1
–3
1

Height (ft)

Time (sec)   page 519

How does a graph represent an event like the path of a basketball?

Nature

page 425

How can you describe the shapes and patterns that appear in nature?

Math is also connected to the other subjects you are studying.
Look on these pages to find examples of how math is connected to:

Science				History				Geography			
p. 44	p. 92	p. 152	p. 174	p. 71	p. 125	p. 144	p. 255	p. 9	p. 13	p. 15	p. 30
p. 253	p. 257	p. 276	p. 284	p. 282	p. 292	p. 303	p. 304	p. 65	p. 93	p. 99	p. 102
p. 328	p. 351	p. 391	p. 397	p. 329	p. 346	p. 349	p. 370	p. 112	p. 153	p. 158	p. 260
p. 412	p. 417	p. 422	p. 483	p. 372	p. 378	p. 395	p. 405	p. 289	p. 333	p. 353	p. 359
p. 520	p. 524	p. 586	p. 607	p. 415	p. 431	p. 458	p. 478	p. 372	p. 375	p. 394	p. 401

PROBLEM SOLVING HAND BOOK

Problems, problems, problems. We run into them every day. We can solve some problems easily and quickly, but there will always be problems that require more effort. If you have ever asked the question, "What do you think?" you'd know that everyone has his or her own way of solving problems.

If you are looking for a job and you're a creative problem solver, then you've got it made—you can think through problems logically, work with others cooperatively, and communicate your thoughts effectively.

Right now your teacher and textbook will guide you to becoming a creative problem solver. In this course you'll explore challenging problems independently and in groups. You'll use problem solving tools such as calculators, computers, even pencil and paper.

The students shown here will be sharing their thoughts with you throughout this textbook. But the key question will always be,

"What do you think?"

1. What do you think creative problem solving is?
2. Give examples of problems that people have to solve every day.

Solving Problems

▶ **Lesson Link**   You've solved many problems in your previous math classes. Now you'll look more closely at well-known methods you can use to solve problems. ◀

Problem Solving

You solve problems every day. A problem such as "how much change should you receive?" is straightforward. Often you can use mathematics to find quick solutions. For example, you can add, subtract, multiply, or divide to find a quick numerical answer.

Problems that involve more thought may have many possible solutions. Finding any solution may be easy, but finding the best solution requires thorough knowledge of the problem. You solve these problems the best way you can. Sometimes it helps to have more than one person solving the same problem because everyone is a unique problem solver.

No matter what problem you are tackling, you need a plan or a strategy for solving it. A plan or strategy will help you to understand the problem, work out a creative solution, and check to see that the solution makes sense.

Problem Solving

Understand
Plan
Solve
Look Back

PROBLEM SOLVING GUIDELINES

① UNDERSTAND the Problem

- What do you know?
- What do you need to find out?

② Develop a PLAN

- Have you ever solved a similar problem?
- What strategies can you use?
- What is an estimate for the answer?

③ SOLVE the Problem

- Do you need to try another strategy?
- What is the solution?

④ LOOK BACK

- Did you answer the right question?
- Is your answer reasonable?

Example

The Arguello's are driving from Denver to Kansas City, a distance of 605 mi. They've been traveling for 5 hr at 55 mi/hr. If they increase their speed to 60 mi/hr, how much longer will it take them to reach their destination?

① UNDERSTAND the Problem

You know that the family has completed part of their drive. *You need to find* out how long the rest of the trip will take.

② Develop a PLAN

You've solved similar problems involving distance, time, and rate. You need to recall that these quantities are related by the formulas $t = d \div r$ and $d = r \times t$, where $d =$ distance, $r =$ average speed, and $t =$ time.

Estimate the answer. After 5 hr, the Arguellos have gone about $5 \times 60 = 300$ mi. They have about 300 mi to go. They need about 5 hr to complete the trip.

One *strategy* is to draw a diagram to help you solve the problem.

③ SOLVE the Problem

After you draw the diagram, you might need to compare it to the formula.

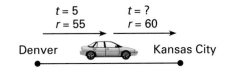

You know that $t = 5$ hr $r = 55$ mi/hr

$d = r \times t = 5 \times 55 = 275$ The family has traveled 275 mi.

Remaining distance $= 605 - 275 = 330$ mi

$t = d \div r = 330 \div 60 = 5.5$ hr needed to complete the trip.

The *solution* is that it will take 5.5 hr. You don't need to *try another strategy.*

④ LOOK BACK

You answered the right question. Because your answer is close to your estimate of 5 hr, *your answer makes sense.*

Check Your Understanding

1. What other strategies could you have used to solve the problem?

2. Why is it important to have a plan before you begin a solution?

3. When would you have to *try another strategy* when solving a problem?

Problem Solving

STRATEGIES

• Look for a Pattern
• Make an Organized List
• Make a Table
• Guess and Check
• Work Backward
• Use Logical Reasoning
• Draw a Diagram
• Solve a Simpler Problem

Look for a Pattern

Sometimes the numbers in a problem form a pattern. To solve the problem, you can find the rule that creates the pattern and use the rule to find the answer. ◄

Example

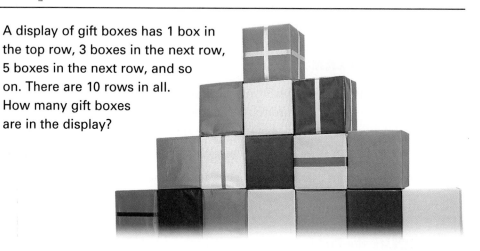

A display of gift boxes has 1 box in the top row, 3 boxes in the next row, 5 boxes in the next row, and so on. There are 10 rows in all. How many gift boxes are in the display?

Look for a pattern using the number of rows and the number of boxes in each row of the gift-box display.

1 row uses **1** box.

2 rows use 1 + 3 = **4** boxes.

3 rows use 1 + 3 + 5 = **9** boxes.

4 rows use 1 + 3 + 5 + 7 = **16** boxes.

Notice the pattern: The total number of boxes is the number of rows multiplied by itself. Use this rule to solve the problem.

The number of boxes in 10 rows is $10 \times 10 = 100$ boxes.

Try It

a. A basketball drops from a height of 76 in. On bounce 1, it rebounds to a height of 38 in. On bounce 2, it rebounds to a height of 19 in. How high does the basketball rebound on bounce 4?

b. The 8 members of a science club are recruiting new members by calling other students. Each science club member calls 12 people. How many phone calls would be made if there were 20 members?

Make an Organized List

Problem Solving

STRATEGIES

• Look for a Pattern
• Make an Organized List
• Make a Table
• Guess and Check
• Work Backward
• Use Logical Reasoning
• Draw a Diagram
• Solve a Simpler Problem

Sometimes a problem asks you to find the number of ways in which something can be done. To solve the problem, list all of the ways and then count them. The key to a correct solution is to organize your list carefully so you do not overlook any possibilities. ◄

Example

Dale and Ali play *Rock, Paper, Scissors.* Each player plays by putting out either a fist (rock), a flat hand (paper), or two fingers (scissors). Paper defeats (covers) rock, rock defeats (dulls) scissors, and scissors defeats (cuts) paper. No one wins if each person plays the same item. How many different ways can Dale and Ali play one game?

Dale	Ali	Winner
Rock	Rock	None
Rock	Paper	Ali
Rock	Scissors	Dale
Paper	Rock	Dale
Paper	Paper	None
Paper	Scissors	Ali
Scissors	Rock	Ali
Scissors	Paper	Dale
Scissors	Scissors	None

• First, list all the results that can occur if Dale plays rock. Ali can play rock, paper, or scissors.

• Next, list all the results that can occur if Dale plays paper. Keep Ali's plays in the same order.

• Finally, list all the results that can occur if Dale plays scissors.

There are 9 possible ways that Dale and Ali can play one game.

Try It

a. A spinner has 3 colors—red, yellow, and blue. If you spin two times, how many different color orders can you get?

b. Neal subscribes to 3 daily newspapers. In how many different orders can he read them?

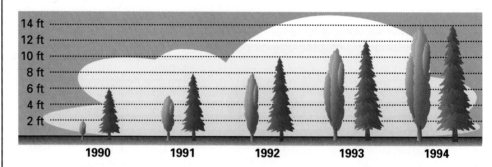

Problem Solving

STRATEGIES

- Look for a Pattern
- Make an Organized List
- **Make a Table**
- Guess and Check
- Work Backward
- Use Logical Reasoning
- Draw a Diagram
- Solve a Simpler Problem

Make a Table

A problem involving a relationship between two sets of numbers can often be solved by making a table. A table helps you organize data so you can see the numerical relationship and find the answer. ◄

Example

In 1990, Beth bought a 6 ft tall redwood seedling. The tree grew 2 ft each year. In 1990, she bought a 2 ft tall willow seedling. The tree grew 3 ft each year. In what year were the trees the same height?

Make a table to organize data about the heights of the trees.

	Year				
	1990	1991	1992	1993	1994
Redwood Height (ft)	6	8	10	12	14
Willow Height (ft)	2	5	8	11	14

The table shows that the amount by which the height of the redwood exceeded the height of the willow decreased each year.

In 1994, both trees were the same height.

Try It

a. Water from an 8,550 ft^3 water tank is used at a rate of 475 ft^3 per day. Water from a 7,200 ft^3 tank is used at a rate of 250 ft^3 per day. If no water is replaced, how much water will be in each tank when the two tanks hold equal amounts?

b. Quality-control personnel in a blue jean sewing plant check every sixteenth pair of jeans for color and every twenty-eighth pair for size. How often is a pair of jeans checked for both color and size?

Guess and Check

Problem Solving

STRATEGIES

- Look for a Pattern
- Make an Organized List
- Make a Table
- Guess and Check
- Work Backward
- Use Logical Reasoning
- Draw a Diagram
- Solve a Simpler Problem

If you're not sure how to solve a problem, make an educated guess at the answer. Check your guess. If it's wrong, revise your first guess by adding or subtracting. Repeat the pattern of *guess-check-revise* until you find the answer. ◄

Example

At a library book sale, Marika used an equal number of quarters and nickels to buy a $1.20 book. How many of each coin did she use?

Guess: Make an educated guess.

3 quarters and 3 nickels

$(3 \times \$0.25) + (3 \times \$0.05) = \$0.90$

Check: The total is too low.

Revise: Add to the first guess.

5 quarters and 5 nickels

$(5 \times \$0.25) + (5 \times \$0.05) = \$1.50$

Check: The total is too great.

Revise: The number is between 3 and 5.

4 quarters and 4 nickels

$(4 \times \$0.25) + (4 \times \$0.05) = \$1.20$

Check: It works.

Marika used 4 quarters and 4 nickels.

Try It

a. In the championship basketball game, Corey scored 25 points total on 2-point goals and 3-point goals. He hit 5 more 2-pointers than 3-pointers. How many of each did he hit?

b. Yolanda drove 600 mi from Castleton to Monroe. She returned to Castleton at a 10 mi/hr slower average speed. She drove 22 hr total. Find her average speed in each direction.

Problem Solving
STRATEGIES

• Look for a Pattern
• Make an Organized List
• Make a Table
• Guess and Check
• Work Backward
• Use Logical Reasoning
• Draw a Diagram
• Solve a Simpler Problem

Work Backward

A problem may give the result of a series of steps and ask you to find the initial value. To solve the problem, you can work backward step-by-step until you get to the beginning. ◄

Example

Laura, Seth, and Keena volunteered to wash a box of test tubes in the chemistry lab. Laura took half the total, Seth took two-thirds of what was left, and Keena took the remaining 8. How many test tubes were in the box?

The problem describes three steps occurring in order:

1. Laura took half the test tubes.

2. Seth took test tubes.

3. Keena took test tubes.

It also tells you the end result of 0 test tubes remaining. To solve the problem, work backward to the beginning.

Step	What Happened	Conclusion
3	Keena took 8 test tubes, leaving none.	Before this step, Seth left 8 test tubes.
2	Seth took two-thirds of the test tubes, leaving 8.	Before this step, Laura left 24 test tubes because 8 is *one-third* of the number Laura left.
1	Laura took half the test tubes, leaving 24.	Before this step, the number of test tubes was *twice* 24, or 48.

The box must have contained 48 test tubes.

Try It

a. Max, Holly, and Kim divided a carton of tennis balls among themselves. Max took half the balls. Holly took three-fourths of what was left. Kim took the remaining 3 balls. How many balls were in the carton?

b. Art is running in a 10 km race. When he has run three times as far as he has already run, he'll be 4 km from the end. How far has he run?

Use Logical Reasoning

Problem Solving STRATEGIES

- Look for a Pattern
- Make an Organized List
- Make a Table
- Guess and Check
- Work Backward
- Use Logical Reasoning
- Draw a Diagram
- Solve a Simpler Problem

To solve a problem using logical reasoning, decide how the facts relate to each other. Then work your way step-by-step to a sensible solution. Be careful not to make conclusions that are not based on facts. ◄

Example

Polly, Ike, and Fred have a dog, a cat, and a parakeet for pets, though not necessarily in that order. Ike is allergic to feathers. The dog owner is Polly's friend and Ike's classmate. Match the owners with their pets.

Take clues one at a time. Use a grid to keep track of your conclusions.

1. Ike is allergic to feathers.

	Dog	Cat	Parakeet
Polly			
Ike			No
Fred			

2. The dog owner is Polly's friend and Ike's classmate.

	Dog	Cat	Parakeet
Polly	No		
Ike	No		No
Fred			

Fred must be the dog owner.

Ike must be the cat owner.

That means Polly owns the parakeet.

	Dog	Cat	Parakeet
Polly	No	No	Yes
Ike	No	Yes	No
Fred	Yes	No	No

Try It

a. Jane, Gus, and Tim visited Canada, Peru, and France. Jane has never been to Europe. Tim plays bridge with the person who visited Canada but not the one who went to France. Match the people with their vacation spots.

b. Tom, Zeno, and Rosa are a farmer, a pilot, and a doctor. Zeno can't tell a pig from a hog. Neither he nor Rosa is a pilot. Match each person with his or her occupation.

Problem Solving

STRATEGIES

• Look for a Pattern
• Make an Organized List
• Make a Table
• Guess and Check
• Work Backward
• Use Logical Reasoning
• Draw a Diagram
• Solve a Simpler Problem

Draw a Diagram

Some problems may involve objects or positions. To solve the problem, draw a diagram and use it to visually identify relationships between the data. Then use the relationships to find the answer. ◄

Example

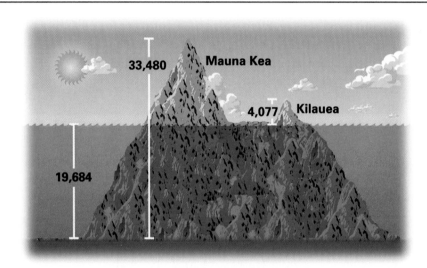

The Hawaiian volcano Mauna Kea is 33,480 ft tall. Also in Hawaii, the volcano Kilauea rises 4,077 ft above sea level. Mauna Kea has 19,684 ft of its height below sea level. How much taller than Kilauea is Mauna Kea?

Draw a sketch to compare the heights.

By looking at the sketch, we can determine by substracting that 13,796 ft of Mauna Kea is above sea level.

$33,480 - 19,684 = 13,796$

Also, $13,796 - 4,077 = 9,719$

Mauna Kea is 9,719 ft taller than Kilauea.

Try It

a. A pilot is 3,800 ft below the clouds. A plane at a lower altitude is 5,500 ft above the ground. The clouds are at 12,000 ft altitude. Find the difference in altitude between the planes.

b. A tree branch divides into 2 branches. Each smaller branch divides into 3 branches. Each of these divides into 5 branches. How many branches of all sizes are there?

Solve a Simpler Problem

Problem Solving STRATEGIES

- Look for a Pattern
- Make an Organized List
- Make a Table
- Guess and Check
- Work Backward
- Use Logical Reasoning
- Draw a Diagram
- Solve a Simpler Problem

A problem may seem very complex. It may contain large numbers or appear to require many steps to solve. Instead of solving the complex problem, try a similar problem that is simpler to solve. After solving the simpler problem, look for shortcuts, patterns, or relationships to solve the original problem. ◄

Example

At the Oh, Grow Up! Nursery, tree seedlings are raised in square plots that are side by side. Each square side is a 1 m section of fence. What is the total length of fence needed for a row of 25 tree plots?

You could sketch all 25 plots and then count the number of 1 m fence sections. That would be very time-consuming. So instead solve the simpler problem for 1, 2, and 3 tree plots.

1 square: ☐   4 m of fence sections are needed.

2 squares: ☐☐   7 m of fence sections are needed.

3 squares: ☐☐☐   10 m of fence sections are needed.

Notice that 4 fence sections are needed for the first square. For all tree plots after that, only three 1 m fence sections are needed.

Of the 25 tree plots, 1 tree plot requires 4 m of fence. The other 24 tree plots will each require 3 m of fence.

$4 + (24 \times 3) = 4 + 72 = 76$

76 m of fence are needed.

Try It

a. When 3 points are marked on a line segment, as in the figure, 3 line segments can be identified. How many segments can be counted if you mark 12 points on a line segment?

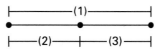

b. Suppose you earned $1 on your first day at a job, $2 the second day, $4 the third day, $8 the fourth day, and so on. How much would your total earnings be after 15 days?

1 Data Analysis

Cultural Link
www.mathsurf.com/8/ch1/people

Entertainment Link
www.mathsurf.com/8/ch1/ent

People of the World

Swahili is a trade and governmental language that is spoken in the Congo region and in East Africa. Swahili number words are shown.

1	moja
2	mbili
3	tatu
4	nne
5	tano
6	sita
7	saba
8	nane
9	tisa
10	kumi

Arts & Literature

Horace was a Roman poet who wrote odes and odes of poems and had something to say about statistics.

"We are just statistics, born to consume resources."

Entertainment

Television makes big bucks on advertising things from what we wear to what we eat. Almost $2 billion was spent on television ads for clothing and food in 1990.

2

Social Studies Link
www.mathsurf.com/8/ch1/social

Science

Between 1980 and 1990 the occurance of measles increased by 14,300 cases. Measles are caused by a virus and usually cause red circular spots on the skin.

Social Studies

To show numbers, Mayans drew dots, lines, and ovals. When an oval is below a number, the result is 20 times larger.

For instance: • = 1;

⚇ = 1 × 20 = 20.

KEY MATH IDEAS

Data can be useful and informative when presented in charts, tables, diagrams, and graphs.

Sometimes a single number, such as the mean, median, or mode, can help you understand the meaning of a set of data.

Surveys are used to collect data for a variety of purposes, such as political elections, advertising, and taste tests.

A sample is the part of the population that participates in a survey.

CHAPTER PROJECT

Problem Solving

Understand
Plan
Solve
Look Back

In this project, you will create a profile of the typical 13- or 14-year-old. You will design a survey to collect all the data needed to draw this profile. Data collected might include favorite subject, teacher, sports, games, hobbies, clubs, music, movies, or food.

Problem Solving Focus

Read each problem and answer the questions about the problem.

Reading the Problem

As you read a problem, you may be overwhelmed by information. Breaking the information into small parts can help you understand what the problem is saying. Ask yourself questions to be sure you understand each part.

1 In skateboard competitions, 5 judges give scores based on 100 points and the highest and lowest scores are thrown out. The remaining 3 scores are averaged to determine the skater's score for the run. Tess' scores were 82, 85, 87, 85, and 84. Mario's scores were 83, 84, 85, 84, and 88. Who won the race?

a. What is the problem about?

b. What is the problem asking?

c. What is the highest score for Tess? For Mario?

d. What is the lowest score for Tess? For Mario?

e. Write and answer a question of your own.

2 The skateboard shop sells custom-made skateboard decks for $50, four wheels for $29, bearings for $16, and trucks for $35. They give a 20% discount on the custom-made board. Ready-made boards cost $99. Which skateboard is less expensive?

a. What is the problem about?

b. What is the problem asking?

c. What is the total cost of the custom-made skateboard before the discount?

d. What is the discount on the custom-made skateboard?

e. Write and answer a question of your own.

Data Presentations

Money In Money Out

Want to make a lot of money? Want to run a successful business? Then invent, make, or produce a product that teenagers will buy. Why? Because teens in the United States spend almost $100 billion each year. Not only do they spend a lot of money, teens also influence how their friends and families spend money.

What do teens spend their money on? It may be the latest music, fashions, or technology—all items that teens frequently know as much, if not more, about than adults.

Where do teens typically get their money? They get it the old-fashioned way—they earn it, by baby-sitting, mowing lawns, delivering newspapers, and doing household chores.

The really amazing thing is that the population of teens in the United States is increasing and has been since 1992. Experts expect the teen population to be about 34,900,000 by the year 2010. That's a lot of teenagers with a lot of money to spend.

1 What is the greatest age difference possible between two teens?

2 How do you think experts forecasted the teen population for the year 2010?

Line Plots and Stem-and-Leaf Diagrams

You'll Learn ...

■ how to understand data with line plots and stem-and-leaf diagrams

... How It's Used

Movie theater managers use stem-and-leaf diagrams to analyze the price of movie tickets across the nation.

Vocabulary

range

line plot

stem-and-leaf diagram

double stem-and-leaf diagram

▶ **Lesson Link**   You have seen how data are used in newspapers and magazines. In this lesson, you will learn ways of using and comparing data. ◀

Explore   Line Plots

Summer's Blockbusters

Summertime isn't just swimming and lemonade, it's also movies. Movie theaters and video stores do their best business in the summer. How many movies did you see this summer?

1. How many movies did each person in your group see in a movie theater? Plot your data as shown in the diagram (one X for each movie).

Movies in a Theater

		X
X		X
X		X
Damion		Shauna

Shauna saw 3 movies in a theater.

2. How many movies on video did each person see? Make a similar plot for this data.

3. Make another plot showing the total number of movies seen by each person in your group.

4. How many students in your group saw fewer than five movies? Between five and ten movies? More than ten movies?

5. Without counting, describe how you can determine by looking at your plot who saw the fewest movies? The most movies?

6. What can you report by looking at your line plots?

Learn   Line Plots and Stem-and-Leaf Diagrams

When working with data it is useful to know the range of the set. The **range** of a data set is the difference between the highest and lowest values.

Between 1950 and 1990, the yearly number of tropical storms worldwide was as low as 2 (in 1982) and as high as 12 (in 1969).

The range of yearly tropical storms is 2 to 12, or 10.

A **line plot** is a display of data that shows how many times each data value occurs. Each time a data value occurs, a mark is made above that value on a number line.

Example 1

A media club had a quiz with the question, "How many cable television networks can you name?" The results were 8, 12, 16, 14, 17, 6, 6, 12, and 13. Make a line plot for the media club's data and report the results.

The range 6 to 17 is used to draw the axis.

Plot 2 Xs above 6 because 2 people each answered "6."

One student got a high score of 17.

Media Club's Cable TV Knowledge

```
  X              X
  X    X         X X X     X X
<-+-+-+-+-+-+-+-+-+-+-+-+->
  6    8   10   12   14   16
```
Television networks

A **stem-and-leaf diagram** uses the digits of the data numbers to show the shape and distribution of a data set. Each data number is separated into a stem and leaf.

Example 2

In the 1995–1996 season, the total number of games won by each team of the Atlantic division of the National Hockey League Eastern Conference (NHL-East) was 45, 41, 41, 39, 38, 37, and 22. Make a stem-and-leaf diagram to see these results.

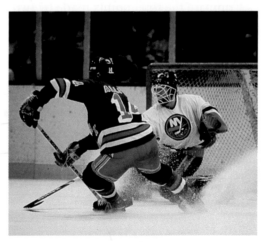

Use the tens digit as the stem. The range of wins is 22 to 45 so stems are 2 to 4. Use the ones digit as the leaf.

Stem	Leaf
2	2
3	7 8 9
4	1 1 5

List ones digits of each stem in increasing order.

37 has a stem of 3 and a leaf of 7.

Two teams had 41 wins.

Remember

In the number 37, 3 is in the tens place and 7 is in the ones place.

(Previous course)

The three strongest teams of the Atlantic NHL division each won over 40 games. The weakest team in the league won only 22 games.

A **double stem-and-leaf diagram** compares two sets of data in one diagram.

Example 3

In the 1995–1996 season, the Pacific NHL-West teams had win totals of 47, 32, 24, 30, 20, 34, and 35. Create a double stem-and-leaf diagram to compare the Atlantic and Pacific NHL teams.

Use the stem-and-leaf diagram from Example 2.

Add a new leaf column to the left of the stem. For each stem list ones digits of Pacific NHL wins in *decreasing* order in the new leaf column.

Stem	Leaf
2	2
3	7 8 9
4	1 1 5

Leaf	Stem	Leaf
4 0	2	2
5 4 2 0	3	7 8 9
7	4	1 1 5

The range of Pacific NHL wins is 20 to 47.

30 has a stem of 3 and a leaf of 0.

The double stem-and-leaf diagram shows that out of both NHL divisions the Atlantic NHL teams won the most games with scores greater than 40 in the 1995–1996 season.

Try It

Compare the total points made by two NBA Chicago Bulls starters, Michael Jordan and Scottie Pippen, during the six-game 1996 finals series. Use a double stem-and-leaf diagram.

Game	1	2	3	4	5	6
Jordan	28	29	36	23	26	22
Pippen	21	21	12	9	14	17

Remember

The number 8 has a tens place value of 0.
(Previous course)

Check | Your Understanding

1. When would you use a line plot? A stem-and-leaf diagram?

2. How can you determine the range of a set of data? Give two ways the range can be expressed.

Practice and Apply

Students in a Pre-Algebra Class

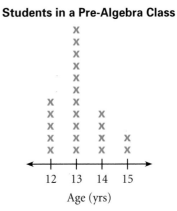

1. **Getting Started**

   a. The line plot represents the ages of students in a pre-algebra class. How many 12-year-olds are there?

   b. What is the range of ages in this class?

   c. What student age is most frequent? Least frequent?

State the range and draw a line plot for each data set.

2. A mother called some piano teachers in the Houston area to ask about prices for half-hour lessons. The prices quoted were $18, $20, $15, $17, $18, $21, and $17.

3. Kids in an arcade were asked, "How much money do you spend in an arcade each week?" Their answers, rounded to the nearest dollar, were $2.00, $3.00, $7.00, $5.00, $2.00, $4.00, $3.00, and $2.00.

4. **Test Prep** Eight gymnastics judges gave Kim scores of 8.9, 9.2, 9.0, 8.8, 9.1, 8.9, 9.2, and 9.1 for her performance on the uneven bars. Which of the following expresses the range of her scores?

   Ⓐ 8   Ⓑ 5   Ⓒ 0.4   Ⓓ 9.2

State the range and draw a stem-and-leaf diagram for each data set.

5. **Science** An aquarium has several species of tropical fish. The populations of each species are 23, 16, 8, 12, 18, 22, and 33.

6. **Geography** The table shows the number of school days per year. (The stem can have two digits.)

Country	Belgium	U.S.	Sweden	Mexico	Scotland	Israel	South Korea	Japan
School Days	160	180	180	180	200	215	220	243

7. Create a double stem-and-leaf diagram to compare nonschool days to school days of the countries listed in Exercise 6. To find the nonschool days of each country, subtract the number of school days from 365.

Problem Solving and Reasoning

8. Math Reasoning When the city schools take a two-week winter holiday, a skating rink gives students under 18 a discount to skate on weekdays. Make a stem-and-leaf diagram using a table which shows the daily number of students that take advantage of this discount. What days are represented in the stem with the most leaves?

Mon.	Tue.	Wed.	Thur.	Fri.	Mon.	Tue.	Wed.	Thur.	Fri.
64	52	57	51	42	44	39	42	52	55

9. Communicate Vicious pooches across the country bite mail carriers. Make a stem-and-leaf diagram of the serious dog bite counts. Write a paragraph about preventing these dog crimes.

Problem Solving TIP

Simply listing data in numerical order can give you a good start.

Houston	117	Chicago	75
Santa Ana	101	Fort Worth	66
South Florida	81	Long Beach	57
Central Florida	76	San Francisco	53
San Jose	75	Oakland	50

10. Critical Thinking Suppose a stem-and-leaf diagram has 2, 3, 4, and 5 listed in the stem column. What can you determine if there is nothing in the leaf column next to the 4?

11. *Journal* A double stem-and-leaf diagram compares two sets of data. Provide a specific situation and reasonable data that would be appropriate to display in a double stem-and-leaf diagram.

Mixed Review

Write each as a number. *[Previous course]*

12. eight million

13. four hundred thirty-seven

14. two thousand six hundred

15. fifty thousand

16. six thousand twenty-two

17. seven million thirty thousand

Add. *[Previous course]*

18. $389 + 267$

19. $295 + 430$

20. $439 + 27 + 64$

21. $8325 + 478$

22. $8376 + 8756$

23. $3740 + 2369$

24. $7345 + 3648$

25. $2669 + 7831$

Measures of Central Tendency

▶ **Lesson Link** ⏐ You know how to display data using line plots and stem-and-leaf diagrams. Now you will learn how to represent data with just one number. ◀

You'll Learn ...

■ how to analyze and represent data using mean, median, and mode

Explore | Mode, Median, and Mean

Middle America

The number of U.S. representatives each state sends to Congress depends on the state's population size. The map shows the number of representatives from the states between the Rocky Mountains and the Mississippi River.

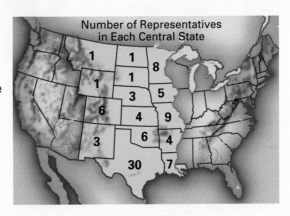

Number of Representatives in Each Central State

... How It's Used

Real estate agents use these numbers to determine how the housing market is behaving.

1. Use the map to create a line plot that shows how many states have the same number of representatives (for example, four states have one representative). Discuss your results.

2. What is the total number of representatives in this central region?

3. What is the greatest number of representatives in one state within this region? The least number of representatives?

4. What would you say is a typical number of representatives for a state in this region of the United States?

5. Suppose each of these 15 states had the same number of representatives and there were a total of 89 representatives in this region. How many representatives would each state have?

Vocabulary

measure of central tendency

mean

median

outlier

mode

Learn | Measures of Central Tendency

A **measure of central tendency** is a single value that summarizes a set of numerical data. The **mean**, or *average*, is the sum of a set of data divided by the number of data.

Example 1

Galileo discovered four large moons of Jupiter in 1610. The diameters of these moons are shown in the table. What is the mean diameter of these moons?

Moon	Moon's Diameter
Europa	3130 km
Io	3640 km
Callisto	4840 km
Ganymede	5270 km

$$\frac{3130 + 3640 + 4840 + 5270}{4} = 4220 \quad \text{Add all data. Divide by number of data.}$$

The mean diameter of Jupiter's large moons is 4220 km.

The **median**, another measure of central tendency, is the middle value of a data set. It is identified when the data are arranged in numerical order. If there is an even number of data values, the median is the mean of the two middle values.

The median can be a better measure of central tendency than the mean when the data set has **outliers**, extreme values separated from most of the data set.

Example 2

An electronics store that wants more young customers sells CD players at the following prices: $350, $275, $500, $325, $100, $375, and $300. What is the median price? Are there any outlier prices?

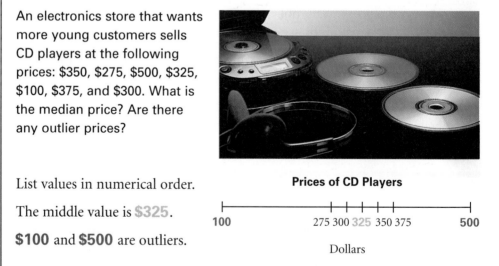

Problem Solving TIP

It can be easier to see an outlier if you plot the data on a number line drawn to scale.

List values in numerical order.

The middle value is $325.

$100 and $500 are outliers.

Prices of CD Players

100   275 300 325 350 375   500

Dollars

The median price for a CD player is $325. The outlier prices are $100 and $500. The store should sell less expensive CD players so young people can afford them.

Example 3

Ten popular brands of berry-flavored sorbet have the following prices per cup: 69¢, 70¢, 59¢, 61¢, 66¢, 67¢, 70¢, 73¢, 66¢, and 93¢. Find the median price of these popular brands.

59, 61, 66, 66, 67, 69, 70, 70, 73, 93   List values in numerical order.

59, 61, 66, 66, 67, 69, 70, 70, 73, 93   There are two middle values.

$\frac{67 + 69}{2} = 68$ Find the mean of the two middle values.

68¢ is the median price per cup of popular brands of berry sorbet.

Example 4

Use your calculator to determine the mean per capita annual income of the following countries.

Guatemala	Tanzania	Indonesia	India	Hungary
$3,350	$580	$3,150	$1,220	$6,050

▶ **Language Link**

"Per capita" means "by heads" in Latin. "Per capita" can mean per person.

Enter 3350 + 580 + 3150 + 1220 + 6050 = *14350*

Enter ÷ 5 = *2870*

The mean per capita income is $2,870.

Try It

Ten people ages 12 to 15 were asked, "How much of your own money do you spend each week?"

The responses were $2, $10, $5, $15, $3, $5, $5, $15, $10, and $20.

Find the mean and median money spent per week by this group.

The **mode** is the *most common* data value. If no value occurs more than once, there is no mode.

The data in Example 3 has two modes, 66¢ and 70¢.

If every value in a set of data only occurs once then there is no mode.

The data in Example 1 has no mode.

Barry Bonds' yearly home run totals from 1987 to 1995 are listed. Would you find the mean, median, or mode to give a summary of his nine year performance?

Year	'87	'88	'89	'90	'91	'92	'93	'94	'95
Home Runs	25	24	19	33	25	34	46	37	33

Sarah thinks ...

I'll find the mean. First I'll add the number of home runs. Then I'll divide by 9, because I added 9 numbers.

$$\frac{25 + 24 + 19 + 33 + 25 + 34 + 46 + 37 + 33}{9} \approx 30.67$$

If I round the answer, the mean is 31 home runs per year.

Daniel thinks ...

I'll find the median and the mode. All I need to do is write the number of home runs in numerical order.

19, 24, 25, 25, 33, 33, 34, 37, 46

It looks like there are two modes: 25 and 33. They both appear twice.

The middle number is 33, so the median is 33.

What do you think?

1. Which mode is closer to the *center* of the data? Explain.

2. Do you think the mean or the median best summarizes the data? Why?

Check | Your Understanding

1. What effect do outliers have on the mean and median of a data set?

2. Describe how to find the median of a data set that has an even number of values.

Practice and Apply

1. **Getting Started** Jerry's test scores for last year's English class were 95, 70, 85, 88, 100, 71, 95, 80, and 90. Find the mean of his test grades.

   a. Find the sum of all of the scores.

   b. How many tests did Jerry take?

   c. Divide the sum by the number of tests to calculate the mean.

Find the mean, median, and mode of each data set.

2. Various brands of skateboards sell for $19.99, $22.99, $59.98, $39.98, $24.99, $27.99, and $29.99.

3. In a stack of paperback books, the total pages of each book are 139, 253, 130, 174, and 204.

4. **Science** Some of the longest times spent in space are 439 days, 115 days, 115 days, and 169 days.

5. **Science** During 1982–1990, the annual number of oil tanker spills worldwide was 9, 17, 15, 9, 8, 12, 13, 31, and 8. Identify the outlier and calculate the mean and median as if the outlier were not in the data set.

Geography The table shows the areas and 1992 populations for five east Asian countries. Use the table in Exercises 6–8.

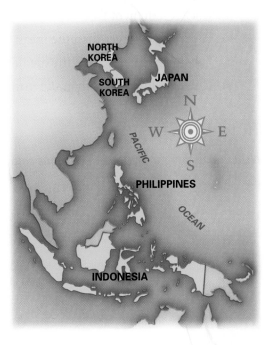

Country	Area (thousands of mi²)	Population (millions)
Indonesia	735	197
Japan	146	125
North Korea	47	22
Philippines	116	67
South Korea	38	44

6. What is the mean area of these countries? Is there an outlier?

7. What is the mean population size?

8. What is the mean population density— that is, population ÷ area?

9. **Test Prep** If a store manager says, "Size 10 is our best-selling women's coat size," what measure of central tendency is being used?

Ⓐ Mean   Ⓑ Median   Ⓒ Mode   Ⓓ Outlier

Problem Solving and Reasoning

10. **Communicate** The top ten American movies from 1980 to 1990 and their gross earnings (to the nearest million dollars) are shown in the table. Is there a relationship between the year of the movie and the movie's gross earnings? Explain.

E.T. (1982)	$400 mil	Back to the Future (1985)	$208 mil
Home Alone (1990)	$286 mil	Beverly Hills Cop (1984)	$235 mil
Ghostbusters (1984)	$221 mil	Raiders of the Lost Ark (1981)	$242 mil
Batman (1989)	$251 mil	The Empire Strikes Back (1980)	$223 mil
Ghost (1990)	$217 mil	Return of the Jedi (1983)	$263 mil

11. **Choose a Strategy** Last year the junior high spirit squad sold five items as homecoming souvenirs to raise money. They sold 61 pom-pons for $1 each, 57 pins for $1 each, 19 cups for $2 each, 45 key chains for $3 each, and 3 T-shirts for $22 each. What was the mean price for a homecoming souvenir? How did outlier prices affect the mean?

12. **Critical Thinking** Create sets of data with at least three values that will make each statement true.

  a. The mode is larger than the mean.

  b. The mean is larger than the median.

  c. The median is larger than the mean.

> ### Problem Solving
> ## STRATEGIES
>
> • Look for a Pattern
> • Make an Organized List
> • Make a Table
> • Guess and Check
> • Work Backward
> • Use Logical Reasoning
> • Draw a Diagram
> • Solve a Simpler Problem

Mixed Review

Write each number in words. *[Previous course]*

13. 856   **14.** 378   **15.** 4826   **16.** 2360

17. 45,600   **18.** 23,867   **19.** 3,746,700   **20.** 2,735,752

Subtract. *[Previous course]*

21. 768 − 42   **22.** 463 − 345   **23.** 634 − 236   **24.** 900 − 678

25. 4637 − 783   **26.** 6040 − 2783   **27.** 7823 − 2975   **28.** 4378 − 3774

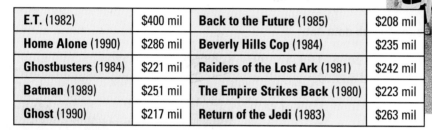

Box-and-Whisker Plots

▶ **Lesson Link**   Now you will use your knowledge of the median to display data graphically. ◀

You'll Learn ...

■ how to analyze and represent the spread and distribution of data using box-and-whisker plots

... How It's Used

Teachers use box-and-whisker plots to understand how students perform on national tests like the PSAT.

Vocabulary

box-and-whisker plot

quartile

lower quartile

upper quartile

Explore | Quartiles

Rolling Sums

Materials: 2 number cubes

1. Roll both number cubes 20 times. Record the sum of each roll.

2. Find the median by listing the data in numerical order. Draw a double line where the median occurs. The ten lowest numbers should be on the left side of this line.

3. Find the median of the ten lowest numbers. Draw a straight line to show where this number would appear. Do the same for the ten highest numbers.

4. You have drawn three lines that divide your data into four parts. Discuss the significance of these four parts.

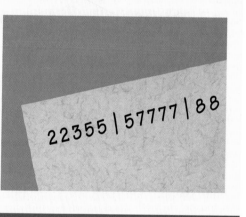

22355 | 57777 | 88

Learn | Box-and-Whisker Plots

A **box-and-whisker plot** is a visual way of showing median values for a set of data.

Quartiles are three numbers that divide a data set into four equal parts. The median is the middle quartile. Take the median of the upper and lower halves of the data set to find the other two quartiles.

Suppose a student scores 97, 80, 85, 72, 65, 94, and 76, on seven quizzes.

65   72   76   80   85   94   97
      ↓   ↓   ↓
      72   80   94

The **lower quartile**, 72, is the median of the lower half of the data set.

The **upper quartile**, 94, is the median of the upper half of the data set.

The whiskers show the range to be 65 to 97.

The median is 80.

The box shows that the middle half of the grades are between **72** and **94**.

Math Quiz Grades

Lower quartile   Median   Upper quartile

65   72 80 94   97

Example 1

Below is a box-and-whisker plot showing the gross earnings of the top 50 movies in 1994. Give the range and median. What does the whisker left of the median show?

1994 Movie Earnings ($ millions)

38.8 91.1
   50.9
26.4   298.9

The range is $26.4 million to $298.9 million.   Look at the whiskers.

The median is $50.9 million.   Look at the middle line in the box.

The whisker left of the median shows that one-quarter of the movies grossed between $26.4 million and $38.8 million.

Try It

One hundred 12 to 15 year olds were asked how many times they had been in a music store within the past 30 days. The results are shown in the box-and-whisker plot.

Number of Times Teens Browse Music Stores

0 2 4   10   20

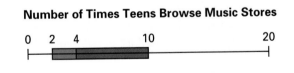

a. What is the range of the data?   **b.** What is the median?

c. What are the lower and upper quartiles?

d. What does the whisker to the right of the median show?

Example 2

When businesses look for employees they often post a classified ad in a big newspaper. The daily price for one line of an ad can vary. Some possible prices are:

$4.20 $4.49 $4.83 $5.24 $5.72 $6.29

$7.01 $7.97 $8.49 $9.73 $10.38 $13.79

$15.31 $16.77

JOB OPPORTUNITIES

HELP WANTED
Great after school job serving ice cream
M – F,   4 – 6 p m
Call 555-CONE

HELP WANTED

Create a box-and-whisker plot of these prices. Between what values does the middle half of the prices fall?

The range of prices is from $4.20 to $16.77.   *Find the range.*

$\dfrac{\$7.01 + \$7.97}{2} = \$7.49$ is the median price   *Find the median.*

$4.20, $4.49, $4.83, $5.24, $5.72, $6.29, $7.01   *Find median of lower half.*

$7.97, $8.49, $9.73, $10.38, $13.79, $15.31, $16.77   *Find median of upper half.*

The lower quartile price is $5.24 and the upper quartile price is $10.38.

The middle half of the prices are between $5.24 and $10.38.

Draw a line showing the range.

Plot the median and the quartiles.

Draw a box between the quartiles.

Write a title.

Daily Prices for an Employment Classified Ad ($)

Lower quartile   Median   Upper quartile
5.24   7.49   10.38
4.20   16.77

Try It

Ten 12 to 15 year olds were asked, "What age would you rather be?" The results were 17, 18, 16, 20, 15, 18, 17, 16, 17, 16. Create a box-and-whisker plot of these desired ages. Between what values does the middle half of the data fall?

Check | Your Understanding

1. How do outliers affect the size of the whiskers on a box-and-whisker plot?

2. In a box-and-whisker plot, how much of the data is in the box? In each whisker? Explain.

Practice and Apply

1. **Getting Started** At a local school's mathematics competition, one team's members obtained scores, in ascending order, of 90, 93, 94, 95, 96, 99, and 100. Follow the steps to prepare a box-and-whisker plot for this data.

   a. Find the highest and lowest scores and draw a line covering the entire range.

   b. Identify the median on the number line.

   c. Identify the lower quartile by finding the median of the lower half of the scores.

   d. Identify the upper quartile by finding the median of the upper half of the scores.

   e. Draw a box from the lower quartile to the upper quartile. Then draw the whiskers.

Sketch a box-and-whisker plot for each set of data. Between what values does the middle half of the data fall?

2. **Science** During the 1980s, the largest major earthquakes around the world registered 7.3, 7.2, 7.7, 7.1, 7.8, 8.1, 7.3, 6.5, 7.3, 6.8, and 6.9 on the Richter Scale.

3. **Consumer** In a mail-order clothing retailer's summer catalog, different models of girls' swimsuits sell for $25, $16, $20, $23, $22, $25, $24, and $20.

4. **Test Prep** What is the upper quartile of the data whose box-and-whisker plot is shown?

   Ⓐ 28   Ⓑ 31   Ⓒ 36   Ⓓ 45

Ages of People in a Ballroom Dancing Class

23   28   31   36   45

5. In 1991, the ten largest U.S. cities had the following burglary rates (per 100,000 people): 1524, 1615, 1858, 2385, 1344, 1507, 2515, 3064, 2432, and 2609. Draw a box-and-whisker plot and discuss the results.

6. The following numbers represent the number of gallons of gas used per automobile in 1993 for each of ten U.S. states: 918, 698, 771, 624, 688, 760, 731, 789, 644, and 614. Draw a box-and-whisker plot. What states might one expect to find at the upper end of the plot?

Problem Solving and Reasoning

7. Communicate Which box-and-whisker plot would typically have longer whiskers: one for a data set with or without outliers? Explain.

8. Medicine Doctors often test for allergies by scratching some of the test substance into the patient's skin and later measuring the size of the resulting wheal, or bump. In one study, a substance produced different-sized bumps on different people. The data are summarized in this plot.

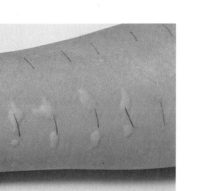

Wheal Size (mm²)

What does this plot suggest? Give more than one interpretation of the data.

9. [Journal] For a box-and-whisker plot, describe in your own words what information you can get from the box, and what information you can get from the whiskers.

10. Number Sense Suppose a box-and-whisker plot displays a data set with 48 values. How many values are represented in the box?

Mixed Review

Multiply. [Previous course]

11. 237 × 78   **12.** 863 × 43   **13.** 326 × 61   **14.** 4362 × 47

15. 7348 × 76   **16.** 375 × 789   **17.** 432 × 636   **18.** 934 × 765

Round as indicated. [Previous course]

19. 43,644, nearest ten   **20.** 78,326, nearest hundred

21. 36,604, nearest thousand   **22.** 63,649, nearest ten

23. 46,351, nearest hundred   **24.** 87,486, nearest thousand

Bar Graphs and Line Graphs

You'll Learn ...

■ how to understand data using bar graphs and line graphs

... How It's Used

News reporters use graphs to help communicate important situations that involve numbers.

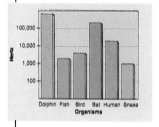

Vocabulary

bar graph

double bar graph

line graph

double line graph

▶ **Lesson Link**   Last year you learned how to create bar graphs and line graphs. Now you will learn some variations of these graphs. ◀

Explore   Line Graphs

Federal Minimum Wages

Year	1955	1960	1965	1970	1975	1980	1985	1990	1995
Wage	$0.75	$1.00	$1.25	$1.45	$2.10	$3.10	$3.35	$3.80	$4.25

The Fair Labor Standards Act of 1938 and its amendments are the reasons our country has a minimum hourly wage.

There have been different minimum wages for different jobs. For example, the wages for farm workers were lower than those of nonfarm workers.

This data shows the minimum wage every five years from 1955 to 1995.

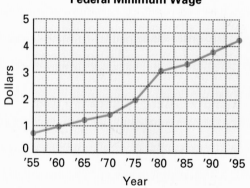

1. In what year was the federal minimum wage the lowest? The highest?

2. What happened to the minimum wage from 1960 to 1965?

3. What was the minimum wage increase between 1975 and 1980?

4. What is the minimum wage now? Did it decrease or increase since 1995? By how much?

5. Discuss how the federal minimum wage might change in the future.

Learn Bar Graphs and Line Graphs

A **bar graph** uses bars to represent the values of a data set. Bar graphs are used to compare data from several situations. Each bar represents a category of data labeled on the horizontal axis. The height of the bars correlate with a number on the vertical axis.

Example 1

People ages 12 to 19 were asked when buying certain products did brand names matter to them.

A bar graph shows the results.

What percent of people prefer a specific brand of jeans? Gum?

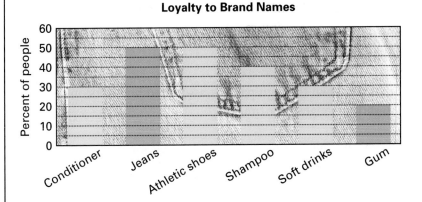

Loyalty to Brand Names

About **50%** think a brand name is important when buying jeans.

About **20%** think a brand name is important when buying gum.

▶ **Industry Link**

Many companies hope that young people will be loyal to their brand. Companies think that when teenagers become adults they will still be loyal to the same brand name.

Try It

The bar graph shows the number of cellular phone subscribers (in thousands) from 1990 through 1994.

a. What year had the least number of subscribers?

b. What year had the greatest number of subscribers?

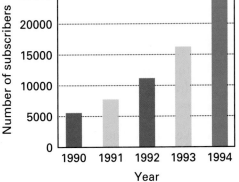

Cellular Phone Subscribers

A **double bar graph** shows two bar graphs together and compares two related data sets.

Example 2

Teenagers who buy music have different tastes from those who don't. Create a double bar graph to see what music style they disagree about most.

Music Style	Rap	Alternative	Country	Top 40
Buyers	81	61	41	61
Nonbuyers	73	46	51	57

The range of both data sets is from 41 to 81.

The bars for buyers and nonbuyers are different colors.

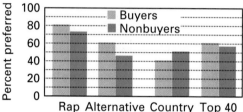

The greatest difference in taste is shown for alternative music. Buyers prefer it more than nonbuyers do.

A **line graph** is a line drawn through pairs of associated numbers on a grid. It is usually used to show changes over time.

Example 3

The table displays U.S. teenagers' income from 1986 to 1994. Display the data in a line graph to determine the year with the most dramatic increase.

Year	'86	'87	'88	'89	'90	'91	'92	'93	'94
Billions of Dollars	$65	$68	$73	$78	$94	$95	$88	$86	$96

The values, $65 billion to $96 billion, must be included in the vertical axis. Draw a break in the vertical axis because it does not start at zero.

Scale vertical axis with dollars and horizontal axis with years.

Plot the income for each year and draw a line through each point.

Label each axis and title the graph.

Teen income increased dramatically from 1989 to 1990.

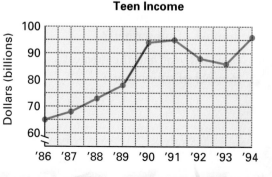

A **double line graph** shows two line graphs together to compare two related data sets.

Example 4

The table and the graphs show some yearly median earnings (in thousands of dollars) for men and women. Compare and contrast the graphs.

Year	1988	1989	1990	1991	1992
Men	26.7	27.3	27.7	29.4	30.4
Women	17.6	18.8	19.8	20.6	21.4

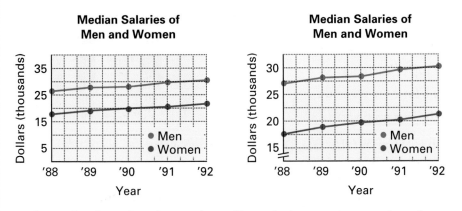

Both graphs show that the men's median salaries were greater than the women's. The graph with the broken scale makes the difference between the salaries seem greater.

Try It

The table shows the number of Soviet and U.S. space launches. Make a double bar graph from the data.

Year	1980	1981	1982	1983	1984	1985
Soviet	89	98	191	98	97	98
United States	13	18	18	22	22	17

Check Your Understanding

1. Display the data of Example 4 in a double bar graph.

2. How is the range of data used in creating a line or bar graph? A double line or double bar graph?

Practice and Apply

1. **Getting Started** Using the bar graph shown, create a line graph that shows the amount of money made by book publishing from 1988 through 1994.

   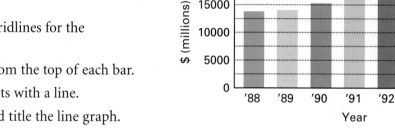

   Earnings of Book Publishing

   a. Draw a grid using the same scale on the vertical axis.

   b. Draw and label gridlines for the horizontal axis.

   c. Plot the points from the top of each bar.

   d. Connect the points with a line.

   e. Label the axes and title the line graph.

2. **Science** Create a bar graph to represent the data. Draw a conclusion about the relationship between life-span and size of animal based on the data.

Animal	Dog	Cat	Rabbit	Guinea Pig	Mouse
Average Life-Span (yr)	12	12	5	4	3

3. **Career** Create a line graph to represent the data. Draw a conclusion about the number of U.S. postmasters after 1994.

Year	1988	1989	1990	1991	1992	1993	1994
Thousands of Postmasters in U.S.	28	27	27	27	26	25	27

4. **Industry** Draw a line graph of the average monthly production of cars (in thousands) in the U.S. from 1986 to 1992. About how many cars were made in 1990?

Year	1986	1987	1988	1989	1990	1991	1992
Cars	474	451	504	567	592	590	626

5. **Test Prep** Which graph would be most appropriate to compare the amounts of money spent by high school boys and girls on food, clothes, transportation, and entertainment?

   Ⓐ Mean   Ⓑ Double line graph

   Ⓒ Bar graph   Ⓓ Double bar graph

Problem Solving and Reasoning

6. **Journal** Explain why a line graph would not be an appropriate choice for displaying the animal life-span data in Exercise 2.

7. **Critical Thinking** The percent of women competing in the Olympic Games has increased since the Games opened in 1896. Data from selected Olympiads are presented in the graph below.

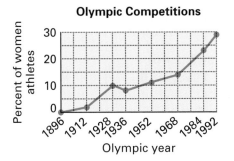

Olympic Competitions

What if someone wanted to present the data using a bar graph instead? Would this method be just as appropriate as a line graph? Explain.

Great Britain's Charlotte Cooper. 1900 Paris Olympics.

United States' Monica Seles. 1996 Atlanta Olympics.

8. **Communicate** What type of graph would be appropriate to present the population of the ten largest states in the United States? Explain.

Mixed Review

Divide. [*Previous course*]

9. 208 ÷ 8   10. 259 ÷ 7   11. 504 ÷ 14   12. 923 ÷ 13   13. 522 ÷ 73

Order from least to greatest. [*Previous course*]

14. 879, 789, 897, 798   15. 735, 4321, 578, 2378   16. 1121, 1211, 1112

17. 4725, 4257, 4527   18. 3100, 3010, 301, 3000   19. 684, 654, 642, 664

Project Progress

Use your survey to prove something about the people in your age group. Ask questions that will give you numerical results and consider the kind of graph that would be most appropriate for your data.

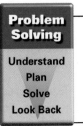

Problem Solving

Understand
Plan
Solve
Look Back

TECHNOLOGY

Using a Spreadsheet • Creating Graphs From Data

Problem: Given the following data set of minimum wages from 1955 to 1997, how could you create a graph that would help you see a trend in the data? Note that the data is given in year-wage pairs.

Data set: 1955, 0.75; 1956, 1.00; 1961, 1.15; 1963, 1.25; 1967, 1.40; 1968, 1.60; 1974, 2.00; 1975, 2.10; 1978, 2.65; 1979, 2.90; 1980, 3.10; 1981, 3.35; 1990, 3.80; 1991, 4.25; 1996, 4.75; 1997, 5.15.

You can use your spreadsheet program to help you create the necessary graph.

1 Enter the data in your spreadsheet as shown.

	A	B
1	Yr.	Minimum wage
2	1955	0.75
3	1956	1.00
4	1961	1.15
5	1963	1.25

Solution: A line or bar graph will show a trend of increasing minimum wages over the years.

2 Using your spreadsheet's built-in graphing capabilities, choose a graph for your data.

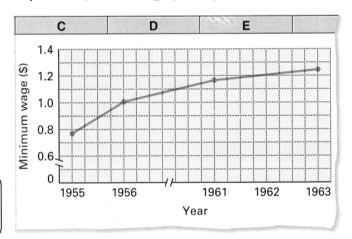

TRY IT

Using your spreadsheet, create a reasonable graph for each of the following data sets:

a. Weekly earnings: Week 1, $12; Week 2, $15; Week 3, $18; Week 4, $21; Week 5, $24.

b. Test Scores: Test 1, 100; Test 2, 95; Test 3, 85; Test 4, 70; Test 5, 60.

ON YOUR OWN

▶ Do you think a spreadsheet automatically gives you the most reasonable graph of your data? Explain.

▶ Which is easier, to generate a graph using a spreadsheet or by hand? Explain.

▶ What kinds of information can you obtain from your graphs?

In this section, you have learned how to create graphs and use them to understand data. In the Connect, you will have a chance to answer a question of your own choosing.

Money in Money out

Materials: Calculator, graph paper

Many people stop at convenience stores to buy soda, gum, candy, or a sandwich. Often people buy things they didn't plan to purchase; this is called "impulse buying."

In a group, talk about how you shop. What do you usually buy when you go shopping? Why would you buy an item on impulse?

Convenience Store Purchases

1. What conclusions can your group draw from the bar graph? Why do you think a broken scale was used?

2. Make two lists of purchases you made in convenience stores in the past month: one of things you bought on impulse and another of things you planned to buy. (Try to list at least five items in each list.)

3. Estimate the price of each item in the lists. Use your calculator to calculate the measures of central tendency for each list. Create a box-and-whisker plot for both of your lists.

4. Create a double bar graph that compares the total you spent on planned purchases and impulse purchases. Compare your graph to those of other members in your group.

5. Use data from the most impulsive and least impulsive shoppers in your group to create a double bar graph.

1. The table shows how the Detroit Tigers placed in the American League baseball teams in the 1930s. Find their mean, median, and mode place finishes during the 1930s. Draw a line plot to show the mode.

Year	1930	1931	1932	1933	1934	1935	1936	1937	1938	1939
Place	5th	7th	5th	5th	1st	1st	2nd	2nd	5th	5th

2. Create a stem-and-leaf diagram for the data: 11, 64, 11, 53, 29, 43, 46.

Geography The table shows data on ten nations of the west African coast.

3. Find the mean area and population of these countries.

4. Create a box-and-whisker plot for the area of these countries.

5. Create a box-and-whisker plot and bar graph for the population of these countries.

6. **Communicate** Describe a possible relationship between the area of one of these African countries and its population. Use your results from Exercises 2–5.

Country	Area (thousands of km^2)	Population (millions)
Senegal	197	8.2
Gambia	11	1.1
Guinea-Bissau	36	1.1
Guinea	246	6.4
Sierra Leone	72	4.6
Liberia	111	2.9
Côte d'Ivoire	322	13.9
Ghana	239	16.9
Togo	57	4.3
Benin	113	5.3

7. **Journal** In 1994, the mean attendance of the Colorado Silver Bullets baseball team's first 44 games was 6595 fans. There were 7462 fans at game 45, the final game. What was the mean attendance for all games? Describe how you solved this problem.

Test Prep

On a multiple choice test, you need to understand the question in order to choose the correct answer.

8. Given the data set 3, 14, 26, 30, 22, 78, 7, and 12, which of the following numbers would best represent the mean of this data?

    Ⓐ 24   Ⓑ 8   Ⓒ 40.5   Ⓓ 14

SECTION **1B**

Using Data to Answer Questions

▶ Social Studies Link ▶ Industry Link ▶ www.mathsurf.com/8/ch1/surveys

Who Asked You ANYWAY?

You are alone in the shopping mall, window-shopping, minding your own business. In the store window you see the reflection of a stranger approaching you with something in his hand. He taps you on the shoulder and you whirl around, your eyes resting on the object in his hand—a clipboard. The stranger is conducting a survey and wants to know what you think.

Your answers and the answers of others surveyed will become data and decisions will be made based on that data. Who makes those decisions and what do they want to know?

One kind of survey is called a product test in which you try a new product and report what you think of it. A taste test is one kind of product test in which you sample different foods and give your reactions. Sometimes you may be paid to participate in a product test.

A good survey requires careful planning beforehand. Sometimes there are questions that research cannot answer, and in those cases, people conducting the survey must use their best judgment.

1 What difficulties might you encounter conducting a survey?

2 What else do you think a survey can be used for?

3 If the first 3 people surveyed like a new product, will most people buy it?

2 Integers

Entertainment Link
www.mathsurf.com/8/ch2/ent

Arts & Literature Link
www.mathsurf.com/8/ch2/art

Entertainment

The greatest loss of yardage in a football game in a single play occurred during the 1929 Rose Bowl. Roy Riegels recovered a fumble and galloped 65 yards in the wrong direction (−65 yards).

People of the World

The average American travels 7753 miles each year by vehicle, not counting trains and planes, more than any other people of the world.

Arts & Literature

In his novel *20,000 Leagues Under the Sea,* written in 1870, Jules Verne describes a ship that could travel great distances under water and stay submerged for long periods of time.

Science Link
www.mathsurf.com/8/ch2/science

Social Studies

The most expensive real estate in the world is found in Japan. A plot of land the size of a piece of notebook paper would cost about $12,000 in Tokyo's central business district, the Ginza.

KEY MATH IDEAS

Integers are whole numbers and their opposites.

The **absolute value** of a number is the distance it is from zero on a number line.

Integers can be added, subtracted, multiplied, and divided.

Integers can be plotted on a **coordinate grid**.

Scientific notation can be used to write very large and very small numbers.

Science

Death Valley, California, is the lowest point in the United States at 282 feet below sea level (-282) and has the highest recorded temperature in the United States at 134°F ($+134$).

CHAPTER PROJECT

Problem Solving
Understand
Plan
Solve
Look Back

In this project, you will create a time line with at least 20 events that have contributed to the development of mathematics throughout history. Use negative numbers to represent B.C. entries.

**Problem
Solving**

Understand
Plan
Solve
Look Back

Problem Solving Focus

Some of the following problems have unnecessary
information. For each problem, state any information
that you think is unnecessary. Do not solve the problems.

Finding Unnecessary Information

Real-life problem
solving often involves
lots of data. You
should understand
that some of the data
is needed to find the
answer but usually
not all of it. Identify-
ing the information
that will not help you
answer the question
is an important step
in finding a solution.

1 The longest suspension bridge
is Humber Bridge in Great
Britain. It is 4626 ft long.
The Verrazano-Narrows Bridge
in New York is 4260 ft long.
The Golden Gate Bridge in
San Francisco is 4200 ft
long. How much longer is the
Humber Bridge than the
Golden Gate Bridge?

2 In January 1989, the toll
on the Golden Gate Bridge
increased from $1 to $2. For
the first 6 months, you could
buy a book of 16 tickets for
$20. How much did each
ticket cost?

3 Since 1989 the toll on the
Golden Gate Bridge increased
from $2 to $3. To motivate
the use of car pools, there is
no toll if there are three or
more people in a car. How
much money can Pat save if
she commutes to work with
two other people?

4 The Lincoln Tunnel in New
York is about twice as long as
the Baytown Tunnel in Texas.
Together they are about
12,300 ft long. About how
long is each tunnel?

Money Makes the World Go Round

Can you imagine our world without money? How would you buy food, clothes, heat, air conditioning? Would there be movies, computers, schools? We use money to purchase things we cannot produce ourselves. Money was developed primarily for trade.

When we think of money, we generally think of coins and paper bills, but early forms of money were quite different. In China, around 3000 B.C., knives and rice were used. In Babylonia, around 2500 B.C., cattle were used. American Indian tribes, in the 1500s and 1600s, used beads and beaver furs.

Paper money was used initially as IOUs or promissory notes. Merchants and goldsmiths would issue the notes. Today, throughout the world, only governments can issue money.

Until the mid 1900s, United States paper money included the words Silver Certificate at the top. This indicated that the bill could be redeemed for silver from the U.S. Treasury. The words Federal Reserve Note have since replaced Silver Certificate on these notes.

1 Give an example of how goods and services could be "priced" if money did not exist.

2 Why might it be troublesome if we also used a 15¢ coin and a 35¢ coin?

3 Would you rather have ten $100 bills or 100,000 pennies? Why?

Integers and Absolute Value

You'll Learn ...

■ to compare and order integers

■ to find the absolute value of integers

... How It's Used

Bank loan officers must compare figures such as income, expenses, profits, and losses to determine whether to approve a loan.

Vocabulary

opposite

integers

positive numbers

negative numbers

absolute value

▶ **Lesson Link** | In Chapter 1, you worked with data in the form of whole numbers, decimals, fractions, and percents. In this chapter you will work with positive and negative numbers. ◀

A number line can be used to display different types of numbers.

Zero is neither positive nor negative.

4 (or +4) is 4 units to the *right* of 0

4 is a positive number

−4 is 4 units to the *left* of 0

−4 is a **negative** number, read as "negative four"

−4 and 4 are opposites

Negative numbers   Positive numbers

$$\xleftarrow{\quad} \; {-4} \;\; {-3} \;\; {-2} \;\; {-1} \;\; 0 \;\; 1 \;\; 2 \;\; 3 \;\; 4 \; \xrightarrow{\quad}$$

Two numbers are **opposites** of one another if they are on opposite sides of zero and the same distance from zero. The opposite of zero is zero.

Explore   Integers

Money Matters

Situations involving money are shown below.

1. For each of the situations, write an opposite event or action.

2. For each pair of opposites that you have noted, which event or action would you assign a negative number to? Why?

3. Name some events or actions that do not involve money that are opposites.

a. Profit of $10

b. Price increased by $4.50

c. Lost $6

d. Stock went up $\frac{1}{8}$ point

e. Markup of $30

f. Earned $0

g. Cut in pay of $25

h. Added $5 to savings

i. Saved $20

Learn | Integers and Absolute Value

Integers are whole numbers and their opposites. This is how we can write the set of all integers:

$$\{\ldots, -5, -4, -3, -2, -1, 0, 1, 2, 3, 4, 5, \ldots\}$$

Positive numbers are numbers greater than zero. **Negative numbers** are numbers less than zero.

Often you have to compare numbers involving integers—temperatures, heights and depths, withdrawals and deposits. Number lines can help you understand how to compare integers.

Integers are greater as you move from left to right on a horizontal number line.

$$\overset{\longleftarrow\!|\!+\!|\!+\!|\!+\!|\!+\!|\!+\!|\!+\!|\!+\!|\!+\!|\!+\!|\!+\!|\!+\!|\!+\!|\!+\!|\!+\!|\!+\!|\!+\!|\!+\!|\!+\!|\!+\!\longrightarrow}{\scriptstyle -10\,-9\,-8\,-7\,-6\,-5\,-4\,-3\,-2\,-1\ \ 0\ \ 1\ \ 2\ \ 3\ \ 4\ \ 5\ \ 6\ \ 7\ \ 8\ \ 9\ \ 10}$$

Integers are greater as you move up on a vertical number line.

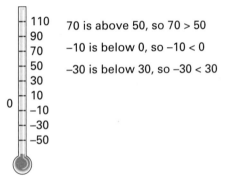

70 is above 50, so 70 > 50

−10 is below 0, so −10 < 0

−30 is below 30, so −30 < 30

Example 1

Which number is greater? Use the number line above to compare.

a. −6 or 4   **b.** −4 or −2

−6 is to the left of 4, so 4 is greater. −2 is to the right of −4, so −2 is greater.

Try It

Which number is greater?

a. −6 or 3   **b.** −$3 or −$9   **c.** 0 or −7

> ▶ **Technology Link**
>
> On many calculators, to enter a negative number you must use the ⊞/⊟ key. To enter −5, press 5 ⊞/⊟.

Sometimes it is more important to know a number's size without its sign.

The **absolute value** of a number is the distance it is from zero. The symbol for absolute value is | |.

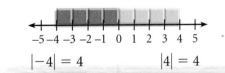

$|-4| = 4$ $|4| = 4$

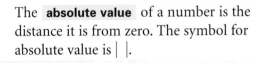

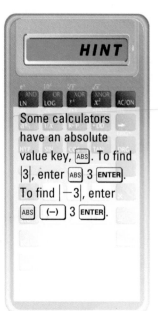

HINT

Some calculators have an absolute value key, [ABS]. To find |3|, enter [ABS] 3 [ENTER]. To find |−3|, enter [ABS] [(−)] 3 [ENTER].

▶ Language Link

The word *currency* comes from the adjective *current,* which means "running or flowing." Currency still flows continually from hand to hand, but now most transactions are electronic— flowing through computer circuits!

Example 2

Which two numbers have an absolute value of 3?

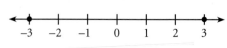

Both 3 and −3 are 3 units from zero, so $|3| = 3$ and $|−3| = 3$.

Try It

What two numbers have an absolute value of 17?

Example 3

Countries' currencies are always fluctuating in relation to each other. The table shows the change in value of $100 in world currencies from 1982 to 1986 with respect to the U. S. dollar. Which two currencies showed the greatest change?

Belgium	3
Canada	−11
Denmark	3
France	−5
West Germany	12
Italy	−9
Japan	48
Netherlands	9
Norway	−13
Sweden	−12
United Kingdom	−16

The number with the largest absolute value is 48, so Japan's currency showed the greatest change.

The number with the next largest absolute value is −16, so the United Kingdom's currency showed the next greatest change.

Try It

Which three countries' currencies showed the least amount of change?

Check | Your Understanding

1. Does every integer have an opposite? Explain.

2. Do you think that a decimal number such as 5.4 has an opposite? Explain.

3. When is the absolute value of a number the number itself?

2-1 Exercises and Applications

Practice and Apply

1. **Getting Started** Follow the steps below to order the following numbers from least to greatest: 2, −4, 0, −1, 3

   a. Draw a number line and graph each number.

   b. Find the number that is graphed farthest to the left. This is the smallest number.

   c. As you move to the right on the number line, the numbers are greater. Put the numbers in order.

Number Sense Name the opposite of each number.

2. 6   **3.** −42   **4.** −111   **5.** 0   **6.** 12

Describe a situation that could be represented by each integer.

7. −25°F   **8.** −10 seconds   **9.** −$60   **10.** 5   **11.** −75

12. What integer is described by the following? The absolute value is 5 and the number is to the left of 0 on a number line.

13. **Test Prep** Which number is an integer?

Ⓐ $-\frac{1}{2}$ Ⓑ 6.2   Ⓒ 0.3   Ⓓ 5

Use >, <, or = to compare each set of numbers.

14. −6 _____ −8   **15.** |$10| _____ |−$10| **16.** −2 _____ 0   **17.** −25°F _____ −10°F

18. −75 _____ −|75| **19.** 8 _____ −14   **20.** −|−3| _____ 0   **21.** −85 _____ −86

Find each absolute value.

22. |218| **23.** |−18| **24.** |0| **25.** |7 − 5|

26. **Science** Temperatures in Verkhoyansk, Russia, have been as low as −90°F and as high as 98°F. Name a temperature lower than −90°F.

27. **Geography** Altitudes can be expressed as integers. For example, the altitude of Mt. Kilimanjaro in Tanzania, Africa, is 19,340 ft. The lowest point of the Dead Sea in Israel is −1312 ft, which means that it is 1312 ft below sea level. Which of these has the greatest absolute value?

28. Consumer This spreadsheet shows income versus expenses for 6 months. Note that expenses appear as negative numbers.

	A	B	C	D	E	F	G
1	Month	Jan.	Feb.	Mar.	Apr.	May	June
2	Income	$4,250	$8,645	$2,398	$4,589	$1,444	$1,624
3	Expenses	−$3,666	−$4,445	−$2,456	−$4,600	−$1,400	−$2,045
4	Profit	$584	$4,200	−$58	−$11	$44	−$421

a. In which months was income greater than expenses? (Hint: Use absolute value.)

b. For which 3 months were profits furthest from 0?

Problem Solving and Reasoning

29. Critical Thinking Suppose you have five positive integers and two negative integers. The mean is:

Ⓐ Negative   Ⓑ Positive   Ⓒ Not enough information

30. **Journal** Is there a greatest negative integer? Can you name it? Is there a smallest positive integer? Explain your answers.

31. Communicate A dollar today doesn't buy as much as it did a few years ago. If the photo accurately represents the value of the dollar, what negative quantity could be associated with the missing portion? Why?

Mixed Review

Identify each sampling as random or nonrandom. *[Lesson 1-5]*

32. For the population of Jonesville residents: A pollster knocks on the doors of all homes on Orchard Avenue.

33. For the population of Watson High School students: A card is made with each student's name, and 40 cards are chosen from a drum.

Construct a corresponding histogram for each stem-and-leaf diagram. *[Lesson 1-6]*

34.

Stem	Leaf
2	46778
3	002235556778
4	011222578
5	25

35.

Stem	Leaf
8	346689
9	012334668
10	24467
11	057

Addition of Integers

▶ Lesson Link In Lesson 2-1, you learned to compare and order integers. In this lesson, you will add integers. Algebra tiles can be used to model integers. Yellow tiles model positive numbers and red tiles model negative numbers. ◀

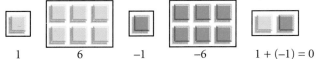

| 1 | 6 | −1 | −6 | 1 + (−1) = 0 |

These tiles form a *zero pair*.

The opposite of a number is called its **additive inverse** .

THE ZERO PROPERTY OF ADDITION

The sum of an integer and its additive inverse is 0.

$a + (-a) = 0$ and $-a + a = 0$

$6 + (-6) = 0$ and $-6 + 6 = 0$

Explore   Adding Integers

Opposites Attract

Materials: Algebra unit tiles
cup

To model addition of integers with algebra tiles, think of addition as putting tiles into a cup.

1. Start with 3 yellow tiles in the cup. Add 4 more yellow tiles. What is the sum? Try other combinations of positive tiles. What is the sign of the sum of two positive numbers?

2. Experiment with the red or negative tiles. Start with 3 red tiles in the cup. Add 4 more red tiles. What is the sum? Try other combinations of red tiles. What is the sign of the sum of two negative numbers?

3. Use both positive and negative tiles. Model the following using the tiles. (Don't forget to remove zero pairs.) What is the sign of your answer in each case?

   a. −5 + 2   **b.** 5 + (−2)   **c.** 2 + (−5)   **d.** −2 + 5

4. Try more examples of adding positive and negative numbers. Make a guess about the sign of the sum of any positive and negative number.

You'll Learn ...

■ to add integers

... How It's Used

Professional golfers must know how to add integers when keeping score.

Vocabulary

additive inverse

commutative property

associative property

In Lesson 2-1, a number line was used to help you understand absolute value and compare and order integers. A number line is also useful when adding.

Example 1

Add.

a. $10 + (-4)$

b. $-3 + 5$

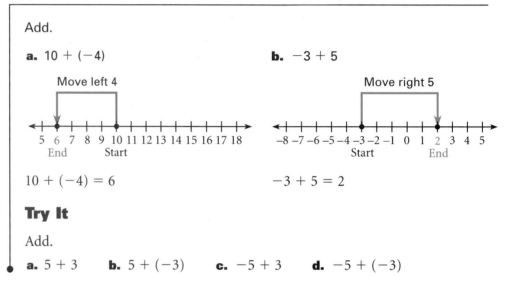

$10 + (-4) = 6$

$-3 + 5 = 2$

Try It

Add.

a. $5 + 3$ **b.** $5 + (-3)$ **c.** $-5 + 3$ **d.** $-5 + (-3)$

You can use absolute value to help you add.

ADDING INTEGERS WITH THE SAME SIGN

- Add the absolute value of the two numbers.
- Use the sign of the numbers.

ADDING INTEGERS WITH DIFFERENT SIGNS

- Subtract the number with the smaller absolute value from the number with the larger absolute value.
- Take the sign of the number with the larger absolute value.

DID YOU KNOW?

In 1775, there were extreme shortages of coins in the British North American colonies, so many other items were declared legal tender.

Example 2

Jolice had a beginning balance of $125.25. Use a calculator to find her ending balance based on the following deposits and withdrawals: $22.50, −$4.50, $5.00, −$10.00.

Enter 125.25 [+] 22.50 [+] 4.50 [+/−] [+] 5.00 [+] 10.00 [+/−] [=] *138.25*.
Her ending balance was $138.25.

When you added whole numbers, you learned the following properties. These properties hold true for integers.

COMMUTATIVE PROPERTY
$a + b = b + a$

ASSOCIATIVE PROPERTY
$(a + b) + c = a + (b + c)$

Example 3

Atoms contain charged particles called protons and electrons. Each proton has a charge of $+1$, each electron has a charge of -1. A sulfur ion has 16 protons and 18 electrons. Represent the net charge using integers.

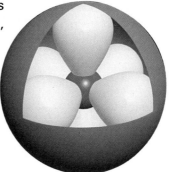

▶ **Chemistry Link**

When an atom has the same number of protons and electrons, it has no charge and is said to be *neutral*.

The charge of the protons can be represented as $+16$ and the charge of the electrons can be represented as -18.

The net charge is found by adding $16 + (-18)$.

$16 + (-18) = -2$.

The net charge of the sulfur ion is -2.

Example 4

Find the sum of $7 + 3 + (-5) + (-7)$.

$7 + 3 + (-5) + (-7)$

$= 7 + (-7) + 3 + (-5)$ Use the commutative property to rewrite the problem.

$= 0 + 3 + (-5)$ 7 and -7 are additive inverses.

$= -2$

Try It

Add.

a. $17 + (-6)$ **b.** $(-9) + -22 + 9$

Check | Your Understanding

1. Does every integer have an additive inverse?

2. When is the sum of two integers with different signs negative?

3. Can the sum of two negative numbers ever be positive? Explain.

2-2 Exercises and Applications

Practice and Apply

1. **Getting Started** Add by using the commutative and associative properties: $-2 + (-4) + 2 + (-3) + 5$.

    a. Group integers that are additive inverses.

    b. Group integers that have the same sign.

    c. Add the numbers in parentheses.

    d. Add the remaining numbers.

Write the addition problem for each model.

2.

3.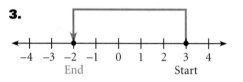

Add.

4. $34 + 28$

5. $-34 + (-28)$

6. $34 + (-28)$

7. $-34 + 28$

8. $95 + 47$

9. $-95 + (-47)$

10. $95 + (-47)$

11. $-95 + 47$

12. $-8 + 8 + (-8)$

13. $-24 + (-100) + (-1)$

14. $-75 + 85 + (-25)$

15. **Test Prep** At 7:00 A.M. the temperature in Paradise, Michigan, was $-7°F$. By noon a front had moved through and the temperature went up 10°F. What is the temperature at noon?

    Ⓐ 3°F   Ⓑ 17°F   Ⓒ $-3°F$ Ⓓ $-17°F$

16. Lee, David, and Bridgit often play miniature golf. Par is the number of strokes it should take you to complete each hole. 4 over par (+4) means it took 4 more strokes. 1 under par (−1) means it took 1 fewer stroke.

    a. Bridgit was 3 under par for the first hole and 1 over par for the second hole. David had scores of −2 and +2 for the first two holes, and Lee had scores of +3 and par. Compare each of their scores to par for the first two holes.

    b. The person with the lowest total is winning after two holes. Who is winning?

Number Sense Decide whether the sum is always, sometimes, or never positive.

17. Two negative numbers **18.** Three positive, one negative number

19. Two positive numbers **20.** Two positive, two negative numbers

21. History In the 1800s, money could not be transferred electronically. Gold bars had to be traded and transported. The North Hope Bank had owed Cheyenne Security Bank 412 gold bars. North Hope sent 85 bars on a stagecoach to Cheyenne Security. Use addition to show how much North Hope still owes.

22. Science The Kelvin temperature scale is sometimes used in science. The formula $K = 273 + C$ relates degrees Kelvin (K) to degrees Celsius (C). Find the Kelvin temperature for each of the following.

  a. $-25°C$ **b.** $0°C$ **c.** $25°C$ **d.** $-32°C$

Problem Solving and Reasoning

23. Journal Explain to a classmate how you can tell, before actually calculating, whether the sum of two integers is positive or negative.

24. Critical Thinking The sum of two integers is -6. One integer is 10 more than the other. What are the integers?

25. Communicate An elevator on the tenth floor goes down 9 floors. Then it goes up 19 floors, down 3, and finally up 12. What floor does it end up on? Explain how you arrived at your answer.

Mixed Review

Make a scatterplot for each data set. Decide whether there is an increasing trend, a decreasing trend, or no trend at all. *[Lesson 1-7]*

26. $(3, 7), (8, 2), (5, 6), (8, 1), (9, 1), (2, 8), (4, 7), (6, 4), (5, 5)$

27. $(1, 6), (5, 6), (7, 4), (6, 5), (2, 5), (4, 5), (9, 6), (8, 5), (3, 4)$

What population would it make most sense to survey for each product?
[Lesson 1-8]

28. Home stereo equipment **29.** Fingernail polish

30. Computer disk drives **31.** Home air-conditioning equipment

In the National Hockey League, players have plus/minus ratings. When a goal is scored, each player on the ice for the goal-scoring team receives +1, and each player on the opposing team receives −1. These points are added through the season.

Example 3

Before the All-Star break, Henri had a plus/minus rating of −18. By the end of the year, his plus/minus rating was 14. What was his plus/minus rating after the All-Star break?

His rating at the end of the year minus his rating before the All-Star break:

$$14 - (-18)$$

His rating after the All-Star break was 32.

Try It

a. Sergei's plus/minus rating was 7 in the first half of the season, but −24 by the end of the season. What was his plus/minus rating in the second half of the season?

b. Early in the fall, the water level in a reservoir was −14 ft with respect to sea level. After the winter rains, the level was 11 ft. How many feet did the water level rise or fall?

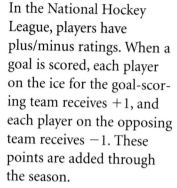

MENTAL MATH

When you subtract a negative number, think of clicking a light switch once to subtract, and again for the minus sign. Two clicks turn the light back **on**, so "minus a minus" is a **plus**.

Check Your Understanding

1. Describe what happens when you subtract the opposite of a number from itself. Use an example in your explanation.

2. Your friend says, "This is great. I don't ever have to subtract again!" Explain what she means.

3. Is the additive inverse used in the subtraction of integers? If so, how and when?

4. If you change a subtraction problem to an addition problem by adding the opposite, will the commutative property hold true? Explain.

Practice and Apply

1. **Getting Started** Write each subtraction as an addition.

   a. $4 - 2 = 4 +$ _____   **b.** $-8 - (-9) = -8 +$ _____   **c.** $-5 - 10 = -5 +$ _____

2. Use your calculator to add or subtract.

   a. $125 - (-40)$ **b.** $125 + 40$ **c.** $-545 + 365$

   d. $-545 - (-365)$ **e.** $-428 + (-467)$ **f.** $-428 - 467$

   g. What do you notice about each pair of problems? Why is this true?

3. **Number Sense** Write each problem as an addition problem. Compute the answer.

   a. $12 - 24$ **b.** $-24 - 12$ **c.** $24 - (-12)$ **d.** $-12 - (-24)$

Add or subtract.

4. $12 - 13$ 5. $-87 + (-61)$ 6. $5 - (-1)$

7. $-55 - 55$ 8. $-1 - 8$ 9. $-18 + 987 - 2$

10. $50 - 80 - (-50)$ 11. $0 - 2$ 12. $101 + 4 - (-5)$

13. $-22 + (-22) - 4$ 14. $7 - 17 - 10$ 15. $400 + 23 + (-3)$

16. **Measurement** A fish finder helps locate fish in deep waters. Your line is at 90 feet, but the finder shows that the fish are 30 feet deeper. Do you let the line out 30 feet? 120 feet? Do you reel it in 30 feet? 60 feet? Explain.

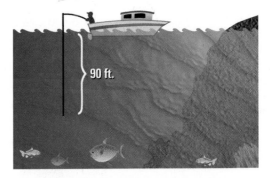

90 ft.

17. **Consumer** Last week, Maria saw a dress priced at $53. The sign in the window said there was $5 off any purchase in the store. She decided to wait for a sale. This week, the dress was priced at $49 but there was no discount. She bought the dress. Should she have waited? Explain.

18. **Social Studies** The national debt, which is in the trillions of dollars, increases by about $650 million a day. It will soon reach $6 trillion. Approximately how much will the debt be one day later?

PRACTICE 2-3

19. Science The planet Venus reaches a temperature of 864°F at the surface, whereas Mercury's temperature may drop to −301°F. What is the difference between the temperatures of the two planets?

20.  Explain how it is possible to subtract a number from 100 and get a result that is greater than 100.

Mercury   Venus

21. **Test Prep** The temperature in Juneau, Alaska, was −10°F. It was predicted to drop 5 degrees. What temperature will it be then?

Ⓐ −5°F   Ⓑ 5°F

Ⓒ 15°F   Ⓓ −15°F

Problem Solving and Reasoning

22. Critical Thinking Find two integers whose difference is −18 and whose sum is 2.

23. Communicate Explain how to fill in the blanks with <, >, or = without actually doing the computations.

a. 28 − (−5) _____ 28 + (−5)   **b.** 35 − 5 _____ 35 − (−5)

24. Critical Thinking The balance on a credit card is calculated monthly.

a. Does a positive balance mean that you owe the company money or that the company owes you money?

b. Does a negative balance mean that you owe the company money or the company owes you money? How might you get a negative balance?

c. Your balance in May was $89.50. In June, $150.25 was charged and a payment of $75.00 was made. What is your June balance?

Mixed Review

Make a stem-and-leaf diagram for each set of data. *[Lesson 1-1]*

25. 32, 41, 53, 42, 46, 58, 34, 38, 42   **26.** 64, 73, 81, 92, 76, 93, 71, 74

Sketch a line graph to represent each set of data. *[Lesson 1-4]*

27.

Year	1990	1991	1992	1993	1994
Profit	483	521	693	875	798

28.

Year	1940	1950	1960	1970	1980
Number	30	42	23	37	32

PROBLEM SOLVING 2-3

Multiplication and Division of Integers

▶ **Lesson Link**   In the last two lessons, you added and subtracted integers. In this lesson, you will learn to multiply and divide integers. ◀

Explore   Multiplying Integers

Product Patterns

Materials: Algebra unit tiles

When modeling multiplication of integers, think of placing (positive) or removing (negative) sets of yellow (positive) or red (negative) tiles.

1. Place 2 sets of 3 red tiles on your layout. How many tiles are there? What is the sign of the product of a positive number and a negative number?

2. Add 2 sets of 3 yellow tiles to the layout to make "zero." Then *remove* 2 sets of 3 red tiles from the layout. How many tiles are left? What product is modeled? What is the sign of the product of two negative numbers?

3. Model each of the following using the tiles.

  a. -3×4 **b.** 3×4 **c.** -3×-4 **d.** 3×-4

You'll Learn ...

■ to multiply and divide integers

... How It's Used

Chemists must calculate with integers to determine whether a reaction will occur when solutions are mixed.

Vocabulary

multiplicative inverse

reciprocal

Learn   Multiplication and Division of Integers

Patterns can often help you discover rules for mathematical computations.

The following patterns suggest rules for multiplying integers.

$3 \times 2 = 6$

$3 \times 1 = 3$

$3 \times 0 = 0$

$3 \times -1 = -3$

$3 \times -2 = -6$

Because of the commutative property, 3×-3 is the same as -3×3.

$-3 \times 2 = -6$

$-3 \times 1 = -3$

$-3 \times 0 = 0$

$-3 \times -1 = 3$

$-3 \times -2 = 6$

The product of two numbers with the **same sign** is **positive**.

$$(+)(+) = (+) \qquad (-)(-) = (+)$$

The product of two numbers with **different signs** is **negative**.

$$(+)(-) = (-) \qquad (-)(+) = (-)$$

Example 1

Earl has a bank account that is charged a $5 service fee for each month that the balance is below $500. Earl's balance was less than $500, and he forgot about the account for 4 months. What has been the overall change in the account balance?

For each of the 4 months, the change in the balance has been −$5. $4 \times -5 = -\$20$. The change in the balance has been −$20.

Try It

ATM withdrawal charges appear as −$1.25 on Amy's bank statement. She made 8 ATM withdrawals. What is the total of the 8 charges?

The associative and commutative properties can help you complete multiplication problems with more than two integers.

MENTAL MATH

Always look to find compatible numbers—numbers that are easy to operate with mentally.

Example 2

Multiply: $-4 \cdot -3 \cdot -25$

Rewrite using the commutative property.

$(-4 \cdot -25) -3$

$= 100 \cdot -3 \qquad (-)(-) = (+)$

$= -300 \qquad (+)(-) = (-)$

If the product of two numbers is 1, each of the numbers is the **multiplicative inverse**, or **reciprocal**, of the other.

THE INVERSE PROPERTY OF MULTIPLICATION

The product of a number and its multiplicative inverse is 1.

$$\frac{a}{b} \cdot \frac{b}{a} = 1$$

Example 3

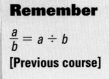

What is the multiplicative inverse of each number?

a. -3 **b.** $\frac{6}{5}$ **c.** $\frac{-4}{7}$

$\frac{1}{-3}$ $\frac{5}{6}$ $\frac{7}{-4}$

Try It

What is the multiplicative inverse of each number?

a. -8 **b.** $\frac{2}{5}$ **c.** $\frac{-8}{3}$

Division and multiplication are inverse operations. $30 \div -6 = -5$ because $-5 \cdot -6 = 30$. $-30 \div -6 = 5$ because $5 \cdot -6 = -30$. Dividing by a number is the same as multiplying by its multiplicative inverse.

$30 \div 6$ is the same as $30\left(\frac{1}{6}\right)$. $\qquad 30 \div (-6)$ is the same as $30\left(\frac{1}{-6}\right)$.

The quotient of two integers is positive if the two integers have the same sign:	$(+) \div (+) = (+)$ $(-) \div (-) = (+)$
The quotient of two integers is negative if the two integers have different signs:	$(+) \div (-) = (-)$ $(-) \div (+) = (-)$

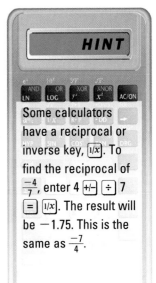

HINT

Some calculators have a reciprocal or inverse key, $\boxed{1/x}$. To find the reciprocal of $\frac{-4}{7}$, enter 4 $\boxed{+/-}$ $\boxed{\div}$ 7 $\boxed{=}$ $\boxed{1/x}$. The result will be -1.75. This is the same as $\frac{-7}{4}$.

Example 4

Yael lost $1200 on 400 shares of stock. How much did each share of stock change in value?

Since $1200 is a loss, the change per share can be written as $-1200 \div 400$. Since $1200 \div 400 = 3$, and a negative number divided by a positive number is negative, the change in value for each share was $-$3$.

Check | Your Understanding

1. Explain whether the following statement is true: $\frac{-3}{-4} = \frac{3}{4}$.

2. Suppose you have a product of four numbers. In all, three are positive and one is negative. What is the sign of the product?

Practice and Apply

1. **Getting Started** Find the product of 13×-6.
   a. Multiply 13×6.
   b. Use the rules for multiplying integers, $(+) \times (-) = (-)$.

Multiply or divide.

2. $6 \cdot 8$
3. $-6 \cdot -8$
4. $-6 \cdot 8$
5. $6 \cdot -8$

6. $(-3)(-5)$
7. $24 \div -2$
8. $-24 \div -2$
9. $-24 \div 2$

10. $24 \div 2$
11. $-2(7)$
12. $\dfrac{-45}{9}$
13. $\dfrac{-46}{-23}$

14. $\dfrac{24}{-8}$
15. $\dfrac{0}{-9}$
16. $\dfrac{45}{5}$
17. $-7 \cdot 20$

18. $-6 \cdot 9 \cdot -5$
19. $-4 \cdot -85 \cdot 0$
20. $-1 \cdot -1 \cdot -1$
21. $3 \times -6 \div 2$

22. $-56 \div 7 \div -4$
23. $0 \div -11 \div -1$
24. $-9 \cdot -5 \div -15$

Number Sense Evaluate.

25. $\left| 2 \times (-7) \right|$
26. $\left| 15 \div (-3) \right|$
27. $\left| -4 \right| \times \left| -7 \right|$
28. $\left| -36 \right| \div \left| -4 \right|$

29. **Test Prep** Marta withdrew $8 a week for 6 weeks from her bank account. Which of the following shows how to find how much her balance changed?
    Ⓐ $-8 + 6$ Ⓑ $-8 - 6$ Ⓒ -8×6 Ⓓ $-8 \div 6$

30. **Measurement** Nancy's watch loses 8 minutes per day. How many minutes will her watch lose in 1 week?

31. Edwin invested in some pretty risky stock. After six months, he had lost $366. Approximately how much did he lose per month on this stock?

32. **Number Sense** Why is the mean of these numbers zero?
    $-1, -3, 3, 1, 2, -2$

33. Use your calculator to compute $-25 \times (-18) \div (-9) \times 48 \div (-24)$.

Santiago, Chile, Stock Exchange

34. Golf An eagle is 2 strokes under par. If you made eagles on 3 holes, how many strokes under par is this?

Problem Solving and Reasoning

35. Communicate Explain which properties could be used to rewrite the following expression so that it is easier to calculate: $4 \cdot -9 \cdot 25$

36. [Journal] How is multiplying integers like multiplying whole numbers? How is it different? How is dividing integers like dividing whole numbers? How is it different?

37. Critical Thinking The temperature has been falling an average of 4° per hour. If the temperature at 12:00 A.M. is 10°F, what do you predict it will be at 6:00 A.M.?

38. [Test Prep] Which multiplication(s) is/are matched with the correct division?

Ⓐ $-16 \times \frac{1}{4}$ and $-16 \div -4$ Ⓑ $-16 \times \frac{-1}{4}$ and $-16 \div 4$

Ⓒ -16×4 and $-16 \div \frac{1}{4}$ Ⓓ -16×-4 and $-16 \div \frac{-1}{4}$

39. Communicate Teo has added a long list of numbers. There are many more negative numbers than positive numbers, but the sum is positive.

a. Do you know whether the mean is positive or negative? Why?

b. Do you know whether the median is positive or negative? Why?

Mixed Review

Find the mean and median of each data set. *[Lesson 1-2]*

40. 18.3, 21.4, 19.3, 8.7, 21.3, 17.4   **41.** 32, 67, 41, 53, 62, 31

42. A stereo manufacturer company surveys customers who have bought its products in the past. How useful will the data be in determining what features need to be added to its products to increase sales? Explain your answer. *[Lesson 1-5]*

Project Progress

When you make your time line, be sure that you have enough room for your range of dates. Subtract the earliest date from the latest date to see how many years your time line will represent.

Problem Solving

Understand
Plan
Solve
Look Back

Evaluating Expressions Using Integers

You'll Learn ...

■ to evaluate expressions involving integers, and to use the distributive property

... How It's Used

Integer expressions are evaluated when college football teams compile game data.

Vocabulary

order of operations

distributive property

► **Lesson Link** | You have worked with expressions with one operation. In this lesson you will work with expressions that involve more than one operation. ◄

Explore | Expressions

Call Your Operator

Materials: Scientific calculator

1. Using the digits for the year (for example, 1998) and any of the operations of $+$, $-$, $\times$, $\div$, write as many expressions as you can. For example,

   $1 \times 9 \div 9 + 8 = 9$ as does $1 \div 9 \times 9 + 8$.

2. Compare your list with others in your group. Can you find expressions that have values equal to all of the numbers 0 to 10?

3. Enter $1 \cdot 9 + 9 \div 8$ into your calculator. What answer do you get? Explain what your calculator did.

4. Enter $(1 \cdot 9 + 9) \div 8$ into your calculator. Do you get the same answer as in Question 3? Explain what your calculator did.

5. Go back to your list of expressions using the digits from the date and $+$, $-$, $\times$, $\div$. Make a new list using the four operations and parentheses. Did you get other values for your expressions?

Learn | Evaluating Expressions Using Integers

When simplifying expressions involving more than one operation, such as $-2 + 3 \times 4$, mathematicians have agreed on an order in which to perform operations so the expression always has the same value. If we need to change the order of operations, grouping symbols such as parentheses and the division bar allow us to do this.

ORDER OF OPERATIONS

Do any operations inside grouping symbols.

Do all multiplications and divisions, from left to right.

Do all additions and subtractions, from left to right.

Example 1

▶ **Technology Link**

Use order of operations to evaluate $-2 + (6 + 4) \div (-2)$.

$-2 + (6 + 4) \div (-2)$

$= -2 + 10 \div (-2)$ Do any operations within the grouping symbols.

$= -2 + -5$ Do all divisions from left to right.

$= -7$ Do all additions from left to right.

Make up a simple example such as $1 + 2 \cdot 3$. If the calculator gives an answer of 7, it has an algebraic operating system. If it gives an answer of 9, it doesn't.

Try It

Use order of operations to evaluate $5 + -30 \div (-6)$.

The **distributive property**, a very important mathematical property, makes use of parentheses.

$2(4 + 5) = 2 \cdot 4 + 2 \cdot 5$

The parentheses show that both the 4 *and* the 5 are multiplied by 2.

THE DISTRIBUTIVE PROPERTY OF MULTIPLICATION OVER ADDITION

In words: Multiplying a sum by a number is the same as multiplying each addend by the number, then adding the products.

In symbols: $a(b + c) = ab + ac$.

Example 2

Test Prep

Use the distributive property to evaluate the expression $-2(-3 - 4)$.

$-2(-3 - 4) = -2(-3 + -4)$ Subtraction is the same as adding the opposite.

$= (-2 \cdot -3) + (-2 \cdot -4)$ Use the distributive property.

$= 6 + 8$ Perform all multiplications from left to right.

$= 14$ Perform additions from right to left.

Look for compatible numbers. To evaluate $7(3.1 + 2.9)$, it is quicker to add first. To evaluate $8(\frac{1}{8} + 1)$, it is quicker to multiply first.

Try It

Use the distributive property to evaluate.

a. $-6(-4 + 8)$ **b.** $-8(100 - 1)$

Use the spreadsheet below to find the total change in inventory value.

	A	B	C	D
1		**Change in**	**Value**	**Change**
2	**Caps**	**Inventory**	**of Each**	**in Value**
3	**Astros caps**	−12	$14	−$168
4	**Rangers caps**	17	$14	$238
5	**Total**	5	$14	

Ashley thinks ...

The value of the Astros caps went down, since −12(14) = −$168. The value of Rangers caps went up, since 17(14) = $238. Adding the values in column D, −168 + 238 = $70. The total change in inventory value is $70.

Seung thinks ...

The total change in cap inventory is −12 + 17, which is 5. The value of each cap is $14. Multiplying the numbers in row 5, the change in inventory value is 5(14) = $70.

What do you think?

If the value of a Rangers cap was $11, would both methods work?

Check Your Understanding

1. Both Juanita and Julio worked the problem 2 + 3 · 4. Juanita got 20 and Julio got 14. Who is correct and why did they get different answers?

2. Is there a distributive property of multiplication over subtraction? Over multiplication? Over division? Explain using examples.

3. Show how the distributive property can help you find the product of 80 and 99 using mental math.

Practice and Apply

1. **Getting Started** Name the operation that should be done first in each expression.

   a. $21 - 2 \times 6$ **b.** $-15(80 + 30)$ **c.** $48 \div 3 \cdot 2$ **d.** $\dfrac{24 + 4}{-4}$

Evaluate each pair of expressions.

2. $15 - 5 + 9$
   $15 - (5 + 9)$

3. $27 - 15 \div 3$
   $27 - (15 \div 3)$

4. $-8 + 2(4 - 4)$
   $-8 + 2 \cdot 4 - 4$

5. $4(6 + -9)$
   $4 \cdot 6 + 4 \cdot (-9)$

6. $-2(4 - 5)$
   $-2 \cdot 4 + (-2) \cdot (-5)$

7. $18 \div -6 \cdot 3$
   $18 \div (-6 \cdot 3)$

8. Use the distributive property to write $5(-2 + 6)$ without parentheses.

Evaluate each expression two different ways.

9. $5(8 + 10)$ 10. $8\left(9 + \dfrac{1}{2}\right)$ 11. $-3(30 - 3)$ 12. $(100 - 2)8$

13. **Consumer** Sara has been saving her money to buy some video games. She has saved $39.24 so far, but she owes each of her twin brothers $5.65. If Sara gets her allowance of $8.50 and pays her brothers, how much money does she have?

Evaluate each expression.

14. $16 \div 4 \cdot (-2) + 6$ 15. $14 - (-8) + 6 \div (-3)$

16. $\dfrac{18 - 9}{9} + (-3)$ 17. $\dfrac{-3(9 + 2)}{-11} + (-2)$

18. **Test Prep** Which is *not* the use of the distributive property for $a(b + c)$?

   Ⓐ $ab - ac$ Ⓑ $ab + ac$ Ⓒ $a(b) + a(c)$ Ⓓ $(a)(b) + (a)(c)$

19. **Measurement** The temperatures for the past week were as follows: $-5°, -4°, -2°, 0°, 10°, 17°, -2°$. What was the mean temperature?

Operation Sense Copy each sentence below. Insert parentheses to make each sentence true.

20. $100 + 24 \div 3 + 1 = 31$ 21. $100 + 24 \div 3 + 1 = 106$

22. $-5 \times 3 + 3 \times 6 = -180$ 23. $-5 \times 3 + 3 \times 6 = -105$

24. Each week the student council has a popcorn and candy sale. The profits for the past month were: $25.00, −$7.25, $23.50, and $26.75.

a. Overall, how much did the student council make on its fund-raiser for the month?

b. If the money is to be divided equally between 3 different committees, how much does each committee get?

25. Science An inch of heavy, wet snow contains 0.2 inches of water, an inch of average snow contains 0.1 inches of water, and an inch of dry, powdery snow contains 0.06 inches of water. If 5 inches of each type of snow falls, how much water is contained in the snow?

Problem Solving and Reasoning

26. Choose a Strategy Carrie wants to bring snack food to the drama club meeting. She decides to buy 15 bagels at $0.50 each and 1 container of cream cheese for $1.50. How much will she spend?

27. Critical Thinking Using only the number 3, the operations $+$, $−$, $\times$, $\div$, and parentheses, write three different expressions that equal 1. You may use the number 3 more than once.

28. [Journal] Explain to a classmate how you would show that you want to add two numbers in an expression before you multiply.

29. Communicate Explain how you could use the distributive property to multiply each of the following mentally.

a. $36 \cdot 101$ **b.** $50 \cdot 99$ **c.** $49 \cdot 13$ **d.** $98 \cdot 42$

> **Problem Solving**
> ## STRATEGIES
> • Look for a Pattern
> • Make an Organized List
> • Make a Table
> • Guess and Check
> • Work Backward
> • Use Logical Reasoning
> • Draw a Diagram
> • Solve a Simpler Problem

Mixed Review

Sketch a box-and-whisker plot for each set of data. *[Lesson 1-3]*

30. 42, 51, 67, 83, 91, 51, 83, 72   **31.** 87, 93, 102, 93, 115, 84, 78, 91

Construct a frequency table for each histogram. *[Lesson 1-6]*

32.

Number (0–9 10–19 20–29 30–39 40–49 50–59 60–69) / Age

33.

Number (1–8 9–16 17–24 25–32 33–40) / Length (in.)

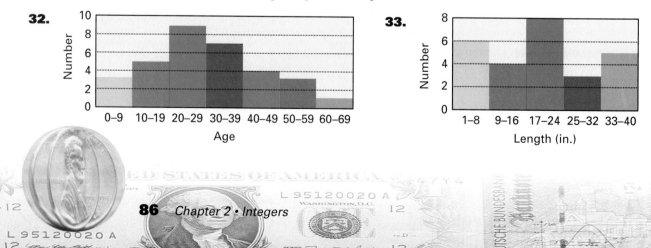

Section 2A Connect

You will now connect your knowledge of integers, order of operations, and the distributive property to solve problems about money.

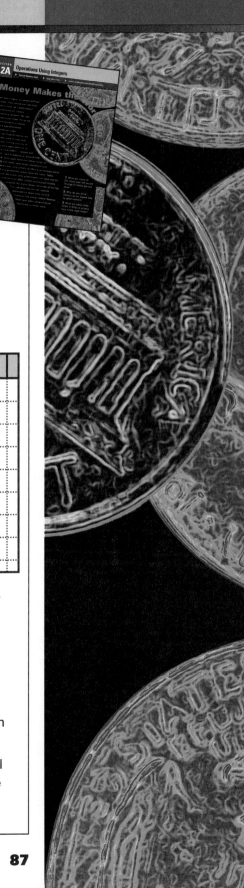

Money Makes the World Go Round

Jill, Jack, Jamie, and Jamal started a lawn-care business. They are a small company that specializes in a select number of tasks. The following spreadsheet lists each job, the charge per job, the expenses per job, the number of jobs done in the first month, and the total tips earned.

1. Copy the chart. Add a column F that shows the total amount made (or lost) on each type of job.

	A	B	C	D	E	
I	Specific Job	Charge	Expenses	Number	Total	
2		per Job	per Job	of Jobs	Tips	
3				Done	Earned	
4	Mow lawn	$10.00	$2.00	27	$67	
5	Edge	$5.00	$3.00	24	$70	
6	Weed gardens	$15.00	$1.00	45	$135	
7	Plant new gardens	$50.00	$10.00	12	$147	
8	Total Earnings					

2. How did you determine the amounts in column F? Write the expression you used.

3. Suppose the numbers in column C were negative? How would your expression change?

4. Find the total amount made (or lost) by the company. Enter this number in cell F 8.

5. If the partners divided the earnings evenly, how would you find each partner's earnings?

6. If the expenses for edging had been $8 per job, what would the total earnings for edging have been? Would it be a good idea to continue to offer this service? Explain your reasoning.

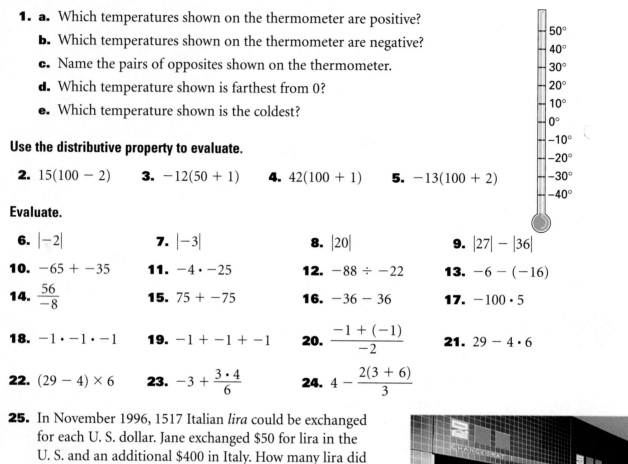

1. a. Which temperatures shown on the thermometer are positive?

   b. Which temperatures shown on the thermometer are negative?

   c. Name the pairs of opposites shown on the thermometer.

   d. Which temperature shown is farthest from 0?

   e. Which temperature shown is the coldest?

Use the distributive property to evaluate.

2. $15(100 - 2)$ **3.** $-12(50 + 1)$ **4.** $42(100 + 1)$ **5.** $-13(100 + 2)$

Evaluate.

6. $|-2|$ **7.** $|-3|$ **8.** $|20|$ **9.** $|27| - |36|$

10. $-65 + -35$ **11.** $-4 \cdot -25$ **12.** $-88 \div -22$ **13.** $-6 - (-16)$

14. $\dfrac{56}{-8}$ **15.** $75 + -75$ **16.** $-36 - 36$ **17.** $-100 \cdot 5$

18. $-1 \cdot -1 \cdot -1$ **19.** $-1 + -1 + -1$ **20.** $\dfrac{-1 + (-1)}{-2}$ **21.** $29 - 4 \cdot 6$

22. $(29 - 4) \times 6$ **23.** $-3 + \dfrac{3 \cdot 4}{6}$ **24.** $4 - \dfrac{2(3 + 6)}{3}$

25. In November 1996, 1517 Italian *lira* could be exchanged for each U. S. dollar. Jane exchanged $50 for lira in the U. S. and an additional $400 in Italy. How many lira did she receive?

26.  Why must there be rules for order of operations for calculations?

Test Prep

When comparing integers with the same sign, think of their placement on a number line. The one that is the farthest to the left is the smaller integer.

27. Which list is sorted from least to greatest?

   Ⓐ $-1, -5, -8, -10$ Ⓑ $-10, -5, -8, -1$ Ⓒ $-10, -8, -5, -1$ Ⓓ None of these

28. Name two situations that would use positive and negative numbers.

Our Planet
Diverse Earth

Have you ever considered how different and diverse the world is? The earth contains an estimated 30 million species of insects and 260,000 species of plants. Although the world population is approximately 5.7 billion, there is only one human species. Yet how different that species can be. Over 3000 different languages are spoken in 191 different countries and 44 dependencies. There are countries with populations in the hundreds of millions and some with populations in the hundreds.

Think of how different the weather is across the earth. Winters in some countries rarely get above freezing, while the temperature on some deserts can rise to 180°F. There are hurricanes with winds of up to 210 mi/hr, tornadoes with even stronger winds, earthquakes that do billions of dollars of damage, and volcanoes whose lava can be as hot as 2012°F. There are also beautiful calm days, perfect for swimming, fishing, hiking, or any of the other forms of exercise and recreation.

1 Name some features of the earth that use large and small numbers.

2 How can the termite population outweigh that of humans?

89

2-6 Integers in the Coordinate System

You'll Learn ...

■ to plot pairs of integers on a coordinate grid

... How It's Used

Cartographers use a coordinate system based on latitudes and longitudes.

Vocabulary

latitude

longitude

coordinate system

x-axis

y-axis

origin

quadrant

ordered pair

x-coordinate

y-coordinate

▶ **Lesson Link** In Chapter 1, you learned how to make a scatterplot by plotting points. In this lesson, you will extend your knowledge to plotting points that involve negative numbers. ◀

To locate places on the earth, we use a system of imaginary lines called **latitude** and **longitude** . The lines that run east and west give the location with reference to the equator. They name the latitude. The lines that run north and south give the location with reference to an imaginary line running through Greenwich, England. They name the longitude. Any point on Earth can be located by its latitude and longitude.

Explore | Coordinates

Finding Your Way

The following map shows the approximate latitudes and longitudes near where 0° latitude and 0° longitude intersect.

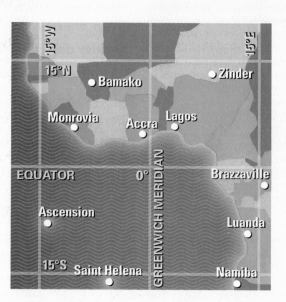

1. What are the approximate latitudes and longitudes of the following?

   a. Lagos   **b.** Namiba

   c. Ascension

2. The following are the approximate latitudes and longitudes of locations shown on the map. Name each location.

   a. Latitude of 13° N, longitude of 8° W

   b. Latitude of 4° S, longitude of 15° E

   c. Latitude of 16° S, longitude of 6° W

   d. Latitude of 14° N, longitude of 8° E

3. Explain how you found the places on the map.

Mapmakers use the system of latitude and longitude to show places on Earth. Mathematicians use a similar system of intersecting number lines to help locate points. Using these intersecting number lines, they create a *coordinate system.*

A **coordinate system** is formed by the intersection of a horizontal number line, the **x-axis**, and a vertical number line, the **y-axis**.

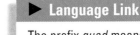

The lines intersect at the **origin**, $(0, 0)$.

The x-axis and the y-axis divide the coordinate grid into four **quadrants**. The axes are not in any quadrant.

Any point can be described by using an **ordered pair** (x, y).

The first coordinate, x, of an ordered pair (x, y), the **x-coordinate**, tells how far to move left or right from the origin along the x-axis.

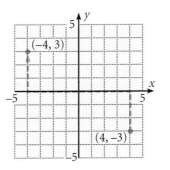

> ▶ **Language Link**
>
> The prefix *quad* means 4, as in quadrilateral (four sides), quadraphonic (4 channels), quadruplets (4 born at the same time), and quadruped (4-legged).

The second coordinate, y, of an ordered pair (x, y), the **y-coordinate**, tells how far to move down or up from the x-axis.

Point T is described by the ordered pair $(-2, -3)$.

Example 1

Plot the points $(-4, 3)$ and $(4, -3)$.

To plot the point $(-4, 3)$, start at the origin. Move 4 spaces to the *left* on the x-axis and 3 spaces *up* from the x-axis.

To plot the point $(4, -3)$, start at the origin. Move 4 spaces to the *right* on the x-axis and 3 spaces *down* from the x-axis.

Try It

Plot each point on a coordinate grid.

a. $(-1, -2)$ **b.** $(-5, 0)$ **c.** $(2, -3)$ **d.** $(-3, 2)$

▶ **Science Link**

A *tsunami,* or tidal wave, may only affect the height of the water by a few feet in the open sea, but the waves can swell up to 120 feet when they hit the shore!

Example 2

High and low tides are usually related to sea level. The points on the graph show the low and high tides, to the nearest foot, for several days. The *x*-coordinate represents low tide and the *y*-coordinate represents high tide. What are the coordinates of point *E*? Describe the low and high tides on that day.

To move from the origin, first move left 1 unit. Because we moved left, the *x*-coordinate is −1.

Then move up 2 units. Because we moved up, the *y*-coordinate is 2.

The point is (−1, 2). The low tide was −1 foot (1 foot below sea level), and the high tide was 2 feet above sea level.

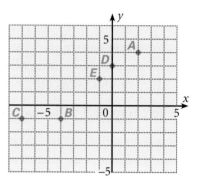

Try It

What are the coordinates of points *A*, *B*, *C*, and *D*? Describe the low and high tides on each day.

Notice the pattern in the signs of the *x*- and *y*-coordinates of all points in a quadrant. This can help you graph points or determine coordinates of an ordered pair on a graph.

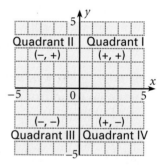

Check Your Understanding

1. Maps of the earth use a coordinate system of latitude and longitude. Does a globe use the same type of coordinate system? Explain.

2. How are the ordered pairs for points on an axis different from those in one of the four quadrants?

3. On a number line the origin is 0. Why is the origin (0, 0) on a coordinate grid?

Practice and Apply

1. **Getting Started** To plot the point $(-2, -4)$;

   a. The -2 tells you to move 2 spaces along the _____ axis.

   b. Should you move right or left? Why?

   c. The -4 tells you to move 4 spaces from the _____ axis.

   d. Should you move up or down? Why?

Plot each point on a coordinate grid.

2. $(5, -2)$ 3. $(-5, 0)$

4. $(-1, -2.5)$ 5. $(3.5, -2.5)$

Find the coordinates of each point.

6. A 7. B 8. C

9. D 10. E 11. F

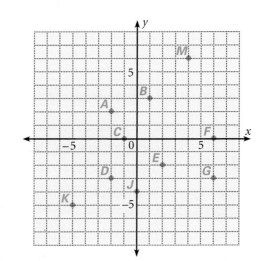

Name the points for each ordered pair.

12. $(4, 6)$ 13. $(6, -3)$

14. $(0, -4)$ 15. $(-5, -5)$

Geography Using the map, locate the approximate latitude and longitude coordinates of the following cities.

16. New York   17. São Paulo

18. Nairobi   19. Bombay

20. **Test Prep** Which city has latitude and longitude coordinates (26° N, 80° W)?

   Ⓐ Munich

   Ⓑ Chicago

   Ⓒ Buenos Aires

   Ⓓ Miami

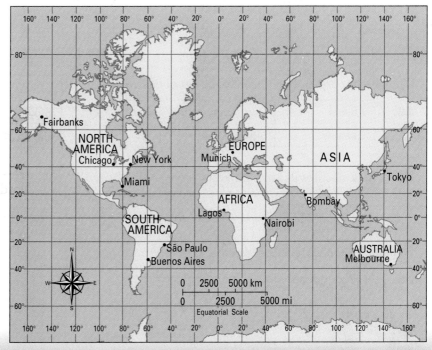

21. Geometry Graph a triangle with vertices $(4, 6)$, $(1, 2)$, and $(4, 0)$. Graph another triangle with vertices $(-4, -6)$, $(-1, -2)$ and $(-4, 0)$. How are the triangles related? How are the coordinates of their vertices related?

Geometry Name the ordered pairs for the vertices of each figure. Name each figure.

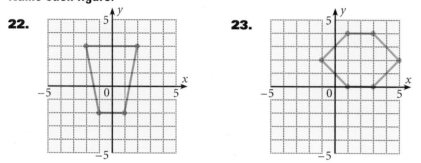

22.   **23.**

Problem Solving and Reasoning

24. Critical Thinking Part of the square is missing. Describe how to graph and connect the appropriate points to complete it.

25. Communicate Without graphing, tell in which quadrant each point lies. Explain your choices.

  a. $(-160, 80)$ **b.** $(22.5, 45)$

  c. $(-416, -400)$ **d.** $\left(2, \dfrac{-1}{2}\right)$

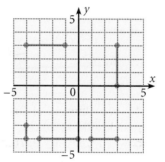

Mixed Review

Sketch a bar graph to represent each set of data. *[Lesson 1-4]*

26.

Animal	Cat	Dog	Bird	Rat	Fish
Quantity	12	18	7	3	10

27.

Student	Abe	Ben	Chao	Deb	Ella
Height (in.)	43	52	46	47	58

28. The stalactites in an underwater cave are measured as follows: 47 in., 8 in., 26 in., $11\frac{1}{2}$ in., $30\frac{3}{4}$ in. What is the range in the lengths of the stalactites? *[Lesson 1-1]*

Find each absolute value. *[Lesson 2-1]*

29. $|-317|$ **30.** $|0|$ **31.** $|7 + 15|$

              32. $|23 - 10|$

TECHNOLOGY

Using a Graphing Utility • Integers and Coordina..

Problem: In which quadrant is each of the following points located: $(-3, -2)$, $(-3, 2)$, $(3, -2)$, and $(3, 2)$?

A graphing calculator's point-on command will help you find the answers.

① Make sure your viewing window has a standard range.

② Starting from the home screen, access your calculator's point-on command.

③ Type in the x- and y-coordinates of the ordered pair $(-3, -2)$. Press "enter." Make note of where the point is plotted.

④ Type in the x- and y-coordinates of each of the other pairs, pressing "enter" each time. Be sure to start from the home screen each time. Make note of where each point is plotted after you press "enter."

Solution: $(-3, -2)$ is in the third quadrant; $(-3, 2)$, is in the second quadrant; $(3, -2)$, is in the fourth quadrant; $(3, 2)$ is in the first quadrant.

TRY IT

a. In which quadrant would $(-2, 3)$ be located?

b. In which quadrant would $(-4, -6)$ be located?

ON YOUR OWN

▶ Why does the viewing range have to be set properly when plotting points?

▶ How do you think the calculator plots points?

▶ If your calculator has a point-off command, what do you think it does?

Powers and Exponents

You'll Learn ...

■ to change numbers from standard notation to exponential notation, and vice versa

... How It's Used

Astronomers use exponential notation to represent great distances.

Vocabulary

exponent

power

▶ **Lesson Link** You have studied multiplication for many years. In this lesson, you will learn shortcuts for multiplying the same number over and over. ◀

Explore | Exponents

What Is Your Calculator Doing?

Materials: Scientific calculator

1. Find the x^2 key.

   a. Enter 4 and then press the x^2 key. What answer do you get? Enter 4 $\times$ 4 $=$. What answer do you get?

   b. Try a few more numbers. What does the x^2 do to any number that you enter?

2. Find the y^x key or the $\wedge$ key.

   a. Enter 4 y^x 3 $=$. What answer do you get? Enter 4 $\times$ 4 $\times$ 4 $=$. What answer do you get?

   b. Compare 2 y^x 4 and 2 $\times$ 2 $\times$ 2 $\times$ 2. Compare 3 $+/-$ y^x 4 and -3 $\times$ -3 $\times$ -3 $\times$ -3 $=$. What does the y^x do to the numbers that you enter?

   c. Enter 3 $+/-$ y^x 3 $=$. Enter 3 $+/-$ y^x 4 $=$. Enter 3 $+/-$ y^x 5 $=$. Enter 3 $+/-$ y^x 6 $=$. Describe any patterns you see with odd exponents and even exponents.

Learn | Powers and Exponents

Using an **exponent** is another way to show repeated multiplication.

Exponential Form	Expanded Form	Words	Value
base 3^5 exponent	$3 \times 3 \times 3 \times 3 \times 3$	Three to the fifth power	243

A **power** is a number that can be written as a product of equal factors.

32 is a power of 2.   32 is the fifth power of 2. $2^5 = 32$

Examples

1 The length of the Appalachian Trail is about 3^7 miles long.

Write 3^7 in standard form.

$3^7 = 3 \times 3 \times 3 \times 3 \times 3 \times 3 \times 3 = 2187$

The Appalachian Trail is about 2187 miles long.

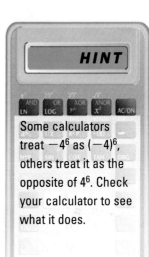

2 Use a calculator to evaluate $(-4)^6$ and -4^6.

$(-4)^6$ is $-4 \times -4 \times -4 \times -4 \times -4 \times -4$. Enter 4 [+/-] [yˣ] 6 [=] *4096*.

-4^6 is the opposite of $4 \times 4 \times 4 \times 4 \times 4 \times 4$. Enter 4 [yˣ] 6 [=] [+/-] *−4096*.

Try It

Evaluate.

a. 5^4 **b.** 15^5 **c.** $(-2)^3$

HINT

Some calculators treat -4^6 as $(-4)^6$, others treat it as the opposite of 4^6. Check your calculator to see what it does.

We can now expand our order of operations to include exponents.

ORDER OF OPERATIONS

Do operations within parentheses or grouping symbols.
Do all exponents from left to right.
Do all multiplications and divisions from left to right.
Do all additions and subtractions from left to right.

Example 3

Evaluate $-2(9 - 6)^2 + 15$.

$-2(9 - 6)^2 + 15$

$-2(3)^2 + 15$ Do operations within parentheses or grouping symbols.

$-2(9) + 15$ Do all exponents from left to right.

$-18 + 15$ Do all multiplications and divisions from left to right.

-3 Do all additions and subtractions from left to right.

Try It

Evaluate.

a. $12 \div 3 \cdot 5 - 4^2$ **b.** $4(1 + 5)^2 \div 8$

c. Most computer fonts have $2^8 - 1$ different characters. Write this number in standard form. How many different characters are there?

Randy and Tanisha played a game where they would receive points based on the number of letters in words they could create by picking alphabet cards one at a time. A one-letter word would be worth 10 points, a two-letter word worth 100 points, a three letter word 1000 points and so on. They wondered how many points would be earned if players could not create a word with the cards they had during their turn.

Tanisha thinks ...

I'll make a chart and follow the pattern. Each time the exponent decreases by 1, the number is divided by 10. Looking at this pattern, I can see that the player would receive one point.

10^4	10,000	10,000
10^3	1,000	10,000 ÷ 10
10^2	100	1,000 ÷ 10
10^1	10	100 ÷ 10
10^0	?	?

Randy thinks ...

I'll use my scientific calculator.

I'll enter 10 $\boxed{y^x}$ 0.

The answer is 1.

What do you think?

What do you think the value of 4^0 is?

▶ Technology Link

Try entering different numbers to the zero power into your calculator. What do you get in each case?

Check Your Understanding

1. If squaring a number always results in a positive number, explain why $-8^2 = -64$.

2. How is 3×6 different from 3^6?

3. Describe what happens when a nonzero number is raised to the zero power.

Practice and Apply

1. **Getting Started** Answer the questions to evaluate 8^4.
   a. What number is the base?
   b. What number is the exponent?
   c. How many times is 8 used as a factor?
   d. Multiply.

2. **Test Prep** What is the exponential form of $-2 \cdot -2 \cdot -2 \cdot -2$?
   Ⓐ -2^4 Ⓑ $(-2)^4$ Ⓒ 2^{-4} Ⓓ $(-2)^{-4}$

Geometry A shortcut to finding the area of a square rather than counting squares is to square the length of a side. Find each area.

3. 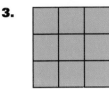   4. 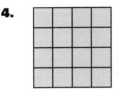   5. 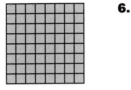   6.

Geometry A shortcut to finding the volume of a cube rather than counting cubes is to cube the length of a side. Find each volume.

7. 8. 9. 10.
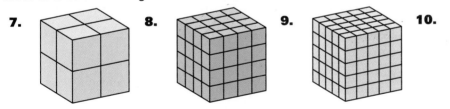

11. **Geography** As the earth rotates each day, a person at the equator moves a distance of $2^2 \cdot 3 \cdot 5^2 \cdot 83$ miles around the earth, but a person at the arctic circle moves $2^2 \cdot 5 \cdot 17 \cdot 29$ miles. What are these distances in standard form?

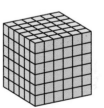

Evaluate.

12. 7^2 13. $(-7)^2$ 14. -7^2 15. 7^0

16. $(0)^4$ 17. $(-1)^3$ 18. $(-5)^0$ 19. $(-2)^4$

20. -10^0 21. 1^3 22. $2(4-2)^3 \div 8$ 23. $(7^2 + 11) - (5^2 + 35)$

24. $(2^4 + 3^2 + 7) \div 8$ 25. $\dfrac{8^2 - 6(4)}{-2}$

26. Patterns Fill in the chart. Describe any patterns that you see. Make a generalization if possible.

Number	Exponential Form	Number of Zeros in Number
1	10^0	0
10	10^1	1
100	10^2	?
1000	?	?
?	10^4	4

Problem Solving and Reasoning

27. Critical Thinking A square deck has an area of 121 square feet. What is the length of one side?

28. Choose a Strategy Each person has 2 parents. Each parent has 2 parents. Each grandparent has 2 parents. How many great-grandparents does a person have? Explain your answer.

Problem Solving STRATEGIES

- Look for a Pattern
- Make an Organized List
- Make a Table
- Guess and Check
- Work Backward
- Use Logical Reasoning
- Draw a Diagram
- Solve a Simpler Problem

Critical Thinking Find each missing number.

29. $?^2 = 64$ **30.** $?^3 = -27$ **31.** $4^? = 64$ **32.** $16 = ?^2$ or $?^4$

33. **Journal** Which do you think is greater, 2^6 or 6^2? Why? Use a calculator to see if your answer is correct.

Mixed Review

Identify each sampling as random or nonrandom. *[Lesson 1-5]*

34. From the population of Smith Junior High School students: Roberta asks the opinion of all the students in her social studies class.

35. From the population of voters in Orange County: Names are selected at random from the local telephone directory.

Add the following integers. *[Lesson 2-2]*

36. $43 + 52$ **37.** $-4 + 10$ **38.** $37 + (-26)$ **39.** $-31 + (-7)$

Scientific Notation Using Positive Exponents

Lesson Link In Lesson 2-7, you worked with exponents. In this lesson, you will use exponents to write large numbers in a different form. ◄

Powers of 10 are very important when using this different notation for large numbers.

$10 = 10^1$, $100 = 10^2$, $1,000 = 10^3$, $10,000 = 10^4$, and so on.

Explore | Scientific Notation

Is One a Lonely Number?

Look for patterns in the table below.

A		B	C
35	=	3.5×10	3.5×10^1
456	=	4.56×100	4.56×10^2
5,678	=	5.678×1000 ?	5.678×10^3 ?
23,456	=	2.3456×10000 ?	2.3456×10^4 ?
432,967	=	4.32967×100000 ?	4.32967×10^5 ?
1,654,763	=	1.654763×1000000 ?	1.654763×10^6 ?

1. Complete column B using powers of 10 in standard notation.

2. Complete column C using powers of 10 in exponential notation.

3. What do you notice about all of the decimals in columns B and C?

4. How are the numbers of zeros in the powers of 10 in column B and the exponents in column C related to the whole numbers in column A?

5. How could you rewrite 11,854,623 to fit the pattern in columns B and C?

6. How could you rewrite 1,000,000,000 and 9,999,999,999 to fit the pattern in column C? What is the same about these two "rewrites?"

7. How could you rewrite 357,000,000 and 35,700,000 to fit the pattern in column C? What is the same about these two "rewrites?"

You'll Learn ...

■ to convert large numbers between standard notation and scientific notation

... How It's Used

Scientific notation makes it easier for geologists to describe features of the earth that involve large numbers.

Vocabulary

scientific notation

Problem Solving TIP

Make a place-value table for large numbers if you need it.

Learn | Scientific Notation Using Positive Exponents

In describing features of the earth, scientists often use powers of 10 to express large numbers in **scientific notation** . In scientific notation, a number is written as a power of 10 times a number whose absolute value is less than 10 but greater than or equal to 1.

$$456{,}000{,}000 = 4.56 \times 10^8 \qquad -287 = -2.87 \times 10^2$$

To write a large number in scientific notation easily, move the decimal point to where you want it, count how many decimal places it moved, and write this as your power of 10. This works because moving the decimal left one place is the same as dividing by 10.

$2053 = 205.3 \times 10^1$ Move the decimal 1 place to the left.

$\quad\ = 20.53 \times 10^2$ Move the decimal another place to the left.

$\quad\ = 2.053 \times 10^3$ It is now in scientific notation.

Example 1

Mandarin, the principal language of China, is the world's most widely spoken language. It is estimated that 844 million people speak Mandarin as their primary language. Write this number in standard and scientific notation.

In standard notation, 844 million is written as 844,000,000.

In scientific notation, 844 million is written as 8.44×10^8.

Try It

Write the following numbers in standard and scientific notation.

a. English: 326 million people   **b.** German: 98 million people

Some numbers are too large for many calculators to display all of the digits. Some calculators automatically display such numbers in scientific notation.

Example 2

The earth is approximately 93 million miles from the sun. What is this distance in feet?

Enter 9.3 $\boxed{\times}$ 10 $\boxed{y^x}$ 7 $\boxed{=}$. The display will read 93000000. Press $\boxed{\times}$ 5280. The display shows *4.9104 11*.

The sun is about 4.9104×10^{11} feet from Earth.

Try It

The core temperature of the sun is estimated to be 15 million degrees Celsius. Find at least two ways to enter this number into your calculator.

Example 3

The following are calculator displays showing numbers in scientific notation. Write these numbers in standard notation.

a. *8.7 E 11*　　**b.** *5.45 10*　　**c.** *−4.5 15*

a. 8.7 E 11 means $8.7 \times 10^{11} = 8.7 \times 100,000,000,000$
= 870,000,000,000

b. 5.45 10 means $5.45 \times 10^{10} = 5.45 \times 10,000,000,000$
= 54,500,000,000

c. −4.5 15 means $-4.5 \times 10^{15} = -4.5 \times 1,000,000,000,000,000$
= −4,500,000,000,000,000

Try It

Write each calculator display in standard notation.
a. *9.6 E 10*　　**b.** *−3.8 12*　　**c.** *1.02 13*

Check　Your Understanding

1. Is there any number that cannot be represented in scientific notation?

2. Why is moving the decimal point left the same as dividing by a power of ten?

3. A number written in scientific notation has two factors. Describe each factor.

Scientific Notation Using Negative Exponents

You'll Learn ...

■ to convert small numbers between standard notation and scientific notation

... How It's Used

Microbiologists work with very small numbers. Scientific notation makes this easier for them.

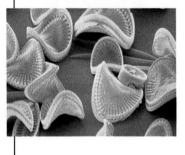

▶ **Lesson Link** In Lesson 2-8, you wrote large numbers in scientific notation using positive exponents. In this lesson you will learn to write very small numbers in scientific notation using negative exponents. ◀

Explore | Negative Exponents

Patterns Everywhere

The following fractions have been written as division problems, as division problems using exponents, and then as decimals.

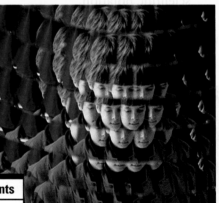

Number	Decimal Form	With Exponents
100	100.0	10^2
10	10.0	10^1
1	1.0	10^0
$\frac{1}{10}$	0.1	?
$\frac{1}{100}$	?	?

1. Continue the table until you reach $\frac{1}{100,000}$. Describe any patterns that you find.

2. How is each number related to the one above it?

3. As you move down the "Decimal Form" column, what happens to the decimal point?

4. As you move down the "With Exponents" column, what happens to the exponents?

5. Describe the relationship, if any, between the exponent and the location of the decimal point.

Negative exponents can be used to write very small numbers much as positive exponents were used to write very large numbers.

To write 0.00345 in scientific notation, move the decimal point to the right until there is only one nonzero digit to the left of the decimal point:

$0.00345 \rightarrow 0003.45$

Count the number of places you moved the decimal. This will be the exponent in the power of 10. Because you moved to the right, it will be negative, -3.

$0.00345 = 3.45 \times 10^{-3}$

Example 1

The DNA in the chromosome of certain bacterium is very thin and is tightly packed inside the cell, twisted and coiled so that it is $\frac{1}{10000}$ cm long. Express this length in scientific notation.

Write 1 ten-thousandth as a decimal.

$\frac{1}{10000} = 0.0001$

0.0001

$00001. \times 10^{?}$

Move the decimal point 4 places to the *right* to get 1.0.

Since the decimal was moved 4 places, the exponent will be -4.

$\frac{1}{10000}$ cm $= 1.0 \times 10^{-4}$ cm.

Single human chromosome

HINT

Many calculators can be placed in scientific notation mode. In this mode, *all* numbers appear in scientific notation.

Example 2

Write 52 millionths in scientific notation.

52 millionths $= 0.000052$ Write in decimal form.

$= 5.2 \times 10^{-5}$ Move the decimal 5 places to the right.

Try It

a. Write 1 millionth in scientific notation.

b. Write 3 hundred-thousandths in scientific notation.

Examples

3 The shortest centipede measures approximately 48 hundredths cm long. Write this in standard and in scientific notation.

In standard notation, 48 hundredths is written as 0.48.

$$0.48 = 4.8 \times 0.1 = 4.8 \times 10^{-1}$$

In scientific notation, 48 hundredths is written as 4.8×10^{-1}.

4 A red blood cell is about 7 hundred-millionths of a cm in diameter. Enter this number into your calculator. There are several different ways to enter it.

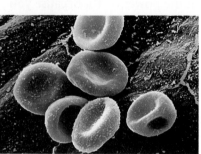

a. Enter 7 $\boxed{\div}$ 100,000,000 $\boxed{=}$.
The display will read *0.00000007*.

b. Enter 7 $\boxed{\times}$ 10 $\boxed{y^x}$ 8 $\boxed{+/-}$ $\boxed{=}$.
The display will read *0.00000007*.

c. Some calculators have an $\boxed{EE}$ or $\boxed{E}$ key.
Enter 7 $\boxed{EE}$ 8 $\boxed{+/-}$. The display will read *7. −08*.

Try It

a. Some viruses are as small as 3 billionths of a cm. Write this number in standard and in scientific notation.

b. Enter 8 millionths into your calculator.

Some numbers are too small for many calculators to display all of the digits. The calculator either displays an error message or automatically displays the numbers in scientific notation.

Check | Your Understanding

1. How is writing a small number in scientific notation similar to writing a large number? How is it different?

2. Why is moving the decimal place to the left the same as multiplying by negative powers of ten? What other operation is the same as multiplying by a negative power of ten? Explain.

3. A small number written in scientific notation is written as two factors. Describe each factor.

2-9 Exercises and Applications

Practice and Apply

1. **Getting Started** Use the following steps to write 35 hundred-thousandths in scientific notation.

   a. Write 35 hundred-thousandths in standard notation.

   b. How many places must the decimal point move? In which direction?

   c. Find the missing exponent: $0.00035 = 3.5 \div 10^{?}$.

   d. Check your answer using a calculator.

2. Which of the following name the same number?

   a. 10^4 **b.** $\dfrac{1}{1000}$ **c.** $\dfrac{1}{10^4}$ **d.** 10^{-4}

3. **Test Prep** Which of the following numbers is greater than 1?

   Ⓐ 0.356   Ⓑ −2.9   Ⓒ 1.00007   Ⓓ 0.9999

Write each number in scientific notation.

4. Forty millionths   5. Four hundred fifty-five hundred-thousandths

Science The following are approximate lengths of very small organisms. Write each in scientific notation.

6. Water fleas: 0.0078 inches

7. *Euglena:* 254 thousandths mm

8. *Mycoplasma laidlawii:* 0.0000000254 inches

9. *Paramecium:* 0.00007 m

Paramecium

Measurement Write each amount in standard notation.

10. Strain of H39 bacteria: 1.0×10^{-16} m   11. A nanosecond: 10^{-9} second

12. Weight of smallest insectivore (insect-eating mammal): 5.2×10^{-2} oz

13. **Science** The human eye can revolve 0.0003 of an arc in 1 minute. Write this number in scientific notation.

Write each calculator display in standard notation.

14. *9.23 E −9*   15. *4.004 −8*

16. *2.5 −05*   17. *−2.1 E −4*

18. Science There are 3.5×10^4 species of mites, which are the largest and most diverse group of arachnids (8-legged insects). An adult spider mite is typically 3.8×10^{-2} in. long. Express each of these numbers in standard notation.

Red spider mite

19. Number Sense Without actually calculating, choose which number in each pair is greater. Explain your answers.

    a. 4.4×10^2 or 4.4×10^{-2}

    b. 1.9×10^{-3} or 1.95×10^{-3}

    c. -1.5×10^{-2} or 1.5×10^{-2}

    d. 9.8×10^{-7} or 1.8×10^{-8}

20. Find at least two ways to enter 2.3 millionths into your calculator.

21. The smallest hole ever drilled was 3.16×10^{-10} meters. Write this number in standard notation.

Problem Solving and Reasoning

22. Communicate Joan said that the number 45.545×10^{-5} is written in scientific notation. Do you agree or disagree? Explain.

23. Critical Thinking Arrange each of the following numbers from greatest to least. Explain your answer.

    a. 1.24×10^{-3} **b.** 2.24×10^{-2} **c.** 1.89×10^{-4} **d.** -2.6×10^{-2}

24. Choose a Strategy The width of a human hair is 7.9×10^{-3} inch. The width of a sheet of paper is approximately 3.0×10^{-3} inches. Which is wider and by how much? Explain how you got your answer.

25. [Journal] Explain how you would determine which is greater, 0.00056 or 5.1×10^{-4}.

Problem Solving STRATEGIES

- Look for a Pattern
- Make an Organized List
- Make a Table
- Guess and Check
- Work Backward
- Use Logical Reasoning
- Draw a Diagram
- Solve a Simpler Problem

Mixed Review

Make a scatterplot for the data set. Decide whether there is an increasing trend, a decreasing trend, or no trend at all. *[Lesson 1-7]*

26. $(3, 9), (5, 4), (7, 3), (6, 4), (4, 6), (3, 4), (6, 8), (5, 2), (8, 6)$

Multiply or divide. *[Lesson 2-4]*

27. $12 \cdot (-4)$ **28.** $(-4)(-10)$ **29.** $-20 \cdot 3$ **30.** $24 \cdot 4$

31. $-32 \div 8$ **32.** $25 \div (-5)$ **33.** $48 \div 8$ **34.** $-100 \div (-10)$

Section 2B Connect

In this Connect, you will look at the diverse features of Earth and represent both the small and large numbers in scientific notation.

Our Diverse Planet Earth

Match each feature of Earth with its measurement.

1. Largest female marine worm		**A.**	0.0128 oz
2. Smallest male marine worm		**B.**	920,000,000°F
3. Heaviest bird egg (ostrich)		**C.**	1×10^{-12} mm
4. Lightest bird egg (hummingbird)		**D.**	39.3 in. long
5. Diameter of a proton		**E.**	326,000,000 mi^3
6. Diameter of an electron		**F.**	2.8×10^{-10} °K
7. Amount of water on the earth		**G.**	0.04 in. long
8. Highest temperature in a lab setting		**H.**	1×10^{-15} mm
9. Lowest temperature in a lab setting		**I.**	5.1 lb

10. Which numbers are written in standard notation? Which are in scientific notation?

11. If a number is in scientific notation, write it in standard notation.

12. If a number is in standard notation, write it in scientific notation.

13. What are the advantages of the two notations?

14. Sort the numbers from least to greatest.

15. If two measurements are written in scientific notation and use the same units, how can you tell which measurement is greater?

16. If two measurements are written in scientific notation but have different units, such as °F and oz, what comparisons can be made between the measurements?

Geography Using the map, locate the approximate latitude and longitude of each of these South American cities.

1. Santiago, Chile   **2.** Caracas, Venezuela

Plot each point. In what quadrant is each point?

3. $(2, -2)$ **4.** $(-3, 0)$ **5.** $(-4, 6)$ **6.** $(-2, -3)$

Find the area or volume of each of the following.

7.   **8.**

9. Journal Explain how -3^2 is different from $(-3)^2$.

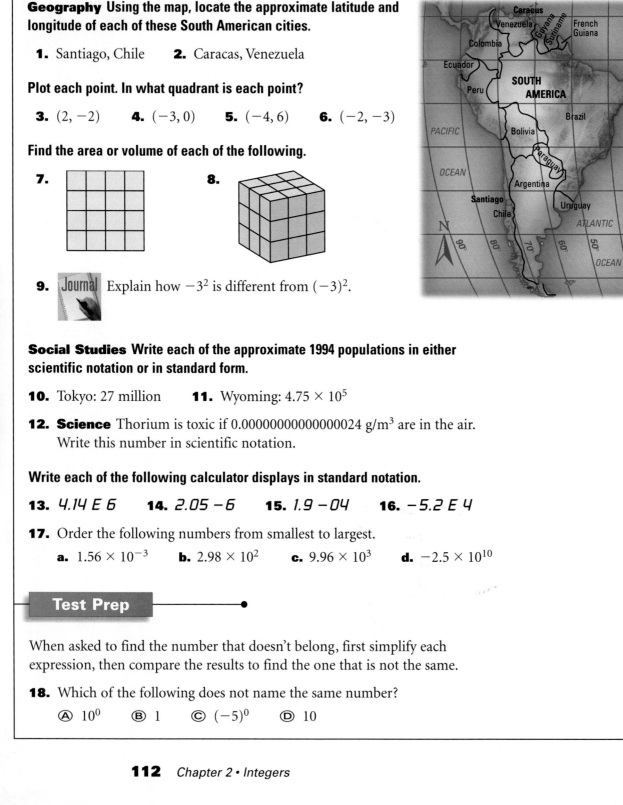

Social Studies Write each of the approximate 1994 populations in either scientific notation or in standard form.

10. Tokyo: 27 million   **11.** Wyoming: 4.75×10^5

12. Science Thorium is toxic if 0.00000000000000024 g/m^3 are in the air. Write this number in scientific notation.

Write each of the following calculator displays in standard notation.

13. *4.14 E 6*   **14.** *2.05 −6*   **15.** *1.9 −04*   **16.** *−5.2 E 4*

17. Order the following numbers from smallest to largest.
   a. 1.56×10^{-3} **b.** 2.98×10^2 **c.** 9.96×10^3 **d.** -2.5×10^{10}

Test Prep

When asked to find the number that doesn't belong, first simplify each expression, then compare the results to find the one that is not the same.

18. Which of the following does not name the same number?
   Ⓐ 10^0 Ⓑ 1 Ⓒ $(-5)^0$ Ⓓ 10

Extend Key Ideas • Patterns and Relationships

Sequences

A *sequence* is a set of numbers arranged in a certain order that can also be shown in a geometric pattern. The numbers in a sequence are called the *terms* of the sequence.

The sequence 1, 3, 6, 10, ..., is called the *triangular numbers*. The first term is 1, the second term is 3, the third term is 6, and so on. The rule for finding any term of the sequence is called the rule for the nth term.

1st term	2nd term	3rd term	4th term	nth term $\dfrac{n(n+1)}{2}$
1	3	6	10	

1 box   **3 boxes**   **6 boxes**   **10 boxes**

To find the fifth term, use $n = 5$, $\dfrac{n(n+1)}{2} = \dfrac{5(5+1)}{2} = 15$.

The fifth term in the sequence of triangular numbers is 15.

1. Find the sixth, seventh, and eighth terms of the sequence above.

2. The rule for the nth term of a sequence is $\dfrac{n(n-1)}{2}$. Give the first five terms of the sequence.

3. Give the rule for the nth term of the sequence of *square numbers* 1, 4, 9, 16, 25, 36. Use dots to draw the geometric pattern for the first five terms of the sequence.

4. Sequences can be used to predict patterns in everyday life. On Monday, the first day of a flu epidemic, three students in the eighth grade were absent. Each day, there was n times as many absences as the day before, until there were 48 on Friday. Find n. How many students were absent on Tuesday, Wednesday, and Thursday?

Graphic Organizer

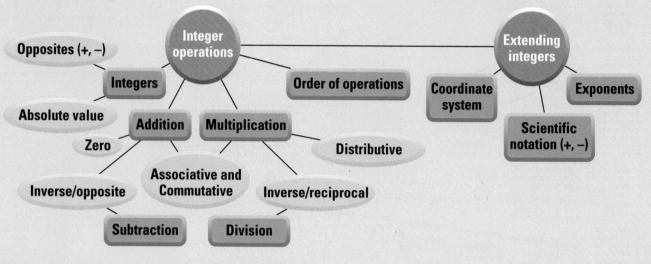

Section 2A Operations Using Integers

Summary

- **Integers** are whole numbers and their opposites.

- The **absolute value** of a number is the distance it is from zero.

- When **adding integers with the same sign,** add the numbers and use the sign of the numbers. When adding **integers with different signs,** subtract the numbers and use the sign of the larger number. Subtracting is the same as adding the opposite.

- The product of two numbers with the same sign is positive. The product of two numbers with different signs is negative. Dividing by a number is the same as multiplying by its multiplicative inverse.

- When simplifying expressions involving more than one operation, follow the **order of operations.**

Review

1. Find $|-43|$.

2. Find $|-8| - 4$.

3. Add $82 + (-25)$.

4. Subtract $-67 - (-101)$.

5. Multiply $16 \times (-9)$.

6. Multiply $-29(-72)$.

7. Divide $-56 \div (-7)$.

8. Evaluate $-2(8 - 4)$.

9. Evaluate $\dfrac{3(18 - (-7))}{5}$.

10. The temperature was $-7°F$ and it went down $17°F$. What was the new temperature?

Section 2B Extending Integers

Summary

■ The **x-axis** and the **y-axis** intersect at the **origin**, and create a **coordinate system**. The two axes divide the system into four **quadrants**, and the location of any point can be described as an **ordered pair** (x, y).

■ A **power**, or **exponent**, is a number that indicates how many times the **base** should be multiplied by itself.

■ Very large and very small numbers written in **standard notation** can be expressed in **scientific notation** as a number between one and ten multiplied by a power of ten.

Review

11. Find the coordinates of each point.

    a. A **b.** B **c.** C

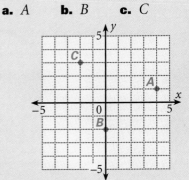

12. Give the coordinates of points A, B, and C.

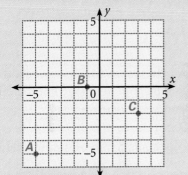

13. Write 4^6 in expanded form.

14. Write $7 \times 7 \times 7 \times 7$ in exponential form.

15. Evaluate 15^1.

16. Evaluate $(-3)^3$.

17. Write three hundred fifty thousand in scientific notation.

18. Write two ten-thousandths in scientific notation.

19. Write 7.25×10^{-5} in standard notation.

20. Write 3.78×10^5 in standard notation.

21. Write 77,600,000 in scientific notation.

22. Write 0.0000034 in scientific notation.

23. An amoeba, a one-celled animal, is approximately 9 millionths of a millimeter in diameter. Express its size in scientific notation.

24. At the Hot Springs in Arkansas, 950,000 gallons of spring water flow each day. Write this number in scientific notation.

Use $<$, $>$, or $=$ to compare each number pair.

1. $5 \;\square\; -7$ **2.** $4 \;\square\; |-4|$ **3.** $|0| \;\square\; |-1|$ **4.** $|2| \;\square\; |-2|$

Add or subtract.

5. $3 + (-2)$ **6.** $-2 + 3$ **7.** $5 + (-7)$ **8.** $-7 + 5$

9. $25 + (-100)$ **10.** $-250 + 65$ **11.** $-250 + (-65)$ **12.** $8 - 27$

13. $-14 - 8$ **14.** $-6 - (-3)$ **15.** $-7 - (-17)$ **16.** $1 - (-8)$

17. $4 - 9 + (-3) - (-8) + 10$ **18.** $-12 - 16 - (-16) - (-12)$

19. The water level in the levee changed from 8 ft above sea level to 13 ft below sea level. How much did the water level rise or fall?

20. Find the coordinates of points A, B, and C.

Multiply or divide.

21. $4(-2)$ **22.** $-6(-5)$ **23.** -1.5×40 **24.** $-60 \div 3$

Evaluate.

25. $\dfrac{4(5 - (-10))}{5}$ **26.** $4 \cdot 5 - (-10) \div 5$ **27.** 9^3 **28.** -2^6

29. A *light year* is the distance light travels in one year. This is approximately 10^{13} kilometers. Write this number in standard notation.

Write each number in scientific notation.

30. two hundred thousand   **31.** 71,077,345   **32.** 0.0035

Write each number in standard notation.

33. 2.37×10^4 **34.** 1.7×10^0 **35.** 6.02×10^{-3}

Performance Task

Many calculators can be set so that numbers appear in *engineering* notation. Engineering notation is similar to scientific notation in that a number is shown as a multiplier and a power of ten. Each of the following is given in engineering notation. Write it in standard and scientific notation.

  a. *12.745 3*   **b.** *387.2257 6*   **c.** *−2.675 3*   **d.** *84 −3*

Multiple Choice

Choose the best answer.

1. What number is not represented in the stem-and leaf diagram below? *[Lesson 1-1]*

Stem	Leaf
7	3 5 9
6	0 2 2 5 7 8
5	1 7 8 8
4	3 6 6 9 9 9

Ⓐ 46   Ⓑ 65   Ⓒ 79   Ⓓ Not here

2. For which data set would the median be the mean of the two middle values? *[Lesson 1-2]*

Ⓐ 1, 3, 7, 10, 12, 16, 19, 20

Ⓑ 2, 6, 10, 13, 15

Ⓒ 8, 15, 20, 22, 27, 27, 29

Ⓓ Not here

3. Which frequency is incorrect? *[Lesson 1-6]*

Color	Tally	Frequency
Brown	⊞⊞ ⊞⊞ IIII	14
Red	⊞⊞ III	8
Yellow	⊞⊞ ⊞⊞ ⊞⊞ ⊞⊞ II	17
Orange	⊞⊞ ⊞⊞ II	12

Ⓐ Brown   Ⓑ Red

Ⓒ Yellow   Ⓓ Orange

4. Wind chill temperatures of less than $-25°F$ are considered dangerous. Which is not less than $-25°$? *[Lesson 2-1]*

Ⓐ $-37°$ Ⓑ $-23°$ Ⓒ $-28°$ Ⓓ $-124°$

5. Which of the following is listed in order from least to greatest? *[Lesson 2-1]*

Ⓐ $-7, 5, 0, -5, 7$

Ⓑ $25, -14, 6, 14, 20$

Ⓒ $-13, -10, -2, 3, 5$

Ⓓ $-9, -6, 3, 0, 6$

6. Which is equivalent to subtracting -6? *[Lesson 2-2]*

Ⓐ Subtracting 6   Ⓑ Adding 6

Ⓒ Adding -6 Ⓓ Not here

7. To graph the point $(-3, 4)$, begin at the origin and: *[Lesson 2-6]*

Ⓐ Move right 3 units and up 4 units.

Ⓑ Move right 3 units and down 4 units.

Ⓒ Move left 3 units and up 4 units.

Ⓓ Move left 3 units and down 4 units.

8. Which expression means "multiply the sum of 5 squared and -9 by -2?" *[Lesson 2-7]*

Ⓐ $-2(5 + (-9))^2$ Ⓑ $-2 \cdot 5^2 + (-9)$

Ⓒ $-2(5^2 + (-9))$ Ⓓ $5^2(-9 + (-2))$

9. Which expression represents 7,500,000 in scientific notation? *[Lesson 2-8]*

Ⓐ 7.5×10^5 Ⓑ 7.5×10^6

Ⓒ 75×10^5 Ⓓ 75×10^6

10. This *Bacillus bacterium* is about 2.4×10^{-3} mm long. In standard notation, this is: *[Lesson 2-9]*

Ⓐ 0.0024 mm

Ⓑ 240 mm

Ⓒ 0.024 mm

Ⓓ Not here

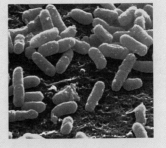

Science

A rattlesnake gains a rattle every time it sheds its skin, about 3 times a year, plus it has about 5 additional rattles from babyhood. To find a rattlesnake's age, you could just count the rattles. Just don't get too close!

Arts & Literature

Samuel Butler (1600–1680) is remembered as a famous English poet and satirist. Butler was not a mathematician. However, from his poem, he should be:

> *"And wisely tell
> what hour
> o'th'day
> The clock
> doth strike,
> by algebra."*

Entertainment

A director must choose music for a movie carefully. Film is run at 24 frames per second. For music that is played at a speed of two beats per second
24 frames of film = 2 beats
48 frames of film = 4 beats.

Variables, Expressions, and Equations

Social Studies

Some mathematicians saw beyond their world, such as Hindu mathematician Brahmagupta. He wrote algebra formulas that helped him with astronomical calculations, such as determining the positions of planets.

KEY MATH IDEAS

Variables, formulas, and algebraic expressions help with computations when two quantities are related mathematically.

Equations are statements that two expressions are equal.

Many equations can be solved by using the Addition Property of Equality and the Multiplication Property of Equality.

People of the World

Grace Hopper, mathematician and U. S. Navy Admiral, codeveloped the Cobol programming language and contributed to the development of modern computers. In 1991, she received the National Medal of Technology.

CHAPTER PROJECT

Problem Solving

Understand
Plan
Solve
Look Back

In this project, you will research number patterns that exist in nature—flowers, sea animals, land animals, and so on—and express these patterns using variable expressions.

119

Problem
Solving

Understand
Plan
Solve
Look Back

Problem Solving Focus

Finding Unnecessary Information

Real-life problem solving often involves lots of data. Some of the data is needed to find the answer, but usually not all of it. You need to under-stand which data will help you answer the question and which will not.

When solving a problem, you need to determine which information is needed to solve the problem, and which information can be ignored. Some of the problems below have unnecessary information. Some problems may not have unnecessary information. For each problem, state the information that you think is unnecessary.

1 Kivi plans to build a display cabinet for his collection of civil war miniature soldiers. It will have five shelves and will be 6 feet high. He has $35.00 to spend on materials and wants the shelves to be spaced evenly. How much space should he leave between each shelf?

2 The collection has over 500 pieces. On Kivi's birthday, his father buys him 4 metal sol-diers and a horse for $45.00. His grandfather gives him $50.00 which Kivi uses to buy 4 identical soldiers. Should Kivi have money left over?

3 Kivi rents a booth at a collec-tors' fair. Visitors pay a $5.00 admission fee and $\frac{1}{4}$ of the profits go to booth renters. Last year's fair was three days and had 1,585 visitors. Expenses averaged $300 a day, and there were 45 booths. How much money did Kivi receive?

4 This year's fair will last 4 days. Kivi will display 250 of his rarest miniatures. If 35 collec-tors display, and the average attendance, expenses, and pay-ment is the same as last year, what will Kivi's share be?

Where Did the Time Go?

On December 31, 1992, 97 people celebrated New Year's Eve in Shannon, Ireland. Shortly after midnight, they boarded a Concorde and flew to Bermuda, arriving at 11:21 P.M. the *previous day* so they could celebrate the New Year's arrival again.

Have you ever traveled to another city where the time is earlier than when you left home? This happens because the world is divided into 24 time zones. Time zones were established so that at approximately noon in any part of the world the sun will be directly overhead. If the whole world used the exact same time, it would be dark at noon in some places.

In the continental United States, there are four time zones: Eastern, Central, Mountain, and Pacific. Because of the rotation of the earth, it is earlier as you move westward. For example, when it is 10 A.M. in New York, it is only 7 A.M. in Los Angeles.

1 Airline schedules use local times. Discuss some advantages and disadvantages of this.

2 Discuss some situations where differences in time zones have led to confusion.

3 Look at a globe near the North and South Poles. What happens to the time zones there? What effect do you think this has?

3-1 Formulas and Variables

You'll Learn ...

■ how to use familiar formulas as an introduction to algebra

... How It's Used

Pilots of small planes use a formula based upon ground temperature to find how high they can fly before ice forms on the wings.

Vocabulary

formula

variable

substitute

constant

▶ **Lesson Link**   You've probably seen mathematical sentences that involve letters, for example, $p = 2l + 2w$. Many of these are useful in everyday life. ◄

Explore Formulas

Letter Fly!

Materials: Calculator (optional)

1. A flight attendant needs to count all the passengers on two planes so that snacks can be served. Each ● represents a passenger. How many snacks are needed?

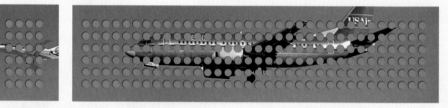

2. Is there a method other than counting that the flight attendant could use to find the number of snacks needed for both planes?

3. How many small boxes are in each rectangle?

4. How is Question 3 similar to Question 1?

5. Try each of the following. Which are easy to compute? Which would take too long to compute without a shortcut method?

   a. Start with 3. Add 7 four times. What is the result?

   b. Start with -4. Add 3 six hundred times. What is the result?

   c. Start with 8. Add 12 six hundred times. What is the result?

6. Describe a shortcut method for finding the answers to Parts b and c in Question 5. Explain why it works.

Many real-world quantities are related mathematically. For example, *distance* equals *rate of speed* multiplied by *time*. In symbols this is $d = rt$.

Multiplication of r by t can be shown several ways:

$$rt \qquad r \times t \qquad r \cdot t \qquad (r)(t)$$

A **formula** such as $d = rt$ states the relationship among unknown quantities represented by **variables** . Here the variables are d, r, and t. To use a formula, you need to **substitute** values for the variables. Some formulas include **constants** . For example, in the formula $p = 2l + 2w$, 2 is a constant. A constant is a number that does not vary.

Examples

1 A popular passenger plane for many years was the Douglas DC-3. It cruises at 160 mi/hr. At this speed how far would it fly in 2.5 hours?

$d = \quad r \quad \cdot \quad t$ Use the formula $d = rt$.

$d = 160 \cdot 2.5$ Substitute known values.

$d = 400$ Multiply to find the unknown value.

The Douglas DC-3 would travel 400 miles in 2.5 hours.

2 How long would it take each plane to fly from New York to Paris, a distance of about 3600 miles? Use the formula $t = \frac{d}{r}$.

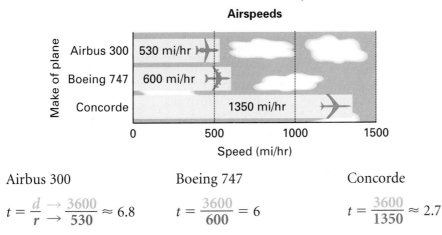

Airspeeds

Make of plane

Airbus 300 — 530 mi/hr
Boeing 747 — 600 mi/hr
Concorde — 1350 mi/hr

0　　　500　　　1000　　　1500
Speed (mi/hr)

Airbus 300

$$t = \frac{d}{r} \to \frac{3600}{530} \approx 6.8$$

Boeing 747

$$t = \frac{3600}{600} = 6$$

Concorde

$$t = \frac{3600}{1350} \approx 2.7$$

The Airbus would take about 6.8 hours, the Boeing 747, 6 hours, and the Concorde about 2.7 hours.

Test Prep

As you divide 3600 by larger numbers, the quotients get smaller.

Remember

The symbol $\approx$ means "is approximately equal to." [Previous course]

Example 3

Pilots sometimes use the temperature formula $T = G - 0.01h$, where G is the ground temperature and T is the temperature at an altitude of h meters. Both temperatures are in degrees Celsius. A pilot takes off when the ground temperature is 10°C and ascends to an altitude of 2000 meters. Is ice likely to form on the wings? Explain.

▶ **Technology Link**

If your calculator shows 19,980 instead of −10, it does not follow the order of operations you learned in Chapter 2! You will need to do the multiplication first.

$T = G - 0.01h$ Use the given formula.

$T = 10 - 0.01(2000)$ Substitute known values.

$T = 10 \boxed{-} 0.01 \boxed{\times} 2000$ Use a calculator to evaluate.

$T = -10$

The air temperature at 2000 meters is −10°C. Since 0°C is the freezing point of water, ice is likely to form on the wings at this altitude.

Try It

a. It is approximately 300 miles from Havana, Cuba, to Miami, Florida. How long would it take each plane to make this trip?

Private plane	120 mi/hr
Bi-plane	215 mi/hr
Commercial plane	460 mi/hr

b. If the ground temperature is 20°C and a pilot ascends to an altitude of 2500 meters, is ice likely to form on the wings? Explain.

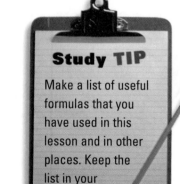

Study TIP

Make a list of useful formulas that you have used in this lesson and in other places. Keep the list in your notebook.

Check | Your Understanding

1. Explain the meaning of a variable in a formula.

2. Why are formulas useful?

3. Kaye used $d = t \cdot r$ rather $d = rt$. Does this formula give the same values for d? Why or why not?

4. The formula for the circumference of a circle is $C = 2\pi r$, where r is the radius of the circle and π is known to be 3.14159265…. Is π a constant or a variable? Why or why not?

Practice and Apply

Getting Started Decide if you would use $d = rt$, $r = \frac{d}{t}$, or $t = \frac{d}{r}$ to answer each question, where d, r, and t stand for *distance, rate of speed,* and *time.* Then answer the question.

1. A plane flies 600 miles in 3 hours. What is its speed?

2. How long would it take a helicopter to rise 6000 feet if it rises at 1500 feet per minute?

3. A motorcycle travels at an average speed of 55 miles per hour for 3 hours. How far does it travel?

4. A 3-toed sloth can run the 100-m dash in 22 minutes. How fast is this in m/min?

Solve each formula for the values given. The purpose of the formula is given.

5. $A = lw$ for $l = 95$ and $w = 37$ (*Area,* given *length* and *width*)

6. $P = 2l + 2w$ for $l = 5\frac{1}{2}$ and $w = 2\frac{1}{4}$ (*Perimeter,* given *length* and *width*)

7. $V = lwh$ for $l = 32$, $w = 14$, and $h = 7$ (*Volume,* given *length, width,* and *height*)

8. $C = 2\pi r$ for $r = 3.2$. Use 3.14 for π (*Circumference,* given the *radius*)

9. $F = 1.8C + 32$ for $C = 20$ (*Fahrenheit* temperature, given *Celsius* temperature)

10. $A = s^2$ for $s = 30$ (*Area* given *side length*)

11. $T = 0.04p$ for $p = \$24.75$ (*Tax* given *price*)

12. $C = np$ for $n = 24$ and $p = \$1.95$ (*Cost* given *number of items* and *price*)

13. **History** Charles Lindbergh was the first person to fly nonstop solo across the Atlantic. In 1927 he flew from New York to Paris, a distance of 3610 miles, in 33.5 hours. What was his average speed?

14. **Meteorology** One general principle is that if t is the time in seconds between a lightning flash and the following peal of thunder, then $d = \frac{1}{5}t$ gives your distance (d) from the lightning flash (in miles). If a person hears thunder 15 seconds after a flash, is the lightning more or less than 10,000 feet away? (1 mile = 5,280 ft)

15. **Consumer** A magazine article says to use the formula $S = 3F - 24$ to find your shoe size, where S is shoe size and F is the foot length in inches. Measure your own foot. Does the formula work for you?

16. **Journal** Describe a calculation you could not easily do without a formula. How does a formula make the calculation easier?

17. **Test Prep** Which formula would give $T = 35$ if 7 is substituted for k?

Ⓐ $T = \dfrac{k}{5}$ Ⓑ $k = T \times 5$ Ⓒ $T = 2k + 21$ Ⓓ $T = (k - 1)^2$

Problem Solving and Reasoning

18. Choose a Strategy The longest parachute jump occurred in 1960 when Captain Joseph Kittinger jumped from a balloon at 102,200 feet. The entire jump took 825 seconds (13.75 minutes). If an object falls without air resistance, the distance it falls, in feet, is related to the time it falls, in seconds, by $d = 16t^2$. Estimate how long it would have taken an object to fall without air resistance from the same height as Kittinger's jump.

19. Communicate The graph shows the maximum recorded speed (without assistance from wind or gravity) for the three fastest birds.

> **Problem Solving**
> ## STRATEGIES
> - Look for a Pattern
> - Make an Organized List
> - Make a Table
> - Guess and Check
> - Work Backward
> - Use Logical Reasoning
> - Draw a Diagram
> - Solve a Simpler Problem

Maximum Airspeeds

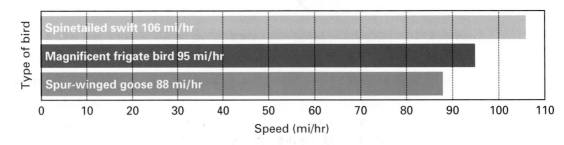

a. Use $t = \dfrac{d}{r}$ to find how long it would take each to fly 500 miles. Round to the nearest hundredth.

b. Do you think these times are reasonable for these birds? Why or why not?

Mixed Review

Make a line plot for each set of data. [Lesson 1-1]

20. 8, 7, 11, 12, 10, 8, 12, 8, 11, 13   **21.** 89, 92, 85, 82, 84, 86, 92, 89, 85

22. A soft drink manufacturer conducts taste tests at a supermarket near the manufacturer's factory. Is this a good test to determine whether to change its soft drink formula? Why or why not? [Lesson 1-8]

Algebraic Expressions and Equations

▶ **Lesson Link** You have already learned how to apply the order of operations and the distributive property to operations with numbers. Now you can apply the same concepts to situations with variables. ◀

Explore Algebraic Expressions

Runaway Runway

1. Airport runway A is 400 feet wide by 4000 feet long. What is its area?

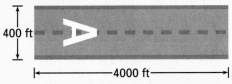

2. Because some planes require longer runways, the airport plans to extend the runway by 1000 feet. What is the area of the added portion?

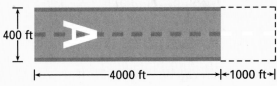

3. Add the area of the original runway and the area of the extension. What is the total area of the runway after it is extended? Can you find this area another way? Explain.

4. Suppose runway B will also be extended, but the length of the extension has not been determined. What is the area of the original runway? What is the area of the extension? Write the total area as the sum of the areas of the original runway and the extension.

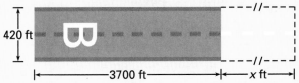

5. Describe the area of the new runway B using the second method you used in Question 3. What is the length? What is the width? Write the area as the product of the length and width.

6. What do you know about the answers to Questions 4 and 5? Why is this true?

You'll Learn ...

■ how to apply algebraic expressions in a wide variety of situations

■ how to solve simple equations

... How It's Used

Physicians use algebraic expressions to determine safe and effective dosage levels of medicines.

Vocabulary

algebraic expression

evaluate

simplify

equation

solve

solution

Learn   Algebraic Expressions and Equations

An expression that involves variables, numbers, and operation symbols is called an **algebraic expression** . To **evaluate** an algebraic expression, substitute values for each variable and **simplify** by applying the order of operations.

Example 1

An airline estimates that each passenger with baggage weighs 224 pounds. A gallon of fuel weighs about 6 pounds. A Boeing 747 can carry 490 passengers and 47,000 gallons of fuel. Approximately how much added weight does the full plane carry?

$224p + 6g$ $224p + 6g$ represents the added weight.

$224(490) + 6(47,000)$ Substitute known values.

$109,760 + 282,000 = 391,760$ Evaluate using the order of operations.

A full Boeing 747 carries almost 400,000 pounds of added weight!

490→P
                490
47000→G
                47000
224P+6G
                391760

You can use a graphics calculator to evaluate expressions. The arrows represent the [STO▶] key, and the results are shown on the right.

An **equation** states that two expressions are equal. $12 = 4 \times 3$ is an equation. Many equations with variables can be made to be true when the correct substitutions are made. Consider $12 = r \times 3$.

Replace r with 7.

$12 = 7 \times 3$

$12 = 21$ false for $r = 7$

Replace r with 4.

$12 = 4 \times 3$

$12 = 12$ true for $r = 4$

To **solve** an equation means to find the replacement that makes the sentence true. This replacement is called the **solution** .

Example 2

a. Solve $m + 2 = 5$.   **b.** Solve $3y = 60$.

You know $3 + 2$ is 5 and $3(20)$ is 60, so the solution to the first equation is $m = 3$, and $y = 20$ is the solution to the second.

Try It

Solve each equation.   **a.** $x + 10 = 30$ **b.** $3x = 24$

Remember

An expression does **not** have an $=$ symbol, but an equation always does.

Equivalent expressions have the same value for the same substitution.

A landscaper has sketched a plan for a large rectangular garden with a flower bed and a rock garden. Write an expression for the area of the flower bed.

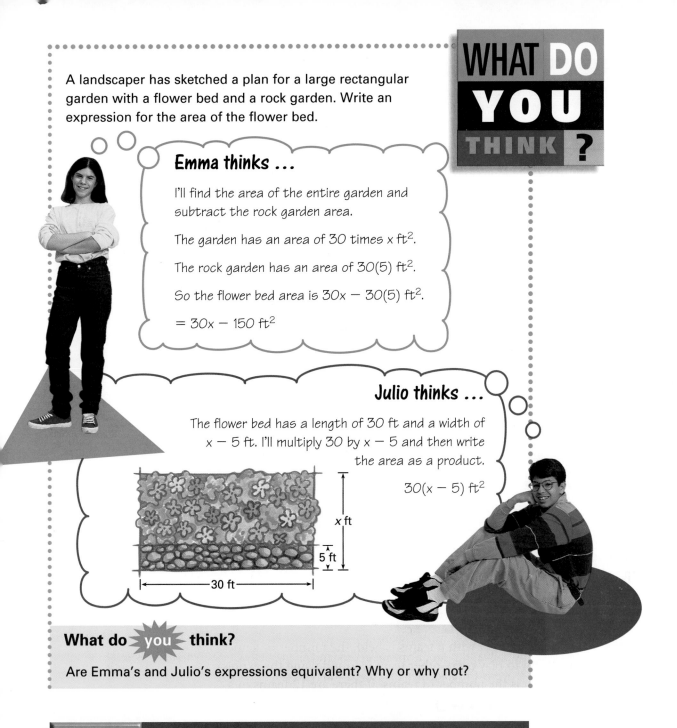

Emma thinks ...

I'll find the area of the entire garden and subtract the rock garden area.

The garden has an area of 30 times x ft^2.

The rock garden has an area of 30(5) ft^2.

So the flower bed area is 30x − 30(5) ft^2.

= 30x − 150 ft^2

Julio thinks ...

The flower bed has a length of 30 ft and a width of x − 5 ft. I'll multiply 30 by x − 5 and then write the area as a product.

30(x − 5) ft^2

x ft

5 ft

30 ft

What do you think?

Are Emma's and Julio's expressions equivalent? Why or why not?

Check | Your Understanding

1. Why can't an algebraic expression be "solved?"

2. How can you evaluate an algebraic expression?

3. Write an expression equivalent to $10(12 + y)$.

4. Write an equation that's true, one that's false, and one that is true when you substitute correctly for a variable. Show the substitution.

Practice and Apply

1. **Getting Started** Follow the steps to evaluate the expression $25x + 40y$ for $x = 10$ and $y = 16$.

   a. Substitute the known values: $25 \cdot 10 + 40 \cdot$ _____

   b. Use the order of operations: $= 250 +$ _____

   c. Simplify: $=$ _____

Evaluate each expression. Remember that operations within parentheses should be done first.

2. $3x + 6y$ for $x = 50$ and $y = 20$

3. $12(x + 3)$ for $x = 25$

4. $12x + 36$ for $x = 2\frac{1}{2}$

5. $12 + 36x$ for $x = 2\frac{1}{2}$

6. $5 + 20y$ for $y = 2.5$

7. $(5 + 20)y$ for $y = 3.8$

8. $18(x + 3y)$ for $x = 10$ and $y = 12$

9. $(18x + 3) \cdot y$ for $x = 10$ and $y = 12$

Solve each equation.

10. $m - 3 = 5$

11. $t + 2 = 9$

12. $9y = 54$

13. $8x = 32$

14. $m = 5(-20)$

15. $r = -2(8 + 2)$

16. $m = 5(-2 + 1)$

17. $z = -\dfrac{45}{9}$

18. **Science** The expression for the mass of a piece of iron, in grams, is $7.9c$, where c is the number of cm^3 of iron. If there are 27 cm^3 of iron, what is its mass?

19. **Sports** When a tournament with n teams is held, the number of games needed for each team to play every other team is found using the expression $\frac{n \cdot (n - 1)}{2}$ where n is the number of teams. If there are 12 teams in a league, how many games are needed?

20. **Test Prep** Which expression always gives the same value as $3(x - 4)$?

    Ⓐ $3x + 4$ Ⓑ $3x - 4$ Ⓒ $3x - 12x$ Ⓓ $3x - 12$

21. **Chance** A coin is flipped r times. $h = \frac{1}{2}r$ represents the average number of times it would land heads up. What is the average number of times it would land heads up if the coin is flipped 25 times?

Problem Solving TIP

If you are not sure which algebraic expression is correct, pick a reasonable number and substitute it in each expression. Which result seems reasonable?

22. Technology Complete the spreadsheet. Entries in column D are obtained by multiplying columns B and C.

	A	B	C	D
1	Fare Class	Number Sold	Ticket Price	Total of Sales
2	First Class	20	$220	
3	Business	17	$140	
4	Economy	81	$98	

Problem Solving and Reasoning

23. **Test Prep** Jill was on hold after making a call and had to listen to the same 30-second ad many times. Which expression would give the number of times she would hear the ad while waiting M minutes?

Ⓐ $30M$ Ⓑ $2M$ Ⓒ $\dfrac{M}{2}$ Ⓓ None of these

24. Critical Thinking Insert parentheses to make each expression equal 0.

a. $12 + 3 \cdot 5 - 75$ **b.** $12 - 3 \cdot 6 - 2$

25. Critical Thinking Alpha Air offers 1.0 frequent flyer mile for each mile traveled on Alpha Air (A), plus 0.5 mile for each mile traveled on Zeta Air (Z).

a. Write an expression for the miles earned on a one-way trip of A miles on Alpha Air and Z miles on Zeta Air. Then write an expression for the miles earned on a round-trip.

b. Alpha Airlines offers a free trip when a passenger earns 7500 frequent flyer miles. Mrs. Yager has already earned 3329 miles. If she flies from Seattle to Chicago to Atlanta and back, will she earn a free trip?

Mixed Review

Find the mean and median of each data set. *[Lesson 1-2]*

26. 8, 15, 17, 21, 34, 27, 31   **27.** 32.6, 42.8, 35.3, 42.8, 49.7

Find each absolute value. *[Lesson 2-1]*

28. $|732|$ **29.** $|78 - 78|$ **30.** $|-521|$ **31.** $|6 + 7|$

32. $|-1 - 3|$ **33.** $|-1 + 3|$ **34.** $|2 + (-2)|$ **35.** $|-2 + (-2)|$

Evaluate each formula for the values given.

1. $t = \frac{d}{r}$ for $d = 150$ and $r = 3$

2. $P = 2l + 2w$ for $l = 55$ and $w = 25$

3. $A = s^2$ for $s = 13$

4. $T = 0.04p$ for $p = \$8.50$

5. A blimp has traveled 179 miles in 3.4 hours. Use $r = \frac{d}{t}$ to find its average speed.

6. One income tax formula is $t = 0.28i$, where i is income and t is the tax paid. What is the tax paid on an income of \$12,150?

Evaluate each expression.

7. $10x + 20y$ for $x = 15$ and $y = 12$

8. $5 + 30y$ for $y = 2.5$

9. $12(x + 5)$ for $x = 3.8$

10. $(14x + 2) \cdot y$ for $x = 8$ and $y = 15$

11. $\dfrac{18(x - 2)}{3}$ for $x = 8$

12. $\dfrac{-8(y - 4)}{8}$ for $y = -4$

Solve each equation. Use number sense or guess and check.

13. $x - 5 = 7$

14. $8y = 64$

15. $y = -\dfrac{36}{4}$

16. $y = 8(-3)$

17. Once an African gray parrot is two weeks old and weighs about 120 g, it increases in weight about 85 g a week for the next few weeks. Write an expression and find the weight of a five-week-old parrot.

18. **Journal** Write a problem situation that involves multiplying and adding. Translate it into an expression and evaluate the expression for a sample value of the variable.

Test Prep

To test if different expressions name the same quantity, you can substitute the same simple number in each expression. Try 0, for example.

19. Which expression is not equivalent to $4x$?

Ⓐ $x + x + x + x$ Ⓑ $x + 3x$ Ⓒ $3x + 1$ Ⓓ $(3 + 1)x$

Watts the Use?

Suddenly, the lights go out, television and computer screens go dark, and you can't remember the last time you saw a flashlight. Without these rare power failures, we would certainly take electric energy for granted.

On November 9–10, 1965, the greatest power failure in history affected 30 million people and left an area of 80,000 square miles in darkness. In New York City, the power failed at 5:27 P.M. and was not restored for more than 13 hours. Can you imagine the resulting chaos—no elevators, no streetlamps, no computers, no television?

We forget that so many things are dependent on electricity. Electricity is a form of energy that can be changed into other forms of energy: heat to keep our homes warm, light for our lamps, sound energy in a stereo, and mechanical energy to turn motors in washing machines and dishwashers.

1 Which of these uses more energy, a 1500-watt hair dryer or a 100-watt lamp? Why?

2 Which appliances do you think require the most electric energy to run for an hour?

3 Which appliances do you think require the most electric energy for the amount of time they are actually in use?

139

Example 3

The largest 24-hour drop in temperature recorded in the United States occurred in Browning, Montana. The temperature dropped 100° to −56°F. What had the temperature been before it began to drop?

Let x = the temperature before the drop. Choose a variable.

$$x - 100 = -56$$ Translate the given information into an equation.

$$x - 100 + 100 = -56 + 100$$ To isolate x, add 100 to each side.

$$x = 44$$

Check: $44 - 100 \overset{?}{=} -56$

$$-56 = -56 \checkmark$$

The temperature had been 44°F before it began to drop.

Try It

Solve each equation.

a. $x + 12 = 30$ **b.** $x - 16 = 5$

c. $540 = 35 + t$ **d.** $x + 45 = -100$

e. $x - 11 = -18$

f. The temperature rose 19° before dawn. The temperature at dawn was 7°F. What had the temperature been?

Check | Your Understanding

1. When Zia checked her solution in the equation $y - 16 = 7$, she got $7 = 7$. Is 7 the solution? Why or why not?

2. When Gordy tried to solve $d - 10 = 5$, he subtracted 5 from both sides. Could he do that? Did it help him solve the problem?

3. In Example 1, the solution shows that you can solve the equation by adding −4 to both sides. This is equivalent to subtracting what number from each side? Why?

Practice and Apply

Getting Started For each balanced scale, what would you do to isolate the unknown weight on one side and still keep the scale balanced?

1.

2.

What is the next step in solving each equation?

3. $x - 5 = 10$ **4.** $x + 4 = 14$ **5.** $-1 = x - 6$ **6.** $7 = x + 4$

Solve each equation. Check your solution.

7. $y - 3 = 12$ **8.** $n + 5 = 11$ **9.** $c - 7 = 8$ **10.** $x + 20 = 32$

11. $m - 17 = 20$ **12.** $p + 35 = 20$ **13.** $a - 1.5 = 4.5$ **14.** $r + 3.8 = 6.2$

15. $r + 13 = 6$ **16.** $13 = m - 7$ **17.** $40 = a + 3$ **18.** $12 = m - 20$

19. $x + 2\frac{1}{2} = 10$ **20.** $x - 3\frac{3}{4} = 7$ **21.** $-1 = n - 33$ **22.** $8 = y + 25$

23. Electricity A three-way lightbulb has three different wattages available as you turn the switch three times in the same direction. The highest wattage is obtained by adding the two lower wattages. If the lowest wattage is 30 watts and the highest wattage is 100 watts, find the middle wattage.

24. Consumer Ordinary incandescent lightbulbs are cheaper, but they do not last as long as fluorescent bulbs. How much longer will a fluorescent bulb last than an incandescent bulb? Is your answer exact or approximate? Explain.

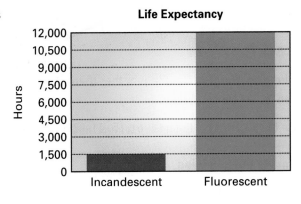

PRACTICE 3-4

25. Sports In bowling, a spare counts 10 points plus the number of pins on the next ball. In the scoresheet shown, the bowler has a score of 157 after a spare and an 8. What had the score been before the spare?

26. Augustus Caesar died in the year 14 A.D. at approximately 76 years of age. Which is the best estimate of the year of his birth?

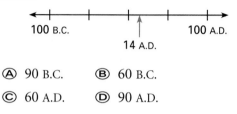

Ⓐ 90 B.C.　　Ⓑ 60 B.C.

Ⓒ 60 A.D.　　Ⓓ 90 A.D.

Problem Solving and Reasoning

27. Critical Thinking
Choose the correct equation, then answer each question.

$500 + x = 5500$

$500 + 5500 = x$

$100 + x = 3000$

$100 + 3000 = x$

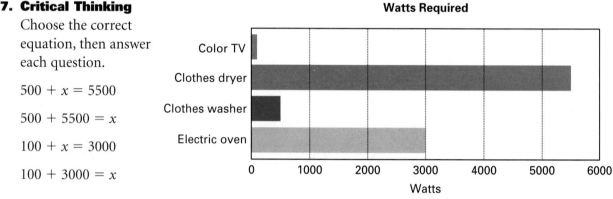

Watts Required

a. How many more watts does a clothes dryer require than a clothes washer?

b. How many more watts does an electric oven require than a color TV?

c. Can you think of any other equation to solve Questions a and b? Explain.

d. What question could be answered using $500 + 5500 = x$?

28. Choose a Strategy Bicycling burns off 6.0 calories per minute, but walking only burns off 3.5 calories per minute. How much longer would it take to burn off 1000 calories by walking than by bicycling?

Mixed Review

Make a scatterplot. Decide whether there is an increasing trend, a decreasing trend, or no trend. *[Lesson 1-7]*

29. $(1, 9), (9, 1), (3, 8), (4, 6), (5, 4), (2, 9), (3, 7), (7, 3), (2, 8), (6, 5)$

Compute the following. *[Lesson 2-3]*

30. $45 - (-28)$　　**31.** $6 + (-2) - (-7)$

32. $-3 - (-5) + 10$　　**33.** $-9 + 8 - (-7)$

Problem Solving

STRATEGIES

- Look for a Pattern
- Make an Organized List
- Make a Table
- Guess and Check
- Work Backward
- Use Logical Reasoning
- Draw a Diagram
- Solve a Simpler Problem

Solving Equations by Multiplying or Dividing

▶ **Lesson Link**   A formula that you have used relating distance, rate of speed, and time is $d = rt$. When you know values for d and t, you can solve for r by using what you know about inverses. ◀

Algebra tiles can be used to model expressions and solve equations.

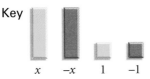

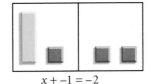

$$x + -1 = -2$$

Any two opposite tiles on the same side of an equation can be removed. Remember that you can add the same quantity to both sides of an equation.

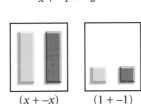

$(x + -x)$ $(1 + -1)$

You'll Learn ...

■ how to solve equations by undoing multiplication or division

... How It's Used

Electricians can determine how much current an appliance will use by solving equations.

Vocabulary

Multiplication Property of Equality

coefficient

Explore   Solving by Multiplying or Dividing

Materials: Algebra tiles

Lonely Tiles

1. What equation is shown by the tiles?

2. To "counteract" the negative tiles on the left in Question 1, how many positive tiles do you need? What tiles do you need to add to both sides? How many? What is the equation's solution?

3. What equation is shown by the tiles?

4. Rearrange the tiles on the right into three equal groups. For each x tile on the left, how many tiles on the right are there?

5. "Divide" each side by three by separating each side into three equal groups. Write the equation that helps you find the value of x. What is the value of x?

6. Model the equation $2x = -8$. How can you find the value of x?

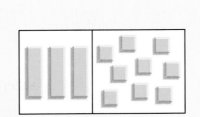

A useful property for solving equations is the **Multiplication Property of Equality**. An equation stays true if you multiply or divide both sides by the same nonzero number.

MULTIPLICATION PROPERTY OF EQUALITY

If $a = b$, then $ac = bc$.

In $4x = 28$, the variable x is multiplied by 4. So 4 is called the **coefficient** of x. In $\frac{x}{4} = 5$, you could rewrite the equation as $\frac{1}{4}x = 5$. So the coefficient of x is $\frac{1}{4}$. Knowing the coefficient can help you isolate the variable.

Examples

1 Solve $4x = 28$.

$$\frac{4x}{4} = \frac{28}{4}$$ Divide both sides by the coefficient, 4, to undo multiplication by 4.

$$x = 7$$

Check: $4(7) \stackrel{?}{=} 28$

$$28 = 28 \checkmark$$

2 In China, $\frac{1}{3}$ of the population owns bicycles. There are about 400,000,000 people with bicycles in China. What is the population?

Let x stand for the population of China. Solve $\frac{1}{3}x = 400,000,000$.

$$\frac{1}{3}x = 400,000,000$$

$$3 \cdot \frac{1}{3}x = 3 \cdot 400,000,000$$ Multiply by 3, the reciprocal of $\frac{1}{3}$.

$$x = 1,200,000,000$$

The population of China is about 1,200,000,000.

Try It

Solve each equation.

a. $8x = 72$ **b.** $\frac{x}{6} = -30$ **c.** $14 = \frac{2}{3}k$

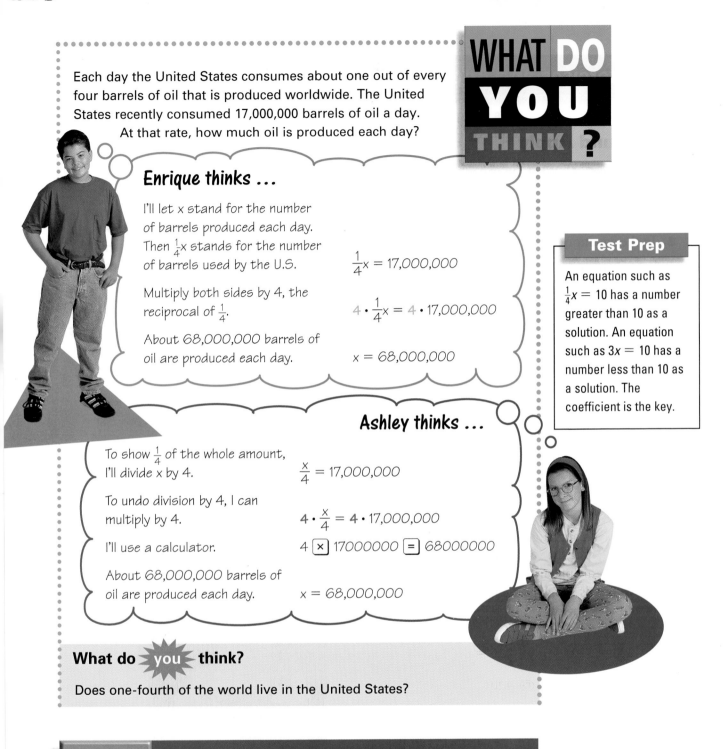

Each day the United States consumes about one out of every four barrels of oil that is produced worldwide. The United States recently consumed 17,000,000 barrels of oil a day. At that rate, how much oil is produced each day?

WHAT DO YOU THINK?

Enrique thinks ...

I'll let x stand for the number of barrels produced each day. Then $\frac{1}{4}x$ stands for the number of barrels used by the U.S.

$$\frac{1}{4}x = 17,000,000$$

Multiply both sides by 4, the reciprocal of $\frac{1}{4}$.

$$4 \cdot \frac{1}{4}x = 4 \cdot 17,000,000$$

About 68,000,000 barrels of oil are produced each day.

$$x = 68,000,000$$

Ashley thinks ...

To show $\frac{1}{4}$ of the whole amount, I'll divide x by 4.

$$\frac{x}{4} = 17,000,000$$

To undo division by 4, I can multiply by 4.

$$4 \cdot \frac{x}{4} = 4 \cdot 17,000,000$$

I'll use a calculator.

4 [×] 17000000 [=] 68000000

About 68,000,000 barrels of oil are produced each day.

$$x = 68,000,000$$

What do you think?

Does one-fourth of the world live in the United States?

Check | Your Understanding

1. When solving equations such as $x - 2 = 40$ or $2x = 40$, how do you know which operation to use to isolate the variable?

2. When would a reciprocal help you solve an equation?

3. Give an example of a division equation that has a negative-number solution.

Solving Two-Step Equations

You'll Learn ...

■ how to solve equations by undoing operations in two steps

... How It's Used

In cutting heating costs, a consumer can use equations to determine how much insulation is needed.

▶ **Lesson Link**   You have already learned to solve equations such as $x + 7 = 20$ and $5x = 15$. By combining the methods you learned for solving such equations, you can solve equations such as $5x + 7 = 37$. To do this, you will use the order of operations in reverse. ◀

Explore   Two-Step Equations

It Could Be Your Undoing!

Materials: Algebra tiles

1. What equation is shown by the model?

2. Take three unit tiles from each side. What operation is represented by removing the three unit tiles from each side? What equation is represented after the tiles are removed?

3. If you separate the remaining unit tiles into two equal groups, what operation is represented? How many unit tiles correspond to each x-tile?

4. What is the solution of the original equation?

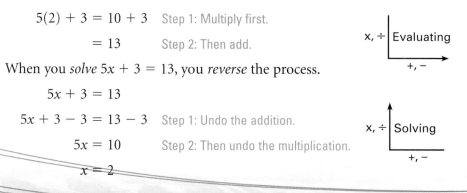

Learn   Solving Two-Step Equations

When you evaluate an expression such as $5x + 3$ for $x = 2$, you substitute 2 for x and use the order of operations.

$$5(2) + 3 = 10 + 3 \quad \text{Step 1: Multiply first.}$$
$$= 13 \quad \text{Step 2: Then add.}$$

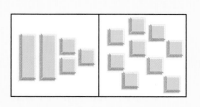

When you *solve* $5x + 3 = 13$, you *reverse* the process.

$$5x + 3 = 13$$
$$5x + 3 - 3 = 13 - 3 \quad \text{Step 1: Undo the addition.}$$
$$5x = 10 \quad \text{Step 2: Then undo the multiplication.}$$
$$x = 2$$

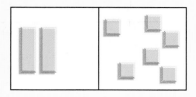

Example 1

Solve $4y - 6 = 50$.

$$4y - 6 = 50$$

$$4y - 6 + 6 = 50 + 6 \quad \text{Add 6 to each side to undo the subtraction.}$$

$$4y = 56 \quad \text{Use the property of additive inverses.}$$

$$\frac{4y}{4} = \frac{56}{4} \quad \text{Divide each side by 4 to undo the multiplication.}$$

$$y = 14$$

Check: $4(14) - 6 \stackrel{?}{=} 50$

$$56 - 6 \stackrel{?}{=} 50$$

$$50 = 50 \checkmark \quad \text{The solution checks.}$$

Remember

$\frac{x}{2}$ and $\frac{1}{2}x$ mean the same thing.

Example 2

In the construction of a townhouse villa, 13 flat-plate solar collectors are installed on the rooftops, one for every two units and three for the clubhouse. How many units are in the villa?

Solve $\frac{x}{2} + 3 = 13$.

$$\frac{x}{2} + 3 = 13 \quad \text{Let } x = \text{ the number of townhouses.}$$

$$\frac{x}{2} + 3 - 3 = 13 - 3 \quad \text{Subtract 3 from each side to undo the addition.}$$

$$\frac{x}{2} = 10 \quad \text{Use the property of additive inverses.}$$

$$2 \cdot \frac{x}{2} = 2 \cdot 10 \quad \text{Multiply both sides by 2 to undo the division.}$$

$$x = 20$$

There are 20 townhouse units in the villa.

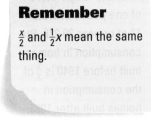

Every 40 minutes the sun delivers as much energy to Earth's surface as all people on Earth use in a year.

Try It

Solve each equation.

a. $5x + 4 = 29$ **b.** $12x - 8 = 70$ **c.** $\frac{n}{3} - 4 = 6$ **d.** $\frac{k}{20} + 5 = 6.5$

28. How many shopping carts will fit completely into the carriage rack shown?

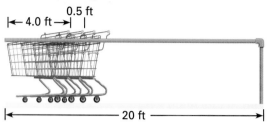

0.5 ft

|← 4.0 ft →|

|← 20 ft →|

29. Write a word problem that could be solved by using the equation $200 = 10x + 50$.

30. A paging service charges $20.00 for activation plus $12.95 a month. Francine paid $123.60 for activation and service. How many months did this cover?

Problem Solving and Reasoning

31. Critical Thinking Peaches are dried at 675 watts at a specified time and then at 450 watts for 40 more hours. If a total of 19.35 kilowatt-hours are used in the process, for how many hours are the peaches dried at 675 watts? (One kilowatt-hour is equivalent to 1000 watts used for one hour.)

32. Math Reasoning The higher the R-value of an insulating material, the more effective it is as an insulator. An external wall of a house should have an R-value of 11 or greater. Suppose an exterior wall is covered with materials having an R-value of 2. How many inches of insulation with an R-value of 3.6 per inch will be needed to achieve a total R-value of 11?

33. Choose a Strategy Suppose you burn a 60-watt lightbulb 24 hours a day, 7 days a week for an entire year. If the cost per kilowatt-hour is 8¢, what is the cost per year? How much would you save by using a fluorescent 13-watt lamp for the same amount of time?

34. Communicate City taxi fare is $2.00 plus $1.50 a mile. If a person was charged $14.00 for a cab ride, how many miles was the ride? Public transportation for the same trip costs $1.25. Discuss the advantages and disadvantages of public transportation over using a cab.

Problem Solving

STRATEGIES

- Look for a Pattern
- Make an Organized List
- Make a Table
- Guess and Check
- Work Backward
- Use Logical Reasoning
- Draw a Diagram
- Solve a Simpler Problem

Mixed Review

Evaluate each expression. *[Lesson 2-5]*

35. $3 + 4 \cdot (-5)$ **36.** $-3(2 + 5)$ **37.** $-5 + \dfrac{3 - (-7)}{5}$ **38.** $\dfrac{-3 + 7}{2} - \dfrac{-5 + 9}{-4}$

Find each power. *[Lesson 2-7]*

39. $(-4)^2$ **40.** 3^5 **41.** 11^3 **42.** $(-2)^5$ **43.** $(-1)^{11}$

Solving Inequalities

► Lesson Link | You know that $3 = 2 + 1$ means the quantities on both sides of the equal sign are equal, and you can solve equations such as $x + 2 = 4$. You also know that $3 > 2$ means that "3 is greater than 2." Now you will see what to do when we replace the $=$ with $>$ in an equation. ◄

Recall that $<$ means "is less than" and $>$ means "is greater than." So $3 < 5$ means "3 is less than 5," and $5 > 3$ means "5 is greater than 3."

You'll Learn ...

■ how to solve inequalities

... How It's Used

A homeowner can use an inequality to determine how many amperes an appliance will use before it overloads the circuit.

Vocabulary

inequality

Explore | Inequalities

Don't Be Crude!

A barrel of crude oil contains 42 gallons. A barrel of crude can provide up to 42 gallons of gasoline. Suppose you are a refiner of crude oil and you make a record of the gasoline refined from a barrel.

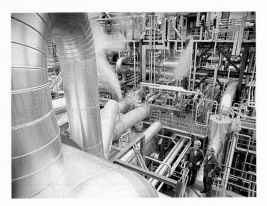

1. Name one possible amount of gasoline in gallons that might be distilled from one barrel.

2. Compare your answer with several others. How many different answers were found?

3. Must each amount be a whole number of gallons? Would 25.50 gallons be reasonable? Is 12.25 gallons a possible amount?

4. Draw a number line. Mark a point to show the greatest amount of gasoline possible for one barrel. Mark another point to show the least amount possible.

5. On the same number line, graph as many points as you can to show possible amounts of gasoline from one barrel. How many points are there?

6. How do you think you could show all possible points on the graph?

Practice and Apply

Getting Started Match each situation with one of the following inequalities: $x > 20$, $x < 20$, $x \le 20$, $x \ge 20$.

1. The maximum current is 20 amperes.

2. The minimum age is 20.

3. The time is more than 20 minutes.

4. The cost is less than $20.

5. **Test Prep** Which inequality could you use to express allowable speeds if the maximum speed is 65 mi/hr?

Ⓐ $x < 65$ Ⓑ $x > 65$ Ⓒ $x \le 65$ Ⓓ $x \ge 65$

Write an inequality for each graph.

6.

7.

Determine whether 10 is a solution for each inequality.

8. $x \ge 10$ **9.** $x + 9 < 19$ **10.** $6x \le 61$ **11.** $3x + 2 < 40$

Solve each inequality. Graph the solution.

12. $x - 5 < 2$ **13.** $x + 3 > 7$ **14.** $x + 7 \le 10$ **15.** $x - 10 \ge 1$

16. $6m > 42$ **17.** $3y \le 15$ **18.** $2v > 20$ **19.** $5p \ge 40$

20. $2w - 1 < 22$ **21.** $4z + 3 \ge 24$ **22.** $6k - 3\frac{1}{2} > 27$ **23.** $10n + 8 \le 74\frac{2}{3}$

24. Consumer A homeowner installs a dishwasher on a circuit that can handle 20 amperes. If 11 amperes are used by other appliances, solve $d + 11 \le 20$ to describe the number of amperes the dishwasher uses.

25. Geography A flood fringe may be defined as an area where the product of the depth of flood waters and the velocity of the water does not exceed 7. If flood waters reach a velocity of 14 ft/sec, how deep can they be for the region to remain a flood fringe?

26. Consumer The minimum recommended R-value for a home ceiling in one area is 19. Fiberglass sheets have an R-value of 3.33 per inch. What is the minimum number of sheets needed? Solve $3.33x \ge 19$.

PRACTICE 3-7

Problem Solving and Reasoning

27. **Math Reasoning** It is estimated that a family can save up to two-thirds of their energy costs by converting from an electric clothes dryer to an energy-efficient gas dryer with electronic ignition. In four years, a family saves $320 by installing a gas dryer, approximately the cost of the new dryer. What is the amount they were spending per year on energy costs for an electric dryer?

28. **Critical Thinking** You can add the same number to both sides of an equation or multiply both sides by the same number, and the equation is still true. Can you always add the same positive or negative number to both sides of an inequality, or multiply both sides by the same number, and still get a true inequality? Explain.

29. **Communicate** For each inequality, describe a real-world situation that could be represented by the inequality.

    a. $x \geq 21$ **b.** $24x < 9.95$

30. **Choose a Strategy** You have made scores of 75 and 82 on your first two tests in Spanish. What scores can you get on your next test if you want an average of at least 80?

Mixed Review

31. Plot the following points on a coordinate grid. *[Lesson 2-6]*

    $(1, -1), (-3, 4), (0, -3), (5, 2), (4, 0), (-4, -3), (2, -4), (-3, -1)$

32. Which ordered pair(s) in Exercise 31 represent(s) points on the *x*-axis? Which represent points on the *y*-axis? *[Lesson 2-6]*

Write each number in standard notation. *[Lesson 2-8]*

33. 7.32×10^7 34. 6.3×10^2 35. 9.3734×10^{12} 36. 8.64×10^6

Write each number in scientific notation. *[Lesson 2-8]*

37. $16,384$ 38. 12^3 39. 144×10^2 40. 5 billion

Problem Solving

STRATEGIES

- Look for a Pattern
- Make an Organized List
- Make a Table
- Guess and Check
- Work Backward
- Use Logical Reasoning
- Draw a Diagram
- Solve a Simpler Problem

Project Progress

Explain some ways you might be able to use a pattern or equation to describe numerical facts about the natural things you are researching. For example, you might use a pattern or equation about a group of spiders to make a conclusion about each spider.

Problem Solving

Understand
Plan
Solve
Look Back

TECHNOLOGY

Using a Spreadsheet • Writing Formulas

Problem: Using the formula $F = 1.8C + 32$, a temperature expressed in degrees Celsius can be converted to degrees Fahrenheit. What Fahrenheit temperature would correspond to the following temperatures expressed in degrees Celsius: 0°, 10°, 20°, 50°, and 100°?

You can use a spreadsheet to generate these conversions quickly.

1 Enter the information into the spreadsheet as shown.

	A	B
1	Celsius	Fahrenheit
2	0	
3	10	
4	20	
5	50	
6	100	

2 In cell B2, enter the formula =1.8*A2+32.

	A	B
1	Celsius	Fahrenheit
2	0	= 1.8*A2 + 32
3	10	
4	20	
5	50	
6	100	

3 Highlight cells B2 through B6, and select the **Fill Down** command for your spreadsheet. The conversions will appear as shown:

	A	B
1	Celsius	Fahrenheit
2	0	32
3	10	50
4	20	68
5	50	122
6	100	212

Solution: The corresponding Fahrenheit temperatures are 32°, 50°, 68°, 122°, and 212°.

TRY IT

Use your spreadsheet to convert from Celsius to Fahrenheit: −5°, 5°, −17.8°, 273.15°, 450°, and 1000°.

ON YOUR OWN

▶ Use your spreadsheet and the formula $C = (F - 32)/1.8$ to convert these Fahrenheit temperatures to Celsius: 0°, 32°, 98.6°, 190°, 240°, 1500°. Use column C to convert the Fahrenheit temperatures back to Celsius.

Section 3B Connect

At the beginning of Section 3B, you learned that electric companies charge by the kilowatt-hour. In this Connect you will use your knowledge of solving equations and inequalities to learn more about how electric companies bill their customers.

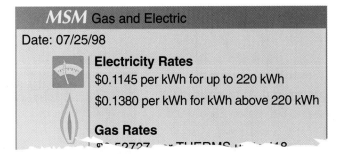

Watts the Use?

One electric company charges its residential customers as follows:

MSM Gas and Electric

Date: 07/25/98

Electricity Rates
$0.1145 per kWh for up to 220 kWh
$0.1380 per kWh for kWh above 220 kWh

Gas Rates

1. Suppose your April bill is $19.10. How many kWh did you use?

2. Suppose your May bill is $25.19. How many kWh did you use?

3. Suppose your June bill is $30.02. How many kWh did you use?

4. What equation did you use for Question 3?

5. In July, the cost for up to 220 kWh will stay the same, but the cost for additional kWh will increase. The utility company assures customers that for 300 kWh, the electric cost should be no more than $35. What rates are possible? Is this reasonable?

6. Why might the rates change at 220 kWh?

7. Try to find an electric bill for your family or someone you know. See how the rate compares with that of the electric company mentioned above. Use the given rates in the bill above and determine how much the bill would be with these rates.

8. Discuss as many ways as you can think of to reduce electric and other energy costs. (Some of them have been mentioned in Section 3B.)

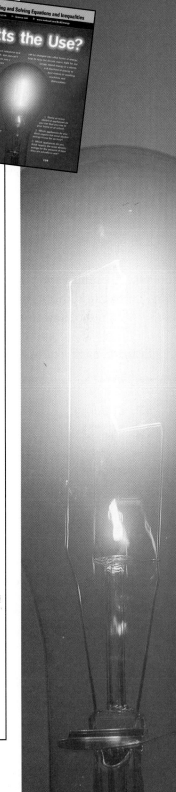

Solve each equation.

1. $a - 5 = 20$ **2.** $z + 3 = 27$ **3.** $x - 2.5 = 12.5$ **4.** $3x = -18$

5. $\frac{1}{3}x = 20$ **6.** $1.5x = 12$ **7.** $\frac{1}{2}x - 10 = 20$ **8.** $3x - 7 = 29$

9. Last month the Archer family paid an electric bill of $22.00. There is a basic service charge of $5.00 plus $0.09 per kilowatt-hour. Solve $0.09x + 5 = 22$ to find how many kilowatt-hours they used.

Solve and graph each inequality.

10. $x - 1 \le 5$ **11.** $2x > 20$ **12.** $\frac{1}{2}x < 3$ **13.** $8x - 3 \ge 13$

14. An adult Panda bear and her cub eat up to 105 pounds of bamboo shoots per day. If the cub eats around 20 pounds of bamboo, how much does the mother eat? Solve $x + 20 \le 105$.

Evaluate each expression for $x = 10$ and $y = 8$. *[Lesson 3-2]*

15. $6x + 3y$ **16.** $(6x + 3) \cdot y$

17. $6(x + y)$ **18.** $6x + 6y$

19. **Journal** Explain why an inequality is used in Exercise 14 rather than an equation.

Test Prep

Remember that words such as *maximum* and *minimum* often mean that either $\le$ or $\ge$ is needed when translating words to an inequality.

20. Which inequality shows the allowable weights if the maximum weight is 2000 pounds?

ⓐ $x < 2000$ ⓑ $x > 2000$ ⓒ $x \le 2000$ ⓓ $x \ge 2000$

21. The inequality $p \ge 40$ means that 40 is

ⓐ Value of p ⓑ Minimum value of p ⓒ Maximum value of p ⓓ None of these

REVIEW 3B

Extend Key Ideas ● Logic

Compound Statements

A compound statement is formed by joining two statements. Statements joined by the word *and* are *conjunctions*. Statements joined by the word *or* are *disjunctions*. Knowing whether a compound statement is a conjunction or disjunction can help you decide whether it is true.

To vote, a person must be a U.S. citizen *and* at least 18 years old. To cash a check, banks require that you have a driver's license *or* a major credit card.

For a conjunction to be true, *both* statements must be true.

U.S. Citizen	At Least 18 Years Old	U.S. Citizen *and* at Least 18 Years Old
True	True	True
True	False	False
False	True	False
False	False	False

To be able to vote, both conditions must be true.

For a disjunction to be true, *only one* of the statements must be true.

To cash a check, at least one condition must be true.

Have a Driver's License	Have a Major Credit Card	Have a Driver's License or a Major Credit Card
True	True	True
True	False	True
False	True	True
False	False	False

Inequalities can be written as conjunctions and disjunctions.

6 is less than 10   *and*   greater than 4. $6 < 10$ *and* $6 > 4$

5 is less than 4   *or*   greater than 4. $5 < 4$ *or* $5 > 4$

$4 < x < 10$ is a special conjunction, meaning $4 < x$ and $x < 10$.

Determine whether each compound statement is a conjunction or a disjunction, and whether it is true or false.

1. A square has four sides and a triangle has three sides.

2. The product of 4 and 6 is 24 or the sum of 4 and 6 is 12.

3. $100 > 10 > 1$ **4.** $5 < 0$ or $-1 > 0$ **5.** $6 < 8$ and $0 > 1$

Interpreting Math Phrases

Many problems that you may want to solve can be represented by one or more algebraic expressions. You should understand that you can use any letter to represent an unknown in an algebraic expression. Then you must determine what operation(s) to use.

Problem Solving Focus

Write an algebraic expression for each situation.

1 Five years older than the Mustang

2 Three times as valuable as a 1965 Corvette

3 Thirty-eight horsepower less than that of a 1952 Olds Rocket Super 88

4 Twelve more classic car museums than last year

5 Twenty-five hundred dollars off the sticker price

6 One-tenth the number of parts stores

7 If Sally's Saturn is y years old, and Victor's Model A Ford is 60 years older, how old is Victor's car?

8 If a equals the speed in miles per hour, what is the speed in miles per minute?

9 If m equals the weight in ounces, what is the weight in pounds?

10 If a car travels 327.6 miles on g gallons of gasoline, what is the number of miles per gallon?

How Much Is That In Dog Years?

Have you ever heard that each year of a dog's life is equal to 7 years of a human's life? If so, did you ever wonder what it means, or whether it is actually true?

This "rule" may have developed from comparing the average life span of a dog to that of a human.

Humans live an average of 75 years. Dogs live an average of 12 years. If you multiply this number by 7, you find that humans should live an average of 84 years by this rule.

Each year of a dog's life certainly does not correspond to 7 years in a human's life. Many dogs are fully grown by a year. But there are few, if any, humans that are grown by age 7!

1 Which is more unusual, a 20-year-old dog or a 140-year-old person?

2 Make a list of possible pets. If you want a pet today that would be alive when you turn 30 years old, which would you choose? (Don't forget, you'll have to take care of it too!)

3 Do you agree that the larger the animal, the longer it generally lives?

171

You can sometimes find the equation relating two variables by looking at a table of their values.

Example 3

A table giving mixtures of potting soil and sand for the bottom of an iguana cage is shown. Find a rule that relates the amount of sand (y) to the amount of potting soil (x). Use it to find the amount of sand you would need for 15 cups of potting soil.

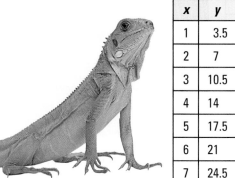

x	y	
1	3.5	When 1 is substituted for x, $y = 3.5$.
2	7	When 2 is substituted for x, $y = 7$.
3	10.5	When 3 is substituted for x, $y = 10.5$.
4	14	When 4 is substituted for x, $y = 14$.
5	17.5	When 5 is substituted for x, $y = 17.5$.
6	21	When 6 is substituted for x, $y = 21$.
7	24.5	When 7 is substituted for x, $y = 24.5$.

In each case $y = 3.5x$. Find the value of y when $x = 15$.

$y = 3.5(15)$ Substitute 15 for x.

$y = 52.5$ Multiply to solve for y.

The value of y when $x = 15$ is 52.5. For 15 cups of potting soil, you would need about 53 cups of sand.

Try It

Find the rule that relates x and y in this table. Then find y when $x = 50$.

x	1	2	3	4	5	6
y	30	60	90	120	150	180

Check Your Understanding

1. How would you make a table for the equation $y = 7x$?

2. How would you make a table for the equation $y = x + 7$? How many solutions does the equation have?

3. A table shows that when $x = 2$, $y = 4$. Does this tell you that the rule relating x and y is $y = 2x$? Explain.

Practice and Apply

1. **Getting Started** Follow the steps below to find the value of y when $x = 5$ in the equation $y = 12x$.

   a. Write the original equation: $y = 12x$

   b. Substitute 5 for x: $y = 12 \times$?

   c. Compute the value of y: $y =$?

Find the value of y when $x = 5$ in each of the following equations.

2. $y = 8x$ **3.** $y = x + 3$ **4.** $y = 40x$ **5.** $y = x - 10$

Complete each table of values.

6.

x	0	1	2	3	4	5
$y = 20x$						

7.

x	0	1	2	3	4	5
$y = -6x$						

8.

x	0	1	2	3	4	5
$y = x + 6$						

9.

x	0	1	2	3	4	5
$y = x - 8$						

Make a table of values for each equation. Use 0, 1, 2, 3, 4, and 5 for x.

10. $y = 15x$ **11.** $y = -10x$ **12.** $y = x + 12$ **13.** $y = x - 15$

Find the rule that relates x and y in each table. Then find y when $x = 20$.

14.

x	y
1	8
2	16
3	24
4	32
5	40

15.

x	y
1	-7
2	-14
3	-21
4	-28
5	-35

16.

x	y
1	10
2	11
3	12
4	13
5	14

17.

x	y
1	-2
2	-1
3	0
4	1
5	2

18. **Test Prep** The table below is represented by which of the lettered equations?

x	0	1	2	3	4
y	0	1	4	9	16

Ⓐ $y = x$ Ⓑ $y = 2x$ Ⓒ $y = x^2$ Ⓓ $y = 3x$

19. Government Each state has two senators and a varying number of representatives in the U.S. Congress. Make a table relating the total number in Congress to the number of representatives for a state.

20. Write a rule that relates the number of chairs to the number of tables.

21. Give examples of two different types of equations.

Problem Solving and Reasoning

22. Critical Thinking

a. Draw the next figure.

b. What rule relates *n*, the figure number, to *d*, the number of dark tiles?

c. What rules relates *n* to *c*, the number of light tiles?

d. What rule relates *n* to *t*, the total number of tiles in each figure?

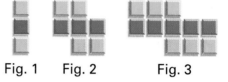

Fig. 1   Fig. 2   Fig. 3

23. Math Reasoning

a. Make a table using the four pairs of values represented on the graph.

b. Write an equation that shows how the maximum number of goldfish is related to the number of gallons of water in an aquarium.

c. Find two other pairs of values from the equation. Explain their meaning.

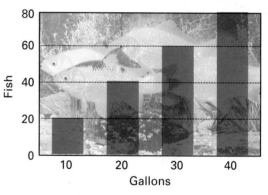

Maximum Number of Fish

Mixed Review

Evaluate each expression. *[Lesson 2-5]*

24. $2(3 + 7)(-5)$

25. $7(8 + 4) - 6(10 + 2)$

26. $\frac{1}{2}(8 + 4) + 17$

27. $8 + 5 - 3(1 + 11)^2$

Express each of the following in exponential form. *[Lesson 2-7]*

28. $3 \times 3 \times 3 \times 3 \times 3$

29. eight to the sixth power

Solutions of Two-Variable Equations

▶ **Lesson Link**   You have learned that equations sometimes have two variables and that such equations may have many solutions. You will now look at solutions and nonsolutions to two-variable equations. ◀

Explore   Solutions of Two-Variable Equations

Want a Polly or a Puppy?

The Dog and Parrot Emporium sells only parrots and puppies. Just for fun, the pet shop owner often takes inventory by counting the number of legs. Find all the different combinations of parrots and puppies that make a total of 24 legs.

1. Make a chart of the values using x for the number of parrots and y for the number of puppies. (Keep in mind the number of legs for each.) Write an expression for the number of legs using these variables.

2. If there are 24 legs in the Dog and Parrot Emporium, can the number of puppies or parrots ever be an odd number? Explain.

3. If there are 24 legs in the Dog and Parrot Emporium, can the number of parrots and puppies be the same? If so, how many of each would there be?

4. Write an equation that states that the number of parrot legs plus the number of puppy legs is 24. Use the variables from the chart.

5. For the pair (2, 7), which number is the x-coordinate and which is the y-coordinate? Is (2, 7) a solution of your equation? How do you know?

You'll Learn ...

■ to determine whether a pair of values is a solution of a two-variable equation

... How It's Used

Bakers are solving two-variable equations when they extend bread recipes to serve large numbers of people.

Problem Solving TIP

Make sure a mathematical solution makes sense in the context of a given problem.

You substituted possible solutions in one-variable equations. If the result was a true statement, the substituted value was a solution. A similar process is used with two-variable equations. A solution of a two-variable equation is an ordered pair.

Remember

You graphed ordered pairs (x, y) in Chapter 2. **[Page 91]**

Example 1

Is the ordered pair (3, 13) a solution of the equation $y = 7 + 2x$?

$y = 7 + 2x$	Write the equation.
$13 = 7 + 2(3)$	Substitute 3 and 13 in the equation for x and y.
$13 = 7 + 6$	Multiply.
$13 = 13$	Add.

Because this is a true statement, (3, 13) is a solution of $y = 7 + 2x$.

You can find solutions to an equation by choosing a value for one variable and solving for the remaining variable.

Remember

Substitute known values for each variable. **[Page 123]**

Example 2

Find two solutions for the equation $2 - 0.5x = y$.

Let $x = 0$.	Select a value for one of the variables.
$2 - 0.5(0) = y$	Substitute the selected value for the variable.
$2 - 0 = y$	Multiply.
$2 = y$	Subtract. (0, 2) is one solution.
Let $x = 2$.	Select another value for one of the variables.
$2 - 0.5(2) = y$	Substitute the selected value for the variable.
$2 - 1 = y$	Multiply.
$1 = y$	Subtract. (2, 1) is another solution.

(0, 2) and (2, 1) are two solutions for $2 - 0.5x = y$.

Try It

a. Determine whether $(-1, 9)$ is a solution of $y = 7 + 2x$.

b. Find two other solutions for $2 - 0.5x = y$.

Example 3

Some people have box turtles as pets. If the turtle and start-up supplies cost $30 and food runs $10 per month, how much will it cost to obtain a box turtle and keep it for 3 months?

Let m = the number of months. Let c = total cost.   Define the variables.

$c = 30 + 10m$ Write an equation showing how the variables are related.

Let $m = 3$.   Select a value for the variable that fits the problem.

$c = 30 + 10(3)$ Substitute the value for the variable.

$c = 30 + 30$ Multiply.

$c = 60$ Add.

It would cost $60 to obtain a turtle and keep it for 3 months.

Try It

a. Refer to Example 3. How much would it cost to obtain a turtle and keep it for a year?

b. It costs about $55 to adopt a dog, and about $70 each month for food, supplies, vet, grooming, and training. How much does it cost to adopt and care for a dog for 2 years?

In some contexts, there are mathematical solutions that do not make sense. In Example 3, a solution of $c = 30 + 10m$ is $m = -3$ and $c = 0$. But owning a turtle for -3 months does not make sense. Also $m = 1000$ would not be reasonable for this situation because turtles only live about 40 years.

Check | Your Understanding

1. How do you know whether an ordered pair is a solution of a two-variable equation?

2. The ordered pair $(3, 2)$ is a solution for a two-variable equation. Write an equation for which this ordered pair would be a solution.

3. Is a formula a two-variable equation? Explain.

You'll Learn ...

■ to graph a two-variable relationship

... How It's Used

Designers often use such graphs to help make decisions.

Vocabulary

linear equation

▶ **Lesson Link** You have learned how to write and find solutions for two-variable equations. In Chapter 2, you learned to graph points on a coordinate plane. Now you will learn to combine two-variable equations with graphing. ◀

Explore | Graphing Two-Variable Relationships

A Full House!

Materials: Graph paper

A pet shop has 12 kennels in which either 1 kitten or 1 puppy is displayed. The shop owner always keeps the kennels filled. But because pets are frequently sold, a puppy is sometimes replaced by a kitten or vice versa.

1. What equation represents the relationship between the number of dogs and cats that are displayed? Let c = the number of cats and let d = the number of dogs.

2. Name all the possible ordered pairs of the form (c, d) that satisfy the equation you wrote in Question 1. For example, one such ordered pair is (11, 1), representing 11 cats and 1 dog.

3. On a sheet of graph paper, graph all the ordered pairs from Question 2. Graph c values on the horizontal axis and d values on the vertical axis.

4. What do you notice about the points you graphed in Question 3?

5. Suppose the number of kennels is increased and there are 8 kittens and 8 puppies. Graph the point (8, 8). Does this ordered pair satisfy the equation you wrote in Question 1? What do you notice about the location of the point in relation to the points you graphed in Question 3?

Learn | Graphing Two-Variable Relationships

You know that a two-variable equation has solutions that are ordered pairs. If you graph the points that represent these ordered pairs and all the points lie on a straight line, the equation is called a **linear equation** .

Linear equations occur frequently in real-world situations. For example, at a pet show there is a basic entrance fee of $3 plus $1 for each event that is entered. If y is the total fee and x is the number of events entered, then $y = x + 3$ shows the relationship between x and y.

► **Language Link**

Notice that the root word of linear is *line*.

Examples

1 The line shown is the graph of the linear equation $y = x + 3$. Two points on the line are labeled *A* and *B*, and one point not on the line is labeled *C*. Which ordered pairs are solutions of the linear equation?

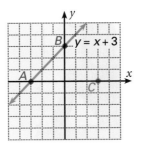

Test each ordered pair by substituting in the equation.

For A $(-3, 0)$	For B $(0, 3)$	For C $(3, 0)$
$y = x + 3$	$y = x + 3$	$y = x + 3$
$0 \overset{?}{=} -3 + 3$	$3 \overset{?}{=} 0 + 3$	$0 \overset{?}{=} 3 + 3$
$0 = 0 ✓$	$3 = 3 ✓$	$0 \neq 6$

The ordered pairs for *A* and *B* are solutions of the linear equation. The ordered pair for *C*, which does not lie on the line, is **not** a solution of the linear equation.

Try It

Use the graph above. Select two points on the line besides *A* and *B* and show that the ordered pairs for those points are solutions of $y = x + 3$. Then select a point that is **not** on the line, and show that its ordered pair is not a solution.

2 Graph the equation $y = 2x$.

Make a table of values. Graph the ordered pairs and connect the points with a line.

x	0	1	2	3
y	0	2	4	6

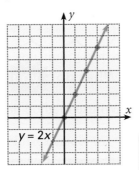

Notice that as the x values increase by 1 each time, the y values increase by 2. For any linear equation, as x values increase by an equal amount, corresponding y values will also increase (or decrease) by an equal amount.

► **Technology Link**

When using the same number many times, such as -3, store it in the memory of your calculator.

Try It

Graph the linear equation $y = -3x$.

17. Geometry When the length of a rectangle is 10 and the width varies, then the perimeter is related to the width.

    a. Make a table showing the relationship between y and x, where x is the width of the rectangle with length 10, and y is the perimeter. Use x values of 1, 2, 3, and 4.

    b. Look at the changes in x values and y values. Is the relationship linear?

    c. Graph the points from the table and connect them.

x m

10 m

Problem Solving and Reasoning

18. Critical Thinking The number of times a cricket chirps per minute (n) is related to the temperature in degrees Fahrenheit (f). A cricket chirps 124 times per minute at 68°F, and 172 times per minute at 80°F. Assume the relationship is linear.

    a. Make a table or graph to determine the temperature when a cricket chirps 140 times and 156 times. (Hint: Remember that in a linear relationship, equal changes in one variable cause equal changes in the other variable.)

    b. For what values do you think this linear relationship holds? Why?

19. Math Reasoning Worms can be used to dispose of organic material in a compost pile. To determine the number of pounds of worms needed, multiply the number of pounds of scraps added to the pile per day by 2. You need 1 ft^3 of space for every pound of worms. Write and graph an equation that relates pounds of scraps per day to ft^3 needed.

Mixed Review

Find the opposite of each number. *[Lesson 2-1]*

20. 72   **21.** -360 **22.** $|-13|$ **23.** $|0.01|$

Write in scientific notation. *[Lessons 2-8 and 2-9]*

24. 28,430,000,000   **25.** 41.07×10^4 **26.** 0.0000625   **27.** 0.094

Project Progress

You may have discovered linear relationships in some of the services you have been researching. You can begin by making tables, developing equations, and sketching graphs to help you with information displays.

Problem Solving

Understand
Plan
Solve
Look Back

At the beginning of this section, you learned that some people use the rule that a "dog" year equals 7 human years. The rule would mean that a 14-year-old dog would correspond to a 98-year-old person.

How Much Is That in Dog Years?

Are there patterns that relate human and dog years? Use what you have learned about patterns and linear relationships to answer the following questions.

1. Assume that a dog's "human age" is just the product of 7 and its actual age. What formula would describe the situation above? Is the formula linear?

2. The oldest dog on record was 29 years old. Using the formula, does this age correspond to the oldest human (121 years old)? Explain.

3. Most dogs are fully grown by the time they are a year and a half old. At what age are humans fully grown? Do the ages correspond, using the formula?

4. Dr. Diane Deads, D.V.M., has the following table on the wall in her waiting room:

Dog Age	1	2	3	4	5	6	7	8	9	10
Human Age	15	27	35	40	44	48	52	56	60	64

Graph this data on a grid. Is it linear? Is any part linear?

5. Would negative values be reasonable on this chart? Explain.

6. Could you describe or make a formula for all or part of this data?

7. Large breeds of dogs generally have short life spans; small breeds have longer life spans. Different breeds also have different developmental stages. How could you take this information into account in developing a conversion table or equation?

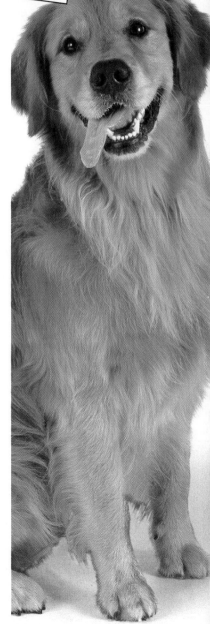

Find the value of *y* for *x* = 8 in each equation.

1. $y = 7x$ **2.** $y = \frac{1}{4}x$ **3.** $y = x - 5$ **4.** $y + x = 10$

Make a table of ordered pairs for each equation. Use 0, 1, 2, 3, and 4 as *x* values.

5. $y = -3x$ **6.** $y = x + 10$ **7.** $y = 2.5x$ **8.** $y = 2x - 1$

Determine whether each ordered pair is a solution of the equation.

9. $y = x + 15$ **a.** $(15, 0)$ **b.** $(0, 15)$ **c.** $(14, 1)$

10. $y = 0.4x$ **a.** $(2, 0.8)$ **b.** $(0.8, 2)$ **c.** $(10, 4)$

Find a rule that relates *x* and *y*. Then find the value of *y* when *x* = 60.

11.

x	0	1	2	3	4	5
y	0	4	8	12	16	20

12.

x	0	1	2	3	4	5
y	4	5	6	7	8	9

13. Graph $y = x + 4$.

14. An animal shelter allows the public to adopt any number of cats for a set fee of $10 plus $15 for each cat to cover the cost of shots.

    a. Write an equation relating the cost, *y*, to *x*, the number of cats adopted. Then make a table of values showing the cost for adopting 1, 2, or 3 cats. Graph the ordered pairs and connect them with a line.

    b. Do the ordered pairs for all points on the line satisfy the equation? Do all these solutions make sense in this situation? Explain.

Test Prep

When you are asked to determine whether an ordered pair is a solution of an equation, remember that the *x*-coordinate appears first in each ordered pair.

15. Which of these ordered pairs is **not** a solution of $y = x - 10$?

    Ⓐ $(0, -10)$ Ⓑ $(10, 0)$ Ⓒ $(0, 10)$ Ⓓ $(5, -5)$

Linear Equations and Inequalities

The rush of wind, the strain of muscles, the cadence matching your heart beat, the road speeding by below you. You must be cycling. Each year, millions take to the roads on bikes. Whether they are with their families or members of bicycle touring clubs, they pursue one goal—to exercise while enjoying the great outdoors.

For some, bicycling may provide the ultimate thrill, like riding down the 10,000-ft slope of Maui's volcano, Haleakala. Or there's the Tour de France, where it takes days to finish the entire course, covering almost 4,000 km.

Do you remember the first time you tried to ride a bike? Perhaps you used training wheels, or someone ran along, holding you up. The bike you learned on was probably a single-speed, built to be used primarily on flat surfaces. Other bicycles, with as many as 21 speeds, allow riders to navigate steep slopes with ease with a click of the finger.

1 How could bicycling behind another rider make it easier to ride fast?

2 Think of hills as slopes. Why is it harder to ride up hills than on flat surfaces?

3 How do gears make climbing a hill easier?

Go Play Outside!

189

Understanding Slope

You'll Learn ...

■ to find the slope of a line

... How It's Used

Land use planners need to calculate slopes to make decisions about runoff.

Vocabulary

slope

rise

run

positive slope

negative slope

▶ **Lesson Link** You have learned to graph equations with two variables, and to determine whether the graph is linear. Now you will learn ways that mathematicians describe these lines. ◀

Explore | Slope

The Ups and Downs of Graphing

Materials: Graph paper
Number cube
Coin (optional)

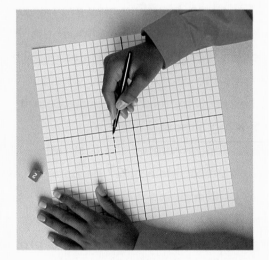

1. On a large sheet of graph paper, draw a coordinate plane with the origin at the center of the page. Label the *x*- and *y*-axes.

2. Flip a coin to see if you should move right (heads) or left (tails). Roll a number cube to determine the number of units you should move, for example, Right 5.

3. Flip the coin again to see if you should move up (heads) or down (tails). Roll the number cube again to determine the number of units you should move, for example, Up 2.

4. Using your results from steps 2 and 3, start at the origin and plot a point.

5. From your point, move the same number of spaces right or left as before, then move up or down as before. Plot a second point.

6. Move and plot several times. What geometric shape is formed by these points? Draw it.

7. Compare your results with those of your classmates.

Beginning skiers use slopes that are not as steep as those used by more advanced skiers. Some lines in the coordinate plane can also be considered "steeper" than others.

Mathematicians use a concept called **slope** to describe the steepness of a line. It relates the vertical change to the horizontal change. These are often called the **rise** and the **run** . When a line slants upward from left to right, it is said to have **positive slope** ; when it slants downward it has **negative slope** .

► **Language Link**

When a variable is used for slope, it is usually the letter *m*. This comes from the French word *monter*, meaning "to climb."

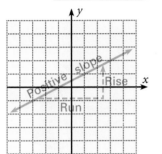

For any line, the rise divided by the run is always the same. This is the slope of the line. A horizontal line has a slope of zero because it has zero rise. A vertical line is said to have no slope.

Example 1

Snow safety experts advise that avalanches are more likely to happen on a hill with a slope of between 0.5 and 1. Is an avalanche likely for Hotgog Hill?

$$\frac{\text{rise}}{\text{run}} = \frac{850}{1275}$$

Dividing to find the slope, 850 $\boxed{\div}$ 1275 $\boxed{=}$ 0.66666667. The slope is between 0.5 and 1, so an avalanche may be likely.

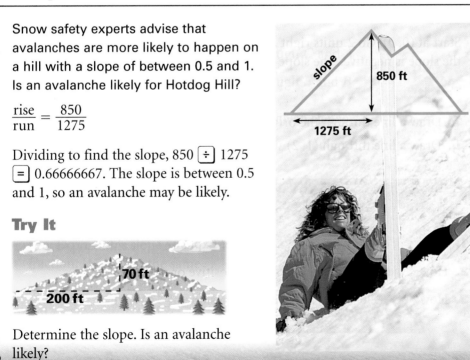

Try It

Determine the slope. Is an avalanche likely?

16. Describe how slope and mountain-biking accidents are related.

Locations of Mountain-Biking Accidents

Uphill 15%

9% Flat

76% Downhill

17. Fine Arts This sculpture is at the NASA Museum in Washington, D. C. What is the slope of the red line shown? Explain how you found it.

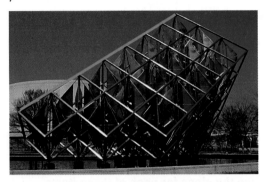

Problem Solving and Reasoning

18. Critical Thinking Patios, driveways, and streets are often designed so they have a slope of about $\frac{1}{48}$ toward their edges. Why would they be designed this way?

Problem Solving TIP

Draw a picture to show the effect of sloped edges.

19. a. Find the missing information for each ski run.

Ski Run	Total Rise	Total Run	Slope
Alpine Meadows	1800 ft	7200 ft	
Diamond Peak	1840 ft	3680 ft	
Bear Valley	1900 ft	4750 ft	
Donner Ski Ranch	750 ft	3000 ft	

b. Communicate Which ski areas would you recommend for advanced skiers? Explain.

20. Critical Thinking Architects use circular or winding stairs in buildings. What is the advantage of this kind of structure?

21. Critical Thinking How would you describe the calculation of the slope of a horizontal line? How would you describe the calculation of the slope of a vertical line?

Mixed Review

Add. *[Lesson 2-2]*

22. $12 + (-12)$ **23.** $-37 + (-4)$ **24.** $43 + 6 - 9$

Solve each formula. *[Lesson 3-1]*

25. $A = bh$, for $b = 7$ and $h = 9$ **26.** $P = 2l + 2w$, for $P = 42$ and $l = 8$

Patterns in Linear Equations and Graphs

▶ **Lesson Link**   You know how to find the slope of a line by looking at its graph. You can also find the slope of a line by looking at its equation. ◀

Explore   Patterns in Linear Equations and Graphs

Materials: Graphing utility

Blizzard of a Graph!

On the ground there was 2 feet of snow. During the night, snow begins falling at 1 foot per hour in some areas, 2 feet per hour in others, and as much as 3 feet per hour in others.

If y is the amount of snow on the ground as it falls, and x is the number of hours it has been falling, then $y = x + 2$, $y = 2x + 2$, and $y = 3x + 2$ describe the relationship between snow on the ground and the number of hours it falls in the three locations.

1. Graph $y = x + 2$, $y = 2x + 2$, and $y = 3x + 2$ using a graphing utility. What do you notice about the steepness of the graphs? Do the graphs share any common points?

2. Graph $y = x + 2$, $y = x - 1$, and $y = x - 3$ using a graphing utility. What do you notice?

3. What is the relationship between the constant added to each x and the point where each graph crosses the y-axis?

4. Do you see any relationships between the coefficient of x and the slope of each line?

You'll Learn …

■ to graph an equation and then find the slope and the intercepts

… How It's Used

Systems used by air-traffic controllers lock planes onto beams generated by linear equations so planes can land safely.

Vocabulary

x-intercept

y-intercept

parallel lines

Remember

To make a table of ordered pairs, substitute different values for *x* and solve for *y*. [Page 173]

You already know that you can find the slope of a line by looking at the graph. You can also determine the **x-intercept** and **y-intercept** by looking at the graph. The *x*-intercept is the *x*-coordinate of the point where the line crosses the *x*-axis, and the *y*-intercept is the *y*-coordinate of the point where the line crosses the *y*-axis.

The slope and *y*-intercept often have meanings in real-world problems.

Example 1

A hockey player receives 2 minutes in the penalty box for each minor penalty. A player already has 4 minutes in minor penalties.

Graph $y = 2x + 4$, find the slope, and *y*-intercept. What are the meanings of the slope and *y*-intercept in the problem?

Make a table of ordered pairs by assigning values to *x* and then finding *y*. Graph the points and connect them with a line. You can choose any values for *x*. Try: -2, 0, and 2.

x	-2	0	2
y	0	4	8

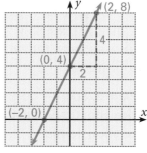

Find the rise and run. Because rise $= 4$ and run $= 2$, the slope $= \frac{4}{2}$ or 2, and the line slants upward. The graph crosses the *y*-axis at 4, the *y*-intercept is 4. The slope matches the 2 minutes he receives for each additional minor penalty. The *y*-intercept means that if he receives no additional penalties, he will have 4 penalty minutes.

Although you can use negative numbers to make the graph, they do not make sense in this problem situation.

Examples

2 Graph $y = \frac{-3}{4}x - 3$. Find the slope, the x-intercept, and the y-intercept.

Make a table of ordered pairs using -4, 0, and 4 as x-values. Graph the points and connect them with a line.

x	-4	0	4
y	0	-3	-6

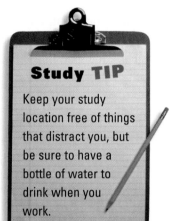

Find the rise and run. Because rise $= -3$ and run $= 4$, the slope $= \frac{-3}{4}$, and the line slants downward. The graph crosses the x-axis at -4 and the y-axis at -3. So the x-intercept is -4 and the y-intercept is -3.

Try It

Graph each equation. Find the slope, the x-intercept, and the y-intercept.

a. $y = 3x - 6$ **b.** $y = \frac{-1}{2}x + 4$

3 Graph $y = 2x - 1$ and $y = 2x + 3$ on the same grid. Then find the slope for each line.

Make a table of ordered pairs for each equation. Graph the points and connect them.

For $y = 2x - 1$

x	-2	0	2
y	-5	-1	3

For $y = 2x + 3$

x	-2	0	2
y	-1	3	7

For each graph, the rise is 4 and the run is 2. So the slope in each case is $\frac{4}{2}$ or 2.

Notice that the lines never intersect no matter how far they are extended. Such lines are called **parallel lines**. Parallel lines have the same slope.

> **Study TIP**
>
> Keep your study location free of things that distract you, but be sure to have a bottle of water to drink when you work.

Check Your Understanding

1. To graph a linear equation, how many points do you need to connect? Why is it a good idea to graph an additional point?

2. When you graph an equation such as $y = \frac{1}{4}x - 2$, can you assign any values to x? Would some values be easier to use than others? Explain.

Practice and Apply

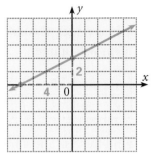

Getting Started

1. The rise is _____ and the run is _____. So the slope is _____.

2. The graph crosses the x-axis at $(-4, 0)$. So the x-intercept is _____.

3. The graph crosses the y-axis at $(0, 2)$. So the y-intercept is _____.

For each line, find the slope, the *x*-intercept, and the *y*-intercept.

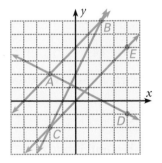

4. Line through A and B

5. Line through C and B

6. Line through A and D

7. Line through C and E

8. Which lines in Exercises 4–7 are parallel? Explain.

Graph each equation. Find the slope, the *x*-intercept, and the *y*-intercept.

9. $y = 2x - 6$

10. $y = x + 8$

11. $y = -x$

12. $y = \frac{1}{5}x$

13. $y = 5x + 2$

14. $y = -\frac{3}{4}x + 2$

15. $y = \frac{1}{2}x - 2$

16. $y = -7x$

17. **Test Prep** The slopes of two lines are given. Which represent parallel lines?

Ⓐ $\frac{6}{3}$ and $\frac{8}{4}$ Ⓑ $\frac{3}{6}$ and $\frac{6}{3}$ Ⓒ $\frac{3}{6}$ and $\frac{-3}{6}$ Ⓓ 4 and $\frac{1}{4}$

18. Peter has just learned how to ski and wants to start out on the beginner's hill. The $\frac{\text{rise}}{\text{run}}$ of the hills are $\frac{723 \text{ ft}}{4820 \text{ ft}}$, $\frac{819 \text{ ft}}{1820 \text{ ft}}$, and $\frac{778 \text{ ft}}{2593 \text{ ft}}$. Determine the slope of each hill. Which one is for beginners?

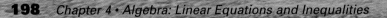

Problem Solving and Reasoning

19. Communicate Marty belongs to a swim club. With a membership fee of $20 per year, the members can swim any number of times for a reduced rate of $2 per swim. Make a graph to show the total cost for varying numbers of swims. Explain how to find a typical cost from the graph.

20. Critical Thinking

a. Is there a way to determine the slope and y-intercept of equations such as $y = 2x - 3$ and $y = -3x + 1$ just by looking at the equation? (Hint: You might use your answers to Exercises 9–16 to help you.)

b. The equation of a line is $y = \frac{2}{3}x + 6$. Predict the slope and the y-intercept without graphing.

c. Communicate Explain how you would change the equation $y = 2x - 3$ so the line will have a greater slope and a smaller y-intercept.

21. Choose a Strategy The formula $h = 450t + 1800$ gives the altitude of a mountain-climbing team t hours after they begin their climb, where h is the height above sea level in feet. At what altitude did they start their climb? How many feet are they climbing per hour?

22. Critical Thinking During winter break, Jerry can earn $12 for every 5 pairs of skis he waxes for the ski shop ($y = \frac{12}{5}x$) or he can earn $18 for every 7 snowboards he waxes ($y = \frac{18}{7}x$). Which job would earn Jerry more money? Explain.

23. Journal Explain how you can determine the slope of a line by looking at its graph; by examining its equation.

> **Problem Solving**
> **STRATEGIES**
> • Look for a Pattern
> • Make an Organized List
> • Make a Table
> • Guess and Check
> • Work Backward
> • Use Logical Reasoning
> • Draw a Diagram
> • Solve a Simpler Problem

Mixed Review

Add or Subtract. *[Lesson 2-3]*

24. $40 - 50$ **25.** $-33 - 13$ **26.** $-42 - (-10)$ **27.** $-9 + 99$

28. A company gives an employee a pension based on the formula $P = \frac{sy}{60}$, where s is the employee's salary, and y is the number of years of employment. What is the pension for an employee with a salary of $40,000 and employed for 18 years? *[Lesson 3-1]*

Solve each equation. *[Lesson 3-2]*

29. $x = 23 + 17$ **30.** $x + 100 = 300$ **31.** $3x = 18$ **32.** $-x = 17$

T E C H N O L O G Y

Using a Graphing Calculator • Parallel Lines

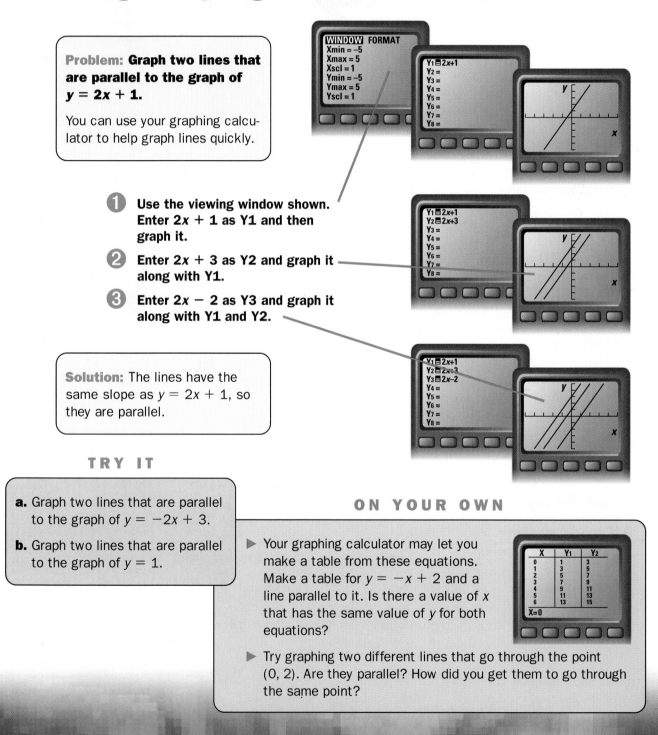

Problem: Graph two lines that are parallel to the graph of $y = 2x + 1$.

You can use your graphing calculator to help graph lines quickly.

1 Use the viewing window shown. Enter $2x + 1$ as Y1 and then graph it.

2 Enter $2x + 3$ as Y2 and graph it along with Y1.

3 Enter $2x - 2$ as Y3 and graph it along with Y1 and Y2.

Solution: The lines have the same slope as $y = 2x + 1$, so they are parallel.

TRY IT

a. Graph two lines that are parallel to the graph of $y = -2x + 3$.

b. Graph two lines that are parallel to the graph of $y = 1$.

ON YOUR OWN

▶ Your graphing calculator may let you make a table from these equations. Make a table for $y = -x + 2$ and a line parallel to it. Is there a value of x that has the same value of y for both equations?

▶ Try graphing two different lines that go through the point $(0, 2)$. Are they parallel? How did you get them to go through the same point?

Pairs of Linear Equations

▶ **Lesson Link**   You have seen how to graph all the solutions of a single linear equation. Now you will learn how to find the solution of a pair of linear equations. ◀

You'll Learn ...

■ to find a single solution of a pair of linear equations

... How It's Used

Firefighters use intersecting lines to pinpoint fire locations.

| **Explore** | **Pairs of Linear Equations** |

Rocking the Boat

Materials: Spreadsheet software (optional)

1. The signs show the cost of renting a boat at two different locations. Copy and complete the table to find the total costs for various times. Extend the table if necessary. Use a spreadsheet program if one is available.

Vistas Boats
$3 + $2/hour

Ray's Rafting
$8 + $1/hour

Hours	Vistas Boats Cost	Ray's Rafting Cost
x	$2x + 3$	$x + 8$
1		
2		
3		
4		

2. Explain why $2x + 3$ is the cost of a boat rental at Vistas Boats, and $x + 8$ is the cost of a boat rental at Ray's Rafting.

3. Which rental arrangement is better if you plan to rent a boat for 1 hour? Why?

4. For what number of rental hours is the cost the same at either place?

5. After how many hours is it cheaper to rent a boat at Ray's Rafting?

6. Do you think that Ray's Rafting will always be cheaper for more than the number of hours you found in Question 5? Why or why not?

Vocabulary

system of linear equations

When two linear equations are considered together, they form a **system of linear equations**. An ordered pair that is a solution of both equations is called a *solution* of the system.

Example 1

Wild World Carnival charges an admission of $10 plus $1 for each ride. Fantastic Fair charges an admission of $6 plus $2 for each ride.

a. Let x be the number of rides and let y be the total cost. Write an equation for the total cost at each park for admission plus x rides. Then make a table to show the cost for various numbers of rides.

b. Is there a number of rides for which the total cost is the same at each park? What ordered pair solves *both* equations that you wrote in Part a?

a. For Wild World Carnival, $y = x + 10$. For Fantastic Fair, $y = 2x + 6$.

Number of Rides	x	0	1	2	3	4	5	6
Wild World Carnival	$y = x + 10$	10	11	12	13	14	15	16
Fantastic Fair	$y = 2x + 6$	6	8	10	12	14	16	18

b. The cost is the same for 4 rides ($14). The ordered pair (4, 14) solves both equations. So (4, 14) is a solution of the system of equations $y = x + 10$ and $y = 2x + 6$.

Try It

a. Suppose Fantastic Fair raises its admission to $8 but still charges $2 a ride. For how many rides would the total cost be the same at both parks?

b. Suppose Fantastic Fair has free admission for a day, but still charges $2 per ride. For how many rides would the total cost be the same at both parks?

Another way to find the solution of a system of linear equations is to graph both equations and find a point that lies on both lines. Then determine the x and y values for that point.

Example 2

Glen needs to decide whether to purchase hang-gliding equipment. If he rents equipment, he will pay $75 for each flight. If he purchases equipment for $200, he will pay $25 for each flight. For what number of flights would each option cost the same?

Let x = number of flights. Let y = total cost.

$y = 75x$ This is the total cost if he rents equipment.

$y = 25x + 200$ This is the total cost if he buys equipment.

Find two or three solutions for each equation and graph each line. Find the point where the lines intersect.

x	$y = 75x$
0	0
2	150

x	$y = 25x + 200$
0	200
2	250

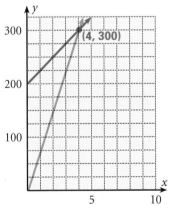

The lines intersect at (4, 300). Check the coordinates for x and y in both equations.

$y = 75x$ $\qquad$ $y = 25x + 200$

$300 \stackrel{?}{=} 75(4)$ $\qquad$ $300 \stackrel{?}{=} 25(4) + 200$

$300 = 300$ ✓ $\qquad$ $300 = 300$ ✓

If Glen makes 4 flights, the total cost would be the same—$300.

Test Prep

You may be able to find a solution of a system using number sense. If you see that Glen pays $50 more per flight if he rents, you might realize that he pays $200 more for 4 flights.

Check | Your Understanding

1. How do you know whether an ordered pair is a solution of a system of two equations?

2. How can you find the solution of a system of equations from a graph?

Linear Inequalities

You'll Learn ...

■ to express two-variable inequalities graphically

... How It's Used

Water testers use inequalities to describe the levels of impurities permitted in drinking water samples.

Vocabulary

linear inequality

boundary line

▶ **Lesson Link**   In Chapter 3, you solved and graphed inequalities with one variable. Now that you can solve equations with two variables, you can see how inequalities with two variables are solved and graphed. ◀

Explore | Linear Inequalities

Which Side Are You On?

Materials: Graph paper and straightedge, or Graphing utility

Imagine yourself kayaking on a beautiful, tree-lined river. As you approach the rapids, you spot a rope supported by buoys dividing the river down the center, marked $y = x - 4$. You must immediately choose one side of the river.

1. Graph the equation $y = x - 4$, which represents the rope dividing the river.

2. Pick any point above the line that you graphed. Decide if the point you chose makes $y = x - 4$, $y > x - 4$, or $y < x - 4$ true. Support your conclusion.

3. Pick any point below the line. Decide if the point you chose makes $y = x - 4$, $y > x - 4$, or $y < x - 4$ true. Support your conclusion.

4. Suppose solutions for $y > x - 4$ indicate the challenging white water rapids and $y < x - 4$ indicates the more manageable side. Lightly shade the side you would choose, sketch your kayak on that side and label it appropriately, either $y > x - 4$ or $y < x - 4$.

Learn | Linear Inequalities

You know that to determine whether a value is a solution of a one-variable inequality, you can substitute and see if the inequality is true. You can do the same for an inequality with two variables.

Examples

1 Is (1, 5) a solution of $y > x + 2$?

$y > x + 2$ Write the inequality.

$5 \overset{?}{>} 1 + 2$ Substitute the ordered pair in the inequality.

$5 > 3 \checkmark$ Check to see if the resulting inequality is true.

The ordered pair $(1, 5)$ is a solution of $y > x + 2$.

When you graph a one-variable inequality, such as $x > 3$, one boundary point ($x = 3$) separates the line into points that are solutions and points that are not.

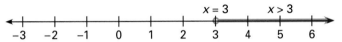

Remember

You know how to graph inequalities on a number line. [Page 156]

When you graph a **linear inequality**, such as $y > x + 2$, a **boundary line** ($y = x + 2$) separates the coordinate plane into points that are solutions and points that are not.

The shaded region is the solution. Instead of an open circle, we can use a dashed line to show that the line is not part of the solution. (For $\geq$ and $\leq$, instead of a closed circle, use a *solid* line.)

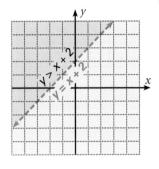

2 Graph the inequality $y \leq 2x - 4$.

First, make a table of values for $y = 2x - 4$.

x	0	2	4
y	−4	0	4

Draw a solid line for $y = 2x - 4$. Choose any point not on the line to see if it is a solution of the inequality. $(0, 0)$ is usually a convenient point. If it is a solution, all points on that side of the line are solutions. If it is not a solution, all points on the other side of the line are solutions.

$0 \leq 2(0) - 4$

$0 \leq -4$ is false. Shade the other side of the graph.

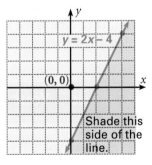

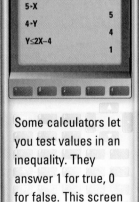

Some calculators let you test values in an inequality. They answer 1 for true, 0 for false. This screen shows that (5, 4) is a solution of $y \leq 2x - 4$.

Try It

Graph $y > x - 2$.

20. **Civics** Votes on proposals often require a two-thirds majority for the proposal to pass. The number of votes in favor must be at least twice the number opposed. Make a graph to show the number of votes required to pass a proposal. Use x as the number opposed, and y as the number in favor.

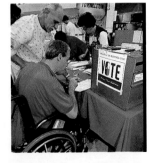

Problem Solving and Reasoning

21. **Communicate** Many communities allow no more than one-fourth of a store's window area to be covered by advertising. Is this storefront window within the law? How did you decide?

22. **Critical Thinking** Graph $y < x + 3$ and $y \geq 2x$ on the same set of axes. Notice that the grid is divided into four regions. Select a point in each region. Substitute the ordered pair for each point into both inequalities. Which region contains the point that solves both inequalities? What is true of all points in that region?

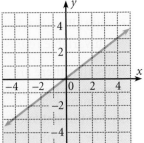

23. **Choose a Strategy** Films are rated by a panel of reviewers. For a film to be rated as a "must see," it must receive between 3 points and 4 points per reviewer. Graph the total points a "must see" film must have. Let x be the number of reviewers.

24. **Math Reasoning** What inequality would produce the graph at the right?

25. **Journal** Compare and contrast graphing a two-variable equation with graphing a two-variable inequality.

Problem Solving
STRATEGIES
• Look for a Pattern
• Make an Organized List
• Make a Table
• Guess and Check
• Work Backward
• Use Logical Reasoning
• Draw a Diagram
• Solve a Simpler Problem

Mixed Review

Express in exponential notation. [Lesson 2-7]

26. $2 \times 2 \times 2 \times 2$ 27. 8×8

28. $7 \times 7 \times 7 \times 7 \times 7 \times 7$ 29. 2 cubed

Solve each equation. [Lesson 3-4]

30. $13 = x + 10$ 31. $x - 23 = 9$ 32. $16 = x - 1$ 33. $x + 8 = 11$

34. $2.4 = x + 1.8$ 35. $x - 0.01 = 0.05$ 36. $\frac{1}{2} = x - 2$ 37. $x + 1\frac{7}{8} = 1\frac{3}{4}$

Section 4B Connect

At the beginning of Section 4B, we discussed bicycles and bicycling. We can use graphs and equations to look at bicycling situations.

Go Play Outside!

Materials: Graph paper or Graphing utility, Colored pencils

Sandy and her brother Mark will be having a bike race. Sandy averages 4 min/mi and Mark averages 6 min/mi. Sandy will give Mark a 5-minute head start.

1. Graph the line $y = 6x$ for Mark's ride and $y = 4x + 5$ for Sandy's. Label the axes appropriately.

2. Find the slope and y-intercept of each line. What do these represent?

3. Find the point where the lines intersect and label it. What does this point represent? What conclusions can you make?

4. Suppose Mark gets to choose how long the race will last, or how far it will go. Identify the part of the graph where Mark would win the race. What conditions should he choose?

5. Suppose Sandy gives Mark a $\frac{1}{2}$ *mile* head start. Use the fact that 4 min/mi is 15 mi/hr and 6 min/mi is 10 mi/hr to graph this situation a different way. Which head start is better for Sandy, 5 min or $\frac{1}{2}$ mi? Why?

Problem Solving Focus

Identifying Missing Information

Evaluating information is an important problem solving skill. However, sometimes some of the necessary information is not given. It is important for you to be able to read the problem and understand if all the information needed to solve the problem is given.

For each problem, identify what additional information would be needed to solve the problem. Some of the problems are not missing information.

1 Ines buys a portable stereo on a time-payment schedule. She makes a down payment of $150 and agrees to pay $75 a month until she pays the full price. Write an equation that shows how long Ines needs to pay the full amount.

2 Ines makes a similar deal on a set of speakers. After a $75 down payment, she will pay $40 a month for 6 months. Write an equation showing how much the speakers will cost.

3 Ines likes to make tapes for her friends. A box of 3 blank cassette tapes costs $6.99 and a box of 10 costs $19.99. Write an equation to find the amount of money it will cost to buy 15 blank cassette tapes.

4 To help pay for her purchases, Ines sells her old stereo to her friend Max for $400. Max will pay part of Ines's payments on the stereo until he has paid off what he owes her. Write an equation showing the number of payments Max needs to make.

SHARING INFORMATION

Throughout time, people have learned to communicate in different ways. Drum beats, smoke signals, sign language—all of these have substituted for the spoken word.

Today, telecommunications are used. They allow people to communicate quickly and over great distances. *Tele* is Greek and means "far off; at a distance."

With the invention of the telegraph around 1837, the speed of communication was almost the speed of light (299,000 km/s, or 186,000 m/s). Alexander Graham Bell's invention of the telephone allowed the human voice, rather than Morse code, to be transmitted.

Radio, television, and the Internet resulted from the desire to make ideas and information known quickly around the world. As the new millennium begins, these telecommunications will probably be replaced by faster methods of communication.

1 How many letters and numbers are used in English?

2 Why might a computer display 186,000 as 186K?

3 Why is typing speed measured in words per minute rather than characters per minute?

Exploring and Estimating Ratios and Rates

You'll Learn ...

■ to estimate ratios and rates from pictures and data

■ to use ratios and rates to compare quantities

... How It's Used

An emergency medical technician (EMT) must be able to estimate pulse rates quickly to determine a course of action.

Vocabulary

ratio

rate

unit rate

▶ **Lesson Link**   In previous chapters, you learned to measure and calculate quantities. In this chapter you will learn to use math to compare quantities. ◀

| **Explore** | Comparisons |

Incomparable!

Decide if each statement is very reasonable, unreasonable, or possibly reasonable. Justify your answers.

1. There are five computers per classroom.

2. There are 15 students for every 12 computers in the middle school.

3. There are twice as many fax machines in the main office as there are in the teacher's lounge.

4. The highest recorded speed for a Morse code message is 75 words per minute.

5. The cost for each minute of a cellular phone call is 28¢.

6. Make a comparison statement that you think is reasonable. Then make a comparison statement that you think is unreasonable. Explain your choices.

| **Learn** | Exploring and Estimating Ratios and Rates |

In your everyday life, you are constantly comparing quantities. A **ratio** is a comparison of two quantities by division. A ratio can be written in three different ways. Because a ratio can usually be written as a fraction, it can be simplified. Suppose there are 15 computers in the math lab and 5 computers in your classroom. This can be written as follows:

$\frac{15}{5}$, or $\frac{3}{1}$ 3 to 1   3:1   The ratio can be read as 3 to 1.

Example 1

Write all of the ratios that can be made using the figure at the right.

1. Shaded area to total area:

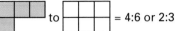 = 4:6 or 2:3

2. Total area to shaded area:

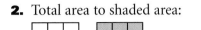 = 6:4 or 3:2

3. Unshaded area to total area:

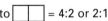 = 2:6 or 1:3

4. Total area to unshaded area:

 = 6:2 or 3:1

5. Shaded area to unshaded area:

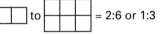 = 4:2 or 2:1

6. Unshaded area to shaded area:

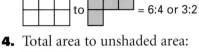 = 2:4 or 1:2

Example 2

The following graph shows the growth in the number of cellular phones since 1984.

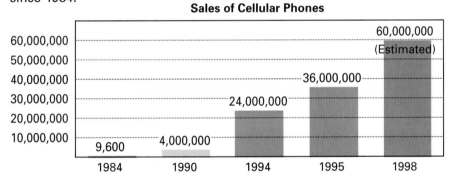

Sales of Cellular Phones

a. Estimate the ratio of the number of phones in 1990 to the number in 1994.

The number in 1990 is approximately 4 million and in 1994 is approximately 24 million. The estimated ratio is 4 to 24. Dividing, this is about 1 to 6.

b. Estimate the ratio of the number of phones in 1998 to the number in 1984.

The estimated number in 1998 is 60 million and in 1984 is about 10 thousand. The estimated ratio is $\frac{60,000,000}{10,000}$. Dividing, this is about 6000:1.

Try It

a. Write all of the ratios that can be made using this figure.

b. Estimate the ratio of the number of cellular phones in 1990 to the number in 1995.

Language Arts Write a ratio comparing the number of vowels to the number of consonants for each word.

9. Ratio   **10.** Rate   **11.** Percent   **12.** Compare   **13.** Fraction

14. Career In 1995, a survey asked 21.2 million American working mothers how they would spend an extra hour.

a. Approximately _____ mothers would spend the hour with a child for every 1 who would spend it with a spouse.

b. Approximately _____ mothers would spend the hour alone for every 1 who would spend it working.

Activity	Numbers of Working Mothers
with their child	9,680,000
alone	6,160,000
sleeping	3,300,000
with spouse	2,200,000
working	440,000

15. Computers A disk drive has 394.3 MB of memory stored and 105.7 MB of memory available. The capacity of the disk drive is the sum of the amount stored and the amount available. Estimate each ratio:

a. Amount stored to capacity

b. Capacity to amount available

c. A 55 MB file is added to the amount stored. Will this affect all the ratios in Parts **a** and **b**? Explain your reasoning.

Problem Solving and Reasoning

16. Communicate When you write a ratio in fraction form, how do you decide which number to use as the denominator?

17. Journal Describe a situation that could be modeled by the ratio 5:2. Explain why this is not the same as modeling it by 2:5.

18. Critical Thinking The ratio of boys to girls in a class of 15 is 2 to 3. How many boys and girls would have to be added in order to have a class of 20 in the ratio of 1 to 1?

Mixed Review

Write each number in scientific notation. *[Lesson 2-9]*

19. 0.00694   **20.** 6 millionths   **21.** $\dfrac{1}{1,000,000,000}$

Solve each equation. *[Lesson 3-5]*

22. $4x = 32$ **23.** $\dfrac{x}{5} = 7$ **24.** $5 = \dfrac{1}{2}k$ **25.** $12 = -2x$

Proportions and Equal Ratios

▶ **Lesson Link**   You have seen that ratios compare two quantities. In this lesson, you will see that a ratio can be compared with another ratio. ◀

Explore Equal Ratios

More Stuffing, Please

Materials: Paper, Envelopes

A company wants to hire students to stuff envelopes neatly and quickly.

1. Determine your group's paper-folding rate (folding a sheet of paper into thirds so it can be stuffed into a legal-sized envelope) in sheets per minute.

2. Determine your envelope stuffing-and-closing rate (inserting a folded sheet and inserting the envelope's flap) in envelopes per minute.

3. Use your data to estimate/calculate the paper-folding and envelope-stuffing rates per hour, 4-hour shift, day, week, year, lifetime.

4. Suppose the company was very impressed with the entire class and hired everyone. How long would it take the class to fold, stuff, and insert the flap for 100,000 pieces of mail? (Could it be done in a year of math classes?)

You'll Learn ...

■ to create and identify equal ratios and rates

■ to express equal ratios and rates in tables

■ to test for proportionality

... How It's Used

Judges often use ratios and proportions to determine degree of responsibility and to award damages.

Vocabulary

equal ratios

proportion

cross product

Learn Proportions and Equal Ratios

Ratios that name the same amount are **equal ratios** . For example, $\frac{3}{6}$ and $\frac{2}{4}$ each represent one half. Here are two ways to find a ratio that is equal to a given ratio.

Multiply the numerator and denominator by the same nonzero number.

$$\frac{3}{1} \times \frac{6}{6} = \frac{18}{6}$$

Divide the numerator and denominator by the same nonzero number.

$$\frac{18}{6} \div \frac{6}{6} = \frac{3}{1}$$

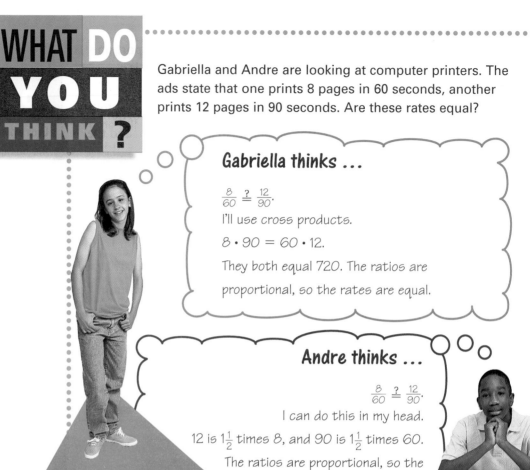

Gabriella and Andre are looking at computer printers. The ads state that one prints 8 pages in 60 seconds, another prints 12 pages in 90 seconds. Are these rates equal?

Gabriella thinks ...

$\frac{8}{60} \overset{?}{=} \frac{12}{90}$.

I'll use cross products.

$8 \cdot 90 = 60 \cdot 12$.

They both equal 720. The ratios are proportional, so the rates are equal.

Andre thinks ...

$\frac{8}{60} \overset{?}{=} \frac{12}{90}$.

I can do this in my head.

12 is $1\frac{1}{2}$ times 8, and 90 is $1\frac{1}{2}$ times 60. The ratios are proportional, so the rates are equal.

MENTAL MATH

Usually if a problem can be done mentally, it is much quicker to do so. Always be on the lookout for numbers that are easy to compute mentally.

What do **you** think?

Suppose the second printer printed 16 pages in 100 seconds. How could you use Andre's method to see if the rates are equal?

Check | Your Understanding

1. How can you tell if two ratios are equal?

2. How can you create two ratios equal to a given ratio?

3. How can you use an equal ratio table if the numbers you are looking for are not in the table?

4. If two quantities always have a proportional relationship and one doubles, what happens to the other quantity? What if one is quartered?

5-2 Exercises and Applications

Practice and Apply

1. **Getting Started** Multiply or divide to find ratios equal to 4:12.

   a. $\dfrac{4 \times 3}{12 \times 3}$ **b.** $\dfrac{4 \times 6}{12 \times 6}$ **c.** $\dfrac{4 \div 4}{12 \div 4}$ **d.** $\dfrac{4 \div 2}{12 \div 2}$ **e.** $\dfrac{4 \times 2}{12 \times 2}$

Complete each table to create ratios equal to the given ratio.

2.

4	8	12	20	24
3				

3.

2				
11	22	33	44	55

4. **Test Prep** A ratio is equal to $\frac{4}{5}$. The denominator is 120. Which of these numbers is the numerator?

   Ⓐ 150   Ⓑ 96   Ⓒ 95   Ⓓ 6

5. **Test Prep** Which of these rates is the same as 5 oranges for $1.55?

   Ⓐ 4 oranges for $1.00   Ⓑ 3 oranges for $1.20

   Ⓒ 8 oranges for $2.48   Ⓓ 10 oranges for $15.50

Check each pair of ratios to see if a proportion is formed. Use = or ≠.

6. $\dfrac{2}{9} \square \dfrac{4}{16}$ 7. $\dfrac{3}{8} \square \dfrac{9}{24}$ 8. $\dfrac{5}{6} \square \dfrac{3}{4}$ 9. $\dfrac{16}{3} \square \dfrac{8}{2}$

10. $\dfrac{10}{4.5} \square \dfrac{20}{9}$ 11. $\dfrac{2.5}{10} \square \dfrac{7.5}{50}$ 12. $\dfrac{\frac{1}{2}}{8} \square \dfrac{1}{16}$ 13. $\dfrac{\frac{1}{3}}{10} \square \dfrac{30}{90}$

14. **Measurement** Fill in the following table of equal rates.

Ounces	32		96	128
Pounds		4	6	

15. **Estimation** The national budget average for public libraries is approximately $100 per 5 residents. A city has 240,000 residents and spends $1,000,000 on its library system. Is this figure about the same as the national average? Justify your answer.

16. **Consumer** If phone calls are 30¢ per minute and are billed in 6 sec (0.1 min) increments, make an equal ratio table with at least six entries.

17. Industry Use cross products to test whether the data transfer times are equal for the following modems: 50 bits at 14,400 bits per second and 120 bits at 34,560 bits per second.

Problem Solving and Reasoning

18. Communication Write two ratios that are not equal. Explain why they are not equal.

19. Journal Describe two ways to tell whether two ratios form a proportion. Use numerical examples to illustrate.

20. Critical Thinking The following table shows operator service charges for various types of calls.

Operator Service Charges	
Customer-Dialed Calling Card Station	$2.50 per call
Operator-Dialed Station	$3.75 per call
Person To Person	$4.50 per call

a. If the charge for two calls was $7.50, what could the service have been? Why? What if there were 3 calls?

b. If the charge for one of these billing categories was $22.50, what could the service have been? Why?

21. Critical Thinking Like proportions, analogies are statements based on comparisons. An example of an analogy is: *1* is to *unicycle* as *2* is to *bicycle.* Select the word that best completes each analogy.

a. *4* is to *rectangle* as *3* is to tricycle/square/recreation/triangle.

b. *Book* is to *library* as photograph/painting/music/math is to *art museum.*

c. *Smoke* is to *fire* as steam/pollution/burn/coffee is to *boiling water.*

d. *Expression* is to *equation* as *ratio* is to graph/variable/numerator/proportion.

Mixed Review

Solve each formula for the values given. *[Lesson 3-1]*

22. $A = lw$ for $l = 17$ in. and $w = 4$ in.   **23.** $A = s^2$ for $s = 11$

24. $P = 2l + 2w$ for $l = 7$ and $w = 9$ **25.** $F = 1.8C + 32$ for $C = 14$

Solve each equation. *[Lesson 3-6]*

26. $\frac{x}{4} - 2 = 11$ **27.** $\frac{x}{9} + 4 = 10$ **28.** $11x - 2 = 97$

Relating Proportions and Graphs

▶ Lesson Link You have learned that two equal ratios form a proportion. In this lesson, you will extend the idea of proportions to graphs. ◀

You'll Learn ...

■ to differentiate proportional and nonproportional relationships graphically

■ to link the constant of proportionality to slope

... How It's Used

Architects must use proportionality in designing building surfaces.

Vocabulary

constant of proportionality

Explore Proportions

Running Rectangles

Materials: Centimeter ruler, Standard paper

1. Take a sheet of paper measuring $8\frac{1}{2} \times 11$ inches and draw a diagonal. Randomly pick and label five points somewhere along the diagonal, being careful to spread the points out.

2. Construct the rectangles that have the selected diagonal point as the upper-right corner. Measure the length and width of each rectangle formed. Make a table of the data.

3. Make a scatterplot from the table.

4. Find the slope between several pairs of points. Describe any patterns that you find.

Learn Relating Proportions and Graphs

In an equal ratio table, you found that any two ratios form a proportion. Other relationships can also be discovered.

Example 3

Graph each relationship, then connect the points with a line. Does either graph show a proportional relationship?

a.

x	2	3	4	6
y	4	6	8	12

b.

x	2	3	4	6
y	4	5	6	8

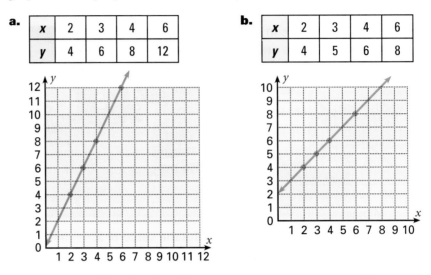

> ▶ **Literature Link**
>
> There are other meanings for the word *proportion*. In Shakespeare's play *Henry IV*, the Archbishop of York describes Northumberland's power as having been "in the first proportion," meaning Northumberland had been very powerful.

In Table **a,** $k = \frac{4}{2} = \frac{6}{3} = \frac{8}{4} = \frac{12}{6} = 2$. Any two pairs of ratios form a proportion. The line connecting the points passes through the origin.

The graph shows a proportional relationship.

In Table **b,** there is no constant of proportionality, because $\frac{4}{2} \neq \frac{5}{3} \neq \frac{6}{4} \neq \frac{8}{6}$. The line connecting the points does not pass through the origin.

The graph does not show a proportional relationship.

Try It

Graph each relationship, then connect the points with a line. Does either graph show a proportional relationship?

a.

Calls (x)	0	3	6	9
Fee (y)	2	3	4	5

b.

Yards (x)	0	1	2	3
Feet (y)	0	3	6	9

Check   Your Understanding

1. How can scatterplots help you find equal ratios?

2. If two quantities are always proportional, what do you know about the slope when the quantities are graphed?

Practice and Apply

1. **Getting Started** For each equation, find one solution. Then find $\frac{y}{x}$.

   a. $y = 3x$ **b.** $y = 10x$ **c.** $y = 0.5x$

Is each table an equal ratio table? If so, find the value of k.

2.

x	2	4	6	8
y	3	5	7	9

3.

x	1	3	5	7
y	6	18	30	42

4.

x	20	30	40	50
y	2	3	4	5

5.

x	1	2	3	4
y	11	22	33	44

6. **Test Prep** If the value of k in $\frac{y}{x} = k$ is 45 and $x = 10$, what is the value of y?

   Ⓐ 4.5   Ⓑ 45   Ⓒ 450   Ⓓ 4500

7. If the value of k in $\frac{y}{x} = k$ is 50 and $y = 250$, what is the value of x?

8. **a.** Using any two points on the graph, calculate the slope of the line. (Note: This will *not* be the slope as it appears on the graph!)

   b. Make a table of values for the graph. Show that k, the ratio of each y to x, is equal to the slope.

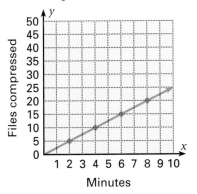

9. This graph shows the price to item ratio of mouse pads. How many mouse pads could you buy for $7? Explain your reasoning.

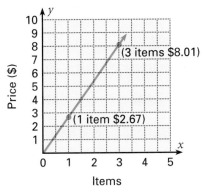

10. **Measurement** Use a cm ruler to measure the width and height of each m. Graph the width on the x-axis and height on the y-axis. Are the ratios of width to height equal?

m m m m

11. Career Tenika works part-time for a telecommunications company. Her weekly pay (p) is based on the number of hours (h) that she works. The graph shows this relationship.

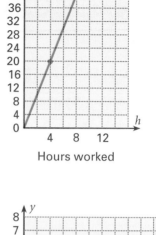

Hours worked

a. Calculate the slope using coordinates of any two points on the line. (Note: This will *not* be the slope as it appears on the graph.)

b. Make a table of values for the graph. Find the value of k.

c. Write a rate equation describing this relationship.

d. Use the equation to find the amount of pay Tenika would get for 17 hr of work.

Problem Solving and Reasoning

12. Communicate Does the graph show a proportional relationship? Explain.

13. Critical Thinking Make a graph of downloading times to show that downloading a 900K file in 6 min is the same rate as downloading a 225K file in 1.5 min.

14. Critical Thinking This graph compares the rates of pay for two different positions at a computer company. What do the two points highlighted on the horizontal line represent? The two points highlighted on the vertical line?

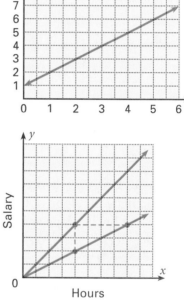

Mixed Review

Evaluate each expression. Let $p = 16$. *[Lesson 3-2]*

15. $3p + 21$ **16.** $\dfrac{p}{4} - 4$ **17.** $7(p + 9)$ **18.** $5 - 2p$

Determine whether 6 is a solution of each inequality. *[Lesson 3-7]*

19. $9x < 63$ **20.** $8x + 2 > 50$ **21.** $5x - 5 \leq 25$ **22.** $4x \geq 12$

Project Progress

Work in small groups to brainstorm issues that are important in your life. On paper, create designs for a class mural that relay a positive message.

Problem Solving
Understand
Plan
Solve
Look Back

Section 5A Connect

In this Connect you will use your knowledge of ratios, rates, and proportions to determine communication costs.

Sharing Information

Even with all the high technology forms of communication these days, people still find creative ways to communicate to people they care about. For instance, you may write notes to your friends and fold the notes in a unique way. Besides calling or writing, some creative ways to communicate are sending balloons, sending a telegram, or even sending a surprise fax.

Choose a few friends you would like to creatively say "hello" to. Choose a method to do this using the charts below. Calculate the cost for sending each "hello." You have $30 to spend and you must spend as much of it as you can.

1. Are the telegram rates proportional?

2. How much do you think a 75-word telegram would cost?

3. If the cost of 1 balloon goes up to $3.00, how much will 10 balloons cost? Why?

Friendly Balloon Bouquets

# of balloons	Price
1	$2.50
5	$11.00
10	$20.50

National Telegram Rates

# of Words	Price
1–15	$15.95
16–25	$22.95
26–35	$31.95
36–50	$41.95

Fast FAX Center Rates

	Send Price	Receive Price
First Page	$1.95	$2.35
Additional Pages	$0.65	$0.75

Write a ratio comparing the number of vowels to the number of consonants for each word.

1. Constant   **2.** Proportional   **3.** Rhythm   **4.** Queuing

Check each pair of ratios to see if a proportion is formed. Use = or ≠.

5. $\frac{2}{4} \square \frac{3}{8}$ **6.** $\frac{5}{6} \square \frac{2.5}{3}$ **7.** $\frac{12}{3} \square \frac{36}{6}$ **8.** $\frac{1.6}{8} \square \frac{8}{4}$

Complete each table to create ratios equal to the given ratio.

9.

4	8	12	20	24
9				

10.

			24	
12	24	36	48	54

11. Computers The bar graph shows the ways students at Hart Middle School use their computers at home.

   a. What is the ratio of use for word processing to budgets?

   b. Which two uses could be described by a ratio of 3 to 5?

   c. Which two uses could be described by a ratio of 3.5 to 4.5?

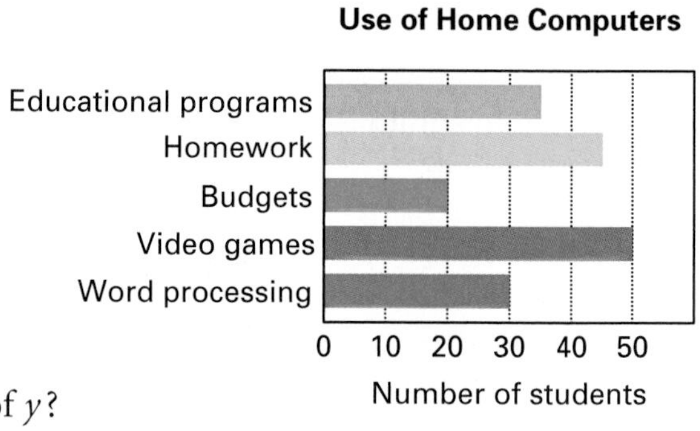

Use of Home Computers

Number of students

12. If the value of k is 87 and $x = 10$, what is the value of y?

Test Prep

When comparing ratios, first write each ratio as a fraction, then use cross products to see if the ratios form a proportion.

13. Ms. Lehr's class found that the ratio of hours spent doing homework with a computer to the hours spent doing it without a computer was 2:5. Which of the following represents the actual number of hours?

   Ⓐ 12 hours with a computer to 35 hours without

   Ⓑ 10 hours with a computer to 20 hours without

   Ⓒ 14 hours with a computer to 35 hours without

   Ⓓ 20 hours with a computer to 70 hours without

Problem Solving Using Proportions

The next time you sit in a movie theater enjoying movies like *Star Wars, Jaws,* and *Independence Day,* think about how these films are made. Huge space ships fly around, a massive shark eats people and ships, and the White House is blown to smithereens. How is it all done? Special effects.

Special effects may be visual or physical. Visual effects artists manipulate what you see with the aid of optical systems found in cameras and projectors. These artists also build models for miniature photography, a key aspect of visual effects; they skillfully photograph the models when it is not possible or practical to use the real thing.

Physical effects artists create the special effects used on the set or on location. They may build special mechanical devices to represent animals, as in *Free Willy.* They also plan and supervise the use of pyrotechnics, the controlled use of fires and explosions.

1 Name a few of your favorite special effects scenes. Do you think miniatures were built, special camera techniques were used, or the scenes were created by computer?

2 To build miniatures, special effects artists keep the dimensions in proportion to the actual object. What do you think this means?

how did they do that?

Solving Proportions

You'll Learn ...

■ to use mental math and cross multiplication to solve proportions

... How It's Used

Technicians need to adjust the rates at which copiers operate.

▶ **Lesson Link**   You have learned to determine if two ratios form a proportion. In this lesson, you will learn to find the values of any missing numbers in a proportion. ◀

Explore   Solving Proportions

Can You Squeeze Them In?

1. Estimate how many people could squeeze, standing, into a 32 ft² area (8 ft by 4 ft). How did you determine your estimate?

2. Use the above data to estimate the answers to the following questions.

　a. Can the entire school fit into this room?

　b. How many people could be squeezed into your school gym?

　c. Can the entire community/town/city fit into your school gym?

　d. How large an area would you need to fit everyone in your city or town?

　e. Could the entire U.S. population fit within your town?

3. Are there other considerations about the number of people that could fit in a given space?

Learn   Solving Proportions

In Lesson 5-2, you learned to determine if two ratios form a proportion by using equal ratios, mental math, and cross products. Sometimes you do not know all of the numbers in a proportion. You can use any of these methods to find the missing number. This is called *solving the proportion.*

Example 1

Leigh's copy machine can make 5 copies of the script in 2 min. She has 20 min to copy a revised script with changes for the cast. How many copies can she make in 20 min?

Define a variable: Let x = number of copies

Set up a proportion: $\dfrac{5 \text{ copies}}{2 \text{ min}} = \dfrac{x \text{ copies}}{20 \text{ min}}$

Use number sense to find x. Think: 2 min $\times$ 10 = 20 min, so 5 copies $\times$ 10 = 50 copies.

She can make 50 copies of the script.

You know that *if* the cross products of two ratios are equal, *then* the ratios form a proportion. The *converse* of this statement is also true:

If two ratios form a proportion, *then* their cross products are equal.

If $\dfrac{a}{b} = \dfrac{c}{d}$, then $ad = bc$.

The property above can help us find missing numbers in a proportion.

Example 2

India produces more feature-length films than any other country, an average of 1800 every two years. If it maintains this rate, how many films could it produce in 25 yr?

Let x = number of films   Define a variable.

$\dfrac{1800 \text{ films}}{2 \text{ yr}} = \dfrac{x \text{ films}}{25 \text{ yr}}$ Set up a proportion.

$1800 \cdot 25 = 2 \cdot x$ Write cross products.

$45{,}000 = 2x$ Multiply.

$\dfrac{45{,}000}{2} = \dfrac{2x}{2}$ Divide both sides by 2.

$22{,}500 = x$ Solve for x.

India would produce 22,500 films in 25 yr.

Try It

For 2 yr, the United States produced approximately 400 films. If it maintains this rate, how many films could be produced in 25 yr?

22. Science About 20 parts in 100 of the Dead Sea is salt. How much salt would be contained in 1 qt (32 oz) of Dead Sea water?

23. Chemistry Two samples containing only carbon and hydrogen are analyzed. If they have the same proportion of carbon and hydrogen, then they are probably the same substance. Do you think they are the same substance? Why?

Problem Solving **TIP**

It does not matter whether you compare carbon with hydrogen or each one with the total.

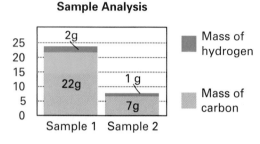

Sample Analysis

24. Gwilym Hughes of Wales has seen 22,188 films in his lifetime. If he has been watching films for 43 yr, estimate the number of films he could see in 80 yr.

Problem Solving and Reasoning

25. Critical Thinking This famous sculpture by Pablo Picasso is located in the city center plaza in Chicago. Before it was constructed in 1966, a maquette, or small model, was first created. The model's height is $41\frac{1}{4}$ in. and its width is 19 in. If the actual sculpture is 50 ft tall, how wide is it?

Algebra Solve each proportion.

26. $\dfrac{5}{x+1} = \dfrac{1}{3}$ **27.** $\dfrac{3}{2x} = \dfrac{1}{2}$ **28.** $\dfrac{x-1}{4} = \dfrac{7}{1}$ **29.** $\dfrac{3x}{4} = \dfrac{5}{2}$

30. Communicate If you know two of the four numbers in a proportion, can you find the other two? Why or why not?

31. Critical Thinking The lengths of the sides of a triangle are in a ratio of 6:5:3. The triangle's perimeter is 56 cm. What is the length of each side?

Mixed Review

Write each distance in scientific notation. *[Lesson 2-8]*

32. Sun to Mercury: 36,000,000 mi   **33.** Earth to the Moon: 238,840 mi

Find the value of *y* if *x* = 7. *[Lesson 4-1]*

34. $y = 4x$ **35.** $y = -6x$ **36.** $y = x + 5$ **37.** $y = x - 2$

Using Unit Rates

▶ Lesson Link You know that rates are ratios that compare quantities that have different units and that unit rates compare to 1. Unit rates are especially useful in solving proportions. ◄

You'll Learn ...

■ to find unit rates and use rate formulas to solve proportion problems

... How It's Used

Camera operators must be able to use rate formulas to determine the speed of the film they need.

Explore   Unit Rates

What Is It for 1?

Materials: Calculator

A movie projector shows 192 frames of an old silent film in 12 seconds.

1. Complete the table.

Frames	16	32	64	144	192
Seconds					12

2. Write and solve a proportion to find how many frames can be shown in 1 second.

3. What does the reciprocal of your answer to **2** represent?

4. How can you use your answer to **2** to find how long it takes to show 48 frames? 80 frames? Any number of frames?

Learn   Using Unit Rates

Rates are ratios that compare quantities that have different units. Recall that a unit rate compares a quantity to 1 unit. Some examples of units rates are 55 miles per hour, 24 shots per roll of film, and $16.95 for each video.

Unit rates can be used to solve proportions and create rate formulas.

Example 1

A movie company has decided to shoot a film in Texarkana, Texas. Sandra is hired as a camera assistant for 12 weeks of filming. For the first 5 weeks she earns $620. At this rate, how much will she make for 12 weeks?

$$\frac{620}{5} = 124$$ Find the unit rate for 1 week. She makes $124 per week.

$$124 \times 12 = 1488$$ Multiply the unit rate by the number of weeks.

Sandra will earn $1488.

Try It

Matt is hired by the same company as a runner for the director. He makes $570 for the first 5 weeks. How much will he earn at the end of 12 weeks?

Example 2

A 16 oz jar of peanut butter costs $2.50. A 12 oz jar is on sale for $1.99. Which is the better buy?

Write the rate for the 16 oz jar as a unit rate per oz.

$$\frac{2.50}{16} = 0.15625$$ The unit rate is slightly less than $0.16 per oz.

Use the unit rate to find a rate formula. Let C = the cost of peanut butter and z = number of oz.

$C = 0.15625z$

Substitute 12 for z to see how much 12 oz would cost at this rate.

$0.15625 \boxed{\times} 12 \boxed{=}$ *1.875*

$C = 1.875$

12 oz would cost about $1.88. This is less than $1.99, so the 16 oz jar is a better buy.

Try It

Morph detergent costs $5.98 for 46 oz; A 75 oz box costs $8.99. Which is the better buy?

Example 3

The rate a movie camera runs is measured in frames per second (fps). The standard projection rate is 24 fps. Use the formula $F = 24s$.

a. How many frames can be filmed in 20 sec?

$F = 24s$	Write the rate equation.
$F = 24(20)$	Substitute 20 for s.
$F = 480$	Multiply.

480 frames could be shot in 20 sec.

b. How long would it take to film 1000 frames?

$F = 24s$	
$1000 = 24s$	Substitute 1000 for F.
$41.67 = s$	Divide each side by 24 to solve for F.

It would take approximately 42 sec to film 1000 frames.

Try It

a. To produce slow motion, the camera rate must be higher than the projection rate. Suppose the camera rate is 48 fps.

Use the formula $F = 48s$. How many frames can be filmed in 60 sec? How long would it take to film 1200 frames?

b. A video camera records at 30 fps. This rate is used when editing video.

What formula would be used to determine the time it takes to record 9000 frames? How long would it take?

DID YOU KNOW?

A camera rate higher than the projection rate creates slow motion; one lower than the projection rate creates fast motion.

Check Your Understanding

1. How can rates be converted to unit rates?

2. What proportion is equivalent to the rate formula $M = 15T$?

3. What operations help you solve rate formulas?

Practice and Apply

1. **Getting Started** If Lorene drove 45 mi in 1.5 hr, how far could she drive in 7 hr?

   a. Find the unit rate by dividing 45 by 1.5.

   b. Use the unit rate and $d = rt$ to find a rate formula where d = distance and t = time.

   c. Substitute 7 for t in the rate formula and solve for d.

Find the unit rate and create a rate formula.

2. $60 for 15 hr
3. 400 words in 10 min
4. 30 students for 3 computers

5. 330 mi in 6 hr
6. 800 m in 25 sec
7. $3 million for 75 days of filming

8. **Estimation** Fifty-nine F-117 jets cost 6 billion dollars to produce. Is 2 million dollars a good estimate for the cost of one F-117? Explain.

9. **Consumer** A 7 lb whole boneless pork roast is advertised for $20.16.

   a. How much does the roast cost per pound?

   b. The ad reads, "You save 71¢ per pound." What was the original price per pound?

10. **Test Prep** Which of the following is a unit rate?

    Ⓐ 1 pizza for 3 students Ⓑ 25 students in a classroom

    Ⓒ 200 mi in 5 hr Ⓓ 27 wins out of 27 games

11. **Industry** The 365 special-effects scenes in *Star Wars* required 3838 separate components. What was the approximate average number of components per special-effects scene?

Consumer Which is the better buy?

12. A 2 lb box of pistachio nuts for $10.99 or a 5 lb box for $30.00

13. A 16 oz box of cereal for $3.49 or a 6 oz box of cereal for $1.25

Special effects scene from *Honey, I Shrunk the Kids*.

14. 15 collector cards for $2.75 or 80 for $13.00

15. $\frac{1}{4}$ lb of coffee for $2.00 or 1 lb for $8.50

16. 20 computer disks for $14.49 or 12 for $9.50

Problem Solving and Reasoning

17. **Communicate** The 102nd-floor observatory of the Empire State Building is at a height of 1250 ft. The 86th-floor observatory is at a height of 1050 ft. Are the floor heights roughly proportional? Explain.

18. **Critical Thinking** A loaf of bread costs $1.29 for 20 slices, a 40 oz jar of peanut butter costs $4.59, and a 22 oz jar of grape jelly costs $1.89. A sandwich uses two slices of bread, about 1.5 oz of peanut butter, and $\frac{3}{4}$ oz of jelly. Determine a reasonable estimate for the cost of a single peanut butter and jelly sandwich.

19. **Journal** Give two examples of real-life situations that involve finding unit rates.

20. **Critical Thinking** For the movie *The Empire Strikes Back*, a camera that could film up to 96 fps was used to film special effects. How many more frames could this camera film in 20 sec than one at the standard rate of 24 fps?

21. **Critical Thinking** Jefferson County School District has approximately 10,000 students and a student-teacher ratio of 25:1.

    a. How many teachers are there?

    b. The school is required to lower the student-teacher ratio to 23:1. Explain how it might do this.

Mixed Review

Write in standard notation. *[Lesson 2-9]*

22. 1.0×10^{-6} **23.** 8.4×10^{-3} **24.** 21 hundred-millionths

Give two solution pairs for each equation. *[Lesson 4-2]*

25. $y = x + 5$ **26.** $2x + 7 = y$ **27.** $x - 6 = y$ **28.** $y = 3x - 1$

Project Progress

Examine the designs for the class mural and vote for your favorite design. Choose a scale to reproduce the design for the wall and plan the completion of the mural.

> **Problem Solving**
> Understand
> Plan
> Solve
> Look Back

Problem Solving Using Rates and Proportions

You'll Learn ...

■ to solve problems with rates and proportions

... How It's Used

Nurses often have to use proportions when preparing intravenous solutions.

▶ **Lesson Link**   You have learned about unit rates and proportions. In this lesson, you will use these concepts to solve problems. ◀

Explore | Rates and Proportions

You Win!

Radio station YDLR, 98.3 FM, is having a giveaway. They will call a listener and say, "You are the YDLR winner! You have your choice: 98.3 pounds of pennies, nickels, dimes, quarters, or half-dollars."

You think you have a chance of being called. You want to get the most money you can, so you search the Internet and find the following information:

Coin	Penny	Nickel	Dime	Quarter	Half-dollar
Number in a pound	146	91	200	80	40

1. Are there one or more coin denominations you would rule out immediately? Why?

2. How much does each type of coin weigh? How did you decide?

3. What is the monetary value of a pound of each type of coin? Which coin denomination gives you the most money? How much is it?

4. Why is there more than one coin denomination in **3**?

5. Write a proportion relating weight and value.

DID YOU KNOW?

Pennies dated before 1981 weigh more than recently minted pennies.

Learn | Problem Solving Using Rates and Proportions

Problem solving skills are important in solving problems relating to rates and proportions. Often, it is best to break down a problem into several steps.

Example

▶ **Science Link**

When an explosion is filmed in close-up to make it look larger, the burst happens too quickly for it to appear believable when filmed at normal speed.

A small special-effects explosion that lasts only $\frac{1}{12}$ sec is filmed with a high-speed camera at a rate of 960 frames per second. When it is shown in the actual film, the scene must last for 5 sec so it appears to be much larger. How many frames are filmed? How many frames per second must be shown?

We have the length of the explosion and the speed at which it is filmed. We want to find the speed at which it must be shown to last 5 sec.

First find out how many frames are filmed. Then use the answer to find the projection rate.

$\frac{1}{12}$ sec · 960 fps = 80 frames filmed.

80 frames must be shown in 5 sec.

$\frac{80}{5} = 16$ Divide.

The rate of projection must be 16 fps.

Try It

A small special-effects bridge collapse that lasts only $\frac{1}{2}$ sec is filmed with a high-speed camera at a rate of 240 fps. When it is shown in the actual film, the scene must last for 4 sec. How many frames are filmed? How many fps must be shown?

Check Your Understanding

1. Can you make a proportion from the Example?

2. Why would it make sense to break a problem into smaller steps?

Practice and Apply

1. **Getting Started** Shooting 15 sec at 24 fps is:

   a. _____ frames altogether;

   b. The same number of frames as _____ sec at 72 fps; and

   c. The same number of frames as 30 sec at _____ fps.

2. An animator makes 80 storyboards, or sketches, for a scene lasting $2\frac{1}{2}$ min. How many storyboards must be made for a 90 min, full-length animated film?

Problem Solving TIP

If you double both the minutes and the number of storyboards, you will have an equal ratio with whole numbers.

3. **Test Prep** Which circles have the same proportion shaded? (Choose all that apply.)

Ⓐ   Ⓑ   Ⓒ   Ⓓ

4. In a movie, large sets are often created so that people appear to be smaller. If a 60 in. tall person appears next to a 96 in. high trash can, but the trash can appears to be 18 in. high in the film, how tall would the person appear to be?

5. **Industry** A television rating of 30 represents about 28.6 million homes. A television rating of 100 represents the total number of households with televisions.

   a. What is the total number of households with televisions?

   b. What does a rating of 1 represent?

6. **History** The Wheel of Life was patented by William Lincoln in 1867. A $2\frac{1}{2}$ ft long strip with 14 still photographs was placed inside the wheel and spun to create movement. How many photographs of this size would a 10 ft long strip have had?

7. **Patterns** Use the numbers 2, 4, 8, 16, 32. Write as many true proportions as you can that use these numbers (only use a number once in each proportion).

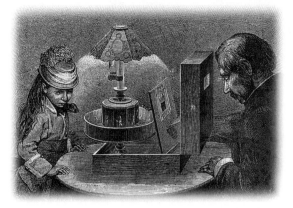

Problem Solving and Reasoning

8. **Communicate** *Proportional representation* gives political parties legislative representation in proportion to the ratio of their popular vote to the total number of votes. The parties in one small country received the following votes. There will be 100 legislators selected. How many Republicrat representatives should be selected? How did you decide?

Party	Votes
Republicrat	17,934
Demican	11,236
Preformed	9,120
Justiced	4,899
Total	43,189

9. **Math Reasoning** When you pedal a bicycle that has gears as shown, turning the pedal around once turns the rear wheel $\frac{52}{18}$ times. How far will the tire roll (turn) when you turn the pedal around once?

10. A worker honey bee collects enough nectar in its lifetime (about 2 months) to make $\frac{1}{10}$ pound of honey.

   a. How much would a colony of 20,000 worker bees collect in this time?

   b. How many 8-ounce ($\frac{1}{2}$ pound) jars of honey are produced?

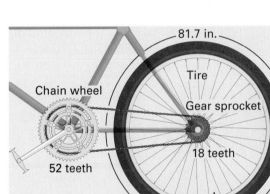

Mixed Review

11. A cheetah can run 105 ft per sec. Use $d = rt$ to find how far it could run in 8 sec as it chases a wildebeest. *[Lesson 3-1]*

Graph each equation. Use 0, 1, 2, and 3 as *x* values. *[Lesson 4-3]*

12. $y = x + 2$ 13. $y = 4x$ 14. $y = 2x - 1$ 15. $y = -2x$

Scale, Scale Drawings, and Models

You'll Learn ...

■ to use scales and create scale drawings

... How It's Used

Special-effects artists often have to create scale models of buildings, people, and animals for their films.

Vocabulary

scale drawing

scale

similar polygons

▶ **Lesson Link**   You have learned how to work with ratios and proportions. Now you will use these concepts to understand scale models and to make scale drawings. ◀

Explore   Scale

A Tangle of Rectangles

Materials: Graph paper or geoboard

1. Make a rectangle on your geoboard or graph paper. Measure the length and width.

2. Make a second larger rectangle that is the same shape but not the same size. Measure the length and width. Find the ratio of the lengths and the ratio of the widths of the two rectangles. What do you notice?

3. Make as many rectangles as you can that are the same shape but not the same size. Measure their lengths and widths. Find the ratios of the lengths and ratios of the widths of any two rectangles. What do you notice?

Learn   Scale, Scale Drawings, and Models

A **scale drawing** shows the shape of an object but not the actual size. A **scale** gives the ratio of the measurements in the drawing to the measurements of the actual object. The drawing length always comes first in the ratio.

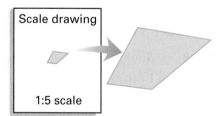

Scale drawing

1:5 scale

The dimensions in the drawing are reduced or enlarged by the same ratio or scale. If the first value of the ratio is smaller, the scale drawing is a reduction; if it is larger, the scale drawing is an enlargement.

Scale is often used when looking at microscopic organisms.

Example 1

The largest bacteria that have been found by microbiologists are called *Epulopiscium* and are about 0.5 mm in length. A scale drawing will be made with a scale of 100 mm:1 mm. What should the length of the bacteria be in the drawing?

$$\frac{\text{scale} \rightarrow}{\text{actual} \rightarrow} \frac{100 \text{ mm}}{1 \text{ mm}} = \frac{x \text{ mm}}{0.5 \text{ mm}} \frac{\leftarrow \text{ scale}}{\leftarrow \text{ actual}}$$

$100 \cdot 0.5 = 1 \cdot x$ Use cross products.

$\quad\quad 50 = x$ Multiply.

The length of the bacteria in the drawing is 50 mm.

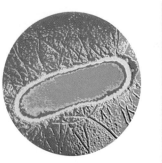

▶ **Science Link**

The first compound microscope was constructed by Zacharias Janssen in 1590. It was very large, and the magnification was just under nine times.

A map is an example of a scale drawing.

Example 2

In the film *Independence Day,* the director chose the Bonneville Salt Flats of Utah to film many of the special effect scenes. The map is drawn to a scale of 1 in. = 40 mi.

a. Approximately how far is it from the Salt Flats to Salt Lake City?

Measure the map length from the Salt Flats to Salt Lake City. It is about $2\frac{1}{4}$ in. Make a proportion of map lengths to actual lengths.

$$\frac{\text{map distance} \rightarrow}{\text{actual distance} \rightarrow} \frac{1 \text{ in.}}{40 \text{ mi}} = \frac{2\frac{1}{4} \text{ in.}}{d \text{ mi}} \frac{\leftarrow \text{ map distance}}{\leftarrow \text{ actual distance}}$$

$1 \cdot d = 40 \cdot 2\frac{1}{4}$ Use cross products.

$\quad d = 90$ Multiply.

Salt Lake City is approximately 90 mi from the Salt Flats.

b. Which city is approximately 15 mi from the Salt Flats?

Wendover is close to the Salt Flats. It is approximately $\frac{3}{8}$ in. away. If 1 in. = 40 mi, then $\frac{3}{8}$ in. is $\frac{3}{8}(40) = 15$ mi. Wendover is approximately 15 mi away.

Scale drawings are often used in blueprints of buildings and models. When making a scale drawing, it is important to choose an appropriate scale.

Example 3

Suppose you want to construct a scale drawing of a model city that will measure 24 ft by 36 ft. Choose a scale that would allow you to draw it on a 12 in. by 16 in. sheet of paper.

If we use 1 in. = 2 ft, the scale drawing would be 12 in. by 18 in. and would not fit.

Try 1 in. = 3 ft.

$$\frac{scale}{actual} \rightarrow \frac{1 \text{ in.}}{3 \text{ ft}} = \frac{x \text{ in.}}{24 \text{ ft}} \leftarrow \frac{scale}{actual}$$ $24 = 3x$, so $8 = x$.

The width would be 8 in.

$$\frac{scale}{actual} \rightarrow \frac{1 \text{ in.}}{3 \text{ ft}} = \frac{x \text{ in.}}{36 \text{ ft}} \leftarrow \frac{scale}{actual}$$ $36 = 3x$, so $12 = x$.

The length would be 12 in.

For a scale of 1 in. = 3 ft, the dimensions would be 8 in. by 12 in. It would fit.

Try It

Suppose you want to construct a scale drawing of a house. The house measures 40 ft by 50 ft. Choose a scale that would allow you to draw it on a 6 in. by 9 in. sheet of paper.

Similar polygons have the same shape but may not have the same size. Their side lengths form proportions. These proportions can help you find a missing length in a pair of similar polygons.

$\frac{3}{6} = \frac{4}{8}$ $\frac{3}{6} = \frac{3.5}{7}$ $\frac{3.5}{7} = \frac{4}{8}$

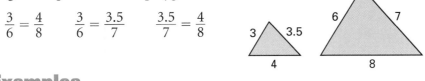

Examples

4 Find the missing value in the pair of similar triangles.

Set up a proportion. $\frac{25}{30} = \frac{45}{n}$

Cross multiply. $25n = 1350$

Solve for n. $n = 54$

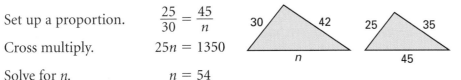

5 Leticia has an 8 in. by 10 in. photo that she will be reducing to fit into a small frame. The width of the reduced photo is $3\frac{1}{2}$ in. What is the height?

$\dfrac{10 \text{ in.}}{x} = \dfrac{8 \text{ in.}}{3\frac{1}{2} \text{ in.}}$

$10 \cdot 3\frac{1}{2} = 8x$ Cross multiply.

$35 = 8x$

$4\frac{3}{8} = x$ Divide.

The height of the reduced photo is $4\frac{3}{8}$ in.

10 in.

8 in. $3\frac{1}{2}$ in.   x in.

Try It

Find the missing value in the pair of similar trapezoids.

Check   Your Understanding

1. What is the advantage of using a scale drawing?

2. What happens to a scale drawing when the scale of 1 in. = 10 ft is changed to 1 in. = 40 ft? When it is changed to 1 in. = 2 ft?

3. How can the scale of a scale drawing or a map be used to help you find the actual size or distance?

4. How could you find the scale on a map that did not have a scale printed on it?

Practice and Apply

1. **Getting Started** Fill in the blanks.

   a. A scale drawing has the same _____ but not necessarily the same _____ of the actual object.

   b. Similar polygons may be different in _____, but have the same _____.

Geography Use the map and a ruler. What is the approximate distance from

2. Seattle to New Orleans?

3. Miami to New York?

4. Which city is approximately 1200 mi from New Orleans?

5. If two cities are approximately $3\frac{1}{2}$ in. apart on the map, what is the actual distance between the two cities?

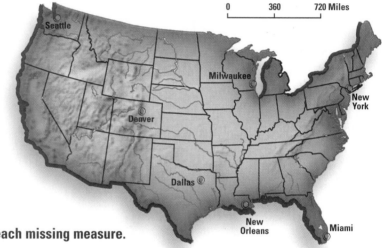

Use the scale 1.5 cm = 10 m to find each missing measure.

	Scale dimension	Actual dimension
6.	0.3 cm	?
7.	?	200 m
8.	4.5 cm	?
9.	?	89.5 m

10. Suppose you need to make a scale drawing of a 14 ft by 18 ft room on a 5 in. by 7 in. index card. What scale would you use?

11. **Science** An insect in a picture is $\frac{1}{4}$ in. long and is labeled "enlarged 8 times." What is the insect's actual length?

12. **Optics** On a pair of binoculars, 7 × 35 means an object appears to be enlarged 7 times, or an object 700 m away appears to be 100 m away (35 means only that the lens has a 35 mm diameter). If an object appears to be 75 m away, how far away is it actually?

13. In the movie *King Kong*, the scale $\frac{3}{4}$ in. = 1 ft was used. If the model was 18 in. tall, how tall was the "actual" Kong?

14. [Test Prep] Miles wants to make a scale drawing of the dinosaur *Brachiosaurus brancai,* which was 46 ft tall and approximately 73 ft long, on a sheet of paper that is $8\frac{1}{2}$ in. by 11 in. Which of the following scales could he use?

Ⓐ 1 in. = 8 ft Ⓑ 1 in. = 5 ft

Ⓒ 1 in. = 3 ft Ⓓ 1 in. = 2 ft

Geometry Find the missing measures in each pair of similar figures.

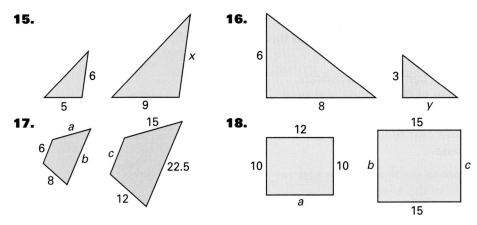

15.

6

5

x

9

16.

6

8

3

y

17.

a

6

b

8

15

c

22.5

12

18.

12

10

a

10

b

15

c

15

Problem Solving and Reasoning

19. [Journal] Why is it important that a road map be drawn to scale?

20. Communicate Explain how scale drawings and similar figures are alike.

21. Critical Thinking The average NBA player is approximately 6 ft 9 in. tall and the basket is 10 ft high. The average eighth grader is 5 ft 5 in. tall. How much should the basket be lowered for the eighth graders to make the ratio of player height to basket height the same?

22. Critical Thinking Two models of the same ship are constructed. One has a scale of 1:2400 and the other a scale of 1:3000. Which scale model is larger? Explain.

Mixed Review

Solve each equation. *[Lesson 3-2]*

23. $x + 7 = -9$ **24.** $2p = 88$ **25.** $5 = \frac{r}{9}$ **26.** $1 = h - 10$

Draw a line through the origin with each of the given slopes. *[Lesson 4-4]*

27. $\frac{2}{3}$ **28.** 3   **29.** $\frac{-1}{2}$ **30.** -2 **31.** 0

TECHNOLOGY

Using the Cabri Geometry Program • Scale Drawings

Problem: How does scaling a triangle using a scale factor of 2 affect the perimeter of the triangle?

1. Use the **Triangle** tool to draw a triangle on the screen.

2. Use the **Distance & Length** measurement tool. Click on a side of the triangle (not on a vertex) to find its perimeter.

3. Use the **Numerical Edit** tool to place the number 2 on the screen.

4. Use the **Point** tool to place a point in approximately the center of the triangle.

5. Now you are ready to scale the triangle. Use the **Dilation** tool. Click on the side of a triangle, on the point in the center, and then on the number 2. You will get a second triangle similar to the one shown.

6. Use the **Distance & Length** tool again to find the perimeter of the new triangle.

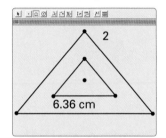

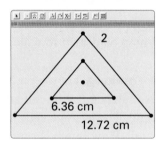

Solution: The perimeter of the scaled triangle is 2 times the perimeter of the original triangle.

TRY IT

Begin with a slightly larger triangle and use 0.5 as the scale factor. How does the perimeter of the new triangle compare to that of the original?

ON YOUR OWN

▶ Repeat the example above, but instead of using the **Distance & Length** tool, use the **Area** tool to find the area of each triangle. Divide the area of the scaled triangle by the area of the original. Is the area of the scaled triangle twice the area of the original?

▶ Repeat with different scale factors.

In this Connect you will use your knowledge of ratios, rates, proportions, and scale drawings to make a model for a special effect in a movie.

How Did They Do That?

Models of rooms on television shows are made before the actual set is created. Before the model is created, a scale drawing of the model is made. Suppose you are starring in your own television show, and the main set is a living room.

This scale drawing shows an incomplete floor plan of a living room. Use a ruler to measure the distances on the drawing to the nearest $\frac{1}{4}$ inch. The actual width of the room's model will be 4 ft and the actual width of the room on the set will be 16 ft.

1. Find the scale of the drawing to the model.

2. Models of the furniture must be created as well. What will the length of the couch be in the model?

3. Find the scale of the model to the actual set.

4. Find the length and width of a chair in your classroom. What size would the chair be for the scale drawing? For the model?

5. Since you will be the star of the show, what size will you be in the model? (use the same scale for height)

6. Complete the scale drawing by personalizing your set for the show.

263

Write and solve a proportion for each of the following situations.

1. How much should 10 bottles of juice cost if 6 cost $1.99?

2. Center Junior High had a win/loss ratio of 3:1. If it won 12 games, how many did it lose?

Solve each proportion. Which method did you use? Why?

3. $\dfrac{4}{5} = \dfrac{x}{100}$
4. $\dfrac{4.5}{8} = \dfrac{6}{x}$
5. $\dfrac{15}{3} = \dfrac{x}{8}$
6. $\dfrac{16}{s} = \dfrac{64}{72}$
7. $\dfrac{\frac{1}{2}}{7} = \dfrac{40}{h}$

Find the unit rate to create a rate formula for each of the following.

8. 27 students per 3 calculators
9. $\dfrac{\$450}{20\ \text{CDs}}$

Find the missing values for each pair of similar figures.

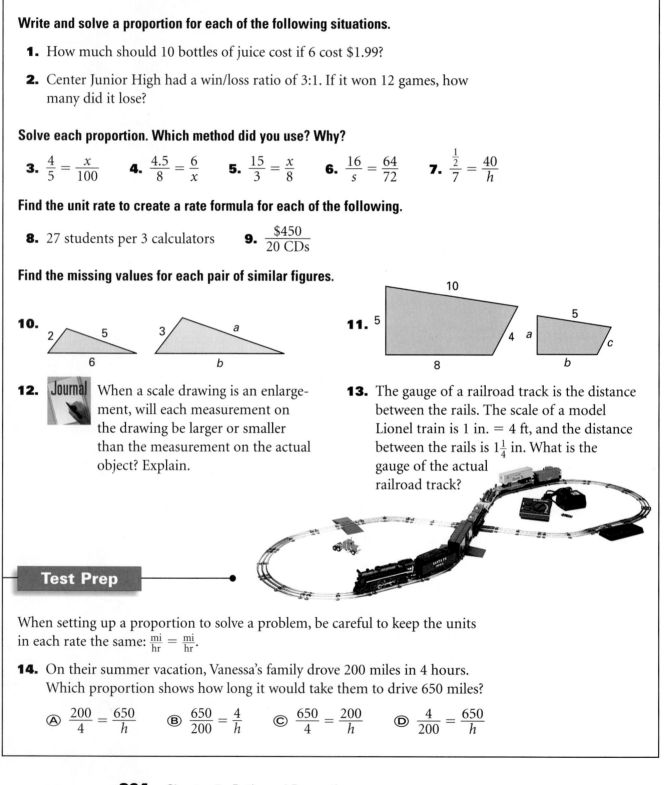

10.

11.

12. **Journal** When a scale drawing is an enlargement, will each measurement on the drawing be larger or smaller than the measurement on the actual object? Explain.

13. The gauge of a railroad track is the distance between the rails. The scale of a model Lionel train is 1 in. = 4 ft, and the distance between the rails is $1\frac{1}{4}$ in. What is the gauge of the actual railroad track?

Test Prep

When setting up a proportion to solve a problem, be careful to keep the units in each rate the same: $\frac{\text{mi}}{\text{hr}} = \frac{\text{mi}}{\text{hr}}$.

14. On their summer vacation, Vanessa's family drove 200 miles in 4 hours. Which proportion shows how long it would take them to drive 650 miles?

Ⓐ $\dfrac{200}{4} = \dfrac{650}{h}$
Ⓑ $\dfrac{650}{200} = \dfrac{4}{h}$
Ⓒ $\dfrac{650}{4} = \dfrac{200}{h}$
Ⓓ $\dfrac{4}{200} = \dfrac{650}{h}$

Fibonacci Sequence

The mathematician Fibonacci lived around 1200 A.D. He wrote a sequence of numbers that follows a certain pattern.

Each number in the Fibonacci sequence is the sum of the previous two numbers (for example, $2 + 3 = 5$, $3 + 5 = 8$). Starting the sequence with a pair of ones, the sequence continues as follows:

$$1, 1, 2, 3, 5, 8, 13, 21, 34, 55, 89, 144, 233, 377, 610, \ldots$$

Use a calculator to complete the table by dividing one number in the sequence by the preceding number. Round to five decimal places. Continue this process up to the fifteenth and fourteenth numbers in the sequence.

Ratio	Decimal
$\frac{1}{1}$	1
$\frac{2}{1}$	2
$\frac{3}{2}$	1.5
$\frac{5}{3}$	1.66667
$\frac{8}{5}$	

Examine the decimal equivalents of the Fibonacci ratios in this table. What happens?

The larger the two consecutive Fibonacci numbers, the closer the ratio of the two numbers will be to the golden ratio. The golden ratio is the ratio of the length to the width of a golden, or "perfect," rectangle; it is approximately 1.61828 to 1.

1.61828   1

Use the golden ratio to set up a proportion to find the following:

a. The length of a golden rectangle with a width of 89 cm

b. The width of a golden rectangle with a length of 2.33 m

c. Examine your answers and refer to the table. What conclusions can you make?

6 Percent

Cultural Link
www.mathsurf.com/8/ch6/people

Entertainment Link
www.mathsurf.com/8/ch6/ent

People of the World

India will soon become the
second country to reach the
1-billion mark in population.
About 16% of the world's
population live in India.

Entertainment

A favorite of scuba divers around
the world, Australia's Great
Barrier Reef extends 1250 miles,
roughly the length of our Atlantic
coastline from Maine to South
Carolina.

Arts & Literature

Of the books published in the
United States, about 11% are
fiction, 6% deal with medicine,
and 2% are sports-related.

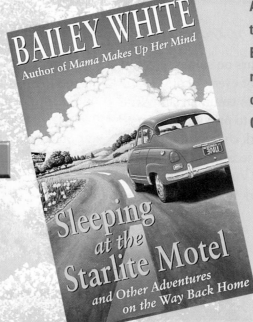

BAILEY WHITE
Author of *Mama Makes Up Her Mind*

Sleeping at the Starlite Motel
and Other Adventures
on the Way Back Home

270

Social Studies Link
www.mathsurf.com/8/ch6/social

Science

Botanists have classified about 240,000 species of plants. However, 11 of these species provide 80% of the food for the world's population.

Social Studies

Norway has the dubious distinction of being a country with one of the highest rates of income tax—65%. Additional personal taxes make it possible for citizens to be charged in excess of 100%.

KEY MATH IDEAS

A **percent** is a ratio that compares a number to 100.

Compatible numbers can be used to help estimate percents.

The percent an amount increases is called the **percent increase**.

The percent an amount decreases is called the **percent decrease**.

Interest is money paid for the use of money. The amount of money deposited or borrowed is called the **principal**. There are two types of interest: **simple interest** and **compound interest**.

CHAPTER PROJECT

Problem Solving

Understand
Plan
Solve
Look Back

In this project, you will examine the time you spend on homework each day. Make a circle graph using a spreadsheet tool. You will write an analysis of your homework schedule and of any changes you may want to make to organize your time more efficiently.

Problem
Solving

Understand
Plan
Solve
Look Back

Problem Solving Focus

For each problem, write down the answer and the arithmetic you used to get the answer. (For example, if you added 5 to 7 to get 12, write "5 + 7 = 12.")

1 Do It Write and Write On stationery stores have a sale. Write On sells pencils at three for forty-five cents. Do It Write sells them for two dollars and seventy-five cents a dozen. Jonah needs a dozen pencils. Which store charges more? How much more?

2 Do It Write sells stationery by the pound. Three pounds cost three dollars and eighty-five cents. Write On's price is one dollar and twenty cents a pound. Ben and Jo will share five pounds. Rounded to the nearest cent, which store has the better buy? How much less is it?

3 Write On matches the advertised prices of Do It Write and gives consumers half the difference in cash. Do It Write advertises Roll-Write ball-point pens at six for two dollars and forty-cents. Write On's ad offers Roll-Write pens at one for fifty cents. Rob buys eight pens at Write On. Rounded to the nearest cent, how much cash does he get?

4 Write On sells magazines. *Sport!* costs two dollars and fifty cents a copy. Reg pays seventeen dollars and fifty cents a year for a monthly subscription. Rounded to the nearest cent, how much less per copy does Reg pay?

YOU ARE WHAT YOU EAT

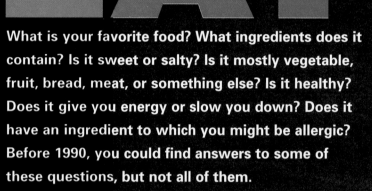

What is your favorite food? What ingredients does it contain? Is it sweet or salty? Is it mostly vegetable, fruit, bread, meat, or something else? Is it healthy? Does it give you energy or slow you down? Does it have an ingredient to which you might be allergic? Before 1990, you could find answers to some of these questions, but not all of them.

Since the Nutrition Labeling and Education Act of 1990, fast-food restaurants have been required to provide nutritional information about the food they serve—hamburgers, French fries, milkshakes, and so on. Nutritional information is also required on items we buy at the grocery store. Every person needs certain amounts of nutrients each day based on his or her recommended caloric intake. The required amount of each nutrient is the daily value and is based on a 2000-calorie diet.

Reading labels on processed foods and learning about the nutritional benefits of foods can help you decide what foods you should eat to get the energy you need for your activities.

1 Describe your favorite food. Give as much nutritional data as you can.

2 Why are labels on food products important?

Percents, Decimals, and Fractions

▶ **Lesson Link** You have represented ratios as fractions and decimals. Now you will learn how to represent a ratio as a percent. ◀

You'll Learn ...

■ to convert among fractions, decimals, and percents

... How It's Used

Advertisers use percents in many of the newspaper ads they create.

Vocabulary

percent

circle graph

| **Explore** | Fractions, Decimals, and Percents |

Calculated Conversions

Materials: Calculator with $F⇄D$ key

Use your calculator to convert fractions, decimals, and percents.

1. Enter 3 ÷ 4 = $F⇄D$. What is displayed?
Press $F⇄D$ again. What is displayed?
Repeat for each fraction.

   a. $\frac{1}{100}$ **b.** $\frac{2}{5}$ **c.** $\frac{5}{4}$ **d.** $\frac{3}{3}$

2. Enter 0.3 $F⇄D$. What is displayed?
Repeat for each decimal.

   a. 1.75   **b.** 0.85   **c.** 0.003   **d.** 2.25

3. Enter 25 $\%$. What is displayed?
Press $F⇄D$. What is displayed?
Repeat for each percent.

   a. 30%   **b.** 45%   **c.** 3%   **d.** 99%

4. What patterns, if any, do you notice?

| **Learn** | Percents, Decimals, and Fractions |

You find percents everywhere—40% off, 95% fat free, sales increase 10%. A **percent** is a ratio that compares a number to 100. *Percent* means "parts per hundred," "hundredths," or "out of every hundred."

We often see percents represented in a **circle graph**, sometimes called a pie chart.

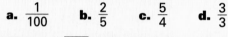

Example 1

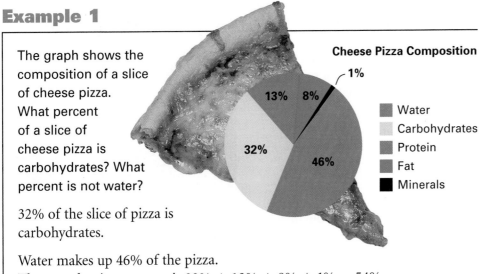

The graph shows the composition of a slice of cheese pizza. What percent of a slice of cheese pizza is carbohydrates? What percent is not water?

Cheese Pizza Composition

1%
13%   8%
32%
46%

- Water
- Carbohydrates
- Protein
- Fat
- Minerals

32% of the slice of pizza is carbohydrates.

Water makes up 46% of the pizza.
The part that is not water is 32% + 13% + 8% + 1% = 54%.

Often we need to find percents from fractions or decimals.

On the label shown, 18 of the 100 calories are from fat. 18 out of 100 can be expressed several ways:

Middle School Popcorn

| Calories: | 100 |
| Calories from Fat: | 18 |

a. Decimal

0.18

b. Ratio

18 to 100

c. Fraction

$\frac{18}{100}$

d. Picture

Each of the expressions can also be represented as a percent.

$$\frac{18}{100} = 0.18 = 18\%$$

When rewriting a ratio as a decimal, as a fraction, or as a percent, it is helpful to think of "parts per hundred," or hundredths.

There are some percents that are used often. These are summarized in the table below. Notice that the fractions are in lowest terms.

Fraction	Percent	Fraction	Percent	Fraction	Percent	Fraction	Percent
$\frac{1}{4}$	25%	$\frac{1}{5}$	20%	$\frac{1}{6}$	$16\frac{2}{3}\%$	$\frac{1}{8}$	$12\frac{1}{2}\%$
$\frac{1}{2}$	50%	$\frac{2}{5}$	40%	$\frac{1}{3}$	$33\frac{1}{3}\%$	$\frac{3}{8}$	$37\frac{1}{2}\%$
$\frac{3}{4}$	75%	$\frac{3}{5}$	60%	$\frac{2}{3}$	$66\frac{2}{3}\%$	$\frac{5}{8}$	$62\frac{1}{2}\%$
1	100%	$\frac{4}{5}$	80%	$\frac{5}{6}$	$83\frac{1}{3}\%$	$\frac{7}{8}$	$87\frac{1}{2}\%$

MENTAL MATH

Because these percents are used so often, it would be wise to memorize the fractional relationships.

Example 2

A gram of fat contains more calories than a gram of protein or carbohydrates. Whole milk is 0.036 fat, however, 0.467 of its calories are from fat.

a. What percent of whole milk is fat?

Rewrite 0.036 as a fraction.

$0.036 = \dfrac{36}{1000}$ Write the decimal as a fraction.

$= \dfrac{36 \div 10}{1000 \div 10}$

$= \dfrac{3.6}{100}$ Divide numerator and denominator by 10.

$= 3.6\%$ Definition of percent.

3.6% of whole milk is fat.

b. What percent of whole milk calories are from fat?

Rewrite 0.467 as a fraction.

$0.467 = \dfrac{467}{1000}$ Write the decimal as a fraction.

$= \dfrac{467 \div 10}{1000 \div 10}$

$= \dfrac{46.7}{100}$ Divide numerator and denominator by 10.

$= 46.7\%$ Definition of percent.

46.7% of whole milk calories are from fat.

Another way to change a decimal to a percent is to move the decimal point two places to the right and add the percent sign:

$0.036 = 0.0\,3\,6 = 3.6\%$ $0.467 = 0.4\,6\,7 = 46.7\%$

Example 3

a. Rewrite $\frac{3}{5}$ as a percent.

Write $\frac{3}{5}$ as a fraction with a denominator of 100.

$\dfrac{3}{5} = \dfrac{3 \cdot 20}{5 \cdot 20} = \dfrac{60}{100} = 0.60 = 60\%$

b. Rewrite $\frac{5}{8}$ as a percent.

Because the denominator is not a factor of 100, divide numerator by denominator to change the fraction into decimal form.

$5 \div 8 = 0.625 = 62.5\%$

Try It

Rewrite each decimal or fraction as a percent.

a. 0.82   **b.** 0.125   **c.** $\dfrac{1}{2}$ **d.** $\dfrac{1}{8}$ **e.** $\dfrac{3}{500}$

You can also convert percents to decimals and fractions. Again, it may be helpful to think of "parts per hundred."

Example 4

Watermelon is 92% water and 6.9% carbohydrates.

a. Rewrite 92% as a fraction and a decimal.

$92\% = \dfrac{92}{100}$ Write as a fraction with denominator 100.

$\dfrac{92}{100} = 0.92$ Write as a decimal.

b. Rewrite 6.9% as a fraction and a decimal.

$6.9\% = \dfrac{6.9}{100}$ Write as a fraction with denominator 100.

$\dfrac{6.9}{100} = \dfrac{6.9 \cdot 10}{100 \cdot 10} = \dfrac{69}{1000}$ Multiply numerator and denominator by 10 to eliminate the decimal.

$\dfrac{69}{1000} = 0.069$ Write as a decimal.

Another way to change a percent to a decimal is to delete the percent sign and move the decimal point two places to the left. For example:

$92\% = 0\,9\,2.\% = 0.92$

$6.9\% = 0\,0\,6.9\,\% = 0.069$

Try It

Rewrite each percent as a fraction and as a decimal.

a. 12%   **b.** 4.5%   **c.** 200%

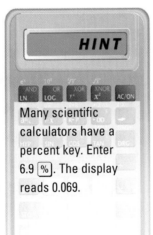

HINT

Many scientific calculators have a percent key. Enter 6.9 %. The display reads 0.069.

Check   Your Understanding

1. How can fractions be changed to percents?

2. How can you tell if a decimal or a fraction will be renamed as a percent greater than 100? Less than 1?

3. Which is greater, 0.6 or 7%? Why?

6-1 Exercises and Applications

Practice and Apply

Getting Started For each figure below, write the fraction, decimal, and percent that describes how much of the figure is shaded.

1. a. Fraction = ?

   b. Decimal = ?

   c. Percent = ?

2. a. Fraction = ?

   b. Decimal = ?

   c. Percent = ?

3. Draw a diagram to show 75%.

4. Use the survey results shown in the circle graph.

   a. What percent of students say they eat out 3–5 times per week?

   b. What percent of students say they eat out no more than 5 times per week?

   c. What percent of students say they eat out at least once a week?

Times Students Eat Out Each Week

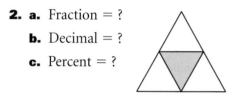

☐	0
☐	1–2
☐	3–5
☐	6–8
☐	9 or more

Write each fraction or decimal as a percent.

5. $\dfrac{4}{5}$　**6.** 0.18　**7.** $\dfrac{6}{5}$　**8.** 0.1667　**9.** 0.0035

Write each percent as a fraction in lowest terms and as a decimal.

10. 0.1%　**11.** 98%　**12.** 13.6%　**13.** 7.5%

14. 25%　**15.** 140%　**16.** 12.5%　**17.** 0.75%

18. **Test Prep** Which shows 345% expressed as a decimal?

   Ⓐ 34.5　Ⓑ 0.345　Ⓒ 3.45　Ⓓ 0.0345

19. Chance If there is about a 1% chance that eating a certain type of food would seriously harm you, would you eat it? Why or why not?

20. Consumer An orange-drink label reads "20% real fruit juice." What fractional part is real fruit juice?

278 *Chapter 6 • Percent*

PRACTICE 6-1

21. Consumer Shoes you need are going on sale. Which sign would you like to see put up? Why?

| 20% off | 15% off | $\frac{1}{4}$% off | 0.5% off |

22. Number Sense The students at Adams Junior High conducted a survey of their favorite lunch foods. The chart displays the results. What percent of the students chose each food?

Favorite Food	Pizza	Chicken	Salad	Hamburger	Tacos	Other
Number of Students	51	10	38	19	30	2

a. Pizza

b. Anything but pizza

c. Tacos

d. Salad

23. Fine Arts To make the color light brown, you mix 7 parts red, 2 parts yellow, and 1 part blue. What percent of the light-brown coloring is red? Yellow? Blue?

Problem Solving and Reasoning

24. **Journal** Explain the differences between 500%, 50%, 5%, and 0.5%.

25. Communicate 90% means 90 out of 100. Explain how a student can score 90% on a test that has only 50 questions.

26. Communicate Explain how to rename a fraction with a denominator of 10 as a percent. Explain how to rename a fraction with a denominator of 1000 as a percent.

27. Math Reasoning A percentile is a point below which a given percent of data lie.

a. What percentile is represented by the median? By the quartiles?

b. Suppose there are 10,000 students taking a test in Alabama. What would it mean to score in the ninety-fifth percentile?

Mixed Review

28. Solve $x + 3 \leq 10$. Graph the solution on a number line. *[Lesson 3-7]*

29. Graph $y = -x - 1$. Find the slope, the x-intercept, and the y-intercept. *[Lesson 4-5]*

22. At Bonnabel Middle School, 372 students were asked to give the time of their school-night curfew. The results are shown in the circle graph. Use the graph to answer the following questions.

School-night Curfews

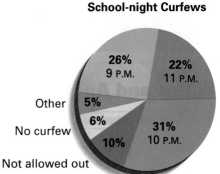

a. What time was the curfew of approximately $\frac{1}{3}$ of the students?

b. Approximately how many students had an 11 P.M. curfew?

Problem Solving and Reasoning

23. Critical Thinking John's tennis coach discovered that when at least 85% of John's first serves are in bounds, John wins the match. In the present match, 73 out of 98 of John's first serves are in bounds. Will he win the match? Explain your reasoning.

24. Critical Thinking The average daily intake of calories is 2000. For a snack, Leandro had yogurt (250 calories) and a small bag of chips (160 calories). Approximately what percent of his total caloric intake did Leandro have?

25. **Journal** Which percents do you think are the easiest to use when estimating? Explain your choices.

26. Communicate Estimate each of the following. Explain how you found your estimate.

a. 148% of 97   **b.** 0.9% of 4230

Mixed Review

Solve each equation. Check your solution. *[Lesson 3-4]*

27. $y - 11 = 8$ **28.** $m + 3 = -1$ **29.** $p - 6 = -8$ **30.** $z + 150 = 72$

31. Graph $y < x - 3$ on a coordinate plane. *[Lesson 4-7]*

Project Progress

Make a chart of the classes in which you have homework and the days of the week. Record the time you spend on each subject each day. Change hr and min to a fraction and to a decimal. For example, 1 hr, 35 min, is $1\frac{35}{60}$ hr $= 1\frac{7}{12}$ hr ≈ 1.58 hr. At the end of the week, estimate what percent of total homework time you spent on each subject.

Problem Solving

Understand
Plan
Solve
Look Back

In this Section you will apply your knowledge of percents to understanding the nutrition facts on a food label.

You Are What You Eat

Examine this nutrition label from a frozen pizza. The serving size and number of servings are given on the label, but the serving size for one person may not be the serving size for another.

1. Decide on a different serving size. Is your serving size larger or smaller than the one shown here?

2. How many servings does the pizza contain now? Is your number of servings larger or smaller than the one shown here? How are the number of servings and the serving size related?

3. Use the original label to find what percent of the total fat is saturated fat.

4. By changing the serving size, what other items on the food label will change?

5. Make a new food label for the serving size you chose.

6. On the original label, total fat was listed as 11 g, or 17%. This means 17% of what number? What are the comparable numbers for your new label?

Nutrition Facts

Serving Size ⅙ pizza (139 g)
Servings Per Container: 6

Amount Per Serving
Calories 320   Calories from Fat 100

	% Daily Value*
Total Fat 11g	**17%**
Saturated Fat 6g	**30%**
Cholesterol 25mg	**8%**
Sodium 870mg	**36%**
Total Carbohydrate 39g	**13%**
Dietary Fiber 3g	**12%**
Sugars 6g	
Protein 3g	

Vitamin A	15%	•	Vitamin C	0%
Calcium	30%	•	Iron	6%

*Percent Daily Values are based on a 2,000 calorie diet. Your daily values may be higher or lower depending on your caloric needs:

	Calories	2,000	2,500
Total Fat	Less than	65g	80g
Sat. Fat	Less than	20g	25g Fat
Cholesterol	Less than	300mg	300mg
Sodium	Less than	2,400mg	2,400mg
Total Carbohydrate		300g	375g
Fiber		25g	30g

Calories per gram:
Fat 9 • Carbohydrate 4 • Protein 4

1. Write the fraction, decimal, and percent that describes how much of one figure is shaded.

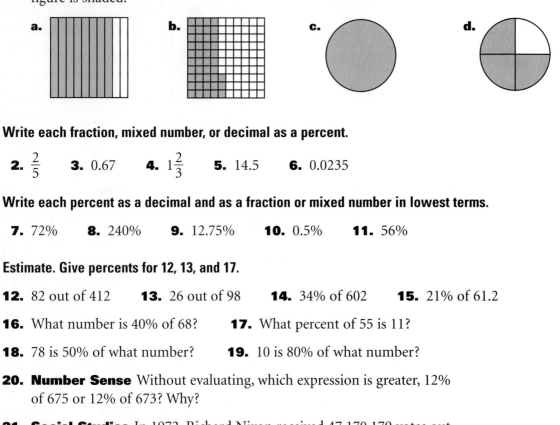

a. b. c. d.

Write each fraction, mixed number, or decimal as a percent.

2. $\frac{2}{5}$ **3.** 0.67   **4.** $1\frac{2}{3}$ **5.** 14.5   **6.** 0.0235

Write each percent as a decimal and as a fraction or mixed number in lowest terms.

7. 72%   **8.** 240%   **9.** 12.75%   **10.** 0.5%   **11.** 56%

Estimate. Give percents for 12, 13, and 17.

12. 82 out of 412   **13.** 26 out of 98   **14.** 34% of 602   **15.** 21% of 61.2

16. What number is 40% of 68?   **17.** What percent of 55 is 11?

18. 78 is 50% of what number?   **19.** 10 is 80% of what number?

20. Number Sense Without evaluating, which expression is greater, 12% of 675 or 12% of 673? Why?

21. Social Studies In 1972, Richard Nixon received 47,170,179 votes out of 77,727,590 cast. Estimate the percent of votes Nixon received.

22. A hairspray label states that it contains 50% alcohol, 40% water, and 14% other ingredients. Is this reasonable? Explain.

Test Prep

Use compatible numbers to estimate percents.

23. In a tennis match, 53 of Cindy's 97 first serves were good. Which is the best estimate of the percent of first serves that were good?

Ⓐ 5%   Ⓑ $\frac{1}{2}$%   Ⓒ 20%   Ⓓ 50%

The Price Is Right

As you look at advertisements in newspapers and magazines and on television, you see examples of how businesses use different techniques to attract customers. They offer sales—Presidents' Day sales, "back-to-school" sales, "going-out-of-business" sales, and so on. Discounts are sometimes given if you make bulk purchases. Many companies will give you "cents off" coupons to encourage you to buy their products instead of those of their competitors or to introduce their new products. Pricing techniques are often used to encourage you to buy their products. An item selling for $99.97, $99.98, or $99.99 is more appealing than one selling for $100.00. Many businesses offer you credit, which allows you to "buy now and pay later." Some companies' products always seem to be on sale, but are the sale prices actually a good buy?

1 Why would a company give a discount for bulk purchases?

2 How can a company afford to offer discounts and coupons for their products?

3 Why do you think a price of $99.99 is more appealing than a price of $100.00?

293

Using a Spreadsheet • Compound Interest

> **Problem:** Which investment strategy will cause your $100 investment to increase the most in 4 years: if you earn 4% interest compounded annually or if you earn 3.75% interest compounded monthly?
>
> A spreadsheet can help you find the answer to this problem.

1 Enter the following information in your spreadsheet as shown.

	A	B	C	D	E	F
1	Year	Amount	Annual Rate	Month	Amount	Monthly Rate
2	0	100		0	100	

2 Enter the following formulas.
In cell C2, enter =.04.
In cell F2, enter =.0375/12.
In cell A3, enter =A2+1.
In cell B3, enter =B2+B2*C$2.
In cell D3, enter =D2+1.
In cell E3, enter =E2+E2*F$2.

	A	B	C	D	E	F
1	Year	Amount	Annual Rate	Month	Amount	Monthly Rate
2	0	100	0.04	0	100	0.003125
3	1	104		1	100.3125	

3 Select cells A3 to F50 and use the **Fill Down** command.

	A	B	C	D	E	F
1	Year	Amount	Annual Rate	Month	Amount	Monthly Rate
2	0	100	0.04	0	100	0.003125
3	1	104		1	100.3125	
4	2	108.16		2	100.6259	
5	3	112.4864		3	100.9404	
6	4	116.9858		4	101.2558	
50	48	657.0528		48	116.1562	

> **Solution:** $100 at 4% interest compounded annually is $116.99; $100 at 3.75% interest compounded monthly is only $116.16.

TRY IT

> Which investment strategy will cause your $100 investment to increase the most in 4 years: if you earn 5% interest compounded annually or if you earn 5% interest compounded quarterly (4 times a year)?

ON YOUR OWN

▶ Which is easier, computing compound interest by calculator or by using a spreadsheet? Explain.

▶ Why must you divide the interest rate by the number of compounding periods?

▶ Why do you have to enter formulas by using the "=" symbol?

In this Section you will connect your knowledge of percents to a situation involving increasing net worth.

The Price Is Right

Materials: Spreadsheet software (optional)

You own a T-shirt company. Your company starts the year with a net worth of $10,000.

1. Place these events in order so that you have the highest net worth at the end of the year.

   a. An increase in sales raises your net worth by 10%.

   b. You must pay $2,000 to repair equipment.

   c. A problem with the shirt manufacturer causes you to lose $5,000.

   d. You collected $15,000 in payments owed.

   e. A decrease in sales causes your net worth to decrease by 10%.

2. Describe the strategy you used.

3. What is your company's net worth at the end?

4. What would the company's net worth have been if the events had occurred in reverse order?

313

Find the percent increase or decrease. Round to the nearest percent.

1. Old: 4000
New: 3000

2. Old: 68
New: 90

3. Old: 990
New: 990

4. Old: $45.62
New: $32.75

5. Old: $0.75
New: $1.00

6. Old: $4250
New: $5000

7. What is the wholesale price of a tape player if the percent increase is 60% and the amount of increase is $65.98?

8. The percent discount is 40%. The amount of discount is $32.75. What is the original price?

9. The cost of a computer is $3562. The cost before taxes is $3298. What is the tax rate?

10. Find the sales tax on a purchase of $125.53 if the tax rate is 7.5%.

11. Find the sale price of a $63 dress at a 30%-off sale.

Test Prep

Tests always include the most common incorrect answers. Be sure you calculate your percent decrease from the *original* amount.

12. The price of a graphing calculator has dropped from $125.00 to $87.50. Which of the following is the percent decrease?

Ⓐ 30% Ⓑ 43% Ⓒ 70% Ⓓ 143%

13. NuVideo has 20%-off ticket price sale. Brian was about to buy an XK VCR with a $239.50 ticket price, but decided on a model that was 25% more than the XK's sale price. How much did he pay?

14. Sales dropped 40% to $5 million last year. What percent increase would return sales to their original level?

15. Find the simple interest paid on a loan of $2000 at 15% for 2 years.

16. **Journal** Write and solve a problem involving sales tax in which the final price is given.

17. **Critical Thinking** The price of an answering machine is reduced 15%. The sales tax is 8%. Is the final cost equal to the original price less 7%? Explain.

18. **Critical Thinking** Nellie gets a discount of 10% on all purchases. This week, her shop is having a 15%-off sale. Nellie gets both discounts. If she buys a VCR, which will give her the best price?

Ⓐ 10% off then 15% off   Ⓑ 15% off then 10%   Ⓒ Take 25% off.   Ⓓ Any of these.

Credit Card Purchases

Yolanda realized when she opened her morning mail that one item would forever change her life. The envelope contained an application for a credit card, which she hurriedly filled out and returned. Soon she received her card and information that she had a credit limit of $1500. It also stated that she would have to pay 18% interest at 1.5% per month on any balance not paid in 30 days.

It didn't take Yolanda long to buy things with her card until she charged to her limit—$1500. Then she realized that she had to pay it off, so she decided not to use the card anymore. The company that issued the card told her that she could make a minimum payment of $20 each month. That's what Yolanda decided to do. That way, she thought she would eventually pay off the entire balance and still have money to spend. But would she?

1. She made her first payment. At 1.5% monthly interest, how much interest was charged for the first month?

2. What was her balance after the first month?

3. She made her second $20 payment. How much interest was charged the second month? What was her balance after the second month?

4. Approximately how long will it take Yolanda to pay off her credit card debt by continuing to make $20 payments?

5. Suppose her payment each month had been $22.17. What would her balance have been after 1 month? After 2 months?

6. What advice would you give Yolanda?

Divisibility Patterns and Prime Factorization

You'll Learn ...

■ to use rules for determining whether a number is divisible by another number

... How It's Used

Egyptologists use divisibility to decipher patterns used in hieroglyphics.

Vocabulary

prime number

composite number

divisible

multiple

factor

prime factor

Fundamental Theorem of Arithmetic

prime factorization

▶ **Lesson Link** You have used patterns to solve problems. Now you will use patterns to determine whether a number divides without a remainder. ◄

A **prime number** is an integer larger than 1 that is only divisible by itself and 1.

Prime numbers: 2, 3, 5, 7, 11, ...

A **composite number** is a positive integer that is not prime. It has factors other than 1 and itself.

Composite numbers: 4, 6, 8, 9, 10, ...

Explore | Primes and Composites

The Chart Is Smart

Materials: Hundred chart

1. Circle 2 and cross out all the other multiples of 2.

2. Circle the next number that has not been crossed out and cross out all of its multiples.

3. Continue this process until all numbers except 1 are either circled or crossed out.

4. Did you use any shortcuts in this process? Describe.

5. Are the circled numbers prime numbers or composite numbers? How do you know?

1	2	3	4	5	6	7	8	9	10
11	12	13	14	15	16	17	18	19	20
21	22	23	24	25	26	27	28	29	30
31	32	33	34	35	36	37	38	39	40
41	42	43	44	45	46	47	48	49	50
51	52	53	54	55	56	57	58	59	60
61	62	63	64	65	66	67	68	69	70
71	72	73	74	75	76	77	78	79	80
81	82	83	84	85	86	87	88	89	90
91	92	93	94	95	96	97	98	99	100

Learn | Divisibility Patterns and Prime Factorization

We say that 15 is **divisible** by 5 because 15 divided by 5 has no remainder.

We say that 15 is a **multiple** of 5 because 15 is divisible by 5.

We say that 5 is a **factor** of 15 because 15 is divisible by 5.

$200 \div 4 = 50$ 4 and 50 are *factors* of 200.

$4 \times 50 = 200$ 200 is a *multiple* of 4 and 50.

Divisibility rules can tell if a given number is divisible by another number.

	Divisibility Rule
2	The ones digit is a *2, 4, 6, 8,* or *0*.
3	The sum of the number's digits is divisible by *3*.
4	As a number, the last two digits are divisible by *4*.
5	The number ends in *5* or *0*.
6	The number is divisible by *2* and *3*.
8	As a number, the last three digits are divisible by *8*.
9	The sum of the number's digits is divisible by *9*.
10	The ones digit is *0*.

Example 1

Enemy X always end their secret messages with a number divisible by 3 and 5, and not 8. A suspicious message ending with 5385 was found. State the divisibility rules that satisfy 5385 to find out if it's from Enemy X.

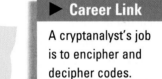

Career Link

A cryptanalyst's job is to encipher and decipher codes.

Divisible by 2, 4, 6, 8, or 10?   5385 is odd so it's not divisible by an even number.

No, because it is not even.   Eliminate the even numbers.

By 5? Yes, because it ends with 5.   Test for divisibility by an odd number.

By 3? Yes, because $5 + 3 + 8 + 5 = 21$ is divisible by 3.

By 9? No, because $5 + 3 + 8 + 5 = 21$ is not divisible by 9.

5385 is divisible by 3 and 5, and not 8, so the message is from Enemy X.

Try It

Is each number divisible by 2, 3, 4, 5, 6, 8, 9, or 10?

a. 38   **b.** 240   **c.** 236   **d.** 345

A **prime factor** of a number is a factor that is a prime number. For example:

List all factors of 36 and identify the primes.   1, 2, 3, 4, 6, 9, 12, 18, 36

2 and 3 are the prime factors of 36.

FUNDAMENTAL THEOREM OF ARITHMETIC

All integers greater than 1 are prime or can be written as a unique product of prime numbers.

Problem Solving and Reasoning

28. Communicate Some say that the average ratio of inches of snow to inches of water is 10 to 1. If the snow is equivalent to $2\frac{7}{8}$ inches of water, how many inches of snow are there? Explain your reasoning.

29. Math Reasoning Will the following calculator key strokes correctly evaluate $\frac{1}{2} \div \frac{3}{4}$? 1 ÷ 2 ÷ 3 ÷ 4 =. Explain your reasoning.

30. Critical Thinking The Great Lakes hold approximately 5439 cubic miles of water. The table shows the fraction of water volume in each lake.

a. Which lake is the largest?   **b.** Smallest?

c. What is the approximate volume of each lake?

Great Lake	Superior	Michigan	Huron	Erie	Ontario
Volume Part	$\frac{53}{100}$	$\frac{11}{50}$	$\frac{4}{25}$	$\frac{1}{50}$	$\frac{7}{100}$

31. Choose a Strategy The product of two positive numbers is greater than one. Can both of these numbers be less than one? Describe your strategy and how you used it.

32. Math Reasoning Multiplication of integers satisfies the *closure property* because if you multiply any two integers the product will be an integer. Does multiplication of even numbers satisfy the closure property? Multiplication of odd numbers? If not, give an example.

Problem Solving STRATEGIES

- Look for a Pattern
- Make an Organized List
- Make a Table
- Guess and Check
- Work Backward
- Use Logical Reasoning
- Draw a Diagram
- Solve a Simpler Problem

Mixed Review

Solve each equation. *[Lesson 3-5]*

33. $9x = 81$ **34.** $\frac{x}{4} = 16$ **35.** $-x = 44$ **36.** $18x = 3$

37. $-5x = 205$ **38.** $20x = -140$ **39.** $x \div 7 = 3$ **40.** $4 \cdot x = 88$

Find the percent of decrease. Round to the nearest whole percent. *[Lesson 6-5]*

41. Price of a video game that was $54.00 and marked down to $36.00

42. If there were 120 apples in the basket and 30 were eaten

43. Price of a skateboard that was $26.00 before sale of $5.00 off

You have learned how to work with rational numbers. Now you will apply what you have learned to understand how water is used by the world.

Will There Be a Drop to Drink?

Materials: Calculator

Some of the most beautiful cities in the world are located near water. The oceans cover at least 70% of Earth's surface.

We've all heard, "Don't leave the water running!!" Why? It must be an important resource.

Use your calculator to compare data about water usage. You will compare how much water is used for industrial, agricultural, and household purposes.

1. The United States gets $\frac{37}{50}$ of its freshwater from surface sources and the other part from underground sources. What part of our freshwater comes from underground?

2. Use the table below to discuss how the former Soviet Union, United States, and China use water. How does each country use its freshwater resources? What fractional part is used for household consumption?

	Industry	Agriculture	Household
Former Soviet Union	$\frac{9}{20}$	$\frac{51}{100}$	?
United States	$\frac{29}{50}$	$\frac{17}{50}$	?
China	$\frac{1}{20}$	$\frac{93}{100}$	?

3. On a worldwide basis water uses are allocated as follows: $\frac{1}{10}$ for domestic use, $\frac{1}{10}$ for industrial use, and $\frac{4}{5}$ for agricultural use. Does this allocation account for all of the world's water usage?

4. Discuss how the world uses water compared to the three countries mentioned above.

Compare each group of numbers and order them on a number line.

1. $-1.07, 1.05, -1$ **2.** $\frac{-2}{3}, \frac{2}{6}, \frac{-1}{3}$ **3.** $1\frac{1}{2}, 1\frac{3}{5}, -1\frac{2}{3}$ **4.** $1.5, -\frac{3}{4}, 1\frac{3}{4}$

Write each fraction as a decimal and determine whether it's terminating or repeating.

5. $\frac{3}{4}$ **6.** $-\frac{5}{6}$ **7.** $11\frac{5}{7}$ **8.** $-\frac{3}{9}$ **9.** $4\frac{7}{10}$

Write each decimal as a fraction or mixed number.

10. -2.34 **11.** 3.005 **12.** -0.451 **13.** $0.\overline{364}$ **14.** $2.\overline{11}$

Calculate.

15. $0.3 + 7.12$ **16.** $8 - 0.00725$ **17.** $3.4 \times (-0.039)$ **18.** $100.46 \div 0.32$

19. $\frac{1}{6} + \left(-\frac{1}{8}\right)$ **20.** $8\frac{1}{2} + 2\frac{3}{4}$ **21.** $3 - 1\frac{3}{8}$ **22.** $\frac{2}{3} - \left(-\frac{5}{7}\right)$

23. $\frac{4}{9} \times \frac{-3}{8}$ **24.** $3\frac{1}{4} \times \frac{6}{7}$ **25.** $5 \div \frac{1}{3}$ **26.** $-4\frac{1}{5} \div -2\frac{2}{3}$

Solve.

27. $\frac{2}{3} = \frac{4}{5} + x$ **28.** $\frac{-3}{4} = -\frac{-1}{3} - x$ **29.** $\frac{6}{7} + \frac{-3}{7} = x$

30. **Journal** A number is divided by -6, multiplied by $\frac{3}{4}$, and added to $6\frac{1}{2}$. The result is 18.5. What is the number? Explain how you solved this problem.

Test Prep

When taking multiple choice tests, express fractions in lowest terms.

31. Tina swam four laps in $3\frac{3}{10}$ minutes. The swim-team record for the distance is $2\frac{9}{10}$ minutes. How far is Tina from matching the team record?

Ⓐ $\frac{1}{10}$ minute   Ⓑ $\frac{1}{5}$ minute   Ⓒ $\frac{3}{10}$ minute   Ⓓ None of these

Irrational Numbers

▶ **Social Studies Link** ▶ **Geography Link** ▶ **www.mathsurf.com/8/ch7/houses**

HOME SWEET HOME

Around the world, people live in a variety of dwellings. Whether the residence is an adobe hut on the plains, a tent in the desert, a high-rise apartment in a big city, or a house in the suburbs, it is called home. Each of these homes is based on an architect's or builder's plan. Building homes involves using numbers such as integers, decimals, or fractions.

People have different homes due to climate, culture, or landscape. In places without trees, you may find a home built of stone or mud. In the forest, you'd be able to find a log cabin. In the southwest United States, the Anasazi people carved their homes into the rock of a mountainside.

1 What are some shapes of homes that you can think of?

2 How would a slope influence the type of home built upon it?

3 How do you think the need for shelter influences mathematics?

363

9. **Test Prep** The Comanche Indians cure buffalo hides and stretch them over a wooden framework to build tepees. If the radius of a tepee is 15 ft and the hides are extended 25 ft up on the slanted sides, how high will the center of the tepee be?

Ⓐ 200 ft   Ⓑ 29 ft   Ⓒ 20 ft   Ⓓ 4.5 ft

Problem Solving and Reasoning

Math Reasoning If the lengths of the sides of a triangle satisfy $a^2 + b^2 = c^2$, the triangle is a right triangle. The longest side is c, the hypotenuse. Does the set of side lengths make a right triangle?

10. 4, 5, 7   **11.** 7, 24, 25   **12.** 20, 21, 29   **13.** 5, 12, 13

14. **Communicate** The ancient Egyptians used ropes tied with knots to form a 3-4-5 triangle to help them with right angles when building the pyramids. Explain how this system would work.

15. **Measurement** A square courtyard with a diagonal walkway has an area of 81 square feet.

   a. Find the length of the sides of the courtyard.

   b. Find the length of the walkway.

16. **Patterns** Use the Pythagorean theorem to find the length of the hypotenuse in right triangles when the legs are integer values of equal length. When do you get an integer length for the hypotenuse?

Mixed Review

Give two solution pairs for each of these equations. *[Lesson 4-2]*

17. $x = 2y$ **18.** $y = x + 4$ **19.** $3x = 5y$ **20.** $y = 3x + 2$

Solve each proportion. *[Lesson 5-4]*

21. $\frac{2}{3} = \frac{44}{x}$ **22.** $\frac{9}{x} = \frac{27,000}{36,000}$ **23.** $\frac{x}{5} = \frac{20}{100}$

24. If a cookie recipe calls for 3 cups of sugar to make 4 dozen cookies, how many cups of sugar are needed to make 10 dozen cookies?

Project Progress	
Look back at your results from the investment period. Look for any use of irrational numbers or square roots.	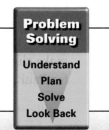

Problem Solving

Understand
Plan
Solve
Look Back

Section 7C Connect

You have learned to use the Pythagorean theorem for right triangles. You will now use the Pythagorean theorem to design parts of a house.

Home Sweet Home

Materials: Calculator

Some people prefer to build or fix up their own house. Measurements and calculations are crucial if you want windows to close, doors to open, stable walls, and straight floors. The Pythagorean theorem can be used for many aspects of building a house.

1. A foundation can keep the wooden frame of a house from rotting after years of rain, wind, and snow. Compare the two foundations shown by determining the depth of each.

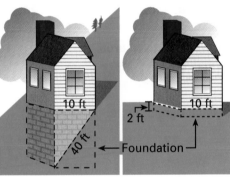

2. The frame of a house is like your body's skeleton. Corner bracing can add strength to a house frame. How long is the entire length of bracing?

3. How long is a part of the bracing that is between two 10-ft-tall wood planks? Explain how you got your answer.

4. Rafters are the parallel beams that support a roof. What is the total length of wood used in the rafters of this roof?

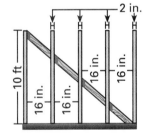

Rafter

5. Draw a sketch of a house that you would build for yourself and describe how you would use the Pythagorean theorem.

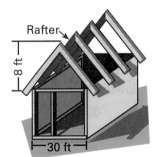

Solving Problems

There is often more than one way to solve a problem. You should use the strategy that works best for you. Trying different strategies can help you decide which one suits your problem-solving style.

Problem Solving Focus

The following problem has already been solved using three different methods.

Three friends buy fresh corn at an outdoor market. Amani buys twice as much corn as Brad. Brad buys three more ears of corn than Chris. All together, Amani, Brad, and Chris buy 17 ears of corn. How much corn does each of them buy?

You know:

- There are 17 ears of corn,
- Amani has twice as many as Brad,
- Brad can't have more than eight ears of corn,
- Chris has three less than Brad.

Guess and Check	Draw a diagram	Logical Reasoning
Guess: 6 ears for Brad. B = 6 A = 6 × 2 = 12 C = 6 − 3 = 3 **Check:** 6 + 12 + 3 = 21 Too big. **Guess:** 5 ears for Brad. B = 5 A = 5 × 2 = 10 C = 5 − 3 = 2 **Check:** 5 + 2 + 10 = 17 It works.	Let ❑ = ears Chris buys. C = ❑ B = ❑ + 3 A = (❑ + 3) + (❑ + 3) You have four ❑'s and three 3's. You have four ❑'s and 9. 17 − 9 = 8 The four ❑'s stand for 8 ears of corn. 8 ÷ 4 = 2 Each ❑ = 2.	■ No one can have more than 17. ■ Amani must have the most. ■ Chris must have the least. ■ The other amounts are based on Brad's amount. So find Brad's amount first. B = 5 A = 5 × 2 = 10 C = 5 − 3 = 2

Solve the following problem. You may use one of the above methods or a method of your own.

1 Four friends work out at a health club. Mark uses the treadmill three times as long as Joan. Allison uses it half as long as David. David uses it 15 minutes longer than Mark. All together, they use the treadmill for 2.5 hours. How long is each person on the machine?

Where am I? Where am I going? How do I get there? If you aren't certain about a location, you can look on a map. It hasn't always been this way.

In the past, people marked trails with stones and noted landmarks such as trees and streams. But snow and rain could interfere with this system. Stars were used for navigation, but that only worked on clear nights.

In 1978, the U.S. Department of Defense said, "We've got to have a system that really works." So since then the government has worked on something called the Global Positioning System, or GPS. There are 24 satellites orbiting the earth connected to a computer system. In a way, you could think

of the satellites as "human-made stars." GPS is accurate enough to give positions, anywhere in the world, within the width of your street, 24 hours a day.

This means that everyone will have the ability to know exactly where they are, all the time. Finally, one of humankind's basic needs will be fulfilled.

Where In The World Am I?

1 GPS is widely used by backpackers and sailors. What other uses can you think of for GPS?

2 GPS allows every square meter of the earth's surface to have a unique address, similar to a coordinate plane. How do you think GPS might change what we know to be a phone book?

Practice and Apply

1. **Getting Started** The highest point in the world is Mount Everest, at 29,028 ft. Express this altitude in miles.

   a. Write the ratio of miles to feet with ft in the denominator.

   b. Multiply the ratio by 29,028 ft.

What U.S. customary unit would you use for each measurement?

2. The volume of earth removed during an archaeological dig

3. The distance traveled in one day by a flock of geese

4. The area of a sail on a sailboat

What metric unit would you use for each measurement?

5. A single dose of cough syrup

6. The distance from the top of a diving board to the water surface

7. The mass of your backpack containing your books

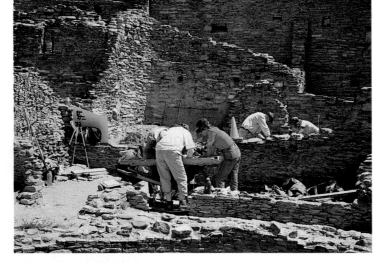

Convert each measurement.

8. 7.8 m to cm	**9.** 2500 L to mL	**10.** 2.5 hr to min
11. 64 oz to lb	**12.** 5 ft 4 in. to in.	**13.** 10 pt to qt

14. **Geography** The area of the United States is 3,536,341 mi^2 and Canada is 3,851,809 mi^2. Which country has a larger area and by how many square miles?

15. **Science** For a geology experiment, a group of students measure the mass of a piece of copper. Their results were 15.64 g, 15.69 g, 15.67 g, 0.01566 kg, and 0.01564 kg. What is the average of the students' measurements?

16. The stopwatch on the right shows the 1995 Boston Marathon record set by Cosmas N'Deti of Kenya in hours, minutes, and seconds. How much time is this in seconds?

17. **Test Prep** Which of these would be an appropriate unit for the area of a rose petal?

   Ⓐ cm²   Ⓑ ft²   Ⓒ mm³   Ⓓ in³

Problem Solving and Reasoning

18. **Critical Thinking** Mont Blanc, the highest peak in the Alps, is 4,807 m above sea level. A climber on Mont Blanc is 88 m from the top. What is her altitude in meters? In kilometers?

19. **Journal** The *cubit* is an ancient unit of measurement defined as the distance from a king's elbow to the tip of his middle finger, about 18 in. What is the problem with this definition? Why do you think standardized measurement units were developed?

20. **Communicate** How would you use proportions to change inches to yards? Give an example.

21. **Measurement** What customary unit would be most appropriate for measuring the area of the GPS display used in agriculture.

22. **Math Reasoning** The Grand Canyon, in Arizona, is 217 miles long. What is this length in yards? Inches? Compare the numerical values of the three measurements. Describe the relationship between these numerical values and the units of measurement associated with them.

Mixed Review

State whether each number is prime or composite. *[Lesson 7-1]*

23. 27   **24.** 91   **25.** 37   **26.** 63

27. 49   **28.** 72   **29.** 1755   **30.** 363

Find the GCF of each pair of numbers. *[Lesson 7-2]*

31. 14, 42   **32.** 16, 64   **33.** 17, 71   **34.** 33, 90

35. 21, 66   **36.** 13, 169   **37.** 82, 16   **38.** 9, 261

Significant Digits and Precision

You'll Learn ...

■ to identify more precise measurements

... How It's Used

Farmers use precise measurements when they analyze the quality of their soil.

Vocabulary

precision

significant digits

▶ **Lesson Link** Now you'll apply what you know about units of measurement to calculate with measurements using significant digits. ◄

Explore | Precision

How Close Can You Get?   **Materials:** Meter stick

1. Measure the distance from the floor to the top of your desk. Record the length to the nearest 1 m, nearest 0.5 m, nearest 1 cm, nearest 0.5 cm, and nearest 1 mm.

2. Compare your measurements with those of others in the group. Did you all get the same numbers? Why or why not?

3. Calculate the height of two desks atop one another using each measurement. (Hint: Multiply by 2.) Do the same for five desks.

4. Which heights are the most exact? Discuss your reasoning.

5. With your group, invent a technique of determining the most accurate measurement from a group of measurements.

Learn | Significant Digits and Precision

The **precision** of a measurement is determined by the unit of measure. The smaller the unit of measure, the more precise the measurement.

Example 1

Determine the more precise height of the national Capitol dome, 287 ft or 96 yd?

Choose the measurement with smaller units.

The foot (ft) is smaller than the yard (yd).

287 ft is the more precise measurement.

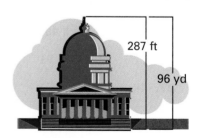

When you compare measurements with the same unit, the more precise measurement can be determined by the decimal places.

Example 2

Using GPS, a geologist finds the distance between two mountain peaks. Which measurement is most precise, 1068 m, 1067.52 m, or 1067.5 m?

Choose the measurement to the smallest decimal place.

1067.52 m is the most precise measurement.

Geologists study movement of the earth's crust by surveying land and mapping altitudes at various locations.

Try It

For each pair of measurements, determine the more precise measurement.

a. 0.5 mi, 2638 ft   **b.** 2 m, 197.5 cm   **c.** 36 in., 35.75 in.

The greatest possible error of any measurement is $\frac{1}{2}$ or 0.5 of the smallest unit used.

The paper clip is 2.8 cm long.

The greatest possible error is $+0.05$ cm or -0.05 cm.

The digits that represent the actual measurement are **significant digits**. The last significant digit in a measurement is an estimated digit. These are rules for determining the number of significant digits.

1. All nonzero digits (1–9) are significant.

2. Zeros between nonzero digits are significant.

3. Zeros to the right of a decimal point and to the right of a nonzero digit are significant.

4. Zeros to the right of a decimal point and to the left of a nonzero digit are not significant.

Example 3

Determine the number of significant digits in each measurement.

a. 420.040 m

4, 2, and 4 are significant.   Apply Rule 1.

All zeros are significant.   Apply Rules 2, 3, and 4.

6 significant digits.

b. 0.00420 m

4 and 2 are significant.

The last zero is significant.

3 significant digits.

Try It

Determine the number of significant digits in each measurement.

a. 0.0050 m   **b.** 3.05607 kg   **c.** 3000 mi   **d.** 11.050 in.

Adding and subtracting measurements require that the answer be as precise as the least precise value of the two measurements.

Example 4

▶ Science Link

An *ornithologist* is someone who studies birds.

To study the toucan, an ornithologist trekked to 6540.75 ft altitude in South America. The ornithologist wants to be at 9455 ft to observe the flocks of toucans. How much higher in altitude does the ornithologist have to go?

The answer will be given to the ones place.

$$\begin{array}{r} 9455. \\ -\ 6540.75 \quad \text{Subtract.} \\ \hline 2914.25 \approx 2914 \end{array}$$

The ornithologist has to climb 2914 ft.

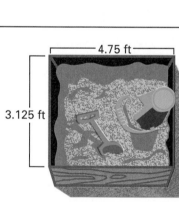

Remember

To round a number, look at the decimal place to the right.

If the digit to the right is ≤ 4, then round down.

If the digit to the right is ≥ 5, then round up.

[Previous course]

Multiplying and dividing measurements require that the answer have as many significant digits as the value in the operation with the least number of significant digits.

Example 5

A rectangular sandbox is built with the lengths 4.75 ft and 3.125 ft. Use significant digits to express the area of the sandbox.

The answer will have 3 significant digits.

Enter: 4.75 $\boxed{\times}$ 3.125 $\boxed{=}$ *14.84375*

The area of the sandbox is 14.8 ft².

4.75 ft

3.125 ft

Try It

Calculate and give the number of significant digits in each answer.

a. 11.4 g + 2.65 g   **b.** 32.06 mL − 22.3 mL

c. 2.3 in. × 20.3 in.   **d.** 32.5 m ÷ 1.5

Check Your Understanding

1. Describe how precision is affected by the unit of measurement used.

2. How do significant digits affect the calculation of measurements?

Practice and Apply

1. **Getting Started** Determine the number of significant digits in 407.050.

   a. Count the number of nonzero digits.

   b. Count the number of significant zeros.

   c. Add the total number of significant digits from **a** and **b**.

Determine the number of significant digits in each measurement.

2. 0.074 m **3.** 0.0056 km **4.** 57.048 mi **5.** 11.050 in.

Determine which measurement is more precise.

6. 1 yd, 37 in. **7.** 235 cm, 230 cm **8.** 18 in., $17\frac{11}{16}$ in. **9.** 0.3 L, 0.25 L

10. **Science** A measurement of 0.088 m is converted to cm. How many significant digits does the measurement have before conversion? How many after?

11. **Industry** A jet pilot completes a test flight which, according to the on-board GPS-based clock, lasts 2.75 hr. Another test flight on the next day lasts 0.55 hr. Using significant digits, how much total flight time did the pilot log for the two days?

Calculate and give each answer with the correct number of significant digits.

12. 8.4 g + 5.20 g **13.** 45 mi − 0.9 mi

14. 9.79 cm × 9.5 cm **15.** 32.8 m × 1.5 m

16. **Test Prep** Determine the most precise measurement.

   Ⓐ 89 ft Ⓑ 89.0 ft Ⓒ 90 ft Ⓓ 88.999 ft

17. **Algebra** The formula for converting temperatures from Fahrenheit to Celsius is $C = \frac{5}{9}(F - 32)$. The normal daily low temperature in Everglades National Park is 56°F. What is this temperature in °C, using significant digits.

18. **Measurement** One leg of a right triangle is measured at 1.38 cm, the other at 0.67 cm. What is the length of the hypotenuse? Use significant digits.

Problem Solving and Reasoning

14. Critical Thinking Name a lake and a city in Mexico that are approximately on the same latitude and 375 miles away from each other.

15. 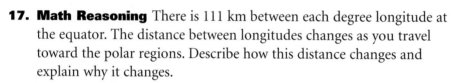 **Journal** What kind of measuring device would you invent to measure distances and directions while traveling? How precise should it be? Make a sketch of it and describe how it would work.

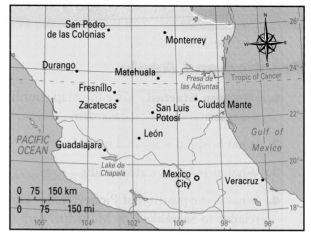

16. Communicate The west coast of Cuba is at 85° W and the east coast of Cuba is at 74° W. If at that latitude, a 5° change in longitude represents about 300 mi, how far is it from coast to coast? Explain your answer.

17. Math Reasoning There is 111 km between each degree longitude at the equator. The distance between longitudes changes as you travel toward the polar regions. Describe how this distance changes and explain why it changes.

18. Algebra Describe the relative position of $(-3, 5)$ with respect to the origin $(0, 0)$ on a coordinate grid.

19. Math Reasoning Kachina hiked 1 mile east, turned right, and walked $\frac{3}{4}$ mile. After a lunch break, she walked in the same direction 1.25 miles, turned left, and continued her hike. What direction is Kachina facing?

20. Math Reasoning A backpacker uses her GPS receiver to find out how much farther she needs to travel. The red dot on the GPS receiver screen shows where she is. The blue dot shows her destination. How far is that point from her current position?

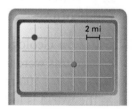

Mixed Review

Find each unit rate. *[Lesson 5-5]*

21. 220 mi in 4 hr   **22.** 18 birds in 9 nests   **23.** $48 for 8 hr

24. $3.99 for 3 lb   **25.** 32 children in 14 homes   **26.** $100 for 10 CDs

Add or subtract. *[Lesson 7-5]*

27. $1.024 + 2.091$ **28.** $0.041 - 0.144$ **29.** $42.1 + 98.156$

30. $\frac{4}{5} + 1\frac{1}{2}$ **31.** $5\frac{1}{3} - 2\frac{2}{3}$ **32.** $9\frac{1}{4} + 2\frac{9}{10}$

Section 8A Connect

You've learned about precision and have converted units of measurement. Now you'll use this knowledge to learn more about GPS.

Where in the World Am I?

The Navstar GPS is controlled by the U.S. military at Falcon Air Force Base in Colorado. In 1995, there were 24 satellites orbiting the earth to enable people all over the world to navigate.

There are two types of Global Positioning Systems. The Precise Positioning Service (PPS) is only for the U.S. Department of Defense. The Standard Positioning Service (SPS) is for the general public.

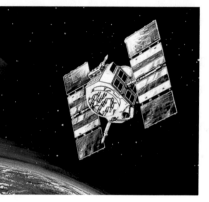

The PPS is encoded and needs a decoder to be used. The SPS is not encoded and is used by fishing boats, cars, airplanes, and backpackers.

Types of GPS		
GPS-Determined Measurements	**PPS Precision**	**SPS Precision**
Distance in any direction N, S, E, or W	Within 17.8 m	Within 100 m
Altitude	Within 27.7 m	Within 156 m
Time (1,000,000,000 ns = 1 sec)	Within 100 ns	Within 340 ns

1. Which GPS service is more precise? Discuss your reasoning.

2. Why would there be two levels of precision for GPS service?

3. One GPS satellite has an orbit approximately 93,305 mi long and completes the orbit in 12 hr. How fast does a GPS satellite travel?

4. Suppose a ship is 200 km east of Boston. If a GPS satellite is 17,500 km directly above Boston, what is the distance between the GPS satellite and the ship? Use the Pythagorean theorem.

5. Some say that a GPS receiver in a backpack could someday help guide blind people. Discuss some other possible applications for GPS.

8-4 Exercises and Applications

Practice and Apply

1. **Getting Started** State whether ∠FDE and ∠BAC are congruent.

   a. Measure ∠FDE. Measure ∠BAC.

   b. Are the measures equal?

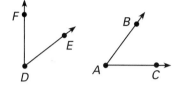

Classify each angle measurement as right, straight, obtuse, or acute.

2. 112° 3. 28° 4. 90° 5. 60° 6. 179.5°

7. 6° 8. 45° 9. 180° 10. 90.5° 11. 140°

Find the measure of the complement of each angle measure.

12. 45° 13. 22° 14. 85° 15. 9.1° 16. 17.6°

Find the measure of the supplement of each angle measure.

17. 120° 18. 39° 19. 90° 20. 175° 21. 60°

Use a protractor to measure each angle.

22. ∠HEK 23. ∠GEK 24. ∠FEG

25. ∠JEF 26. ∠FEK 27. ∠HEF

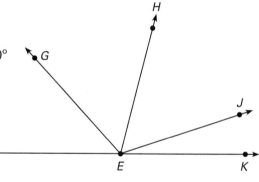

Identify each as a ray, line, or line segment and draw each.

28. $\overline{RS}$ 29. $\overrightarrow{TV}$ 30. $\overleftrightarrow{ST}$ 31. $\overrightarrow{RV}$

32. **Science** Gypsum, a mineral found in North America, is shown at the right. What kind of angles do you see?

33. **Test Prep** Two sides of a square meet to form what kind of angle?

   Ⓐ Acute Ⓑ Obtuse Ⓒ Right Ⓓ Straight

34. What is the measure of the two resulting angles after a 120° angle is bisected?

35. What is the measure of the two resulting angles after a 314° angle is bisected?

36. History Measure the obtuse angle above the entrance to Saint Peter's Basilica, constructed during the 1500s in Rome.

Problem Solving and Reasoning

37. Math Reasoning Pilots often use the numbers on a clock face to indicate angles. "Twelve o'clock" means "dead ahead." Suppose one pilot radios another, "Bogies at two o'clock!" At what angle have enemy planes been spotted?

38. **Journal** In Al Held's 1992 acrylic painting *Ima Ima II* how many acute angles can you find? How many obtuse angles? How many right angles? How do you think the kinds of angles in the painting affect the mood the painting creates?

39. Communicate Explain how to construct two line segments, one 6 cm and the other 3.5 cm long, meeting to form a 30° angle.

40. Math Reasoning A wheel has six equally spaced spokes that form six congruent angles. If each of these angles is to be bisected, what will the angle measure be between spokes?

Geometry In the figure at the right, $m\angle ACB = 140°$.

41. Algebra Two angles are supplementary. One angle measures x degrees, the other y degrees. Write an equation expressing that these angles are supplementary, and solve this equation for y. Find y if $x = 71°$.

42. What is $m\angle ACD$? What is $m\angle BCE$?

43. How are $\angle ACD$ and $\angle BCE$ related?

Mixed Review

Solve each rate and proportion. [*Lesson 5-6*]

44. $0.60 each cup = _____ for 8 cups

45. 60 mi/hr = _____ mi in 4 hr

46. _____ ft per sec = 36 ft in 9 sec

47. $24 for 3 hr = _____ per hr

Add or subtract, writing each answer in lowest terms. [*Lesson 7-5*]

48. $\frac{3}{5} + \frac{1}{4}$ **49.** $5\frac{2}{3} - 2\frac{2}{3}$ **50.** $6.902 + 0.53$ **51.** $36.17 - 8.66$

Example 2

In the diagram, $\overleftrightarrow{AC} \parallel \overleftrightarrow{DF}$.

Find $m\angle DYE$.

$\angle AXE$ and $\angle CXE$ are supplementary angles.

$m\angle AXE = 180° - m\angle CXE = 180° - 68° = 112°$

$\angle AXE$ and $\angle DYE$ are corresponding angles so $\angle AXE \cong \angle DYE$.

$m\angle DYE = 112°$

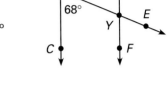

When two lines intersect they form two pairs of **vertical angles** . Vertical angles are congruent.

Angles *1* and *3*, and *2* and *4* are vertical angles.

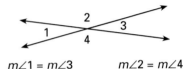

$m\angle 1 = m\angle 3 \qquad m\angle 2 = m\angle 4$

Example 3

Use the diagram to determine $m\angle 2$.

Identify the angle vertical to $\angle 2$.

$\angle 2$ and $\angle 4$ are vertical angles, so $m\angle 2 = 158°$.

$m\angle 2 = 158°$

$m\angle 1 = 22° \qquad m\angle 4 = 158°$

Try It

In the diagram, $\overline{PQ} \parallel \overline{RS}$. Find each angle measure.

$m\angle 2 = 146°$

a. $m\angle 4$ **b.** $m\angle 6$ **c.** $m\angle 5$

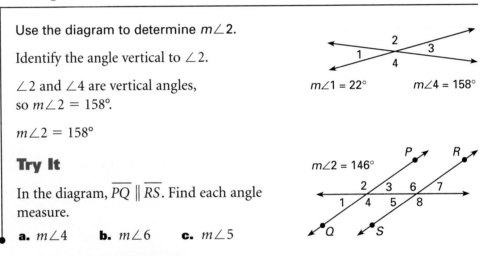

Check | Your Understanding

1. Describe a situation in which alternate interior angles formed by a transversal are not congruent.

2. What does the definition of *parallel* tell you about the distance between parallel lines?

3. Suppose a transversal is perpendicular to two parallel lines. What are the angle measures for all interior and exterior angles? Explain.

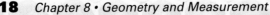

8-5 Exercises and Applications

Practice and Apply

1. **Getting Started** $\overleftrightarrow{XT} \parallel \overleftrightarrow{BW}$. Find the measures of all angles in the diagram.

   a. Identify all angles with a measure of 60°.

   b. Identify all angles with a measure of 120°.

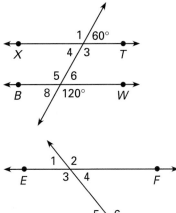

In the figure shown at right, $\overleftrightarrow{EF} \parallel \overleftrightarrow{GH}$. Use the figure for Exercises 2–10.

2. Name all alternate interior angles.

3. Name all alternate exterior angles.

4. Name two pairs of corresponding angles.

5. Name two pairs of vertical angles.

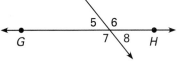

If $m\angle 6 = 130°$, find each angle measure.

6. $m\angle 5$ 7. $m\angle 7$ 8. $m\angle 3$ 9. $m\angle 2$ 10. $m\angle 1$

In the figure on the right, $\overleftrightarrow{ST} \parallel \overleftrightarrow{UV}$. Use the figure to find the measure of each angle.

11. $m\angle 4$ 12. $m\angle 1$

13. What kind of angles are $\angle 2$ and $\angle 8$?

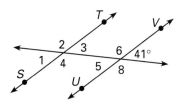

14. **Test Prep** How many angles are formed when a transversal crosses three parallel lines?

   Ⓐ 8   Ⓑ 6   Ⓒ 12   Ⓓ 16

15. **Science** Movement along a fault usually causes earthquakes. What is the angle of the fault plane to the layers in the side of the hill?

Complete each statement to make it true.

16. _____ lines intersect at a 90° angle.

17. _____ lines never intersect.

18. A _____ intersects a line segment at 90° and divides it into two equal lengths.

19. Vertical angles are always _____.

20. Geography In midtown Manhattan, almost all streets are either parallel or perpendicular—except for Broadway. What kind of angles are formed at the intersection of Broadway and 7th Avenue?

Problem Solving and Reasoning

21. Journal When you see a rainbow, the sun is behind you and the rain is in front of you. The points in the red arc of a rainbow form a 42° angle with the sun's rays. Use words such as *parallel*, *transversal*, and *alternate interior angles* to describe what is happening in the diagram.

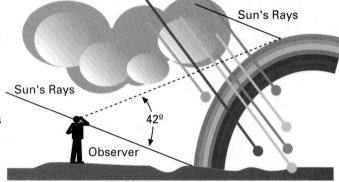

22. Communicate If two lines are both perpendicular to the same line, what is the relationship between those two lines? Explain.

23. Measurement $\overleftrightarrow{KP} \parallel \overleftrightarrow{VF}$. Find the measure of each numbered angle.

24. Geometry $\overleftrightarrow{KP} \parallel \overleftrightarrow{VF}$. Find the sum of the angles of the triangle. How does this sum relate to a straight angle?

Mixed Review

Solve each proportion. *[Lesson 5-7]*

25. $\dfrac{1 \text{ in.}}{40 \text{ ft}} = \dfrac{x \text{ in.}}{160 \text{ ft}}$ **26.** $\dfrac{1 \text{ in.}}{x \text{ mi}} = \dfrac{3 \text{ in.}}{36 \text{ mi}}$ **27.** $\dfrac{2 \text{ cm}}{1 \text{ km}} = \dfrac{10 \text{ cm}}{x \text{ km}}$

Multiply or divide, then write each answer in lowest terms. *[Lesson 7-6]*

28. $\dfrac{1}{2} \times \left(-\dfrac{4}{9}\right)$ **29.** $\dfrac{7}{8} \div \dfrac{8}{9}$ **30.** 5.072×1.54 **31.** $5.2\overline{)9.256}$

PROBLEM SOLVING 8-5

Project Progress

As you learn more about a culture, find out how it charted the stars and planets. A culture's knowledge of astronomy can be related to its knowledge of geometry.

Problem Solving

Understand
Plan
Solve
Look Back

Polygons

▶ Lesson Link You've learned about line segments and angles. Now you're ready to learn about shapes made from them. ◀

A **polygon** is a closed figure formed by three or more points joined by line segments (sides). A **vertex** of a polygon is a point at which two sides intersect.

Explore Polygons

Getting in Shape

Materials: Geoboard™, Rubber bands

1. Wrap a rubber band around any three pegs on the Geoboard™ to outline a polygon with three sides.

2. How many unique three-sided polygons can you outline?

3. How many vertices does a three-sided polygon have?

4. How many unique four-sided polygons can you outline?

5. How many vertices does a four-sided polygon have?

6. How many unique five-sided polygons can you outline? How many six-sided polygons?

7. How many vertices do five- and six-sided polygons have?

8. Discuss the relationship between number of sides and number of vertices a polygon has.

Learn Polygons

A polygon is classified by the number of sides it has.

Number of Sides	3	4	5	6	7	8
Polygon	Triangle	Quadrilateral	Pentagon	Hexagon	Heptagon	Octagon
Example						

You'll Learn ...

■ to classify polygons

... How It's Used

People who make stained glass use polygons in their designs.

Vocabulary

polygon
vertex
triangle
quadrilateral
pentagon
hexagon
heptagon
octagon
Venn diagram
equilateral triangle
isosceles triangle
scalene triangle
parallelogram
rectangle
rhombus
square
trapezoid
diagonal
regular polygon
convex polygon
concave polygon

A **Venn diagram** shows a relationship by visually grouping things into sets.

Three important types of triangles are shown in the Venn diagram to the right.

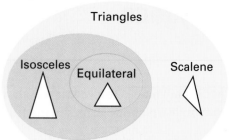

An **equilateral triangle** has three congruent sides.

An **isosceles triangle** has at least two congruent sides.

A **scalene triangle** has no congruent sides. All sides have different lengths.

A triangle has the same number of congruent sides as it has congruent angles.

The sum of a triangle's angle measures always equals 180°.

▶ **Science Link**

Humpback whales belong to the order of Cetacea. Members of Cetacea are mammals that live in the ocean.

Example 1

An isosceles triangle can be seen in the shape of the tail on a humpback whale. What is the length of $\overline{FG}$?

$m\overline{FG} = m\overline{DF}$ because $\triangle DFG$ is isosceles.

$m\overline{FG} = 6.6$ ft

Example 2

In the scalene triangle shown, find the missing angle measure.

$32° + 76° + x = 180°$ Write an equation.

$\qquad 108° + x = 180°$ Add.

$\qquad\qquad x = 72°$ Subtract 108° from both sides.

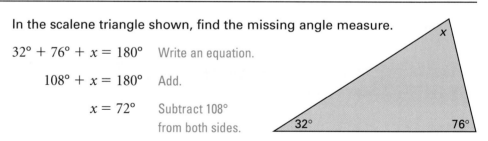

Try It

$\triangle ABC$ is equilateral.

a. Determine the length of $\overline{BC}$.

b. Determine the length of $\overline{AC}$.

c. Determine all angle measures of triangle ABC.

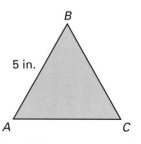

A Venn diagram can show the types of quadrilaterals.

A **parallelogram** is a quadrilateral with two pairs of parallel sides.

A **rectangle** is a quadrilateral with four right angles.

A **rhombus** is a parallelogram with four equal sides.

A **square** is a rectangle with four equal sides.

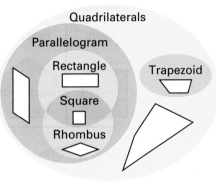

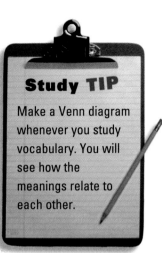

A **trapezoid** is a quadrilateral with exactly one pair of parallel sides.

The Venn diagram shows that a rectangle is a type of parallelogram.

Example 3

Determine $m\angle ABC$ in parallelogram $ABCD$.

A parallelogram has two pairs of parallel sides, so $\overline{AB} \parallel \overline{CD}$ and $\overline{AD} \parallel \overline{BC}$.

$\angle ADC \cong \angle BCK \cong \angle PBR \cong \angle ABC$
They are all corresponding or vertical angles.

$m\angle ADC = m\angle ABC = 56°$

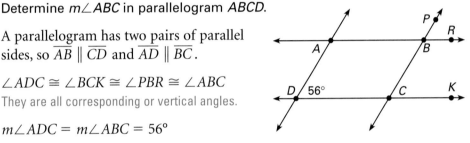

A **diagonal** of a polygon connects two vertices that do not share a side.

Example 4

In the trapezoid:

$\angle ADC \cong \angle BCD$ and $\angle DAB \cong \angle CBA$.

Measure $\angle ACD$ and $\angle BDC$ formed by the diagonals, $\overline{AC}$ and $\overline{BD}$.

$m\angle ACD = 54°$ and $m\angle BDC = 54°$

Try It

a. Determine $m\angle RST$ in parallelogram $QRST$.

b. Determine $m\angle TQR$ in parallelogram $QRST$.

c. Identify the diagonal line segment.

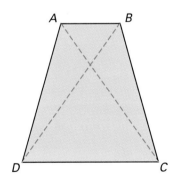

Practice and Apply

1. **Getting Started** Draw a base plan using the illustration shown.

a. Draw the top view.

b. Count the number of cubes in each column and label each square in the view.

2. Draw the right, front, and top views for the 3-D object shown.

3. Draw a base plan for the cube tower shown.

4. This chair design is called the Kubus Chair. Draw a base plan for it.

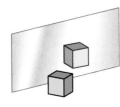

5. **Science** Amethyst, the February birthstone, is a purple type of quartz crystal. The crystal shown is rectangular. Draw a net for a rectangular prism.

6. **Test Prep** Which net would make the solid shown?

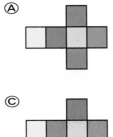

Ⓐ

Ⓑ

Ⓒ

Ⓓ

History Shown is a photograph of Ft. McHenry in Baltimore, Maryland, where Francis Scott Key wrote "The Star-Spangled Banner" during the War of 1812.

7. Draw a top view of Ft. McHenry.

8. What general shape does this remind you of?

Problem Solving and Reasoning

9. Critical Thinking Which net matches the 3-D figure?

Ⓐ
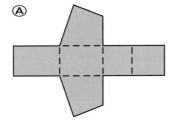

Ⓑ
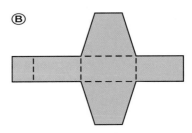

10. Patterns Construct a solid shape by gluing or taping together a copy of the net shown. What do you get?

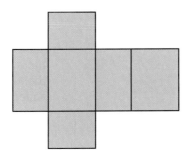

11. Math Reasoning Gems can be cut in different ways. The picture shows the top view of one type of faceted cut. Sketch how you think the right and front views look.

12. Communicate A ziggurat is a type of pyramid with terraces. The photo at the right shows Chichén Itzá, the Mayan ziggurat. Describe how you would draw a net for this shape?

Mixed Review

Draw a line through the origin with the given slope.
[Lesson 4-4]

13. $\frac{5}{8}$ **14.** 3 **15.** -1 **16.** $-\frac{1}{2}$

Identify each number as rational or irrational. *[Lesson 7-8]*

17. $\sqrt{10}$ **18.** $0.\overline{6}$ **19.** $\sqrt{19}$ **20.** $\sqrt{225}$ **21.** 0.2323

TECHNOLOGY

Using Geometry Software • Drawing Side and Top Views

Problem: Construct the top and side views of a square nut.

You can use dynamic geometry software to help with this exercise.

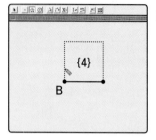

1. Use the **Regular Polygon** tool to construct a square. Use the **Measure** menu to find the length of each side and the measure of each angle.

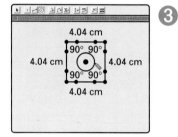

3. Use the **Circle** tool to draw a circle inside the square. The circle will have the same center as the square. Hide the diagonal line segments and you'll have the top view of your square nut.

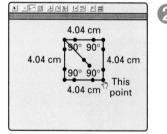

2. Use the **Segment** tool to draw two diagonals between opposite pairs of vertices. This shows the center of the square.

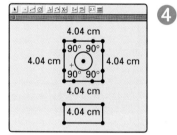

4. Draw a rectangle with length the same as a side of the square. This is the side view of the square nut.

Solution: Length measurements may vary.

ON YOUR OWN

TRY IT

What would the top and side views of a hexagonal nut look like?

► How do you think the geometry software calculates the lengths of the sides of your construction?

► Is it easier to construct these views using geometry software or by hand? Explain.

► How do you think an architect's design program can help you construct these views?

Section 8B Connect

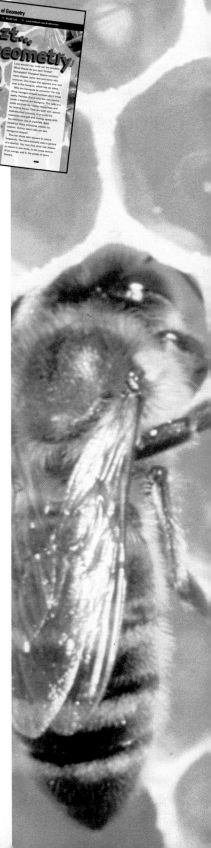

In this section, you'll have a chance to apply your creativity to what you've learned about flat and three-dimensional shapes.

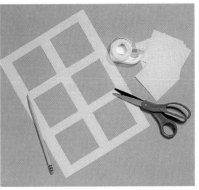

Bzzzt... Beeometry

Materials: Paper, Scissors, Tape

Draw six congruent squares on a sheet of paper, in order to construct a net for a "geometry cube."

You will design the net with drawings and labels from Exercises 1–6.

1. On one square, draw a line, line segment, or a ray.

2. On another square, draw any angle and label its measure.

3. On another square, draw parallel or perpendicular lines.

4. On another square, draw parallel lines with a transversal and label all angle measurements.

5. On another square, draw any polygon and include its classification.

6. On the last square, write "roll again."

7. How many pairs of parallel lines are on your net?

8. How many pairs of perpendicular lines are on your net?

9. How many acute angles are on your net? Obtuse angles?

10. How many right angles are on your net?

11. Classify all of the polygons on your net.

12. Cut out your net and use tape to make a "geometry cube."

13. All the group members will roll their cubes. If a cube lands on "roll again," then that player must roll the cube again.

14. When all cubes say other than "roll again," each player must create a drawing that uses each figure shown on the cubes.

Use the illustration to classify each angle as right, straight, obtuse, or acute.

1. ∠ABD　　**2.** ∠DBF　　**3.** ∠FBC

4. ∠EBF　　**5.** ∠ABE　　**6.** ∠ABC

7. Find the angle measure complementary to 57.5°.

8. Find the angle measure supplementary to 108°.

$\overleftrightarrow{EF} \parallel \overleftrightarrow{GH}$. **If** $m\angle 3 = 130°$, **find each angle measure.**

9. $m\angle 2$　　**10.** $m\angle 7$　　**11.** $m\angle 6$　　**12.** $m\angle 8$

Match each pair of angles with the angle classification.

13. ∠6 and ∠7　　**A.** Alternate interior angles

14. ∠5 and ∠4　　**B.** Alternate exterior angles

15. ∠1 and ∠8　　**C.** Corresponding angles

16. ∠3 and ∠7　　**D.** Vertical angles

Identify the polygon in each photograph. Be as specific as possible.

17.　　**18.**　　**19.**　　**20.**

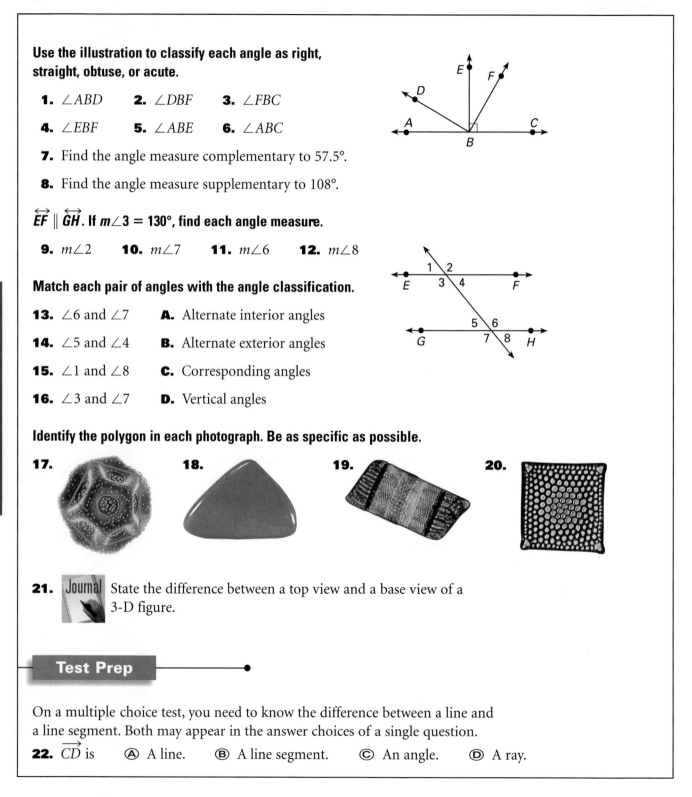

21. **Journal** State the difference between a top view and a base view of a 3-D figure.

Test Prep

On a multiple choice test, you need to know the difference between a line and a line segment. Both may appear in the answer choices of a single question.

22. $\overrightarrow{CD}$ is　　Ⓐ A line.　　Ⓑ A line segment.　　Ⓒ An angle.　　Ⓓ A ray.

Slopes of Parallel and Perpendicular Lines

Slope is the ratio of the change in y-coordinates to the change in x-coordinates.

On the first graph notice that $\overleftrightarrow{AB} \parallel \overleftrightarrow{CD}$. If you determine the slopes of $\overleftrightarrow{AB}$ and $\overleftrightarrow{CD}$, you will find they are equal.

$slope = \frac{rise}{run}$ slope of $\overleftrightarrow{AB} = \frac{-3}{-6} = \frac{1}{2}$

slope of $\overleftrightarrow{CD} = \frac{-3}{-6} = \frac{1}{2}$

$\overleftrightarrow{AB}$ and $\overleftrightarrow{CD}$ have the same slope and are parallel.

So …
- If lines have equal slope, lines are parallel.
- If lines are parallel, lines have equal slope.

On the second graph notice that $\overleftrightarrow{EF} \perp \overleftrightarrow{GH}$.

If you determine the slopes of $\overleftrightarrow{EF}$ and $\overleftrightarrow{GH}$, you will find that the product of their slopes is −1.

$slope = \frac{rise}{run}$ slope of $\overleftrightarrow{EF} = \frac{-9}{6} = \frac{-3}{2}$

slope of $\overleftrightarrow{GH} = \frac{6}{9} = \frac{2}{3}$

The product of the slopes is $\frac{-3}{2} \times \frac{2}{3} = \frac{-3 \times 2}{2 \times 3} = \frac{-6}{6} = -1$. So …

- If the product of the slopes = −1, lines are perpendicular.
- If lines are perpendicular, the product of the slopes = −1.

Find the slope to determine whether the lines are $\parallel$ or $\perp$.

1. Determine whether $\overleftrightarrow{AB}$ and $\overleftrightarrow{CD}$ are $\parallel$ or $\perp$.
   a. Plot the points $A(-4, 5)$, $B(3, 7)$, $C(-5, -2)$, and $D(2, 0)$.
   b. Draw lines $\overleftrightarrow{AB}$ and $\overleftrightarrow{CD}$.
   c. Find the slopes of $\overleftrightarrow{AB}$ and $\overleftrightarrow{CD}$.
   d. Are they $\parallel$ or $\perp$?

2. Determine whether $\overleftrightarrow{EF}$ and $\overleftrightarrow{GH}$ are $\parallel$ or $\perp$.
   a. Plot the points $E(-4, 7)$, $F(3, 0)$, $G(-4, -2)$, and $H(6, 8)$.
   b. Draw lines $\overleftrightarrow{EF}$ and $\overleftrightarrow{GH}$.
   c. Find the slopes of $\overleftrightarrow{EF}$ and $\overleftrightarrow{GH}$.
   d. Are they $\parallel$ or $\perp$?

435

9 Area and Volume

Arts & Literature Link
www.mathsurf.com/8/ch9/arts

Entertainment Link
www.mathsurf.com/8/ch9/ent

Arts & Literature

The cubism art movement was largely attributed to European artists Pablo Picasso and George Braque.

Entertainment

Yokohama City, Japan, is the home of the world's largest Ferris Wheel, which boasts a diameter of 328 feet.

People of the World

Indian mathematician, Srinivasa Ramanujan (1887–1920), developed a formula for calculating a decimal approximation for π. Sixty-seven years after his death, computers, using a formula very similar to his, calculated the value of π to more than 100 million decimal places.

Social Studies Link
www.mathsurf.com/8/ch9/social

Science

The circumference of Earth is 24,830 miles. Using a unit of measure called *stadia,* Eratosthenes (276 – 195 B.C.) estimated the circumference of Earth to be about 24,811 miles, based on the distance between two Egyptian cities.

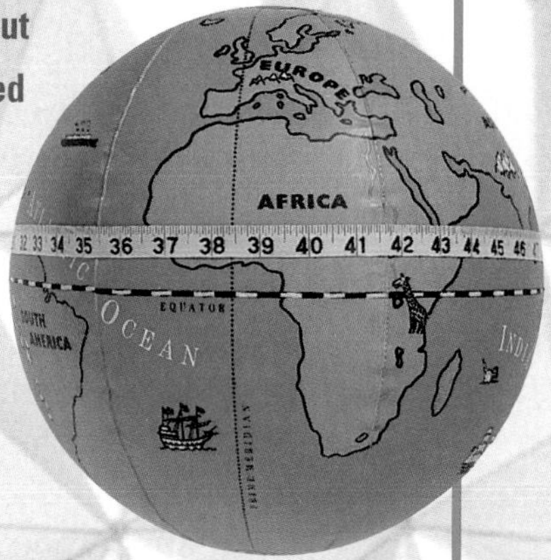

Social Studies

The perimeter of the base of the Great Pyramid of Khufu in Egypt, divided by twice its height, results in the value 3.14, remarkably close to the value of π.

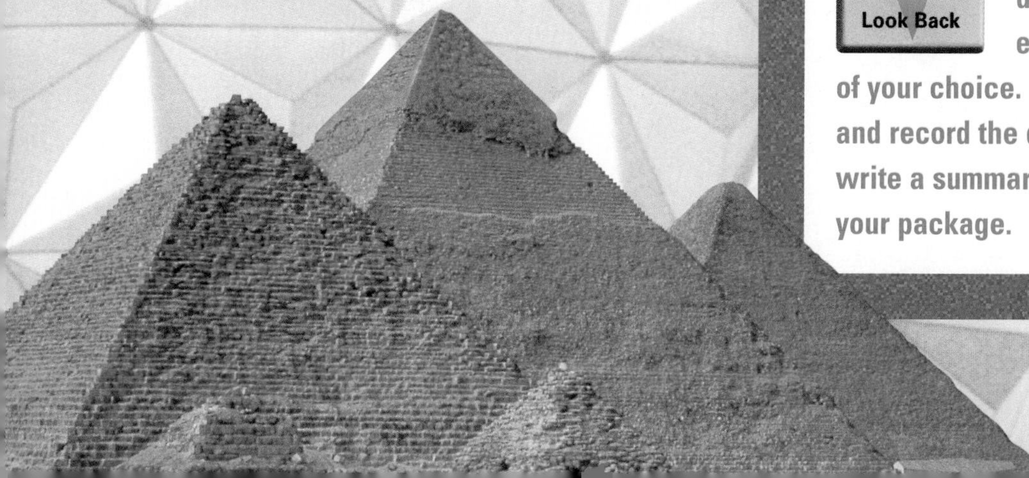

KEY MATH IDEAS

Perimeter and **area** are measurements of a two-dimensional figure.

Surface area and **volume** are measurements of a three-dimensional figure.

Prisms, cylinders, pyramids, and **cones** are all three-dimensional figures.

Both two-dimensional and three-dimensional figures can be dilated using a scale factor.

CHAPTER PROJECT

Problem Solving

Understand
Plan
Solve
Look Back

In this project, you will design and make the most efficient package for an item of your choice. You'll first measure the item and record the dimensions. You will also write a summary of how you decided on your package.

Problem
Solving

Understand
Plan
Solve
Look Back

Problem Solving Focus

Checking
for a
Reasonable
Answer

When you look back
to check your answer
to a problem, it is
important to evaluate
whether rounding is
reasonable. Deciding
whether to round
up or down often
depends upon com-
mon sense and what
you are asked to
solve.

Each of the problems below gives the answer, but the answer may not be accurate enough for the situation. State if each answer is "close enough," "too low," or "too high," and explain why.

1 After graduation, the Whitman Middle School invites the graduates and their guests to a celebration banquet. Long tables are set up in the gymnasium for the banquet. Each table holds 25 people. If 1539 people attend the banquet, how many tables are there? **Answer: 61**

2 The printing company delivers the yearbooks in boxes that contain 48 books each. There are 538 graduates. If each one gets a book, how many boxes will be delivered?
Answer: 11

3 Each graduate receives a souvenir pin with the name of the school and the year of their graduation. The pins are packed in boxes of a dozen, and cost $28.00 a box. Individual pins cost $3.00. How many boxes should the school buy? **Answer: 44 plus 10 individual pins**

4 The day before graduation, the school takes all the graduates to an amusement park. They are taken to the park in buses that each hold 24 people. An adult chaperone will ride on each bus. How many buses should the school request?
Answer: 22

Perimeter, Area, and Surface Area

▶ Fine Arts Link ▶ Literature Link ▶ www.mathsurf.com/8/ch9/theater

The Great Stage

Radio City Music Hall opened on December 27, 1932, as the first building of Rockefeller Center in New York City. S. L. "Roxy" Rothafel conceived the building and was determined to make Radio City the world's biggest theatrical environment in his time. Rothafel designed the interior of the music hall to feature a golden arch and ceiling that gives the appearance of a huge sunset.

Virtually everything about Radio City is big and impressive. The stage itself is still one of the largest and best equipped theatrical stages in the world. The stage measures 144 feet wide by 60 feet deep. It features a revolving turntable, 43 feet in diameter, and three stage elevators, each 70 feet long. Each elevator is capable of being lowered 27 feet into the basement or raised 13 feet above the level of the stage. In fact, the elevator system—and the hydraulics that run it—became the design prototype for the elevators in U.S. aircraft carriers during World War II.

1 What mathematical measurements might the original architects and engineers have used to design Radio City Music Hall?

2 What mathematical measurements of the great stage might set designers for a production company want to know? How might these be used?

3 How might mathematics be used in producing a 45-minute stage show?

443

9-1 Perimeter and Area of Polygons

▶ **Lesson Link** You've looked at units of measurement and many kinds of polygons. Now you'll determine perimeter and area of polygons. ◀

The **perimeter** (*p*) is the distance around a figure.

The perimeter of the figure to the right is 35 centimeters.

Explore Perimeter

Side by Side

Materials: Geometry software

1. Use your geometry software to draw regular polygons with 3, 4, 5, and 6 sides. Make two different polygons for each number of sides.

2. On paper, make a table with the following headings: Number of Sides, Regular Polygon, Side Length, and Perimeter.

Number of Sides	Regular Polygon	Side Length	Perimeter

3. For each regular polygon, measure the length of a side and the perimeter. Use these measurements to complete the table.

4. Look for a pattern in the data from your table. In a regular polygon, what is the relationship between the number of sides, the side length, and the perimeter? State the rule for this relationship.

5. Test your rule to see if it works with regular polygons that have more than 6 sides.

Learn Perimeter and Area of Polygons

You can calculate the perimeter of any figure by adding all the side lengths.

You can calculate the perimeter of rectangles and squares using a formula.

The perimeter of a rectangle is two times the base (*b*) plus two times the height (*h*).

$$p = 2b + 2h = 2(b + h)$$

The perimeter of a square is four times the length of a side (*s*).

$$p = 4s$$

Example 1

A large theater will have an orchestra pit, where a full orchestra will play the music for a musical or opera. What is the perimeter of the orchestra pit shown?

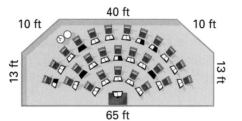

Add all side lengths.

$$10 + 40 + 10 + 13 + 65 + 13 = 151 \text{ ft}$$

The perimeter of the orchestra pit is 151 ft.

Examples

2 Use a formula to find the perimeter of the rectangle.

$$p = 2(b + h)$$

$$p = 2\left(8\frac{1}{4} + 5\frac{3}{4}\right) = 2 \cdot (14) = 28$$

The perimeter is 28 in.

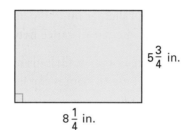

$5\frac{3}{4}$ in.

$8\frac{1}{4}$ in.

3 Find the perimeter of the L-shaped figure.

First, find *x*. $x = 15 - 3$

$$x = 12$$

$$p = 3 + 4 + x + 3 + 15 + 7$$

$$p = 3 + 4 + 12 + 3 + 15 + 7 = 44$$

The perimeter is 44 m.

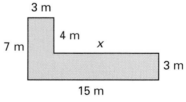

3 m

4 m

7 m

x

3 m

15 m

Try It

a. Use a formula to find the perimeter of the square.

0.53 in.

b. Find the perimeter of the L-shaped figure.

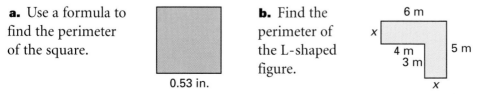

6 m

x

4 m

3 m

5 m

x

The **area** (A) of a polygon is the number of square units contained in that polygon. You can calculate the area of rectangles and squares using a formula.

The area of a rectangle is the base (b) times the height (h). $A = b \cdot h$

The area of a square is the length of a side (s) squared. $A = s^2$

Example 4

The New York State Theater has scenery-storage areas in each wing. Each is 40 ft by 35 ft. What is the area of one of these storage areas?

$A = b \cdot h$

$A = 40 \cdot 35$ Substitute and solve.

$A = 1400 \text{ ft}^2$

35 ft

40 ft

You can use the formula for the area of a rectangle to find the area of other polygons.

In a parallelogram, the height (h) is the perpendicular distance between the bases (b).

The area of a parallelogram is the length of the base (b) times the height (h): $A = b \cdot h$.

b h

h h

b b

Example 5

Find the area of the parallelogram.

$A = b \cdot h$

$A = 13.5 \cdot 7.5$ Substitute and solve.

$A = 101.25 \text{ cm}^2$

13.5 cm

7.5 cm

Try It

Find the area of each polygon.

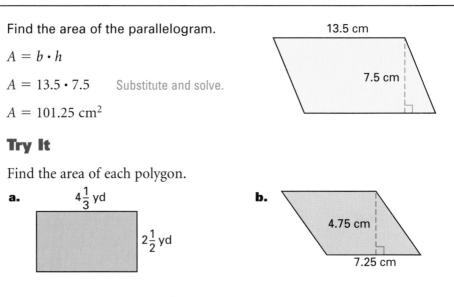

a. $4\frac{1}{3}$ yd

$2\frac{1}{2}$ yd

b. 4.75 cm

7.25 cm

The height of a triangle is the perpendicular distance between the base and the opposite vertex.

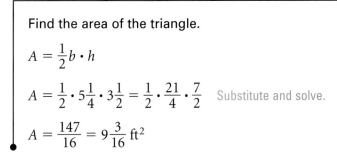

The area of a triangle is $A = \frac{1}{2}b \cdot h$.

The area of a triangle is $\frac{1}{2}$ the area of a rectangle or parallelogram.

Example 6

Find the area of the triangle.

$A = \frac{1}{2}b \cdot h$

$A = \frac{1}{2} \cdot 5\frac{1}{4} \cdot 3\frac{1}{2} = \frac{1}{2} \cdot \frac{21}{4} \cdot \frac{7}{2}$ Substitute and solve.

$A = \frac{147}{16} = 9\frac{3}{16}$ ft^2

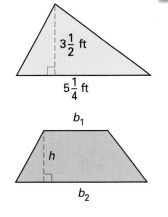

The area of a trapezoid is $A = \frac{1}{2}h(b_1 + b_2)$.

Example 7

Find the area of the trapezoid.

$A = \frac{1}{2}h(b_1 + b_2)$

$A = \frac{1}{2} \cdot 12(10 + 15)$ Substitute and solve.

$A = \frac{1}{2} \cdot 12 \cdot 25 = 150$ cm^2

Try It

Find the area of each polygon.

a.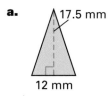

b.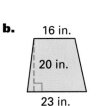

Check Your Understanding

1. Describe the difference between the perimeter and the area of a polygon.

2. Which formula would you use to find the area of a rhombus?

Practice and Apply

1. **Getting Started** Find the area of the triangle.

a. Use the formula $A = \frac{1}{2}b \cdot h$.

b. Solve.

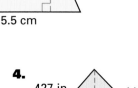

4 cm

5.5 cm

Find the perimeter and area of each polygon.

2.
$h = 16$ in.
$b = 21$ in.

3.
6.25 cm

4.
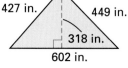
427 in.   449 in.
318 in.
602 in.

5.
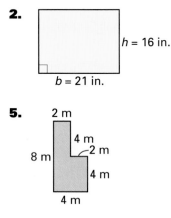
2 m
4 m
8 m   2 m
4 m
4 m

6.
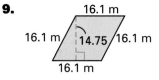
$2\frac{3}{4}$ ft $1\frac{1}{2}$ ft
$4\frac{1}{4}$ ft

7.
6 cm   7.2 cm
5 cm
8 cm

8.
4.65 cm
5 cm
3.5 cm   4.1 cm
10.2 cm

9.
16.1 m
16.1 m   14.75   16.1 m
16.1 m

10.
4.8 cm
12.4 cm

11.
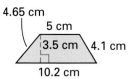
4.5 cm
5.25 cm   5.25 cm
5.25 cm

12.
$5\frac{1}{4}$ ft
$3\frac{3}{4}$ ft
$4\frac{1}{2}$ ft
$5\frac{1}{4}$ ft

13.
$3\frac{1}{3}$ ft
$3\frac{1}{3}$ ft

14. Science A halogen floor light is designed to give maximum light in a triangular shape. What is the area of maximum light for this bulb?

15. Career A set designer wants to make a parlor room 16 ft by 24 ft.

a. How much tape does he need to mark out the room on the stage?

b. How much carpet does he need to cover the whole floor?

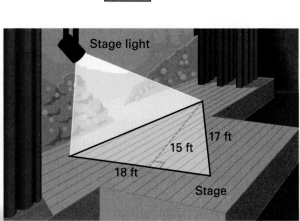

Stage light

17 ft
15 ft
18 ft

Stage

16. **Test Prep** Niambi is carpeting the floor of her room, which is 9 ft by 13 ft. How much carpet will she have to buy to cover the entire floor?

ⓐ 22 ft ⓑ 117 ft² ⓒ 44 ft² ⓓ 484 ft

Use the figure to the right for Exercises 17–19.

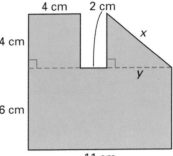

17. What is the value of y? What is the value of x?

18. Find the areas of the square, the rectangle, and the triangle. Find the total area.

19. Find the perimeter of the figure.

Problem Solving and Reasoning

Algebra Find the missing dimension in each figure.

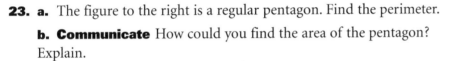

20. 10.8 cm
$A = 63.72$ cm² h

21. 15 ft b
$A = 555$ ft²

22. s
s
$A = 21.16$ m²

23. a. The figure to the right is a regular pentagon. Find the perimeter.

b. Communicate How could you find the area of the pentagon? Explain.

24. Critical Thinking Draw a polygon made by connecting a trapezoid, a triangle, and a parallelogram. Label the bases and heights. Find the perimeter and the total area of your figure.

25. Choose a Strategy A stage crew wants to design a room that is 48 m².

a. List four pairs of possible dimensions.

b. Which of your dimensions has the smallest perimeter? The largest?

Mixed Review

Write each fraction or decimal as a percent. *[Lesson 6-1]*

26. $\frac{3}{4}$ **27.** 0.09 **28.** $\frac{9}{5}$ **29.** 1.42 **30.** 0.0038

Use the Pythagorean theorem ($c^2 = a^2 + b^2$) to decide whether each set of lengths would make a right triangle. *[Lesson 7-9]*

31. 2, 3, 5 **32.** 3, 4, 5 **33.** 6, 8, 10 **34.** 5, 7, 11

Scale and Area

You'll Learn ...

■ to dilate rectangles and predict the resulting perimeters and areas

... How It's Used

Directors need to be aware of the area of a scene to plan the movement of the actors and location of scenery and props.

Vocabulary

dilation

scale factor

▶ Lesson Link You know how to find perimeter and area of some polygons. Now you'll see how scaling a polygon affects the perimeter and area. ◀

Explore Scaling a Rectangle

Expanding Dimensions

Materials: Dynamic geometry software

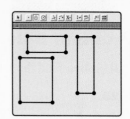

1. Draw three small rectangles. Measure the base, height, perimeter, and area of each rectangle.

2. Record your measurements in three tables, each with four columns.

3. Drag one base of each rectangle until you double the height. Record the new dimensions in your table.

4. Drag one height of each rectangle until you double the base. Record the new perimeter and area. How do the perimeter and area measurements of each rectangle compare?

Base	Height	Perimeter	Area

5. Discuss any conclusions regarding what you found about doubling the dimensions, perimeter, and area.

Learn Scale and Area

A **dilation** is a proportional reduction or enlargement of a figure. The ratio of the original and new dimensions is called the **scale factor** .

$$\frac{10}{4} = 2.5 \qquad \frac{5}{2} = 2.5$$

The scale factor is 2.5 for the dilation.

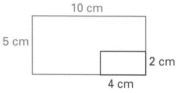

You can use the scale factor to find the dimensions of the dilated figure. The blue triangle is dilated by a scale factor of $\frac{2}{3}$.

$h = \frac{2}{3} \cdot 4 = 2.\overline{6}$ cm $b = \frac{2}{3} \cdot 3 = 2$ cm

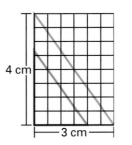

4 cm

3 cm

Examples

1 A theater-in-the-round is where the stage is in the middle of the audience. A model of this stage will be made by reducing it by a scale factor of $\frac{1}{10}$. Find the area and perimeter of the model's main stage.

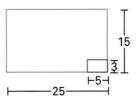

6 ft

9 ft

First, find the base and height.

$b = \frac{1}{10} \cdot 9 = \frac{9}{10}$ $h = \frac{1}{10} \cdot 6 = \frac{6}{10} = \frac{3}{5}$

$p = 2\left(\frac{9}{10}\right) + 2\left(\frac{3}{5}\right) = \frac{9}{5} + \frac{6}{5} = \frac{15}{5} = 3$ Find the perimeter.

$A = \left(\frac{9}{10}\right) \cdot \left(\frac{3}{5}\right) = \frac{27}{50}$ Find the area.

The model will show the main stage with $p = 3$ units and $A = \frac{27}{50}$ units^2.

2 The rectangle shown will be dilated by a scale factor of 5.25. Find the resulting perimeter and area.

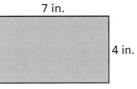

7 in.

4 in.

First, find the base and height.

$b = 5.25 \cdot 7 = 36.75$ in. $h = 5.25 \cdot 4 = 21$ in.

$p = 2(36.75) + 2(21) = 115.5$ in.   Find the perimeter.

$A = (36.75) \cdot (21) = 771.75$ in^2.   Find the area.

Try It

Determine the scale factor used to dilate the blue rectangle.

15

3

5

25

Example 3

Use a spreadsheet to observe the effect on the perimeter and area if a 3 in. by 5 in. rectangle is dilated by a scale factor of 3.

Find *b* and *h* for each dilated rectangle.

9 in. ⊤ 3 in. ⊥ ⊢5 in.⊣ ⊢——15 in.——⊣

Use $p = 2(b + h)$ and $A = b \cdot h$

The perimeter increases by a factor of 3.

The area increases by 3^2, or 9 times.

	A	B	C	D
	Base	Height	Perimeter	Area
1				
2	5	3	16	15
3	15	9	48	135
4	45	27	144	1215
5	135	81	432	10935

A pattern of dilated rectangles emerges with scale factors 1, 2, and 3.

Scale Factor	Perimeter	Area
1	$1 \cdot 15 = 15$	$1^2 \cdot 15 = 15$
2	$2 \cdot 15 = 30$	$2^2 \cdot 15 = 60$
3	$3 \cdot 15 = 45$	$3^2 \cdot 15 = 135$

Scale Factor	*p*	*A*
1	$1 \cdot p$	$1^2 \cdot A$
2	$2 \cdot p$	$2^2 \cdot A$
3	$3 \cdot p$	$3^2 \cdot A$

This pattern can be used for any polygon.

You can use this fact to find the new perimeter or area of any dilation.

For a dilation with scale factor *x*,

1. The new perimeter is $x \cdot p$, and

2. The new area is $x^2 \cdot A$.

Example 4

A community theater wants to enlarge its thrust stage by a scale factor of 1.25. What will the new area of the thrust stage be?

$A = (1.25)^2 \cdot (13 \cdot 8)$

$= (1.5625) \cdot (104) = 162.5 \text{ ft}^2$

The new area will be 162.5 ft².

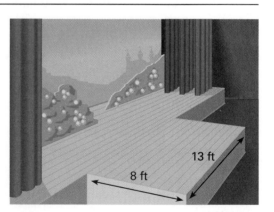

13 ft

8 ft

Try It

Find the new area and perimeter of a 4 m by 5 m rectangle that is dilated by a scale factor of $1\frac{3}{4}$.

An 8 cm by 6 cm rectangle is dilated by a scale factor of $\frac{1}{2}$. Find the perimeter and area of the new rectangle.

6 cm

8 cm

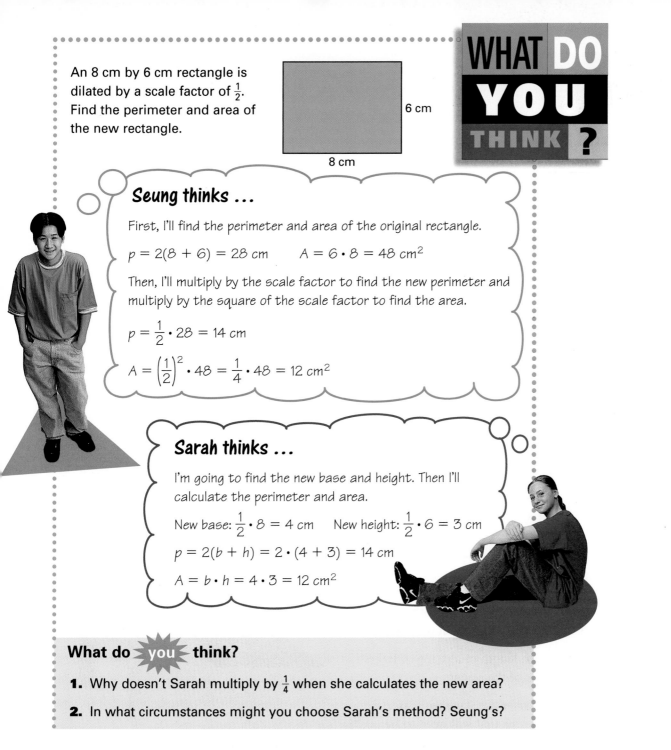

Seung thinks ...

First, I'll find the perimeter and area of the original rectangle.

$p = 2(8 + 6) = 28$ cm $A = 6 \cdot 8 = 48$ cm²

Then, I'll multiply by the scale factor to find the new perimeter and multiply by the square of the scale factor to find the area.

$p = \frac{1}{2} \cdot 28 = 14$ cm

$A = \left(\frac{1}{2}\right)^2 \cdot 48 = \frac{1}{4} \cdot 48 = 12$ cm²

Sarah thinks ...

I'm going to find the new base and height. Then I'll calculate the perimeter and area.

New base: $\frac{1}{2} \cdot 8 = 4$ cm   New height: $\frac{1}{2} \cdot 6 = 3$ cm

$p = 2(b + h) = 2 \cdot (4 + 3) = 14$ cm

$A = b \cdot h = 4 \cdot 3 = 12$ cm²

What do you think?

1. Why doesn't Sarah multiply by $\frac{1}{4}$ when she calculates the new area?

2. In what circumstances might you choose Sarah's method? Seung's?

Check Your Understanding

1. What is a dilation?

2. What happens when you dilate a figure by a scale factor less than 1? Greater than 1? Equal to 1?

Practice and Apply

1. **Getting Started** Find the area of the triangle when it is dilated by a scale factor of 4.

   a. Multiply each dimension by the scale factor 4.

   b. Use the formula $A = \frac{1}{2}b \cdot h$, using the new dimensions.

   6 cm

   4.2 cm

Find the perimeter and area of each polygon after the given dilation.

2. Scale factor = 3

   5 cm

   3.2 cm

3. Scale factor = 4.8

   4 ft   5 ft

   3 ft

4. Scale factor = 0.5

   12 in.

   12 in.

5. Scale factor = 1.5

   4 m   5 m

   9 m

6. Scale factor = $\frac{1}{10}$

   7.7mm

   8.6 mm

   8.6 mm

7. Scale factor = 0.25

   10.4 cm

   12 cm   12 cm

   12 cm

Fine Arts A Shakespearean theater group wants to buy material for its new rectangular stage. On the model, the stage is 40 cm by 100 cm. The scale factor reads 25.

8. What is the minimum length of a string of lights around the perimeter of the stage?

9. The group wants to cover the stage with special flooring. What is the area that will need to be covered?

10. **Science** The rectangular cells of an onion are viewed under a microscope that enlarges each cell by the scale factor 360. If each plant cell appears to be 6 cm, what is the size of the specimen?

PRACTICE 9-2

11. **Test Prep** Determine the scale factor of a dilation of the red figure to the blue figure.

Ⓐ 2.5   Ⓑ 2   Ⓒ $\frac{1}{2}$ Ⓓ 6.25

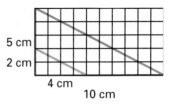

5 cm
2 cm
4 cm
10 cm

Problem Solving and Reasoning

Number Sense Decide whether the scale factor will produce a dilation that is an enlargement or a reduction.

12. Scale factor = $\frac{3}{4}$ **13.** Scale factor = 4.5   **14.** Scale factor = 0.01

15. **Math Reasoning** Using the right triangle as shown, what is the effect on the perimeter and area if you double only one of the two dimensions?

16. **Communicate** Create a rectangle and describe the effects on the perimeter and area if you double only one of its dimensions.

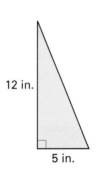

12 in.

5 in.

The background curtains on the stage of a theater are 1250 ft². The production company wants to make a model of the stage using a scale factor of $\frac{1}{25}$.

17. **Measurement** Find the area of the curtains in the model.

18. **Patterns** What is a possible set of dimensions for the curtains in the stage model?

19. **Journal** Write an explanation of how to find the perimeter and area of a polygon after a dilation by scale factor = k.

Mixed Review

Solve each. *[Lesson 6-2]*

20. What number is 15% of 90?   **21.** 40% of 200 is what number?

22. What percent of 39 is 13?   **23.** 100 is 25% of what number?

Convert each unit. *[Lesson 8-1]*

24. 3 hr to min   **25.** 150 cm to m   **26.** 42 kg to g   **27.** 196 in. to ft

---

Project Progress

Identify the shapes that your item exhibits, such as squares, circles, triangles, or pentagons. Measure the perimeter and area of the sides of your chosen item.

Problem Solving

Understand
Plan
Solve
Look Back

Circles

You'll Learn ...

■ to find the area and circumference of circles

... How It's Used

Set builders often work with the measurements of circular objects for the stage.

Vocabulary

circumference

center

radius

diameter

π (pi)

inscribed

circumscribed

▶ **Lesson Link** You've seen how to measure the distance around a polygon and its area. Now you'll do the same for circles. ◀

The distance around a circle is the **circumference** (C).

The **center** of a circle is a point that is the same distance from all points on the circle.

A **radius** (r) of a circle is the segment or distance from the center of the circle to any point on the circle.

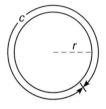

Explore A Circle's Ratio

Circle Search

Materials: Dynamic geometry software

1. Draw a circle. Draw a line segment from the circle to its center to show the radius.

2. Measure the radius (r), circumference (C), and area (A) of the circle. Make a table to record the data. Leave space for a total of nine columns in your table.

3. Drag the circle until it is about $\frac{1}{2}$ of its original area. Record the results in your table. Drag the circle again, but double the original area.

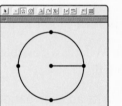

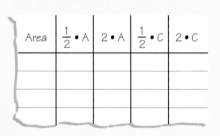

Area	$\frac{1}{2} \cdot A$	$2 \cdot A$	$\frac{1}{2} \cdot C$	$2 \cdot C$

4. Drag the circle until it has about $\frac{1}{2}$ of its original circumference. Record the results in your table. Drag the circle again, but double the original circumference.

5. Label the last two columns of your table $\frac{C}{2r}$ and $\frac{A}{r^2}$. Calculate these ratios and record them in your table. How do these two ratios compare?

6. From the data in your table, discuss any relationships between the radius, circumference, and area of a circle.

The **diameter** of a circle is the segment or distance of the segment that passes through the center and has both endpoints on the circle.

$2r = d$

r r

Example 1

Find the diameter of a circle with radius $2\frac{3}{4}$ in.

$d = 2r = 2\left(2\frac{3}{4}\right)$

$d = \frac{2}{1} \cdot \frac{11}{4} = \frac{22}{4} = 5\frac{1}{2}$ in.

The diameter is $5\frac{1}{2}$ in.

$2\frac{3}{4}$ in.

For every circle, the ratio of the circumference to the diameter is represented by the Greek letter **π (pi)**. In calculations, $\pi \approx 3.14$ is often used.

$\frac{C}{d} = \pi$ Solve the ratio to find the circumference formula.

$C = \pi d = \pi(2r)$ $d = 2r.$

$C = 2\pi r$ The formula for circumference is $C = 2\pi r.$

Example 2

Radio City Music Hall, where the Rockettes perform, features a revolving turntable 43 ft in diameter. Find the circumference of Radio City Music Hall's turntable.

$C = 2\pi r = \pi d$

$C \approx (3.14) \cdot 43 = 135.02$ ft

The circumference is ≈ 135 ft.

Remember

$\approx$ means "approximately equal to." [Previous course]

Try It

a. Find the radius of a circle with diameter 3.46 m.

b. Find the circumference of a circle with diameter 3.46 m.

3.46 m

$$\frac{A}{r^2} = \pi \qquad \text{π is also the ratio of the area of a circle to the radius squared.}$$

$$A = \pi r^2 \qquad \text{The formula for the area of a circle is } A = \pi r^2.$$

Example 3

In the mid-1800s, the Blackfoot people used 6 buffalo skins to build tepees that had 10 ft diameter floors. What is the floor area of a tepee this size?

First, find the radius. $5 \text{ ft} = r$

$A = \pi r^2$

$A = \pi(5)^2 = 25\pi \text{ ft}^2$

$\approx (25 \cdot 3.14) \text{ ft}^2$

$A \approx 78.5 \text{ ft}^2$

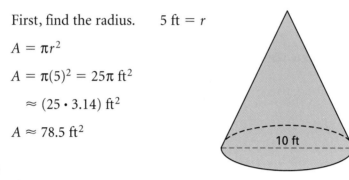

10 ft

A polygon inside a circle with all its vertices on the circumference is **inscribed** in the circle.

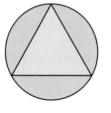

A polygon out-side a circle with one point of each side on the circle is **circumscribed** about the circle.

Example 4

Determine whether the pentagon circumscribes or inscribes the circle.

The pentagon is inside the circle and all the vertices are on the circumference. The pentagon is inscribed in the circle.

Try It

a. Find the area of a circle with $r = 4$ cm.

b. Does the square circumscribe the circle?

Check | Your Understanding

1. How are perimeter and circumference alike? How are they different?

2. What are the two ratios that equal π?

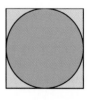

Practice and Apply

1. [Getting Started] Find the area of the circle shown. Use $\pi = 3.14$.

a. Find the radius. **b.** Find the area.

8 cm

Sketch each figure.

2. Square inscribed in a circle   **3.** Pentagon circumscribed about a circle

Find the circumference of each circle. Use $\pi = 3.14$.

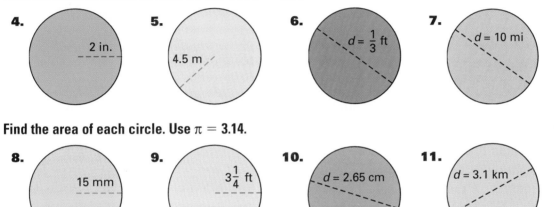

4. 2 in.

5. 4.5 m

6. $d = \frac{1}{3}$ ft

7. $d = 10$ mi

Find the area of each circle. Use $\pi = 3.14$.

8. 15 mm

9. $3\frac{1}{4}$ ft

10. $d = 2.65$ cm

11. $d = 3.1$ km

12. Science The earth's circumference is approximately 25,000 mi. Find the approximate diameter of the earth.

25,000 mi

13. Career A costume designer is making costumes for an Elizabethan play. An actress's neck has a 14 in. circumference. The ruff (collar) will be made from a circle with a 6.2 in. radius. How much lace is needed to accent the circumference of the ruff?

Queen Elizabeth I of England (1533–1603)

14. Algebra A circle has an area of 42 cm². Write an equation and solve for r, the radius.

15. Geography In the U.S. Midwest some farmers use a circular irrigation method. Suppose the length of an irrigation arm is 500 ft. What is the area of the irrigated circle?

16. [Test Prep] A circle has a radius of 4.5 m. Which is the best approximation for the area of this circle?

Ⓐ 20.25 m²   Ⓑ 20.25π m²

Ⓒ 63.6 m²   Ⓓ 63.6π m²

Problem Solving and Reasoning

17. Communicate A theater owner wants to design a Greek style semicircular stage with a radius of 30 ft. Explain how to find the perimeter and area of the stage. Include an illustration.

18. Number Sense Investigate what happens to the perimeter and area of a circle when you double the radius. Give an example and write about your conclusions.

19. [Journal] TV and FM radio signals have a line-of-sight range, which means mountains can interfere. A radio tower has a broadcast range with a 23 mi radius. How much area does the broadcast cover?

Theater of Dionysos in Athens, Greece

20. Math Reasoning A regular pentagon, hexagon, and octagon circumscribe a circle with a radius of 5 in. Which polygon has an area measurement closest to the area of the circle. Explain.

21. Geometry A hexagon is inscribed in the circle.

　a. Find the area of the triangle.

　b. Find the area of the hexagon.

　c. Find the area of the circle.

　d. Find the area of the shaded region.

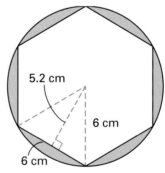

5.2 cm

6 cm

6 cm

Mixed Review

Estimate each percent. *[Lesson 6-3]*

22. 34 out of 198   **23.** 67 out of 97   **24.** 49 out of 76   **25.** 2 out of 19

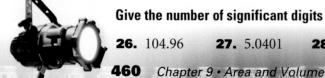

Give the number of significant digits in each number. *[Lesson 8-2]*

26. 104.96   **27.** 5.0401   **28.** 0.0006   **29.** 105   **30.** 20.40

Surface Area of Prisms and Cylinders

9-4

▶ **Lesson Link** You know how to find the area of flat figures, such as polygons and circles. Now you'll learn about the surface area of 3-D figures. ◀

A **polyhedron** is a 3-D figure that is composed of polygons. Each polygon surface is called a **face**.

The **edge** of a polyhedron is where two faces meet.

A **vertex** of a polyhedron is the intersection of three or more faces.

Three Polyhedrons

Five faces:
4 triangles
1 square

Six faces:
6 rectangles

Ten faces:
2 octagons
8 rectangles

The **surface area** (SA) of a polyhedron is the sum of the areas of all the faces.

You'll Learn ...

■ to find surface area of prisms and cylinders

... How It's Used

Interior designers use surface area to figure the amount of material to cover solid objects.

Vocabulary

polyhedron

face

edge

vertex

surface area

prism

base

cylinder

Explore Prisms

Surfing the Surface

Materials: Four sheets of 8.5 in. by 11 in. paper, Tape, Scissors

1. Find the area of one sheet of paper.

2. Make 3-D figures using one sheet of paper for each.

   Figure a: Roll paper so opposite edges can be taped together.

   Figure b: Fold paper into equal thirds and tape edges together.

   Figure c: Fold paper into equal fourths and tape edges together.

Figure 2a

Figure 2b

Figure 2c

3. Is the surface area of each of these figures greater than, less than, or equal to the area of the original sheet of paper? Explain.

4. What shapes are needed to complete the surface of each figure? Draw these shapes and calculate their areas. Tape them onto the appropriate figures.

5. Rank the three solids in total surface area from least to greatest. Justify your ranking.

A **prism** is a polyhedron that has two congruent faces that are parallel polygons. Each parallel, congruent face is called a **base**.

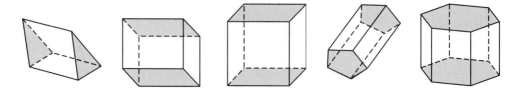

A net helps you find the surface area because it shows all faces as flat polygons.

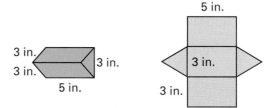

Example 1

Find the surface area of the rectangular prism.

First, sketch a net; then find the area of each face. There are three different rectangular faces.

Two faces are 30 cm by 24 cm.

$A = b \cdot h = 30 \cdot 24 = 720 \text{ cm}^2$

Two faces are 30 cm by 5 cm.

$A = b \cdot h = 30 \cdot 5 = 150 \text{ cm}^2$

Two faces are 24 cm by 5 cm.

$A = b \cdot h = 24 \cdot 5 = 120 \text{ cm}^2$

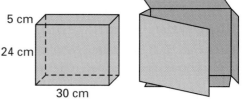

The surface area of the rectangular prism is

$SA = 2(720 + 150 + 120) = 1980 \text{ cm}^2.$

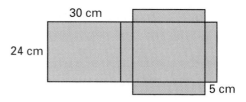

Try It

Find the surface area of a rectangular prism that is 1 in. by 2 in. by 3 in.

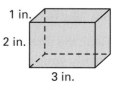

Example 2

A 24 in. wide ramp from a stage to the audience floor needs to be built. The stage is 6 in. above the audience floor. The ramp will extend 8 in. away from the stage. What is the surface area of the ramp?

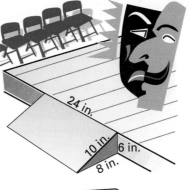

> **Career Link**
>
> Large theater companies have house crews that consist of carpenters, electricians, and other craftspeople to help design and build the setting for a performance.

Find the area of each face.

Each triangle has $b = 8$ in. and $h = 6$ in.

$A = \frac{1}{2}(b \cdot h) = \frac{1}{2}(8 \cdot 6) = \frac{1}{2}(48) = 24$ in^2

One face is 6 in. by 24 in. with $A = 144$ in^2.

One face is 8 in. by 24 in. with $A = 192$ in^2.

One face is 10 in. by 24 in. with $A = 240$ in^2.

The surface area is

$SA = 2(24) + 144 + 192 + 240 = 624$ in^2.

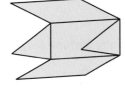

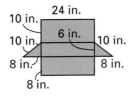

A **cylinder** is a 3-D figure with two congruent circles for bases.

Notice the base of the rectangle is the circumference of a circle. The height of the rectangle is the height of the cylinder.

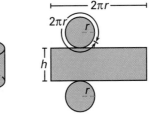

Try It

a. Find the area of each circle of the cylinder.

b. Find the area of the cylinder's side.

c. Find the surface area of the cylinder.

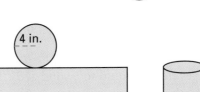

Check Your Understanding

1. How many length measurements do you need to find the surface area of a prism? A cylinder? Draw a diagram to explain.

2. How many faces would a pentagonal prism have? A hexagonal prism?

Practice and Apply

1. **Getting Started** Find the surface area of the
rectangular prism.

   a. Draw the net for the prism. Label the dimensions
   for each face.

   b. Find the area of each face.

   c. Find the sum of the areas.

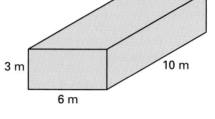

3 m   10 m   6 m

Sketch a net for each, then find the surface area.

2. 5.4 m   6.5 m   1.8 m

3. 4.3 in.   5 in.   5 in.   12 in.   5 in.

4. 3.5 cm   7.2 cm

5. $2\frac{1}{2}$ ft $2\frac{1}{2}$ ft $2\frac{1}{2}$ ft

6. 9 m   12 m

7. 5 yd $2\frac{1}{4}$ yd $6\frac{1}{2}$ yd

8. **Literature** A decorative platform is being constructed for
a performance of *Hansel and Gretel*. Which shape would
have the greater surface area, a cube 4 ft on each side or a
rectangular prism that is 8 ft by 4 ft by 2 ft?

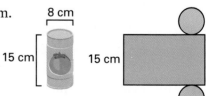

9. **Science** Water changes from a liquid to a solid at 32°F, the
freezing point. Each section in an ice cube tray is $1\frac{1}{2}$ in. by
1 in. by 1 in. How much surface area does an ice cube from
this tray have?

10. **Test Prep** A can has a diameter of 8 cm and a height of 15 cm.
Find the area of paper for a label to cover the curved side.

   Ⓐ 3014.4 cm²   Ⓑ 120 cm²

   Ⓒ 188.4 cm²   Ⓓ 376.8 cm²

8 cm   15 cm   15 cm

11. What is the surface area of a box that is 12 in.
by $7\frac{1}{2}$ in. by 4 in?

12. The box for a videotape is 19 cm tall, 10.5 cm long, and 2.5 cm wide. It is open on one of the long and narrow sides so that the tape can be put in. What is the surface area of the box?

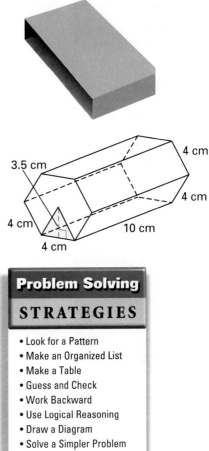

Problem Solving and Reasoning

13. Geometry Find the surface area of the hexagonal prism.

14. Number Sense Find the surface area of a cylinder with 3 m height and 1 m radius. Also, find the surface area of a cylinder with 1 m height and 3 m radius. How does the formula πr^2 affect these results?

3.5 cm
4 cm
4 cm
4 cm
4 cm
10 cm

15. Choose a Strategy A cereal company is making a jumbo-size box by doubling the dimensions of its midsize box which is 12 in. by 8 in. by 2 in. How much more cardboard will be needed to make the jumbo size?

> ### Problem Solving
> ## STRATEGIES
>
> • Look for a Pattern
> • Make an Organized List
> • Make a Table
> • Guess and Check
> • Work Backward
> • Use Logical Reasoning
> • Draw a Diagram
> • Solve a Simpler Problem

Math Reasoning Determine a shortcut formula for finding the surface area.

16. A cube   **17.** A rectangular prism

18. *Journal* Invent a possible surface-area problem that a set designer for a movie or play might have to solve.

19. The diameter of cylinder A is half that of cylinder B. Both have the same height.

    a. Communicate Predict which will have the greater total surface area, one of cylinder B or two of cylinder A? Explain.

    b. Critical Thinking Which do you think would hold more, one of cylinder B or two of cylinder A? Why?

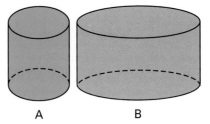

A   B

Mixed Review

Find the percent increase for each. *[Lesson 6-4]*

20. Old: 1420
New: 1562

21. Old: 12.9
New: 25.8

22. Old: $9.88
New: $14.82

Classify each angle as right, straight, obtuse, or acute. *[Lesson 8-4]*

23. 130°   **24.** 45°   **25.** 90°   **26.** 180°   **27.** 25°

9-5 Surface Area of Pyramids and Cones

You'll Learn ...

■ to find the surface area of pyramids and cones

... How It's Used

Model builders know how to make polyhedrons such as pyramids and cones.

Vocabulary

pyramid

height

slant height

▶ **Lesson Link**   You've worked with polyhedrons called prisms; now you'll work with polyhedrons called pyramids. ◄

A **pyramid** is a polyhedron with one base—all the other faces are triangles. The shape of the base is used to name the pyramid.

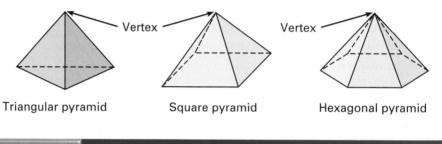

Triangular pyramid   Square pyramid   Hexagonal pyramid

Explore   Surface Area of a Pyramid

Build Your Own Pyramid

Materials: 2 sheets of 8.5 in. by 11 in. paper, Scissors, Tape, Ruler

1. Cut an 8.5 by 8.5 in. square from your sheet of paper.

2. Fold the square along each of the two diagonals, one at a time.

3. Cut out one of the V-shaped sections. Tape the cut edges together to make the pyramid.

4. Cut and attach a shape to fit on the uncovered face. Determine the surface area of your pyramid.

Step #2   Step #3

Learn   Surface Area of Pyramids and Cones

The **height** of a pyramid is the perpendicular distance from the base to the opposite vertex.

The **slant height** is the perpendicular distance from the edge of the base to the opposite vertex.

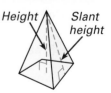

You can find the surface area of a pyramid by looking at its net.

For a square pyramid, notice that the slant height is the height of a triangular face. The base of each triangular face is a side of the square.

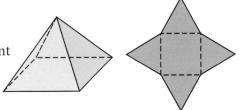

Example 1

In a play such as *Joseph and the Amazing Technicolor Dreamcoat,* which has a scene in Egypt, a square pyramid might be part of the set.

A square pyramid for a stage could have a height of 3 ft and a base area of 64 ft².

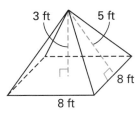

Find the surface area of this pyramid.

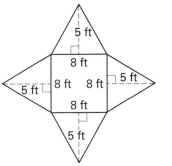

The pyramid base is a square with area 64 ft².

The pyramid has four triangular faces.

$$A = \frac{1}{2}b \cdot h = \frac{1}{2}(8 \cdot 5) = 20 \text{ ft}^2$$

The surface area of the pyramid is

$A = 64 + 4(20) = 144 \text{ ft}^2.$

Try It

a. What kind of pyramid is shown?

b. What is the height of the pyramid?

c. Use the Pythagorean theorem ($c^2 = a^2 + b^2$) to find the slant height of the pyramid.

d. What is the area of the triangular face?

e. What is the surface area of the pyramid?

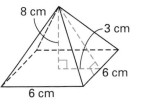

Remember

The Pythagorean theorem ($c^2 = a^2 + b^2$) can be used to determine the length of a side in a right triangle: *a* and *b* are legs and *c* is the hypotenuse.
[Page 374]

A triangular pyramid has four triangular faces. Only one of them is the base of the pyramid. The slant height of the pyramid is the height of a triangular face that is not the base.

Example 2

The triangular pyramid has an equilateral triangle base and three other faces. What is the surface area of this pyramid?

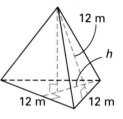

First, find the area of the base.

Use the Pythagorean theorem to find h.

$a^2 + b^2 = c^2$

$h^2 + 6^2 = 12^2$

$h^2 = 12^2 - 6^2$

$h^2 = 108$

$h \approx 10.4$ m

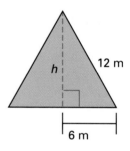

So $A = \frac{1}{2}bh$

$A \approx \frac{1}{2}(12)(10.4)$ Substitute.

$A \approx 62.4$ m^2

Find the area of one of the three congruent triangles.

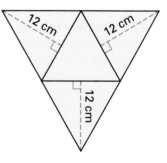

$A = \frac{1}{2}b \cdot h$

$A = \frac{1}{2}(12 \cdot 12) = 72$ m^2

The surface area of the triangular pyramid is

$SA \approx 62.4 + 3(72) = 278.4$ m^2.

Try It

a. What is the slant height of the pyramid?

b. Use the Pythagorean theorem ($a^2 + b^2 = c^2$) to find the height of the triangular base.

c. What is the area of a triangular face?

d. What is the surface area of the pyramid?

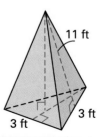

A **circular cone** is a 3-D figure with a circular base and one vertex.

To find the surface area of a cone, you find the area of the base and the area of the curved surface.

The area of the curved surface is $A = \frac{1}{2}Cs$.

The area of the base is $A = \pi r^2$.

The surface area of a cone is $SA = \left(\frac{1}{2}Cs\right) + \pi r^2$.

s = slant height

Example 3

Denise needs to make a model of a cinder cone volcano for a school play. The cone should be 4 ft tall, the base 4 ft in diameter, and the slant height about 4.48 ft. She needs to know the surface area of the cone in order to buy wire mesh to make the frame. What is the surface area of this cone?

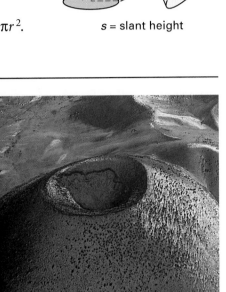

Area of curved surface $= \frac{1}{2}Cs$

$A = \frac{1}{2}(2\pi \cdot 2)4.48 \approx 28.13 \text{ ft}^2$

Area of base $= \pi r^2$

$A = \pi(2)^2 \approx 12.56 \text{ ft}^2$

$SA \approx 28.13 + 12.56$ Take the sum to find the surface area.

$\approx 40.69 \text{ ft}^2$

Denise needs approximately 40.69 ft^2 of wire mesh.

4 ft

Check Your Understanding

1. What is the difference between the slant height and the height of a pyramid or cone?

2. How can you tell by looking at a net whether the solid is a prism, a pyramid, a cone, or a cylinder?

Practice and Apply

1. **Getting Started** Find the surface area of the triangular pyramid with the net shown.

   a. How many faces does the pyramid have?

   b. What is the area of the pyramid's base?

   c. What is the area of each of the other faces?

   d. Take the sum of the areas of the faces and the base to determine the surface area of the pyramid.

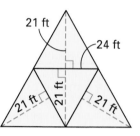

For each figure, find **a. The slant height.** **b. The surface area.**

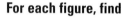

2.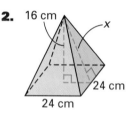

3.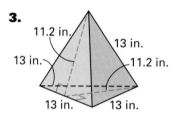

4.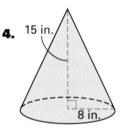

5. An amusement park wants a square pyramid in its Ancient Wonders theme area. The pyramid is to be 8 ft high and have a 12 ft wide square base. What is the surface area of the pyramid that will be built?

6. A triangular pyramid has an equilateral triangle with side length of 4 ft for a base. The height of the pyramid is 3.2 ft and the slant height is approximately 3.4 ft. What is the approximate surface area of this pyramid?

7. **Test Prep** Which do you need to find the area of the base of a cone?

   Ⓐ π   Ⓑ Radius

   Ⓒ Slant height   Ⓓ A and B

8. **Fine Arts** In a staged version of *Sleeping Beauty*, the princess wears a cone-shaped headpiece 18 in. tall. It is constructed of cardboard and wrapped with velvet fabric. How much fabric is needed to cover the cone if the actress's head has a 22 in. circumference?

Shakespeare's *Richard III*, 1949

9. **Social Studies** Sioux tepees are cone-shaped. If the diameter of a tepee is 18 ft and the height is 12 ft, how much buffalo hide is needed to cover the outside surface?

10. **Algebra** A square pyramid has a total surface area of 176 yd². If the slant height is 7 yd and the area of the base is 64 yd², then what is the height of the pyramid? Round your answer to the nearest hundredth place.

Problem Solving and Reasoning

11. **Communicate** Your classmate is confused about the difference between the height of a pyramid and the slant height. Describe the difference between the two.

For Exercises 12 and 13, refer to the square pyramid and cone of the same height, with the diameter of the cone's base equal to the side of the square base of the pyramid.

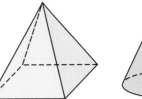

12. **Math Reasoning** Which is greater, the perimeter of the square base or the circumference of the circular base?

13. **Critical Thinking** Which do you think has the greater surface area? Explain.

14. **Journal** What would happen to the surface area of a pyramid if you double its height? Give an example and explain.

15. **Number Sense** How many faces does a hexagonal pyramid have? Octagonal pyramid? Describe the number pattern.

Mixed Review

Find the slope, *x*-intercept, and *y*-intercept for each equation. *[Lesson 4-5]*

16. $y = 2x - 1$ 17. $y = x + 3$ 18. $y = \frac{1}{2}x + 2$ 19. $y = -2x$

20. $y = -x + 1$ 21. $y = 3x + 0$ 22. $y = -0.5x - 2$ 23. $y = 4x - 5$

$\overleftrightarrow{AB} \parallel \overleftrightarrow{CD}$. Use the diagram on the right to answer the questions. *[Lesson 8-5]*

24. Find the measures of all angles in the diagram.

25. Identify all interior angles.

TECHNOLOGY

Using Geometry Software • Measuring Polygons

Problem: Construct a triangle. What are its perimeter and area?

You can use geometry software to answer this question.

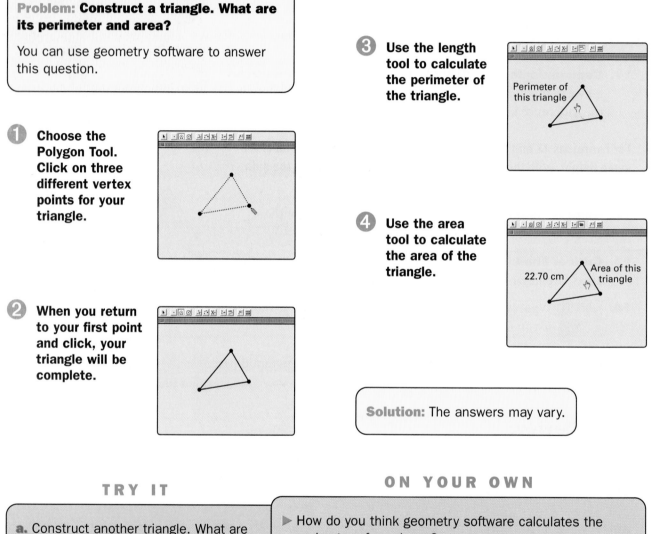

① **Choose the Polygon Tool. Click on three different vertex points for your triangle.**

② **When you return to your first point and click, your triangle will be complete.**

③ **Use the length tool to calculate the perimeter of the triangle.**

Perimeter of this triangle

④ **Use the area tool to calculate the area of the triangle.**

22.70 cm   Area of this triangle

Solution: The answers may vary.

TRY IT

a. Construct another triangle. What are its perimeter and area?

b. Construct a quadrilateral. What are its perimeter and area?

ON YOUR OWN

▶ How do you think geometry software calculates the perimeter of a polygon?

▶ Is it easier to find the area of a polygon using geometry software rather than a formula? Explain.

▶ Describe what would happen to the area of your triangle if you moved one of the vertices.

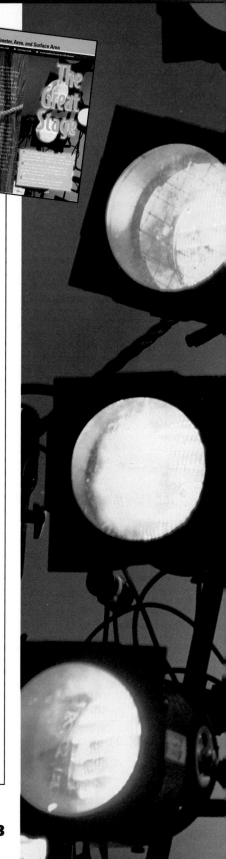

In the beginning of Section 9A, you learned about a historical American theater hall. Now you will design a stage set for a play.

The Great Stage

Materials: Drawing paper, Ruler, Compass, Drawing pens

You and your group are in charge of designing a stage set for a school play.

The producer wants an archway that looks like a palace entrance. The archway must have a semicircular (half-circle) top and cylindrical columns for support.

You must also design rectangular steps up to a doorway in the arch.

You must decide the quantity of various materials you will use to make this archway. Do this by using what you know about area, perimeter, and surface area.

1. Each person in the group draws a sketch of each part of the design: each column, the semicircle, and the stairs. Each drawing should show the actual dimensions of the props and the drawing scale.

2. Calculate the material needed to cover the surface area of all the props.

3. Decide on the materials you would use to cover these props; for example, paint, fabric, paper, tile, and so on.

4. Make a list of the amount of materials you'll need to cover the props.

5. Decide on a layout of the stage and draw a top view of this stage plan including the props you have just designed.

6. Draw the front view of your stage plan. Identify a story line that would be appropriate for your design.

Fill in the appropriate vocabulary term for each sentence.

1. The distance around a polygon is the _____.

2. The _____ of a circle is π times the diameter.

3. A _____ has two parallel polygons that are the same size and shape.

4. A reduction of a geometric figure by a scale factor is a _____.

5. **Journal** Explain the difference between a prism and a pyramid and the difference between a cylinder and a cone.

Find the perimeter/circumference and area for each figure.

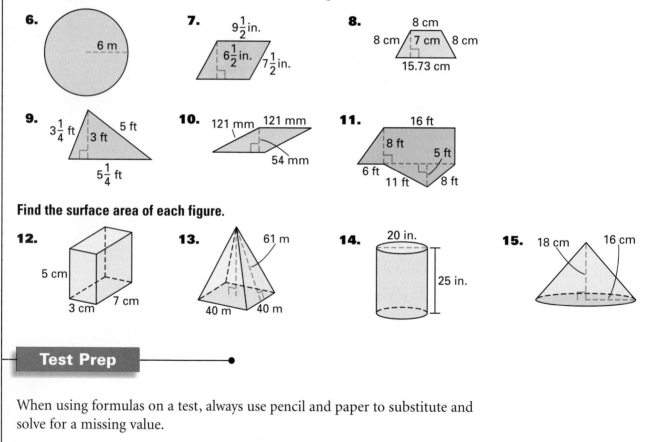

6. 6 m

7. $9\frac{1}{2}$ in. $6\frac{1}{2}$ in. $7\frac{1}{2}$ in.

8. 8 cm, 8 cm, 7 cm, 8 cm, 15.73 cm

9. $3\frac{1}{4}$ ft, 5 ft, 3 ft, $5\frac{1}{4}$ ft

10. 121 mm, 121 mm, 54 mm

11. 16 ft, 8 ft, 5 ft, 6 ft, 11 ft, 8 ft

Find the surface area of each figure.

12. 5 cm, 3 cm, 7 cm

13. 61 m, 40 m, 40 m

14. 20 in., 25 in.

15. 18 cm, 16 cm

Test Prep

When using formulas on a test, always use pencil and paper to substitute and solve for a missing value.

16. The diameter of a bicycle wheel is 18 in. What is its circumference?

ⓐ 21.52 in.   ⓑ 28.52 in.   ⓒ 56.52 in.   ⓓ 85.52 in.

REVIEW 9A

Volume

Deliveries

The Big

The year was 1907 and business in the United States was flourishing. Few people had telephones or cars, so how were messages and packages delivered? Jim Casey, an enterprising 19-year-old from Seattle, had an idea. He borrowed $100, started the American Messenger Company, and hired other teenagers to work for him.

Jim's company did very well because of his old-fashioned values: customer courtesy, reliability, round-the-clock service, and low rates. Jim had an idea that no one else had thought of — consolidated delivery. Packages to be delivered to one neighborhood were put into a single delivery vehicle. This saved time and money.

During the 1930s Jim's company changed its name to United Parcel Service or UPS. This company now delivers over 12 million documents and packages around the world.

1 What mathematics might a package-delivery company use to keep delivery going accurately and on time?

2 Why might delivery companies set limits on overall dimensions and weight of packages?

Volume of Rectangular Prisms

You'll Learn ...

■ to determine the volume of rectangular prisms

... How It's Used

Volume tells you how much space a package occupies and how much it might weigh. Weight and space are important factors for a delivery company.

You'll Learn ...

■ to determine the volume of rectangular prisms

... How It's Used

Volume tells you how much space a package occupies and how much it might weigh. Weight and space are important factors for a delivery company.

Vocabulary

volume

▶ **Lesson Link**   You've learned how to find the surface area of rectangular prisms. Now you'll find the volume of rectangular prisms. ◀

The **volume** is the number of cubic units in a solid.

The volume of this solid is 1 cm³.

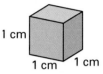

Explore   **Filling a Rectangular Prism**

Fill It Up!

Materials: Centimeter cubes, 8.5 in. by 11 in. paper, Tape, Centimeter ruler

1. Make two different rectangular prisms (without bases) by folding two 8.5 in. by 11 in. sheets of paper into equal fourths: one using the longer side and one using the shorter side. Tape the edges to form the prism.

2. Make a layer of unit cubes to cover the base of each rectangular prism.

   a. How tall is a single layer of cubes?

   b. How many cubes cover each base?

3. For each prism, how many cubes are needed to make two layers? Three layers? Four layers? Make a table to record your data.

4. a. How tall is each rectangular prism (in centimeters)?

   b. How many layers are needed to fill each prism?

5. How many cubes would fill each prism?

Learn   **Volume of Rectangular Prisms**

The volume of a prism is found by multiplying the area of the base (*B*) by the prism height (*h*).

$V = B \cdot h$

The area of the base of a polyhedron is shown by B. The length of the base of a polygon is shown by b.

Example 1

A next-day delivery service delivers a package with dimensions 12 in. by 7 in. by 30 in. What is the volume of the package?

First, draw the prism and label the dimensions.

Find the area of the rectangular base.

$B = 12 \cdot 30 = 360 \text{ in}^2$

$V = B \cdot h$

$V = 360 \cdot 7$

$V = 2520 \text{ in}^3$

The volume is 2520 in³.

7 in.   30 in.   12 in.

Example 2

Find the height of a rectangular prism with volume 72 cm³ and base dimensions 6 cm by 3 cm.

First, find the area of the rectangular base.

$B = 6 \times 3 = 18 \text{ cm}^2$

Then use the volume formula to solve.

$V = B \cdot h$

$72 = 18 \cdot h$

$4 = h$

3 cm   6 cm

The prism has a height of 4 cm.

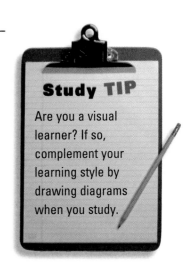
Try It

Find the volume of each figure.

a.

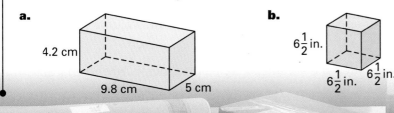

4.2 cm

9.8 cm   5 cm

b.

$6\frac{1}{2}$ in.

$6\frac{1}{2}$ in. $6\frac{1}{2}$ in.

You can find the volume of some irregularly-shaped solids by breaking the figure into rectangular prisms.

Example 3

► History Link

In 1720, it took the postal service three days to deliver a parcel from Philadelphia to New York (almost 100 miles).

Speedy Delivery, Inc., charges by volume for irregularly-shaped packages. If it charges $170.63 for a package with the dimensions shown, how much do they charge per in^3?

This solid is composed of two rectangular prisms.

Find the volume of each rectangular prism.

Find the volume of the bottom prism, V_{bottom}.

$V_{bottom} = (8)(3)(3)$

$V_{bottom} = 72 \text{ in}^3$

Find the volume of the top prism, V_{top}.

$V_{top} = (4.5)(3.5)(3)$

$V_{top} = 47.25 \text{ in}^3$

Find the total volume: $V_{bottom} + V_{top}$.

$V_{bottom} + V_{top} = 72 + 47.25 = 119.25 \text{ in}^3$

$\dfrac{170.63}{119.25} \approx \$1.43 \text{ per in}^3$

Try It

Find the volume of the figure shown.

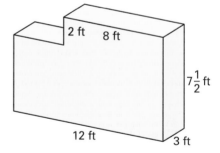

Check Your Understanding

1. Would the volume of a package change if you measured it in cubic centimeters instead of cubic inches? Explain.

2. Describe the difference between the surface area and volume of a rectangular prism.

3. In formulas for area and volume, describe the difference between b and B. Give examples of how b and B are used.

Practice and Apply

1. **Getting Started** Find the volume of the rectangular prism.

   a. Multiply the length and width to determine the area of the base.

   b. Multiply the area of the base by the height.

Find the volume of each figure.

2.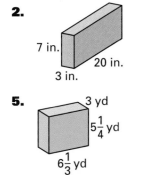
7 in. 20 in. 3 in.

3.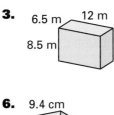
6.5 m 12 m 8.5 m

4.
15 cm 15 cm 15 cm

5.
3 yd $5\frac{1}{4}$ yd $6\frac{1}{3}$ yd

6.
9.4 cm 9.4 cm 9.4 cm

7.
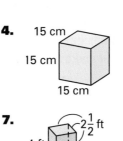
4 ft $2\frac{1}{2}$ ft $1\frac{1}{2}$ ft $3\frac{1}{4}$ ft

Problem Solving TIP

Drawing a diagram is helpful when solving volume problems. Remember to label the dimensions.

Sketch each figure, then find its volume.

8. A box of granola cereal that measures 23 cm by 8 cm by 35 cm

9. A fly-casting pool in the park that is 30 ft wide, 40 ft long, and 5 ft deep

10. **Test Prep** A cube-shaped storage container measures $1\frac{1}{2}$ ft on each side. What is the volume of 6 such containers?

  Ⓐ $3\frac{3}{8}$ ft³   Ⓑ $20\frac{1}{4}$ ft³   Ⓒ $4\frac{1}{2}$ ft³   Ⓓ None of these

11. **Geography** Falan paid $38.40 to ship a package by air from Washington, D.C., to his family in Bombay, India. The package was 18 in. by 24 in. by 20 in. What did he pay per cubic in?

12. **Number Sense** A box has base dimensions of 32 ft by 16 ft and its volume is 6144 ft³. What is the height of this box?

13. **Algebra** The formula for the volume of a sphere is $\frac{4}{3}\pi r^3$ where r is the radius of the sphere. What is the volume of a sphere where $r = 3$ cm?

PRACTICE 9-6

14. Science The concrete in bridges expands in the hot sun. To prevent the road from buckling, engineers build gaps, called expansion joints, between segments of the road. What is the total volume of an expansion joint that is 25 ft by 1 ft by 4 in?

Problem Solving and Reasoning

15. Algebra Draw a cube with a side length of 5 cm. Find its volume. Write a formula for finding the volume of a cube.

16. Communicate Which formula do you prefer to use in finding the volume of a rectangular prism: $V = B \cdot h$ or $V = l \cdot w \cdot h$? Explain.

Patterns The chart at the right has been started to list all the possible sets of whole-number dimensions that make a rectangular prism with a volume of 36 ft³.

L	W	H	V
1	2	18	36
			36
			36

17. Copy and complete the chart.

18. Find the surface area of each prism.

19. Which set of dimensions has the greatest surface area? The least?

20. Critical Thinking An airline reserves some of its cargo space for shipping packages but limits the size of packages. A corrugated box is 48 in. by 18 in. by 36 in. Redesign the box so that it has the same volume but less surface area.

21. Math Reasoning A rectangular box has dimensions of 18 in. by 6 in. by 6 in. A large coffee table book has dimensions of 18 in. by 9 in. by 4 in. Find the volume of each and determine whether the book will fit in the box. Explain.

22. Estimation Seth can't fit everything in his 5040 in³ suitcase. Use the photograph to estimate the volume of clothes he's trying to pack.

Mixed Review

Check to see if the point is a solution of both equations. *[Lesson 4-6]*

23. Point $(2, -3)$

$y = x - 5$

$y = 2x - 7$

24. Point $(1, 3)$

$y = 2x + 1$

$y = 4x - 1$

25. Point $(-4, 1)$

$y = 3x + 13$

$y = -x - 5$

Find the sum of the angle measures for each polygon. *[Lesson 8-6]*

26. Triangle   **27.** Octagon   **28.** Pentagon   **29.** Square

DELIVERED

Scale and Volume

▶ **Lesson Link**   Now that you know about volume of a rectangular prism, you'll see how volume is affected when dimensions are scaled up or down. ◀

Explore   Scaling a Rectangular Prism

Which Dimension?   **Materials:** Spreadsheet software

Examine the effect on the volume of a rectangular box if you multiply one of its dimensions by a scale factor.

	A	B	C	D	E
1	Scale Factor	Length	Width	Height	Volume
2	1	4	3	2	?
3	2	8	3	2	?
4	3	12	3	2	?

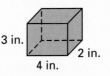
3 in.   2 in.
4 in.

... How It's Used

Package design involves the scaling of boxes up or down to see the effect on volume, which in turn affects weight and cost of shipping.

1. Use a spreadsheet to make a table similar to the one shown. Apply scale factors 1 through 5 to the length of the box. Find each volume.

2. How do the new volumes compare to the original volume?

3. Predict the volume of the box if the length is scaled by a factor of 6.

4. Make another table, but this time hold the length constant and apply the scale factor to the width. How do the resulting volumes compare to those in the first table?

5. Make a third table, this time applying the scale factor to height only. How do the resulting volumes compare to the two previous tables?

6. Make a conclusion about scaling one dimension of a rectangular box.

Learn   Scale and Volume

The volume of a rectangular prism is affected when its length measurements are scaled. The change of volume depends on whether one, two, or three dimensions are scaled.

When one dimension of a rectangular prism is scaled, multiply the original volume by the scale factor to find the volume of the scaled prism.

When two dimensions of a rectangular prism are scaled, multiply the original volume by the square of the scale factor to find the volume of the scaled prism.

Example 1

A delivery service charges 1¢ per in^3 for foam filler to package fragile items. Suppose a breakable parcel that was originally in a 6 in. by 4 in. by 4 in. box needed to be put in a larger box. Determine the ratio of the volume of the larger box to the volume of the original box.

The volume of the original box is 96 in^3.

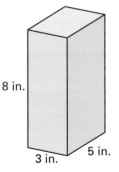

a. How much is the foam filler if one 4 in. dimension is tripled?

The box is 6 in. by 12 in. by 4 in.

The volume of foam filler is
$V = 6 \cdot 12 \cdot 4$

$V = 288$ in^3.

The cost of foam filler for a 6 in. by 12 in. by 4 in. box is $2.88.

Since $288 \div 96 = 3$, the volume of the larger box is 3 times greater than the original box.

b. How much is the foam filler if both 4 in. dimensions are tripled?

The box is 6 in. by 12 in. by 12 in.

The volume of foam filler is
$V = 6 \cdot 12 \cdot 12$

$V = 864$ in^3.

The cost of foam filler for a 6 in. by 12 in. by 12 in. box is $8.64.

Since $864 \div 96 = 9$, the volume of the larger box is 9 times greater than the original box.

Try It

a. Find the volume of a 3 in. by 5 in. by 8 in. rectangular box.

b. Find the volume of the same box after one dimension has been increased by a scale factor of 4.

c. Find the volume of the same box after two dimensions have been increased by a scale factor of 4.

8 in.

3 in.   5 in.

A dilation of a three-dimensional figure changes all three dimensions by the scale factor. The blue rectangular prism is a dilation of the red rectangular prism.

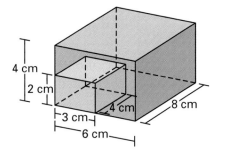

You can find the scale factor by using the ratio of any two corresponding dimensions.

$$\frac{4}{2} = 2 \qquad \frac{6}{3} = 2 \qquad \frac{8}{4} = 2$$

The scale factor of the dilation is 2.

The volume of the red prism is 24 cm³. So, $24 \cdot 2^3 = 24 \cdot 8 = 192$, since the scale factor is 2. The volume of the blue prism is 192 cm³.

When a prism is dilated, the volume is multiplied by the cube of the scale factor.

Example 2

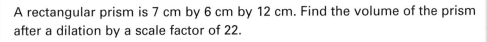

A rectangular prism is 7 cm by 6 cm by 12 cm. Find the volume of the prism after a dilation by a scale factor of 22.

The original volume

$V = 7 \cdot 6 \cdot 12$

$V = 504 \text{ cm}^3$

The volume of the dilation

$V = (22)^3 \cdot 504$

$V = 5{,}366{,}592 \text{ cm}^3$

6 cm

12 cm   7 cm

▶ **Science Link**

The pupil is in the iris of the eye. In dim light, the iris dilates to let more light into the eye.

Try It

A rectangular prism has a volume of 43 ft³. Find the volume after the dilation.

a. Scale factor = 5   **b.** Scale factor = $\frac{1}{2}$

The pattern will work for the dilation of any prism with volume V.

Scale Factor	Volume of Dilated Prism
1	$1^3 \cdot V$
2	$2^3 \cdot V$
3	$3^3 \cdot V$
...	...
n	$n^3 \cdot V$

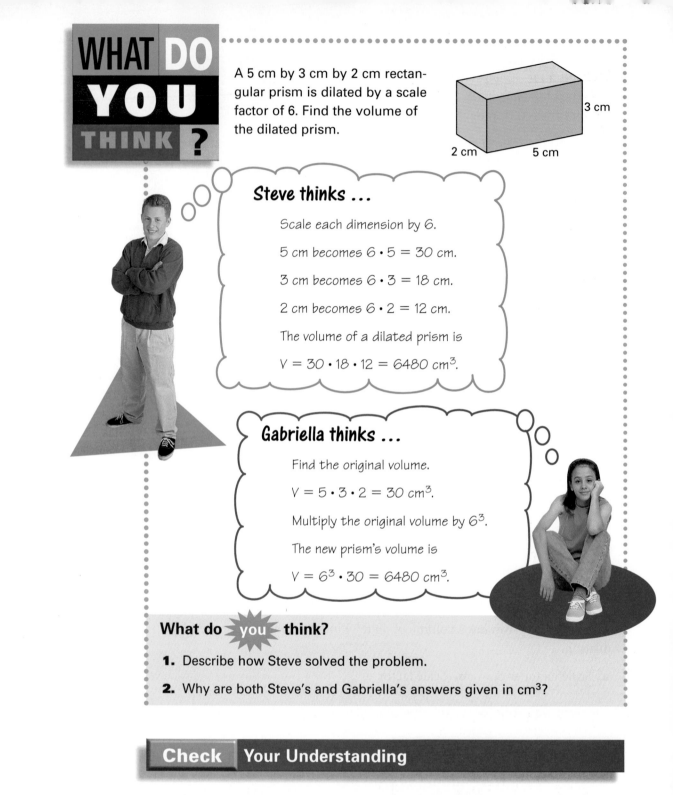

WHAT DO YOU THINK?

A 5 cm by 3 cm by 2 cm rectangular prism is dilated by a scale factor of 6. Find the volume of the dilated prism.

3 cm

2 cm   5 cm

Steve thinks ...

Scale each dimension by 6.

5 cm becomes $6 \cdot 5 = 30$ cm.

3 cm becomes $6 \cdot 3 = 18$ cm.

2 cm becomes $6 \cdot 2 = 12$ cm.

The volume of a dilated prism is

$V = 30 \cdot 18 \cdot 12 = 6480$ cm^3.

Gabriella thinks ...

Find the original volume.

$V = 5 \cdot 3 \cdot 2 = 30$ cm^3.

Multiply the original volume by 6^3.

The new prism's volume is

$V = 6^3 \cdot 30 = 6480$ cm^3.

What do you think?

1. Describe how Steve solved the problem.

2. Why are both Steve's and Gabriella's answers given in cm^3?

Check | Your Understanding

1. If you want to scale two dimensions of a rectangular prism, does it matter which pair of dimensions you scale? Explain.

2. What happens to the volume of a rectangular prism when you dilate it by a scale factor greater than 1? Less than 1?

DELIVERED

Practice and Apply

1. **Getting Started** Find the volume of a rectangular prism of 360 ft^3 after a dilation of $\frac{1}{2}$.

a. Find $\left(\frac{1}{2}\right)^3$.

b. Multiply this by 360 to find the new volume.

Find the volume of each prism after scaling one dimension by the indicated scale factor.

2. Scale factor = 8

3. Scale factor = $\frac{1}{3}$

4. Scale factor = 0.5

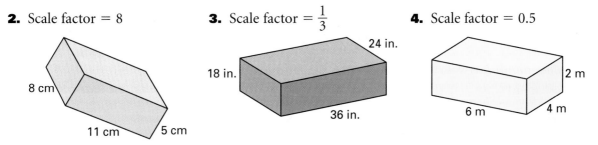

8 cm · 11 cm · 5 cm

24 in. · 18 in. · 36 in.

2 m · 6 m · 4 m

Find the volume of each figure after the dilation.

5. Scale factor = 3

6. Scale factor = 0.8

7. Scale factor = 2

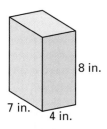

8 in. · 7 in. · 4 in.

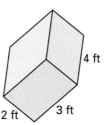

4 ft · 2 ft · 3 ft

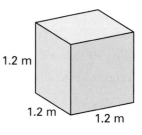

1.2 m · 1.2 m · 1.2 m

8. **Science** Alkaline earth metals are found in many sea shells. A researcher ships some abalone shells to the lab. The delivery company charges $1.25 per cubic ft for next-day delivery. What will a $1\frac{3}{4}$ ft × $1\frac{1}{2}$ ft × 2 ft package cost for next-day service?

9. **Test Prep** What is the scale factor between a cubic box that exactly fits a $3\frac{1}{2}$ in. diameter softball and one that exactly fits a 9 in. diameter basketball?

Ⓐ 3   Ⓑ $31\frac{1}{2}$ Ⓒ $\frac{7}{18}$ Ⓓ $2\frac{4}{7}$

PRACTICE 9-7

10. Measurement Find the volume of the figure to the right after a dilation of 2.5.

11. Number Sense Find the volume of the figure to the right after a dilation with a scale factor of 10. Do the same for a dilation with a scale factor of $\frac{1}{10}$. Find the ratio of these volumes.

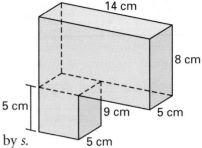

12. Algebra Write a volume formula for a box with $V = 214 \text{ cm}^3$ after

    a. One dimension is scaled by s.   **b.** Two dimensions are scaled by s.

    c. Three dimensions are scaled by s.

Problem Solving and Reasoning

13. You have a package 24 in. by 18 in. by 12 in. to ship. E-Z Shipping charges by volume $0.002 per in^3, whereas Speedy Shipping charges by surface area $0.005 per in^2.

    a. Which company is cheaper for this package?

    b. Communicate Will this be true for all shapes of packages? Explain.

14. Patterns A manufacturing company wants you to design a box with 4 times the volume of its standard 12 in. × 6 in. × 4 in. box. Find as many whole-number solutions as you can.

15. Choose a Strategy Sally wants to make a scale model of a long hut 45 ft by 25 ft by 10 ft for a social studies project.

    a. Choose a scale factor for her. Why did you select it?

    b. Find the surface area of the model hut.

    c. Find the volume of the model hut.

Problem Solving
STRATEGIES

- Look for a Pattern
- Make an Organized List
- Make a Table
- Guess and Check
- Work Backward
- Use Logical Reasoning
- Draw a Diagram
- Solve a Simpler Problem

Mixed Review

Test whether each point is a solution of the inequality. *[Lesson 4-7]*

16. $y > 2x - 5$ **a.** $(2, -3)$ **b.** $(4, 5)$ **c.** $(1, -2)$

17. $y \le 3x + 1$ **a.** $(2, 7)$ **b.** $(-2, -6)$ **c.** $(4, -13)$

18. How many cubes are needed to build a tower with this base plan? *[Lesson 8-7]*

19. How many of the cubes can be seen from a front view of the tower? *[Lesson 8-7]*

20. How many cubes can be seen from a side view of the tower? *[Lesson 8-7]*

4	5	4
3	4	3
2	3	2
1	2	1

Side

Volume of Prisms and Cylinders

▶ **Lesson Link**   You've learned how to find the volume of rectangular prisms. Now you'll find the volume of other prisms and cylinders. ◀

Explore   Volume of a Cylinder

Volume in the Round

Materials: 2 sheets of 8.5 in. by 11 in. paper, Tape, Centimeter cubes, Centimeter ruler

1. Make two different cylinders, each from a sheet of paper. Roll one along the longer side and the other along the shorter side. Tape the sides together for each one.

2. Make a layer of unit cubes to cover the circular base of each cylinder.

   a. Estimate the number of cubes needed to cover each base.

   b. Calculate the area of each base by measuring the radius and then using $A = \pi r^2$ (use cm^2). Compare this result with your estimate.

3. **a.** Using cm, how tall is a single layer of cubes?

   b. For each cylinder, how many cubes are needed for two layers? Three layers? Four layers?

4. **a.** Using cm, how tall is each cylinder?

   b. Estimate how many layers of cubes are needed to completely fill each cylinder. Describe how you made the estimate.

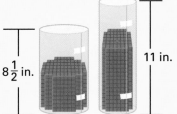

$8\frac{1}{2}$ in.   11 in.

5. How many cubes will completely fill each cylinder? Discuss why you think the numbers differ.

You'll Learn ...

■ to find the volume of prisms and cylinders

... How It's Used

Packages come in shapes of prisms and cylinders. The volume of these packages determine space needed for shipping.

Learn   Volume of Prisms and Cylinders

The volume of prisms and cylinders can be found by taking the product of the base area (B) and the height (h). $V = B \cdot h$

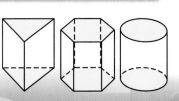

For a triangular prism, the area of the base $B = \frac{1}{2}(b \cdot h)$. You may recognize this as the formula for the area of a triangle.

$B = area\ of\ a\ prism\ base$ and $b = length\ of\ a\ triangular\ base$.

Also, there are two heights to consider—the height of the triangle and the height of the prism. Both of them are represented by the variable h.

Example 1

Posters can be sent through the mail in boxes that are triangular prisms. Find the volume of the triangular box.

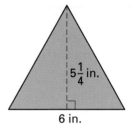

$5\frac{1}{4}$ in.
$38\frac{1}{4}$ in.
6 in.

First, find the area of the triangular base (B).

$$B = \frac{1}{2}(b \cdot h)$$

$$B = \frac{1}{2}(6 \cdot 5\frac{1}{4}) = 15\frac{3}{4} \text{ in}^2$$

$5\frac{1}{4}$ in.

6 in.

Use B to find the volume.

$$V = B \cdot h$$

$$V = 15\frac{3}{4} \cdot 38\frac{1}{4}$$

$$V = 15.75 \cdot 38.25$$

$$V = 602.4375 \text{ in}^3$$

The volume is 602.4375 in³.

Try It

a. What is the height of the triangular base.

b. What is the area of the triangular base.

c. What is the volume of the prism.

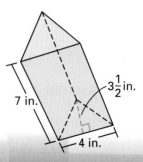

7 in.
$3\frac{1}{2}$ in.
4 in.

For a cylinder, the area of the base $B = \pi r^2$, where $r = $ radius. The volume of a cylinder then is $V = Bh = (\pi r^2)h$.

Example 2

Find the volume of the cylinder.

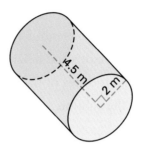

First, find the area of the base (B).

$B = \pi \cdot r^2$

$B = \pi \cdot (2)^2 \approx 12.56 \text{ m}^2$

Use B to find the volume.

$V = B \cdot h$

$V \approx 12.56 \cdot 4.5$

$V \approx 56.52 \text{ m}^3$

The volume is 56.52 m^3.

Try It

Find the volume of each cylinder.

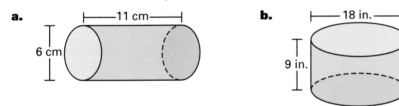

a. 11 cm, 6 cm

b. 18 in., 9 in.

Check   Your Understanding

1. A stack of 40 nickels is $2\frac{1}{2}$ in. tall. The diameter of a nickel is $\frac{13}{16}$ in. Describe how you would find the volume of the stack of nickels.

2. Describe the similarities and differences between finding the volume of a prism and a cylinder.

3. Explain how to find the volume of a prism or cylinder with a height of zero.

4. Based on what you know about finding the volume of a triangular prism, describe how you would find the volume of a hexagonal prism.

▶ **Language Link**

A *numismatist* is someone who studies or collects coins, money, and medals.

Practice and Apply

1. **Getting Started** A cylinder has a diameter of 5 m and a height of 6 m.
   a. Sketch the cylinder and label the radius and height.
   b. Use the formula $A = \pi r^2$ to find the area of the base (use 3.14 for π).
   c. Multiply by the height to find the volume.

Find the volume of each solid, using 3.14 for π.

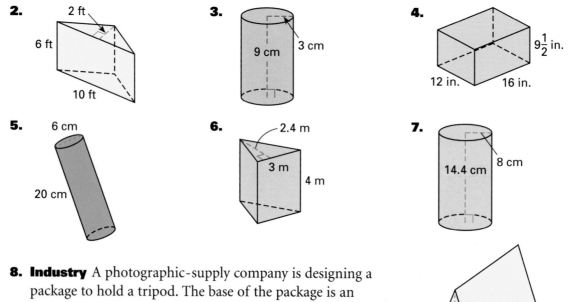

2.
2 ft
6 ft
10 ft

3.
9 cm
3 cm

4.
$9\frac{1}{2}$ in.
12 in.
16 in.

5.
6 cm
20 cm

6.
2.4 m
3 m
4 m

7.
14.4 cm
8 cm

8. **Industry** A photographic-supply company is designing a package to hold a tripod. The base of the package is an isosceles triangle with a base of 15 in. and a height of 20 in. The length of the package is 22 in. What is the volume of this package?

20 in.
15 in.
22 in.

9. **Science** A *hotbed* is a bed of soil that is enclosed in glass. The heat trapped under the glass is useful for raising seedlings. A hotbed forms the shape of a triangular prism that is 1.2 m long. The triangular base has a height of 0.3 m and a base length of 0.5 m. What is the volume of this hothouse?

10. | Test Prep | A grain silo shaped like a cylinder is 30 ft tall and 8 ft in diameter. To the nearest hundred ft³, how many cubic ft of grain can the silo hold?

Ⓐ 75,400 ft³   Ⓑ 82,400 ft³   Ⓒ 1,500 ft³   Ⓓ 7,500 ft³

Problem Solving and Reasoning

Operation Sense Find the volume of the shaded region in each figure.

11.

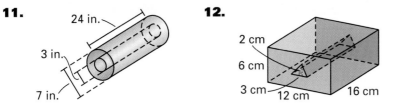

24 in.

3 in.

7 in.

12.

2 cm

6 cm

3 cm   12 cm   16 cm

13. Geometry A hotel in Detroit is shaped like a cylinder with a diameter of 35 m and a height of 230 m.

a. To the nearest m³, what is the volume of the building?

b. The curved surface is covered with glass. How much glass is there on the surface of the hotel?

14. | Journal | A classmate is confused about the difference between the height of the triangle in the base of a triangular prism and the height of the prism. Write an explanation with an illustration to help clarify the two heights.

15. Communicate The base areas of a triangular, rectangular, and hexagonal prism are equal. Which prism do you think has the greatest volume? The least? Explain.

Mixed Review

Find the coordinates of each point. *[Lesson 2-6]*

16. *A*   **17.** *B*

18. *C*   **19.** *D*

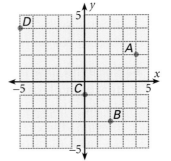

Complete each table of values. *[Lesson 4-1]*

20.

x	0	1	2	3	4	5
y = x + 7						

21.

x	0	1	2	3	4	5
y = −3x						

Volume of Pyramids and Cones

You'll Learn ...

■ to find the volume of pyramids and cones

... How It's Used

A CAD operator creates drawings and 3-D models of motorcycles, cars, airplanes, and other things that require detailed engineering and design.

▶ **Lesson Link** You've found the volume of prisms and cylinders. Now you'll use that knowledge to find the volume of pyramids and cones. ◀

Explore | **Cone to Cylinder**

Cups and Cones

Materials: Scissors, Tape, Centimeter ruler, 2 sheets of 11 in. by 17 in. paper, Compass, Centimeter cubes

1. Use a compass to draw a circle with a 12.7 cm radius. Use a ruler to draw a radius on your circle. Cut out the circle.

2. Cut along the radius line that you drew.

3. Pull one edge of the cut radius until you produce a cone with a 15.2 cm diameter circular base. Use tape to keep this cone in place.

4. Measure the height of the cone.

5. Cut out a rectangle that will make a cylinder with the same height as the cone. The cylinder should also have the same diameter as the cone's base.

6. Calculate the volume of the cylinder by measuring the dimensions.

7. Estimate the volume of the cone by filling it with centimeter cubes. Record the estimate.

8. Place the cone inside the cylinder so that both of their circular bases are on the tabletop. Estimate the volume between the cylinder and the cone by filling the space with centimeter cubes. Record the estimate.

9. Discuss the relationship between the volume of the cylinder and the volume of the cone.

Learn | Volume of Pyramids and Cones

The volume of a cone is $\frac{1}{3}$ the volume of a cylinder.

$V_{cone} = \frac{1}{3}(B \cdot h)$ where B is the area of the base and h is the height.

Example 1

Find the volume of the cone.

First, find the area of the circular base (B).

$B = \pi \cdot r^2$

$B = \pi \cdot 6^2 \approx 113.04 \text{ cm}^2$

Use B to find the volume.

$V = \frac{1}{3}(B \cdot h)$

$V \approx \frac{1}{3}(113.04) \cdot 8$

$V \approx 301.44 \text{ cm}^3$

The volume is about 301.44 cm³.

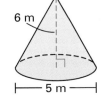

8 cm

6 cm

Try It

Find the volume of the cone.

6 m

5 m

The formula used to find B, the area of a figure's base, will depend on the shape of the base.

Finding the area of the square base will be different than finding the area of a triangular base.

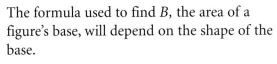

h

The volume of a pyramid is related to the volume of its related prism.

For a prism with volume $V = B \cdot h$, the related pyramid has volume $V = \frac{1}{3}(B \cdot h)$.

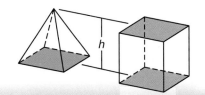

h

Example 2

Find the volume of the pyramid.
Let h_t = *height of the triangle.*

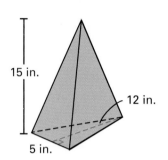

$$V = \frac{1}{3}B \cdot h$$

$$V = \frac{1}{3}\left(\frac{1}{2}b \cdot h_t\right) \cdot h$$

$$V = \frac{1}{3}\left(\frac{1}{2}(5 \cdot 12)\right) \cdot 15$$

$$V = \frac{1}{3}(30) \cdot 15 = 150 \text{ in}^3 \qquad \text{The volume of the pyramid is } 150 \text{ in}^3.$$

15 in.   12 in.   5 in.

Example 3

Find the volume of the pyramid.

$$V = \frac{1}{3}B \cdot h$$

$$V = \frac{1}{3}(9^2) \cdot h$$

$$V = \frac{1}{3}(81) \cdot 25$$

$$V = \frac{1}{3}(81) \cdot 25 = 675 \text{ cm}^3 \qquad \text{The volume of the pyramid is } 675 \text{ cm}^3.$$

25 cm   9 cm   9 cm

Try It

Find the volume of each pyramid.

a. 5 m   5 m   6 m

b. 12 in. $h = 7$ in.   9 in.

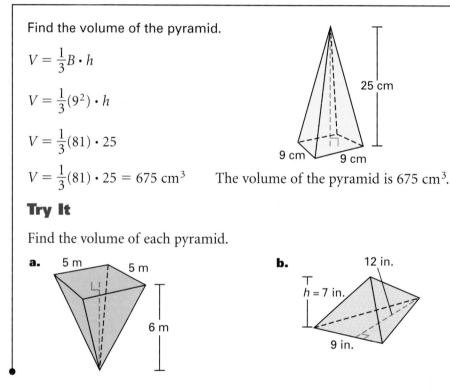

Check | Your Understanding

1. How are the volumes of pyramids and cones similar?

2. Given a cone that has a height of 18 cm and a circular base with a diameter of 8 cm, describe the cylinder that has 3 times the volume of that cone.

3. As the height of a pyramid increases does the slant height increase? Explain.

Practice and Apply

1. **Getting Started** Find the volume of the pyramid.
   a. Find the area of the base.
   b. Multiply the base area by the height and divide by 3 to find the volume.

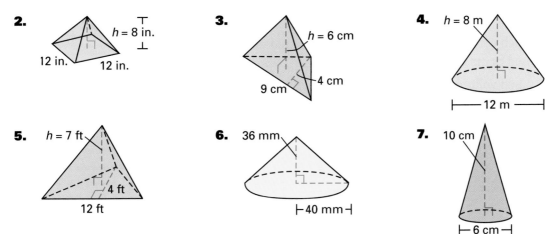

Find the volume of each solid. Use 3.14 for π.

2. $h = 8$ in.
   12 in. 12 in.

3. $h = 6$ cm
   9 cm, 4 cm

4. $h = 8$ m
   12 m

5. $h = 7$ ft
   4 ft
   12 ft

6. 36 mm
   40 mm

7. 10 cm
   6 cm

8. **Geography** The Great Pyramid of Khufu in ancient Egypt was a square pyramid 147 m high, with each side of the base 230 m. To the nearest m^3, how much lime-stone rock made up the pyramid?

9. **Algebra** A cone with height of 25 mm is 3685 mm^3. What is the radius of the base?

10. **Number Sense** Two square pyramids are each 10 inches tall. One pyramid has a 25 in^2 base and the other has a 64 in^2 base. Which pyramid has the greater volume?

11. **Science** The funnel at the right is used to put coolant, a mixture of antifreeze and water, in the radiator of a car. What is the maximum volume of coolant that the funnel can hold?

12. **Test Prep** An ice-cream company sells a prepackaged sugar cone with a 6 cm diameter with ice cream, fudge, and nuts filled to the top of the cone. To the nearest cm, what is the volume of this cone if it is 14 cm tall?
    (A) 301 cm^3 (B) 151 cm^3 (C) 603 cm^3 (D) 132 cm^3

14.5 cm
12 cm
11 cm
1.5 cm

PRACTICE 9-9

Problem Solving and Reasoning

13. **Math Reasoning** Which solid has a greater volume, the pyramid or cone?

14. **Communicate** Suppose you know the dimensions of a cone but have forgotten the formula for the volume of a cone. Describe a way you could find the volume.

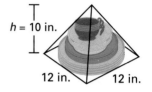

15. **Algebra** Write an equation and use the Pythagorean theorem to find the height of a cone that has a slant height of 15 in. and a radius of 9 in.

16. **Critical Thinking** A dinnerware factory packs its dinnerware in a pyramid-shaped box.

   a. How much cardboard is saved by using a pyramid design over a square-based prism design?

   b. How much volume is saved?

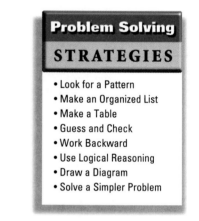

17. **Choose a Strategy** A manufacturer of cone-shaped hats wants to ship each hat in a cylinder with the same diameter and height. How much packing filler is needed for each cylinder to completely fill the package?

Problem Solving

STRATEGIES

• Look for a Pattern
• Make an Organized List
• Make a Table
• Guess and Check
• Work Backward
• Use Logical Reasoning
• Draw a Diagram
• Solve a Simpler Problem

Mixed Review

Evaluate. *[Lesson 2-7]*

18. -5^2 **19.** 4^3 **20.** $(-2)^5$ **21.** 8^2 **22.** -6^0

Determine if each ordered pair is a solution of the equation. *[Lesson 4-2]*

23. $y = 4x$ **a.** $(2, 8)$ **b.** $(4, -16)$

24. $x = y + 1$ **a.** $(7, 6)$ **b.** $(3, 2)$

25. $y = 3x - 2$ **a.** $(1, 1)$ **b.** $(2, -4)$

Project Progress

You should know the volume of your chosen item. Be able to describe the relationship between the dimensions of your package and the dimensions of your item. Also, look back on how you decided on the final package.

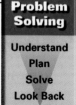

Problem Solving

Understand
Plan
Solve
Look Back

PROBLEM SOLVING 9-9

Section 9B Connect

In the beginning of Section 9B, you learned how some teenagers started what is today one of the largest package-delivery companies in the world. Now you will use your knowledge of volume to solve packaging problems involved in operating a business of your own.

The Dig on Deliveries

Materials: Calculator

You and your friends have a part-time job buying used stereo-sound components and shipping them to a relative in another state who refurbishes and resells them.

The boxing, foam packing, and shipping costs come out of your pay of $25 per component. You have the three components to ship (see photos). Your local post office has the box sizes shown in the lower right chart to use for shipping.

Woofer-tube   Sub-woofer   Band-pass enclosure

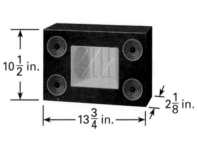

$9\frac{1}{2}$ in. $\leftarrow$ 8 in. $\rightarrow$ $12\frac{1}{2}$ in. $\leftarrow$7 in.$\rightarrow$ $10\frac{1}{2}$ in. $\leftarrow$ $13\frac{3}{4}$ in. $\rightarrow$ $2\frac{1}{8}$ in.

1. Determine the volume, to the nearest in³, of each sound component.

2. Choose the box size to ship each component. (You may ship more than one component per box.) Determine the volume of foam packing needed for each box.

3. The foam packing material is $0.99 per ft³. If a delivery company charges $0.002 per in³ for shipping, what is the total cost of boxing, packing, and shipping for the three components? How much profit did you make?

2 in. x 10 in. x 13 in.	$1.75
10 in. x 12 in. x 15 in.	$2.25
10 in. x 14 in. x 20 in.	$2.50
12 in. x 16 in. x 24 in.	$3.25
16 in. x 20 in. x 24 in.	$3.50

Section 9B Review

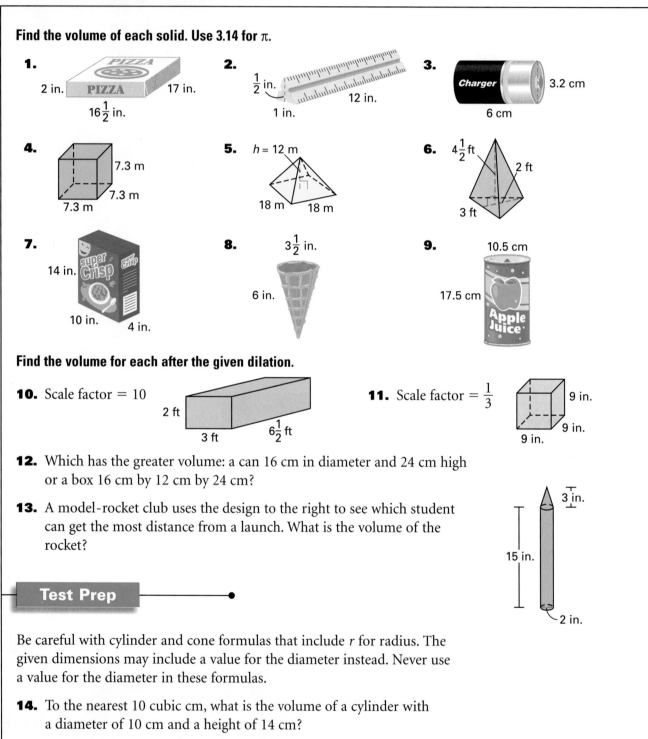

Find the volume of each solid. Use 3.14 for π.

1.
PIZZA
2 in.   PIZZA   17 in.
$16\frac{1}{2}$ in.

2.
$\frac{1}{2}$ in.   12 in.
1 in.

3.
Charger   3.2 cm
6 cm

4.
7.3 m
7.3 m
7.3 m

5. $h = 12$ m
18 m   18 m

6. $4\frac{1}{2}$ ft   2 ft
3 ft

7.
14 in.   super Crisp
10 in.   4 in.

8. $3\frac{1}{2}$ in.
6 in.

9. 10.5 cm
17.5 cm   Apple Juice

Find the volume for each after the given dilation.

10. Scale factor = 10
2 ft
3 ft $6\frac{1}{2}$ ft

11. Scale factor = $\frac{1}{3}$
9 in.
9 in.
9 in.

12. Which has the greater volume: a can 16 cm in diameter and 24 cm high or a box 16 cm by 12 cm by 24 cm?

13. A model-rocket club uses the design to the right to see which student can get the most distance from a launch. What is the volume of the rocket?

3 in.

15 in.

2 in.

Test Prep

Be careful with cylinder and cone formulas that include r for radius. The given dimensions may include a value for the diameter instead. Never use a value for the diameter in these formulas.

14. To the nearest 10 cubic cm, what is the volume of a cylinder with a diameter of 10 cm and a height of 14 cm?

   Ⓐ 440 cm^3 Ⓑ 4400 cm^3 Ⓒ 1100 cm^3 Ⓓ 7700 cm^3

Comparing Areas of Map Projections

A map shows the earth's surface on a plane. If the earth were flat, it would be easy to represent its surface on a flat sheet of paper. But the earth is a sphere, and a spherical surface is not easily flattened. A **map projection** is an attempt to represent a spherical surface as a flat surface.

Use the facts that Greenland has an area of 840,050 mi^2 and Canada has an area of 3,851,809 mi^2 to compare the following two representations of the earth.

The **cylindrical projection** was originally ideal for navigation and is still used today. The lines of longitude and latitude appear as straight lines that intersect at right angles. The North and South Poles are greatly exaggerated.

The **conic projection** usually shows latitude lines as parts of circles, and longitude lines radiate from the North or South Pole.

Cylindrical projection

Conical projection

Try It

1. Look up *map projection* in an encyclopedia or atlas. Why is the cylindrical projection most accurate for areas located on the equator?

2. Imagine that you are a sailor navigating from the coast of Brazil to Greenland. Describe an advantage of using the cylindrical projection.

3. Compare the cylindrical and conic projections to a globe. If you wanted to compare the areas of the seven continents, which projection would you use? Why?

4. Describe how the areas of Greenland and Canada compare on each of the above projections.

Graphic Organizer

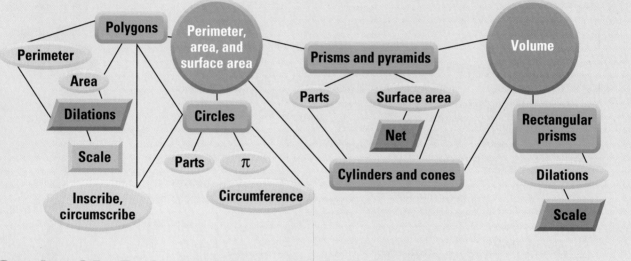

Section 9A   Perimeter, Area, and Surface Area

Summary

- The **perimeter** (p) is the distance around a figure.

- The **area** (A) of a polygon is the number of square units it contains. Area of a rectangle $= bh$, area of a square $= s^2$, and area of a triangle $= \frac{1}{2}bh$.

- The distance around a circle is the **circumference**. The **radius** is the distance from the **center** to any point on the circle. The **diameter** $= 2r$. π **(pi)** is used to calculate the area of a circle.

- A **polyhedron** is a 3-D figure composed of polygonal **faces** that meet at **edges**. A **vertex** of a polyhedron is the intersection of three or more faces. **Prisms, cylinders, pyramids,** and **cones** are polyhedrons.

- The **surface area** (SA) of a polyhedron is the sum of the areas of all the faces. A net can be helpful in finding the surface area of a polyhedron.

Review

1. Find the perimeter and area of each polygon.

   a.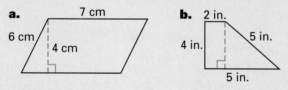
   7 cm
   6 cm
   4 cm

   b. 2 in.
   4 in.
   5 in.
   5 in.

2. Find the perimeter and area of

   a. The polygon in Exercise 1a after a dilation of a scale factor of 3.

   b. The polygon in Exercise 1b after a dilation of a scale factor of $\frac{2}{5}$.

3. For the circle shown, find the circumference and the area.

8.3 cm

4. One of the rings in a three-ring circus has a circumference of 141.3 ft. Find the diameter of the ring.

5. Find the surface area of each figure.

a.

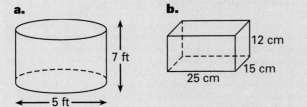
7 ft
◄— 5 ft —►

b.

12 cm
15 cm
25 cm

6. Find the slant height and the surface area.

a.

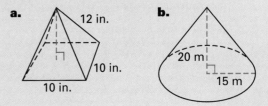
12 in.
10 in.
10 in.

b.

20 m
15 m

Section 9B   Volume

Summary

■ The **volume** of a solid measures the space it occupies.

■ Volume (V) of a prism or cylinder $= B \cdot h$, and volume (V) of a pyramid or cone $= \frac{1}{3}B \cdot h$ where $B =$ area of the figure's base.

■ In a dilation with a scale factor of x, the volume of the solid is multiplied by x^3.

Review

7. Find the volume of each solid.

a.

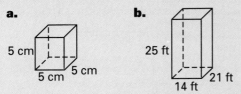
5 cm
5 cm
5 cm

b.

25 ft
14 ft
21 ft

8. Find the volume of each solid.

a.

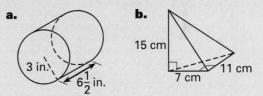
3 in.
$6\frac{1}{2}$ in.

b.

15 cm
7 cm
11 cm

9. a. Sketch a triangular prism with height 4 cm where the triangle has a base 10 cm and height 6 cm. Then find its volume.

b. Sketch a cone with diameter 8 in. and height 5 in. Then find its volume.

10. a. Find the volume of the solid in Exercise 7a after scaling two dimensions by a scale factor of $\frac{1}{5}$.

b. Find the surface area and volume of the solid in Exercise 7b after a dilation of a scale factor of 7.

11. Find the volume of a triangular prism where $B = 3$ m^2 and

a. $h = 4.5$ m

b. $h = 9$ m

12. Find the volume of a cylinder where $B = 12$ ft^2 and

a. $h = 2$ ft

b. $h = \frac{1}{2}$ ft

1. Refer to the parallelogram shown below.

  a. Find the perimeter and area.

  b. Find the perimeter and area after a dilation of a scale factor of 4.

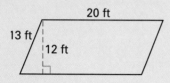

2. Refer to the triangle shown below.

  a. Find the perimeter and area.

  b. Find the perimeter and area after a dilation of a scale factor of $\frac{3}{4}$.

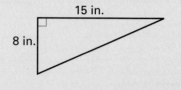

3. Find the diameter, area, and circumference of the circle at the right.

4. Which shows **a.** **b.** a square circumscribed about a circle.

5. Refer to the rectangular prism shown below.

  a. Sketch a net of the prism.

  b. Find the surface area of the prism.

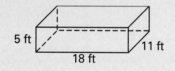

6. Refer to the cylinder shown below.

  a. Find the surface area of the cylinder.

  b. Find the volume of the cylinder.

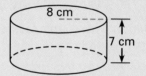

7. Refer to the pyramid shown below. Find the slant height and surface area of the pyramid.

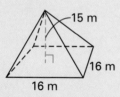

8. A disposable paper cup has the shape of a cone with diameter 5 cm and height 6 cm. How much water does the cup hold?

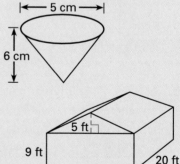

9. A simplified drawing of Monique's house is shown at the right.

  a. What is the volume of the house?

  b. Monique plans to paint her house. How much surface area will she cover? (Do not include the roof or the floor.)

Performance Task

Make a chart showing a drawing of every kind of 3-D figure you have learned. Label each figure with its name. Show formulas for surface area and volume of each figure.

Cumulative Review Chapters 1–9

Test Prep

Performance Assessment

Choose one problem.

THINK GLOBALLY, ACT LOCALLY

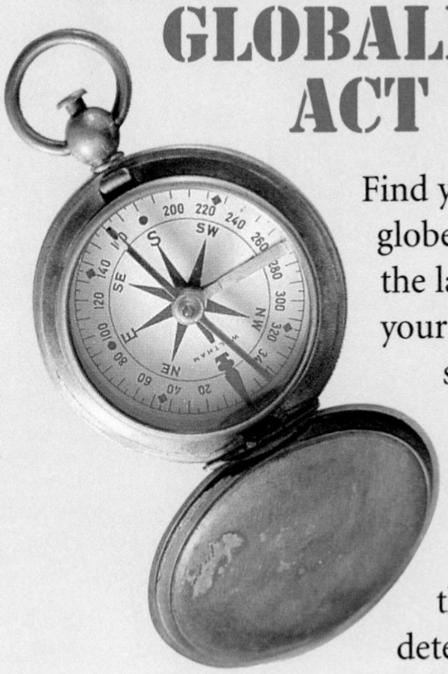

Find your home location on a globe of the earth. Determine the latitude and longitude of your home. Then draw a map showing the region that is within 5° latitude north or south, and within 5° longitude east or west of your home. Use the scale of the globe to determine the perimeter and area of this region.

BUILDING A CUBE THE HARD WAY

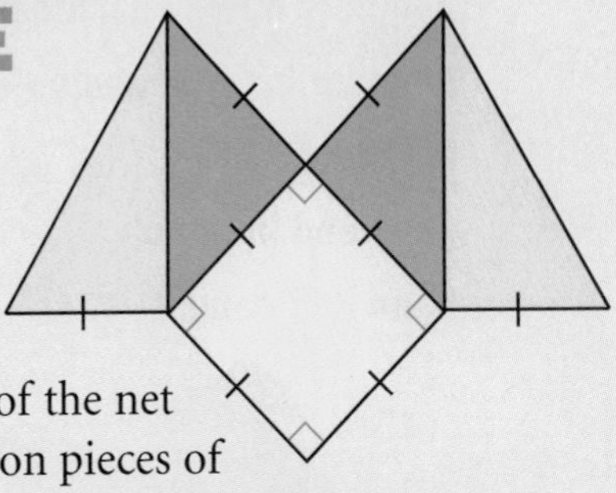

Make three copies of the net shown at the right on pieces of stiff paper. The sides shown with tick marks are all the same length. Make the patterns as large as you can, but all the same size. Cut out each net. Fold and tape each one to make three figures. Put the three figures together to make a cube. How does this three-dimensional puzzle relate to the formula for the volume of a pyramid?

Roll-to-Roll CARPETING

Dena bought a 10 ft by 8 ft piece of lime green carpet that is 1 in. thick. When the carpet is rolled up it forms a cylinder 10 ft long and $1\frac{1}{2}$ ft in diameter. What is the volume of this roll of carpet and about how many layers of carpet are there in the cylinder?

How Much Is Money?

You'll need a quarter, dime, nickel, and penny. Find the area of the circular base of each coin. Now find the height of each coin. Use this information to find the volume of each coin. Compare the ratios of coin value to volume.

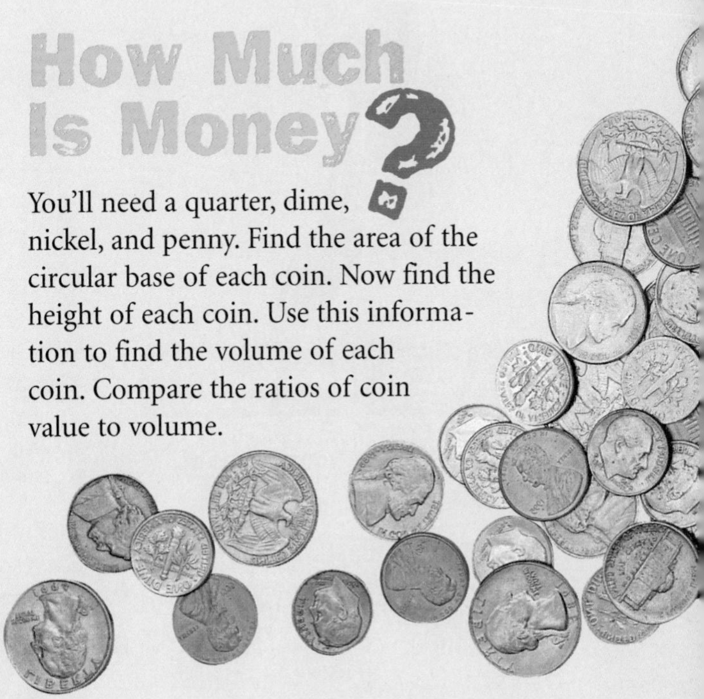

Entertainment Link
www.mathsurf.com/8/ch10/ent

Science Link
www.mathsurf.com/8/ch10/science

Entertainment

Jugglers now use mathematics to describe *siteswaps*—how high a pin goes and in which hand it is caught.

Science

Jupiter's four largest moons—Callisto, Io, Europa, and Ganymede—were discovered by Galileo in the year 1609.

Arts & Literature

The graph of the frequencies of the 12-step chromatic scale forms an exponential curve. High C has double the frequency of middle C.

and Relationships

➤ **Social Studies Link**
www.mathsurf.com/8/ch10/social

People of the World

Astronomer Annie Jump Cannon (1863–1941) published a catalog listing more than 1000 stars according to their color spectra. It took ten volumes to contain the catalog.

Social Studies

The shape of the flag of the United States was determined in 1959 by executive order of President Dwight Eisenhower. Federal standards require that the ratio of its width to its length must be 1:1.9.

KEY MATH IDEAS

A function is a relationship that gives one output value for each input value.

The input is the independent variable and the output is the dependent variable.

The graph of a linear function is a line.

The graph of a quadratic function is nonlinear; it is a curve called a parabola.

An expression such as $2x^4 - 3x + 2$ is a polynomial.

Like terms have the same variable raised to the same exponent.

CHAPTER PROJECT

Problem Solving
Understand
Plan
Solve
Look Back

Find a situation you would like to model with an equation or function; for example, the height of a baseball over time as it leaves the bat, the thickness of a book given the number of pages, the value of a doll given its age. As you learn about the various models in this chapter, decide which is the best for your situation. Try to find a way to use the model for the situation you chose.

Problem Solving

Understand
Plan
Solve
Look Back

Checking for a Reasonable Answer

When you look back, it is important to check your answer to a problem to make sure that it is reasonable. Sometimes you may find that your answer is mathematically correct, but makes no sense in the real world.

Problem Solving Focus

Read each problem and its answer. Show why each is mathematically correct. Then explain whether the answer is reasonable or not.

❶ Lois and Jack have the same birthday, but Jack is 15 years older than Lois. The sum of their ages is 9. How old is each one of them?
Answer: Jack is 12, Lois is −3

❷ Tyra bought Jack a tie and Lois a bracelet. The bracelet was on sale, but was $39 more than Jack's tie. The bill totaled $25. How much was each gift?
Answer: Bracelet $32, tie −$7

❸ There is a snowstorm on the day of their birthday party. When the guests arrive, the temperature is 12°F. By the time they leave, the storm causes a temperature drop of 18°F. What is the temperature then? **Answer: −6°F**

❹ Jack makes hot soup for his guests. He empties 3 cans of soup concentrate into a pot, adds 3 cans of milk and warms the soup. He pours an 8 oz cup of soup for Lois, leaving 40 oz of soup in the pot. How much does a can hold? **Answer: 8 oz**

❺ The entire party lasted two hours. If they spent 40 minutes making and eating soup, 20 minutes opening gifts, 45 minutes looking at pictures, and 25 minutes playing in the snow, how much time was left for eating cake?
Answer: −10 minutes

A World in Motion

Motion, the act or process of changing position, surrounds us in our daily lives. Earth rotates on its axis and around the sun. When we fly kites, the wind, which is air in motion, makes our kites soar into the sky or fall to the ground. Periodic motion can be seen in the pendulum of a grandfather clock as it swings and repeats its movement regularly and exactly. We observe and experience motion in our own movements as well as in those of others, such as in a handshake, the blink of an eyelid, a walk around the block.

The graceful movements of a dancer, a football quarterback running for a touchdown, a child running in the park—each is an example of motion. Imagine a bird flying to its nest, a dog running to greet its owner, a cat licking its paws. Motion occurs each time we move or observe movement.

1 How do you think motion is affected by gravity?

2 What do you think is meant by slow motion? Motion picture? Range of motion?

3 When you are sitting still in class, is motion occurring? Explain.

507

Functions

▶ **Lesson Link** In previous lessons, you looked at many different relationships between numbers. In this lesson, you will look at one of these relationships in which one number depends on another number. ◀

If you put whole carrots into a food processor and use the "slice" blade, you know that the result will always be sliced carrots. The result depends on the vegetable you put in and the type of blade used.

A machine that performs a duty can be used to represent relationships in mathematics. We *input* a value, apply a *rule*, and get an *output* value.

You'll Learn ...

■ to recognize a function and to find the input and output values of a function

... How It's Used

Computer graphics artists use functions to add effects such as shading to their artwork.

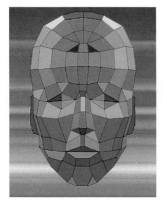

Vocabulary

function

Explore | Functions

What's My Rule?

| Input 4 | What's my rule? | Output 4 |

1. Here is a "rule" machine. Find as many rules as possible that will give you the output value for the given input value.

2. When the input is 4, what output does each rule give?

3. Compare your output values for an input value of 4 to another person's output values. Try to guess the rules the other person used.

4. If you used the same rule, is it possible to get two different output values if you both use 6 as the input value?

Learn | Functions

When each input value for a rule results in exactly one output value, this special relationship is called a *function*. A **function** is a relationship in which an output value depends on an input value, and gives only one output for each input. Two different input values can have the same output value, but two different output values cannot have the same input value.

Example 1

Ashley's salary as a dance instructor depends on the number of hours she works. If she is paid $7 an hour, what is her salary for 8 hours? 15 hours? 25 hours? If her salary was $133, how many hours did she work? Is her salary a function of the hours she works?

Input	Rule: Multiply by 7	Output
8	8 × 7	56
15	15 × 7	105
25	25 × 7	175

For 8 hours, her salary is $56. For 15 hours, her salary is $105. For 25 hours, her salary is $175.

To reverse multiplying by 7, you can divide by 7: 133 ÷ 7 = 19. She worked 19 hours for $133.

Yes, her salary is a function of her hours worked. For each number of hours (input), there is only one value for her salary (output).

Try It

Denika is Ashley's assistant. She earns $5.50 an hour. How much does she make for 20 hours? Is her salary a function of her hours worked? If she earned $55.00, how many hours did she work?

> ### MENTAL MATH
>
> Only SIDO rules out a function (Same Input, Different Output). These situations are okay for functions: Same input, same output; Different input, same output.

Example 2

Is the cost a function of the number of items? Explain.

Input (items)	4	9	1	8	4
Output (cost)	$2.00	$4.00	$0.50	$4.00	$3.00

4 items may cost $2, or 4 items may cost $3 (for the input 4, there is more than one output). So cost is not a function of the number of items.

Try It

Is the price a function of the number of Buddy Biscuits? Explain.

Buy 4, and the 5th one is free!

Biscuits	1	2	3	4	5
Price	$0.75	$1.50	$2.25	$3.00	$3.00

Example 3

Country western line dancing had a rise in popularity in 1996. The number of dancers in each row is related to the length of the dance floor. Examine the table below. Is the relationship a function? If so, what's the rule? Explain.

Floor Length (ft) Input	Dancers per Row Output
12	4
15	5
24	8
39	13

If you divide each input value by 3, you get the output value.

$12 \div 3 = 4$

$15 \div 3 = 5$

$24 \div 3 = 8$

$39 \div 3 = 13$

There is only one output value for each input value, so the relationship is a function. The rule is "Divide the input value by 3 to get the output value."

Try It

Is the relationship a function? If so, what is the rule? Explain your answer.

a.

Input	2	5	0	6	4
Output	4	25	0	36	16

b.

Input	1	2	3	2	1
Output	10	20	30	40	50

Check Your Understanding

1. What is special about a function? Give an example of a relationship that *is* a function. Give an example of a relationship that *is not* a function.

2. The x^2 key on a calculator squares the number that you input. Is this a function? Explain.

3. Why is the rule "Round a number to the nearest 10" a function, but the rule "Round a number" is not?

10-1 Exercises and Applications

Practice and Apply

1. **Getting Started** Answer each question for the given function machine.

   a. What number is the input value?

   b. What number is the output value?

   c. What is the rule?

   d. If you input 6, what is the output?

   | 4 | Multiply by 3 and subtract 4 | 8 |

For the function machine shown, find the output value for each input value.

2. Input of 4   3. Input of −1

4. Input of 10   5. Input of 0

   | Input | Multiply by 4 and add 1.75 | Output |

For the function machine shown, find the input value for each output value.

6. Output of 1   7. Output of 4

8. Output of 9   9. Output of −4

   | Input | Divide by 4 | Output |

What is a possible rule for the input and output shown in each table?

10.

Input	Output
−1	−2
0	0
1	2
2	4

11.

Input	Output
5	9
7	13
9	17
11	21

12.

Input	Output
7	0
6	0
5	0
4	0

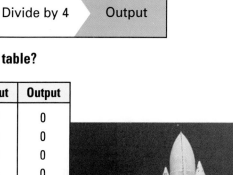

13. **Test Prep** Which situation does **not** describe a function?

   Ⓐ Distance traveled given the rate of speed.

   Ⓑ Distance traveled given the time it takes.

   Ⓒ Distance traveled given the age of the commander.

   Ⓓ They are all functions.

14. **Geometry** Is the area of a circle a function of its diameter?

15. An average person skiing cross country at 6 mi/hr burns about 13.5 calories per min.

a. Write a rule for how many calories would be burned by skiing 6 mi/hr. Use the rule to find the number of calories burned in 15 min; 20 min; 30 min; 45 min.

b. To burn 300 calories, approximately how long must Donna ski?

c. Does the number of calories burned depend on the number of minutes spent skiing? Does the relationship describe a function? Explain.

16. Chemistry There are three different forms, or *isotopes*, in which hydrogen atoms occur. Is the number of neutrons a function of the number of protons?

	Protons	Neutrons
Hydrogen-1 (protium)	1	0
Hydrogen-2 (deuterium)	1	1
Hydrogen-3 (tritium)	1	2

Problem Solving and Reasoning

17. Communicate A flare is launched straight up from the ground. The table shows the relationship of the height above the ground with respect to time. Is the relationship a function? Explain.

Time (sec)	0	1	2	3	4	5
Height (m)	0	20	30	30	20	0

18. Journal If you are given the output of a function, would there be only one input?

Critical Thinking Guess my rule.

19.

If You Say ...	−2	−1	1	2
I Say ...	2	1	1	2

20.

If You Say ...	3	5	6	10
I Say ...	8	24	35	99

Mixed Review

Find the percent decrease for each. *[Lesson 6-5]*

21. From 100 to 77   **22.** From 1000 to 977   **23.** From 0.3 to 0.21   **24.** From 1000 to 10

25. Draw a net for the number cube shown. (Note that numbers on opposite faces add up to 7.) *[Lesson 8-7]*

Linear Functions

▶ **Lesson Link**   You have learned about special relationships called functions. In this lesson, you will represent functions in different ways. ◀

Explore   Linear Functions

Is It Possible?

Materials: Graphing utility

1. Using a graphing utility, press ⌊ Y= ⌋ and enter the equation Y=1.5X−1. Press ⌊GRAPH⌋ to graph the equation. Use one of the ⌊ZOOM⌋ key options to get an integer window.

2. Press ⌊TRACE⌋. What point is shown?

3. Move along the line by pressing the left and right arrow keys. What happens to the value of *x*? Is it possible to find two points on the graph with the same *x*-coordinate but with different *y*-coordinates?

4. Graph another linear equation. Use the trace feature again. Can you find two different *y* values for the same *x*-coordinate on this graph?

... How It's Used

A printer uses linear functions to determine costs of large print jobs.

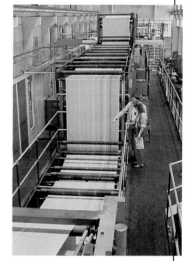

Learn   Linear Functions

You have used function machines to enter an input, perform a function, and receive an output. The value of the output depended on the value of the input.

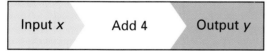

| Input *x* | Add 4 | Output *y* |

If we let *x* represent the input and *y* the output, this relationship can be represented by the function rule $x + 4 = y$ or $y = x + 4$. The output (y) depends on the input (x).

When the value of *y* depends on the value of *x*, *y* is a function of *x* and is called the **dependent variable** ; *x* is called the **independent variable** .

In graphing, we use the horizontal axis (*x*-axis) for the independent variable and the vertical axis (*y*-axis) for the dependent variable.

Vocabulary

dependent variable

independent variable

linear function

The equation $y = 3x + 2$ is a statement that the expressions y and $3x + 2$ are equal. The function $y = 3x + 2$ means the value of y is given by the rule $3x + 2$.

Examples

1 Graph the equation $y = 3x + 2$. Does it describe a function? Is it linear?

Make a table of input and output values.

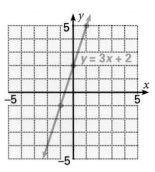

Input	Function Rule	Output
x	$3x + 2$	y
-1	$3(-1) + 2$	-1
0	$3(0) + 2$	2
1	$3(1) + 2$	5

The equation is a function, because each input (x) value has a single output (y) value. It is a **linear function** because the graph is a line.

2 The swim team is sponsoring a swim-a-thon to raise money. Paula's pledges totaled $3 for each lap completed.

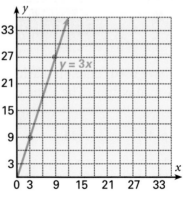

a. Write and graph the rule that relates the money pledged to the number of laps completed. If after fifteen minutes, Paula had raised $27, how many laps did she complete?

Let y = the money pledged and x = number of laps completed; the rule is then $y = 3x$.

Locate the output, or dependent value, 27 on the y-axis. Find the approximate corresponding x value: $x = 9$ laps.

b. Does the rule describe a function? Explain.

The rule describes a function because for each input value there is only one output value.

Try It

a. Graph $y = -2x$. Does it describe a linear function? Explain.

b. The Spanish club is selling T-shirts as a fund-raiser. The T-shirts sell for $4 each. Write and graph the rule that relates the money earned to the number of T-shirts sold. If after one day James had collected $36, how many T-shirts did he sell? Does the rule describe a function? Explain.

In the weightless conditions aboard a space station, the height of a pushed pencil can be modeled by a linear function of the time since it was released. A pencil pushed downward from a height of 120 cm drops 2.5 cm per second. Make a set of output values for the function $y = -2.5x + 120$.

Tanisha thinks ...

I can find output values by using the tables in a calculator. If I enter $-2.5x$ [+] 120 as the function Y_1 and look at the table formed, I can find the output values.

```
Y₁ = -2.5X + 120
Y₂ =
Y₃ =
Y₄ =
Y₅ =
Y₆ =
Y₇ =
Y₈ =
```

X	Y₁
0	120
1	117.5
2	115
3	112.5
4	110
5	107.5
6	105

X = 0

The output values are 120, 117.5, 115, 112.5, and so on.

Daniel thinks ...

I noticed that 120 is the y-intercept. I can just subtract 2.5 for each increase of 1 in the x values.

x	0	1	2	3	4	5
y	120	117.5	115	112.5	110	107.5

–2.5 –2.5 –2.5 –2.5 –2.5

What do you think?

What method would you use if you wanted to know how long it would take for the pencil to hit the floor? Why?

Check | Your Understanding

1. How can you use the graph of a function to find the input value for a given output value?

2. How can you tell from a table if a relationship is a function?

3. Is the graph $y = \frac{1}{2}x - 5$ the graph of a linear function? Explain.

PRACTICE 10-2

Practice and Apply

1. **Getting Started** Given the function rule $y = x + 3$,

   a. What is the dependent variable?

   b. What is the independent variable?

   c. Find the output values for the following input values: $x = -5$, $x = 0$, $x = 5$.

Given the following function rules, complete the table of values.

2. $y = 2x - 6$

Input (x)	Output (y)
−1	
0	
1	
2	
3	

3. $y = -x + 10$

Input (x)	Output (y)
−1	
0	
1	
2	
3	

4. $y = 3x - 5$

Input (x)	Output (y)
−1	
0	
1	
2	
3	

5. **Test Prep** Which number is the input value for $y = 1.5x - 4$, if the output value is 2?

   Ⓐ −1   Ⓑ 4   Ⓒ 1   Ⓓ $1\frac{1}{3}$

Graph each linear equation. Does the equation describe a function?

6. $y = -x + 8$ **7.** $y = 2x - 1$ **8.** $y = 3$ **9.** $x = 3$

10. **Consumer** Some airlines offer in-flight phones. The total cost to use the in-flight phone on one airline is $8 + $2 per min.

    a. Find a rule and make a table of values for the cost of 6 different call lengths.

    b. Is this relationship a function?

    c. Is the total cost dependent on the number of minutes used?

11. **Science** The distance the fastest marine animal, a killer whale, can travel is a function of the time traveled. The killer whale travels approximately 34.5 mi/hr.

    a. Write an equation to show the relationship between distance and time.

    b. Use your equation to find how far the whale can travel in 2 hr, 6 hr, and 10 hr.

Does each table of values represent a function? Explain your answer.

12.

Input (x)	Output (y)
−1	1
0	0
1	1
2	1
3	1

13.

Input (x)	Output (y)
−2	8
−1	4
0	0
−1	−4
−2	−8

14.

Input (x)	Output (y)
0	0
100	10
100	−10
400	20
400	−20

15. Jenny is placing an ad in the newspaper classifieds to sell her snowboard. The cost of the ad is $18 plus $6.50 for each line.

a. Write an equation that relates the cost (c) of an ad in the classifieds to the number of lines (n) in the ad.

b. Make a graph relating these values.

c. Is the cost of the ad a function of the number of lines it has?

Problem Solving and Reasoning

16. Critical Thinking Isaac wondered if airlines base ticket prices on the distance flown. He found the approximate mileage between some cities and round-trip fares.

a. Is ticket price a function of distance? Explain.

b. What other things might affect the cost of a ticket?

Cities	Distance (mi)	Price ($)
Chicago-Baltimore	675	298
Denver-Los Angeles	1050	445
Jacksonville-Charleston	675	189
Knoxville-Buffalo	675	442
Milwaukee-Boston	1050	895
Tampa-Pittsburgh	1050	189

17. Journal Give an example of a function in your everyday life. Explain why it is a function and define the dependent and independent variables.

Mixed Review

18. Start with 1000. What is the result of a 27% decrease followed by a 30% increase? *[Lesson 6-6]*

Find the perimeter and area of each polygon. *[Lesson 9-1]*

19. An equilateral triangle with sides 4 in. long

20. A 2 m by 6 m rectangle

21. A parallelogram with base 23 cm and height 10 cm

10-3

Quadratic Functions

You'll Learn ...

■ to represent quadratic functions as graphs, tables, and equations

... How It's Used

Projectile motion, the motion in a launched fireworks display, can be modeled using quadratic equations.

Vocabulary

nonlinear function

quadratic function

parabola

▶ **Lesson Link** You have studied linear functions. In this lesson, you will extend many of the ideas that you learned about linear functions to another type of function. ◀

Explore Quadratic Functions

Ups and Downs

Materials: Graphing calculator

1. Graph $y = x^2$ using the standard graphing calculator screen. Is this graph a function? Explain.

2. Where is the value of y increasing? Where is it decreasing?

3. Trace along the graph (or evaluate) to find y when x is 4. Then trace along the graph to find y when x is -4.

4. Trace along the graph to find a negative value for y. How does the function equation help to explain your findings?

5. Change the function to $y = x^2 - 4$ and graph. Does this change your answer to Question 4? Explain.

Learn Quadratic Functions

You have already learned about linear functions; in this lesson you will look at a **nonlinear function** called a **quadratic function** . A quadratic function is a function in which the highest power of x is 2. The following are examples of quadratic functions.

$$y = x^2 \qquad y = -x^2 \qquad y = 2x^2 \qquad y = 4x^2 - 6 \qquad y = x^2 + 2x + 1$$

The graph of a linear function is a straight line; this is because equal changes in x result in equal changes in the value of y. Recall that the change in y divided by the change in x is the slope.

The graph of a quadratic function is a ∪ or upside-down ∪-shaped curve, called a **parabola** .

For quadratic functions, equal changes in x do not result in equal changes in the value of y.

Look at the graph of the quadratic function representing the height of a ball thrown into the air. As x increases by 1, y changes by different amounts.

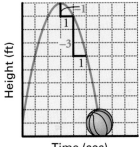

Height (ft)

Time (sec)

Examples

1 Make a table and graph for $y = 2x^2 + 4$. Use both positive and negative values for x. What happens to the y value as the x value increases?

x	y
−2	12
−1	6
0	4
1	6
2	12

$y = 2x^2 + 4$

As the values of x increase, the values of y decrease until $x = 0$; then they begin to increase again.

2 Graph each function. How are the graphs alike? How are they different?

a. $y = x^2$ and $y = -x^2$

b. $y = x^2$ and $y = x^2 + 3$

$y = x^2$
$y = -x^2$

$y = x^2 + 3$
$y = x^2$

a. Both graphs are parabolas. $(0, 0)$ is part of both graphs. They are both symmetric about the y-axis.

The graph of x^2 opens upward, whereas the graph of $-x^2$ opens downward.

b. Both graphs are parabolas, open upward, and are symmetric about the y-axis.

The y-intercept of the graph of x^2 is $y = 0$, whereas the y-intercept of the graph of $x^2 + 3$ is $y = 3$.

Try It

a. Make a table and graph for $y = 2x^2 - 4$.

b. Graph $y = x^2$ and $y = 2x^2$. How are the graphs alike? How are they different?

Sometimes when we are working real-world problems, some values do not make sense in the problem. The part of a graph that solves a problem may not look like a whole parabola.

Example 3

A pilot drops supplies to scientists working at an Antarctic Substation. Ignoring air resistance, if the drop is made from 800 ft, the function $h = -16t^2 + 800$, where t is time in sec and h is height in ft, will model the situation. Make a table and a graph using $t = 0$ to 8 sec. Could you use negative values for t or h? Why was the graph not a complete parabola?

Time (sec)	Height (ft)
0	800
1	784
2	736
3	656
4	544
5	400
6	224
7	16
8	−224
9	−496

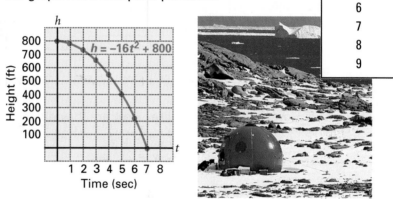

You could use negative values for t and h to see the entire graph, but it would not make sense in the problem to use negative values for time or height. Because the negative values were not used, the graph was not a parabola.

Try It

A pilot drops food to a village from a height of 500 ft. Ignoring air resistance, the function $h = -16t^2 + 500$, where t is time in sec and h is height in ft, will model the situation. Make a table and a graph using $t = 0$ to 6 sec.

Check | Your Understanding

1. How does a quadratic function differ from a linear function?

2. How does multiplying x^2 by -1 affect the graph of a quadratic function?

3. Compare the graphs of $y = x^2 - 2$ and $y = x - 2$. How are they alike? How are they different?

4. When can you ignore negative values of x? Why?

Practice and Apply

Getting Started Which are graphs of linear functions? Which are graphs of quadratic functions? Which are neither?

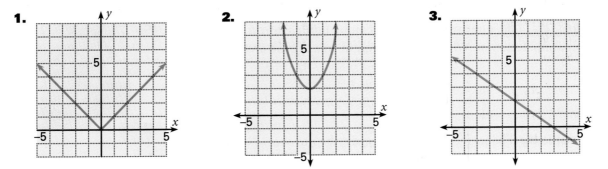

1. **2.** **3.**

Graph each set of functions and describe the similarities and differences within the set of graphs.

4. $y = x^2$, $y = x^2 + 3$, and $y = x^2 - 3$ **5.** $y = x^2$, $y = 2x^2$, $y = 4x^2$, and $y = 8x^2$

6. $y = x^2$ and $y = -x^2$ **7.** $y = 2x^2$ and $y = -2x^2$

Match each graph with the function that describes it.

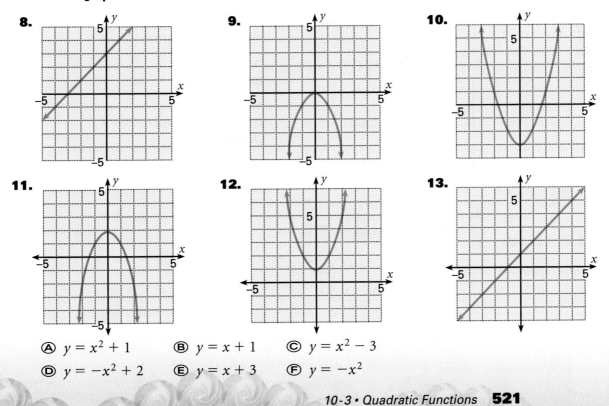

8. **9.** **10.**

11. **12.** **13.**

ⓐ $y = x^2 + 1$ ⓑ $y = x + 1$ ⓒ $y = x^2 - 3$

ⓓ $y = -x^2 + 2$ ⓔ $y = x + 3$ ⓕ $y = -x^2$

14. **Science** A toy rocket was launched into the air. The function $h = 50t - 5t^2$ models this situation, where h = height in m and t = time in sec.

a. When is the rocket 105 m in the air? Explain.

b. What happens at 10 sec?

15. **Test Prep** The area of a square can be modeled by a quadratic function. Which is the function rule for the area of a square?

Ⓐ $y = 4x$ Ⓑ $y = x \cdot x \cdot x \cdot x$

Ⓒ $y = x^2$ Ⓓ $y = 4x^2$

16. **Geometry** The formula $d = \frac{n^2 - 3n}{2}$ gives the number of diagonals (d) for a polygon with n sides.

a. How many diagonals does a square have?

b. How many diagonals does a hexagon have?

c. How many diagonals does an octagon have?

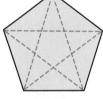

Problem Solving and Reasoning

17. **Communicate** Ossie dropped a pebble into a canyon. He heard it hit the ground 5 sec later. The function $h = -16t^2$ will model this situation. Time (t) is in sec, height (h) is in ft. Graph the function. If the pebble hits the ground in 5 sec, how deep is the canyon? Why is the value negative?

18. **Critical Thinking** Answer each question about the functions.

i. $y = 4x^2$ **ii.** $y = -4x^2$

iii. $y = x^2 + 2$ **iv.** $y = 2 - x^2$

a. Which graph(s) will open upward? How do you know?

b. Which graphs pass through the point $(0, 0)$? How do you know?

c. Which graphs are symmetric about the y-axis?

19. **Journal** How can you tell the shape of a parabola from its function rule?

Mixed Review

Solve each equation. *[Lesson 3-2]*

20. $x + 5 = 12$ 21. $y - 10 = 17$ 22. $\frac{1}{3}p = 4$

23. Find the perimeter of a triangle with side lengths of 9 cm, 8 cm, and 5 cm after it is dilated by a scale factor of 3. *[Lesson 9-2]*

Other Functions

▶ **Lesson Link** In the last lesson, you looked at one type of nonlinear function, a quadratic function. In this lesson, you will look at other types of nonlinear functions. ◀

Explore   Other Functions

Which Is Which?

Which graph do you think is appropriate for each situation? Explain your reasoning.

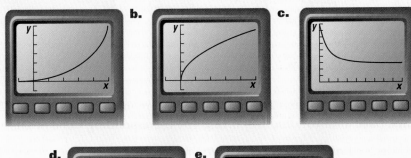

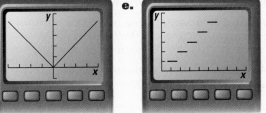

1. The temperature of a cup of cocoa that cools quickly at first, then more and more slowly as it reaches room temperature.

2. The size of a bacteria colony doubles every hour.

3. The length of the side of a square increases as the enclosed area increases linearly.

4. The output value is the input value rounded to the nearest integer.

5. The distance of a train from the station as it approaches the station and then passes the station.

You'll Learn …

■ to graph and evaluate other types of functions

… How It's Used

The rate that carbon 14 decays is an exponential function that helps paleontologists determine the age of a fossil.

Vocabulary

exponential function

step function

In all linear and quadratic functions, a variable was raised to an exponent.

In many nonlinear functions, the exponent will be a variable. These nonlinear functions, such as $y = 2^x$, are called **exponential functions** .

Examples

1 Graph the function $y = 0.5^x$ for $x \geq 0$. What is the value of y when x is 2? What is x when y is 0.125?

You can use a graphing utility.

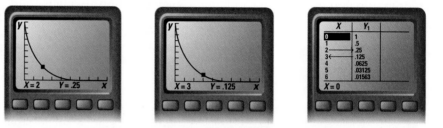

Trace to 2 on the x-axis and find the corresponding value of y, $y = 0.25$. Then trace until you find $y = 0.125$. The corresponding value of x is 3.

2 A colony of bacteria is being grown in a laboratory. The lab technicians begin with a single bacterium. Every hour, the number of bacteria doubles. How long will it take the colony to number 1000?

You can find the answer from a table or a graph.

Hours (x)	0	1	2	3	4	5	6	7	8	9	10
Number (y)	1	2	4	8	16	32	64	128	256	512	1024

The function $y = 2^x$ can be used to model this situation. Using a graphing utility, trace to find x when y is approximately 1000.

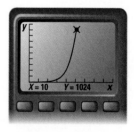

The colony will number 1000 in approximately 10 hr.

Try It

a. Graph the function $y = 0.9^x$. What is the approximate value of y when x is 4? What is the value of x when y is approximately 0.8?

b. Suppose the number of bacteria triples every hour. The function $y = 3^x$ can be used to model this situation. How long will it take the colony to number 5000?

Functions can also be made up of pieces or steps. In a **step function**, different rules may be applied to different input values. The graph of a step function is not connected.

Example 3

Wind speeds are usually given to the nearest 10 mi/hr. Graph the function that rounds a number to the nearest 10.

Numbers ending in 5 or more round up. Make a table.

x	3	5	8	14	15	18	20	24	25	34
y	0	10	10	10	20	20	20	20	30	30

The value of y is 10 for any value of $x \geq 5$ but less than 15, so this part of the graph is a flat segment.

Because 14.99 rounds to 10, whereas 15 rounds to 20, we use an open circle at (15, 10) to show that the point is not included.

Try It

Graph the function that rounds a number to the nearest 100.

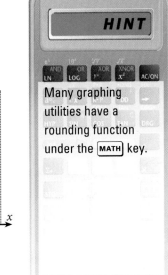

HINT

Many graphing utilities have a rounding function under the MATH key.

Check   Your Understanding

1. Explain the difference between the functions $y = x^2$ and $y = 2^x$.

2. How are the graphs of $y = 2^x$ and $y = 0.5^x$ alike? How are they different?

3. How can you tell from the equation that a function is exponential?

Practice and Apply

Getting Started Match each function to its graph.

1. $y = 2x$ **2.** $y = x^2$ **3.** $y = 2^x$ **4.** $y =$ round down to the whole number

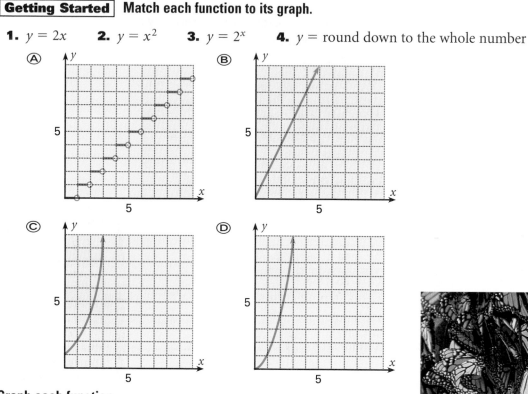

Ⓐ   Ⓑ   Ⓒ   Ⓓ

Graph each function.

5. $y = 1.5^x$ **6.** $y = 1.5x$ **7.** $y = 4x$ **8.** $y = 4^x$

9. Suppose the population of butterflies on an island doubles in size each year. If there are 1,000 butterflies now, in how many years will there be 1,000,000 butterflies? Show how this is modeled by $y = 1,000 \cdot 2^x$.

10. John bought a new bank. The first day, he put two pennies in it. Each day he doubled the number of pennies he put in. The equation $y = 2^x$ models this situation.

   a. Graph the equation.

   b. On what day did John add $0.64?

      c. What was the first day John added more than $2.00 to the bank?

11. **Consumer** Ready Rent-All rental charges for a VCR are as follows.

Rental Time	Rental Fee
1 day or portion thereof	$10.00
Over 1 day, up to 3 days	$20.00
Over 3 days up to 5 days	$35.00

   a. Graph the function.

   b. What kind of function is this?

Identify each function as linear, quadratic, exponential, or step.

12. $y = 0.6^x$ **13.** $y = 0.6x^2$ **14.** $y =$ round to nearest ten   **15.** $y = 6x$

16. **Test Prep** The equation $y = x^2 - 5$ describes which type of function?

ⓐ Linear   ⓑ Quadratic   ⓒ Exponential   ⓓ Step

17. Tabitha's mom started a savings account to help pay for her college education. She deposited $1000 and is receiving 7% interest compounded annually on her money. The function $A = 1000(1.07)^t$ will show the balance (A) after t years.

a. How much money is in the account after 5 years?

b. Approximately how many years will it take to have a balance of $2000?

18. **Chance** What are the chances that a 90% free-throw shooter will make the next 10 free throws in a row? Graph 0.9^x and find y when x is 10.

Problem Solving and Reasoning

19. **Choose a Strategy** As the value of x increases, what happens to each value?

a. $2x$ **b.** x^2 **c.** 2^x **d.** 0.2^x

20. **Journal** Give an example of a step function you might see in your everyday life. Why is it a step function?

Communicate **Without graphing, describe each graph.**

21. $y = 5^x$ **22.** $y = \left(\frac{1}{2}\right)^x$

> **Problem Solving**
> ## STRATEGIES
> • Look for a Pattern
> • Make an Organized List
> • Make a Table
> • Guess and Check
> • Work Backward
> • Use Logical Reasoning
> • Draw a Diagram
> • Solve a Simpler Problem

Mixed Review

Write an expression for each situation. *[Lesson 3-3]*

23. Twice a number, subtracted from 10   **24.** Three times a number, plus 3

Find the circumference and area of a circle with each given radius. *[Lesson 9-3]*

25. $r = 6$ m   **26.** $r = 18$ mm   **27.** $r = 2.9$ m   **28.** $r = 87$ cm

Project Progress

Sketch and label a graph for the situation you chose. Compare your sketch to the graphs of the function models you have seen. Rule out any that do not work.

> **Problem Solving**
> Understand
> Plan
> Solve
> Look Back

TECHNOLOGY

Using a Graphing Calculator • Graphing Functions

Problem: The distance from Kansas City, Missouri, to Denver, Colorado, is 600 mi. How long will it take to make the trip at different rates of speed?

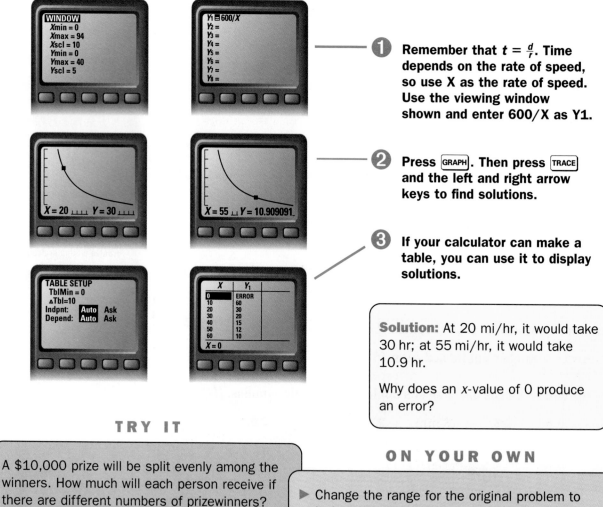

① Remember that $t = \frac{d}{r}$. Time depends on the rate of speed, so use X as the rate of speed. Use the viewing window shown and enter 600/X as Y1.

② Press GRAPH. Then press TRACE and the left and right arrow keys to find solutions.

③ If your calculator can make a table, you can use it to display solutions.

Solution: At 20 mi/hr, it would take 30 hr; at 55 mi/hr, it would take 10.9 hr.

Why does an *x*-value of 0 produce an error?

TRY IT

A $10,000 prize will be split evenly among the winners. How much will each person receive if there are different numbers of prizewinners? Graph the solutions.

ON YOUR OWN

▶ Change the range for the original problem to include negative numbers for *x* and *y*. Describe the shape of the graph. Trace to the left of 0. What are some other solutions? Do these make sense in the problem situation?

Section 10A Connect

In this Connect, you will combine your knowledge of the different types of functions.

The World in Motion

Materials: Graphing utility

Kirt estimated that as a pelican swooped down toward the water, it was about 20 ft high, then 12, then 8, then 5, then 3. Then it stayed very close to the water as it flew. He used his graphing utility and found several possible function models for its height over time based upon the initial height.

He started with time at 0 sec.

    a. $y = -4x + 20$ **b.** $y = x^2 - 8x + 20$ **c.** $y = 20(0.6)^x$

1. Graph each function.

2. Which are good models for the height of the pelican? Which are not? Which do you feel is the best model? Why?

3. Do you think a step function would be a good model? Why or why not?

4. Suppose the pelican flew down to the water and immediately back up again. How would your answer to Question 2 change?

For the function machine shown, find each missing value.

1. Input -1 output ___

2. Input ___ output -8

3. Input 4 output ___

4. Input ___ output -6

5. Input 3 output ___

6. Input ___ output 100

| Input | Multiply by 2 and subtract 8 | Output |

Test Prep

Use inverse operations to find the input value of a function.

7. Which is the input value for $y = 5x$ if the output value is -30?

Ⓐ -150 Ⓑ 6 Ⓒ -6 Ⓓ 5

Sketch an example of a graph for each type of function.

8. Linear   **9.** Quadratic   **10.** Exponential   **11.** Step

12. If y is a function of x, name the dependent variable and the independent variable.

Is y a function of x? Explain.

13.

x	−1	0	1	2	3
y	1	0	1	2	3

14.

x	−2	−1	0	−1	−2
y	8	4	0	−4	−8

15. Graph $y = x$, $y = x^2$, and $y = 4^x$. Describe the similarities and differences.

16. Geology Antarctic glaciers flow approximately 0.0005 km/hr. Write an equation to show the relationship between distance and time. Find how far a glacier travels in a week.

17. Science The height of a penny dropped into a well is modeled by the function $h = -16t^2$, where time (t) is in sec and height (h) is in ft.

a. Make a table of values and graph the function, using $t = 1$ to 8 sec.

b. If the penny hits bottom in 4 sec, how deep is the well? Why is the value of h negative?

18. A bank offers a 6% annual-interest savings account. The function $A = 1000(1.06)^t$ gives the balance (A) after t years. If $1000 is invested, how much money is in the account after 5 years? Approximately how many years will it take to have a balance of $2000?

Polynomials

WHICH CAME FIRST?

When we think of animals living today that are direct descendants of dinosaurs, we probably think of alligators, lizards, komodo dragons, or rhinoceroses. But we probably don't think of birds.

The earliest bird fossil found was that of Archaeopteryx, a bird that lived about 140 million years ago. It had wings with both feathers and claws, teeth, and a dinosaur-like tail. It could barely fly, and may even have climbed trees.

Today's birds are also varied in shape and form. From the ostrich, to the penguin, to the burrowing owl, to the peacock, nature has given birds colors and abilities of which we can only dream.

1 What do you think distinguishes birds from other classes of vertebrates?

2 35% of a bird's weight is in the flight muscles. Estimate the weight of the flight muscle in a 6-lb bird.

3 Only 16% of Archaeopteryx' weight was in the flight muscles. What affect might this have had?

531

Polynomials

▶ **Lesson Link**
You have learned about linear functions and several nonlinear functions. Now you will learn about another type of nonlinear function. ◀

You'll Learn ...

■ to evaluate polynomials

... How It's Used

Computer programmers use polynomials to program 3-D graphics for video games.

Vocabulary

polynomial

term

monomial

binomial

trinomial

degree

Explore | **Polynomials**

Let's Box!

1. Find the area of each square end of the box pictured above.

2. Find the area of the rectangular faces.

3. Find the surface area of the box by adding the areas of all the faces.

4. If the square ends had side length *x* units, write an expression that would give the surface area of the box.

5. How does the surface area change as the length of the side of the square changes? Explain your answer.

▶ **Language Link**

Poly- means many or too many.

Learn | **Polynomials**

A **polynomial** is an algebraic expression that is the sum of one or more parts, called **terms** . Each term is a signed number, a variable, or a number multiplied by a variable or variables. The variables can have whole-number exponents.

Polynomial: $-2x^3 - 4x^2 + 3x + 1$

Terms: $\quad -2x^3 \quad -4x^2 \quad 3x \quad 1$

Some polynomials have special names.

monomial: $x,$ $2x^3,$ -2 **Monomials** have one term.

binomial: $x + 1,$ $2x^3 - 7x$ **Binomials** have two terms.

trinomial: $x + 3x^2 - 4x^3,$ $x^2 - 4x + 3$ **Trinomials** have three terms.

The **degree** of a polynomial with one variable is the value of the largest exponent of the variable that appears in any term.

$2x^3, 2x^3 - 7,$ and $-4x^3 + 3x^2 + x$ have degree 3

$x^2 - 4x + 3$ has degree 2

x and $x + 4$ each have degree 1

-2 has degree 0

Polynomials are usually written with the term that has the highest degree first, the next highest second, and so on. This is called writing a polynomial in descending order.

$x^4 + 3x - 2x^6 + 5$ written in descending order is $-2x^6 + x^4 + 3x + 5.$

Examples

1 Write the polynomial $x^5 + 2x - 6x^3 + 2x^2$ in descending order. What is the degree of the polynomial?

$x^5 - 6x^3 + 2x^2 + 2x$ The term with the highest degree is x^5, then $-6x^3$, then $2x^2$, and finally $2x$.

Because the largest exponent is 5, the degree of the polynomial is 5.

2 The height of a sagging highwire x m from the end can be modeled by the polynomial $15 + 0.00025x^3 - 0.375x - 0.005x^2 + 0.000004x^4$. Write this polynomial in descending order. What is the degree of the polynomial?

$0.000004x^4 + 0.00025x^3 - 0.005x^2 - 0.375x + 15$ The exponents are in order.

Since the largest exponent is 4, the degree of the polynomial is 4.

Try It

Write the trinomial $x + 2 - 4x^2$ in descending order. What is the degree of the polynomial?

Polynomials can be evaluated by replacing the variables with the given numbers and using the order of operations to simplify the expression.

Examples

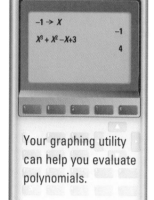

Your graphing utility can help you evaluate polynomials.

3 Evaluate $x^3 + x^2 - x + 3$ for $x = -4$.

$(-4)^3 + (-4)^2 - (-4) + 3$ Substitute -4 for x in the polynomial.

$= -64 + 16 + 4 + 3$ Simplify powers, then add or subtract.

$= -41$

4 The volume of a cube can be represented by the function $V = s^3$, where V = volume and s = the length of a side. Find the volume of a cube with each given side length.

a. 3 in.   **b.** 1.5 in.   **c.** 2 cm

Substitute the given side length into the equation $V = s^3$.

a. $V = (3)^3 = 27$. The volume of the cube is 27 in³.

b. $V = (1.5)^3 = 3.375$. The volume of the cube is 3.375 in³.

c. $V = (2)^3 = 8$. The volume of the cube is 8 cm³.

Try It

a. Evaluate $x^3 - x^2 + x + 5$ for $x = 0$ and $x = -3$.

b. The volume of a hemispheric birdbath is a function of the length of its radius and can be represented by the function $V = \frac{2}{3}\pi r^3$, where V = volume and r = the length of the radius. Find the volume of a birdbath with each given radius length. Use $\pi = 3.14$.

i. 1 ft   **ii.** 4 ft   **iii.** 2.25 m

Study TIP

Understanding common prefixes and suffixes can help you learn the meanings of unfamiliar words.

Check   Your Understanding

1. What do the prefixes *mono-*, *bi-*, *tri-*, and *poly-* mean?

2. How do you determine the degree of a polynomial?

3. Are the polynomials $3x^2 - 2 + x - x^3$ and $x - 2 - x^3 + 3x^2$ the same? How do you know?

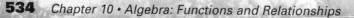

Practice and Apply

1. **Getting Started** State the number of terms in each polynomial expression.
   a. $-2x^2 + 3x + 1$ b. $4x$ c. $-2x^3 + 6$

Identify each expression as a monomial, binomial, or trinomial.

2. $0.75y$ 3. $a + 3 - 4a^2$ 4. $2b^5$ 5. $x + 12$ 6. $3x^3 + 2x^2 + 9$

Write each polynomial expression in descending order, then find the degree of each polynomial.

7. $4 + 2x$ 8. $2x + 4x^2 - 3$ 9. $x^2 - x^3 - x^4$ 10. $2x + 4x^3 + 1$

Evaluate each polynomial for $x = -3$.

11. $3x + 6$ 12. $x^2 + 3x - 3$ 13. $3x^2 - 4x + 12$ 14. $x^3 - 3$

Evaluate each polynomial for $g = 2$ and for $g = 10$.

15. $g - g^2 + g^3$ 16. $g^2 - 9g$ 17. $5 - g$ 18. $25g^2 - 4$

19. **Geometry** The surface area of a cylinder with a height of 12 in. is given by $2\pi r^2 + 24\pi r$. Find the surface area of a cylinder with a radius, r, of 2 in.

20. **Language Arts** The words *monomial, binomial, trinomial,* and *polynomial* use the prefixes *mono-, bi-, tri-,* and *poly-*. Find some other words that use these prefixes and give their meanings.

21. **Test Prep** Which of the following is the degree of the polynomial $5 + 3x^4 - 2x^5 + x^8$?
    Ⓐ 18   Ⓑ 8   Ⓒ 5   Ⓓ 4

22. **Patterns** Evaluate each polynomial in the table for $x = 0, 1, 2,$ and 3. Describe the pattern that is formed.

	$x = 0$	$x = 1$	$x = 2$	$x = 3$
$x + 1$				
$x^2 + 2x + 1$				
$x^3 + 3x^2 + 3x + 1$				
$x^4 + 4x^3 + 6x^2 + 4x + 1$				

23. **Geometry** At Epcot Center in Orlando, Florida, the Spaceship Earth is built in the shape of a sphere with a diameter of approximately 165 ft. Use $\pi = 3.14$ to answer each question.

  a. Use the formula $S = 4\pi r^2$, where S = surface area and r = radius, to find the approximate surface area.

  b. Using the formula $V = \frac{4}{3}\pi r^3$, where V = volume and r = radius, find the approximate volume.

24. **Science** Niels Bohr's model of the atom shows that electrons rotate around the nucleus in a series of orbits called *shells*. $2x^2$ represents the number of electrons in each shell, where $x = 1$ in the first shell, $x = 2$ in the second shell, and so on. How many electrons could be orbiting the nucleus in the fourth shell of an atom?

Problem Solving and Reasoning

25. **Critical Thinking** The Birdseed Box uses boxes that are the same length, width, and height. Write an expression that will give the total volume of any number of boxes.

26. **Journal** Give some examples of expressions that are polynomials. Give some examples of expressions that are not polynomials and explain why they are not.

27. **Math Reasoning** The differences between terms of this sequence form a pattern.

    sequence: 0 1 3 6 10 15
    differences: 1 2 3 4 5

    Evaluate $\frac{2n^3 + 3n^2 + n}{6}$ for $n = 0, 1, 2, 3,$ and 4 to create a sequence. Describe the pattern in the differences.

Mixed Review

Solve each equation. *[Lesson 3-4]*

28. $x + 20 = 55$ 29. $88 = x - 17$ 30. $x + 4\frac{1}{2} = 5\frac{1}{2}$ 31. $x - 40 = 140$

Find how much fabric is needed to cover each object. *[Lesson 9-4]*

32. The cover of a photo album that is 10 in. by 13 in. by 3 in.

33. A gift box that is 28 cm by 28 cm by 16 cm and its lid that is 28 cm by 28 cm by 2 cm

Adding Polynomials

▶ **Lesson Link** In the last lesson, you were introduced to polynomials. In this lesson, you will learn to add polynomials. ◀

Explore   Adding Polynomials

Family Reunion

Materials: Algebra tiles

1. What expression is modeled by the tiles?

2. What expression is modeled by the tiles?

3. Model the two sets of tiles above with your tiles. Combine the two sets. Remove any zero pairs. What expression remains?

4. Model $x^2 + 4x - 3$ with algebra tiles. Model $4x - 2x^2 + 1$ with more algebra tiles. Combine the two sets and remove any zero pairs. What expression remains?

5. When you combine algebra tiles, do you combine x^2 tiles with x tiles? x tiles with unit tiles? How can you apply this to adding expressions?

Learn   Adding Polynomials

Recall from the last lesson that polynomials contain terms. **Like terms** are terms that have the same variable raised to the same exponent.

For the polynomial $3x^2 + 4x^3 - 6x + 2 - 8x^3 - 2x^2$, $3x^2$ and $-2x^2$ are like terms because both contain the variable x raised to the second power; $4x^3$ and $-8x^3$ are like terms because both contain the variable x raised to the third power. Like terms can be combined using the distributive property.

$$3x^2 + -2x^2 = (3 + -2)x^2 = 1x^2 \qquad 4x^3 + -8x^3 = (4 + -8)x^3 = -4x^3$$

You'll Learn ...

■ to add polynomials

... How It's Used

Many irregularly-shaped pieces were used to renovate the Statue of Liberty.

Sometimes you will have to add polynomials in order to find the area of irregular figures.

Vocabulary

like terms

simplified

A polynomial is **simplified** when it contains no like terms.

Examples

1 Simplify each expression.

a. $1 + 4x + 3x^2 - 5x$ **b.** $3w^2 + (-6w) + 4w^2 - 2w$

a. $3x^2 + 4x - 5x + 1$ List the terms in descending order.

$\quad = 3x^2 + (4 - 5)x + 1$ Group like terms.

$\quad = 3x^2 + -1x + 1$ Combine like terms.

$\quad = 3x^2 - x + 1$ $-1x = -x.$

b. $3w^2 + 4w^2 + (-6w) - 2w$ List the terms in descending order.

$\quad = (3 + 4)w^2 + (-6 - 2)w$ Group like terms.

$\quad = 7w^2 + (-8)w$ Combine like terms.

$\quad = 7w^2 - 8w$

When combining like terms, just think of x^2 as apples, x as oranges, integers as bananas, and so on.
You can only add apples to apples and oranges to oranges.

2 Add the polynomials $2x^2 - 4x - 8$, $-x^2 + 2$, and $x - 3$.

$(2x^2 - 4x - 8) + (-x^2 + 2) + (x - 3)$

$= 2x^2 - 4x - 8 + -x^2 + 2 + x - 3$ Write without parentheses.

$= (2x^2 - x^2) + (-4x + x) + (-8 + 2 - 3)$ Group like terms.

$= x^2 + (-3x) + (-9)$ Combine like terms to simplify.

$= x^2 - 3x - 9$

Polynomials can also be added vertically in columns. If there is a term missing in one of the polynomials, it can be replaced by 0 as a placeholder.

x^2	x	constant	
$2x^2$	$- 4x$	$- 8$	Arrange terms in descending order.
$-1x^2$	$+ 0x$	$+ 2$	Group like terms by aligning them vertically.
$+ 0x^2$	$+ x$	$- 3$	

$\quad 1x^2 \quad + (-3x) \quad + (-9) \; = x^2 - 3x - 9$ Combine like terms and simplify.

Try It

Simplify each expression.

a. $5x^2 + 12x + 2x^2 - 5x + 1$

b. $-6n^2 - 3n + 2n + (-5)n^2 - 9$

c. Add $5x^2 + 2x - 4$, $5x - 2x^2$, and $x - 6$.

Example 3

Find an expression for the floor area of the chicken coop. If x is 20 ft, what is the area?

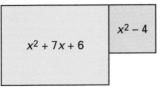

To find the floor area, add the polynomials.

$(x^2 + 7x + 6) + (x^2 - 4)$

$(x^2 + x^2) + 7x + (6 - 4)$ Group like terms.

$2x^2 + 7x + 2$ Combine like terms.

or

$(x^2 + 7x + 6)$ Arrange terms in descending order.

$\underline{+ (x^2 + 0x - 4)}$ Group like terms by aligning them vertically.

$2x^2 + 7x + 2$ Combine like terms.

When x is 20:

$2(20)^2 + 7(20) + 2$

$= 2(400) + 140 + 2$

$= 942$

The chicken coop has an area of 942 ft^2.

Try It

Find an expression for the area of the total region. What is the area when $x = 10$?

$x^2 - 4x - 5$ $x^2 + 5x - 6$

Check   Your Understanding

1. Give an example of like terms and of terms that are not alike. Explain.

2. Can the sum of two binomials be a trinomial? Explain.

3. When you write a polynomial in descending order, what in the expression is descending?

Practice and Apply

1. | Getting Started | Fill in the blanks.

To simplify the polynomial $4p + 3p^2 - p + 5p^2$, write the polynomial in _____ order. Then combine _____ by using the _____ property.

Simplify each, if possible. If the expression cannot be simplified, write "already simplified." Write answers in descending order.

2. $2x^2 - 4x + 8x^3 + x$

3. $4y^2 + 2y$

4. $4p - 3$

5. $2m^2 - 8m + 5m + 5m^2$

6. $5b^2 - 4b + 2b^3 + (-3)b$

7. $5a - 4a + 3a + 6$

Find each polynomial sum. Write the answers in simplest form.

8. $(2m - 6m^2) + (-2m^2 - 2m + 1)$

9. $(2x) + (-2x^2 - 2x + 1)$

10. $(-y^3 + 3y) + (4y^2 + 3y - 1)$

11.
$$\begin{array}{r} 5x^2 + 6x + 2 \\ + 8x^2 - 2x - 9 \\ \hline \end{array}$$

12.
$$\begin{array}{r} 5z^2 + 3z - 1 \\ + -3z + 1 \\ \hline \end{array}$$

13.
$$\begin{array}{r} x^2 + 3x - 6 \\ + 3x^2 - 4x + 15 \\ \hline \end{array}$$

14. Measurement The volume of a tennis ball can is approximately 620 cm^3. A tennis ball has a diameter of approximately 6.68 cm.

a. Use the formula for the volume of a sphere, $V = \frac{4}{3}\pi r^3$, to find the approximate volume of a tennis ball. Use $\pi = 3.14$.

b. How many tennis balls do you think will fit into one can? Explain your reasoning.

15. | Test Prep | Which of the following pairs of terms are like terms?
ⓐ x^2 and $3x^2$　　ⓑ x^3 and $3x$　　ⓒ $7x$ and 7　　ⓓ x^2 and y^2

16. Consumer Carpet is sold for $9.95 per square yd. To find the area of her family room, Marjorie used the formula $A = x^2 + 2x$, where A = area in yd^2 and x = length of the room = 3 yd. How much did it cost Marjorie to carpet her family room?

17. A zoo built an aviary for its exotic birds. The total volume includes the flight space, x^3, an exercise room, $5x^2$, a private loft, $4x^2$, and a nesting box, $7x$. Write the polynomial that represents the total volume of the aviary, then simplify it. Evaluate the polynomial for $x = 6$ ft.

18. If you know the cube of a counting number x, x^3, you can find the cube of the next counting number by adding $3x^2 + 3x + 1$. The cube of 5 is 125. Show how you can add polynomials and evaluate to find 6^3.

Geometry Find the total area of each figure.

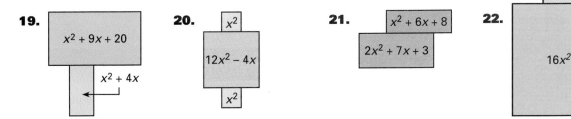

19.
$x^2 + 9x + 20$
$x^2 + 4x$

20.
x^2
$12x^2 - 4x$
x^2

21.
$x^2 + 6x + 8$
$2x^2 + 7x + 3$

22.
x^2
$16x^2$

Problem Solving and Reasoning

23. Critical Thinking Write an expression that contains four terms and simplifies to $2x$.

24. [Journal] Is simplifying an equation the same as solving it? Explain.

25. Communicate Jennifer simplified the expression $4x + 3x$ to $7x^2$. Was she correct? Explain your reasoning.

26. Choose a Strategy Find the missing term.

$$(3x^2 - 6x) + (\underline{} - 2x^2) = x^2 - 8x$$

27. Critical Thinking When asked to simplify $x^2 + x^2$, four students got the following answers. Who is correct? What do you think each of the students did to get their answer?

a. Willard's answer is x^4. **b.** Bryant's answer is $2x^4$.

c. Katie's answer is $2x^2$. **d.** Matt's answer is x^2.

Problem Solving
STRATEGIES

- Look for a Pattern
- Make an Organized List
- Make a Table
- Guess and Check
- Work Backward
- Use Logical Reasoning
- Draw a Diagram
- Solve a Simpler Problem

Mixed Review

Solve each equation. *[Lesson 3-5]*

28. $14x = 84$ **29.** $27 = \frac{3}{4}x$ **30.** $\frac{x}{5} = -60$ **31.** $7.1x = 63.9$

Find each surface area. *[Lesson 9-5]*

32.
10 cm
6 cm

33.
9.5 cm
1.5 cm

You'll Learn ...

■ to subtract polynomials

... How It's Used

A carpenter subtracts polynomials when calculating the amount of material needed to construct the walls if space is left for doors and windows.

▶ **Lesson Link** In the last lesson, you learned to add polynomials. In this lesson, you will learn to subtract polynomials. ◀

Explore | Subtracting Polynomials

The Buddy System

Materials: Algebra tiles

1. What expression is modeled?

2. What would remain if you subtracted or removed 1 x^2 tile and 1 negative x tile?

3. What would remain if you added 1 negative x^2 tile and 1 positive x tile to the original expression? Remember to remove zero pairs.

4. Compare the results from Steps 2 and 3. Why did this happen?

5. What would remain if you added 1 negative x^2 tile, 3 positive x tiles, and 1 negative unit tile to the original expression? Explain.

Learn | Subtracting Polynomials

Recall from previous work with algebra tiles that the following are additive inverses and make up zero pairs.

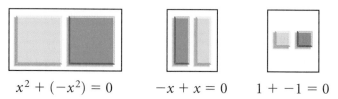

$$x^2 + (-x^2) = 0 \qquad -x + x = 0 \qquad 1 + -1 = 0$$

In Chapter 2, you learned that the opposite of a number is called its additive inverse. When you add a number to its additive inverse, you get zero. The additive inverse of 3 is -3; of x^3, $-x^3$; of $-5x^2$, $5x^2$. You also learned that subtraction of integers is the same as adding the opposite.

$a - b$ is the same as $a + (-b)$.

Examples

1 Find the additive inverse of the polynomial $x^2 + 4x - 8$.

$-(x^2 + 4x - 8)$ Take the opposite of the polynomial.

$= -(x^2 + 4x + -8)$ Change subtraction to adding the opposite.

$= -x^2 + -4x + 8$ Take the opposite of each term in the polynomial.

$= -x^2 - 4x + 8$

When you subtract polynomials, add the opposite or additive inverse.

2 Subtract $(6x^3 + 2x^2 - 5) - (x^3 - 3x^2 + 7)$.

$(6x^3 + 2x^2 - 5) + -(x^3 - 3x^2 + 7)$ Add the opposite of the second polynomial.

$= (6x^3 + 2x^2 + -5) + -(x^3 + -3x^2 + 7)$ Change subtracting to adding the opposite.

$= (6x^3 + 2x^2 + -5) + (-x^3 + 3x^2 + -7)$ Find the opposite of all terms in the parentheses.

$= (6 + -1)x^3 + (2 + 3)x^2 + (-5 + -7)$ Group like terms.

$= 5x^3 + 5x^2 + -12$ Combine like terms.

$= 5x^3 + 5x^2 - 12$

As with addition, subtraction can be done vertically.

$(6x^3 + 2x^2 - 5) + -(x^3 - 3x^2 + 7)$ Add the opposite of the second polynomial.

$= (6x^3 + 2x^2 + -5) + -(x^3 + -3x^2 + 7)$ Change subtracting to adding the opposite.

$= (6x^3 + 2x^2 + -5) + (-x^3 + 3x^2 + -7)$ Find the opposite of all terms in the parentheses.

$$\begin{array}{r} (6x^3 + 2x^2 + -5) \\ + (-x^3 + 3x^2 + -7) \\ \hline 5x^3 + 5x^2 + -12 \end{array}$$ Group like terms by aligning them vertically.

     Combine like terms.

$= 5x^3 + 5x^2 - 12$

Try It

a. Find the additive inverse of $-2x^3 + 1$.

b. Subtract $(4x^3 + 6x^2 - 2x) - (2x^3 - 8x + 5)$.

> **Remember**
>
> You can use the distributive property of multiplication to remove parentheses when simplifying polynomials. **[Page 83]**

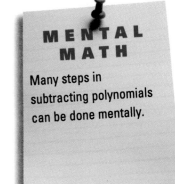

MENTAL MATH

Many steps in subtracting polynomials can be done mentally.

Examples

3 At For the Birds, the annual revenue from selling a macaw cage at a price (*p*) is given by $-4p^2 - 100p + 4,200$. The cost is $-1,300p + 60,000$. Profit is revenue minus cost. What is the profit function for selling the cages? What is the profit when cages are sold for $150? For $200?

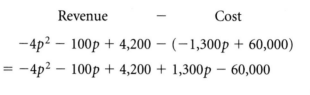

$$\text{Revenue} \qquad - \qquad \text{Cost}$$

$$-4p^2 - 100p + 4,200 - (-1,300p + 60,000)$$
$$= -4p^2 - 100p + 4,200 + 1,300p - 60,000 \qquad \text{Change subtracting to adding the opposite.}$$

$$= -4p^2 + (-100 + 1,300)p + (4,200 - 60,000) \qquad \text{Group like terms.}$$
$$= -4p^2 + 1,200p - 55,800 \qquad \text{Combine like terms.}$$

The profit function is $-4p^2 + 1,200p - 55,800$. Evaluate.

$$-4p^2 + 1,200p - 55,800 \qquad\qquad -4p^2 + 1,200p - 55,800$$
$$= -4(150)^2 + 1,200(150) - 55,800 \qquad = -4(200)^2 + 1,200(200) - 55,800$$
$$= -90,000 + 180,000 - 55,800 \qquad = -160,000 + 240,000 - 55,800$$
$$= 34,200 \qquad\qquad\qquad = 24,200$$

The annual profit is $34,200 when cages are priced at $150; $24,200 when they are priced at $200.

4 Find the unknown side length.

Add the known lengths of the sides.

$$(x^2 + 4) + (2x^2 - 4x) + (3x + 1) + (2x - 3)$$
$$= 3x^2 + x + 2$$

Subtract from the given perimeter.

$$(4x^2 + 2) - (3x^2 + x + 2) = x^2 - x$$

The length of the unknown side is $x^2 - x$.

(Pentagon figure labeled: $x^2 + 4$, $2x^2 - 4x$, $3x + 1$, $2x - 3$, $p = 4x^2 + 2$)

Try It

a. The annual revenue from selling parakeets at a price *p* is given by $-70p^2 - 25p + 200$. The cost is $-1520p + 500$. What is the profit function for selling the parakeets? What is the profit when parakeets are sold for $10?

b. The perimeter is $7x^2 + 3x + 8$. Find the unknown side length.

(Quadrilateral figure labeled: $5x + 4$, $5x^2 + 9$, $2x^2 - 8x$)

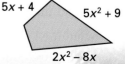

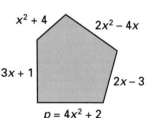

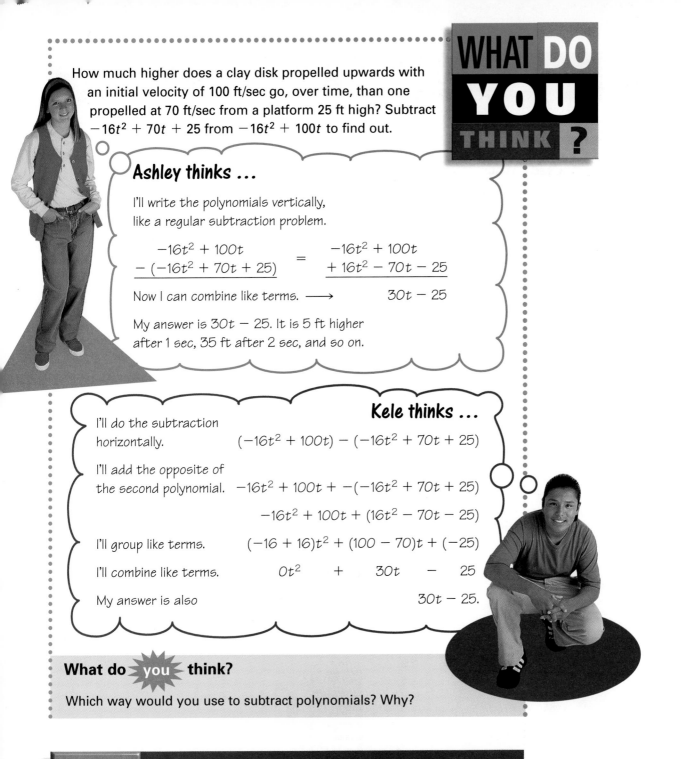

How much higher does a clay disk propelled upwards with an initial velocity of 100 ft/sec go, over time, than one propelled at 70 ft/sec from a platform 25 ft high? Subtract $-16t^2 + 70t + 25$ from $-16t^2 + 100t$ to find out.

Ashley thinks ...

I'll write the polynomials vertically, like a regular subtraction problem.

$$\begin{array}{r} -16t^2 + 100t \\ -\,(-16t^2 + 70t + 25) \end{array} = \begin{array}{r} -16t^2 + 100t \\ +\,16t^2 - 70t - 25 \end{array}$$

Now I can combine like terms. ⟶ $30t - 25$

My answer is $30t - 25$. It is 5 ft higher after 1 sec, 35 ft after 2 sec, and so on.

Kele thinks ...

I'll do the subtraction horizontally.
$$(-16t^2 + 100t) - (-16t^2 + 70t + 25)$$

I'll add the opposite of the second polynomial.
$$-16t^2 + 100t + -(-16t^2 + 70t + 25)$$
$$-16t^2 + 100t + (16t^2 - 70t - 25)$$

I'll group like terms.
$$(-16 + 16)t^2 + (100 - 70)t + (-25)$$

I'll combine like terms.
$$0t^2 \quad + \quad 30t \quad - \quad 25$$

My answer is also $30t - 25$.

What do you think?

Which way would you use to subtract polynomials? Why?

Check   Your Understanding

1. How are addition and subtraction of polynomials related?

2. How do you find the additive inverse of a polynomial expression?

3. Add a polynomial expression and its inverse. Explain your result.

PRACTICE 10-7

Practice and Apply

1. **Getting Started** Write the additive inverse of each monomial.

    a. $-x^3$ **b.** $4x^2$ **c.** $2x$ **d.** $-7x^5$ **e.** 27

Find the additive inverse of each polynomial.

2. $3x^3 - 5x^2 + (-x) + 2$ **3.** $x^4 - 2$ **4.** $4x^2 - 12x + 9$

5. $3x^3 - (-2x)$ **6.** $-4x^3 + 7x^2 + 13x - 2$ **7.** $-x^5 + 2x + 9x^3 - 3$

Subtract Write your answers in simplest form.

8. $(5x^2 + 6x + 2) - (8x^2 - 2x - 9)$ **9.** $(2x) - (-2x^2 - 2x + 1)$

10. $(-y^3 + 3y) - (4y^2 + 3y - 1)$ **11.** $(2m - 6m^2) - (-2m^2 - 2m + 1)$

12. $(3m^2 + 3m - 5)$
      $-\ (3m^2 + 3m - 5)$

13. $(4v^3 - 3v^2 + 1)$
      $-\ (2v^3 + 5v^2 - 6v + 2)$

14. $(5g^2 + 4g - 7)$
      $-\ (2g^2 + 3g - 5)$

15. $(5a^3 - 4a^2 + 2a + 3)$
      $-\ (4a^3 + 2a^2 + 6)$

Geometry Find an expression for the area not covered by the bird.

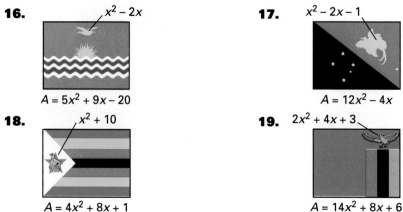

16. $x^2 - 2x$
     $A = 5x^2 + 9x - 20$

17. $x^2 - 2x - 1$
     $A = 12x^2 - 4x$

18. $x^2 + 10$
     $A = 4x^2 + 8x + 1$

19. $2x^2 + 4x + 3$
     $A = 14x^2 + 8x + 6$

20. **Test Prep** Which of the following polynomials is the additive inverse of the polynomial $2x^2 - 4x + 7$?

     Ⓐ $-2x^2 - 4x + 7$ Ⓑ $2x^2 + 4x + 7$

     Ⓒ $-2x^2 + 4x + -7$ Ⓓ $-2x^2 - 4x - 7$

Geometry Find the missing side length, based on the perimeter of each figure.

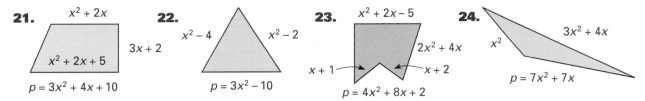

21.
$x^2 + 2x$
$3x + 2$
$x^2 + 2x + 5$
$p = 3x^2 + 4x + 10$

22.
$x^2 - 4$ $x^2 - 2$
$p = 3x^2 - 10$

23.
$x^2 + 2x - 5$
$2x^2 + 4x$
$x + 1$ $x + 2$
$p = 4x^2 + 8x + 2$

24.
$3x^2 + 4x$
x^2
$p = 7x^2 + 7x$

25. Physics How much higher does a disc propelled upwards with an initial velocity of 40 m/sec go, over time, than one propelled at 30 m/sec from a platform 8 m high? Subtract $-5t^2 + 30t + 8$ from $-5t^2 + 40t$.

Problem Solving and Reasoning

26. Critical Thinking Find two monomials with a difference of $4x^3$.

27. Communicate Josie simplified the expression $4x - 3x$ and got an answer of 1. Was she correct? Explain your reasoning.

28. Critical Thinking What would you subtract from $8x^2$ to get $-18x^2$?

29. *Journal* What conclusion can you make about two polynomials with a difference of zero? Explain your answer.

30. Critical Thinking Find the missing term.

$$(-2x^2 - 4x) - (\text{\_\_\_\_} - 3x^2) = x^2 - 8x$$

31. A *matrix* is a rectangular array of numbers. It can be used to add or subtract polynomials. The first two rows show the aligned coefficients of $x^3 - x^2 + 2x - 4$ and $2x^3 - 3x^2 + 5$. The third row shows the sum of each pair of corresponding coefficients. Use a matrix to subtract $x^5 - 3x^2 + 2$ from $3x^5 + 2x^4 - 2x + 3$.

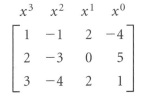

$$\begin{array}{cccc} x^3 & x^2 & x^1 & x^0 \\ \begin{bmatrix} 1 & -1 & 2 & -4 \\ 2 & -3 & 0 & 5 \\ 3 & -4 & 2 & 1 \end{bmatrix} \end{array}$$

Mixed Review

32. A heron weighing 2 kg eats 340 g of food daily. What percent of its weight does it eat daily? *[Lesson 6-2]*

Determine the prime factorization of each. *[Lesson 7-1]*

33. 90   **34.** 256   **35.** 87   **36.** 101   **37.** 375

Find the volume of each. *[Lesson 9-6]*

38.
7.25 in.
7.25 in.
7.25 in.

39.
3.8 m
10.2 m   6 m

Multiplying Polynomials and Monomials

You'll Learn ...

■ to multiply polynomials and monomials

... How It's Used

Astrophysicists often multiply numbers in scientific notation.

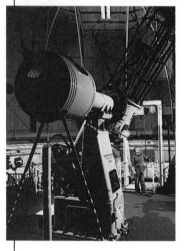

► Lesson Link In the last two lessons, you added and subtracted polynomials. In this lesson, you will learn to multiply polynomials and monomials. ◄

Explore   Multiplying Polynomials and Monomials

It's Powerful!

Compound microscopes use two or more lenses to expand the size of an image. Understanding how to multiply powers will give you an idea of how much an image can be expanded when lenses are used together.

1. Multiply 2^3 by 2^4. What is the product?

2. Is the result a power of 2? Write the result as a power of 2.

3. How does the product appear to relate to the exponents in 2^3 and 2^4?

4. Test your conjecture on the product of 3^2 and 3^4.

5. Suppose you multiply 2^3 and 100^4. Would you be able to relate the product to the exponents in the same way? Explain.

Remember

Exponential form is a base with an exponent that tells how many times the base is used as a multiplier. **[Page 97]**

Learn   Multiplying Polynomials and Monomials

Recall that 5^2 is the same as $5 \cdot 5$, and 5^4 is the same as $5 \cdot 5 \cdot 5 \cdot 5$.

To multiply $5^2 \cdot 5^4$, think $(5 \cdot 5)(5 \cdot 5 \cdot 5 \cdot 5)$. This is 5^6.

When you multiply two powers with the same base, add their exponents.

MULTIPLYING POWERS WITH LIKE BASES

In words: When multiplying powers with like bases, add their exponents.

In symbols: $a^m \cdot a^n = a^{m+n}$ **Example:** $x^4 \cdot x^5 = x^{4+5} = x^9$

Example 1

a. Multiply $6^7 \times 6^8$.

$$6^7 \times 6^8 = 6^{7+8} = 6^{15}$$

b. Multiply 2×2^5. (Note that 2 is 2^1.)

$$2^1 \times 2^5 = 2^{1+5} = 2^6$$

The methods for multiplying numerical bases, such as 6 and 2 above, can help you multiply monomials.

Example 2

a. Multiply x by x^4.

x is x^1.

$$x^1 \cdot x^4 = (x)(x \cdot x \cdot x \cdot x) = x^{1+4} = x^5$$

b. Multiply $2x^2(3x^3)$.

$$2x^2 \cdot 3x^3 = 2 \cdot 3(x \cdot x)(x \cdot x \cdot x) = 6x^{2+3} = 6x^5$$

Try It

Multiply.

a. $5^2 \times 5^4$ **b.** $8^3 \times 8^0$ **c.** $x^5(x^3)$ **d.** $4x^3 \cdot -8x^3$

Because you can multiply a monomial times a monomial, the distributive property can help you multiply a monomial times a polynomial.

Example 3

a. Multiply $5x^2$ by $2x^3 + 6$.

$5x^2(2x^3 + 6) = 5x^2 \cdot 2x^3 + 5x^2 \cdot 6$ Use the distributive property.

$= 10x^{3+2} + 30x^2$ Multiply monomials.

$= 10x^5 + 30x^2$ Simplify.

b. Multiply $-5x^4$ by $3x + 5 - 2x^3$.

$-5x^4(3x + 5 - 2x^3)$

$= -5x^4 \cdot 3x + -5x^4 \cdot 5 + -5x^4 \cdot -2x^3$ Use the distributive property.

$= -15x^{4+1} + -25x^4 + 10x^{4+3}$ Multiply monomials.

$= -15x^5 - 25x^4 + 10x^7$ Simplify.

Try It

a. Multiply $-2x^2$ by $5x^4 + 6x$.   **b.** Multiply $2x^2$ by $3x^2 + 5x - 1$.

In Chapter 2, you studied scientific notation. The rules for multiplying powers can help you multiply two numbers written in scientific notation.

Examples

4 The smaller the bird, the faster it needs to flap its wings to stay airborne. A hummingbird flaps its wings 1.5×10^3 times per min. How many times would it flap its wings if it could stay airborne for a year (5.256×10^5 min)?

$(1.5 \times 10^3)(5.256 \times 10^5)$

$= (1.5 \cdot 5.256) \times (10^3 \cdot 10^5)$ Group numbers and bases together.

$= 7.884 \qquad \times \qquad 10^8$ Multiply the numbers, add the exponents.

A hummingbird would flap its wings 7.884×10^8 times, or approximately 800 million times in a year.

5 A light year, the distance light travels in a year, is 5.87×10^{12} miles. A parsec is 3.26×10^0 light years. Multiply to find how many miles are in a parsec. Write the answer in scientific notation.

$(5.87 \times 10^{12}) \times (3.26 \times 10^0)$

$= (5.87 \cdot 3.26) \times (10^{12} \cdot 10^0)$ Group numbers and bases together.

$\approx 19.1 \times 10^{12}$ Multiply. Add exponents.

$\approx 1.91 \times 10^{13}$ Rewrite in scientific notation.

There are about 1.91×10^{13} miles in a parsec.

Try It

a. Multiply 7×10^4 by 5×10^6. Write the answer in scientific notation.

b. In 1995, the estimated population of the U. S. was 2.6×10^8. Each person's share of the national debt is about $\$1.9 \times 10^4$. What is the national debt?

Check | Your Understanding

1. Explain how to multiply two powers with the same base.

2. Why can't you simplify the product of w^3 and x^2?

3. When multiplying $-2x^3$ by a polynomial, how do you know what the sign of each term will be?

10-8 Exercises and Applications

Practice and Apply

1. **Getting Started** Use these steps to multiply x^4 by x^3.
   a. Write x^4 as the product of factors. _____ • _____ • _____ • _____.
   b. Write x^3 as the product of factors. _____ • _____ • _____.
   c. Count the total number of x factors. _____.
   d. $x^4 \cdot x^3 =$ _____.

Multiply.

2. $7^2 \cdot 7^7$ 3. $4^1 \cdot 4^6$ 4. $c^3 \cdot c^6$ 5. $2r^2 \cdot 3r^4$ 6. $(-4r^3)(5r^2)$

7. $(-3d^6)(8d^4)$ 8. $(-s^2)(-s^2)$ 9. $(4f^6)(5f^9)$ 10. $8y^2 \cdot y^0$

11. $9b^3 \cdot \frac{1}{3}b^2$ 12. $4y^2(-3y^5 - 6)$ 13. $-6t(1 - t^2)$ 14. $-2s^7(s^2 + 2s - 1)$

15. $5g^4(3g^3 - 2g^2 + 5g + 8)$ 16. $-\frac{1}{2}a^2(10a - 8)$ 17. $m(2m + 4)$

18. **Test Prep** Which monomial is the product of $-5x^3 \cdot -5x^3$?
    Ⓐ $-10x^3$ Ⓑ $25x^3$ Ⓒ $25x^6$ Ⓓ $-10x^6$

Multiply each of the following. Write your answers in scientific notation.

19. $(3.2 \times 10^4) \cdot (3.1 \times 10^5)$ 20. $(1.3 \times 10^2) \cdot (2.7 \times 10^6)$ 21. $(5.1 \times 10^3) \cdot (1.6 \times 10^3)$

22. Find an expression for the area of each region and the total area of the figure. Simplify if possible.

$2x$ | $3x + 1$ | $5x - 2$ | 4 | $4x + 5x + 3$

23. **Journal** Why do you add exponents when you multiply powers with the same base?

24. Find the volume of the bird house.

25. If each person's share of the national debt is 1.9×10^4 dollars, how much of the debt are the people in the following states responsible for?
    a. Florida: population 1.3×10^7
    b. Oklahoma: population 3.1×10^6
    c. Wyoming: population 4.5×10^5
    d. California: population 3.1×10^7

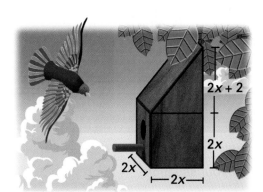

$2x + 2$
$2x$
$2x$
$2x$

26. Geometry Multiply to find an expression for the volume of the box. Simplify if possible.

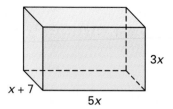

$3x$

$x + 7$

$5x$

Problem Solving and Reasoning

27. Math Reasoning What is $(3^2)^3$? (Think of it as $3^2 \cdot 3^2 \cdot 3^2$.) What is the expanded product $(a^2)^3$?

28. Critical Thinking Find an expression for the surface area of the figure at the right.

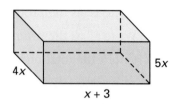

$5x$

$4x$

$x + 3$

29. Communicate When you multiplied powers with like bases, you added exponents.

a. What do you think you would do when dividing powers with like bases?

b. Try your conjecture on $\dfrac{2^3}{2^2}$

Mixed Review

Find the GCF of each set of numbers. *[Lesson 7-2]*

30. 40, 56   **31.** 125, 175   **32.** 18, 48   **33.** 63, 15, 126

Find the volume of each after the dilation. *[Lesson 9-7]*

34. Scale factor = 0.5

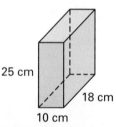

25 cm

18 cm

10 cm

35. Scale factor = 4

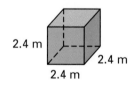

2.4 m

2.4 m

2.4 m

36. Scale factor = $\dfrac{1}{3}$

1 in.

12 in.

9 in.

Project Progress

Decide on a model. (You might also try graphing some polynomial functions, such as $y = x^3$, before you decide.) Explain how the model you chose fits or does not fit your situation.

Problem Solving

Understand

Plan

Solve

Look Back

In this Connect, you will link your knowledge of polynomials.

Which Came First?

Materials: Centimeter cubes

Stacked boxes of eggs are to be marked "fragile." Suppose all visible sides are marked. How many boxes will be marked on 1 side? On 2 sides? Use cubes to simulate the exercise.

1. Build a 2 by 2 by 2 cube. How many small cubes did you use? If all the visible faces are marked, how many cubes will have 3 marked faces? 2 marked faces? 1 marked face? 0 marked faces? Copy the table and complete the column for the 2 by 2 by 2 cube.

2. Build a 3 by 3 by 3 cube. Complete the column for this cube. Then build a 4 by 4 by 4 cube, and so on, to finish the table. Describe any patterns you see in the table.

	Dimensions			
	$2 \times 2 \times 2$	$3 \times 3 \times 3$	$4 \times 4 \times 4$	$5 \times 5 \times 5$
Number of boxes				
Number with 3 Sides Marked				
Number with 2 Sides Marked				
Number with 1 Side Marked				
Number with 0 Sides Marked				

3. For an $n \times n \times n$ cube of boxes, how many boxes are there? If all visible faces of the $n \times n \times n$ cube are marked, match the number of boxes to the correct expression.

   a. The total number of boxes   **i.** 8

   b. The number with 3 marked sides   **ii.** $12(n - 2)$

   c. The number with 2 marked sides   **iii.** n^3

   d. The number with 1 marked side   **iv.** $(n - 2)^3$

   e. The number with 0 marked sides   **v.** $6(n - 2)^2$

4. In a 20 by 20 by 20 cube, how many boxes would be unmarked?

Identify each polynomial expression as a monomial, binomial, trinomial, or none of these. Explain your choice.

1. $4x^2 + x$ **2.** $4x + x^5 + 2$ **3.** $-2x^3$ **4.** $x^3 + x^2 - x + 3$

Find the degree of each polynomial expression. Write the polynomial expression in descending order.

5. $-6 + 8x$ **6.** $2x^3 + 3x^2 - 9$ **7.** $x^2 - x - x^5$ **8.** $28x$ **9.** $x^7 - 3$

Simplify each if possible. If the expression cannot be simplified, write "already simplified." Write your answer in descending order.

10. $-6x^2 - 3x + 8x^3 + 2x$ **11.** $8x^2 + 8x$

12. $-6y^3 + 4y + -3y^3 - 5y$ **13.** $8x - 2x + 4x + 5$

14. $(2x^2 - 5x + 2) + (-4x^2 - 3x)$ **15.** $(2x) - (-2x^2 - 2x + 1)$

16. $\begin{array}{l} (5x^2 + 3x + 1) \\ + (3x^2 + 4x - 5) \end{array}$ **17.** $\begin{array}{l} (5p^2 + 3p - 7) \\ - (4p^2 + 5p + 2) \end{array}$

18. $a(a^7)$ **19.** $x^2 \cdot x^4$ **20.** $3y(y^2 + 2y - 4)$ **21.** $4x^2 \cdot -5x^8$

22. $-2m^2(2m - 6)$ **23.** $(y + 3)y$ **24.** $x^5 \cdot y^5$ **25.** $x^3(x^2 + 5)x$

26. The function $h = -5(t^2 - 5t + 10)$ can be used to find the approximate height of a launched flare in t sec. Write this function another way.

Test Prep

When asked to multiply numbers in scientific notation, remember to group numbers together and bases together, then add exponents.

27. Which is the product of 1.2×10^6 and 4.1×10^8?

   Ⓐ $5.3 \cdot 10^{14}$ Ⓑ $4.92 \cdot 10^2$

   Ⓒ $4.92 \cdot 10^{14}$ Ⓓ $4.92 \cdot 10^{48}$

28. Multiply to find the expression for each area. Add; Simplify if possible.

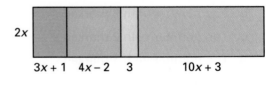

$2x$ $3x + 1$ $4x - 2$ 3 $10x + 3$

Variation

When a situation can be modeled by a linear function, where y divided by x is constant, y varies directly with x. This is called **direct variation.** If one quantity is doubled, the other is doubled. For example:

Stamps (x)	1	2	3	4	5
Price (y)	0.32	0.64	0.96	1.28	1.60

$\frac{y}{x} = 0.32$. The price varies directly with the number of stamps.

But if the *product* of x and y is constant, the variables are *inversely* related. If one quantity is doubled, the other is halved. This is **inverse variation.** For example:

Gallons Used (x)	1	2	3	4	5
Miles per Gallon (y)	120	60	40	30	24

The product of x and y is 120.

Are the quantities in each of the following directly related or inversely related?

1. Your cost for a field trip depends on the number of students who sign up.

2. The number of snacks needed for the swim team depends on the number of swimmers.

3. The time it takes to read *Don Quixote* depends on the number of pages you read each day.

4. In the 1500s, when Michelangelo was commissioned to paint the ceiling of the Sistine Chapel, he spent about 216 weeks only inches away from the vast panorama. How many artists would have been needed in order to complete the painting of the ceiling in 18 weeks? In 4 weeks?

Chapter 10 Assessment

1. For the function machine shown,

   In   Subtract 15   Out

   a. Find the output value for an input of 12.

   b. Find the input value for an output of 31.

2. What is a possible rule for the input and output shown in the table?

Input	5	7	9	11
Output	−11	−15	−19	−23

3. For the function rule $y = 4x - 7$, complete the table of values.

x	−1	0	1	2	3
y					

4. Is the area of a house (in ft^2) a function of the number of rooms in the house? Explain.

5. Graph the function $y = 1.25x$.

6. Graph each pair of functions and describe the similarities and differences.

   a. $y = x^2 - 3$ and $y = 3 - x^2$

   b. $y = -4x^2$ and $y = -x^2$

7. A call costs 15¢ for the first min, 10¢ for each additional min. The time is rounded to the next whole number before the charge is calculated. Graph the price as a function of time.

8. Graph the equation $y = -x + 4$. Does the equation describe a linear function?

9. Evaluate $2x^3 - 3x - 8$ for $x = 5$.

10. Write the polynomial $2x - 3x^4 + 1 + 7x^6$ in descending order and give its degree.

11. Find the additive inverse of the polynomial $-6x^2 + 12x - 5$.

Simplify, if possible. Write your answer in descending order.

12. $7 + 3x - 5x^3 + 6x$

13. $(5z^2 - 4) + (-3z^2 + 2z - 5)$

14. $(5r^3 - 2r + 5) - (7r^2 + 3r - 2)$

15. $7p^2 \cdot 3p^5$

16. $x(3x^3 - 4x^2 + 7x)$

17. $8u^5(5u^3 + 4u^2 - 3u - 2)$

18. Multiply $(4.8 \times 10^7) \cdot (1.2 \times 10^{10})$. Write your answer in scientific notation.

Find the area of each shaded region.

19.

$2x^2 - 5x - 2$

$A = 5x^2 + 3x - 4$

20.

$3x$

$2x^2 - 8x + 7$

Performance Task

A flare is shot upwards at 40 m/sec. The height after t sec is given by $h = 40t - 5t^2$. Sketch a graph of this function. Label your graph to show when the flare is rising, when it is falling, and when it hits the ground.

Multiple Choice

Choose the best answer.

1. Which pair of ratios does **not** form a proportion? *[Lesson 5-2]*

  Ⓐ $\frac{88}{121} \overset{?}{=} \frac{48}{66}$ Ⓑ $\frac{81}{36} \overset{?}{=} \frac{54}{24}$

  Ⓒ $\frac{15}{35} \overset{?}{=} \frac{24}{56}$ Ⓓ $\frac{28}{40} \overset{?}{=} \frac{55}{75}$

2. 64 is 8% of which number? *[Lesson 6-2]*

  Ⓐ 5.12   Ⓑ 12.5   Ⓒ 80   Ⓓ 800

3. Find the quotient $\frac{5}{7} \div \frac{3}{14}$. Write the answer in lowest terms. *[Lesson 7-6]*

  Ⓐ $\frac{70}{21}$ Ⓑ $\frac{13}{14}$ Ⓒ $\frac{10}{3}$ Ⓓ $\frac{15}{98}$

4. How many sides does a pentagon have? *[Lesson 8-6]*

  Ⓐ 4   Ⓑ 5   Ⓒ 6   Ⓓ 7

5. For the pyramid shown, which of the following is equal to 384? *[Lessons 9-5, 9-7]*

  Ⓐ Slant height

  Ⓑ Surface area

  Ⓒ Volume

  Ⓓ Both B and C

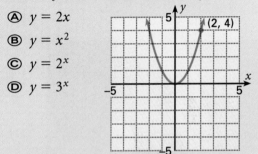

6. A circle has a diameter of 7 in. Find the approximate area of the circle. *[Lesson 9-3]*

  Ⓐ 38.5 in²   Ⓑ 44.0 in²

  Ⓒ 22.0 in²   Ⓓ 153.9 in²

7. Find the volume of a 6 ft by 4 ft by 5 ft rectangular prism. *[Lesson 9-6]*

  Ⓐ 15 ft³   Ⓑ 120 ft³

  Ⓒ 40 ft³   Ⓓ 20 ft³

8. What is a possible rule for the input and output shown in the table? *[Lesson 10-1]*

Input	6	7	8	9
Output	14	17	20	23

  Ⓐ $y = x + 8$ Ⓑ $y = \frac{1}{3}(x + 4)$

  Ⓒ $y = 3x - 4$ Ⓓ $y = x - 8$

9. Which function is shown in the graph below? *[Lessons 10-2, 10-3, 10-4]*

  Ⓐ $y = 2x$

  Ⓑ $y = x^2$

  Ⓒ $y = 2^x$

  Ⓓ $y = 3^x$

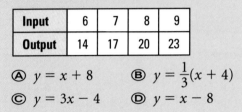

10. Which of the following is a polynomial of degree 2? *[Lesson 10-5]*

  Ⓐ $5x + 3$ Ⓑ $2x^3 + 7x - 4$

  Ⓒ $3x^2$ Ⓓ $7x^3 - 6x + 2$

11. Which of the following shows $(3x^2 + 7x - 3) + (8x^2 + 5)$ in simplest form? *[Lesson 10-6]*

  Ⓐ $11x^2 + 7x + 2$

  Ⓑ $8x^2 + 3x^2 + 7x + 2$

  Ⓒ $-5x^2 + 7x - 8$

  Ⓓ $11x^2 + 7x - 8$

12. Find the additive inverse of $4x^3 + 2x - 5$. *[Lesson 10-7]*

  Ⓐ $4x^3 - 2x + 5$ Ⓑ $-4x^3 - 2x + 5$

  Ⓒ $-4x^3 + 2x - 5$ Ⓓ $-4x^3 - 2x - 5$

13. Find the product of $2x^3 \cdot 5x^4$. *[Lesson 10-8]*

  Ⓐ $7x^{12}$ Ⓑ $7x^7$ Ⓒ $10x^{12}$ Ⓓ $10x^7$

Similarity, Congruence, and

Entertainment Link
www.mathsurf.com/8/ch11/ent

Arts & Literature Link
www.mathsurf.com/8/ch11/arts

Entertainment

A knowledge of angles and reflections is essential to successful billiard players, as they must frequently bank their shots to avoid moving their opponents' ball.

Arts & Literature

The works of Dutch artist M. C. Escher (1898–1972) consist almost entirely of interlocking, infinitely repeating designs called tessellations, which are based on translations, rotations, and reflections.

Circle Limit III by M. C. Escher.
©1996 Cordon Art-Baarn-Holland.
All rights reserved.

People of the World

Despite having asthma, Jackie Joyner-Kersee achieved world records in the heptathalon. Great athletes like her often do weight lifting training which can strengthen muscles symmetrically.

Transformations

Science Link
www.mathsurf.com/8/ch11/sci

Science

A periscope uses reflections in two mirrors, enabling the viewer to see above the line of sight. The mirrors are parallel to each other and at a 45° angle to the horizon line.

KEY MATH IDEAS

Two figures are similar if they have the same shape but not necessarily the same size. Two figures are congruent if they have the same shape and size.

For an angle in a right triangle with measure *x*, the trigonometric ratios sin, cos, and tan can be used to find the length of a side.

A line of symmetry divides a figure into two identical halves.

A tessellation is a pattern of repeated figures that covers a plane.

Social Studies

The Japanese have long perfected the art of paper folding, called *origami,* which is a striking application of the many properties of reflections.

CHAPTER PROJECT

Problem Solving

Understand
Plan
Solve
Look Back

In this project, using a 3 in. by 5 in. card, you will make a hypsometer—a device for measuring tall objects. You will use it to measure the height of a building. After you have made the hypsometer, align it with the top and bottom of the building. Determine the distance between you and the building and you'll be able to find the height of the building. Explain how this works after you've tried it.

Problem Solving Focus

**Problem
Solving**

Understand
Plan
Solve
Look Back

Checking the Rules of the Problem

After you have solved a problem, look back to make sure you followed the rules of the problem. If you followed all the rules, then your answer is probably correct.

Each problem below has three answers. State which of the three answers is correct, and which rule the other two answers didn't follow.

❶ At the Winthrop Fair, there is an apple-bobbing contest. Each contestant has two minutes to bob for apples. The one who gets the most wins. Mary, Colin, LuAnn, and Jamie enter. Mary comes up with twice as many apples as Colin. Between them, Colin and LuAnn get two fewer than Mary. Jamie gets half as many as LuAnn. All together, the four bobbers get 15 apples. How many did each get?

Answer #1	Answer #2	Answer #3
M = 8	M = 8	M = 8
C = 6	C = 2	C = 4
L = 6	L = 2	L = 2
J = 3	J = 1	J = 1

❷ Jamie met Marsha, Albert, and Seena at the fair. They all went over to the ticket booth, where they bought tickets to use on all of the rides at the fair. Jamie bought 3 times as many tickets as Marsha, but he gave $\frac{1}{3}$ of them to his little brother. Albert bought half as many tickets as Jamie. Seena bought 5 more tickets than Marsha. Marsha bought 6 fewer tickets than Albert. All together, they bought 83 tickets. How many did each person buy?

Answer #1	Answer #2	Answer #3
J = 24	J = 36	J = 18
M = 8	M = 12	M = 6
A = 12	A = 18	A = 12
S = 13	S = 17	S = 11

Bridge building is part art, part science. Engineers use science (including math!) to make sure that bridges can support the weight of the vehicles and pedestrians using them. Architects working with engineers use their artistic instincts and training to create bridges that are not only strong but pleasing to the eye.

Both strength and attractiveness are usually enhanced by a property called symmetry, which in the case of bridges means that one side is the mirror image of the other. When a symmetric bridge is made up of numerous triangles (as many bridges are), the triangles come in pairs: Each triangle on one side of a bridge has an identical twin on the other—another triangle congruent to the first one, as a mathematician would say. Later in this chapter, you will be learning more about symmetry. First, though, you will learn about congruency as well as similarity, different ways in which two triangles (and other shapes) can be alike.

Un·a·bridged

1 Why might a bridge with matching triangles on each side be stronger than one where the triangles on each side are different?

2 Why might a bridge with all vertical and horizontal bracing be less stable?

Similar Figures

▶ Lesson Link You've seen the results of scaling a rectangle. Now you'll see how angle and side measurements correspond on scale drawings. ◀

You'll Learn ...

■ to identify similar figures

... How It's Used

Sign makers use similar figures as repetitive design elements in their work.

Vocabulary

similar

corresponding angles

corresponding sides

similarity ratio

Explore   Similar Polygons

The Size Factor

Materials: Dynamic geometry software, $8\frac{1}{2}$ in. by 11 in. paper

1. With the geometry software, draw a polygon with 3, 4, or 5 sides.

2. On paper, make a table with as many columns as the polygon has sides. Label the first column "side 1," the second, "side 2," and so on.

3. Measure each side of the polygon using the measure tool, and record your measurements in your table. Use the dilate tool to shrink or enlarge your polygon. Notice that the side measurements change.

▶	·	⁄	⊙	⅄	·⌐ X⊣ ?··

Pointer

Rotate

Dilate

Rotate and Dilate

4. Record the new measurements in the appropriate columns.

5. In each column, find the ratio between the old and new measurements. What do you notice? Why do you think you got these results?

6. Use the dilate tool again and record a third set of measurements. Find the ratios between the second and third measurements for each table column. What do you notice?

7. Do you think the dilation changed the angle measurements?

Learn   Similar Figures

Two figures are **similar** if they have the same shape but not necessarily the same size.

$\triangle ABC \sim \triangle XYZ$ means $\triangle ABC$ is similar to $\triangle XYZ$.

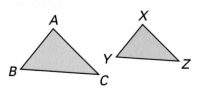

In similar figures, corresponding angles are congruent.

∠MLO and ∠SRU are corresponding angles.

In similar figures, pairs of **corresponding sides** have equal length ratios.

$\overline{TU}$ and $\overline{NO}$ are corresponding sides.

When viewing two similar figures, we see that one is a scale drawing of the other.

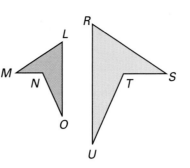

The ratio between corresponding side lengths of similar figures is the **similarity ratio**. The similarity ratio of similar figures can be compared to the scale factor of scale drawings.

Example 1

A cantilever bridge has two cantilevers that extend from both sides of a waterway. These two cantilevers meet at the middle of the waterway.

△QSR ~ △DEF. Find the similarity ratio of the two figures.

$\overline{QR}$ and $\overline{DF}$ are corresponding sides. Identify corresponding sides.

$\dfrac{m\overline{QR}}{m\overline{DF}} = \dfrac{85 \text{ ft}}{100 \text{ ft}} = \dfrac{17}{20}$ Take the ratio of their lengths.

The similarity ratio of △QSR and △DEF is $\dfrac{17}{20}$.

Example 2

The hexagons are similar. Find $m\angle XST$.

∠FAB and ∠XST are corresponding angles.

So $m\angle XST = 137°$.

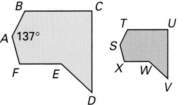

Try It

PQRS ~ BCDE

a. Find the similarity ratio of figure PQRS to figure BCDE.

b. Find the measure of ∠PQR.

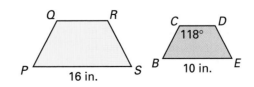

If pairs of corresponding angles are congruent, the triangles are similar.

Remember

A dilation of a figure produces a similar figure. The scale factor of a dilation can be compared to the similarity ratio of similar figures. **[Page 448]**

Example 3

Determine whether $\triangle ABC$ and $\triangle DEF$ are similar.

$\angle CAB \cong \angle FDE$

$\angle ACB \cong \angle DFE$

$\angle ABC \cong \angle DEF$

All corresponding angles are congruent.

$\triangle ABC \sim \triangle DEF$

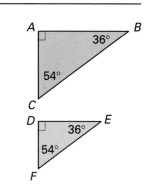

Example 4

Are the figures similar?

$\frac{1}{3}$ and $\frac{3}{5}$ are ratios for two pairs of corresponding sides.

$\frac{1}{3} \neq \frac{3}{5}$. The figures are not similar.

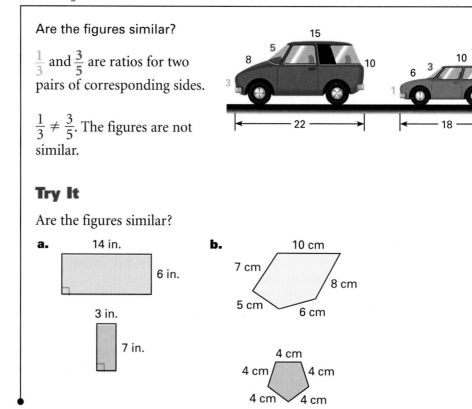

Try It

Are the figures similar?

a. 14 in. 6 in. 3 in. 7 in.

b. 10 cm 7 cm 8 cm 5 cm 6 cm

4 cm 4 cm 4 cm 4 cm 4 cm

Check | **Your Understanding**

1. If the ratio between all corresponding sides of two figures is 1, are the figures similar? Explain.

2. Are any two regular pentagons similar? Explain.

Practice and Apply

1. **Getting Started** Decide whether the triangles are similar.

   a. Write a proportion for the corresponding sides.

   b. Determine if the cross products are equal.

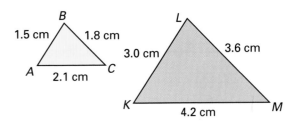

Decide whether each pair of figures is similar.

2.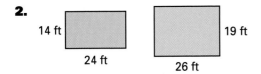

3.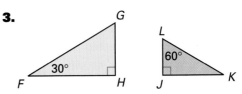

4. The two trapezoids are similar.

   a. Find x.

   b. Find the measure of $\angle 1$.

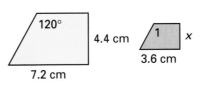

5. **Industry** The main span of New York's Brooklyn Bridge is 1595 ft long. On a blueprint for the bridge, the span measures 31.9 in. What is the scale factor of the blueprint?

6. **Measurement** The two jeans pockets are similar. Find x, the length of the top of the smaller pocket.

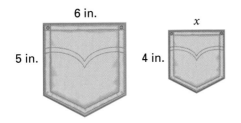

7. **Test Prep** Given that triangles ABC and DEF are similar, what is the length of side $\overline{BC}$ on $\triangle ABC$?

   Ⓐ 28 mi   Ⓑ 35 mi

   Ⓒ 14 mi   Ⓓ 42 mi

PRACTICE 11-1

8. Quadrilateral I was shrunk and flipped to make quadrilateral II. Find the similarity ratio of I to II.

9. Algebra Write an algebraic expression that represents the area of the dilation of a square with an area of 64 unit^2, where the scale factor is x.

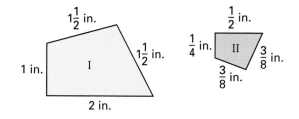

Problem Solving and Reasoning

10. Journal Are all squares similar? Are all rectangles similar? Which polygons do you think will always be similar?

11. Communicate The photo of the Pont de Brotonne in France shows how the cables that support the roadway are directly connected to the towers. A fan pattern is shown by the cables connecting several points of the roadway to several points on the tower. Tell how you know that the triangles formed by the cables on one side of a tower are not similar.

12. Technology Using geometry software, draw a polygon and dilate it by a scale factor of 2. Then measure the area of each polygon using the area tool. Calculate the ratio of the two areas. What is the area ratio for a scale factor of 3?

13. Math Reasoning Draw a conclusion about dilating figures using a scale factor less than 1 versus using a scale factor greater than 1. Give an example to support your conclusion.

Mixed Review

List all factors for each number and identify the prime factors. *[Lesson 7-1]*

14. 45   **15.** 66   **16.** 81   **17.** 48   **18.** 100

For the rule "add 5," find the output value for each input value. *[Lesson 10-1]*

19. 7   **20.** 5.5   **21.** 0.01   **22.** $\frac{3}{4}$ **23.** -22

Congruent Figures

▶ **Lesson Link** You know how to identify similar polygons. Now you'll work with polygons with the same size and shape. ◀

Explore Congruent Polygons

Congratulations! They're Twins!

Materials: Paper, Ruler, Protractor, Compass

1. On a sheet of paper, draw a polygon with 6, 7, or 8 sides. Do this so no one can see your work.

2. With your group, take turns describing your figure as the others try to draw an identical figure. You can use length and angle measurements to describe your figure.

3. When describing your figure, what did you say to make it easier for those who are drawing? What units of measurement did you use?

4. When taking your turn to draw, what did you find most helpful?

You'll Learn ...

■ to identify congruent figures

... How It's Used

The art of jewelry-making exhibits the use of congruent shapes.

Vocabulary

congruent polygons

Learn Congruent Figures

Congruent polygons have the same shape and size.

To indicate congruence, write $ABCD \cong NMLK$.

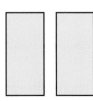

Congruent

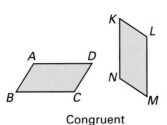

Congruent

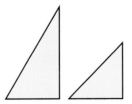

Not congruent

Corresponding angles of congruent figures are congruent.

$\angle DCB \cong \angle KLM$ in the congruent parallelograms.

Corresponding sides of congruent figures are congruent.

$\overline{AD} \cong \overline{NK}$ in the congruent parallelograms.

You can determine whether two figures are congruent by matching a tracing or comparing measurements.

Example 1

Determine whether the two figures are congruent.

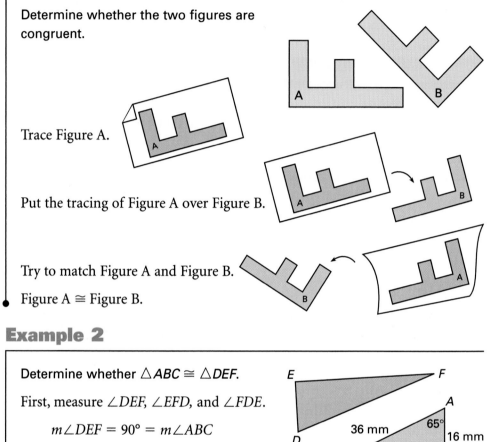

Trace Figure A.

Put the tracing of Figure A over Figure B.

Try to match Figure A and Figure B.

Figure A ≅ Figure B.

Example 2

Determine whether △*ABC* ≅ △*DEF*.

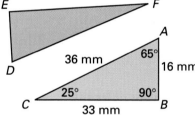

First, measure ∠*DEF*, ∠*EFD*, and ∠*FDE*.

$m\angle DEF = 90° = m\angle ABC$

$m\angle EFD = 20° \neq m\angle BCA$

$m\angle FDE = 70° \neq m\angle CAB$

Measure $\overline{EF}$, $\overline{DF}$, and $\overline{DE}$.

$m\,\overline{EF} = 37 \text{ mm} \neq m\,\overline{BC}$

$m\,\overline{DF} = 40 \text{ mm} \neq m\,\overline{AC}$

$m\,\overline{DE} = 13 \text{ mm} \neq m\,\overline{AB}$

All corresponding parts are not congruent. △*ABC* and △*DEF* are not congruent.

Try It

Determine whether the squares are congruent.

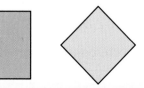

Example 3

Determine whether the two hexagons are congruent.

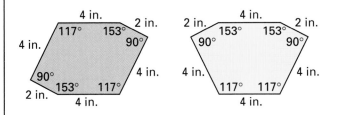

They both have the same angle and side length measures, but the measurements do not occur in the same order. The hexagons are not congruent.

If two figures are congruent and you know the measurements of one, you can find the measurements of the other figure.

Example 4

Trapezoids *ABCD* and *EFGH* are congruent. Find the length of $\overline{FG}$.

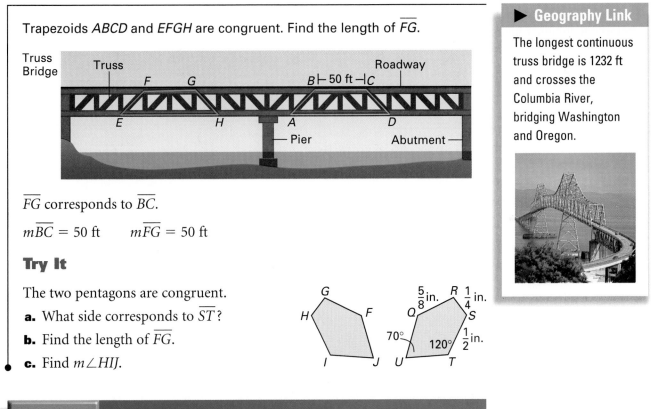

► **Geography Link**

The longest continuous truss bridge is 1232 ft and crosses the Columbia River, bridging Washington and Oregon.

$\overline{FG}$ corresponds to $\overline{BC}$.

$m\overline{BC} = 50$ ft $m\overline{FG} = 50$ ft

Try It

The two pentagons are congruent.

a. What side corresponds to $\overline{ST}$?

b. Find the length of $\overline{FG}$.

c. Find $m\angle HIJ$.

Check Your Understanding

1. Are any two regular hexagons congruent? Are they similar? Explain.

2. If all the angles of an octagon are congruent to the angles of another octagon, are the octagons congruent? Explain.

Practice and Apply

1. **Getting Started** Determine whether the parallelograms are congruent.

   a. Measure the corresponding sides.

   b. Measure the corresponding angles.

The two pentagons are congruent.

2. Find $m\angle STP$.

3. Find $m\overline{XY}$.

Determine whether each pair of figures is congruent.

4.

5.

6. **Test Prep** Two of the figures shown are congruent. Which are they?

   Ⓐ 2 and 4   Ⓑ 1 and 3

   Ⓒ 1 and 2   Ⓓ 3 and 4

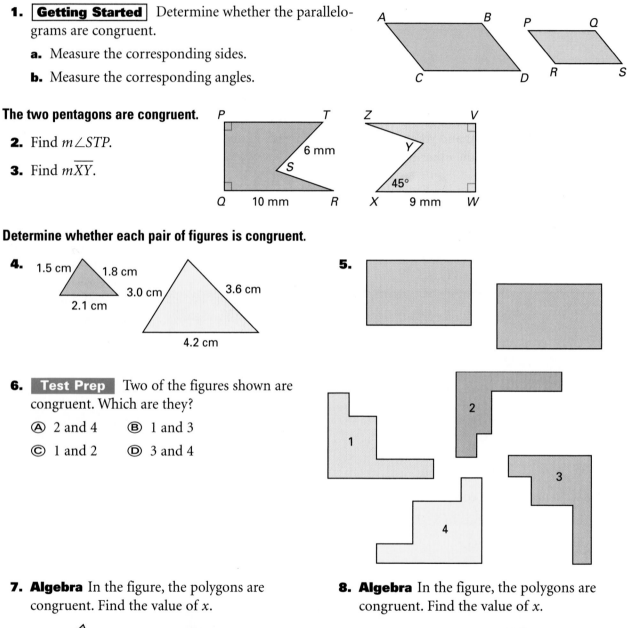

7. **Algebra** In the figure, the polygons are congruent. Find the value of x.

8. **Algebra** In the figure, the polygons are congruent. Find the value of x.

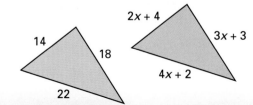

9. **Geometry** Construct a polygon congruent to the one shown, and describe how you did it. Label the vertices and the corresponding sides.

Problem Solving and Reasoning

10. **Communicate** The photograph shows the Forth Rail Bridge, a cantilever bridge in Scotland. Terry thinks that the highlighted triangles on the bridge are not congruent because they don't appear to be the same size in the photo. Explain the error in Terry's reasoning.

11. **Technology** With geometry software, construct a triangle congruent to the one shown. Measure the length of each side. Then move the vertices around until all side measures match those in the figure. (You may not be able to match them exactly; just do your best.) Now measure the angles inside the triangle, rounding to the nearest degree. How did the corresponding angles compare?

12. **Math Reasoning** If you are checking two triangles for congruency, do you need to measure every side and every angle? If not, how many measurements do you need?

13. What steps would you perform to construct a copy of this regular octagon? Is there more than one way to do it?

Mixed Review

Find the GCF for each pair of numbers. [Lesson 7-2]

14. 13, 52   15. 16, 24   16. 28, 49   17. 20, 50   18. 15, 40

Decide whether each equation describes a function. [Lesson 10-2]

19. $y = 2$ 20. $y = 3x + 2$ 21. $y = -4x$ 22. $y = |x + 1|$

Triangle Congruence

▶ **Lesson Link** Now that you've learned about congruent figures, you're ready to take a closer look at triangles and ways of showing their congruence. ◀

You'll Learn ...

■ to identify congruent triangles

... How It's Used

A percussionist can have a set of triangles. If the triangles are not congruent, then they will produce different pitches.

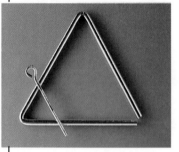

Vocabulary

Side-Side-Side

Side-Angle-Side

Angle-Side-Angle

Side-Angle-Angle

Explore | **Congruent Triangles**

Stone Bridges

Below is an illustration of a stone bridge with the wooden framework used to build it. The people who built the bridge set up the wooden framework to support the stones as the bridge was built.

Because the sketch is not drawn to scale, you only know the measurements shown. You will determine whether triangles that appear to be congruent are congruent.

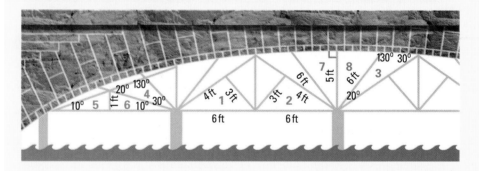

1. With triangles 1 and 2, all corresponding sides are congruent. Are the triangles congruent? Explain.

2. With triangles 3 and 4, all corresponding angles are congruent. Are the triangles congruent? Explain.

3. With the measurements given for triangles 5 and 6, do you know if they are congruent? Explain.

4. With the measurements given for triangles 7 and 8, do you know if they are congruent? Explain.

5. Discuss the minimum information necessary to determine whether or not two triangles are congruent.

Learn | Triangle Congruence

You don't need every measurement to know that two triangles are congruent. Small marks are used to signify that corresponding parts are congruent.

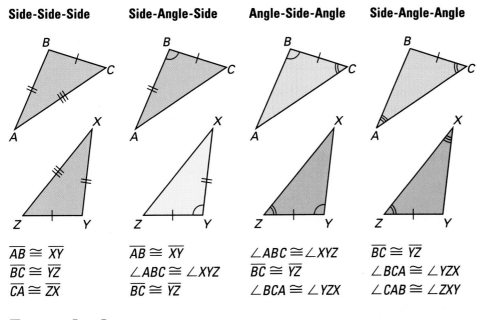

Side-Side-Side

$\overline{AB} \cong \overline{XY}$
$\overline{BC} \cong \overline{YZ}$
$\overline{CA} \cong \overline{ZX}$

Side-Angle-Side

$\overline{AB} \cong \overline{XY}$
$\angle ABC \cong \angle XYZ$
$\overline{BC} \cong \overline{YZ}$

Angle-Side-Angle

$\angle ABC \cong \angle XYZ$
$\overline{BC} \cong \overline{YZ}$
$\angle BCA \cong \angle YZX$

Side-Angle-Angle

$\overline{BC} \cong \overline{YZ}$
$\angle BCA \cong \angle YZX$
$\angle CAB \cong \angle ZXY$

Example 1

Are the triangles congruent? If so, state the rule that justifies your answer.

Yes, because of the Side-Side-Side rule.

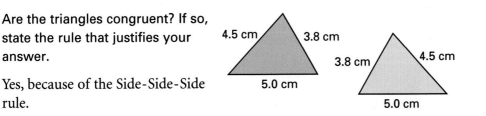

Try It

Bascule bridges, as seen along the Chicago River, open upward to let ships pass. Suppose the dimensions are as labeled.

Are the two triangles congruent? If so, state the rule that justifies your answer.

Test Prep

Use initials to help remember facts for a test.

SSS = Side-Side-Side

SAS = Side-Angle-Side

ASA = Angle-Side-Angle

SAA = Side-Angle-Angle

Example 2

Are the triangles congruent? If so, state the rule that justifies your answer.

Yes, because of the Side-Angle-Side rule.

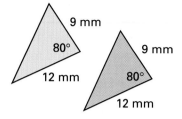

Example 3

Are the triangles congruent? If so, state the rule that justifies your answer.

No. The length measurements "2 m" do not appear on corresponding sides.

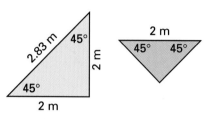

Try It

History Link

Completed in May of 1937, the Golden Gate Bridge in California spans 6450 ft. That's more than a mile!

Suspension bridges, such as the Golden Gate Bridge in San Francisco, are used to span long distances.

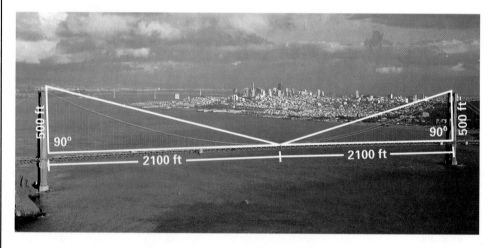

Are the two triangles shown in this bridge congruent? If so, state the rule that justifies your answer.

Check Your Understanding

1. Why isn't there an Angle-Angle-Angle rule? Explain.

2. Suppose you know that four parts of a triangle are congruent to four corresponding parts of another triangle. Is this enough information to know that the triangles are congruent? Explain.

Practice and Apply

1. **Getting Started** $\triangle GHI \cong \triangle SQR$ and $\overline{HI}$ corresponds to $\overline{QR}$.

   a. $\overline{HG}$ corresponds to _____.

   b. $\overline{IG}$ corresponds to _____.

   c. $\angle H$ corresponds to _____.

   d. $\angle I$ corresponds to _____.

   e. $\angle G$ corresponds to _____.

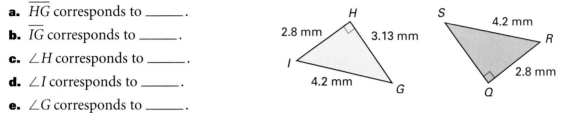

2. For each pair, what rule tells you that the two triangles are congruent?

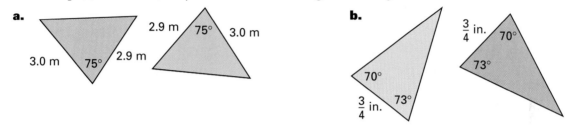

State whether each pair of triangles has congruence; if it does, give the rule that justifies your answer.

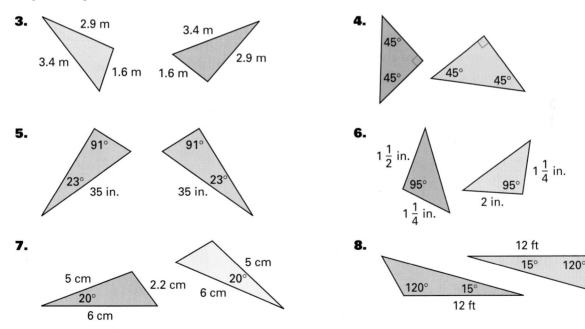

3.

4.

5.

6.

7.

8.

9. For each rule, draw a pair of triangles that satisfy it.

   a. Side-Side-Side   b. Angle-Side-Angle   c. Side-Angle-Side

10. [Test Prep] How far is it from Cauchy Square to the Weierstrasse?

Ⓐ 0.20 km

Ⓑ 0.17 km

Ⓒ 0.10 km

Ⓓ Insufficient information

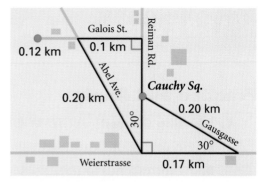

11. Career A surveyor at this native-plant preservation area concludes that the fences on the right and left sides of the land are the same length. State the rule used to determine this.

Problem Solving and Reasoning

12. Communicate Refer to the two triangles and find $m\overline{EF}$ if you can; if not, explain why not.

13. Math Reasoning The three angles of one triangle are congruent to the three angles of a second triangle. Are the triangles congruent? Explain.

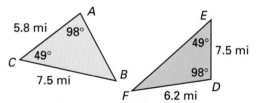

14. Critical Thinking Truss bridges are built over canyons and rivers. The parts of the trusses are arranged in the form of triangles, as in the portion shown. Make a similar shape out of line segments. Then, taking as few measurements as possible (including at least one angle), finish your truss by adding a left half that is the mirror image of the right. What is the minimum number of measurements you need?

Mixed Review

Find the LCM for each pair of numbers. *[Lesson 7-3]*

15. 6, 20   **16.** 35, 40   **17.** 2, 10   **18.** 5, 12   **19.** 4, 15

Graph each function and decide whether it is linear or quadratic. *[Lesson 10-3]*

20. $y = x^2 + 1$ **21.** $y = 4x$ **22.** $y = -x^2$ **23.** $y = (-x)^2$

Trigonometry

▶ **Lesson Link** You've seen various ways of finding missing side lengths of triangles. Now you'll learn another way. ◀

The longest side of a right triangle is the hypotenuse. You can refer to the two other sides in relationship to an acute angle.

The side next to ∠1 is the **adjacent leg** . The side across from ∠1 is the **opposite leg** .

You'll Learn ...

■ to use ratios in order to find missing side lengths of a right triangle

... How It's Used

Navigators continuously calculate to determine the distance between their ship and their destination.

Explore Trigonometric Ratios

Finding the Right Ratio

Materials: Dynamic geometry software, $8\frac{1}{2}$ in. by 11 in. paper

1. With the software, draw three similar right triangles. In each triangle, label one acute angle 1, 2, and 3.

2. On a sheet of paper, make a table with six columns labeled "angle," "opposite," "adjacent," "hypotenuse," " $\frac{opposite}{hypotenuse}$," and " $\frac{adjacent}{hypotenuse}$."

3. Record the measures of ∠1, ∠2, and ∠3 in the "angle" column.

4. Use the measure tool to find the length of each side of all three triangles and record your measurements in the table.

5. Use the measurements from Steps 3 and 4 to calculate and record the ratios for the remaining columns. Do you notice a pattern? Explain.

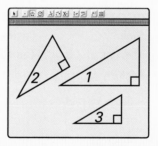

Vocabulary

adjacent leg

opposite leg

trigonometric ratios

sine

cosine

tangent

Learn Trigonometry

As you have already learned, when triangles have two pairs of congruent angles and a corresponding pair of congruent sides, the triangles are congruent.

Now you will learn how to find the other sides of right triangles.

Example 1

Use the right triangle shown to answer each.

a. Name the hypotenuse. Answer: $\overline{AC}$

b. Name the leg opposite $\angle CAB$. Answer: $\overline{BC}$

c. Name the leg adjacent to $\angle CAB$. Answer: $\overline{AB}$

Try It

a. Name the hypotenuse.

b. Name the leg opposite $\angle MKL$.

c. Name the leg adjacent to $\angle MKL$.

For any right triangle, the lengths of the hypotenuse, an adjacent leg, and an opposite leg may be compared by using three common **trigonometric ratios** .

TRIGONOMETRIC RATIOS

Sine	Cosine	Tangent
The sine of x is	The cosine of x is	The tangent of x is
$\sin(x) = \frac{\text{opposite}}{\text{hypotenuse}}$	$\cos(x) = \frac{\text{adjacent}}{\text{hypotenuse}}$	$\tan(x) = \frac{\text{opposite}}{\text{adjacent}}$

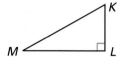

Example 2

For the triangle shown, evaluate the trigonometric ratios for $\angle CAB$.

$$\sin \angle CAB = \frac{\text{opposite}}{\text{hypotenuse}} = \frac{3}{5} = 0.6$$

$$\cos \angle CAB = \frac{\text{adjacent}}{\text{hypotenuse}} = \frac{4}{5} = 0.8$$

$$\tan \angle CAB = \frac{\text{opposite}}{\text{adjacent}} = \frac{3}{4} = 0.75$$

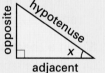

$$\sin \angle CAB = 0.6 \qquad \cos \angle CAB = 0.8 \qquad \tan \angle CAB = 0.75$$

Try It

Use the triangle in Example 2 to answer each question.

a. What is the sine ratio of $\angle ACB$?

b. What is the tangent ratio of $\angle ACB$?

Example 3

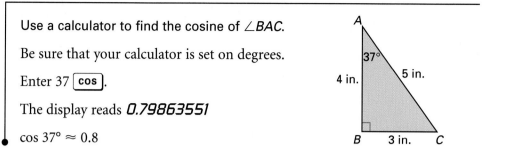

Use a calculator to find the cosine of $\angle BAC$.

Be sure that your calculator is set on degrees.

Enter 37 $\boxed{\cos}$.

The display reads *0.79863551*

$\cos 37° \approx 0.8$

Using trigonometric ratios, we can find the unknown side lengths of a right triangle using one acute angle and one known side length.

Example 4

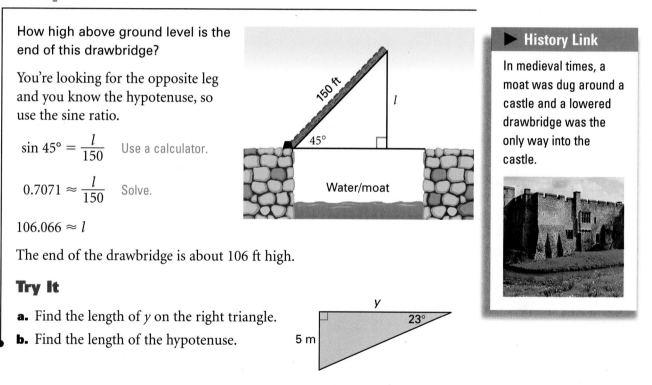

How high above ground level is the end of this drawbridge?

You're looking for the opposite leg and you know the hypotenuse, so use the sine ratio.

$\sin 45° = \dfrac{l}{150}$ Use a calculator.

$0.7071 \approx \dfrac{l}{150}$ Solve.

$106.066 \approx l$

The end of the drawbridge is about 106 ft high.

Try It

a. Find the length of y on the right triangle.

b. Find the length of the hypotenuse.

► **History Link**

In medieval times, a moat was dug around a castle and a lowered drawbridge was the only way into the castle.

Check Your Understanding

1. If you know the sine of one angle in a right triangle, what two sides do you know the ratio for? Explain.

2. What happens when you use your calculator to find the sine, cosine, and tangent of 90°?

3. How can the sine ratio for a given angle be the same no matter how big the triangle?

Practice and Apply

1. **Getting Started** Find the length of side $\overline{PQ}$ on the triangle shown.

   a. Is $\overline{QR}$ opposite or adjacent to $\angle QPR$?

   b. Is $\overline{PQ}$ opposite or adjacent to $\angle QPR$?

   c. Which ratio, sine, cosine, or tangent, compares the side opposite to the side adjacent?

   d. Use the ratio from 1c above to find the length of $\overline{PQ}$.

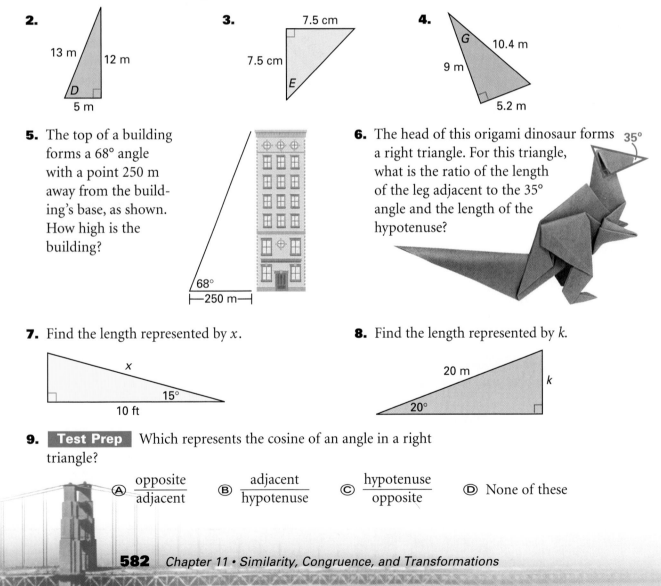

Use the lengths of the sides to write and evaluate the sine, cosine, and tangent ratios for each of the labeled angles.

2.

   13 m 12 m
   D
   5 m

3.   7.5 cm

   7.5 cm
   E

4.   G   10.4 m

   9 m
   5.2 m

5. The top of a building forms a 68° angle with a point 250 m away from the building's base, as shown. How high is the building?

   68°
   ├─250 m─┤

6. The head of this origami dinosaur forms a right triangle. For this triangle, what is the ratio of the length of the leg adjacent to the 35° angle and the length of the hypotenuse?   35°

7. Find the length represented by x.

   x
   15°
   10 ft

8. Find the length represented by k.

   20 m
   k
   20°

9. **Test Prep** Which represents the cosine of an angle in a right triangle?

   Ⓐ $\dfrac{\text{opposite}}{\text{adjacent}}$ Ⓑ $\dfrac{\text{adjacent}}{\text{hypotenuse}}$ Ⓒ $\dfrac{\text{hypotenuse}}{\text{opposite}}$ Ⓓ None of these

10. **Science** A model rocket travels straight up from its launch pad. At a point, there is a 55° angle. Determine the distance between the nose of the rocket and the launch pad.

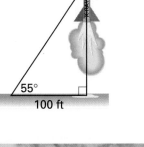

55°
100 ft

Problem Solving and Reasoning

11. **Critical Thinking** The New River Gorge Bridge in West Virginia has the world's longest single steel span, arching 876 ft above the river. The bridge forms a 30° angle with the side of the gorge. How long is the bridge?

12. **Communicate** Suppose two right triangles have a pair of congruent acute angles. Are the triangles similar? Are they congruent? Explain.

13. **Geometry** Construct a right triangle with a 60° angle. Then measure all three sides. Use your calculator to find the sine, cosine, and tangent of 60°.

14. **Choose a Strategy** A right triangle has a 15° angle and the adjacent side is 6 ft. A classmate calculates that the length of the opposite leg is 1.6 ft and the hypotenuse is 7 ft. Check your classmate's calculations and make corrections if necessary.

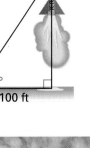

30°

876 ft

Problem Solving

STRATEGIES

• Look for a Pattern
• Make an Organized List
• Make a Table
• Guess and Check
• Work Backward
• Use Logical Reasoning
• Draw a Diagram
• Solve a Simpler Problem

Mixed Review

Write each as a fraction or mixed number in lowest terms. *[Lesson 7-4]*

15. 2.02   16. 0.05   17. 4.24   18. 1.33   19. 9.9

Identify each function as linear, quadratic, exponential, or step. *[Lesson 10-4]*

20. $y = 0.5x^2$ 21. $y = 0.5^x$ 22. $y = 5$ 23. $y = 5x$

Project Progress

Stand the 3 in. by 5 in. card on the 3 in. side. Cut a slit the width of one ruler above the bottom of the card. Fold the longer flap vertically so it makes a right angle. Along the crease of the flap, mark $\frac{1}{2}$ in. lengths. Tape the ruler-width part of the card onto a ruler.

Problem Solving

Understand
Plan
Solve
Look Back

Indirect Measurement

You'll Learn ...

■ to apply your knowledge of geometry and trigonometric ratios

... How It's Used

Paleontologists use indirect measurement to figure out what the size of a living dinosaur was based on bone measurements.

▶ Lesson Link You've seen how to find the side lengths of right triangles using trigonometric ratios. Now you'll apply these ratios to real-world situations. ◀

Explore | Indirect Measurement

It's Not What You Know, It's Where You Know It

Materials: Dynamic geometry software, $8\frac{1}{2}$ in. by 11 in. paper

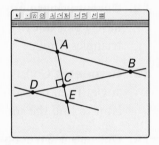

1. Draw two parallel lines. Draw two transversals that are perpendicular to each other.

2. Label all intersection points.

3. On paper, make a table with three columns. Label the columns "part," "measurement," and "reason."

4. In the first column of your table, list all sides and all angles of both triangles that appear in your drawing.

5. Measure all angles and all side lengths of these two triangles. Enter the results in the second column of your table.

6. Find as many other side and angle measurements as you can and enter them in your table's second column. For each measurement, use the third column of your table to briefly state how you got the measurement.

7. Discuss the results with your group. How many angle measurements could you find? How many side measurements?

8. What was listed most frequently in the third column of your table?

Learn | Indirect Measurement

Sometimes a length can't be measured with a ruler. Often you can find the measurement indirectly.

When solving a problem with similar triangles, you can use the similarity ratio.

Example 1

Part of a bridge roadway is 150 m long. On its scale model, the corresponding length is 2 m. On the same model, a cable from the roadway to the top of a tower is almost 2.17 m. How long is the actual cable?

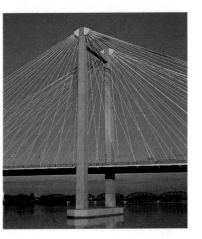

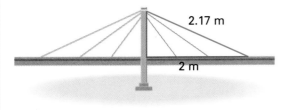

The triangles on the bridge and model are similar.

$\frac{150}{2} = 75$ Use a ratio to find the scale factor.

$75 \cdot 2.17 = 162.75$ m

The cable is almost 163 m long.

Example 2

Megan, who is 5 ft tall, stands in the shadow of a redwood tree. Megan is 388 ft from the tree and her shadow is 7 ft long. If the tip of Megan's shadow and the tree's shadow are at the same point on the ground, how tall is the tree?

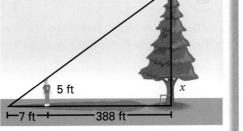

The diagram shows the similar triangles.

$7 + 388 = 395$ ft   Find the length of the tree's shadow.

$\frac{x}{395} = \frac{5}{7}$ Set up a proportion and solve.

$x \approx 282$

The tree is approximately 282 ft tall.

▶ **Literature Link**

Author John Steinbeck referred to redwood trees as "ambassadors from another time."

Try It

Find the length of the base of the larger triangle. The triangles are similar.

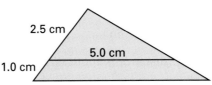

Example 3

$\triangle TSR \sim \triangle TUV$. Find the length of $\overline{RT}$.

Identify the corresponding sides.

$\overline{UV}$ corresponds to $\overline{SR}$.

$\overline{VT}$ corresponds to $\overline{RT}$.

$\dfrac{x}{56} = \dfrac{15}{52.5}$ Set up a proportion and solve.

$x = 16$

The length of $\overline{RT}$ is 16 mm.

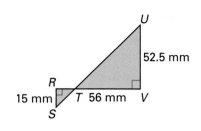

Try It

In the figure, the triangles are similar.

Find x.

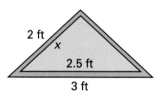

When you solve a problem with right triangles, you can use trigonometric ratios.

Example 4

A person on a boat sees a seagull perched on a bridge 22° above the horizon. The boat is 800 ft from the bridge. How far is the seagull from the passenger?

The passenger's line of vision forms a hypotenuse.

The adjacent side is 800 ft with respect to the 22° angle.

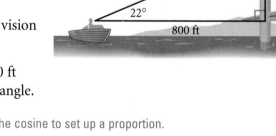

$\cos 22° = \dfrac{800}{h}$ Use the cosine to set up a proportion.

$0.927 \approx \dfrac{800}{h}$ Use a calculator to find cos 22°.

$0.927 \cdot h \approx 800$ Solve.

$h \approx 863$

The distance is about 863 ft.

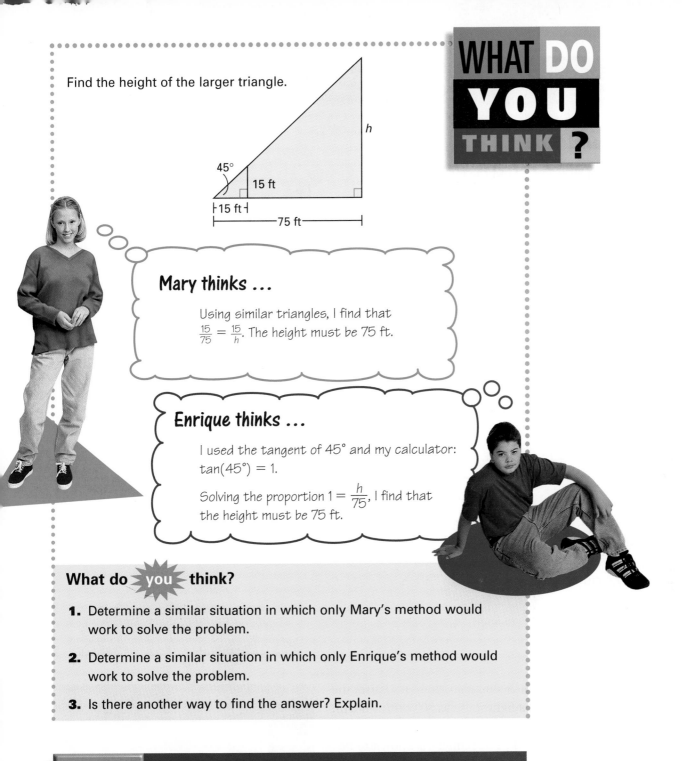

Find the height of the larger triangle.

45°

15 ft

15 ft

75 ft

h

Mary thinks ...

Using similar triangles, I find that $\frac{15}{75} = \frac{15}{h}$. The height must be 75 ft.

Enrique thinks ...

I used the tangent of 45° and my calculator: $\tan(45°) = 1$.

Solving the proportion $1 = \frac{h}{75}$, I find that the height must be 75 ft.

What do you think?

1. Determine a similar situation in which only Mary's method would work to solve the problem.

2. Determine a similar situation in which only Enrique's method would work to solve the problem.

3. Is there another way to find the answer? Explain.

Check Your Understanding

1. Suppose a real-world problem requires the height of some object that can't be measured directly. Which method is easier to use, similarity ratios or trigonometry? Explain.

2. What do we mean by indirect measurement?

Practice and Apply

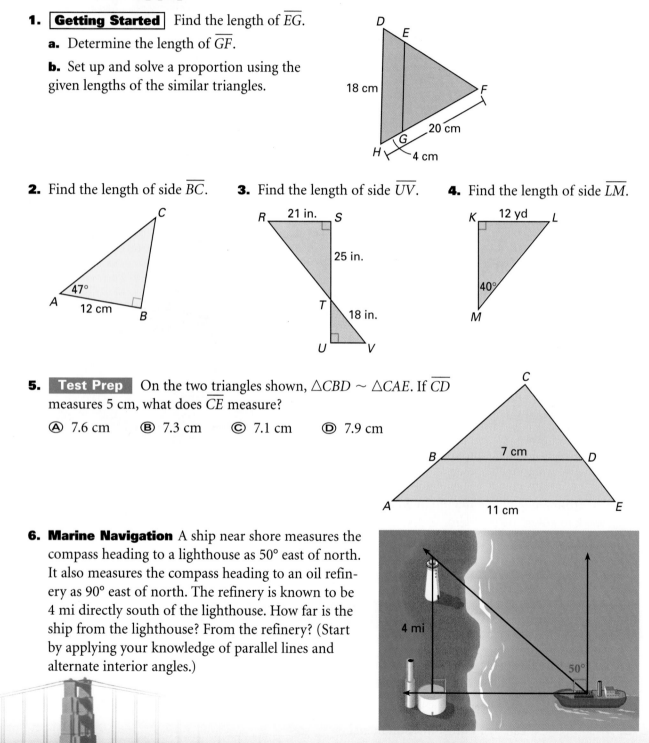

1. **Getting Started** Find the length of $\overline{EG}$.

   a. Determine the length of $\overline{GF}$.

   b. Set up and solve a proportion using the given lengths of the similar triangles.

2. Find the length of side $\overline{BC}$.

3. Find the length of side $\overline{UV}$.

4. Find the length of side $\overline{LM}$.

5. **Test Prep** On the two triangles shown, $\triangle CBD \sim \triangle CAE$. If $\overline{CD}$ measures 5 cm, what does $\overline{CE}$ measure?

   Ⓐ 7.6 cm   Ⓑ 7.3 cm   Ⓒ 7.1 cm   Ⓓ 7.9 cm

6. **Marine Navigation** A ship near shore measures the compass heading to a lighthouse as 50° east of north. It also measures the compass heading to an oil refinery as 90° east of north. The refinery is known to be 4 mi directly south of the lighthouse. How far is the ship from the lighthouse? From the refinery? (Start by applying your knowledge of parallel lines and alternate interior angles.)

Problem Solving and Reasoning

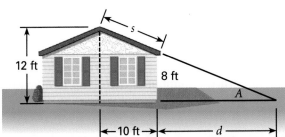

7. **Algebra** A surveying team plots two points, P_1 and P_2, 550 yd apart. It then plots two more points, P_3 and P_4, and measures four angles, as shown. How far apart are P_3 and P_4?

8. **Patterns** The points $A(1, 1)$; $B(4, 1)$; and $C(4, 5)$ form a triangle when connected. Compare the slope of $\overline{AC}$ to the tangent of $\angle CAB$.

Communicate Use the diagram of the house to answer these questions.

9. Suppose you know that $\angle A$ measures 22°. How can you find s?

10. Suppose instead of $m\angle A$, you know that $d = 20$ ft. Explain how you could find s.

11. How many similar triangles are identified? Describe where they are.

12. **Estimation** The rope between a parasailer and the boat is 600 ft long and forms a 30° angle with the water. About how far above the water is the parasailer?

13. **Number Sense** Suppose you use a trigonometric ratio to find a length measurement on a bridge. Why will your measurement be only an approximation?

14. **Math Reasoning** Draw a right triangle with a 45° angle. Find the cos 45° and sin 45° and use your drawing to explain their relationship.

Mixed Review

Add or subtract. Write each answer in lowest terms. *[Lesson 7-5]*

15. $0.219 - 0.043$ **16.** $128.6 + 204.7$ **17.** $\dfrac{5}{8} - \dfrac{3}{16}$ **18.** $3\dfrac{7}{8} + 4\dfrac{6}{8}$

Write each polynomial expression in descending order and find its degree.
[Lesson 10-5]

19. $2x + 5 - 3x^2$ **20.** $x^4 + 4x - 2x^2$ **21.** $3x - x^2 - x^3 - 3$ **22.** $x^5 + x^{10}$

T E C H N O L O G Y

Using a Search Engine • Searching the World Wide Web

Problem: Search for documents related to music, then search for documents about music and not opera. What is the difference between the number of documents found in each search?

Search engines have different ways to search. For example, typing "music NOT opera" or "music–opera" are just two possible ways to search for music except for opera. Learn how your favorite search engine works so you can answer the question.

1 After you've learned what you need to know about a search engine, search for music. Record the number of matching documents found.

Search!

Search! found **1362470** documents about: **music**. Documents **1–10** sorted by **confidence**

65% **Music**   Sort by Site

2 Search for music except for opera using the appropriate keystrokes. Record the number of matching documents.

Search!

Search! found **1277440** documents about: **music NOT opera**. Documents **1–10** sorted by **confidence**

57% **Music NOT Opera**   Sort by Site

Solution: The music except for opera search had 85,030 less documents than the music search.

ON YOUR OWN

TRY IT

a. What would you type if you're looking for information about boats that don't have sails?

b. If you wanted information about all mammals except for whales, what would you type in your search?

▶ Describe how *not* affects a search. Why does the number of matching documents decrease?

▶ Search engines usually use commands that act like the words *or, and,* and *not.* Give three examples of a search each using one of these words.

Section 11A Connect

At the beginning of Section 11A, you saw that geometry is used in the design and construction of bridges. Now you'll construct a model of your own bridge design using what you know about geometry.

Un·a·bridged

Materials: Toothpicks, Scissors, Tape, Ruler

Before bridges are built in the real world, scale models are made using proportions. You can build a model bridge out of toothpicks.

Your group is a team of people hired to design and build a bridge.

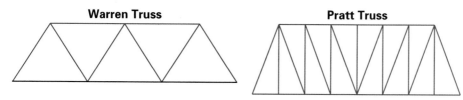

Warren Truss   Pratt Truss

1. Decide on a bridge design that includes congruent and similar triangles. Choose from the two designs shown, or make your own.

2. Determine the toothpick measurements for the model bridge. Use your ruler, scissors, and tape to construct the necessary lengths.

3. When you are finished constructing your model bridge, count the pairs of similar triangles. How many pairs can you find? How do you know that these are similar pairs? Do the same for congruent triangles.

4. How many pairs of congruent triangles can you find? How do you know that they are congruent?

5. How many right triangles are used in your bridge? Are they all congruent to each other? How do you know?

6. Push gently on your bridge. Can it support a load? Would the result have been different if you had based your bridge on parallelograms instead of triangles? Explain.

7. Is there a place on your bridge where both sides are mirror images of each other? If so, where is it and what would your bridge be like without this feature?

1. The trapezoids are similar. Find the length represented by *x*.

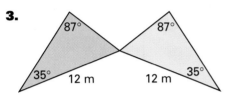

8 in.

53°

12 in.

x

9 in.

2. Measure to determine if the two pentagons are congruent.

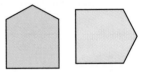

State whether each pair is congruent and the rule that justifies your answer.

3.

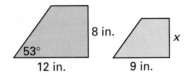

87° 87°

35° 12 m 12 m 35°

4.

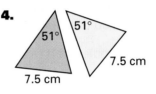

51° 51°

7.5 cm

7.5 cm

5. A lens casts a 3 in. image of a tree onto a sheet of paper. The image is 5 in. from the lens, and the lens is 10 ft from the tree. Find the object's size.

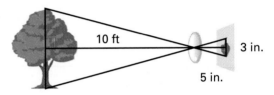

10 ft 3 in.

5 in.

6. **Journal** Suppose you're given the hypotenuse length of a right triangle and the measure of one of the acute angles. How would you use this information to prove congruence to another triangle by the Angle-Side-Angle method?

7. A tornado watcher spots the top of a funnel cloud 14° above the horizon as the funnel crosses a lake 2.5 mi away. How high is the top of the funnel to the nearest 10 ft?

Test Prep

On a multiple choice test, be careful not to confuse similar figures and congruent figures. Also, when finding a missing part of similar triangles, check to make sure the proportion is set up correctly.

8. △*ABC* ~ △*DEF*. What is the length of $\overline{EF}$?

Ⓐ 3.75 in. Ⓑ 1 in.

Ⓒ 4.4 in. Ⓓ 5.4 in.

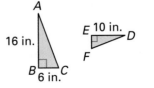

A

16 in.

E 10 in. *D*

F

B 6 in. *C*

Doing What Comes Naturally

"He's a born comedian." "She was born to be in the Olympics." When people say things like that, they mean that you were born with certain abilities.

The use of geometric shapes and patterns in centuries-old Native American art is an example of talents with which the artisan seemed to be born. We can be fairly certain he or she never studied geometry as you are doing.

Native American artisans have found that a repeating pattern is especially fitting when the work already involves repetition. The repetition involved in the work includes adding rows of colored threads to a woven blanket or sewing rows of beads to a decorative vest. A repeating design usually consists of repetitions of the same basic shape. The differences between shapes—their location and orientation—are related to transformations of the shapes.

1 What shapes do you see in this Native American design?

2 Choose a shape of your own and draw a design by repeating your shape.

11-6 Transformations and Congruence

You'll Learn …

■ to move all the points of a figure and still have a congruent shape

… How It's Used

Transformations are the basis for patterns in art and architectural design.

Vocabulary

transformation

reflection

rotation

center of rotation

angle of rotation

translation

▶ **Lesson Link** You've seen many types of polygons. Now you will explore what happens when polygons are flipped or moved. ◀

A **transformation** is an operation that affects all points of a figure, such as a slide, flip, or turn.

You've seen your reflection in a mirror or in water. In math, a **reflection** is a transformation that flips a figure over a line.

A reflection is congruent to the original figure.

Reflection

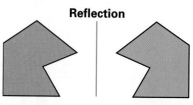

Explore | Reflections

Time to Reflect

Materials: Dynamic geometry software

1. Display the *x*- and *y*-axes and draw a rectangle in the first quadrant.

2. Use the reflection tool to reflect the rectangle with respect to the *y*-axis.

3. Find the coordinates of each vertex of both rectangles. Identify corresponding vertices.

4. Is there a pattern between the *x*-coordinates of the corresponding corners? The *y*-coordinates?

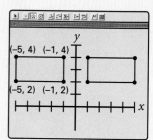

5. Draw a polygon, reflect it with respect to the *x*-axis, and find the pattern between the coordinates of corresponding vertices. What can you conclude about reflections with respect to the *y*-axis? The *x*-axis?

Learn | Transformations and Congruence

A **rotation** is a transformation that turns a figure about a point called a **center of rotation**. The **angle of rotation** is the angle of the turn. A rotated image of a figure is congruent to the original figure.

The transformation of a figure is labeled using prime notation for the corresponding vertices. For example, *A* corresponds to *A'*.

Example 1

The origin is the center of rotation. Rotate trapezoid *ABCD* clockwise 90° and 270° and give the vertex coordinates for each.

Use $\overline{CD}$ as a guide to rotate the trapezoid. $D(0, 0)$ is the center of rotation.

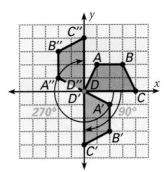

$A'B'C'D'$ is the result of the 90° rotation.

$A'(2, -1)$ $\quad$ $B'(2, -3)$ $\quad$ $C'(0, -4)$ $\quad$ $D'(0, 0)$

$A''B''C''D''$ is the result of the 270° rotation.

$A''(-2, 1)$ $\quad$ $B''(-2, 3)$ $\quad$ $C''(0, 4)$ $\quad$ $D''(0, 0)$

Try It

This pattern is from the Native American baskets of British Columbia. Rotate the figure clockwise 180° and 360°. Use the origin as the center of rotation and find the vertex coordinates.

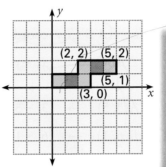

▶ History Link

The swamps and forests of British Columbia, Canada, were a great resource for many regional tribes known for their basket weaving.

A transformation that slides all points of a figure the same distance in the same direction is called a **translation**. All *x*- and *y*-coordinates of a translated figure change by adding or subtracting. A translated image of a figure is congruent to its original figure.

Example 2

The vertices of a triangle are $A(2, 5)$, $B(4, 2)$, and $C(0, 2)$.

Give the vertices of $\triangle ABC$ translated to the right 4 units and **up 2**.

On the *x*-axis, "right" is a positive direction, so add 4 to each *x*-coordinate.

On the *y*-axis, "up" is a positive direction, so **add 2** to each *y*-coordinate.

Locate points *A*, *B*, *C* and draw $\triangle ABC$.

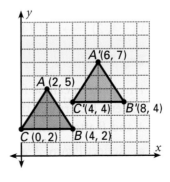

$\triangle ABC$	$(x + 4, y + 2)$	$\triangle A'B'C'$
↓	↓	↓
$A(2, 5)$ →	$(2 + 4, 5 + 2)$ →	$A'(6, 7)$
$B(4, 2)$ →	$(4 + 4, 2 + 2)$ →	$B'(8, 4)$
$C(0, 2)$ →	$(0 + 4, 2 + 2)$ →	$C'(4, 4)$

Label corresponding vertices A', B', and C'.

The coordinates of $\triangle A'B'C'$ are $A'(6, 7)$, $B'(8, 4)$, and $C'(4, 4)$.

Practice and Apply

1. **Getting Started** Rotate the blue image clockwise 90°. What are the new coordinates? Use the origin as the center of rotation.

   a. Turn the figure to the right so the vertex on the origin stays there.

   b. Plot the new vertex coordinates.

   c. Identify the new vertex coordinates.

2. What transformation of the blue T-shirt gives the yellow T-shirt?

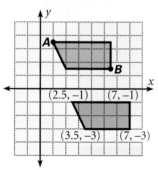

3. What transformation of the pink shoe gives the yellow shoe?

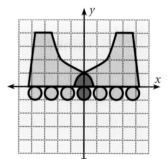

4. **Geometry** Find the coordinates of points *A* and *B* on the trapezoid that has been translated 1.5 units left and 4.5 units up.

5. Across which axis was the figure reflected?

6. **Social Studies** The Yurok people of northern California wove intricate baskets using plants such as sourgrass. On the basket, what transformations do the parallelograms and triangles exhibit?

7. **Test Prep** Some of these happy faces are transformations of each other. Which two are translations of each other?

    Ⓐ 2 and 3   Ⓑ 3 and 7   Ⓒ 2 and 7   Ⓓ 4 and 6

Problem Solving and Reasoning

8. **Algebra** The blue rhombus has been reflected across the y-axis. Give a general rule for changing coordinates (x, y) of the blue rhombus into corresponding coordinates on the green one.

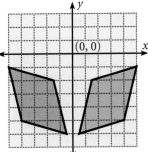

Critical Thinking What transformations, if any, will turn each collection of shapes into a math word you've recently learned? (Turning the book and using a mirror may help you decide.)

9. ROTATE   **10.** REFLECT   **11.** TRANSLATE

12. **Journal** Describe how two different transformations can result in the same image and provide an example.

13. **Math Reasoning** Is there a transformation that changes a parallelogram into a trapezoid? Explain.

14. **Communicate** Explain the difference between reflections and rotations. Provide a sketch as an example.

Mixed Review

Multiply or divide. Write each answer in lowest terms. *[Lesson 7-6]*

15. 26.9×14.2 **16.** 0.081×-0.9 **17.** $\frac{4}{7} \times \frac{4}{9}$ **18.** $12 \times \frac{5}{6}$

19. $2.04 \div 3$ **20.** $44 \div \frac{1}{4}$ **21.** $9\frac{1}{3} \div \frac{3}{28}$ **22.** $-4.5 \div -2.25$

Add. Simplify if possible. *[Lesson 10-6]*

23. $(2x^2 + 4x + 5) + (x^3 + 5x^2 - 4x - 7)$ **24.** $(8p^5 - p^2) + (2p^5 + 4p^3 + 11)$

Transformations and Similarity

You'll Learn ...

■ to transform a figure and have a shape that is similar to but not congruent to the original

... How It's Used

Photo developers create similar figures when creating enlargements.

▶ **Lesson Link** You've seen how transformations result in congruent figures. Now you'll use a transformation that results in a figure that is similar to but not congruent to the original. ◄

Explore | Dilations

This Is Getting Expansive

Materials: Graph paper, Ruler

This design is adapted from Sioux art. It represents six directions: east (red), west (yellow), north (blue), south (black), up, and down.

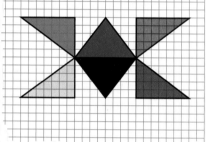

1. Copy this figure onto graph paper.

2. On another piece of graph paper, draw a scale drawing of this design using a scale factor of 2.

3. Is each of the six triangles of the dilated design congruent to its corresponding triangle of the original design? Is it similar? Explain.

Learn | Transformations and Similarity

The coordinates of a dilation on the coordinate plane can be determined by multiplying every coordinate by the scale factor.

Example 1

Use a scale factor of 2 to dilate $\triangle ABC$. Give the vertex coordinates of the dilation.

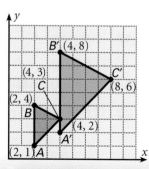

$$
\begin{array}{ccc}
\triangle ABC & (2 \cdot x, 2 \cdot y) & \triangle A'B'C' \\
\downarrow & \downarrow & \downarrow \\
A(2, 1) \rightarrow & (2 \cdot 2, 2 \cdot 1) \rightarrow & A'(4, 2) \\
B(2, 4) \rightarrow & (2 \cdot 2, 2 \cdot 4) \rightarrow & B'(4, 8) \\
C(4, 3) \rightarrow & (2 \cdot 4, 2 \cdot 3) \rightarrow & C'(8, 6)
\end{array}
$$

A scale factor greater than 1 causes an enlargement, whereas a positive nonzero scale factor less than 1 causes a reduction.

▶ **Language Link**

The prefix *non-* means "not."

So "*x* is a nonzero number" means $x \neq 0$.

Example 2

Use a scale factor of $\frac{1}{3}$ to dilate Figure *KLMN*. Give the coordinates of the vertices that correspond to *KLMN*.

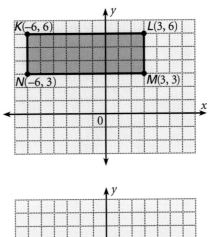

Find the new vertex coordinates, then plot the dilated figure.

$$KLMN \qquad \left(\frac{1}{3} \cdot x, \frac{1}{3} \cdot y\right) \qquad K'L'M'N'$$

$$\downarrow \qquad\qquad \downarrow \qquad\qquad \downarrow$$

$$K(-6, 6) \rightarrow \left(\frac{1}{3} \cdot -6, \frac{1}{3} \cdot 6\right) \rightarrow K'(-2, 2)$$

$$L(3, 6) \quad \rightarrow \left(\frac{1}{3} \cdot 3, \frac{1}{3} \cdot 6\right) \quad \rightarrow L'(1, 2)$$

$$M(3, 3) \quad \rightarrow \left(\frac{1}{3} \cdot 3, \frac{1}{3} \cdot 3\right) \quad \rightarrow M'(1, 1)$$

$$N(-6, 3) \rightarrow \left(\frac{1}{3} \cdot -6, \frac{1}{3} \cdot 3\right) \rightarrow N'(-2, 1)$$

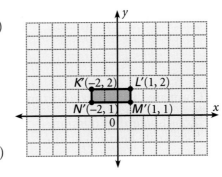

Try It

Find the new vertex coordinates after each dilation.

a. Use a scale factor of 2.5.

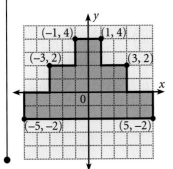

b. Use a scale factor of $\frac{2}{3}$.

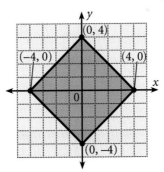

Example 3

The point *A'*(4, 12) is on a polygon that has been dilated by a scale factor of 4. What are the coordinates of the corresponding point *A*?

$(4 \div 4, 12 \div 4) \rightarrow A(1, 3)$ Divide *A'* coordinates by 4.

If you have a figure and its dilation and you know the coordinates of corresponding vertices, then you can find the scale factor of the dilation.

► **Geography Link**

Native American tribes of the Northwest are known for using animal designs in wood carvings. They also used animal names for geometric designs, such as "snake track" or "grasshopper."

Example 4

The design shown here is one of many from Northwest American tribes that are based on diagonal lines.

Find the scale factor of the dilation by comparing corresponding vertices.

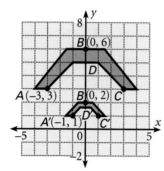

Compare the x- or y-coordinates of $A(-3, 3)$ and $A'(-1, 1)$.

$$\frac{\text{coordinate after dilation}}{\text{coordinate before dilation}} = \frac{-1}{-3} = \frac{1}{3}$$

The scale factor of the dilation is $\frac{1}{3}$.

Try It

a. Find the scale factor of the dilation of Figure A to Figure B.

b. Find the scale factor of the dilation of Figure B to Figure A.

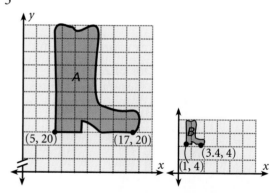

Check | Your Understanding

1. Before drawing a dilation, how can you tell whether it will be an enlargement or a reduction?

2. If Figure X is a dilation of Figure Y, can Y also be a dilation of X? Explain.

3. What happens to the coordinates of a figure after a dilation of a scale factor of 1?

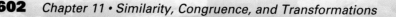

Practice and Apply

1. ⎡Getting Started⎤ Which two figures are dilations of each other?

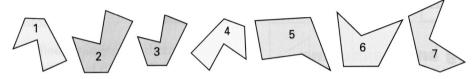

2. Trapezoid 2 is a dilation of trapezoid 1. Classify the dilation as a reduction or an enlargement, and find the scale factor.

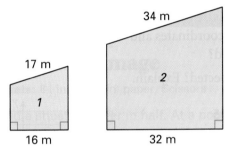

3. The smaller hand is a dilation of the larger hand. Classify the dilation as a reduction or an enlargement, and find the scale factor.

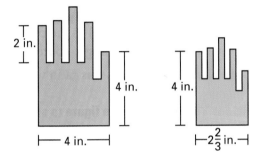

4. a. Use a scale factor of $\frac{1}{3}$ to dilate pentagon *ABCDE*. Find the coordinates of the vertices of the dilation.

b. Graph pentagon $A'B'C'D'E'$.

5. ⎡Test Prep⎤ Which of the following properties does *not* remain the same after a dilation?

Ⓐ Angle measure   Ⓑ Side length

Ⓒ Orientation   Ⓓ Shape

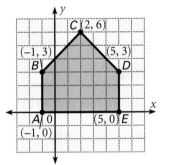

6. Complete the sentence: Two figures with the same shape but different sizes are _____ but not _____.

7. An image on a photo can be considered a dilation of the figure on a negative. A typical negative is $1\frac{1}{4}$ in. by $\frac{7}{8}$ in. What is the scale factor if the photo is 6 in. by 4.2 in?

8. A figure on a coordinate grid includes the points $K(-3, 5)$; $L(2, 0)$; and $M(4, 2)$. What are the coordinates of the corresponding points after a dilation of:

a. 3   **b.** 0.6   **c.** $\frac{1}{4}$ **d.** 2.5

Covering the Plane

You'll Learn ...

■ to create endless patterns using transformations

... How It's Used

Fabric designers make one pattern that, when translated, creates a continuous pattern that can be printed on many yards of fabric.

Vocabulary

tessellation

▶ **Lesson Link**   You'll use what you know about transformations that produce congruent figures to cover flat surfaces in interesting and attractive patterns. ◄

Explore | **Tessellations**

Seeing Double, Triple, Quadruple ...

Materials: Graph paper, Power polygons

1. Trace the outline of one shape onto graph paper. Trace more outlines of that shape to make a pattern without gaps or overlaps.

2. Use another polygon to make another pattern without gaps or overlaps.

3. When did you use translations? Rotations?

4. Describe how the properties of each shape affected your use of translations or rotations.

5. Use both shapes together to draw another pattern without gaps or overlaps.

Learn | **Covering the Plane**

A **tessellation** is a repeating pattern of figures that covers a plane (flat surface) without gaps or overlaps.

Example 1

Is the woven thunderbird design from the Winnebago tribe a tessellation?

No, because there are gaps between the thunderbird shapes.

Example 2

Is the design made by M. C. Escher, the artist, a tessellation?

Yes, because there are no gaps or overlaps.

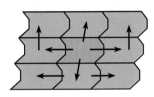

Symmetry Drawing E20 by M. C. Escher.
©1996 Cordon Art-Baarn-Holland.
All rights reserved.

Many tessellations are made by rotating, reflecting, or translating one shape again and again.

Example 3

What transformation is used to make this tessellation of an octagon?

Translations are used.

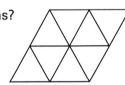

Some tessellations use more than one transformation.

Example 4

Does this tessellation display any of the transformations?

a. Translations   **b.** Rotations   **c.** Reflections

Check for each transformation.

Translations are shown.   Rotations are shown.   Reflections are shown.

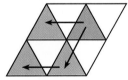 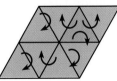 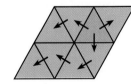

Try It

Does this tessellation display any of the transformations?

a. Translations

b. Rotations

c. Reflections

Drawing by Ryan Evans from *Tessellation Winners: Original Student Art,*
The Second Contest (Palo Alto, CA: Dale Seymour Publications, 1994).
Copyright © 1994 by Dale Seymour Publications.

Triangles and quadrilaterals tessellate, but many shapes don't. To find out whether a shape tessellates, you have to experiment. For example,

Some irregular pentagons do; Regular pentagons don't.

When a shape is tessellated, you can find the total area of the tessellation by multiplying the area of a single shape by the number of shapes used.

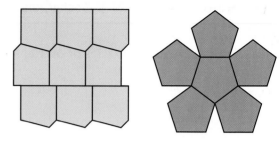

Remember

Dividing by a fraction requires you to multiply by the fraction's reciprocal. **[Page 357]**

Example 5

A kitchen floor is 6 ft by 10 ft = 60 ft². The tiles used to cover the floor are squares with $\frac{1}{2}$ ft side lengths. How many tiles are needed to cover the floor?

$\left(\frac{1}{2}\right)^2 = \frac{1}{4}$ Find the area of one tile.

$60 \div \frac{1}{4} = x$ Divide by $\frac{1}{4}$.

$60 \cdot 4 = 240$ Multiply by the reciprocal of $\frac{1}{4}$.

About 240 tiles are needed to cover the kitchen floor.

Try It

A 24 inch by 60 inch counter will be covered by square tiles with 4-inch side lengths. How many tiles are needed? Tiles can be cut to fit if necessary.

Check Your Understanding

1. Can any shape create a tessellation? Explain.

2. If you know the area of a shape used to tessellate a surface and the number of shapes used, can you always calculate the area of the tessellation? Explain.

3. If someone gives you two different shapes and asks whether or not they can form a tessellation, describe what steps you would take to answer their question.

4. Can you use more than one transformation to create a tessellation? Explain and provide an example.

Practice and Apply

1. **Getting Started** State whether each pattern will tessellate.

   a. **b.** **c.**

   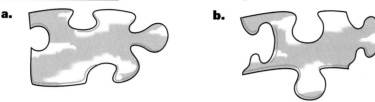

2. Use eight translations of the figure to produce a tessellation.

   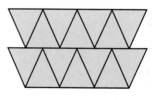

3. **a.** Which regular polygons tessellate?

   b. Explain why regular pentagons do not tessellate.

4. **Test Prep** Which transformation would have to be used for the tessellation shown?

   Ⓐ Translation Ⓑ Rotation

   Ⓒ Reflection Ⓓ Dilation

5. **History** Tiles on floors or ceilings often form tessellations. The Alhambra in Spain, built around 1300, is an elaborate example of Islamic architecture. How many square tiles with 6 in. sides would it take to cover a wall with an area of 1000 ft²?

6. **a.** Name and draw a polygon that will tessellate.

   b. Name and draw a polygon that will not tessellate.

   c. Name and draw two polygons that can tessellate together.

7. Name the figures used in each tessellation.

   a. **b.** **c.**

   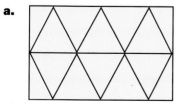
   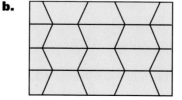

Social Studies A tribe from British Columbia called these designs the mouth and the fish net.

8. What polygons are used?

9. Can the patterns be produced using
   a. Only translations?   b. Only rotations?
   c. Only reflections?   d. A combination?

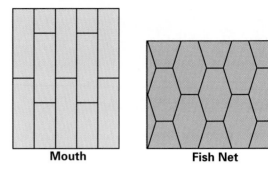

Mouth   Fish Net

Problem Solving and Reasoning

10. **Journal** This pattern is created using a rhombus and a parallelogram. Can this tessellation be created using only reflections and translations? Explain.

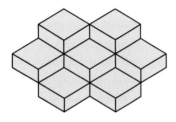

11. **Communicate** A flooring contractor has 175 tiles that are 6 in. by 6 in. for covering a kitchen floor that is 15 ft by 10 ft. Does he have enough tiles? Explain.

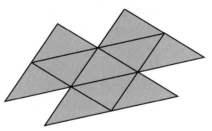

12. **Patterns** You can tessellate any triangle or quadrilateral using 180° rotations around the midpoints of the sides. This pattern starts with an obtuse triangle. Do the same thing with an acute triangle and a trapezoid and sketch the result for each.

13. **Math Reasoning** Find five letters of the alphabet that tessellate. (*Hint:* You can draw the letters.)

Mixed Review

Find the missing side length for each right triangle. *[Lesson 7-9]*

14.
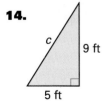
c   9 ft
5 ft

15.
a   24 in.
18 in.

16.
b
10 m   6 m

Solve each proportion. *[Lesson 5-4]*

17. $\frac{4}{5} = \frac{x}{100}$ 18. $\frac{2.5}{20} = \frac{7.5}{x}$ 19. $\frac{6}{7} = \frac{21}{x}$ 20. $\frac{4.3}{8.6} = \frac{x}{50}$

Section 11B Connect

At the beginning of Section 11B, you saw how Native American arts and crafts repeat shapes to make patterns. You'll design your own pattern by using various transformations.

Doing What Comes Naturally

The Pueblo people of the American Southwest are known for their pottery. Pottery made by the Zuni, Laguna, and Acoma tribes display many patterns, including geometric designs and natural shapes such as birds and lizards.

Symmetry and transformations are frequently used in the paintings on their pottery.

1. Look at the photo and notice the symmetry. Discuss the types of symmetry you see. Is there a type of symmetry that every piece has?

2. Now discuss the types of transformations you see and how often they appear. Point out tessellations if you see any.

3. With your group, design a pattern to put on a traditional Native American object (pottery, tepee, rug, mask, beadwork, jewelry, blanket). Start by dividing the object into four equal areas.

4. Each of the four areas will have a unique shape.

   Area 1: Shape with exactly one line of symmetry.

   Area 2: Shape with exactly three lines of symmetry.

   Area 3: Shape with point symmetry.

   Area 4: Shape with any symmetry you like.

5. Apply a different transformation to each of the four shapes. Rotate, translate, reflect, and dilate.

6. If any of the shapes make a tessellation, that area of your piece will be filled with that tessellation. Do you think a dilation will tessellate?

7. Sketch some plans for your design.

Graphic Organizer

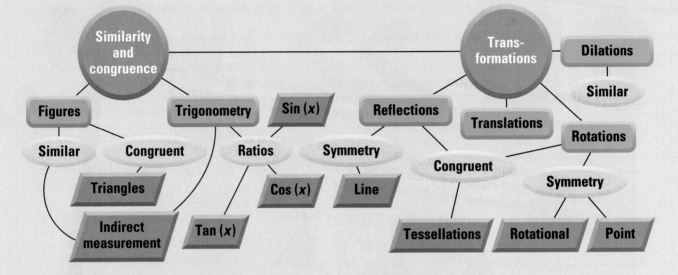

Section 11A Similarity and Congruence

Summary

- Two figures are **congruent** ($\cong$) if they have the same shape and size. Two figures are **similar** ($\sim$) if they have the same shape but not necessarily the same size. Corresponding angles and corresponding sides appear in both congruent and similar figures.

- You can use the **Side-Side-Side, Side-Angle-Side, Angle-Side-Angle,** and **Side-Angle-Angle** rules to determine congruence of two triangles.

- For an acute angle in a right triangle, the **adjacent leg** is the leg next to the angle and the **opposite leg** is opposite the angle.

- The **trigonometric ratios sine, cosine,** and **tangent** can be used for **indirect measurement** of triangles.

Review

1. The two pentagons are similar. Find the length x and the measure of $\angle 1$.

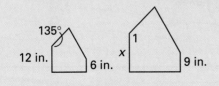

2. State whether the triangles are congruent; if they are, give the rule that justifies your answer.

3. Are the figures congruent?

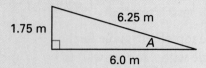

4. Calculate each trigonometric ratio.

  a. sin 60°   **b.** cos 30°   **c.** tan 45°

5. Use the lengths of the sides to write and evaluate the sine, cosine, and tangent ratios for the labeled angle.

6. In the figure, △PQR is similar to △TSR. Find the length of $\overline{RT}$.

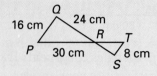

Section 11B   Transformations

Summary

■ A **transformation** is a change in a figure that could be a **reflection, translation, rotation,** or **dilation.**

■ A figure has **symmetry** if it coincides with itself after a transformation. Three types of symmetry are: **line symmetry, rotational symmetry,** and **point symmetry.**

■ A **tessellation** is a repeating pattern of figures that covers a plane without gaps or overlaps.

Review

7. A figure has vertex coordinates $K(0, 0)$; $L(3, 1)$; $M(2, 4)$; and $N(0, 5)$. Find the coordinates of K', L', M', and N' after each transformation.

  a. Reflection across the x-axis

  b. Reflection across the y-axis

  c. Rotation 90° counterclockwise

8. △ABC is translated 4 units right and 1 unit down. Find the coordinates of A', B', and C'.

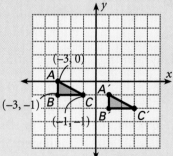

9. Which transformation has occurred? Are the figures similar? Congruent?

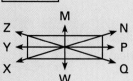

10. Which are lines of symmetry?

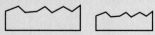

11. Can this tessellation be made using only rotations of a single triangle?

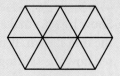

Entertainment

The object of Mancala, an African stone game, is to get more stones than the opponent. At each turn, players must consider the possible combinations of moves that can be made.

People of the World

In 1968, Shirley Chisholm was the first African-American woman elected to Congress. A former teacher, she fulfilled her pledge to her community to support education. This required her to analyze data to compare the possible ways of allocating funds.

Social Studies

At weddings, the custom of throwing the bridal bouquet to the unmarried female guests began in France in the 1300s. The chance of catching the bouquet depends on the number of people trying to catch it.

Science

Following much experimentation with various combinations of Siamese and Persian cats, breeders developed a new breed of long-haired cat—the much-sought-after Himalayan.

Arts & Literature

Three-line symbols called *trigrams*, commonly found in Asian art, are made of combinations of solid and broken lines. The ones on this flag symbolize heaven, earth, fire, and water. The Counting Principle can be used to determine how many ways these three-line symbols can be made.

KEY MATH IDEAS

You can count the number of ways a series of events can occur by using a tree diagram or the Counting Principle.

A permutation, or arrangement, is an ordered selection of objects. A combination is a selection of objects without regard to order.

The probability, or theoretical probability, of an event is the likelihood that the event occurs.

Experimental probability is the number of times the event occurs divided by the number of trials. Geometric probability is calculated by comparing areas, lengths, or other measures.

Conditional probability is the probability that event B will occur, given that event A has already occurred. The events may be independent events or dependent events.

CHAPTER PROJECT

Problem
Solving

Understand
Plan
Solve
Look Back

Create a game that involves permutations and/or combinations. Use your knowledge of probability to make the game interesting. You may want to use cards, coins, spinners, number cubes, or just select numbers or objects from a hat. You might want the game to involve several players, or it could be a game of solitaire.

Checking for a Reasonable Answer

We often need to use calculators to solve problems with large numbers. But it is easy to enter incorrect numbers, forget parentheses, or miss a digit when writing the answer from the calculator screen. So it is important to look back at the reasonableness of your answer. Estimation and common sense are good guides to reasonableness.

Problem Solving Focus

Kirk is a volunteer for an environmental organization. These are some situations he has encountered.

State if each answer is "close enough," "too low," or "too high." Explain.

❶ An acre, 43,560 ft², is set aside for a grove of trees. If the grove is a square region, how long should each side of the grove be?
Answer: 660 ft

❷ A tree is 150 ft tall and has a diameter of 12 ft. The portion of usable wood from the tree is $\frac{4}{5}$. What is the usable-wood volume of the tree?
Answer: 1085 ft³

❸ There are estimates that rain forests are being cut down at the rate of 100 acres per minute. At this rate, how many acres are being cut down in a month?
Answer: 4,320,000 acres

❹ Recycled paper is called "postconsumer." It costs $2.60 to produce 1000 sheets of 100% postconsumer paper and $3.20 to produce 1500 sheets of 20% postconsumer recycled filler paper. How much more does the 100% recycled paper cost to produce per sheet?
Answer: $0.05

SWIFTER, HIGHER, STRONGER

Thousands of people in the stadium, and millions more around the world, are cheering you on. The starter gun sounds, every muscle in your body strains, your lungs search desperately for air, and before you know it, you cross the finish line victorious. You're an Olympic champion, and the national anthem sounds as you accept the accolades of your country and the world. In the future, what do you think will be remembered about the Olympic Games held in Atlanta? The American gymnast who vaulted with an injured ankle and enabled her team to win the gold? The decathlon winner who, four years earlier, though favored to win, hadn't even qualified? Or the gold-medal swimmer who, because of exercise-induced asthma, sometimes passed out during vigorous workouts? Perhaps the individuals themselves won't be remembered. Maybe what will be remembered is their dedication and courage to perform their very best and never give up.

1 The number of women athletes in the 1992 Barcelona Games was 2708. In the Atlanta Games four years later, the number rose to 3779. What percent of increase is this?

2 In the Atlanta Games, Turkey's 141-pound Naim Suleymanoglu lifted 413 pounds. How many times his weight did he lift?

17. Chance To win a game, you must guess 6 numbers from the numbers 1–53. They must match 6 randomly selected numbers. Why is this game virtually impossible to win?

18. In Olympic diving, 7 judges award a score for each dive. The high and low scores are removed. In how many ways can 2 judges' scores be removed?

19. **Test Prep** A flower shop carries 12 types of flowers and sells a special Crazy 8 birthday bouquet using your choice of 8 different flowers. How many different ways can 8 flowers be selected?

Ⓐ 96   Ⓑ 495   Ⓒ 12^8 Ⓓ 40,320

Problem Solving and Reasoning

20. Critical Thinking How many ways can you give 10 swim-team members a snack if you have 12 snacks and each swimmer is to receive 1?

21. Communicate Suppose you select a group from 10 people. What size group has the most ways of being selected? Explain.

22. Choose a Strategy How many ways can groups of from 0 to 12 items be chosen from 12 items?

23. Math Reasoning How many different ways can you select 3 players from 10 for one basketball team, and then 3 from the remaining 7 for another team?

> **Problem Solving**
> # STRATEGIES
> • Look for a Pattern
> • Make an Organized List
> • Make a Table
> • Guess and Check
> • Work Backward
> • Use Logical Reasoning
> • Draw a Diagram
> • Solve a Simpler Problem

Mixed Review

Is the table an equal ratio table? If so, find the value of k, where $\frac{y}{x} = k$. *[Lesson 5-3]*

24.

x	3	6	9	12
y	4	7	10	13

25.

x	2	4	6	8
y	3	6	9	12

Determine whether each pair of figures is congruent. *[Lesson 11-2]*

26.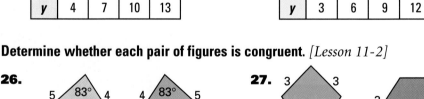

27.

> **Project Progress**
>
> Think about whether you want your game to involve permutations, combinations, or both. Which would make the game more difficult?

> **Problem Solving**
> Understand
> Plan
> Solve
> Look Back

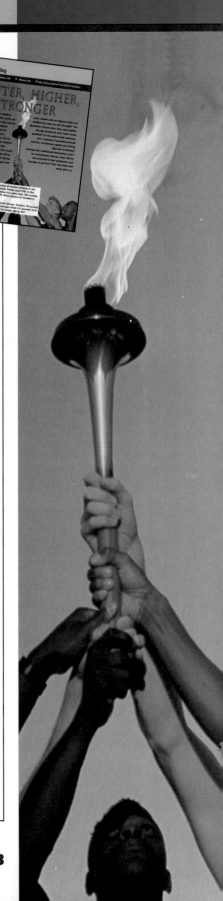

You have seen many examples of counting situations. In this Connect, you will compute the combinations and permutations associated with the Olympic Games.

Swifter, Higher, Stronger

The interlocked rings of the Olympic symbol represent Africa, the Americas, Asia, Australia, and Europe.

1. In how many ways could the colors of the Olympic symbol have been arranged among the rings?

2. Let each group in the room be a "nation" in the Olympics. In how many orders can the groups march in the opening ceremonies?

3. In how many ways can the teams win gold, silver, and bronze in the first event? (Assume that each team can win no more than 1 medal.)

4. If only the top 3 teams can compete in the all-around competition, how many ways can they be arranged?

5. If the rules are changed and the top 4 teams can compete in the all-around competition, how many ways can they now be arranged?

6. In how many ways can the gold medal be awarded if each team competes in the first 5 events?

7. If 10 events are to be held, in how many different ways can the events be ordered?

8. Use one of the situations explored here. Show that choosing a group (combination), then ordering the group (permutation) is the same as selecting and ordering a group (permutation).

Evaluate.

1. $8!$ **2.** $12!$ **3.** $(10 - 3)!$ **4.** $(3!)(3!)$ **5.** $\dfrac{10!}{2!}$

6. $4(3!)$ **7.** $\dfrac{8!}{6!}$ **8.** $\dfrac{7!}{(7 - 4)!}$ **9.** $\dfrac{8!}{3! \times 5!}$ **10.** $\dfrac{6!}{2!(6 - 4)!}$

11. Make an organized list or tree diagram showing the possible outcomes of tossing 3 coins.

12. Make a tree diagram to show the possible outcomes of spinning the spinner twice.

How many ways can the letters in each of these words be arranged if no letter is used twice? The letters do not have to form a word.

13. SILVER   **14.** MEDALIST   **15.** WRESTLING

16. Consumer On his vacation, Fred wanted to take 6 tours, but he was having trouble deciding in what order to take them. How many different ways could he go on the tours?

17. Olympics In the heptathlon, there are 7 events—hurdles, high jump, shot put, 200 m dash, javelin throw, long jump, and 800 m run. These events are held in a certain order. How many different ways could these 7 events be ordered?

18. Civics A candidate will visit 9 of the 50 states the week before the election. How many ways can this be done? Write in factorial notation.

19. Olympics Mark Spitz won 7 gold medals in swimming at the 1972 Olympic Games in Munich. If he wanted to display the medals in a row on his wall, how many different ways could he arrange them?

20. Journal Compare selecting 3 items from 7 if the selection is a permutation to selecting 3 items from 7 if the selection is a group.

Test Prep

Think about whether order is important.

21. For an international flight, how many different ways can 5 flight attendants be selected from 10 flight attendants?

ⓐ 10×5 ⓑ $10!$ ⓒ $\dfrac{10!}{5!}$ ⓓ $\dfrac{10!}{5! \times 5!}$

HAPPY BIRTHDAY, BABY

How many birthdays has the average person had? Actually, just one. All the other days you celebrate as birthdays are the anniversaries of that day. But "Happy Anniversary to You" is too difficult to sing, so we call them all birthdays.

You undoubtedly share this day with someone famous. Born February 17? Michael Jordan shares your birthday. Born May 16? So were Janet Jackson, Pierce Brosnan, and Tori Spelling.

We celebrate the birthdays of people important to our country, such as George Washington and Martin Luther King, Jr., with national holidays.

The day on which different people celebrate their birthdays is sometimes filled with coincidences. Five presidents were either born on, or died on, July 4.

Were you born alone or along with a brother or sister? When you were born, you had …

– 1 chance in 80 of being a twin,
– 1 chance in 6400 of being a triplet,
– 1 chance in 512,000 of being a quadruplet,
– 1 chance in 40,960,000 of being a quintuplet.

1 Of 250 million Americans, about how many were born on April 15?

2 Martin Luther King, Jr.'s birthday is celebrated on the third Monday in January. Does this always fall on his birthday? Why do you think this is done?

3 Which has the greater chance of occurring, being born a twin or a quintuplet?

645

You'll Learn ...

■ to compute probability

... How It's Used

Probability is used to predict the place a hurricane will occur.

Vocabulary

experiment

outcomes

sample space

event

probability

▶ **Lesson Link** You have worked with methods for counting possible outcomes. Now you will learn to compute the chance that an outcome will happen. ◀

Explore   Probability

It's a Sure Thing

1. Draw a number line similar to this one.

| 0 | 0.1 | 0.2 | 0.3 | 0.4 | 0.5 | 0.6 | 0.7 | 0.8 | 0.9 | 1 |

If 0 indicates that something is impossible and 1 indicates that something is a sure thing, label points along this line that would show the chance of the following events occurring.

a. Rolling a 6 in a single roll of a number cube

b. Getting heads on a single flip of a coin

c. Selecting a pair of matching socks from a drawer, without looking, if there are two pairs of socks in the drawer

d. Drawing a card containing a vowel from a set of 10 cards containing the first 10 letters of the alphabet

e. Rolling a number other than 6 in a single roll of a number cube

2. Provide a rationale for each of your selections of position. Does each person in your group have the points in the same order?

3. Describe events you could place at 0 and at 1.

Learn   Probability

Suppose you toss a coin as an **experiment**. The coin can land on heads or tails, so there are two equally likely results or **outcomes** possible.

The set of all possible outcomes of an experiment is the **sample space**. Usually we are interested in the chance of a particular **event** occurring. This is called the **probability** of the event.

Probability can be expressed as a decimal, fraction, ratio, or percent.

$$P(\text{event}) = \frac{\text{number of outcomes in the event}}{\text{number of outcomes in the sample space}}$$

Examples

1 Jason and Alexander are playing a game with a number cube. If Jason rolls a *3 or more* on his next roll, he wins the game.

What are the outcomes in the sample space? Outcomes satisfying the event *3 or more*?

What is the probability of the event *3 or more*?

Sample space: 6 outcomes → 1, 2, 3, 4, 5, 6

Event *3 or more*:   4 outcomes →   **3, 4, 5, 6**

The probability of Jason rolling a *3 or more* on his next roll is $\frac{4}{6}$, or $\frac{2}{3}$.

2 Nicole likes to try to guess a person's birthday. What is the probability that she can guess the correct month of Jessica's birthday on the first try? Assume that it is equally likely for a person to have been born in any month.

There are 12 months in the year, so the number of outcomes in the sample space is 12. Jessica's birthday could only be during 1 month, so the number of outcomes in the event is 1.

$$P(\text{guessing correct month}) = \frac{1}{12}$$

Try It

For each situation, what are the outcomes in the sample space? What is the probability of the event?

a. If Alexander rolls a *5 or more* on his next roll of a number cube, he wins the game.

b. Will the next large Pacific earthquake occur *on a weekend*? (Assume that it is equally likely to occur on any day of the week.)

► **Science Link**

The Ring of Fire surrounds the entire Pacific Ocean with earthquake activity. It is the most active earthquake zone in the world.

The probability of an event occurring is always written as a number from 0 to 1.

When it is impossible for an event to occur, the probability is 0. When an event is certain to occur, the probability is 1.

Impossible   Certain

$$0 \qquad \frac{1}{4} \qquad \frac{1}{2} \qquad \frac{3}{4} \qquad 1$$

Example 3

Suppose you get one spin on the spinner at the right. What is the probability that the spinner will land on ...

a. Red   **b.** Red or blue   **c.** Green   **d.** *Not* red

a. $P(\text{red}) = \frac{2}{5}$

b. $P(\text{red or blue}) = 1$ (certain)

c. $P(\text{green}) = 0$ (impossible)

d. $P(\textit{not} \text{ red}) = \frac{3}{5}$

You can see that the probability of red plus the probability of *not* red is 1. The sum of the probability of an event occurring and the event *not* occurring is 1.

Remember

A **prime number** is an integer larger than 1 that is only divisible by itself and 1. **[Page 324]**

Try It

Find the probability that one roll of a number cube results in a

a. Prime number

b. Composite number

c. Number > 5

d. Number < 7

e. Fraction between 1 and 2

Check   Your Understanding

1. Explain the difference between an outcome and an event. Can an outcome be an event?

2. How does a probability of 25% compare with a probability of 0.4? With a probability of $\frac{1}{4}$?

3. If events A and B account for all of the possibilities in the sample space, what do you know about $P(B)$? Why?

Practice and Apply

1. **Getting Started** Find the probability of rolling a 2 on a number cube.

   a. List all of the outcomes in the sample space.

   b. How many outcomes are in the sample space?

   c. How many outcomes of rolling a 2 are in the sample space?

   d. Write a ratio using answers from **b** and **c** to find the probability.

   e. Express the probability as a fraction, decimal, and percent.

2. **History** Two U.S. Presidents, James Polk and Warren Harding, were both born on November 2. What is the probability of 2 people with November birthdays sharing the same birthday? (November has 30 days.)

List all outcomes in each sample space.

3. Rolling a number cube

4. Drawing a marble from a bag with 3 red, 2 green, and 3 blue marbles

Express the probability as a fraction, decimal, and percent.

5. Rolling an even number on a single roll of a number cube

6. Drawing a red sock out of a drawer that contains only red socks

7. Going to math class on New Year's Day

8. That a person's birthday is not on the fourth of July

9. **Test Prep** Which has the greatest probability of occurring?

   Ⓐ Tossing heads on a coin toss

   Ⓑ Tossing heads or tails on a coin toss

   Ⓒ Tossing a 6 on a number cube

   Ⓓ Not tossing a 6 on a number cube

10. On Jim's birthday, he chose a pet from a litter of dalmations. They were so cute, he just closed his eyes and picked one. If there were 3 males and 2 females, what are the chances that Jim's puppy is female?

11. **Science** Chromosomes determine whether a child is male or female. The probability of having 13 children that are all male is $\frac{1}{8192}$. What is the probability of having 13 children that are **not** all male?

The yellow and green sectors of the spinner are each $\frac{1}{4}$ of the spinner area.

12. What is the probability of spinning red?

13. Which two colors have equal probability?

14. What is the probability of not spinning green?

15. Number Sense Suppose you randomly select answers on a test. What is the probability of selecting the correct answer in each situation?

    a. Multiple choice question with 4 choices

    b. True-false question

16. Chance The *odds* of an event happening is the ratio of the ways it can happen to the ways it *cannot* happen. What are the odds of rolling a 3 with one number cube?

Problem Solving and Reasoning

17. Math Reasoning Two of these cakes are identical. Which are they? Suppose you had chosen two of them randomly. What is the probability that you would have chosen the two identical cakes?

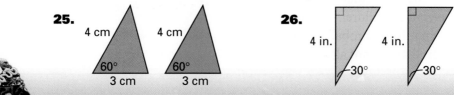

Critical Thinking Answer "always," "sometimes," or "never."

18. An event that is certain _____ has a probability of 1.

19. An impossible event _____ has a probability of 1.

20. Communicate Explain the difference between *possible* and *probable*.

21. Journal Explain why the probability of an event can never be greater than 1. Give an example of an event that has a probability of 1.

Mixed Review

Sketch each figure and find its volume. *[Lesson 9-6]*

22. A suitcase measuring 18 in. by 32 in. by 8 in.

23. A dumpster measuring 2 m by 1.5 m by 1.5 m

24. A box that is 3 cm by 4 cm by 3 cm

Are the triangles congruent? If so, state the rule that justifies your answer. *[Lesson 11-3]*

25. 4 cm 60° 3 cm   4 cm 60° 3 cm

26. 4 in. 30°   4 in. 30°

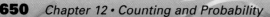

Experimental and Geometric Probability

▶ **Lesson Link** You have learned how to compute probabilities. Now you will see if what is likely to happen *does* happen. ◀

Explore | Experimental Probability

Putting a Spin on It

Materials: Shiny new nickels

1. Working in your groups, determine whose birthday is the latest in his or her birth month (for example, in a group in which students were born on the 12th, 3rd, 24th, and 19th, the 24th is the latest). Call this number *n.*

2. You will be spinning a nickel *n* times (24 times for the above). Write down how many times you expect to get heads.

3. Spin the nickel *n* times. Record the number of times you get heads. Is this the number you expected?

4. Divide the number of heads by the number of spins. Round to the nearest hundredth and write this as your probability.

5. What is the highest group probability? The lowest?

6. Tally the class results (total heads, total spins), and divide to find the class probability. Is this closer to what you expected?

... How It's Used

Food manufacturers use market testing and probability to determine whether a recipe will be successful.

Vocabulary

theoretical probability

experimental probability

trial

geometric probability

Learn | Experimental and Geometric Probability

Sometimes it is easy to calculate the actual, or **theoretical probability** , of an event. When you roll a number cube, it is clear that each side has a $\frac{1}{6}$ probability of coming up. But for other situations, you may need to estimate the probability from survey or experimental data. The probability calculated by this method is called **experimental probability** .

The best way to understand experimental probability is to use it in a situation in which we know the theoretical probability and then compare the two.

Each time you perform an experiment, it is called a **trial** .

Example 1

a. What is the theoretical probability of rolling each possible sum when rolling a pair of number cubes?

Using the Counting Principle, there are $6 \times 6 = 36$ possible outcomes. You can draw a diagram or make an organized list to see all possible sums.

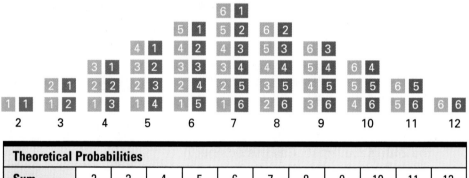

Theoretical Probabilities											
Sum	2	3	4	5	6	7	8	9	10	11	12
Outcomes	1	2	3	4	5	6	5	4	3	2	1
Percent	2.8	5.6	8.3	11.1	13.9	16.7	13.9	11.1	8.3	5.6	2.8

b. To find the experimental probabilities, roll a pair of number cubes 50 times and keep track of the sums that appear.

One student obtained these results:

Experimental Probabilities											
Sum	2	3	4	5	6	7	8	9	10	11	12
Outcomes	2	4	3	5	7	8	9	5	4	3	0
Percent	4	8	6	10	14	16	18	10	8	6	0

c. Compare these experimental results to the theoretical percents for sums from 2 through 12.

The percents of the experimental and theoretical probabilities are close. They would be much closer if the student had used a large number of trials.

Try It

a. What is the theoretical probability of tossing 2 heads, 1 head, and 0 heads when tossing a pair of coins?

b. To find the experimental probability, toss a pair of coins 50 times. Keep track of the number of times each result occurs.

c. Compare your experimental results to the theoretical percents.

In many situations, it may be difficult or impossible to find the theoretical probability, so experimental methods are necessary.

Example 2

At many birthday parties, it is traditional to fill a piñata with treats and hang it from a tree. After being blindfolded and spun around a few times, guests are given 2 chances to break the piñata open with a bat or stick. When it breaks, there is a free-for-all for the treats.

El Burro manufactures piñatas. It would like the probability that a solid hit with the bat breaks the piñata to be about 8%. The company brings in children to test piñatas.

Complete the table to find the probability that a hit breaks each type of piñata. Which piñatas are ready to sell?

▶ Language Link

In Spanish, *piñata* means "pot." Originally, a clay pot was used to hold the treats, but now piñatas are made from wire, cardboard, and papier-maché.

Piñata Type	Number of Hits	Piñatas Broken	P(Hit Breaks Piñata)
Dragon	107	18	?
Bull	216	8	?
Burro	254	19	?

Dragon $P = \frac{18}{107} \approx 16.8\%$; bull $P = \frac{8}{216} \approx 3.7\%$; burro $P = \frac{19}{254} \approx 7.5\%$.

The burro piñatas are ready to sell.

Try It

Quality control is important in many businesses. BrightLights makes candles. BrightLights will tolerate a 0.5% defective rate for each package of candles (missing wicks, chips, and so on). Tests were run in different factories.

Complete the table to find the probability that a box contains defective candles. Which factories passed the inspection?

Factory	Number with Defects	Number of Packages Checked	P(Box Contains Defective Candles)
San Antonio	20	4534	?
Tulsa	27	5324	?
Uvalde	10	1095	?

If the number of packages produced at the San Antonio factory were 10,000 a day, how many would you predict would contain defective candles?

► **History Link**

In 1582, Pope Gregory XIII corrected the calendar, adjusting leap year to occur every 4 years—except for years divisible by 100, unless it is also divisible by 400.

Another way to determine probability is by using geometric models and comparing areas, lengths, or other measures. This is called **geometric probability**.

Example 3

A small prize is placed randomly in the birthday cake. It can be anywhere in the cake with equal likelihood. What is the probability that the prize is under one of the **iced edges**?

The area of the entire rectangle is 36 in. × 24 in. = 864 in². The center area is **30 in. × 18 in.**, or 540 in², so the area under the icing is 864 − **540 = 324 in².**

The probability that the prize is in an edge piece is $\frac{324}{864}$.

324 ÷ 864 = **0.375**, or 37.5%.

Try It

A small prize is placed randomly in the birthday cake. It can be anywhere in the cake with equal likelihood. What is the probability that the prize is under one of the flowers?

Check Your Understanding

1. Explain the difference between theoretical and experimental probability. Are probabilities quoted by doctors theoretical or experimental? Is geometric probability theoretical or experimental?

2. Carinna says that an experimental probability can exceed 1. Is this true? If so, give an example.

3. Suppose a quality-control tester at BrightLights tested 20 boxes, found defective candles in 1, and said the factory failed the test. Is this fair?

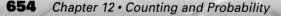

Practice and Apply

Getting Started Decide whether each probability is theoretical or experimental.

1. The probability that a bowler makes a strike is 30%.

2. The probability that a number cube lands on 6 is $\frac{1}{6}$.

3. Two coins are tossed 100 times. Two heads come up 23 times.

4. For his grandmother's 100th birthday celebration, Jeremy's mother asked him to find out what flavor cake each guest would prefer so she could begin cutting the 4 delicious cakes.

a. What is the probability that a guest selected chocolate?

b. What is the probability that a guest would choose lemon?

c. What is the probability that the next guest would request a flavor other than carrot cake?

Flavor of Cake	No. of Requests
Chocolate	62
White	28
Carrot	22
Lemon	14

5. Geometry A player throws a marker onto the game board. It lands in a random location.

a. What is the probability of its landing in the triangle?

b. What is the probability of its landing outside the triangle?

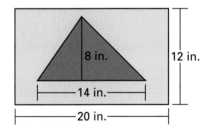

Toss 3 coins 50 times and make a table to record your results. Use the data to find the experimental probability of each event.

6. Tossing 3 heads and no tails   **7.** Tossing 2 heads and 1 tail

8. Compare the experimental probability of tossing 3 heads and no tails with the theoretical probability.

9. Geometry A particle travels around the perimeter of the hexagon and stops at a random location. What is the probability that it lands on the shortest side?

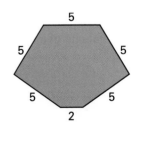

10. The day before her birthday, Shirin begged her mother to let her open one of her 7 gifts. With her mother's permission, she picked one to open, hoping it would be the radio she knew her father had bought her. Two of the packages were too small to be a radio. What is the probability that Shirin picked the radio?

11. Problem Solving Cliff surveyed his class to find the day of the month each person was born and organized his data in a stem-and-leaf diagram.

Stem	Leaf
0	1 3 5 7 7 8 8 9
1	1 1 3 5 6 7 7 7 8 9
2	0 0 1 2 2 3 4 6 6 7 8 9
3	0 0 1

   a. What is the probability that a student was born on the 17th?

   b. What is the probability that a student was born after the 29th?

   c. What is the probability that a student was not born on the 4th?

12. **Test Prep** Estimate the probability that a person was born in May.

   Ⓐ 8.5%   Ⓑ 12%   Ⓒ $\frac{11}{12}$ Ⓓ 60.1%

Problem Solving and Reasoning

13. Communicate Of 1000 patients, 600 were given a new medicine, and the rest were given a placebo (which has no effect). Of those given the medicine, 300 said their condition had improved, compared to 50 who received the placebo. Would you say the medicine is effective? Why?

14. Journal 7 candles from a box of 24 regular candles were switched with "magic" candles that don't blow out. When Perry tried to blow out his 12 birthday candles, 5 of them remained lit. Compare the theoretical probability to the experimental probability that a candle would not blow out.

15. Critical Thinking If the theoretical probability of an event is 1, can the experimental probability be less than 1?

16. Math Reasoning What is the probability that the price of a birthday cake exceeds the median price for all birthday cakes? Explain.

Mixed Review

Find the volume of each prism after a dilation with a scale factor of 2. *[Lesson 9-7]*

17. 2 ft, 3 ft, 6 ft

18. 2 m, 2 m, 2 m

19. 8 in., 5 in., 5 in.

20. Evaluate the trigonometric ratios for $\angle BAC$. *[Lesson 11-4]*

10, *B*, 26°, *A*, 4.4, 9, *C*

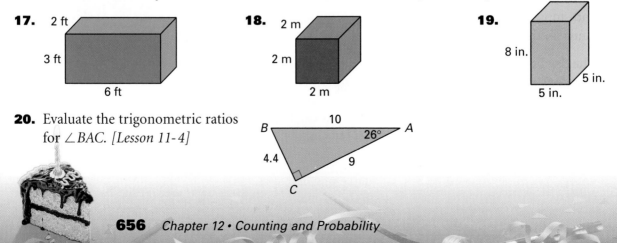

Conditional Probability

▶ **Lesson Link** You have learned to compute probabilities of single events. Now you will learn how additional information and conditions affect probabilities. ◀

You'll Learn …

■ to understand what affects the probability of an event

… How It's Used

Planning a large event requires considering many "what-ifs"—conditions and probabilities—so that risk is minimized.

Vocabulary

conditional probability

Explore Conditional Probability

Food for Thought

Suppose that you have the following information about meal orders at a class function. You are working in the kitchen handing out meals on plates.

	Chicken	Vegetarian
Boys	73	11
Girls	52	29
Teachers	4	3

1. What is the probability that a person ordered a vegetarian meal? What is the probability that any meal is for a teacher?

2. Is a vegetarian meal more likely to be for a boy, a girl, or a teacher? Is a chicken meal more likely to be for a boy, a girl, or a teacher?

3. Suppose a girl needs a meal. Is she more likely to have ordered chicken or vegetarian? Would you have been more sure or less sure of the meal selection if the person had been a boy? Why?

4. Suppose the first three teachers order a vegetarian meal. How sure would you be of the choice for the next teacher's meal?

Learn Conditional Probability

In many real-world situations, knowledge of one event affects your decisions about a second event. This is true in probability situations also. Often additional information leads to a more accurate ability to find the theoretical probability of an event.

Example 1

Suppose that you toss 2 coins. The first coin comes up heads.

a. What is the probability that you will toss 2 heads?

If you did not know anything about the first coin, the probability of 2 heads would be $\frac{1}{4}$. Because you know that the first coin is heads, then the sample space is reduced. There are now only 2 possible outcomes in the sample space. The probability of 2 heads, given that the first coin came up heads, is $\frac{1}{2}$.

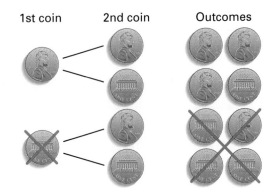

1st coin   2nd coin   Outcomes

b. What is the probability that you will toss 2 tails?

Because the first coin came up heads, the probability that you will toss 2 tails is 0.

Try It

Suppose you roll two number cubes. The first cube comes up 1.

a. What is the probability that the sum of the two number cubes is 6?

b. What is the probability that the sum of the two number cubes is 8?

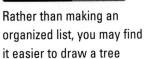

Problem Solving TIP

Rather than making an organized list, you may find it easier to draw a tree diagram to find the theoretical probability.

Conditional probability is the probability that, given that event A has already occurred, event B will occur. The fact that event A has already occurred reduces the sample space for calculating the conditional probability of B.

Example 2

Vanessa Mae, youngest person to record the Tchaikovsky and Beethoven Violin Concertos, shares a birthday with the legendary violinist Nicolò Paganini. Paganini was born in October of 1782.

a. What is the probability that you could guess her birthday randomly?

Since you know her birthday is in October, a month with 31 days, the probability is $\frac{1}{31}$.

b. What is the probability that she was born in a month that has exactly 30 days?

Because October has 31 days, the probability that she was born in a month with 30 days is 0.

Example 3

Movie reviewers Gene Siskel (born January 26) and Roger Ebert (born June 18) give each film they review "thumbs up" or "thumbs down." The table shows their ratings of 213 movies they reviewed between September 9, 1995, and July 27, 1996.

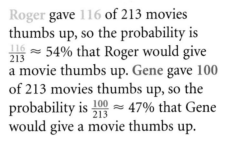

a. What is the probability that Roger would give a movie thumbs up? That Gene would give a movie thumbs up?

	Roger 👍	Roger 👎	Total
Gene 👍	80	20	100
Gene 👎	36	77	113
Total	116	97	213

Roger gave 116 of 213 movies thumbs up, so the probability is $\frac{116}{213} \approx 54\%$ that Roger would give a movie thumbs up. Gene gave 100 of 213 movies thumbs up, so the probability is $\frac{100}{213} \approx 47\%$ that Gene would give a movie thumbs up.

b. If Gene gives a movie thumbs up, what is the probability that Roger would too?

If **Gene** gives a movie thumbs up, the sample space is reduced. The probability is $\frac{80}{100}$, or 80%, that Roger would give it thumbs up too.

c. If Gene gives a movie thumbs down, what is the probability that Roger would give it thumbs up?

If **Gene** gives a movie thumbs down, the probability is $\frac{36}{113} \approx 32\%$ that Roger would give it thumbs up.

> ► **Career Link**
>
> To become a movie critic, you can study film criticism at a university.

Try It

The results of a student survey are shown. First find the totals.

	Like Math	Don't Like Math
Calculators used in class	56	34
Calculators not used in class	35	25

a. What is the probability that a student selected at random would like math?

b. If you know that a student uses calculators in class, what is the probability that the student would like math?

Conditional probability can be shown geometrically. You know that a specific happening occurred in one region and you want to know the probability that it would occur in a smaller or intersecting region.

In the figure, the probability of a point being in square B is $\frac{1}{16}$. But if we know that the point is somewhere within square A, then the probability that the point is in square B is now $\frac{1}{4}$.

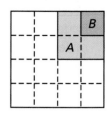

Example 4

Given that a point is inside the rectangle *RSTU,* what is the probability that it is inside square *ABCD*?

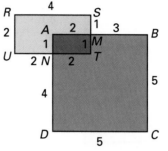

Because you know that the point is in rectangle *RSTU,* then it could possibly be in the rectangle *AMTN.* This rectangle is $\frac{1}{4}$ of the area of *RSTU,* so the probability that the point is in *ABCD* is $\frac{1}{4}$, or 0.25.

Try It

a. Given that a point lies in square *ABCD* above, what is the probability that it is inside rectangle *RSTU*?

b. What is the probability that a point within the large circle is also within the shaded region? Given that the point is within the small circle, what is the probability that it is within the shaded region?

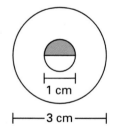

Check | Your Understanding

1. Do new conditions always change the probability of an event? Explain.

2. Give an example of probability that increases given some condition. Give an example of probability that decreases given some condition.

3. Two number cubes are thrown. The first number cube shows a 2. What is the probability that the sum of the two number cubes is 9? Why?

Practice and Apply

1. **Getting Started** Suppose you spin the spinner twice.

   a. Make a tree diagram or an organized list to show the possible outcomes.

   b. How many possible outcomes are there?

   c. If the first spin lands on red, now how many possible outcomes are there?

   d. What is the probability that both spins will land on red?

2. Suppose you spin the spinner 3 times. What is the probability that it lands on green all 3 times?

Suppose that a fly lands on a checkerboard square. What is the probability that it lands…

3. On a red square?

4. On a square in the third row?

5. On a red square in the third row?

6. If you know that the fly landed on a black square, what is the probability that it landed on the bottom right corner square?

7. You roll a pair of number cubes in a board game. If the first cube comes up a 6, find the probability that the sum of the two number cubes is

   a. 6   **b.** 7   **c.** Greater than 10   **d.** Greater than 6

The graph shows the percent of people who have lost a job for various reasons.

8. **Career** Two employees are let go from an electronics company. What is the probability that both are let go due to negative attitudes?

9. **Math Reasoning** This graph represents 5000 people. About how many people were let go because they could not get along with others?

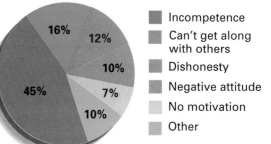

10. February 29 is sometimes referred to as Sadie Hawkins Day. Sadie was a character in Al Capp's comic strip *Li'l Abner*. Suppose one small spot on the comics page misprinted. If *Li'l Abner* was $\frac{1}{3}$ page and the Sadie Hawkins panel was $\frac{1}{6}$ of the comic strip, what is the probability that the misprint was on the Sadie Hawkins panel?

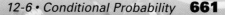

11. Consumer You are planning a pizza party and need a pizza parlor to provide the food. The results of the research on customer satisfaction of various pizza delivery services in your area are shown below.

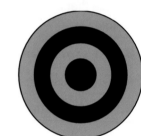

	Satisfied	Not Satisfied	Total
Jay & Dee	12	6	18
The Coloseum	32	10	42
Peet-sa!	15	20	35
Total	59	36	95

What is the probability that if you choose a delivery service randomly from the ones shown …

a. You will be satisfied?

b. You will be satisfied if you choose The Coloseum?

c. What is the probability that a person who was surveyed rated the Coloseum?

Problem Solving and Reasoning

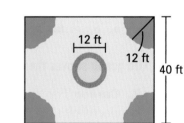

12. Geometry If the inner circle has a radius of 2 in. and each ring has a width of 2 in., what is the probability of hitting a bull's-eye if a person's dart has hit in one of the black areas?

Critical Thinking Suppose a parachutist lands in the rectangular region shown.

13. What is the probability that the parachutist will land in a safe (light green) area, away from the corner trees and central fountain?

14. Communicate If she misses the trees, what is the probability that she will land in the safe area? Explain your strategy. What is the relationship between the sections of trees and the fountain?

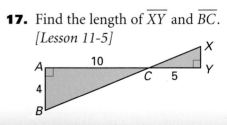

Mixed Review

Find the volume of each solid. Use 3.14 for π. *[Lesson 9-8]*

15. 5 in. 12 in. 3 in. 12 in.

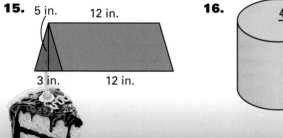

16.

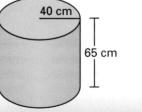

40 cm 65 cm

17. Find the length of $\overline{XY}$ and $\overline{BC}$. *[Lesson 11-5]*

A 10 C 5 X Y 4 B

Dependent and Independent Events

▶ **Lesson Link** You have learned about how one event can change the probability of another event. Now you will learn about whether one event can depend on another. ◀

Explore Probability and Dependency

Point of No Return

Materials: Paper bag
3 Algebra tiles
Tape or dry marker

Mark the red side of two tiles and the yellow side of the third tile with tape or dry marker.

1. Without looking, take 1 tile out of the bag and record whether the red or yellow side is marked. Return the tile to the bag.

2. Take a second tile out of the bag and record whether the red or yellow side is marked.

3. As a class, make a table of the experimental outcomes.

		Second Tile	
		Red	Yellow
First Tile	Red		
	Yellow		

4. Repeat the experiment, but this time do not replace the tile.

5. Describe the effect of the first draw on the second draw in each case.

... How It's Used

Electricians need to know when flows of electricity are independent from each other before they begin work.

Vocabulary

compound events
independent events
dependent events
multiplication property

Learn Dependent and Independent Events

Events that contain more than one outcome are called **compound events**. Sometimes the occurrence of one event affects the probability of a second event; sometimes it has no effect. If there is no effect, we say that the events are **independent events**.

If the events are not independent, the second event is a **dependent event**. You have considered several such situations in dealing with conditional probability earlier.

Example 1

Are these events independent?

a. The first roll of a number cube is 5, and the sum of the first two rolls is 4.

The second event is dependent on the first since the probability of rolling a sum of 4 changes to 0.

b. It is sunny and a movie theater changes its movies.

The fact that the sky is sunny has no effect on a theater changing its movies. The events are independent.

c. One person was born on May 27th and another was born on May 27th.

The birthday of the second person does not depend on the birthday of the first person. The events are independent.

Try It

Are these events independent?

a. It is raining and the parade is canceled.

b. You wear a Yankee cap, and the Yankees win.

If events A and B are independent events, then the probability of both A and B occurring is given by $P(A \text{ and } B) = P(A) \times P(B)$. This property for independent events is known as the **multiplication property**.

You could show the situation geometrically. If the probability of event A is $\frac{2}{5}$ and the probability of event B is $\frac{3}{4}$, then the probability of both event A and event B is $\frac{2}{5} \times \frac{3}{4} = \frac{6}{20}$, or $\frac{3}{10}$.

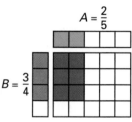

Example 2

Find the probability of flipping a coin and getting tails and then tossing a number cube and getting a number greater than 1.

The result of the coin flip does not influence the result of tossing the number cube. The probability of getting tails and tossing a number greater than 1 is $P(\text{tails, and roll} > 1) = \frac{1}{2} \times \frac{5}{6} = \frac{5}{12}$, or about 42%.

This can be shown by a tree diagram as well.

There are 12 possible outcomes; 5 satisfy the conditions, so the probability is $\frac{5}{12}$.

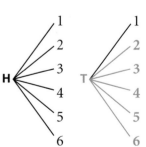

Example 3

Suppose you select a student at random. The probability that the student is either sex is 0.5 and the probability that the student is left-handed is 0.06. What is the probability that the student is a left-handed male?

$P(\text{male and left-handed}) = 0.5 \times 0.06 = 0.03$. The probability of selecting a left-handed male is 3%.

Try It

At Artistes, 80% of the customers are female, and 43% make a purchase. What is the probability that a customer is a woman who makes a purchase?

When drawing a card from a deck, whether or not you replace each card affects the probability.

Example 4

a. A card is drawn and replaced. A second card is drawn. What is the probability that the first card is red and the second is blue?

b. Two cards are drawn (the first card is not replaced). What is the probability that the first card is red and the second is blue?

a. First card: $P(R) = \frac{4}{7}$ Second card: $P(B) = \frac{1}{7}$
$P(\text{red and blue}) = \frac{4}{7} \times \frac{1}{7} = \frac{4}{49} \ (\approx 8.2\%)$

b. First card: $P(R) = \frac{4}{7}$ Second card: $P(B) = \frac{1}{6}$
$P(\text{red and blue}) = \frac{4}{7} \times \frac{1}{6} = \frac{4}{42} \ (\approx 9.5\%)$

Try It

Two cards are drawn. What is the probability that both will be green if the first card is replaced? If it is not replaced?

Check Your Understanding

1. How is the independence of events important to a person using probability?

2. Why can you use the multiplication property to find the probability associated with a pair of independent events?

3. For event A, the probability is $\frac{1}{2}$; for B it is $\frac{1}{3}$; and for A and B, $\frac{1}{5}$. Would you say A and B are independent events? Explain?

Practice and Apply

1. **Getting Started** A number cube is tossed two times. Find P(even number, 6).

   a. Find the probability of rolling an even number.

   b. Find the probability of rolling a 6.

   c. Multiply the two probabilities and express your answer as a percent.

State whether each pair of events is independent or dependent.

2. A number cube is rolled twice.

3. Choose a marble, replace it, and choose a second marble.

4. Two children are born into a family—a girl, then a boy.

5. Your birthday is today and you have a birthday party.

Suppose that two marbles are drawn from the bag. The first marble is replaced before the second is drawn. Find each probability.

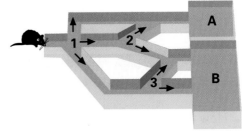

6. P(blue, yellow)   7. P(blue, blue)   8. P(green, **not** green)

Suppose that two marbles are drawn from the bag. The first marble is *not* replaced before the second is drawn. Find each probability.

9. P(blue, yellow)   10. P(blue, blue)   11. P(green, **not** green)

In the maze, a mouse picks his paths at random and continues toward the rooms marked A and B.

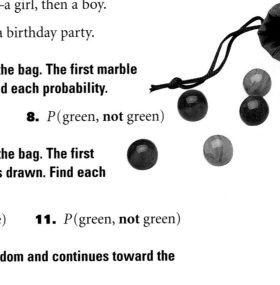

12. If the mouse reaches **2**, what is the probability that he ends in room A?

13. If the mouse reaches **3**, what is the probability that he ends in room B?

14. What is the probability that the mouse shown ends in room A? In room B?

15. **Industry** Suppose a security system and its backup each have a 97% chance of functioning correctly. If the systems are independent, what is the probability that they both fail?

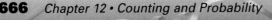

16. **Test Prep** You buy a box of 50 birthday candles that has 10% red, 30% blue, 30% green, 20% yellow, and 10% white candles. If you pull 2 candles from the box, what is the probability that they are both blue?

Ⓐ 8.6%　　Ⓑ 9%　　Ⓒ 15%　　Ⓓ 60%

17. You won a prize on your birthday.

a. If the prizes are chosen at random, what is your chance of winning the concert tickets?

b. If the first-place winner chose the graphing calculator, what are your chances of winning the concert tickets now?

PRIZES!

Concert Tickets

Graphing Calculator

Computer Game

3 Music CDs

Dinner for 2

Problem Solving and Reasoning

18. **Critical Thinking** Two different letters are selected from the word BIRTHDAY. The first letter is not replaced.

a. What is the probability that at least one letter is a vowel?

b. If the first letter selected is R, what is the probability that at least one letter is a vowel?

c. If the first letter selected is A, what is the probability that at least one letter is a vowel?

19. **Communicate** Explain how you could use the Counting Principle to find the probability of a compound event.

20. **Chance** You toss a coin three times and each time it comes up heads. What is the probability that it will come up heads on the fourth toss?

Mixed Review

Find the volume of each solid. Use 3.14 for π. *[Lesson 9-9]*

21.

11 in.

2.5 in.

22.

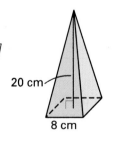

20 cm

8 cm

23. What are the coordinates of the point $(-1, -2)$ after being translated 2 units right and 4 units up? *[Lesson 11-6]*

Project Progress

Think about the probabilities you would want for your game. Can you use permutations or combinations to help you design your game?

Problem Solving

Understand

Plan

Solve

Look Back

TECHNOLOGY

Using a Graphing Calculator • Simulation

Problem: Simulate how often people arrive at a checkout counter. Estimate the probability that at least 2 people will show up at the same time within a 5-minute period.

You can use a graphing or scientific calculator to do this.

Suppose that the number of people arriving at a checkout counter each minute is given by the probabilities shown in the table.

Generate a random probability with your calculator. Find out how many people this represents using the last column of the table.

1 Complete the table (look for a pattern).

Number Arriving	Probability	Use
0	0.5	0 to 0.5
1	0.25	0.5 to 0.75
2	0.13	0.75 to 0.88
3	0.07	
4	0.05	

2 Press MATH, then choose **PRB** and **rand**. When you press ENTER twice, you get a random number between 0 and 1. Because this number is between 0.5 and 0.75, it represents 1 customer arriving.

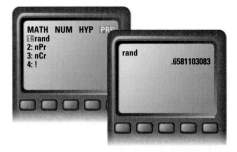

3 Pressing ENTER 4 more times gives you 5 "minutes." For the numbers shown, 1, 1, 0, 0, and 0 customers arrived at the register. Two or more people did **not** show up within the same minute.

Solution: Generate several more 5-minute periods and record whether 2 or more people show up. To estimate the probability, divide the total number of times 2 or more people show up by the total number of 5-minute periods.

TRY IT

Suppose the probability that a basketball player makes a free throw is 0.710. Use a simulation to estimate the probability that she makes 3 out of 3 free throws.

ON YOUR OWN

► Try to simulate spins of a spinner numbered from 0 to 10.

Section 12B Connect

In the Connect, you will apply your knowledge of probability to a famous birthday problem.

Happy Birthday, Baby

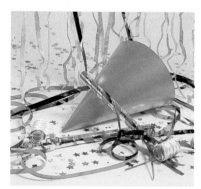

Your mission: Get through the room without finding two people with the same birthday. It should be easy, true? After all, there are 366 possible birthdays and only 20 to 30 of you.

Don't ask birthdays yet!

1. You will be the first student. Begin with one other student. What is the probability that you two share a birthday? Is this experimental or theoretical probability?

2. Assuming that you two do not share a birthday, how many birthdays remain that are open (not one of your birthdays)?

3. Add a third person. Does the birthday match either of your birthdays?

4. Continue adding a person at a time. What's happening to the probability of any pair sharing a birthday? Is the chance of each new person sharing a birthday with the others independent of the number of people already there?

5. Did you succeed in your mission? If there was a match, how many people did it take? How many matches were there in your class? Are you surprised?

6. If there were 370 people in the room, would there have to be a pair that share a birthday? Why?

Section 12B Review

Identify the sample space for each experiment, find the number of outcomes satisfying each event, and find the probability of each event.

1. Rolling a number cube with faces numbered 1 through 6. Events:

   a. Rolling a 5   **b.** Rolling a multiple of 2   **c.** Rolling a 7

2. Drawing a marble from a bag of 4 red, 2 green, and 3 blue marbles. Events:

   a. Drawing a red marble   **b.** Not drawing a blue marble

3. If you toss two number cubes, what are the following probabilities?

   a. $P(\text{sum of } 2)$ **b.** $P(\text{sum} > 9)$ **c.** $P(\text{sum of } 6, 7, \text{ or } 8)$

4. You draw two marbles from a bag of 3 red, 2 green, and 3 blue marbles. Find the probability if the first marble is replaced. Then find the probability if it is not replaced.

   a. $P(\text{red, then green})$ **b.** $P(\text{red, then red})$ **c.** $P(\text{red, then \textbf{not} red})$

5. What is the probability of spinning yellow?

6. What is the probability of **not** spinning red?

7. If you spin the spinner twice, what is the probability of spinning red, then yellow?

8. If the first spin lands on red, what is the probability that both spins will land on red?

9. If one person is selected from a group to serve on a committee, does that affect the probability of the next selection? Why or why not?

10. **Journal** Compare and contrast independent and dependent events.

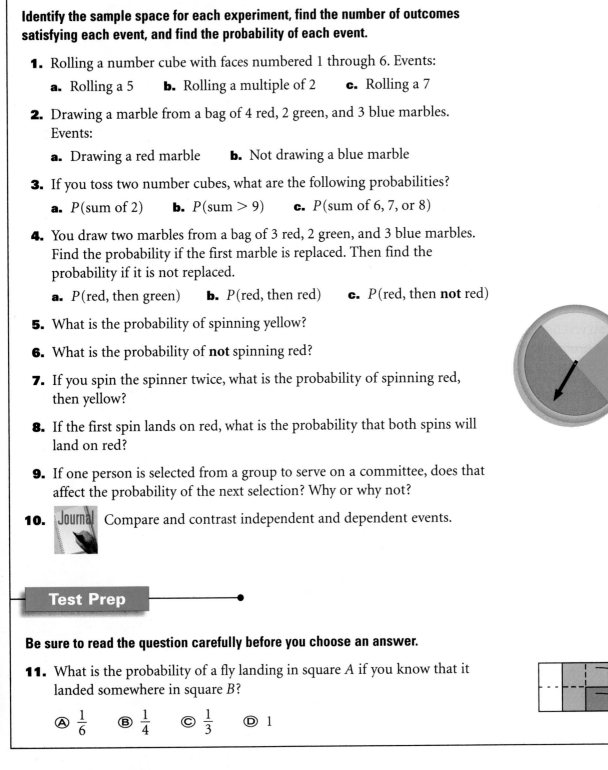

Test Prep

Be sure to read the question carefully before you choose an answer.

11. What is the probability of a fly landing in square *A* if you know that it landed somewhere in square *B*?

    Ⓐ $\dfrac{1}{6}$ Ⓑ $\dfrac{1}{4}$ Ⓒ $\dfrac{1}{3}$ Ⓓ 1

Probability of *A* OR *B*

When a number cube is rolled, it can't come up 2 and 5 at the same time. These are called *mutually exclusive* events—if one happens, the other can't happen. The probability of rolling a 2 OR rolling a 5 is just the sum of the probabilities.

In general, the probability of two mutually exclusive events is
$P(A \text{ OR } B) = P(A) + P(B)$.

Of 100 students, 90 take math, 80 take science. What is the probability that a student is taking math OR science (or both)?

If we were to simply add their probabilities, the result is greater than 1:

$$P(\text{math OR science}) \stackrel{?}{=} P(\text{math}) + P(\text{science})$$
$$\stackrel{?}{=} 0.9 + 0.8$$
$$\stackrel{?}{=} 1.7$$

But they are not mutually exclusive; you *can* take both math and science. You can see how adding in this case counts those taking math AND science twice:

To avoid this, the one extra math AND science group must be subtracted:

$$P(\text{math OR science}) = P(\text{math}) + P(\text{science}) - P(\text{math AND science})$$

Assuming that taking math and taking science are independent events:

$$P(\text{math AND science}) = 0.9(0.8)$$

So $P(\text{math OR science}) = 0.9 + 0.8 - 0.9(0.8) = 1.7 - 0.72 = 0.98$.

The probability that a student would take math or science is 0.98.

Try It

a. Two number cubes are rolled. What is the probability that either the first or second cube gives a 4?

b. What is the probability that, on a single draw, a heart or an ace will be picked from a deck of 52 cards? *Hint:* There are 13 hearts, 4 aces, and 1 ace of hearts.

1. Carmen's is having an outfit special. Buyers can choose one of 3 shirts, pants in one of 5 colors, and shoes in one of 2 styles. How many different outfits can a buyer choose?

2. The lunch special at Earl's Eatery includes soup or salad, and a choice of pasta, quiche, or sandwich. How many different lunch specials can be ordered?

3. Evaluate each expression.

   a. $7!$ b. $\dfrac{8!}{5!}$ c. $\dfrac{6!}{2!(6-2)!}$

4. How many ways can the letters of the word PHONE be arranged?

5. A disc jockey has chosen 6 songs he wants to play, but there is only enough time for 3 of them before the news. How many different ways can he select and order the 3 songs?

6. The debate club has 11 members.

   a. Find the number of ways to choose a committee of 3 members.

   b. Find the number of ways to choose 8 members to go on a trip.

7. What is the probability that a student chosen at random was born in March? Give your answer as a fraction, decimal, and percent. *Hint:* March has 31 days.

8. A pencil is chosen at random from 7 red, 3 blue, and 4 green pencils. List the possible outcomes in the sample space. What is the probability that the chosen pencil is green?

9. Cecilia rolled a number cube 60 times. Her results are shown. Give the experimental probability of rolling a 2.

Result	1	2	3	4	5	6
Number of Rolls	12	9	10	11	8	10

10. A wire is bent to make a trapezoid, as shown at the right. Find the probability that an ant crawling along the wire is on the 5 cm side.

    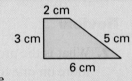

11. Find the probability that the ant in Exercise 10 is on the 6-cm side, given that it is on one of the two parallel sides.

12. Julio was born on the 30th day of the month. Find the probability that he was born in October. *Hint:* All months except February have at least 30 days.

13. A card is drawn at random from a deck of 52 cards containing 13 diamonds. It is replaced and the cards are shuffled, and then a second card is drawn. Find the probability that both cards are diamonds. Are these *independent* or *dependent* events?

14. What would your answers be in Exercise 13 if the first card is **not** replaced?

Performance Task

Show several ways to find the number of 4-letter combinations from the word SAMPLE. Then write down all of the combinations in an organized list.

Multiple Choice

Choose the best answer.

1. If the value of k in $\frac{y}{x} = k$ is 8 and $x = 4$, what is the value of y? *[Lesson 5-3]*

Ⓐ 2   Ⓑ 16   Ⓒ 32   Ⓓ 64

2. Holly's Appliance Depot buys an oven for $600 and sells it for $750. What is the percent increase? *[Lesson 6-4]*

Ⓐ 20%   Ⓑ 25%

Ⓒ 80%   Ⓓ 125%

3. Which number is divisible by 9? *[Lesson 7-1]*

Ⓐ 6,829,269   Ⓑ 4,286,484

Ⓒ 9,238,832   Ⓓ 5,757,365

4. Find the angle supplementary to 73°. *[Lesson 8-4]*

Ⓐ 27°   Ⓑ 107°   Ⓒ 117°   Ⓓ 163°

5. Find the area of a circle with a diameter of 12 cm. Use 3.14 for π. *[Lesson 9-3]*

Ⓐ 37.68 cm^2 Ⓑ 75.36 cm^2

Ⓒ 113.04 cm^2 Ⓓ 452.16 cm^2

6. Subtract the polynomials. *[Lesson 10-7]*
$(2x^2 - 4) - (5x^2 + 3x + 4)$

Ⓐ $-3x^2 - 3x - 8$ Ⓑ $-3x^2 - 3x$

Ⓒ $-3x^2 + 3x - 8$ Ⓓ $-3x^2 + 3x$

7. What rule shows that the triangles are congruent? *[Lesson 11-3]*

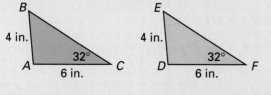

Ⓐ Angle-Side-Angle   Ⓑ Side-Angle-Side

Ⓒ Side-Angle-Angle   Ⓓ None of these

8. $\triangle PQR$ is similar to $\triangle TSR$. Find the length of $\overline{TR}$. *[Lesson 11-5]*

Ⓐ 28.8 cm

Ⓑ 31.5 cm

Ⓒ 41.14 cm

Ⓓ 45 cm

9. What kinds of symmetry are in this figure? *[Lesson 11-8]*

Ⓐ Line symmetry

Ⓑ 90° rotational symmetry

Ⓒ Point symmetry

Ⓓ A and C

Ⓔ A, B, and C

10. A pizza parlor offers 3 sizes and 8 toppings. How many different 1-topping pizzas can be ordered? *[Lesson 12-1]*

Ⓐ 8   Ⓑ 24   Ⓒ 56   Ⓓ 336

11. A test requires students to choose 3 of the 5 essay questions. How many ways can the 3 questions be chosen? *[Lesson 12-3]*

Ⓐ 10   Ⓑ 15   Ⓒ 20   Ⓓ 60

12. Arlene flipped a coin 100 times and got 48 heads and 52 tails. What is the experimental probability of flipping tails? *[Lesson 12-5]*

Ⓐ $\frac{12}{25}$ Ⓑ $\frac{12}{13}$ Ⓒ $\frac{13}{25}$ Ⓓ $\frac{1}{2}$

13. You roll a number cube twice. What is the probability that you get a 4 on the first roll and an odd number on the second roll? *[Lesson 12-7]*

Ⓐ $\frac{1}{36}$ Ⓑ $\frac{1}{12}$ Ⓒ $\frac{1}{4}$ Ⓓ $\frac{2}{3}$

Chapter Review

1. Construct a line plot for the data set 43, 39, 51, 45, 40, 39, 49, 47, 42, 50, 39, 42, 44.

2. Make a stem-and-leaf diagram for the data set 28, 14, 29, 26, 35, 26, 19, 15, 19.

3. Find the mean, median, and mode of the data values 50.3, 41.2, 59.0, 46.7, 41.2, and 45.4.

4. Construct a box-and-whisker plot for the data set 3, 7, 2, 9, 4, 5, 2, 1, 0, 6.

5. Make a bar graph to show that a sandwich costs $4.00, a dessert $2.00, a drink $1.50, and a candy bar $0.50.

6. Describe a method for taking a random sample of customers in a bookstore.

7. Make a line graph for the following running times (in sec): 84 on September 5, 93 on September 10, 87 on September 15, and 82 on September 20.

8. Would a random selection of 200 people watching a movie premiere be a random sample of the population of moviegoers? Explain.

9. Read the bar graph to determine the number of each item in the music store.

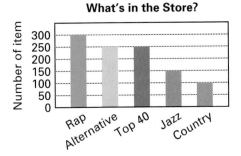

10. Read the line graph to determine the number of alternative CDs purchased by the music store each year.

11. Create a frequency table for the data set 4, 2, 5, 3, 2, 6, 5, 4, 5, 6, 2, 6, 4, 2.

12. Create a frequency table for the data set 1.5, 1.1, 0.8, 1.4, 0.9, 1.1, 1.5, 1.0, 1.3, 0.9, 1.5, 1.0, 1.3, 1.2.

13. Make a frequency table showing four occurrences each of 9.3 and 5.7, two of 1.5, and one each of 6.4 and 7.7.

14. Create a scatterplot and draw a trend line for the data set (1982, 10.3), (1984, 8.4), (1986, 11.4), (1988, 10.0), (1990, 13.5), and (1992, 14.2).

15. The U.S. government collected individual income taxes totaling $240 billion in 1980, $330 billion in 1985, $470 billion in 1990, and $590 billion in 1995 (estimated). Create a scatterplot and draw a trend line if possible.

16. One day in July, the temperature during the day was 89°F at 1:00 P.M., 92°F at 2:00 P.M., 94°F at 3:00 P.M., 96°F at 4:00 P.M., and 95°F at 5:00 P.M. Create a scatterplot for the data.

Chapter 2 Review

1. Find the absolute value of −93.

2. Find $|15| + |-23|$.

Compute.

3. −37 + (−29)

4. 73 + (−41)

5. −63 − 22

6. −38 − (−84)

7. −12 × 8

8. −54(−19)

9. 84 ÷ (−7)

10. −273 ÷ (−13)

11. 7 × −6

12. −4(12 − 19)

13. 4 × 11 − 56 ÷ (−8)

14. $5 - \dfrac{4(14 - 9)}{2}$

15. The temperature was −18°F and it went down 7°. What was the new temperature?

Give the coordinates of each point.

16. A

17. B

18. C

19. D

20. E

21. F

22. Write 8^4 in expanded form.

23. Write 12^5 in expanded form.

24. Write 9 × 9 × 9 × 9 × 9 × 9 in exponential form.

25. Write 2 × 2 × 2 × 2 in exponential form.

Evaluate.

26. $(-5)^3$

27. -4^0

28. -8^2

29. 1^8

Write each number in scientific notation.

30. Forty-two million

31. Seven thousandths

32. 835,000

33. 0.00000091

34. Write 6.31×10^6 in standard notation.

35. Write 2.97×10^{-4} in standard notation.

36. A microgram is 0.000001 g. Express this weight in scientific notation.

37. Venus is 67,200,200 mi from the sun. Express this distance in scientific notation.

38. The population of New Orleans, Louisiana, was 1,240,000 in 1990. Write this number in scientific notation.

39. A milligram in the metric system equals 0.0000022 lb. Write this number in scientific notation.

CHAPTER REVIEW

1. Using w for weeks and d for days, write a formula for the number of weeks in d days.

2. Find the area of a triangle with base 6.4 m and height 8.8 m. Use the formula $A = \frac{1}{2}bh$, where b is the base and h is the height.

3. Write an algebraic expression for "$12.50 each, plus $2.00 shipping and handling."

4. Simplify the expression $6(b - 3)$.

5. Evaluate the expression $5x + 2y$ for $x = -2$ and $y = 4$.

6. Evaluate the expression $-6x + 5y$ for $x = 3$ and $y = -2$.

Solve each equation.

7. $23 = m + 36$ **8.** $\frac{x}{3} = 12$ **9.** $z - 9 = 4$ **10.** $4y = 28$

11. The Pizza-n-More restaurant sells submarine sandwiches for $6 each and charges $2 for delivery. With $20, how many subs can you buy?

12. Are $x - 2$ and $4x$ equivalent expressions? Justify your answer.

Solve each equation.

13. $n - 40 = 47$ **14.** $x + 31 = 78$ **15.** $y \times 6 = 3.3$ **16.** $10 = \frac{2x}{3}$

17. $2.4 = 16z$ **18.** $7 = \frac{h}{42}$ **19.** $4x + 18 = 34$ **20.** $2x - 12 = 12$

21. The maximum height h (in ft) of an object thrown straight up from an initial height of a (in ft) with velocity v (in ft/sec) is given by the formula $h = a + \frac{v^2}{64}$. Find the initial height when $h = 36$ ft and $v = 32$ ft per sec.

Solve each inequality.

22. $y + 21 < 49$ **23.** $7.9 \geq \frac{2b}{5}$ **24.** $x - 14 > 32$ **25.** $12 \leq \frac{1}{2}y$

26. $w + (-2) \geq 32.5$ **27.** $\frac{k}{3} < 2.76$ **28.** $67 \geq h + 5$ **29.** $13 > \frac{3f}{6}$

Solve each inequality, then graph the solution.

30. $10 + 2x \leq 4$ **31.** $2y - 8 \geq -2$ **32.** $7 < \frac{x}{2}$ **33.** $3x - 1 > 3$

34. $\frac{x}{3} < 4$ **35.** $4x - 7 \leq 5$ **36.** $17 + 3x > 20$ **37.** $y + 14 < 12$

Chapter 4 Review

1. Find the value of y when $x = -2$ in the equation $y = -3x$.

2. Make a table of values for the equation $y = x - 9$. Use 0, 1, 2, 3, 4, and 5 for x.

3. Find the rule that relates x and y in the table. Then find y when $x = 28$.

x	1	2	3	4	5
y	4	8	12	16	20

4. Determine whether each ordered pair is a solution of $y = \frac{3}{2}x - 2$.

   a. $(2, 5)$ b. $\left(3, \frac{5}{2}\right)$ c. $(6, 9)$ d. $(8, 10)$

5. Give two solutions for the equation $y = 4x + 1$.

6. Graph the equation $y = 2x - 3$. Use 0, 1, 2, and 3 as x values.

7. A towing company charges a fee of $50 plus $2 per mile to tow a car. Graph the price charged. Use x for the number of miles towed.

8. Draw a line through the origin with the given slope.

   a. -2 b. $\frac{3}{4}$ c. $-\frac{1}{2}$

9. Graph the equation $y = -\frac{1}{4}x + 1$. Find the slope, the x-intercept, and the y-intercept.

10. For each line, find the slope, the x-intercept, and the y-intercept.

    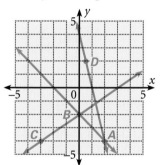

    a. Line through A and B
    b. Line through B and C
    c. Line through A and D

11. For each line, find the slope, x-intercept, and y-intercept.

    a. $y = 5x - 2$

    b. $y = -x + 1$

    c. $y = x - \frac{1}{2}$

Solve each system of equations by graphing.

12. $y = 2x + 3 \qquad y = -\frac{1}{2}x - 2$

13. $y = x + 2 \qquad y = 2x + 1$

14. Econo Taxi charges $2 per trip plus $2 per mi. Super Taxi charges $5 per trip plus $1 per mi. For what number of mi is each cost the same?

Graph each inequality.

15. $y \geq 3x - 2$

16. $y < -\frac{1}{2}x - 1$

17. $y \leq x + 2$

18. $y > 2x - 1$

1. Write the ratio 5 to 6 as a fraction.

2. Draw a picture to show a ratio 4:3 of circles to squares.

3. Write all the ratios that can be made using the figure at the right.

4. Jean drives 248 mi in 4 hr and Paul drives 392 mi in 7 hr. Use cross products to determine whether these rates are equal.

5. Is the table an equal ratio table? If so, find the value of k.

x	6	12	18	24	30
y	5	10	15	20	25

6. Complete the table to create ratios equal to the given ratio.

5			20		30
8	16	24		40	

7. If the value of k in $\frac{y}{x} = k$ is 12 and $x = 25$, what is the value of y?

8. If the value of k in $\frac{y}{x} = k$ is 3 and $y = 12$, what is the value of x?

Solve each proportion.

9. $\dfrac{84}{48} = \dfrac{63}{m}$

10. $\dfrac{36}{81} = \dfrac{x}{324}$

11. $\dfrac{x}{102} = \dfrac{72}{136}$

12. $\dfrac{17}{x} = \dfrac{8}{32}$

13. Find the unit rate and create a rate formula for a rate of $1540 in 7 weeks.

14. Julie types 251 words in 4 min. Estimate how many words she would type in 15 min.

15. The ratio of jackets to shirts sold by Carla's Clothing Store is 6:17. In a two-week period, the store sold 136 shirts. About how many jackets were sold?

16. Last year, Central School had 420 students and 24 teachers. This year, there are 490 students. If the student-teacher ratio remained the same, how many teachers are there this year?

17. A scale drawing of a house is 3 in. tall and 13 in. across. If the scale is 1 in. = 4 ft, what are the dimensions of the actual house?

18. Find the missing measures in the pair of similar figures.

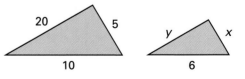

19. Find the unit rate for each situation.

a. $7.20 buys 18 candy bars

b. $0.50 for 100 paper clips

c. Traveled 120 miles in 2 hours

Chapter 6 Review

1. Use the information in the circle graph.

   a. What percent of the students watch 1 hr of television or less per day?

   b. What percent of the students watch 2 to 3 hr of television per day?

   c. What percent of the students watch 3 or more hr of television per day?

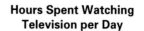

Hours Spent Watching Television per Day

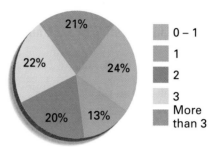

- 0 – 1
- 1
- 2
- 3
- More than 3

2. Write the fraction, decimal, and percent that describe how much of the figure is shaded.

3. Estimate the percent of the shaded region.

4. What number is 65% of 280?

5. Estimate 55% of 342.

6. Of the people at a concert, 12% bought a T-shirt after the show. If 156 people bought T-shirts, how many people were at the concert all together?

7. Find the total cost of a $110 stereo when its price is increased by 12%.

8. Estimate 37% of 248.

9. 15 is 24% of what number?

10. Pete's Boutique buys a sweatshirt for $24.95 and sells it for $39.95. What is the percent of increase?

11. A video normally sells for $29.95. Find its price during a 20%-off sale.

12. Abdul bought a book priced at $22.95. What was the tax rate if he had to pay $24.67 with tax?

13. Sharon earned $260 in simple interest on an investment in 5 yr. If the interest rate was 8%, what was her principal?

14. The price of a plane ticket can vary depending on the time of travel. Find the percent decrease for a ticket with a price of $210 in June and $145 in September.

15. Sal receives a discount on all purchases at the store where he works. He buys a radio for which the store originally paid $49.60. The store marked the price up 25% for retail, but Sal's price is $49.60. What percent discount did he receive?

16. Gina has a car valued at $4500. She sells it at an auction at an increase of 19%, but the auctioneer took 5% of the selling price. What amount did Gina receive when she sold her car?

Chapter 7 Review

1. Determine whether 184 is divisible by 2, 3, 4, 5, 6, 7, 8, 9, or 10.

2. Use a factor tree to determine the prime factorization of 504.

Determine the prime factorization of each number.

3. 21

4. 68

5. 117

6. 136

7. Find the GCF of 48 and 66.

8. Use prime factorization to find the GCF of 60 and 294.

9. Write the fraction $\frac{72}{104}$ in lowest terms.

10. Find the LCM of 24 and 30.

11. In one classroom, $\frac{4}{7}$ of the students are wearing T-shirts and $\frac{1}{3}$ of the students with T-shirts are wearing jeans. What fraction of the students are wearing both a T-shirt and jeans?

12. Rebecca does aerobics every three days and weight training every four days. Today she did both. In how many days will Rebecca again do both aerobics and weight training on the same day?

13. Write $\frac{14}{33}$ as a decimal and determine whether it is repeating or terminating.

14. Replace $\square$ with $>$, $<$, or $=$ to compare 10.9119 $\square$ 10.912.

15. Write 0.62 as a fraction in lowest terms.

16. Subtract $98.24 - 24.351$.

17. Add $4\frac{5}{8} + 11\frac{1}{2}$.

18. Divide $3\frac{4}{5} \div 5\frac{1}{6}$.

Write each decimal as a fraction in lowest terms.

19. 0.56

20. 76.892

21. $0.\overline{33}$

22. $1.\overline{64}$

23. Use prime factorization to find the LCM of 35 and 84.

24. Use prime factorization to find the GCF of 26 and 78.

Determine each square root.

25. $\sqrt{81}$

26. $-\sqrt{121}$

27. $\pm\sqrt{144}$

28. $-\sqrt{625}$

29. State whether 169 is a perfect square.

30. Find the square root of $\frac{36}{225}$.

31. Find the two consecutive integers that $\sqrt{89}$ is between.

32. What is the side length of a square with area 48 ft²?

33. Find $\pm\sqrt{361}$.

34. Find the missing side length for the right triangle.

1. Convert 16 pt to qt.

2. Convert 6.2 m to cm.

3. What metric unit would you use for the mass of a bicycle?

4. Determine which measurement is more precise, 6 m or 605 cm.

5. Calculate 12.34 ft × 3.194 ft with the correct number of significant digits.

6. Find the complementary and supplementary angle measures for a 73° angle.

7. What are the latitude and longitude of Munich?

8. What is the position of Berlin relative to Frankfurt?

9. Classify 60° as a right, straight, obtuse, or acute angle.

10. In the figure shown,

   a. Which lines are parallel?

   b. Which lines are perpendicular?

   c. Which angle is a supplement to ∠A?

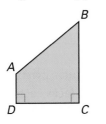

11. In the figure shown,

   a. Which angle is obtuse?

   b. Which angle is acute?

   c. Which angle is 90°?

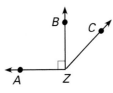

12. Draw the top view for the cube tower.

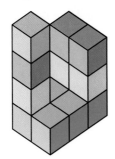

13. Classify the shape of this polygon by the number of sides. Then find the sum of the angle measures. [Hint: $180°(k - 2)$]

CHAPTER REVIEW

1. Find the perimeter and area of each polygon.

a.

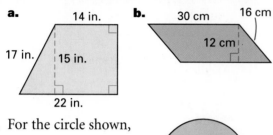

14 in.

17 in.　15 in.

22 in.

b.

30 cm　16 cm

12 cm

2. Find the perimeter and area of

　a. the polygon in Exercise 1a after a dilation by a scale factor of $\frac{3}{2}$.

　b. the polygon in Exercise 1b after a dilation by a scale factor of $\frac{3}{4}$.

3. For the circle shown, find the circumference and the area.

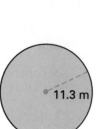

11.3 m

4. Katie wears a ring that has a circumference of 2.36 in. Find the diameter of the ring.

5. Find the surface area of each figure.

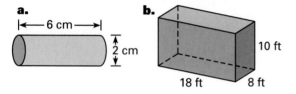

a.

6 cm

2 cm

b.

10 ft

18 ft　8 ft

6. Find the slant height and the surface area of each figure.

a.

15 in.

8 in.

b.

18 ft　18 ft

13.5 ft

18 ft　18 ft

7.8 ft

7. Find the volume of each solid.

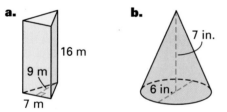

a.

16 m

9 m

7 m

b.

7 in.

6 in.

8.　a. Find the volume of the solid in Exercise 7a after scaling two dimensions by a scale factor of $\frac{1}{4}$.

　b. Find the surface area and volume of the solid in Exercise 7b after a dilation by a scale factor of 3.

9. Sketch a cylinder with a diameter of 3 in. and a height of 4 in. Then find its volume.

10. Sketch a triangular prism 6 cm in height. The triangular faces each have a base of 8 cm and a height of 4 cm. Then find its volume.

11. Find the volume of each solid.

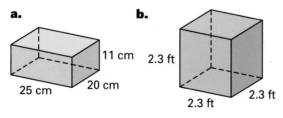

a.

11 cm

25 cm　20 cm

b.

2.3 ft

2.3 ft

2.3 ft

12. A circular cone has a base area of 12 in². Find the volume of the cone if it's height is:

　a. 3 in.

　b. 12 in.

Chapter 10 Review

1. For the function machine shown,

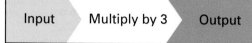

   a. Find the output value for an input of 4;

   b. Find the input value for an output of -15.

2. What is a possible rule for the input and output shown in the table?

Input	3	5	7	9	10
Output	5	9	13	17	19

3. For the function rule $y = -4x - 1$, complete the table of values.

x	-1	0	1	2	3
y					

4. A ball is dropped from a height of 240 ft. Its height after t sec is given by $h = -16t^2 + 240$. Graph the function. When did the ball hit the ground?

5. Graph the functions $y = x^2$ and $y = x^2 - 2$ and explain their differences.

6. Graph the equation $y = 2x + 4$. Does the equation describe a linear function?

7. A car rental company charges $35 for each day or portion thereof. Graph this function.

8. Write the polynomial expression $4x^2 - 7x^4 + 2x - 1 + x^3$ in descending order. Find the degree of the polynomial.

Evaluate each expression for the given value of the variable.

9. $g^2 - 4g$ for $g = 2$ **10.** $2x^2 + 5x - 7$ for $x = -4$ **11.** $x^3 - x^2 + 6x - 2$ for $x = -3$

Simplify each expression. Write the resulting polynomial in descending order.

12. $3 - 6x + x^2 + x - 12 + 4x^3$

13. $2x - 9 + 4x^2 - x + 17$

Add or subtract each polynomial. Write each answer in simplest form.

14. $(y^2 - 7y + 4) + (3y^2 - y - 9)$

15. $(x^2 + 8x - 11) + (2x^2 + 3x - 1)$

16. $(-y^2 + 5y) - (2y^2 - 3y + 8)$

17. $(x^3 + 2x^2 - x + 4) - (x^3 - 2x^2 - 2x + 10)$

18. Find the total area of the region.

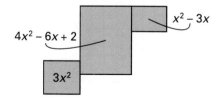

19. The perimeter is $3x^2 - 4x + 9$. Find the missing side length.

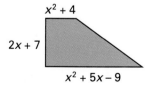

20. Find the area of a rectangle with a width of $3x + 4$ and a length of $2x^2$. Write the answer in lowest terms.

21. Multiply $-\frac{1}{3}t^2(3 - 12t)$.

1. The two trapezoids are similar. Find the length x and the measure of ∠A.

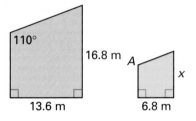

2. Are the figures congruent?

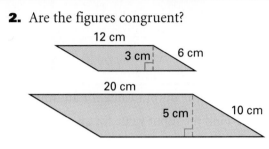

3. State whether the triangles are congruent; if they are, give the rule that justifies your answer.

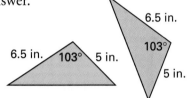

4. Use the lengths of the sides to write and evaluate the sine, cosine, and tangent ratios for the labeled angle.

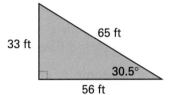

5. In the figure, △DEF is similar to △GHF. Find the length of $\overline{GH}$.

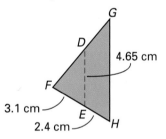

6. Which are lines of symmetry?

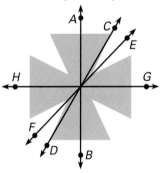

7. Which transformation has occurred? Are the figures similar? Congruent?

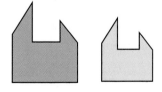

8. The trapezoid was reflected across the y-axis. Find the coordinates of points A and B.

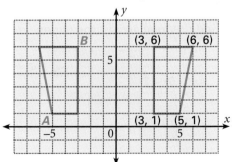

9. Can this tessellation be made using only rotations of a single polygon?

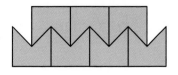

Chapter 12 Review

1. Make a tree diagram to show the possible results of spinning both spinners.

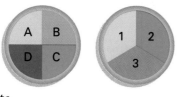

2. There are 6 different types of sandwiches and 5 different drinks. How many choices are there if only one sandwich and one drink are allowed?

3. Evaluate.

   a. $(4!)(2!)$ **b.** $(8 - 5)!$ **c.** $\dfrac{9!}{3!(9 - 3)!}$

4. How many ways can the letters of the word CAPTION be arranged?

5. Ten people are running in a race. How many ways can runners place first, second, and third?

6. A pizza parlor offers 12 different toppings for its pizzas. How many ways can a customer select 5 toppings for a pizza?

7. An office has 200 employees. How many ways can 15 employees be chosen to attend a conference? Use factorial notation for your answer.

8. What is the probability of rolling an odd number on one toss of a number cube?

9. What is the probability that a card chosen from a 52-card deck is one of the 13 hearts?

10. The probability that a tennis player will win a match is 60%. What is the probability that the player will lose the match?

11. Roll a pair of number cubes 25 times. Record the sums that appear and calculate the experimental probability of rolling sums greater than 9.

12. A dart is thrown at the target shown. What is the probability that the dart lands in a red area?

13. What is the probability that a card chosen from a 52-card deck is an ace, given that it is a diamond?

14. You roll a pair of number cubes and the first one comes up 5. What is the probability that the sum of the two number cubes is less than 8?

15. A drawer contains 6 black socks, 5 white socks, and 2 brown socks. Two socks are chosen in order. Find P(black, brown) if

    a. the first sock is replaced before choosing the second.

    b. the first sock is not replaced.

16. A gumball machine contains 16 blue, 22 white, 12 yellow, and 25 green gumballs. Find the probability of

    a. getting one white followed by one blue gumball.

    b. getting two yellow gumballs.

17. State whether Exercise 15 involves *independent* or *dependent* events.

18. A number cube is rolled twice. Find the probability that 4 is rolled both times.

Geometric Formulas

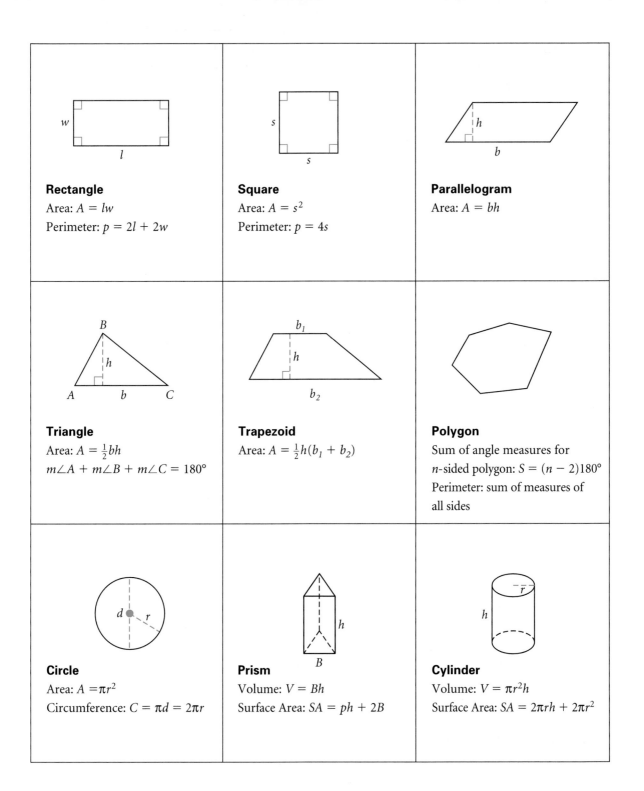

Rectangle
Area: $A = lw$
Perimeter: $p = 2l + 2w$

Square
Area: $A = s^2$
Perimeter: $p = 4s$

Parallelogram
Area: $A = bh$

Triangle
Area: $A = \frac{1}{2}bh$
$m\angle A + m\angle B + m\angle C = 180°$

Trapezoid
Area: $A = \frac{1}{2}h(b_1 + b_2)$

Polygon
Sum of angle measures for
n-sided polygon: $S = (n - 2)180°$
Perimeter: sum of measures of
all sides

Circle
Area: $A = \pi r^2$
Circumference: $C = \pi d = 2\pi r$

Prism
Volume: $V = Bh$
Surface Area: $SA = ph + 2B$

Cylinder
Volume: $V = \pi r^2 h$
Surface Area: $SA = 2\pi rh + 2\pi r^2$

Measurement Conversion Factors

Metric Measures of Length
1000 meters (m) = 1 kilometer (km)
100 centimeters (cm) = 1 m
10 decimeters (dm) = 1 m
1000 millimeters (mm) = 1 m
10 cm = 1 decimeter (dm)
10 mm = 1 cm

Area
100 square millimeters = 1 square centimeter
(mm^2) (cm^2)
$10,000 \ cm^2 = 1$ square meter (m^2)
$10,000 \ m^2 = 1$ hectare (ha)

Volume
1000 cubic millimeters = 1 cubic centimeter
(mm^3) (cm^3)
$1000 \ cm^3 = 1$ cubic decimeter (dm^3)
$1,000,000 \ cm^3 = 1$ cubic meter (m^3)

Capacity
1000 milliliters (mL) = 1 liter (L)
1000 L = 1 kiloliter (kL)

Mass
1000 kilograms (kg) = 1 metric ton (t)
1000 grams (g) = 1 kg
1000 milligrams (mg) = 1 g

Temperatures in Degrees Celsius (°C)
0°C = freezing point of water
37°C = normal body temperature
100°C = boiling point of water

Time
60 seconds (sec) = 1 minute (min)
60 min = 1 hour (hr)
24 hr = 1 day

Customary Measures of Length
12 inches (in.) = 1 foot (ft)
3 ft = 1 yard (yd)
36 in. = 1 yd
5280 ft = 1 mile (mi)
1760 yd = 1 mi
6076 ft = 1 nautical mile

Area
144 square inches = 1 square foot
(in^2) (ft^2)
$9 \ ft^2 = 1$ square yard (yd^2)
$43,560 \ sq \ ft^2 = 1$ acre (A)

Volume
1728 cubic inches = 1 cubic foot
(cu in.) (cu ft)
27 cu ft = 1 cubic yard (cu yard)

Capacity
8 fluid ounces (fl oz) = 1 cup (c)
2 c = 1 pint (pt)
2 pt = 1 quart (qt)
4 qt = 1 gallon (gal)

Weight
16 ounces (oz) = 1 pound (lb)
2000 lb = 1 ton (T)

Temperatures in Degrees Fahrenheit (°F)
32°F = freezing point of water
98.6°F = normal body temperature
212°F = boiling point of water

TABLES

Symbols

$+$	plus or positive	$\llcorner$	right angle
$-$	minus or negative	$\perp$	is perpendicular to
$\cdot$	times	$\parallel$	is parallel to
$\times$	times	AB	length of $\overline{AB}$; distance between A and B
$\div$	divided by	$\triangle ABC$	triangle with vertices A, B, and C
$\pm$	positive or negative	$\angle ABC$	angle with sides $\overrightarrow{BA}$ and $\overrightarrow{BC}$
$=$	is equal to	$\angle B$	angle with vertex B
$\neq$	is not equal to	$m\angle ABC$	measure of angle ABC
$<$	is less than	$'$	prime
$>$	is greater than	a^n	the nth power of a
$\leq$	is less than or equal to	$|x|$	absolute value of x
$\geq$	is greater than or equal to	$\sqrt{x}$	principal square root of x
$\approx$	is approximately equal to	π	pi (approximately 3.1416)
$\%$	percent	(a, b)	ordered pair with x-coordinate a and y-coordinate b
$a{:}b$	the ratio of a to b, or $\frac{a}{b}$	$P(A)$	the probability of event A
$\cong$	is congruent to	$n!$	n factorial
$\sim$	is similar to		
$\circ$	degree(s)		
$\overleftrightarrow{AB}$	line containing points A and B		
$\overline{AB}$	line segment with endpoints A and B		
$\overrightarrow{AB}$	ray with endpoint A and containing B		

Squares and Square Roots

N	N^2	$\sqrt{N}$	N	N^2	$\sqrt{N}$
1	1	1	51	2,601	7.141
2	4	1.414	52	2,704	7.211
3	9	1.732	53	2,809	7.280
4	16	2	54	2,916	7.348
5	25	2.236	55	3,025	7.416
6	36	2.449	56	3,136	7.483
7	49	2.646	57	3,249	7.550
8	64	2.828	58	3,364	7.616
9	81	3	59	3,481	7.681
10	100	3.162	60	3,600	7.746
11	121	3.317	61	3,721	7.810
12	144	3.464	62	3,844	7.874
13	169	3.606	63	3,969	7.937
14	196	3.742	64	4,096	8
15	225	3.873	65	4,225	8.062
16	256	4	66	4,356	8.124
17	289	4.123	67	4,489	8.185
18	324	4.243	68	4,624	8.246
19	361	4.359	69	4,761	8.307
20	400	4.472	70	4,900	8.367
21	441	4.583	71	5,041	8.426
22	484	4.690	72	5,184	8.485
23	529	4.796	73	5,329	8.544
24	576	4.899	74	5,476	8.602
25	625	5	75	5,625	8.660
26	676	5.099	76	5,776	8.718
27	729	5.196	77	5,929	8.775
28	784	5.292	78	6,084	8.832
29	841	5.385	79	6,241	8.888
30	900	5.477	80	6,400	8.944
31	961	5.568	81	6,561	9
32	1,024	5.657	82	6,724	9.055
33	1,089	5.745	83	6,889	9.110
34	1,156	5.831	84	7,056	9.165
35	1,225	5.916	85	7,225	9.220
36	1,296	6	86	7,396	9.274
37	1,369	6.083	87	7,569	9.327
38	1,444	6.164	88	7,744	9.381
39	1,521	6.245	89	7,921	9.434
40	1,600	6.325	90	8,100	9.487
41	1,681	6.403	91	8,281	9.539
42	1,764	6.481	92	8,464	9.592
43	1,849	6.557	93	8,649	9.644
44	1,936	6.633	94	8,836	9.695
45	2,025	6.708	95	9,025	9.747
46	2,116	6.782	96	9,216	9.798
47	2,209	6.856	97	9,409	9.849
48	2,304	6.928	98	9,604	9.899
49	2,401	7	99	9,801	9.950
50	2,500	7.071	100	10,000	10

Trigonometric Ratios

Degrees	Sin	Cos	Tan	Degrees	Sin	Cos	Tan
0°	0.0000	1.0000	0.0000				
1°	0.0175	0.9998	0.0175	46°	0.7193	0.6947	1.0355
2°	0.0349	0.9994	0.0349	47°	0.7314	0.6820	1.0724
3°	0.0523	0.9986	0.0524	48°	0.7431	0.6691	1.1106
4°	0.0698	0.9976	0.0699	49°	0.7547	0.6561	1.1504
5°	0.0872	0.9962	0.0875	50°	0.7660	0.6428	1.1918
6°	0.1045	0.9945	0.1051	51°	0.7771	0.6293	1.2349
7°	0.1219	0.9925	0.1228	52°	0.7880	0.6157	1.2799
8°	0.1392	0.9903	0.1405	53°	0.7986	0.6018	1.3270
9°	0.1564	0.9877	0.1584	54°	0.8090	0.5878	1.3764
10°	0.1736	0.9848	0.1763	55°	0.8192	0.5736	1.4281
11°	0.1908	0.9816	0.1944	56°	0.8290	0.5592	1.4826
12°	0.2079	0.9781	0.2126	57°	0.8387	0.5446	1.5399
13°	0.2250	0.9744	0.2309	58°	0.8480	0.5299	1.6003
14°	0.2419	0.9703	0.2493	59°	0.8572	0.5150	1.6643
15°	0.2588	0.9659	0.2679	60°	0.8660	0.5000	1.7321
16°	0.2756	0.9613	0.2867	61°	0.8746	0.4848	1.8040
17°	0.2924	0.9563	0.3057	62°	0.8829	0.4695	1.8807
18°	0.3090	0.9511	0.3249	63°	0.8910	0.4540	1.9626
19°	0.3256	0.9455	0.3443	64°	0.8988	0.4384	2.0503
20°	0.3420	0.9397	0.3640	65°	0.9063	0.4226	2.1445
21°	0.3584	0.9336	0.3839	66°	0.9135	0.4067	2.2460
22°	0.3746	0.9272	0.4040	67°	0.9205	0.3907	2.3559
23°	0.3907	0.9205	0.4245	68°	0.9272	0.3746	2.4751
24°	0.4067	0.9135	0.4452	69°	0.9336	0.3584	2.6051
25°	0.4226	0.9063	0.4663	70°	0.9397	0.3420	2.7475
26°	0.4384	0.8988	0.4877	71°	0.9455	0.3256	2.9042
27°	0.4540	0.8910	0.5095	72°	0.9511	0.3090	3.0777
28°	0.4695	0.8829	0.5317	73°	0.9563	0.2924	3.2709
29°	0.4848	0.8746	0.5543	74°	0.9613	0.2756	3.4874
30°	0.5000	0.8660	0.5774	75°	0.9659	0.2588	3.7321
31°	0.5150	0.8572	0.6009	76°	0.9703	0.2419	4.0108
32°	0.5299	0.8480	0.6249	77°	0.9744	0.2250	4.3315
33°	0.5446	0.8387	0.6494	78°	0.9781	0.2079	4.7046
34°	0.5592	0.8290	0.6745	79°	0.9816	0.1908	5.1446
35°	0.5736	0.8192	0.7002	80°	0.9848	0.1736	5.6713
36°	0.5878	0.8090	0.7265	81°	0.9877	0.1564	6.3138
37°	0.6018	0.7986	0.7536	82°	0.9903	0.1392	7.1154
38°	0.6157	0.7880	0.7813	83°	0.9925	0.1219	8.1443
39°	0.6293	0.7771	0.8098	84°	0.9945	0.1045	9.5144
40°	0.6428	0.7660	0.8391	85°	0.9962	0.0872	11.4301
41°	0.6561	0.7547	0.8693	86°	0.9976	0.0698	14.3007
42°	0.6691	0.7431	0.9004	87°	0.9986	0.0523	19.0811
43°	0.6820	0.7314	0.9325	88°	0.9994	0.0349	28.6363
44°	0.6947	0.7193	0.9657	89°	0.9998	0.0175	57.2900
45°	0.7071	0.7071	1.0000	90°	1.0000	0.0000	

TABLES

Glossary

absolute position   Location given as coordinates. [p. 402]

absolute value   A number's distance from zero, represented by $|\ |$. Example: $|-8| = 8$. [p. 63]

acute angle   An angle measuring less than 90°. [p. 412]

Addition Property of Equality   If $a = b$, then $a + c = b + c$. [p. 141]

additive inverse   A number's opposite. The sum of additive inverses is zero. Example: 5 and -5 are additive inverses of each other. [p. 67]

adjacent leg   For an acute angle on a right triangle, the leg lying on one of the angle's sides. [p. 579]

algebraic expression   An expression involving variables, numbers, and operation symbols. Example: $2x + 17$. [p. 128]

alternate angles   Two angles formed by a transversal and each of the lines it crosses, on opposite sides of the transversal, either both interior or both exterior. [p. 417]

angle   A figure formed by two lines meeting at one point. [p. 410]

angle bisector   A line, segment, or ray that divides an angle into two congruent angles. [p. 413]

angle of rotation   The angle through which a figure turns during a rotation. [p. 594]

Angle-Side-Angle (ASA)   A rule used to determine whether triangles are congruent by comparing corresponding parts. [p. 575]

area   The number of square units contained in a figure. [p. 446]

arrangement   The order in which people, letters, numbers, or other things appear. [p. 631]

Associative Property (of Addition)   The fact that grouping does not affect the sum of two or more numbers. Example: $(a + b) + c = a + (b + c)$. [p. 69]

Associative Property (of Multiplication)   The fact that grouping does not affect the product of two or more numbers. Example: $(ab)c = a(bc)$.

bar graph   A graph using bars to represent the values of a data set. [p. 23]

base   On a three-dimensional figure, the top or bottom. [p. 462]

binomial   A two-term polynomial. [p. 533]

boundary line   On a graph of a linear inequality, the line separating points that are solutions from points that are not. [p. 207]

box-and-whisker plot   A visual way of showing median values for a data set. [p. 17]

center   The point that is the same distance from all points on a circle. [p. 456]

center of rotation   The point about which a rotation turns a figure. [p. 594]

circle   A plane figure whose points are all the same distance from its center. [p. 457]

circle graph   A graph in the form of a circle cut into wedges, also called a pie chart. [p. 274]

circular cone   A three-dimensional figure with a circular base and one vertex. [p. 469]

circumference   The distance around a circle. [p. 456]

circumscribed   A polygon with exactly one point of each side on the circumference of a circle. [p. 458]

coefficient   A constant by which a variable is multiplied. Example: in $12y$, 12 is the coefficient. [p. 146]

combination   A selection of objects from a set, without regard to order. [p. 638]

common denominator   A denominator that is the same for two or more fractions. [p. 345]

common factor   A factor shared by two numbers. Example: 7 is a common factor of 28 and 42. [p. 330]

common multiple   A multiple shared by two numbers. Example: 12 is a common multiple of 2 and 3. [p. 335]

Commutative Property (of Addition)   The fact that order does not affect the sum of two or more numbers. Example: $a + b = b + a$. [p. 69]

Commutative Property (of Multiplication)   The fact that order does not affect the product of two or more numbers. Example: $ab = ba$.

complementary   Two angles whose measures add up to 90°. [p. 412]

composite number An integer larger than 1 that is not prime. [p. 324]

compound event Event containing more than one outcome. Example: rolling first a 3 and then an even number with a number cube. [p. 663]

compound interest Interest based on both principal and previous interest. [p. 308]

compound statement A logical statement formed by joining two or more statements. [p. 163]

concave polygon A polygon with one or more diagonals lying outside the figure. [p. 424]

conditional probability The probability that an event B will occur, given that event A has already occurred. [p. 658]

cone A solid with one circular base. [p. 469]

congruent Two figures with the same shape and size. [p. 413]

conic projection A map projection that uses a cone shape to represent a spherical surface. [p. 499]

conjunction A logical set of statements joined by the word *AND*. [p. 163]

constant A number that does not vary. [p. 123]

constant of proportionality The quantity $\frac{y}{x}$ for two variables x and y whose ratio is constant. [p. 235]

convex polygon A polygon with all diagonals lying inside the figure. [p. 424]

coordinate system A set of intersecting number lines used to locate points. [p. 91]

coordinates A pair of numbers used to locate a point on the coordinate plane. [p. 235]

corresponding angles Matching angles on similar figures. The angles on the same side of a transversal that intersects two or more lines. [p. 417]

corresponding sides Matching sides on figures. [p. 565]

cosine For an acute angle x on a right triangle, the cosine of x is $\cos(x) = \frac{\text{adjacent leg}}{\text{hypotenuse}}$. [p. 580]

Counting Principle If a situation can occur in m ways, and a second situation can occur in n ways, then these things can occur together in $m \times n$ ways. [p. 627]

cross multiplication Multiplying opposite numerators and denominators of two ratios. [p. 243]

cross product The product of a numerator of one ratio with the denominator of another. [p. 229]

cube A 6-sided prism whose faces are congruent squares. [p. 479]

cylinder A three-dimensional figure with two parallel, congruent circles for bases. [p. 463]

cylindrical projection A map projection that uses a cylinder shape to represent a spherical surface. [p. 499]

degree For a polynomial, the value of the largest exponent of a variable. Example: the degree of $7x - x^3$ is 3. [p. 533]

dependent events Events for which the occurrence of one affects the probability of the other. [p. 663]

dependent variable The output variable for a function. [p. 513]

diagonal On a polygon, a segment connecting two vertices that do not share a side. [p. 423]

diameter The length of the segment that passes through the center of a circle and has both endpoints on the circle. [p. 457]

dilation A proportional reduction or enlargement of a figure. [p. 450]

direct variation When two variables are related by a constant ratio. [p. 555]

disjunction A logical set of statements joined by the word OR. [p. 163]

Distributive Property The fact that $a(b + c) = ab + ac$. [p. 83]

divisible Can be divided by another integer without remainder. [p. 324]

double bar graph A combination of two bar graphs, comparing two related data sets. [p. 24]

double line graph A combination of two line graphs, comparing two related data sets. [p. 25]

double stem-and-leaf diagram A stem-and-leaf comparison of two sets of data in a single diagram. [p. 7]

edge A segment where two faces of a polyhedron meet. [p. 461]

endpoint A point at the end of a line segment or ray. [p. 411]

equal ratios Ratios naming the same amount. Example: $\frac{6}{2}$ and $\frac{3}{1}$. [p. 227]

equation A statement that two numerical or variable expressions are equal. [p. 128]

equilateral triangle A triangle with three congruent sides. [p. 422]

equivalent equations Equations that are true for exactly the same variable replacements. [p. 141]

equivalent expressions Two expressions that always have the same value for the same substitutions. [p. 164]

evaluate To substitute values for variables in an expression and then simplify by applying the order of operations. [p. 128]

event A set of outcomes. Example: when a number cube is rolled, an event may be an even number turns up. [p. 646].

experiment In probability, any activity involving chance, like a coin flip. [p. 646]

experimental probability An estimated probability based on data from experiments or surveys. [p. 651]

exponent A raised number showing repeated multiplication. Example: $5^3 = 5 \cdot 5 \cdot 5$, where 3 is the exponent. [p. 96]

exponential function A nonlinear function in which an exponent is a variable. [p. 524]

exterior angles Angles formed by a transversal and the lines it crosses, outside of those lines. [p. 417]

face One of the polygon surfaces composing a polyhedron. [p. 461]

factor An integer that divides another integer without remainder. Example: 6 is a factor of 42. [p. 324]

factor tree A diagram showing how a whole number breaks into its prime factors. [p. 326]

factorial The product of all positive integers less than or equal to a number. Example: 6 factorial = $6! = 6 \cdot 5 \cdot 4 \cdot 3 \cdot 2 \cdot 1$. [p. 633]

formula A statement of a relationship among unknown quantities. Example: $P = 2(b + h)$. [p. 123]

frequency The number of times something occurs in a survey. [p. 38]

frequency table A table showing classes of things, a tally, and the frequency with which things occur. [p. 38]

function An input-output relationship giving only one output for each input. [p. 508]

Fundamental Theorem of Arithmetic All integers greater than 1 can be written as an unique product of prime numbers. [p. 325]

geometric probability A probability based on comparing measurements of geometric figures. [p. 654]

golden rectangle Rectangle with a length to width ratio of approximately 1.618. [p. 265]

greatest common factor (GCF) The largest number that is a common factor. Example: 15 is the GCF of 45 and 60. [p. 330]

height On a pyramid, the perpendicular distance from the base to the (opposite) vertex. [p. 466]

heptagon A seven-sided polygon. [p. 421]

hexagon A six-sided polygon. [p. 421]

histogram A type of bar graph where the categories are numeric. [p. 38]

hypotenuse The side opposite the right angle in a right triangle. [p. 374]

identity For any operation, the number that keeps another number the same. 0 is the additive identity, since $a + 0 = a$, 1 is the multiplicative identity since $a \times 1 = a$. [p. 141]

independent events Events for which the occurrence of one has no effect on the probability of the other. [p. 663]

independent variable The input variable for a function. [p. 513]

inequality A mathematical sentence involving $<$, $>$, $\le$, or $\ge$. [p. 156]

inscribed A polygon with all its vertices on the circumference of a circle. [p. 458]

integers Whole numbers and their opposites: ... $-3, -2, -1, 0, 1, 2, 3, ...$. [p. 63]

interest Money paid for the use of money. [p. 308]

interior angles Angles formed by a transversal and the lines it crosses, between those lines. [p. 417]

inverse variation When two variables are related by a constant product. [p. 555]

irrational number A number, such as $\sqrt{2}$, that cannot be expressed as a repeating or terminating decimal. [p. 370]

isosceles triangle A triangle with at least two congruent sides. [p. 422]

latitude A measurement in degrees east or west from the prime meridian. [p. 90]

least common multiple (LCM) The smallest number that is a common multiple. Example: 48 is the LCM of 12 and 16. [p. 335]

like terms Terms in which the same variable is raised to the same exponent. Example: $3x^2$ and $9x^2$ are like terms. [p. 537]

line A one-dimensional figure extending forever in both directions. [p. 411]

line graph A line drawn through pairs of associated numbers on a grid, usually to show changes in data over time. [p. 24]

line of symmetry   The line that divides a figure with line symmetry into two identical halves. [p. 605]

line plot   A display of data that uses stacked X's to show how many times each data value occurs. [p. 7]

line segment   Part of a straight line, with two endpoints. [p. 411]

line symmetry   A figure has line symmetry if one half is the mirror image of the other. [p. 605]

linear equation   An equation for which the graph is a straight line. [p. 182]

linear function   A function whose graph is a straight line. [p. 514]

linear inequality   A mathematical sentence involving $<$, $>$, $\leq$, or $\geq$ whose graph is a region with a straight-line boundary. [p. 207]

longitude   A measurement in degrees north or south from the equator. [p. 90]

lower quartile   The median of the lower half of a data set. [p. 18]

mean   The sum of a set of data values, divided by the number of values. [p. 11]

measure of central tendency   A single value summarizing a set of numerical data. [p. 11]

median   The middle value of a data set, when the values are arranged in numerical order. [p. 12]

metric system   A system of measurement based on the meter, the gram, and the liter. [p. 390]

mode   The most common value in a data set. [p. 13]

monomial   A one-term polynomial. [p. 533]

multiple   A product of a given integer and some other integer. Example: 35 is a multiple of 5, since $5 \cdot 7 = 35$. [p. 324]

multiplication property   If A and B are independent events, then the probability of both occurring is given by $P(A \text{ and } B) = P(A) \cdot P(B)$. [p. 664]

Multiplication Property of Equality   If $a = b$, then $ac = bc$. [p. 146]

multiplicative inverse   If the product of two numbers is 1, each number is the multiplicative inverse of the other. Example: 6 and $\frac{1}{6}$ are multiplicative inverses. [p. 78]

mutually exclusive   If either event A or B occurs, then the other cannot occur. [p. 671]

negative number   A number less than zero. [p. 63]

negative slope   The slope of a line slanting downward. [p. 191]

negative square root   The opposite of the principal square root of a number. [p. 369]

net   A pattern that could be folded to create a three-dimensional figure such as a prism. [p. 462]

nonlinear equation   An equation whose graph is a curve rather than a line. [p. 213]

nonlinear function   A function for which equal changes in x do not result in equal changes in y. [p. 518]

obtuse angle   An angle measuring more than 90° but less than 180°. [p. 412]

octagon   An eight-sided polygon. [p. 421]

opposite leg   For an acute angle on a right triangle, the leg lying across from the angle. [p. 579]

opposites   Two numbers on opposite sides from zero and the same distance from zero, such as 3 and -3. [p. 62]

Order of Operations   The rules telling what order to do operations in: Do any operations inside grouping symbols, exponents, multiplications and divisions and additions and subtractions. [pp. 83, 97]

ordered pair   A pair of numbers, such as $(-2, 8)$, used to describe a point in a coordinate system. [p. 91]

origin   The point $(0, 0)$ in a coordinate system, where the x-axis and y-axis intersect. [p. 91]

outcome   One of the possible equally likely results of an experiment. [p. 646]

outlier   An extreme value in a data set, separated from most of the other values. [p. 12]

parabola   A U-shaped or upside-down U-shaped curve, the graph of a quadratic function. [p. 518]

parallel lines   Lines in a plane that never intersect. On a graph, lines with the same slope. [p. 197]

parallelogram   A quadrilateral with two pairs of congruent sides. [p. 423]

pentagon   A five-sided polygon. [p. 421]

percent   A ratio comparing a number to 100. Example: 63% means $\frac{63}{100}$. [p. 274]

percent decrease   The decrease in an amount expressed as a percent of the original amount. [p. 300]

percent increase   The increase in an amount expressed as a percent of the original amount. [p. 294]

perfect square   A number with an integer square root. [p. 364]

perimeter The distance around a figure. [p. 444]

permutation An arrangement in which order is important. [p. 631]

perpendicular Lines forming a right angle. [p. 416]

perpendicular bisector A line, segment, or ray that is perpendicular to a line segment and divides the line segment into two congruent parts. [p. 416]

pi (π) The ratio of a circle's circumference to its diameter: 3.14159265... . [p. 457]

point symmetry Point symmetry is a kind of rotational symmetry. A figure has point symmetry if it rotates onto itself after a rotation of 180°. [p. 607]

polygon A figure formed by three or more points joined by line segments. [p. 421]

polyhedron A three-dimensional figure composed of polygons. [p. 461]

polynomial An algebraic expression that is the sum of one or more terms. [p. 532]

population The collection of all things to be studied in a survey. [p. 32]

positive number A number greater than zero. [p. 63]

positive slope The slope of a line slanting upward. [p. 191]

power A number that can be written as a product of equal factors (or, in other words, as an integer with an integer exponent). Example: $32 = 2^5$. [p. 96]

precision The exactness of a measurement, determined by the unit of measure. [p. 396]

prime factor A prime number that divides another integer without remainder. [p. 325]

prime factorization A number written as a product of prime factors. Example: $120 = 2^3 \cdot 3 \cdot 5$. [p. 326]

prime number An integer larger than 1 divisible only by itself and one. The primes start with 2, 3, 5, 7, 11, ... [p. 324]

principal An amount of money deposited or borrowed, on which interest is paid. [p. 308]

principal square root The positive square root of a number. [p. 369]

prism A polyhedron with vertical sides whose bases are congruent and parallel. [p. 462]

probability The chance that a particular event can occur. [p. 646]

proportion An equation stating that two ratios are equal. [p. 229]

pyramid A polyhedron with one base, on which all other faces are triangles meeting at a single point. [p. 466]

Pythagorean Theorem For every right triangle, the sum of the squares of each leg equals the square of the hypotenuse. [p. 374]

quadrant One of the four regions into which the x- and y-axes divide the coordinate grid. [p. 91]

quadratic function A function where the value of x is squared. The graph of a quadratic function is a parabola. [p. 518]

quadrilateral A four-sided polygon. [p. 421]

quartile One of the numbers dividing a data set into equal fourths. [p. 17]

radical sign $\sqrt{}$, the symbol for the square root of a number. [p. 364]

radius The distance from the center of a circle to any point on the circle. [p. 456]

random sample A sample chosen in such a way that every member of the population has an equal chance of being included. [p. 33]

range The difference between the highest and lowest values in a data set. [p. 6]

rate A ratio in which two quantities using different units of measure are compared. Example: 76 dollars per 8 hours. [p. 224]

ratio A comparison of two quantities by division. [p. 222]

rational number A number that can be written as a ratio of two integers, such as $\frac{2}{3}$. [p. 344]

ray Part of a straight line, with just one endpoint. [p. 411]

real numbers All rational and irrational numbers. [p. 370]

reciprocal One divided by a number. The number and its reciprocal are multiplicative inverses. [pp. 78, 357]

rectangle A quadrilateral with four right angles. [p. 423]

reflection A transformation that flips a figure over a line. [p. 594]

regular polygon A polygon with all sides and all angles congruent. [p. 424]

relative position Location given in relationship to another place. [p. 402]

repeating decimal A decimal with a repeating digit or group of digits on the right, like 5.787878... . [p. 345]

rhombus A parallelogram with four sides of equal length. [p. 423]

right angle An angle measuring 90°. [p. 412]

right triangle A triangle with one right angle. [p. 374]

rise For a line on a graph, the vertical change for a given horizontal change, or run. [p. 191]

rotation A transformation that turns a figure about a point. [p. 594]

rotational symmetry A figure has rotational symmetry if it rotates onto itself after a rotation of less than 360°. [p. 606]

run For a line on a graph, the horizontal change used to find the vertical change, or rise. [p. 191]

sample The part of the population examined in a survey. [p. 32]

sample space The set of all possible outcomes of an experiment. [p. 646]

scale The ratio of measurements in a scale drawing to the measurements of the actual object. [p. 256]

scale drawing A drawing showing the shape of an object exactly, but not the actual size. [p. 256]

scale factor The ratio of new dimensions to old dimensions after a dilation. [p. 450]

scalene triangle A triangle with no congruent sides. [p. 422]

scatterplot A graph showing a set of points based on two data sets. [p. 43]

scientific notation Writing a number as a power of 10 times a number whose absolute value is less than 10 but greater than or equal to 1. Example: $0.097 = 9.7 \times 10^{-2}$. [p. 102]

sequence A patterned arrangement of numbers. [p. 113]

Side-Angle-Angle (SAA) A rule used to determine whether triangles are congruent by comparing corresponding parts. [p. 575]

Side-Angle-Side (SAS) A rule used to determine whether triangles are congruent by comparing corresponding parts. [p. 575]

Side-Side-Side (SSS) A rule used to determine whether triangles are congruent by comparing corresponding parts. [p. 575]

significant digits In a measured quantity, the digits representing the actual measurement. [p. 397]

similar Having the same shape but not necessarily the same size. [p. 259]

similarity ratio The ratio between corresponding side lengths on similar figures. [p. 565]

simple interest Interest based on principal alone. [p. 308]

simplified A polynomial containing no like terms. [p. 538]

simplify To reduce the complexity of an expression by applying the order of operations. [p. 128]

simulation An experimental model used to find probability. [p. 668]

sine For an acute angle x on a right triangle, the sine of x is $\sin(x) = \frac{\text{opposite leg}}{\text{hypotenuse}}$. [p. 580]

slant height On a pyramid, the perpendicular distance from one edge of the base to the vertex. [p. 466]

slope For a line on a graph, the rise divided by the run. [p. 191]

solution The variable replacement making an equation true. [p. 128]

solution of a system The variable replacements making all equations in a system true. [p. 202]

solve To find the variable replacement that makes an equation true. [p. 128]

sphere A solid whose points are all the same distance from its center. [p. 479]

square A rectangle with four sides of equal length. [p. 423]

square root The square root of N is the number that when multiplied by itself gives N. Example: 9 is the square root of 81. [p. 364]

stem-and-leaf diagram A display of data that uses the digits of the data numbers to show the shape and distribution of the data set. [p. 7]

step function A function in which different rules are applied to different input values. The graph of a step function is made up of unconnected pieces. [p. 525]

straight angle An angle measuring 180°. [p. 412]

substitute To replace a variable with a specific value. [p. 123]

supplementary Two angles whose measures add up to 180°. [p. 412]

surface area On a polyhedron, the sum of the areas of the faces. [p. 461]

survey A study that requires collecting and analyzing information. [p. 32]

symmetry A figure has symmetry if it coincides with itself after some transformation. [p. 605]

system of linear equations Two or more linear equations considered together. [p. 202]

tally A quick record of a count taken during a survey. [p. 38]

tangent For an acute angle x on a right triangle, the tangent of x is $\tan(x) = \frac{\text{opposite leg}}{\text{adjacent leg}}$. [p. 580]

term A number in a sequence. [p. 113]

terminating decimal A number with a fixed number of digits. [p. 345]

terms A part of a polynomial containing a variable with a whole-number exponent and coefficient. [p. 532]

tessellation A repeating pattern of figures that covers a plane without gaps or overlaps. [p. 610]

theoretical probability The actual probability of an event. The ratio of the number of equally likely outcomes in the event to the number in the sample space. [p. 651]

transformation A movement of points that affects all points of a figure. [p. 594]

translation A transformation that slides all points of a figure the same distance in the same direction. [p. 595]

transversal A line crossing two or more other lines. [p. 417]

trapezoid A quadrilateral with exactly one pair of parallel sides. [p. 423]

tree diagram A tree-like diagram on which each branch shows a possible outcome of a situation. [p. 626]

trend A pattern formed by points on a scatterplot. [p. 43]

trend line A line that approximately "fits" points forming a trend in a scatterplot. [p. 43]

trial One experiment. [p. 652]

triangle A three-sided polygon. [p. 421]

trigonometric ratios Ratios of the side lengths of a right triangle, related to the measures of the triangle's acute angles. [p. 580]

trinomial A three-term polynomial. [p. 533]

unit rate A rate in which the second number in the comparison is one unit. Example: 300 million meters per second. [p. 224]

U.S. customary units A system of measurement units, including the inch, the pound, and the gallon, widely used in the United States. [p. 390]

upper quartile The median of the upper half of a data set. [p. 18]

variable A symbol, such as x, that represents an unknown quantity. [p. 123]

Venn diagram A visual aid that shows relationships by grouping things into sets. [p. 422]

vertex On an angle or a polygon, the point where the two sides intersect. On a polyhedron, the intersection point of three or more faces. [pp. 410, 421, 461]

vertical angles Angles on opposite sides of the intersection of two lines. [p. 418]

volume The number of cubic units in a solid. [p. 476]

x-axis The horizontal number line in a coordinate system. [p. 91]

x-coordinate The first number in an ordered pair used to locate a point in a coordinate system. [p. 91]

x-intercept The x-coordinate of the point where a graph crosses the x-axis. [p. 196]

y-axis The vertical number line in a coordinate system. [p. 91]

y-coordinate The second number in an ordered pair used to locate a point in a coordinate system. [p. 91]

y-intercept The y-coordinate of the point where a graph crosses the y-axis. [p. 196]

Zero Property of Addition The sum of an integer and its additive inverse is 0. [p. 67]

Selected Answers

Chapter 1

1-1 Try It

Leaf	Stem	Leaf
	0	9
	1	2 4 7
9 8 6 3 2	2	1 1
6	3	

1-1 Exercises & Applications

1. a. 5 **b.** 3 or 12–15 **c.** 13; 15
3. Range: $2 to $7

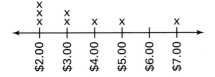

5. Range: 8 to 33

Stem	Leaf
0	8
1	2 6 8
2	2 3
3	3

7.

Leaf	Stem	Leaf
2	12	
	13	
5	14	
0	15	
5	16	0
	17	
5 5 5	18	0 0 0
	19	
5	20	0
	21	5
	22	0
	23	
	24	3

9.

Stem	Leaf
5	0 3 7
6	6
7	5 5 6
8	1
10	1
11	7

13. 437 **15.** 50,000
17. 7,030,000 **19.** 725 **21.** 8803
23. 6109 **25.** 10,500

1-2 Try It

Mean: $9; Median: $7.50

1-2 Exercises & Applications

1. a. 774 **b.** 9 **c.** 86 **3.** Mean:
180; Median: 174; Mode: None
5. Outlier: 31; Revised mean:
≈ 11.4; Revised median: 10.5
7. Mean: 91 million people **9.** C
11. Mean: $5.80 **13.** Eight hun-
dred fifty-six **15.** Four thousand
eight hundred twenty-six
17. Forty-five thousand six hundred
19. Three million seven hundred
forty-six thousand seven hundred
21. 726 **23.** 398 **25.** 3854
27. 4848

1-3 Try It (Example 1)

a. 20 or 0–20 **b.** Median: 4
c. Lower quartile: 2; Upper quartile:
10 **d.** One-quarter of the 12- to 15-
year-olds have been to a music store
between 10 and 20 times.

1-3 Try It (Example 2)

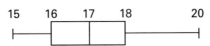

Between 16 and 18

1-3 Exercises & Applications

1. a. 100; 90 **b.** 95 **c.** 93 **d.** 99
e.

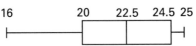

3. Between 20 and 24.5

5.

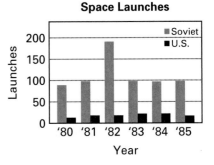

Possible answer: The middle half of
the data has a range of 1524 to
2515. **7.** With outliers **11.** 18,486
13. 19,886 **15.** 558,448
17. 274,752 **19.** 43,640
21. 37,000 **23.** 46,400

1-4 Try It (Example 1)

a. 1990 **b.** 1994

1-4 Try It (Example 4)

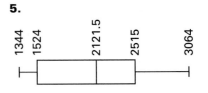

1-4 Exercises & Applications

1.

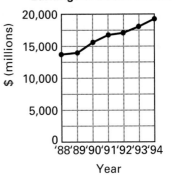

3.

Number of Postmasters in U.S.

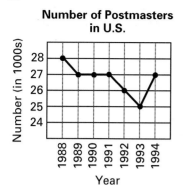

Probably stayed the same.   **5.** D
7. Yes; all the data would still be shown.   **9.** 26   **11.** 36   **13.** 7 R11
15. 578, 735, 2378, 4321   **17.** 4257, 4527, 4725   **19.** 642, 654, 664, 684

Section 1A Review

1. Mean: 3.8; Median: 5; Mode: 5

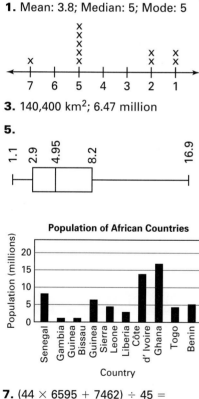

3. 140,400 km^2; 6.47 million

5.

Population of African Countries

7. (44 × 6595 + 7462) ÷ 45 = (about) 6614 fans

1-5 Try It

a. 679   **b.** No: a person who is on-line had a better chance of being surveyed than a person who is not.

1-5 Exercises & Applications

1. City households; 2301   **3.** U.S. state governors; Random
5. Country music fans; Not random
7. No; Sample is too small.
9. a. Women   **b.** 7244   **11.** No; Possible answers: Only people who respond to surveys responded.
13. Possible answer: Advertisers want to influence buyers, not users.
15. 56,460   **17.** 974,352

1-6 Try It (Example 1)

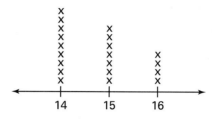

1-6 Try It (Example 2)

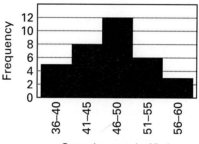

Speed range (mi/hr)

1-6 Exercises & Applications

1. a.

1993 Population

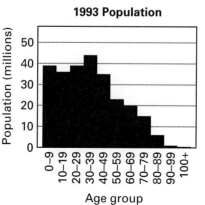

Age group

b. No, the frequency table gives intervals instead of exact ages.
c. A histogram

5.

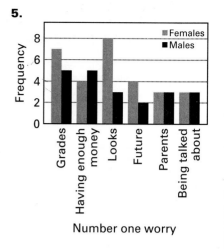

Number one worry

7. 2,066,592   **9.** 5,975,692
11. 1,758,591   **13.** 1,367,888
15. Mean: ≈ 55.44; Median: 64
17. Mean: 75.5; Median: 75.5

1-7 Try It (Example 1)

As the total waste increases, the amount recycled increases.

1-7 Try It (Example 2)

a. No   **b.** No relationship

1-7 Exercises & Applications

1. a. No trend   **b.** Yes, positive
c. Yes, negative
3.

NASA's Budget

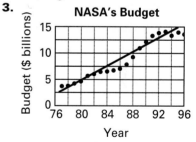

Year

$17 billion   **5.** D   **9.** Yes
11. 891,488   **13.** 15,251,067,288
15. 77,732,551,971

1-8 Try It

a. How many hours do you spend on homework each week?
b. Possible answer: Pick names randomly.   **c.** Possible answer: A box-and-whisker plot.

1-8 Exercises & Applications

1. a. U.S. teenagers   **b.** To get U.S. teenagers to buy more of the company's shoes.   **c.** No, since New Yorkers might have different music tastes than the rest of the country.
3. Possible answer: What sports do you participate in?   **5.** Possible answer: How many TVs are in your home?   **7.** B   **11.** 32,768
13. 161,051   **15.** 7,311,616

Section 1B Review

1. a. Not random; Every 1st through 49th car.   **b.** Not random; Students who aren't the student's friends.
3.

Wait time (sec)	Frequency
0–60	4
61–120	6
121–180	3
181–240	1
241 +	1

Yes; The average wait time is about 112 seconds.   **5.** D

Chapter 1 Summary & Review

1.

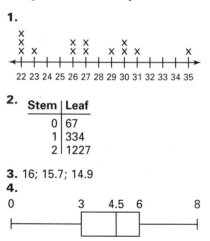

2.

Stem	Leaf
0	67
1	334
2	1227

3. 16; 15.7; 14.9
4.

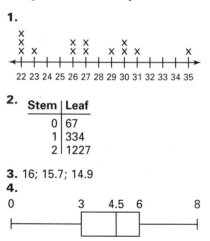

5.

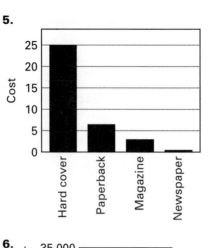

6.

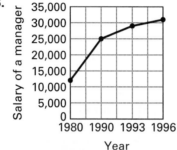

7. Answers may vary.   **8.** No, not all American adults read *TV Guide*.
9. Fiction: 1400; Non-Fiction: 1600; Reference: 1200; Multimedia: 500; Periodicals: 200   **10.** 1985: 200 books; 1986: 250 books; 1987: 300 books; 1988: 400 books; 1989: 300 books; 1990: 200 books

11.

0	1
1	1
2	3
4	1
5	3
6	2
7	2

12.

1	1
2	1
3	3
5	2
6	1
7	3
9	2

13.

1.57	2
2.45	1
2.74	1
5.35	3
7.39	1

14.

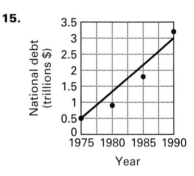

15.

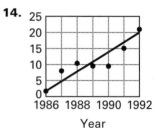

16.

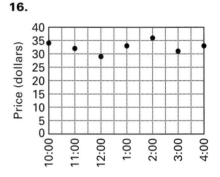

2-1 Try It (Example 1)

a. 3   **b.** −$3   **c.** 0

2-1 Try It (Example 2)

17, −17

2-1 Try It (Example 3)

Belgium, Denmark, France

2-1 Exercises & Applications

1. a.

b. −4 **c.** −4, −1, 0, 2, 3 **3.** 42
5. 0 **7.** Possible answer: Temperature on a winter day is 25° below zero. **9.** Possible answer: Owe $60. **11.** Possible answer: Deducted 75 points. **13.** D **15.** =
17. < **19.** > **21.** > **23.** 18
25. 2 **27.** 19,340 ft **29.** C
31. Possible answer: −$0.08
33. Random

2-2 Try It (Example 1)

a. 8 **b.** 2 **c.** −2 **d.** −8

2-2 Try It (Example 4)

a. 11 **b.** −22

2-2 Exercises & Applications

1. a. −2 + 2 + (−4) + (−3) + 5
b. (−2 + 2) + [(−4) + (−3)] + 5
c. 0 + (−7) + 5 **d.** −2 **3.** 3 + −5 = −2 **5.** −62 **7.** −6 **9.** −142
11. −48 **13.** −125 **15.** A
17. Never **19.** Always **21.** 327 gold bars **25.** It will be on the 29th floor. (Maybe the 30th floor because many buildings do not have a 13th floor.)
27. No trend

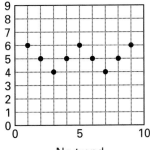

No trend

29. Women **31.** People who live in warm climates.

2-3 Try It (Example 2)

a. −12 **b.** −12 **c.** 12 **d.** 12

2-3 Try It (Example 3)

a. −31 **b.** Rose 25 ft

2-3 Exercises & Applications

1. a. −2 **b.** 9 **c.** −10 **3. a.** 12 + −24 = −12 **b.** −24 + −12 = −36
c. 24 + 12 = 36 **d.** −12 + 24 = 12
5. −148 **7.** −110 **9.** 967 **11.** −2
13. −48 **15.** 420 **17.** No
19. 1165°F **21.** D **23. a.** >; 5 is added on the left. **b.** <; 5 is added on the right.
25.

Stem	Leaf
3	2 4 8
4	1 2 2 6
5	3 8

2-4 Try It (Example 1)

−$10.00

2-4 Try It (Example 3)

a. $\frac{1}{-8}$ **b.** $\frac{5}{2}$ **c.** $\frac{3}{-8}$

2-4 Exercises & Applications

1. a. 78 **b.** −78 **3.** 48 **5.** −48
7. −12 **9.** −12 **11.** −14 **13.** 2
15. 0 **17.** −140 **19.** 0 **21.** −9
23. 0 **25.** 14 **27.** 28 **29.** C
31. $61 loss per month **33.** 100
35. Commutative **37.** −14°F
39. a. Positive **b.** Negative
41. $47\frac{2}{3}$; 47

2-5 Try It (Example 1)

10

2-5 Try It (Example 2)

a. −24 **b.** −792

2-5 Exercises & Applications

1. a. Multiplication **b.** Addition
c. Division **d.** Addition **3.** 22, 22
5. −12, −12 **7.** −9, −1 **9.** 90
11. −81 **13.** $36.44 **15.** 20
17. 1 **19.** 2° **21.** 100 + 24 ÷ (3 + 1) = 106 **23.** −5 × (3 + 3 × 6) = −105 **25.** 1.8 in. **27.** Possible answers: 3 ÷ 3 = 1; $\frac{3 + 3}{3 + 3}$ = 1; 3 − 3 + 3 ÷ 3 = 1 **29. a.** 36(100 + 1)
b. 50(100 − 1) **c.** (50 − 1)13
d. (100 − 2)42
31.

78   85.5   92 97.5   115

33.

Length (in.)	Frequency
1–8	6
9–16	4
17–24	8
25–32	3
33–40	5

Section 2A Review

1. a. 10°, 20°, 30°, 40°, 50° **b.** −10°, −20°, −30°, −40° **c.** 10°, −10°; 20°, −20°; 30°, −30°; 40°, −40° **d.** 50°
e. −40° **3.** −612 **5.** −1,326 **7.** 3
9. −9 **11.** 100 **13.** 10 **15.** 0
17. −500 **19.** −3 **21.** 5 **23.** −1
25. 682,650 **27.** C

2-6 Try It (Example 1)

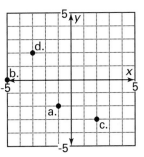

2-6 Try It (Example 2)

A is (2, 4); The low tide was 2, the high tide was 4.

B is (−4, −1); The low tide was −4, the high tide was −1.

C is (−7, −1); The low tide was −7, the high tide was −1.

D is (0, 3); The low tide was 0, the high tide was 3.

2-6 Exercises & Applications

1. a. *x* **b.** Left; −2 is negative.
c. *x* **d.** Down; −4 is negative.
2–5.

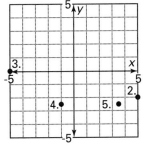

b. $f = 2g$, where g is the number of gallons and f is the maximum number of fish. **25.** 12 **27.** -419 **29.** 8^6

4-2 Try It (Examples 1–2)

a. No **b.** Possible answer: (4, 0), (6, −1)

4-2 Try It (Example 3)

a. $150 **b.** $1735

4-2 Exercises & Applications

1. a. Yes **b.** Yes **c.** No **3. a.** Yes **b.** No **c.** Yes **5. a.** No **b.** No **c.** Yes **7. a.** No **b.** Yes **c.** Yes **9. a.** No **b.** No **c.** Yes **11–17.** Possible answers given: **11.** (0, 2), (1, 3) **13.** (0, 3), (1, 5) **15.** (0, 2), (2, 12) **17.** (1, 8), (2, 7) **19.**

Number of Toppings	Price
1	$ 8.25
2	$ 9.00
3	$ 9.75
4	$10.50

21. Possible answer: (20, 12), (30, 13), (40, 14) **23. a.** $y = \frac{1}{4}x$ **b.** 75 pounds **c.** 800 pounds **25.** They are all ordered pairs in which the x-coordinate and y-coordinate are equal. **27.** 46 **29.** 0 **31.** C

4-3 Try It (Example 1)

Possible points on line: (2, 5) and (4, 7)
For (2, 5), $5 = 2 + 3$
For (4, 7), $7 = 4 + 3$
Possible point not on line: (0, 5)
For (0, 5), $5 \neq 0 + 3$

4-3 Try It (Example 2)

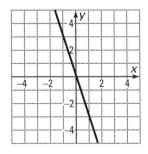

4-3 Exercises & Applications

1. 1; 2; Does
a.

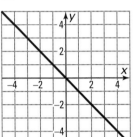

b. Yes

3.

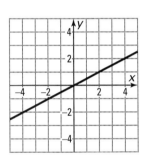

5.

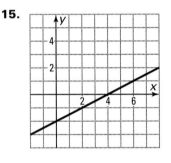

7.

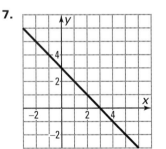

9.

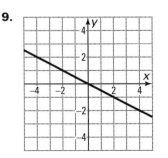

11.

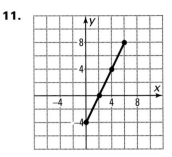

Graph is linear.

13.

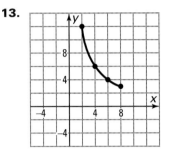

Graph is not linear.

15.

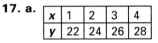

17. a.

x	1	2	3	4
y	22	24	26	28

b. Yes

c.

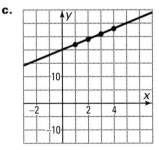

706

19. $c = 2p$, where c is cubic feet of space needed and p is pounds of scraps added per day.

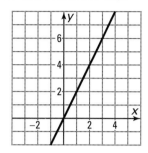

21. 360   **23.** −0.01   **25.** 4.107×10^5 **27.** 9.4×10^{-2}

Section 4A Review

1. 56   **3.** 3

5.

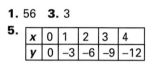

x	0	1	2	3	4
y	0	−3	−6	−9	−12

7.

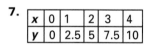

x	0	1	2	3	4
y	0	2.5	5	7.5	10

9. a. No   **b.** Yes   **c.** No
11. $y = 4x$; 240

13.

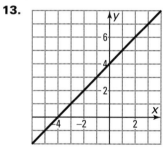

15. C

4-4 Try It (Example 1)

0.35; No

4-4 Try It (Example 2)

−2

4-4 Try It (Example 3)

a.

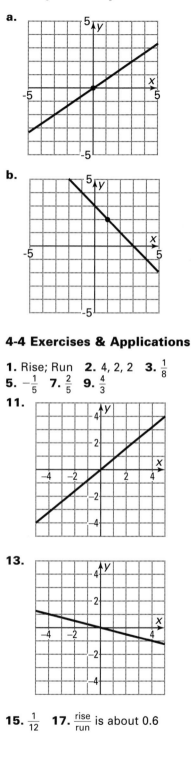

b.

4-4 Exercises & Applications

1. Rise; Run   **2.** 4, 2, 2   **3.** $\frac{1}{8}$
5. $-\frac{1}{5}$ **7.** $\frac{2}{5}$ **9.** $\frac{4}{3}$
11.

13.

15. $\frac{1}{12}$ **17.** $\frac{\text{rise}}{\text{run}}$ is about 0.6

19. a. $\frac{1}{4}, \frac{1}{2}, \frac{2}{5}, \frac{1}{4}$ **b.** Diamond Peak and Bear Valley   **21.** Horizontal: $\frac{\text{rise}}{\text{run}} = \frac{0}{\text{run}} = 0$; Vertical: $\frac{\text{rise}}{\text{run}} = \frac{\text{rise}}{0}$, and division by 0 is not defined.

23. −41   **25.** $A = 63$

4-5 Try It

a. 3; 2; −6

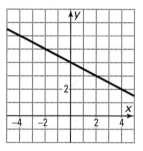

b. $-\frac{1}{2}$; 8; 4

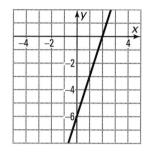

4-5 Exercises & Applications

1. 2; 4; $\frac{1}{2}$ **2.** −4   **3.** 2   **5.** 2; −1; 2
7. 1; 0; 0
9. 2; 3; −6

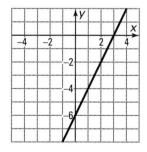

11. −1; 0; 0

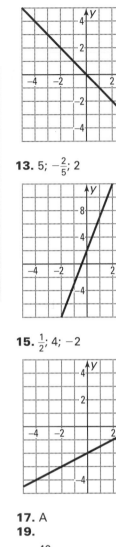

13. 5; $-\frac{2}{5}$; 2

15. $\frac{1}{2}$; 4; −2

17. A

19.

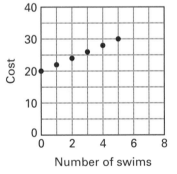

21. 1800 ft; 450 ft per hr **25.** −46
27. 90 **29.** 40 **31.** 6

4-6 Try It

a. 2 rides **b.** 10 rides

4-6 Exercises & Applications

1. a. Yes **b.** Yes

3.

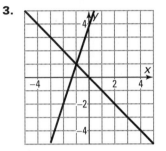

(−1, 1)

5.

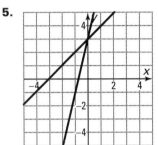

(0, 3)

7.

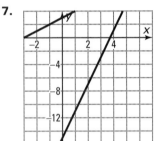

(6, 9)

9.

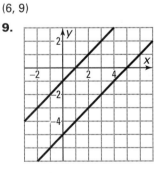

No solution

11.

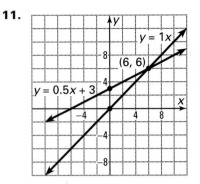

Each side has 6 oz on it. **13.** For 5
times, the cost is the same either
way. For 6 times, the cost is $55 for
the first plan, but $60 for the second.
So she should take the first plan.
15. The cost is $48 in either case. It
doesn't matter. **17.** −48 **19.** −8
21. $D + 4$ **23.** $2p + 17$

4-7 Try It (Examples 1–2)

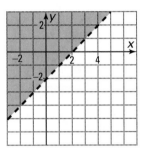

4-7 Try It (Example 3)

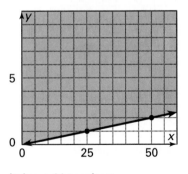

At least 11 teachers

4-7 Exercises & Applications

1. D **2.** C **3.** A **4.** B **5. a.** No
b. No **c.** No

7.

9.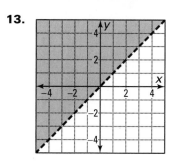

11.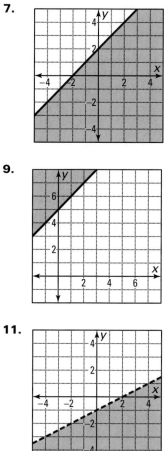

13.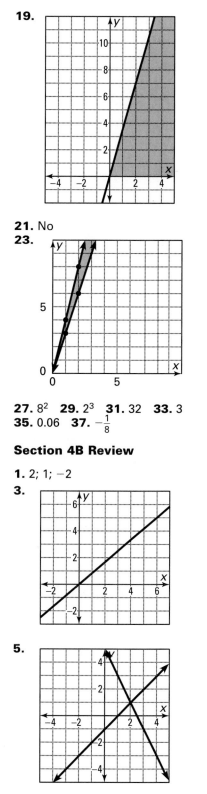

15. y = teachers, x = students

17. $n \geq 4x$, where n is the number of calories and x is the weight in grams.

19.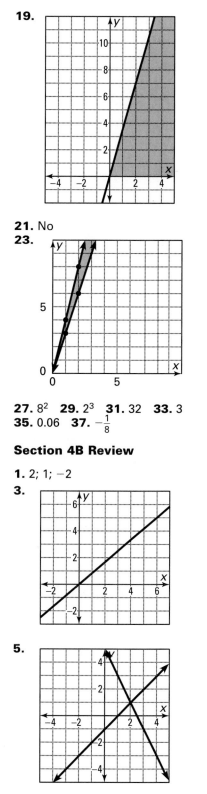

21. No

23.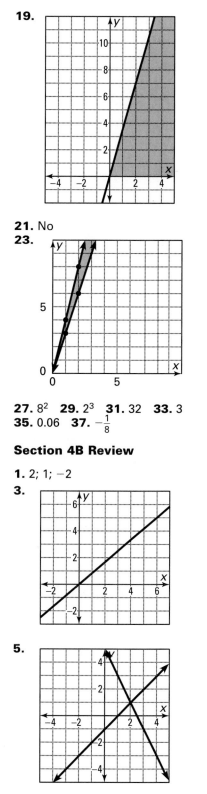

27. 8^2 **29.** 2^3 **31.** 32   **33.** 3
35. 0.06   **37.** $-\frac{1}{8}$

Section 4B Review

1. 2; 1; −2

3.

5.

(2, 1)

7.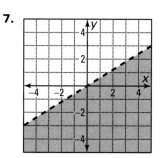

9. $y > 2x$

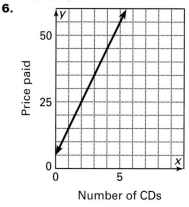

11. Substitute the coordinates for the ordered pair into the equation or inequality. If the resulting statement is true, the ordered pair is a solution.

Chapter 4 Summary & Review

1. $y = -15$

2.

x	0	1	2	3	4	5
y	4	5	6	7	8	9

3. $y = -7x$; $y = -161$ **4. a.** No
b. Yes   **c.** No   **5.** Possible answer: (0, 15), (5, 0)

6.

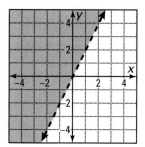

Price paid / Number of CDs

7. a.

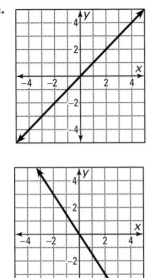

b.

8. a. Slope $-\frac{1}{2}$; x-intercept -2; y-intercept -1 **b.** Slope $-\frac{3}{2}$; x-intercept 2; y-intercept 3 **c.** Slope 2; x-intercept $-\frac{3}{2}$; y-intercept 3

9. Slope $\frac{3}{5}$; x-intercept 5; y-intercept -3

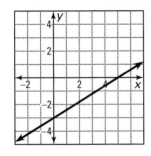

10.

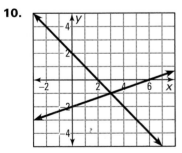

$(3, -1)$ **11.** 8 months

12. a.

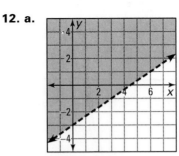

b.

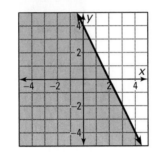

Cumulative Review
Chapters 1–4

1. B **2.** D **3.** D **4.** B **5.** C **6.** B
7. B **8.** C **9.** A **10.** C **11.** C
12. A **13.** B **14.** D **15.** B

Chapter 5

5-1 Try It (Examples 1-2)

a. 4 to 9; 5 to 9; 4 to 5; 5 to 4; 9 to 4; 9 to 5 **b.** 1:9

5-1 Try It (Example 3)

a. ≈ 0.82 **b.** $\approx 62{,}500{,}000$

5-1 Exercises & Applications

1. a. 3:4 **b.** 4:7 **c.** 7:4

3. a.

b.

5. No **7. a.** 8:25 **b.** 21:7 or 3:1
c. 25 to 7; 7 to 25 **9.** 3:2 **11.** 2:5
13. 3:5 **15. a.** 4:5 **b.** 5:1 **c.** Yes;
When amount of stored memory
increases, available memory

decreases. **19.** 6.94×10^{-3}
21. 1×10^{-9} **23.** $x = 35$
25. $x = -6$

5-2 Try It (Examples 1-2)

a. 3; 5; 20; 150

b.

Tickets	20	40	60
Cost ($)	5	10	15

$\approx \$11$

5-2 Try It (Example 3)

a. No **b.** Yes

5-2 Exercises & Applications

1. a. $\frac{12}{36}$ **b.** $\frac{24}{72}$ **c.** $\frac{1}{3}$ **d.** $\frac{2}{6}$ **e.** $\frac{8}{24}$
3. 4; 6; 8; 10 **5.** C **7.** = **9.** $\neq$
11. $\neq$ **13.** $\neq$ **15.** No **17.** Yes,
$\frac{50}{14{,}400} = \frac{120}{34{,}560}$ **21. a.** Triangle
b. Painting **c.** Steam
d. Proportion **23.** $A = 121$
25. $F = 57.2$ **27.** $x = 54$

5-3 Try It (Example 1)

a. $\frac{4}{1}, \frac{8}{2}, \frac{12}{3}, \frac{16}{4}, \frac{20}{5}$ **b.** 40; 80
c. If y = number of pages and x = time, $y = 4x$.

5-3 Try It (Example 2)

a. $k = 2$
  x 5 10 15
  y 10 20 30

b. 2; They are the same.

5-3 Try It (Example 3)

a. The graph does not show a proportional relationship.

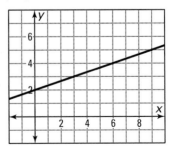

b. The graph shows a proportional relationship.

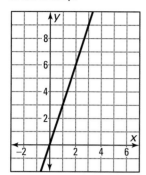

5-3 Exercises & Applications

1. a. $\frac{y}{x} = 3$ **b.** $\frac{y}{x} = 10$ **c.** $\frac{y}{x} = 0.5$
3. Yes, $k = 6$ **5.** Yes, $k = 11$ **7.** 5
9. 2; 2 cost \$5.34 and 3 cost \$8.01
11. a. 5   **b.** $k = 5$ **c.** $p = 5h$
d. \$85.00
13.

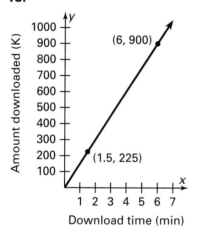

15. 69   **17.** 175   **19.** Yes   **21.** Yes

Section 5A Review

1. $2:6 = 1:3$ **3.** 1:5   **5.** $\neq$ **7.** $\neq$
9. 18, 27, 45, 54   **11. a.** 3:2
b. Word proc. to video games.
c. Educ. programs to homework.
13. C

5-4 Try It

5000 films

5-4 Exercises & Applications

1. a. 7×3 **b.** 21   **c.** 21   **d.** $5\frac{1}{4}$
3. $\frac{12}{x} = \frac{8}{2.50}$ **5.** 75   **7.** 12   **9.** B

---

11. D   **13.** 8   **15.** 31   **17.** 20
19. 8   **21.** C   **23.** No; $\frac{2}{22} \neq \frac{1}{7}$
25. ≈ 23 ft   **27.** $x = 3$ **29.** $x = 3\frac{1}{3}$
31. 24 cm, 20 cm, 12 cm
33. 2.3884×10^5 **35.** -42 **37.** 5

5-5 Try It (Example 1)

\$1,368

5-5 Try It (Example 2)

75 ounces for \$8.99

5-5 Try It (Example 3)

a. 2880 frames; 25 seconds
b. $F = 30s$; 300 seconds (5 min)

5-5 Exercises & Applications

1. a. 30   **b.** $d = 30t$ **c.** $d = 30 \cdot 7$;
$d = 210$ mi   **3.** 40 words per
minute; $W = 40m$ **5.** 55 miles per
hour; $M = 55h$ **7.** \$40,000 per day;
$C = 40,000d$ **9. a.** \$2.88 per lb
b. \$3.59 per lb   **11.** ≈ 10.5 **13.** A
6 oz box for \$1.25   **15.** $\frac{1}{4}$ lb for \$2.00
17. Yes; The average height of each
floor is about 12.2 ft   **21. a.** about
400   **b.** Hire 35 more teachers
23. 0.0084   **25.** Possible answers:
(1, 6); (2, 7)   **27.** Possible answers:
(1, –5); (2, –4)

5-6 Try It

120 frames; 30 fps

5-6 Exercises & Applications

1. a. 360   **b.** 5   **c.** 12   **3.** A and B
5. a. ≈ 95.3 million   **b.** $\approx 953,000$
7. $\frac{2}{4} = \frac{4}{8}$, $\frac{4}{8} = \frac{8}{16}$, $\frac{8}{16} = \frac{16}{32}$, $\frac{2}{8} = \frac{16}{32}$, $\frac{2}{8} =$
$\frac{4}{16}$, $\frac{4}{16} = \frac{8}{32}$, $\frac{2}{8} = \frac{8}{32}$, $\frac{2}{16} = \frac{4}{32}$, $\frac{4}{8} = \frac{16}{32}$
and all reciprocals of these.
9. 236 in.   **11.** 840 ft

5-7 Try It (Example 3)

Possible answer: 1 in. = 10 ft

5-7 Try It (Examples 4-5)

12.5

5-7 Exercises & Applications

1. a. Shape; Size   **b.** Sizes; Shape
3. 1200 mi   **5.** ≈ 2520 mi   **7.** 30 cm
9. 13.425 cm   **11.** $\frac{1}{32}$ in.   **13.** 24 ft
15. 10.8   **17.** $b = 15$, $c = 9$, $a = 10$
21. About 24 in.   **23.** $x = -16$
25. $r = 45$

Section 5B Review

1. $\frac{10 \text{ bottles}}{x} = \frac{6 \text{ bottles}}{1.99}$; $x = \$3.32$
3. 80   **5.** 40   **7.** 560   **9.** Possible
answer: $P = 22.5n$ **11.** $a = 2.5$;
$b = 4$; $c = 2$ **13.** 5 ft

Chapter 5 Summary & Review

1. $\frac{3}{7}$

2.
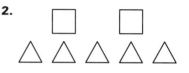

3. Red area to total area: 2:5. Total
area to red area: 5:2. Blue area to
total area: 3:5. Total area to blue
area: 5:3. Red area to blue area: 2:3.
Blue area to red area: 3:2.   **4.** Not
equal   **5.** No

6.

4	8	12	16	20	24
5	10	15	20	25	30

7. $x = 60$ **8.** $u = 77$ **9.** 3 gallons
per hour; $g = 3h$, where g is the
number of gallons and h is the number of hours.   **10.** About 350 mi.
11. 231 pairs of blue shoes.
12. 5166 comedy videos.   **13.** 7.5 ft
tall and 17.5 ft across.   **14.** $x = 12$;
$z = 22.5$

Chapter 6

6-1 Try It (Example 3)

a. 82%   **b.** 12.5%   **c.** 50%
d. 12.5%   **e.** 0.6%

6-1 Try It (Example 4)

a. $\frac{12}{100} = \frac{3}{25}$; 0.12   **b.** $\frac{45}{1000} = \frac{9}{200}$;
0.045   **c.** $\frac{200}{100} = 2$; 2.00

6-1 Exercises & Applications

1. a. $\frac{74}{100} = \frac{37}{50}$ **b.** 0.74 **c.** 74%
2. a. $\frac{1}{4}$ **b.** 0.25 **c.** 25%
3. Possible Answer:

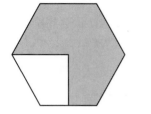

5. 80% **7.** 120% **9.** 0.35% **11.** $\frac{49}{50}$; 0.98 **13.** $\frac{3}{40}$; 0.075 **15.** $\frac{7}{5} = 1\frac{2}{5}$; 1.40 **17.** $\frac{3}{400}$; 0.0075 **19.** No; The risk is too high. **21.** 20% off; It is the largest reduction. **23.** 70%; 20%; 10% **25.** 90% of 50 = 45; The student answered 45 correctly. **27. a.** 50%; 25%, 50%, and 75%. **b.** You scored better than 9500 students.

6-2 Try It (Example 3)

1. a. 12.5% **b.** 36 **c.** 90

6-2 Try It (Example 4)

3200 oz = 200 lb

6-2 Exercises & Applications

1. $\frac{12}{x} = \frac{40}{100}$ **3.** 4 **5.** 22 **7.** $33\frac{1}{3}$% **9.** 200% **11.** 20 **13.** 1.25 **15.** 435 students **17. a.** 16 passengers **b.** 104 **c.** U.S. **19.** 1% **21.** Iron **23.** 30% **25.** $\frac{(a + b + c + d)}{4}$; Answers may vary.

6-3 Try It (Example 1)

a. 180 **b.** 60

6-3 Try It (Example 2)

About 80 or 90 mg

6-3 Try It (Example 3)

a. About $33\frac{1}{3}$% **b.** About 250 students

6-3 Try It (Example 4)

About 35–40%. The top part is about 25%. The bottom part is half of that or 13%. 25% + 13% = 38%.

6-3 Exercises & Applications

1. a. $\frac{1}{3}$ **b.** $\frac{1}{5}$ **c.** $\frac{1}{100}$ **d.** $\frac{1}{10}$ **3.** 25% **5.** 98% **7.** 14 **9.** 4 **11.** 30% **13.** 67% **15.** > **17.** < **19.** 0.3 g **21.** B **23.** It cannot be determined. About 75% of his serves are in bounds. **27.** $y = 19$ **29.** $p = -2$
31.

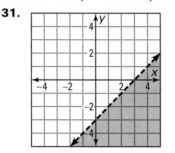

Section 6A Review

1. a. $\frac{4}{5}$; 0.8; 80% **3.** 67% **5.** 1450% **7.** 0.72; $\frac{18}{25}$ **9.** 0.1275, $\frac{51}{400}$ **11.** 0.56, $\frac{14}{25}$ **13.** 25% **15.** 12 **17.** 20% **19.** 12.5 **21.** About 60% **23.** D

6-4 Try It (Examples 1-2)

a. ≈ 50% **b.** $79.13

6-4 Try It (Example 3)

4593

6-4 Exercises & Applications

1. a. $1.20 **b.** $17.19 **c.** $17.19 **3.** 100% **5.** 17% **7.** 14% **9.** $909.42 **11.** $21 **13.** ≈162 cm **15.** January **17.** ≈ 596% **21. a.** 1.2 oz **b.** 1.44 oz **c.** 12% **23.** 3:5; 3:8; 5:3; 5:8; 8:3; 8:5

6-5 Try It (Example 1)

$12.23

6-5 Try It (Example 2)

20%

6-5 Try It (Example 3)

$279.75

6-5 Exercises & Applications

1. a. 78% **b.** 70% **c.** 80% **d.** 60% **3.** 8% **5.** 18% **7.** 9% **9.** $1.91 **11.** 29 **13.** $31.25 **15.** C **19. a.** $78.80; $80.38 **21.** = **23.** =

6-6 Try It (Example 2)

a. $81.72 **b. i.** $38.40 **ii.** $42.00

6-6 Try It (Example 3)

20%

6-6 Exercises & Applications

1. a. 150% **b.** $90 **c.** $90; $133\frac{1}{3}$% **d.** $120 **3.** 25 **5.** 75 **7.** 100 **9.** 2 **11.** $49.94 **13.** $121.50 **15.** $100.31 **17.** 25% **19. a.** 1350 **b.** About 11% **21.** 12 notes **23.** 37.5% **25.** $y = 19$ **27.** $a = -3$ **29.** $p = -\frac{1}{3}$ **31.** 17.4 **33.** 0.1

Section 6B Review

1. 25% decrease **3.** 0% (neither) **5.** 33% increase **7.** $109.97 **9.** 8% **11.** $44.10 **13.** $239.50 **15.** $600 **17.** No

Chapter 6 Summary & Review

1. $\frac{4}{5}$; 0.8; 80% **2. a.** 16% **b.** 24% **c.** 60% **3.** 161 **4.** 75 **5.** 225 **6.** About 20% **7.** About 10% **8.** About 40 **9.** About 37.2% **10.** 6.5% **11.** $24.36 **12.** $221 **13.** About 75% **14.** $2400 **15.** $139,872 **16.** About 23.1%

Cumulative Review
Chapters 1–6

1. B **2.** A **3.** B **4.** D **5.** C **6.** B **7.** B **8.** C **9.** A **10.** C **11.** C **12.** D **13.** C **14.** B **15.** B **16.** A

Chapter 7

7-1 Try It (Example 1)

a. 2 only **b.** 2, 3, 4, 5, 6, 8, 10 **c.** 2, 4 **d.** 3, 5

7-1 Try It (Example 2-3)

a. $2 \times 3 \times 3 \times 3$ **b.** $2 \times 2 \times 3 \times 11$
c. $2 \times 2 \times 59$ **d.** $2 \times 3 \times 59$

7-1 Exercises & Applications

1. Prime **3.** Composite **5.** Prime
7. 3, 9 **9.** 2 **11.** 3, 9 **13.** 2
15. 2, 4, 8 **17.** 1, 2, 4, 8, 11, 22, 44,
88 **19.** 1, 2, 4, 5, 10, 20, 25, 50, 100
21. $2 \times 3 \times 3 \times 3$ or 2×3^3 **23.** 2^7
25. $2 \times 2 \times 5 \times 11$ or $2^2 \times 5 \times 11$
27. $3 \times 5 \times 5 \times 5$ or 3×5^3
29. 5×101 **31.** D **33.** $n = 81$
35. $w = 1250$ **37.** $2^3 \times 3^2 \times 5$
39. 34 **41.** Possible answers: $3 = 2^2 - 1$; $7 = 2^3 - 1$; $31 = 2^5 - 1$
43. Possible answers: 24, 36, 48, 600
45. B **50.** 37.5 hr or 37 hours and 30 minutes

7-2 Try It (Example 2)

a. 6 **b.** 7 **c.** 4

7-2 Try It (Examples 3-4)

a. 5 **b.** $\frac{3}{4}$

7-2 Exercises & Applications

1. a. 1, 3, 9, 27 **b.** 1, 3, 5, 9, 15, 45
c. 1, 3, 9 **d.** 9 **3.** 4 **5.** 7 **7.** 9
9. 30 **11.** 8 **13.** 4 **15.** 14 **17.** 5
19. 12 **21.** 2 **23.** $\frac{2}{5}$ **25.** $\frac{1}{4}$
27. $\frac{9}{10}$ **29.** $\frac{2}{3}$ **31.** $\frac{6}{11}$ **33.** 210,
512, 915, 972 **35.** $18 = 2 \times 3^2$
37. A **39.** Possible answers: 4 and
7; 15 and 16; 9 and 20. **41.** 1; Yes
43. Slope = 2; x-intercept = 2;
y-intercept = -4. **45.** Slope = -3;
x-intercept = $\frac{8}{3}$; y-intercept = 8.
47. Slope = -7; x-intercept = 0;
y-intercept = 0.

7-3 Try It (Example 2)

a. 30 **b.** 147 **c.** 9384

7-3 Try It (Example 4)

a. $\frac{6}{21}$ and $\frac{14}{21}$ **b.** $\frac{28}{48}$ and $\frac{15}{48}$

7-3 Exercises & Applications

1. a. 8, 16, 24, 32, 40, 48, 56, 64, 72,
80 **b.** 12, 24, 36, 48, 60, 72, 84, 96,
108, 120 **c.** 24, 48, 72 **d.** 24

3. 40 **5.** 60 **7.** 144 **9.** 60 **11.** 84
13. 88 **15.** 744 **17.** 60 **19.** 7000
21. 3432 **23.** $\frac{4}{6}$ and $\frac{1}{6}$ **25.** $\frac{3}{8}$ and $\frac{6}{8}$
27. $\frac{20}{36}$ and $\frac{15}{36}$ **29.** $\frac{45}{60}, \frac{40}{60}$, and $\frac{42}{60}$
31. $\frac{28}{252}, \frac{72}{252}$, and $\frac{105}{252}$ **33.** Every 90
days. **35.** A **37.** Multiply the two
numbers; their product is the LCM.
38. Possible answers: A 10 3 6 rectangle **41.** $(-3, 8)$ **43.** $(4, -1)$
45. 176% **47.** 0.5% **49.** 320%
51. 0.3% **53.** 640% **55.** 275%
57. 0.2%

Section 7A Review

1. 2, 3, 6, 9 **3.** 2, 4, 5, 8, 10 **5.** 2, 4
7. $5^2 \times 19$ **9.** $2^4 \times 3^2$ **11.** GCF, 1;
LCM, 36 **13.** GCF, 3; LCM, 120
15. $\frac{3}{5}$ **17.** $\frac{3}{7}$ **19.** $\frac{2}{3}$ **21.** 12
23. 24 **27.** A

7-4 Try It (Example 3)

a. $0.8\overline{3}$; Repeating **b.** 0.125;
Terminating **c.** 0.75; Terminating

7-4 Try It (Example 4)

a. $\frac{15}{100}$ or $\frac{3}{20}$ **b.** $2\frac{6}{10}$ or $2\frac{3}{5}$ **c.** $\frac{46}{1000}$ or
$\frac{23}{500}$

7-4 Try It (Example 5)

a. $2\frac{13}{99}$ **b.** $\frac{8}{33}$

7-4 Try It (Example 6)

a. $-4\frac{1}{3} < -4.3$ **b.** $2.07 < 2\frac{1}{7}$

7-4 Exercises & Applications

1. a. 210 **b.** $-\frac{140}{210}, \frac{175}{210}, \frac{0}{210}, -\frac{120}{210}$,
$\frac{189}{210}, -\frac{42}{210}, \frac{35}{210}$ **c.** $-\frac{140}{210}, -\frac{120}{210}, -\frac{42}{210}$,
$\frac{0}{210}, \frac{35}{210}, \frac{175}{210}, \frac{189}{210}$ **3.** < **5.** < **7.** >
9. < **11.** 0.44; Terminating
13. $0.\overline{285714}$; Repeating **15.** $\frac{9}{20}$
17. $4\frac{14}{25}$ **19.** $2\frac{1}{3}$
21.

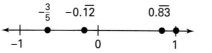

23. The sea cow **25.** Ana

27. 3.14084507; 3.14285714
29. $\frac{3}{8}$ **31.** Possible answer: $\frac{11}{50}$
33. Possible answer: $-\frac{62}{72}$ **35.** $12 + n$
37. $36k$ **39.** 150 **41.** 40

7-5 Try It (Example 1)

a. 111.63 **b.** 36.75 **c.** 527.05
d. 3.74

7-5 Try It (Example 3)

a. $2\frac{1}{2}$ **b.** $5\frac{5}{6}$

7-5 Try It (Example 4)

a. $-5\frac{1}{4}$ **b.** $14\frac{5}{24}$

7-5 Exercises & Applications

1. a. $\frac{24}{30}, \frac{25}{30}$ **b.** $\frac{49}{30}$ **c.** $1\frac{19}{30}$
3. -160.713 **5.** 164.14 **7.** $-\frac{1}{4}$
9. $-\frac{2}{15}$ **11.** $10\frac{2}{5}$ **13.** $4\frac{4}{7}$
15. $-14\frac{43}{60}$ **17.** $n = -1\frac{1}{2}$ **19.** $n = 11\frac{1}{4}$ **21.** 3.29 miles per second
23. $\frac{1}{20}$ **25.** B **29.** $x = \frac{3}{4} + \frac{3}{8} - 1\frac{1}{4} = -\frac{1}{8}$ **31.** $x = 17$ **33.** $k = -54$
35. $r = -4.9$ **37.** $n = -2.2$
39. 43%

7-6 Try It (Example 1)

a. -3.6 **b.** 56.1697

7-6 Try It (Example 2)

a. 2.24 **b.** $-68.\overline{18}$

7-6 Try It (Example 3)

a. $-3\frac{31}{48}$ **b.** 22

7-6 Try It (Example 4)

a. 4 **b.** $4\frac{1}{2}$

7-6 Exercises & Applications

1. a. $\frac{13}{4}$ **b.** $\frac{78}{4}$ **3.** 0.0072 **5.** 0.032
7. $\frac{1}{9}$ **9.** $-2\frac{1}{3}$ **11.** $\frac{1}{6}$ **13.** $1\frac{67}{115}$
15. $\frac{9}{14}$ **17.** $1\frac{2}{7}$ **19.** 150 **21.** $\frac{5}{114}$

23. ≈ 4,524,518 square miles
25. $\frac{1}{4}$ × 100 gallons **27.** A **29.** No
31. No; Possible answer: If both of the numbers are < 1, their product would have to be < 1. **33.** $x = 9$
35. $x = -44$ **37.** $x = -41$ **39.** $x = 21$ **41.** 33% **43.** 19%

Section 7B Review

1.

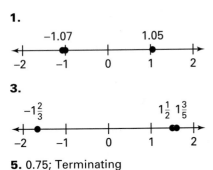

3.

5. 0.75; Terminating
7. 11.$\overline{714285}$; Repeating
9. 4.7; Terminating **11.** $3\frac{1}{200}$
13. $\frac{364}{999}$ **15.** 7.42 **17.** −0.1326
19. $\frac{1}{24}$ **21.** $1\frac{5}{8}$ **23.** $-\frac{1}{6}$ **25.** 15
27. $x = -\frac{2}{15}$ **29.** $x = \frac{3}{7}$ **31.** D

7-7 Try It (Example 1)

a. Yes **b.** No **c.** Yes **d.** No

7-7 Try It (Example 2)

a. 12 **b.** 21 **c.** 50 **d.** 91

7-7 Try It (Example 3)

a. 3 and 4; 3.2 **b.** 4 and 5; 4.6
c. 5 and 6; 5.5 **d.** 8 and 9; 8.9

Try It (Example 4)

a. $\frac{5}{8}$ **b.** $\frac{10}{25}$ **c.** $\frac{11}{18}$ **d.** $\frac{6}{15}$

7-7 Exercises & Applications

1. a. $\frac{\sqrt{9}}{\sqrt{144}}$ **b.** $\frac{3}{12}$ **c.** $\frac{1}{4}$ **3.** Yes
5. No **7.** 5 and 6 **9.** 8 and 9
11. 5 and 6 **13.** $1\frac{1}{2}$ **15.** $\frac{3}{5}$
17. ≈ 230.22 meters **19.** 9, 10
21. 12 in. **23.** 7.5 seconds
25. 8 feet **27.** Possible answers:
$(1 \cdot 2 \cdot 3 \cdot 4) + 1 = 25 = 5^2$; $(2 \cdot 3 \cdot 4 \cdot 5) + 1 = 121 = 11^2$; $(3 \cdot 4 \cdot 5 \cdot 6) + 1 = 361 = 19^2$; $(5 \cdot 6 \cdot 7 \cdot 8) + 1 =$

$1,681 = 41^2$; $(6 \cdot 7 \cdot 8 \cdot 9) + 1 = 3025 = 55^2$ **29.** Yes **37.** $\frac{11}{66}$ **39.** $\frac{3 \text{ ft}}{1 \text{ yd}}$

7-8 Try It

a. Irrational **b.** Rational; −30
c. Rational; ±74 **d.** Irrational

7-8 Exercises & Applications

1. a. 9.7467943 **b.** Irrational
3. Irrational **5.** Irrational
7. Irrational **9.** Irrational
11. Rational **13.** 3.873 **15.** 9.950
17. 15.875 **19.** 44.721 **21.** 21.354
23. ≈ 5.48 in. **25.** 6.5 m **27.** 22 ft × 22 ft **29.** A **31.** 1; 4: 1, 2, 4; 9: 1, 3, 9; 16: 1, 2, 4, 8, 16; 25: 1, 5, 25; 36: 1, 2, 3, 4, 6, 9, 12, 18, 36; 49: 1, 7, 49; 64: 1, 2, 4, 8, 16, 32, 64; 81: 1, 3, 9, 27, 81; 100: 1, 2, 4, 5, 10, 20, 25, 50, 100. Possible answers: They all have an odd number of factors.
33. 38.3 miles; No; They would see about 54.2 miles. **35.** $y = 39$
37. $y = 17$
39.

x	0	1	2	3	4	5
y	−3	−2	−1	0	1	2

41.

x	0	1	2	3	4	5
y	−4	−3	−2	−1	0	1

7-9 Try It (Example 1)

a. $c = 5$ in. **b.** $h \approx 17.69$ cm

7-9 Try It (Example 2)

a. $a \approx 9.16$ m **b.** $a \approx 10.39$ ft

7-9 Try It (Example 4)

a. $a \approx 5$ in. **b.** $c \approx 8.367$ m

7-9 Exercises & Applications

1. a. $12^2 + 16^2 = c^2$ **b.** $144 + 256 = c^2$; $400 = c^2$ **c.** $c = 20$ cm
3. $a \approx 21.07$ **5.** ≈ 7.2 ft **7.** 1600 ft
9. C **11.** Yes **13.** Yes **15. a.** 9 ft
b. ≈ 12.728 ft **17.** Possible answers: (2, 1); (6, 3) **19.** Possible answers: (10, 6); (15, 9)
21. $x = 66$ **23.** $x = 1$

Section 7C Review

1. No **3.** No **5.** Yes **7.** ≈ 8.25
9. $\frac{2}{5}$ **11.** −6 **13.** ±3.5 **15.** −3

17. Rational **19.** Rational
21. ≈ 5.66 in. **23.** 21 cm
25. ≈ 2.06 ft **27.** $m = 15$

Chapter 7 Summary & Review

1. Divisible by 2, 3, 6, and 9
2. $924 = 2^2 \times 3 \times 7 \times 11$ **3.** 3 **4.** $\frac{3}{4}$
5. 75 **6.** 60 **7.** 0.1875;
Terminating **8.** 3.806 > 3.8059
9. $\frac{3}{25}$ **10.** 18.478 **11.** $5\frac{1}{18}$ **12.** $\frac{57}{80}$
13. No **14.** $\frac{5}{6}$ **15.** 7 and 8
16. ≈ 5.657 cm **17.** ± 23 **18.** −27

Chapter 8

8-1 Try It (Examples 1-2)

a. 32,000 m **b.** ≈ 1.96 mi

8-1 Try It (Example 3)

a–d. Possible answers: **a.** mL
b. min **c.** lb **d.** kg

8-1 Try It (Example 4)

a–d. Possible answers: **a.** m^2
b. mm^3 **c.** g **d.** mi

8-1 Exercises & Applications

1. a. $\frac{1 \text{ mi}}{5280 \text{ ft}}$ **b.** ≈ 5.5 mi **3.** mi
5. mL **7.** kg **9.** 2,500,000 mL
11. 4 lb **13.** 5 qt **15.** 15.66 g
17. A **21.** in^2 **23.** Composite
25. Prime **27.** Composite
29. Composite **31.** 14 **33.** 1
35. 3 **37.** 2

8-2 Try It (Example 2)

a. 2638 ft **b.** 197.5 cm **c.** 35.75 in.

8-2 Try It (Example 3)

a. 2 **b.** 6 **c.** 1 **d.** 5

8-2 Try It (Example 5)

a. 14.1 g; 3 **b.** 9.8 mL; 2 **c.** 47 in.; 2 **d.** 22 m; 2

8-2 Exercises & Applications

1. a. 3 **b.** 3 **c.** 6 **3.** 2 **5.** 5
7. 235 cm **9.** 0.25 L **11.** 3.30 hr

13. 44 mi   **15.** 49 m²   **17.** 13° C
19. 42,600 m   **23.** 21   **25.** 55
27. 104   **29.** 60
31.

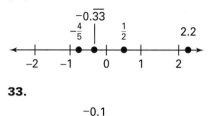

33.

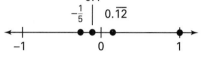

35. $2\frac{17}{100}$ **37.** $\frac{1}{2}$

8-3 Try It (Example 2)

a. 4 blocks east   **b.** $c - 17$

8-3 Try It (Examples 3-4)

a. Brazil   **b.** 30° N, 90° W

8-3 Exercises & Applications

1. 10C   **3.** Salt Lake City Municipal
Airport No. 2   **5.** Northeast   **7.** 4°
latitude; ≈ 1° longitude   **9.** Mt.
Everest   **11.** About 395 mi
13. About 200 mi   **15.** Answers
may vary   **17.** Possible answer:
Distance between longitude lines
decrease as you get closer to the
north and south poles because they
all intersect at the poles.   **19.** East
21. 55 mi/hr   **23.** $6 per hr
25. ≈ 2.3 children per home
27. 3.115   **29.** 140.256   **31.** $2\frac{2}{3}$

Section 8A Review

1. Liter   **3.** cm²   **5.** ≈ 4.08 hr
7. 2,500,000 mL   **9.** 28 oz   **11.** 1
13. 3   **15.** 1.89 L   **17.** 3499 in.
19. 13.6 g   **21.** 93 cm²   **23.** China
25. C

8-4 Try It (Example 1)

a. 145°   **b.** 52°

8-4 Try It (Example 2)

Acute

8-4 Try It (Examples 3-4)

a. 47.3°   **b.** 72°

8-4 Exercises & Applications

1. a. 53°; 53°   **b.** Yes   **3.** Acute
5. Acute   **7.** Acute   **9.** Straight
11. Obtuse   **13.** 68°   **15.** 80.9°
17. 60°   **19.** 90°   **21.** 120°
23. 135°   **25.** 162°   **27.** 105°
29.
31.

33. C   **35.** 157°   **37.** 60°   **41.** $x + y = 180$; $y = 180 - x$; $y = 109°$
43. They are congruent. The same
two lines form the sides for both
angles.   **45.** 240   **47.** $8   **49.** 3
51. 27.51

8-5 Try It (Example 1)

∠DQK and ∠GRL; ∠KQE and ∠FRL

8-5 Try It (Examples 2-3)

a. 146°   **b.** 146°   **c.** 34°

8-5 Exercises & Applications

1. a. 4; 6; 8   **b.** 1; 3; 5   **3.** 1 and 8; 2
and 7   **5.** Possible answers: 1 and 4;
2 and 3; 5 and 8; 6 and 7   **7.** 130°
9. 130°   **11.** 139°   **13.** Alternate
exterior angles   **15.** 47°   **17.** parallel   **19.** congruent   **23.** $m\angle 3 = 75°$;
$m\angle 4 = 55°$; $m\angle 5 = 50°$; $m\angle 6 = 125°$;
$m\angle 7 = 130°$ **25.** $x = 4$ **27.** $x = 5$
29. $\frac{63}{64}$ **31.** 1.78

8-6 Try It (Examples 1-2)

a. 5 in.   **b.** 5 in.   **c.** 60°, 60°, 60°

8-6 Try It (Examples 3-4)

a. 114°   **b.** 114°   **c.** $\overline{QS}$

8-6 Try It (Examples 5-6)

Regular convex hexagon

8-6 Exercises & Applications

1. a. 84°   **b.** 96°   **3.** Irregular convex hexagon   **5.** Irregular convex
octagon   **7.** False   **9.** True   **11.** 71°
13. 61°   **15.** 720°   **17.** 1080°

19. a. Triangles and rectangles
b. Pentagons and hexagons   **21.** n
23. A concave polygon must have at
least 4 sides.
25.

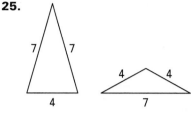

The length of the third side could be
4 in. or 7 in.; There are two possible
triangles.   **31.** 7   **33.** 13   **35.** 4
37. $\frac{3}{11}$

8-7 Try It

a. 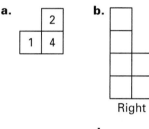 **b.** Right

c. Front   **d.** Top

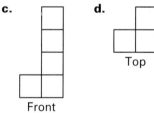

8-7 Exercises & Applications

1. a. **b.**

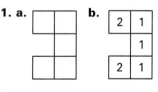

3.

5. Possible answer:

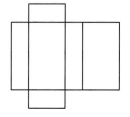

7.

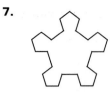

9. A **17.** Irrational **19.** Irrational
21. Rational

Section 8B Review

1. Acute **3.** Acute **5.** Right
7. 32.5° **9.** 130° **11.** 130°
13. d **15.** b **17.** Pentagon
19. Parallelogram **21.** Their
shapes are the same but the base
plan has the number of units
stacked up written on it.

Chapter 8 Summary & Review

1. Liter **2.** 192 oz **3.** 438 ft
4. 36.1 cm^2 **5.** 40° N; 83° W
6. About 235 mi south
7. Complement: 52°; Supplement:
142°
8.

3	4	3	4
1	2	3	4

9. a. $\overline{AB}$ and $\overline{CD}$ **b.** $\overline{AB}$ and $\overline{BC}$ or
$\overline{BC}$ and $\overline{CD}$ **c.** $\angle D$ **10.** Obtuse
11. 540°

Cumulative Review, Chapters 1-8

1. C **2.** B **3.** A **4.** C **5.** B **6.** A
7. D **8.** A **9.** C **10.** C **11.** D
12. A **13.** C **14.** C **15.** D **16.** A

Chapter 9

9-1 Try It (Examples 2–3)

a. 2.12 in. **b.** 22 m

9-1 Try It (Example 5)

a. $10\frac{5}{6}$ yd^2 **b.** 34.4375 cm^2

9-1 Try It (Example 7)

a. 105 mm^2 **b.** 390 in^2

9-1 Exercises & Applications

1. a. $A = (\frac{1}{2})(5.5) \cdot 4$ **b.** $A = 11$ cm^2
3. 25 cm; 39.0625 cm^2 **5.** 24 m;
24 m^2 **7.** ≈ 35.2 cm; ≈ 52 cm^2
9. 64.4 m; 237.475 m^2 **11.** 15.75
cm; 11.8125 cm^2 **13.** $13\frac{1}{3}$ ft; $11\frac{1}{9}$ ft^2
15. a. 80 ft **b.** 384 ft^2 **17.** 5; ≈ 6.4
19. ≈ 47.4 cm **21.** 37 ft **23. a.** 20
cm **b.** Find the area of the triangle
and multiply it by 5. **25. a.** 6 by 8,
4 by 12, 3 by 16, and 2 by 24
b. 6 m by 8 m; 2 by 24 **27.** 9%
29. 142% **31.** No **33.** Yes

9-2 Try It (Examples 1–2)

5

9-2 Try It (Example 4)

$p = 31\frac{1}{2}$ m and $A = 61\frac{1}{4}$ m^2

9-2 Exercises & Applications

1. a. $b = 16.8$ cm; $h = 24$ cm
b. 201.6 cm^2 **3.** 57.6 ft; 138.24 ft^2
5. 42 m; 81 m^2 **7.** 9 cm; 3.9 cm^2
9. 250 m^2 **11.** A **13.** Enlargement
15. Perimeter increases slightly, but
the area doubles. **17.** 2 ft^2 **21.** 80
23. 400 **25.** 1.5 m **27.** $16\frac{1}{3}$ ft

9-3 Try It (Example 2)

a. 1.73 m **b.** ≈ 10.86 m

9-3 Try It (Example 4)

a. ≈ 50.24 cm^2 **b.** Yes

9-3 Exercises & Applications

1. a. 4 cm **b.** ≈ 50.24 cm^2
3.

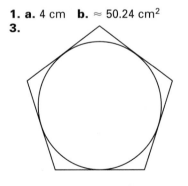

5. ≈ 28.26 m **7.** ≈ 31.4 mi
9. ≈ 33.17 ft^2 **11.** ≈ 7.5 km^2

13. ≈ 39 in. **15.** ≈ 785,000 ft^2
17. The circumference for a full
circle would be 188.4 ft, so for a
semicircle the perimeter would be
half of that plus 60 ft, or 154.2 ft;
The area of a full circle would be
2826 ft^2, so the area of a half-circle
would be 1413 ft^2. **21. a.** 15.6 cm^2
b. 93.6 cm^2 **c.** ≈ 113.04 cm^2
d. 19.4 cm^2 **23.** 70% **25.** 10%
27. 5 **29.** 3

9-4 Try It (Example 1)

22 in^2

9-4 Try It (Example 2)

a. $A ≈ 50.2$ in^2 **b.** $A ≈ 150.7$ in^2
c. $SA ≈ 251$ in^2

9-4 Exercises & Applications

1. a.

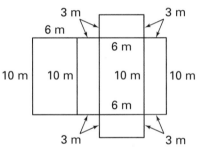

b. $3 \times 6 = 18$, $3 \times 10 = 30$, and
$6 \times 10 = 60$ **c.** 216 m^2
3. 201.5 in^2

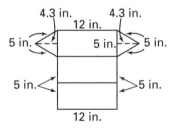

5. $37\frac{1}{2}$ ft^2

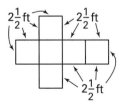

7. $116\frac{3}{4}$ yd

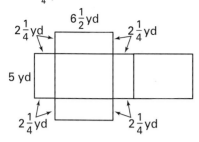

9. 8 in² **11.** 336 in² **13.** 324 cm²
15. 816 in² **17.** 2(*bh* + *hw* + *bw*)
19. a. Cylinder B; It has the same
area on its side as two cylinder As
put together, and it has more area
on the ends. **b.** Cylinder B; Two
cylinder As could be put inside it
with room to spare. **21.** 100%
23. Obtuse **25.** Right **27.** Acute

9-5 Try It (Example 1)

a. Square pyramid **b.** 8 cm
c. ≈ 8.5 cm **d.** ≈ 25.5 cm²
e. ≈ 138 cm²

9-5 Try It (Example 2)

a. 11 ft **b.** ≈ 2.6 ft **c.** ≈ 16.5 ft²
d. ≈ 53.4 ft²

9-5 Exercises & Applications

1. a. 4 **b.** 252 ft² **c.** 252 ft² each
d. 1008 ft² **3. a.** 11.2 in. **b.** 291.2
in² **5.** 384 ft² **7.** D **9.** ≈ 423.9 ft²
11. Possible answer: The height is
like one of the legs of a right triangle and the slant height is like the
hypotenuse. **13.** The pyramid
15. 7, 9; If the base of a pyramid
has *k* sides, then the pyramid has
k + 1 faces. **17.** 1, −3, 3 **19.** −2,
0, 0 **21.** 3, 0, 0 **23.** 4, $\frac{5}{4}$, −5
25. 2, 3, 4, 5

Section 9A Review

1. Perimeter **3.** Prism **7.** 34 in.;
$61\frac{3}{4}$ in. **9.** $13\frac{1}{2}$ ft; $7\frac{7}{8}$ ft² **11.** 59 ft;
192 ft² **13.** 6480 m² **15.** 2014 cm²

9-6 Try It (Example 2)

a. 205.8 cm³ **b.** $274\frac{5}{8}$ in³

9-6 Try It (Example 3)

246 ft³

9-6 Exercises & Applications

1. a. 12 **b.** 60 **3.** 663 m³
5. $99\frac{3}{4}$ yd³ **7.** $27\frac{13}{16}$ ft³
9. 6000 ft³

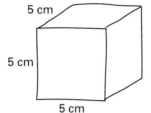

11. $\frac{4}{9}$ of a cent per in³
13. ≈ 113.04 cm³
15. 125 cm³; *V* = *s*³

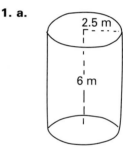

17–18.

L	W	H	V	A
1	1	36	36	146
1	2	18	36	112
1	3	12	36	102
1	4	9	36	98
1	6	6	36	96
2	2	9	36	80
2	3	6	36	72
3	3	4	36	66

19. The prism with dimensions
1 in. × 1 in. × 36 in. has the greatest
surface area. The prism with dimensions 3 in. × 3 in. × 4 in. has the
least. **21.** Both items have a volume of 648 in³. The book will not fit
in the box because of its 9 in. length.
23. Yes **25.** No **27.** 1080°
29. 360°

9-7 Try It (Example 1)

a. 120 in³ **b.** 480 in³ **c.** 1920 in³

9-7 Try It (Example 2)

a. 5375 ft³ **b.** 5.375 ft³

9-7 Exercises & Applications

1. a. $\frac{1}{8}$ **b.** 45 ft³ **3.** 5184 in³
5. 6048 in³ **7.** 13.824 m³ **9.** D
11. 785,000 cm³; 0.785 cm³, $\frac{1}{1,000,000}$
13. a. Speedy Shipping **b.** No;
E-Z Shipping would be cheaper for
a 10 in. × 10 in. × 10 in. package,
for example. **15. a.** Possible
answer: $\frac{1}{30}$, which makes the
model 18 in. long—a suitable size
for a class project. **b.** 404 in² not
including the floor **c.** 720 in³
17. a. Yes **b.** Yes **c.** Yes **19.** 13

9-8 Try It (Example 1)

a. $3\frac{1}{2}$ in. **b.** 7 in² **c.** 49 in³

9-8 Try It (Example 2)

a. ≈ 310.86 cm³ **b.** ≈ 2289.06 in³

9-8 Exercises & Applications

1. a.

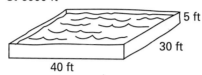

b. ≈ 19.625 m² **c.** ≈ 117.75 m³
3. ≈ 254.34 cm³ **5.** ≈ 565.2 cm³
7. ≈ 2893.824 cm³ **9.** 0.09 m³
11. ≈ 753.6 in³ **13. a.** 221,174 m³
b. 25,277 m² **15.** The tallest prism
will have the greatest volume; The
shortest will have the least; Since
the volume of a prism is the base
area times the height, the volume
will be proportional to height.
17. (2, −3) **19.** (−5, 4)

9-9 Try It (Example 1)

V ≈ 39.25 m³

9-9 Try It (Example 3)

a. 50 m³ **b.** 126 in³

9-9 Exercises & Applications

1. a. $12\frac{1}{4}$ ft² **b.** $16\frac{1}{3}$ ft³ **3.** 36 cm³

5. 56 ft³ **7.** ≈ 94.2 cm³ **9.** ≈ 11.9 mm **11.** 680 cm³ (This is only an approximation, since part of the cone actually sticks into the cylinder.) **13.** The pyramid **15.** $h^2 + 81 = 225$ $h = 12$ in. **17.** 6280 cm³ **19.** 64 **21.** 64 **23. a.** Yes **b.** No **25. a.** Yes **b.** No

Section 9B Review

1. 561 in³ **3.** ≈ 48.2304 cm³ **5.** 1296 m³ **7.** 560 in³ **9.** ≈ 1515 cm³ **11.** 27 in³ **13.** 50.24 in³

Chapter 9 Summary & Review

1. a. $p = 26$ cm; $A = 28$ cm² **b.** $p = 16$ in.; $A = 14$ in² **2. a.** $p = 78$ cm; $A = 252$ cm² **b.** $p = 6.4$ in.; $A = 2.24$ in² **3.** $C ≈ 52.1$ cm; $A ≈ 216$ cm² **4.** ≈ 45 ft **5. a.** ≈ 149.2 ft² **b.** 1710 cm² **6. a.** $s = 13$ in.; $SA = 360$ in² **b.** $s = 25$ m; $SA ≈ 1884$ m² **7. a.** $V = 125$ cm³ **b.** $V = 7350$ ft³ **8. a.** $V ≈ 184$ in³ **b.** $V = 192.5$ cm³ **9. a.** $V = 120$ cm³

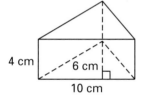

b. $V ≈ 83.7$ in³

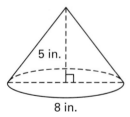

10. a. $V = 5$ cm³ **b.** $SA = 114,562$ ft²; $V = 2,521,050$ ft³ **11. a.** $V = 13.5$ m³ **b.** $V = 27$ m³ **12. a.** $V = 24$ ft³ **b.** $V = 6$ ft³

Chapter 10

10-1 Try It (Example 1)

$110; Yes; 10 hours

10-1 Try It (Example 2)

Yes; For any given number of Buddy Biscuits, there is only one price.

10-1 Try It (Example 3)

a. Yes; Input n yields output n^2
b. No; There are two output values for 1 and two output values for 2.

10-1 Exercises & Applications

1. a. 4 **b.** 8 **c.** Multiply by 3 and subtract 4 **d.** 14 **3.** −2.25 **5.** 1.75 **7.** 16 **9.** −16 **11.** Multiply by 2 and subtract 1 **13.** C **15. a.** Calories burned = minutes × 13.5; 202.5; 270; 405; 607.5 **b.** About 22 min **c.** Yes; Yes; Each input value yields only one output. **17.** Yes; For any given time there is only one height **19.** Take the absolute value. **21.** 23% **23.** 30%

10-2 Try It (Example 2)

a. Yes; The graph is a straight line.
b. Money earned = $4 × number of shirts sold; 9 shirts; Yes; The number of shirts determines the amount of money earned.

10-2 Exercises & Applications

1. a. y **b.** x **c.** $y = -2$, $y = 3$, $y = 8$ **3.** 11, 10, 9, 8, 7 **5.** B **7.** Yes **9.** No **11. a.** $d = 34.5t$ **b.** 69 mi, 207 mi, 345 mi **13.** No; Inputs −1 and −2 each have two output values. **15. a.** $c = 6.5n + 18$ **c.** Yes **19.** 12 in., $4\sqrt{3} ≈ 6.9$ in² **21.** Perimeter can't be determined, 230 cm²

10-3 Try It (Examples 1–2)

a.
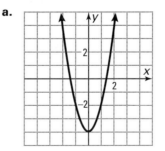

b.
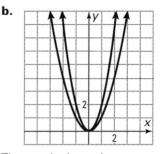

The graphs have the same general shape, but the $2x^2$ graph is skinnier.

10-3 Try It (Example 3)

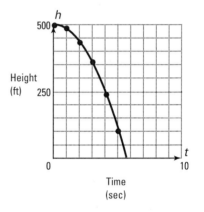

10-3 Exercises & Applications

1. Neither **3.** Linear
5.
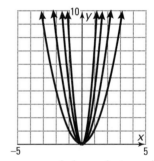

Same general shape, but varying widths.
7.
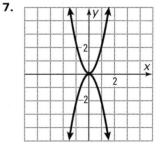

Same shape, but one opens up and one opens down.

9. F **11.** D **13.** B **15.** C
17. The canyon is 400 ft deep; The value is negative because the function represents height measured from the canyon's rim. **21.** 27
23. 66 cm

10-4 Try It (Examples 1–2)

a.

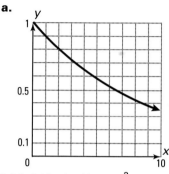

0.66, 2.12 **b.** About $7\frac{3}{4}$ hours

10-4 Try It (Example 3)

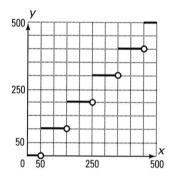

10-4 Exercises & Applications

1. B **3.** C

5.

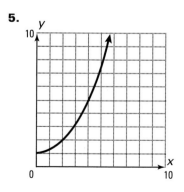

7.

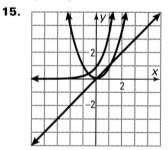

9. There will be $1000 \times 2^1 = 2000$ butterflies after 1 year, $1000 \times 2^2 = 4000$ butterflies after 2 years, $1000 \times 2^3 = 8000$ butterflies after 3 years, and $1000 \times 2^{10} = 1,024,000$ butterflies after 10 years. **11. b.** Step
13. Quadratic **15.** Linear
17. a. $1402.55 **b.** 11 years
19. a. Increase **b.** Decrease for $x < 0$, increase for $x > 0$
c. Increase **d.** Decrease
21. Exponential, increasing
23. $10 - 2n$ **25.** 12π m, 36π m²
27. 5.8π m, 8.41π m²

Section 10A Review

1. -10 **3.** 0 **5.** -2 **7.** C
13. Yes; Each x value corresponds to only one y value.

15.

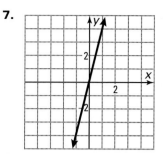

Similar: All three functions are increasing to the right of the origin. Different: $y = x$ is a straight line, $y = x^2$ curves up at both ends (and so is decreasing to the left of the origin), and $y = 4^x$ is nearly flat on the left and curves up on the right.

17. a.

Time (sec)	Height (ft)
0	0
1	-16
2	-64
3	-144
4	-256
5	-400
6	-576
7	-784
8	-1024

b. 256 ft; Height is measured from ground level.

10-5 Try It (Examples 1–2)

$-4x^2 + x + 22$

10-5 Try It (Examples 3–4)

a. 5, -34 **b. i.** ≈ 2.09 ft³
ii. ≈ 134 ft³ **iii.** ≈ 23.8 m³

10-5 Exercises & Applications

1. a. 3 **b.** 1 **c.** 2 **3.** Trinomial
5. Binomial **7.** $2x + 4$; 1 **9.** $-x^4 - x^3 + x^2$; 4 **11.** -3 **13.** 51 **15.** 6;
910 **17.** 3; -5 **19.** 175.9 in²
21. B **23. a.** 85,486 ft²
b. 2,350,879 ft³ **25.** $V = ns^3$ where s is the side length and n is the number of boxes. **27.** 0, 1, 5, 14, 30; The differences are the perfect squares 1, 4, 9, 16. **29.** 105
31. 180 **33.** 3584 cm²

10-6 Try It (Examples 1–2)

a. $7x^2 + 7x + 1$ **b.** $-11n^2 - n - 9$
c. $3x^2 + 8x - 10$

10-6 Try It (Example 3)

$2x^2 + x - 11$; 199

10-6 Exercises & Applications

1. a. Descending **b.** Like terms
c. Distributive **3.** Already simplified **5.** $7m^2 - 3m$ **7.** $4a + 6$
9. $-2x^2 + 1$ **11.** $13x^2 + 4x - 7$
13. $4x^2 - x + 9$ **15.** A **17.** $x^3 + 5x^2 + 4x^2 + 7x$; $x^3 + 9x^2 + 7x$;
582 ft³ **19.** $2x^2 + 13x + 20$
21. $3x^2 + 13x + 11$ **23.** Possible answer: $4x - 3x + 2x - x$
25. No; Should be $7x$

27. a. Incorrect; Added exponents, forgot to add coefficients.
b. Incorrect; Added exponents.
c. Correct; Added coefficients but not exponents. **d.** Incorrect; Forgot to add coefficients. **29.** 36 **31.** 9
33. ≈ 30.8 cm^2

10-7 Try It (Examples 1–2)

a. $2x^3 - 1$ **b.** $2x^3 + 6x^2 + 6x - 5$

10-7 Try It (Example 3–4)

a. $-70p^2 + 1495p - 300$; $7650
b. $6x - 5$

10-7 Exercises & Applications

1. a. x^3 **b.** $-4x^2$ **c.** $-2x$ **d.** $7x^5$
e. -27 **3.** $-x^4 + 2$ **5.** $-3x^3 - 2x$
7. $x^5 - 2x - 9x^3 + 3$ **9.** $2x^2 + 4x - 1$ **11.** $-4m^2 + 4m - 1$
13. $2v^3 - 8v^2 + 6v - 1$ **15.** $a^3 - 6a^2 + 2a - 3$ **17.** $11x^2 - 2x + 1$
19. $12x^2 + 4x + 3$ **21.** $x^2 - 3x + 3$
23. $x^2 + 4$ **25.** $10t - 8$ **27.** No; She dropped the variable.
31. $2x^5 + 2x^4 + 3x^2 - 2x + 1$
33. $2 \cdot 3^2 \cdot 5$ **35.** $3 \cdot 29$ **37.** $3 \cdot 5^3$
39. 232.56 m^3

10-8 Try It (Example 2)

1. a. 5^6 **b.** 8^3 **c.** x^8 **d.** $-32x^6$

10-8 Try It (Example 3)

a. $-10x^6 - 12x^3$
b. $6x^4 + 10x^3 - 2x^2$

10-8 Try It (Examples 4–5)

a. 3.5×10^{11} **b.** 4.94×10^{12}

10-8 Exercises & Applications

1. a. $x \cdot x \cdot x \cdot x$ **b.** $x \cdot x \cdot x$ **c.** 7
d. x^7 **3.** 4^7 **5.** $6r^6$ **7.** $-24d^{10}$
9. $20f^{15}$ **11.** $3b^5$ **13.** $-6t + 6t^3$
15. $15g^7 - 10g^6 + 25g^5 + 40g^4$
17. $2m^2 + 4m$ **19.** 9.92×10^9
21. 8.16×10^6 **25. a.** 2.47×10^{11}
b. 5.89×10^{10} **c.** 8.55×10^9
d. 5.89×10^{11} **27.** $3^6 = 729$; a^6
29. a. Subtract exponents
b. $2^1 = \frac{8}{4} = 2$ **31.** 25 **33.** 3
35. 884.736 m^3

Section 10B Review

1. Binomial, two terms.
3. Monomial, one term. **5.** 1; $8x - 6$ **7.** 5; $-x^5 + x^2 - x$ **9.** 7; $x^7 - 3$
11. Already simplified **13.** $10x + 5$
15. $2x^2 + 4x - 1$ **17.** $p^2 - 2p - 9$
19. x^6 **21.** $-20x^{10}$ **23.** $y^2 + 3y$
25. $x^6 + 5x^4$ **27.** C

Chapter 10 Summary & Review

1. a. -18 **b.** 4 **2.** Multiply by 3 and add 1.
3. Yes

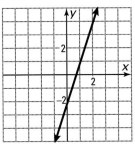

4. Answers may vary.

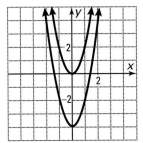

5. 64 ft

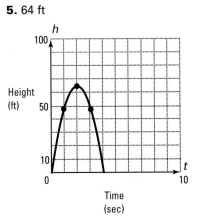

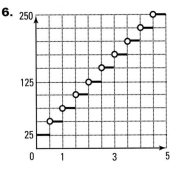

7. $-4x^3 - 7x^2 + 3x + 5$ **8. a.** 18
b. 12 **9.** $5x^3 - 5x^2 - 3x + 14$
10. $4p^2 - 1$ **11.** $4x^2 + 2x + 5$
12. $x^2 - x - 5$ **13.** $6x^3 - 9x^2 - 2x + 15$ **14.** $g^2 + 8g + 3$
15. $6x^3 - 15x^2$ **16.** 4.14×10^{14}
17. $-15u^5 + 21u^4 - 12u^3$

Cumulative Review
Chapters 1–10

1. D **2.** D **3.** C **4.** B **5.** D **6.** A
7. B **8.** C **9.** B **10.** C **11.** A
12. B **13.** D

Chapter 11

11-1 Try It (Example 2)

a. $\frac{8}{5}$ **b.** 118°

11-1 Try It (Example 4)

a. Yes **b.** No

11-1 Exercises & Applications

1. a. $\frac{1.5}{3.0} = \frac{1.8}{3.6}$ **b.** Yes, $(1.5)(3.6) = (3.0)(1.8) = 5.4$ **3.** Yes **5.** 1 in.:50 ft **7.** A **9.** $64x^2$ **11.** Each cable forms a different angle measurement where it intersects the road.
15. Factors: 1, 2, 3, 6, 11, 22, 33, 66; Prime factors: 2, 3, 11 **17.** Factors: 1, 2, 3, 4, 6, 8, 12, 16, 24, 48; Prime factors: 2, 3 **19.** 12 **21.** 5.01
23. -17

11-2 Try It (Example 2)

No

11-2 Try It (Example 4)

a. $\overline{HI}$ **b.** $\frac{5}{8}$ in. **c.** 120°

11-2 Exercises & Applications

1. a. The corresponding sides are not congruent.   **b.** The corresponding angles are congruent.   **3.** 6 mm
5. Yes   **7.** 8   **11.** They are congruent.   **15.** 8   **17.** 10
19. Yes   **21.** Yes

11-3 Try It (Example 1)

No.

11-3 Try It (Example 3)

Yes; The SAS rule.

11-3 Exercises & Applications

1. a. $\overline{QS}$ **b.** $\overline{RS}$ **c.** $\angle Q$ **d.** $\angle R$
e. $\angle S$ **3.** Yes; The SSS rule.
5. Yes; The SAA rule.   **7.** Yes; The SAS rule   **9. a–c.** Answers may vary.   **11.** The SAS rule.   **13.** Not necessarily; The triangles are the same shape (i.e., similar) but not necessarily the same size.   **15.** 60
17. 10   **19.** 60

11-4 Try It (Example 1)

a. $\overline{KM}$ **b.** $\overline{ML}$ **c.** $\overline{KL}$

11-4 Try It (Example 2)

a. $\frac{4}{5}$ **b.** $\frac{4}{3}$

11-4 Try It (Example 4)

a. ≈ 11.78 m   **b.** ≈ 12.79 m

11-4 Exercises & Applications

1. a. Opposite   **b.** Adjacent
c. Tangent   **d.** ≈ 38.87 in.   **3.** $\sin = \frac{1}{\sqrt{2}}$, $\cos = \frac{1}{\sqrt{2}}$, $\tan = 1$ **5.** ≈ 618.8 m
7. ≈ 10.4 ft   **9.** B   **11.** ≈ 3035 ft
13. $\sin(60°) \approx 0.866$, $\cos(60°) = 0.5$, $\tan(60°) \approx 1.732$ **15.** $2\frac{1}{50}$ **17.** $4\frac{6}{25}$
19. $9\frac{9}{10}$ **21.** Exponential
23. Linear

11-5 Try It (Example 2)

7 cm

11-5 Try It (Example 3)

$1.\overline{66}$ ft

11-5 Exercises & Applications

1. a. 16 cm   **b.** $m\overline{EG} = 14.4$ cm
3. ≈ 11.58 in.   **5.** D   **7.** ≈ 387.32 yd
9. Possible answer: Since $\angle A$ is congruent to the corresponding angle of the triangle for which s is the hypotenuse and 10 ft is the length of the adjacent side of that angle, solve the equation $\frac{10}{s} = \cos(22°)$.   **11.** 4
13. Because most trigonometric ratios are irrational numbers, the results involving them are approximate rather than exact.   **15.** 0.176
17. $\frac{7}{16}$ **19.** $-3x^2 + 2x + 5$; 2
21. $-x^3 - x^2 + 3x - 3$; 3

Section 11A Review

1. 6 in.   **3.** Yes, SAA   **7.** 3290 ft

11-6 Try It (Example 1)

$(-2, -2)$, $(-5, -2)$, $(-5, -1)$, $(-3, 0)$; $(2, 2)$, $(5, 2)$, $(5, 1)$, $(3, 0)$

11-6 Try It (Examples 3-4)

a. $(-3, 1)$; $(-1, 1)$; $(-3, 4)$; $(-1, 4)$
b. $(-1, -2)$; $(-4, -2)$; $(-1, -3)$; $(-2, -3)$; $(-2, -5)$; $(-4, -4)$

11-6 Exercises & Applications

1. a.

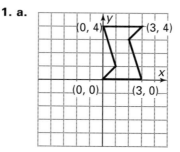

c. $(0, 0)$, $(0, 4)$, $(3, 4)$, $(3, 0)$
3. Rotation   **5.** The y-axis   **7.** C
9. A reflection   **11.** No transformations of the word "TRANSLATE" as a whole will work. Each letter must be reflected and rotated separately.
13. No; A parallelogram and a trapezoid are not congruent.
15. 381.98   **17.** $\frac{16}{63}$ **19.** 0.68
21. $87\frac{1}{9}$ **23.** $x^3 + 7x^2 - 2$

11-7 Try It (Example 2)

a. $(-12.5, -5)$; $(-7.5, 5)$; $(-2.5, 10)$; $(2.5, 10)$; $(7.5, 5)$; $(12.5, -5)$
b. $(-2\frac{2}{3}, 0)$; $(0, 2\frac{2}{3})$; $(2\frac{2}{3}, 0)$; $(0, -2\frac{2}{3})$

11-7 Try It (Example 4)

a. $\frac{1}{5}$ **b.** 5

11-7 Exercises & Applications

1. 2 and 3   **3.** Reduction, $\frac{2}{3}$ **5.** B
7. ≈ 4.8 **9.** The result will be a lizard 11.75 cm long and 6.25 cm wide.   **11.** 12   **13. a.** The quotient is 2 in every case.   **b.** Yes
15. $E'' = (8, 0)$, $F'' = (10, 6)$, $G'' = (5, 8)$, $H'' = (0, 6)$, $I'' = (2, 0)$ **17.** $\frac{2}{3}$
19. $\frac{8}{9}$ **21.** $2x^3 - 4x^2 + 2x - 5$
23. $-x^2 - 5x - 2$

11-8 Try It (Example 3)

a. Four   **b.** Yes; 90°

11-8 Try It (Example 5)

Rotational and point symmetries

11-8 Exercises & Applications

1. a. $\overleftrightarrow{BY}$ **b.** $\overrightarrow{PX}$ **c.** $\overleftrightarrow{QW}$ **3.** C
5. 120°, 240°, 360°   **7.** Ten
9. Horizontal line through E.
11. No lines of symmetry.   **13.** Yes; Yes; The deer in the top two rows are congruent.   **15.** You can't because the deer in each row are looking in different directions.   **19.** Irrational   **21.** Rational   **23.** 5.762×10^{14} **25.** 5.39×10^7

11-9 Try It (Example 4)

a. Yes   **b.** Yes   **c.** No

11-9 Try It (Example 5)

90

11-9 Exercises & Applications

1. a. No   **b.** Yes   **c.** No
3. a. Triangles, squares, hexagons.

b. Possible answer: They do not fit together to cover the plane without gaps or overlaps. **5.** 4000
7. a. Equilateral triangles
b. Trapezoids **c.** Regular hexagons
9. a. Yes **b.** Yes **c.** No **d.** Yes
15. ≈ 15.9 in. **17.** $x = 80$ **19.** 24.5

Section 11B Review

1. a. Rotation **b.** Translation
c. Reflection **3.** For each point (x, y) the reflected point is $(-x, y)$.
5. Possible answer: Give up translation, which can be replaced by two successive rotations with different axis points, or by two reflections with parallel reflection lines. The other option: Give up rotation, which can be replaced by two successive reflections using intersecting reflection lines. **7.** B

Chapter 11 Summary & Review

1. $x = 18$ in.; $m\angle 1 = 135°$

2. Congruent by SAA **3.** Not congruent **4. a.** ≈ 0.87 **b.** ≈ 0.87

c. 1 **5.** $\sin \angle A = \frac{1.75}{6.25}$; $\cos \angle A = \frac{6}{6.25}$; $\tan \angle A = \frac{1.75}{6}$ **6.** 15 cm

7. a. $K'(0, 0)$; $L'(3, -1)$; $M'(2, -4)$; and $N'(0, -5)$ **b.** $K'(0, 0)$; $L'(-3, 1)$; $M'(-2, 4)$; and $N'(0, 5)$ **c.** $K'(0, 0)$; $L'(-1, 3)$; $M'(-4, 2)$; and $N'(-5, 0)$

8. $A'(1, -1)$, $B'(1, -2)$, $C'(3, -2)$

9. Dilation; Yes; No **10.** $\overleftrightarrow{MW}, \overleftrightarrow{PY}$

11. Yes

Chapter 12

12-1 Try It (Example 1)

Possibilities are: Flight 1 return A, flight 1 return b, flight 1 return C, flight 2 return A, flight 2 return B, flight 2 return C, flight 3 return A, flight 3 return B, flight 3 return C, flight 4 return A, flight 4 return B, flight 4 return C.

12 pairs

12-1 Try It (Example 2)

360

12-1 Try It (Example 3)

3600

12-1 Exercises & Applications

1. a. Possibilities are: Pork and Swiss on wheat, pork and Swiss on rye, pork and American on wheat, pork and American on rye, pork and jack on wheat, pork and jack on rye, beef and Swiss on wheat, beef and Swiss on rye, beef and American on wheat, beef and American on rye, beef and jack on wheat, beef and jack on rye. **b.** 12 **3. a.** 40 **b.** 18 **c.** 20

5.

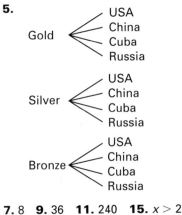

7. 8 **9.** 36 **11.** 240 **15.** $x > 2$

17. $x \le 4$ **19.** ≈ 24.6 in^2

12-2 Try It (Example 1)

40,320

12-2 Try It (Example 2)

a. 24 **b.** 24 **c.** 30,240

12-2 Try It (Example 3)

a. 181,440 **b.** 60 **c.** 60; 120; 120

12-2 Exercises & Applications

1. a. Possibilities are: Justin, Butch, Rod; Justin, Rod, Butch; Butch, Justin, Rod; Butch, Rod, Justin; Rod, Justin, Butch; Rod, Butch, Justin
b. 6 **c.** 3! **3.** 720 **5.** 3,628,800

7. 30,240 **9.** 7 **11.** 120 **13.** 120
15. 5040 **17.** 1 in 6 **19.** $\frac{1}{6}$
21. a. 14,400 **b.** 120 **23.** LULL has repeated letters; SALT has 4! = 24 arrangements, and PEPPER has 3! = 6. **25.** No; Order is not important. **27.** No **29.** Yes

12-3 Try (Example 1)

Abby / Bonita / Chantall
Abby / Bonita / Dani
Abby / Bonita / Eleni
Abby / Chantall / Dani
Abby / Chantall / Eleni
Abby / Dani / Eleni
Bonita / Chantall / Dani
Bonita / Chantall / Eleni
Bonita / Dani / Eleni
Chantall / Dani / Eleni
10 combinations

12-3 Try It (Example 3)

15

12-3 Exercises & Applications

1. Yes **2.** No **3.** Yes **4.** No
5. $\frac{96!}{24! \times 72!}$ **7.** 252 **9.** 10 **11.** 10
13. 792 **15.** Yes **17.** The chances of winning are 1 in $\frac{53!}{6! \times 47!}$, or 1 in 22,957,480. **19.** B **21.** 5 people, since the value of $\frac{10!}{r!(10 - r)!}$ peaks when r is half of 10.

23. 4200 **25.** Yes; $k = \frac{3}{2}$ **27.** No

Section 12A Review

1. 40,320 **3.** 5040 **5.** 1,814,400
7. 56 **9.** 56 **11.** 3 heads, 2 heads and 1 tail, 2 tails and 1 head, 3 tails
13. 720 **15.** 362,880 **17.** 5040
19. 5040 **21.** D

12-4 Try It (Examples 1–2)

a. 1, 2, 3, 4, 5, 6; $\frac{1}{3}$ **b.** Sun, Mon, Tues, Wed, Thur, Fri, Sat; $\frac{2}{7}$

12-4 Try It (Example 3)

a. $\frac{1}{2}$ **b.** $\frac{1}{3}$ **c.** $\frac{1}{6}$ **d.** 1 **e.** 0

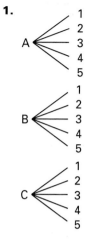

12-4 Exercises & Applications

1. a. 1, 2, 3, 4, 5, 6 **b.** 6 **c.** 1 **d.** $\frac{1}{6}$
e. $\frac{1}{6}$; 0.1666...; $16\frac{2}{3}$% **3.** 1, 2, 3, 4, 5,
6 **5.** $\frac{1}{2}$, 0.5, 50% **7.** 0, 0, 0%
9. B **11.** $\frac{8191}{8192}$ **13.** Yellow, green
15. $\frac{1}{4}$; $\frac{1}{2}$ **17.** First in top row, third
in bottom row; 1 in 36 **19.** Never
25. Yes

12-5 Try It (Example 1)

a. 2 heads: $\frac{1}{4}$; 1 head: $\frac{1}{2}$; 0 heads: $\frac{1}{4}$
b. Answers may vary. **c.** There
should be $\approx$ 25% of 2 heads, 50% of
1 head, and 25% of 0 heads.

12-5 Try It (Example 2)

San Antonio is the only one that
passed; You would expect to find
defective candles in $\approx$ 44 boxes out
of 10,000.

12-5 Try It (Example 3)

$\frac{4}{27}$

12-5 Exercises & Applications

1. Experimental **2.** Theoretical
3. Experimental **5. a.** $\frac{7}{30}$ **b.** $\frac{23}{30}$
7. About $\frac{3}{8}$ **9.** $\frac{2}{27}$ **11. a.** $\frac{1}{11} \approx$ 9%
b. $\frac{1}{11} \approx$ 9% **c.** 1 **13.** Yes **15.** Yes
17. 288 ft^3 **19.** 1600 in^3

12-6 Try It (Example 1)

a. $\frac{1}{6}$ **b.** 0

12-6 Try It (Example 3)

a. $\frac{91}{150} \approx$ 60.7% **b.** $\frac{28}{45} \approx$ 62.2%

12-6 Try It (Example 4)

a. $\frac{2}{25}$ **b.** $\frac{1}{18}$; $\frac{1}{2}$

12-6 Exercises & Applications

1. a. red, red blue, blue yellow,
yellow green, green red, blue
blue, red yellow, red green, red
red, yellow blue, yellow yellow,
blue green, blue red, green
blue, green yellow, green green,
yellow **b.** 16 **c.** 4 **d.** $\frac{1}{16}$ **3.** $\frac{1}{2}$
5. $\frac{1}{16}$ **7. a.** 0 **b.** $\frac{1}{6}$ **c.** $\frac{1}{3}$ **d.** 1
9. 800 people **11. a.** $\frac{59}{95} \approx$ 62.1%
b. $\frac{32}{42} \approx$ 76.2% **c.** $\frac{42}{95} \approx$ 44.2%
13. $100 - \frac{9\pi}{100} \approx$ 72% **15.** 90 in^3
17. $XY = 2$; $BC \approx$ 10.77

12-7 Try It (Example 1)

a. Dependent **b.** Independent

12-7 Try It (Example 3)

34.4%

12-7 Try It (Example 4)

a. $\frac{4}{49}$ **b.** $\frac{2}{42}$

12-7 Exercises & Applications

1. a. $\frac{1}{2}$ **b.** $\frac{1}{6}$ **c.** $\approx$ 8.3%
3. Independent **5.** Dependent
7. $\frac{1}{4}$ **9.** $\frac{1}{10}$ **11.** $\frac{4}{15}$ **13.** 1
15. 0.09% **17. a.** 1 in 5 **b.** 1 in 4
21. 71.96 in^3 **23.** (1, 2)

Section 12B Review

1. Sample space: 1, 2, 3, 4, 5, 6
a. 1 outcome; Probability: $\frac{1}{6}$ **b.** 3
outcomes; Probability: $\frac{1}{2}$ **c.** 0 outcomes; Probability: 0 **3. a.** $\frac{1}{36}$ **b.** $\frac{1}{6}$
c. $\frac{4}{9}$ **5.** $\frac{1}{4}$ **7.** $\frac{1}{8}$ **9.** Yes; There is
one less person left to pick from.
11. D

Chapter 12 Summary & Review

1.

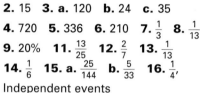

2. 15 **3. a.** 120 **b.** 24 **c.** 35
4. 720 **5.** 336 **6.** 210 **7.** $\frac{1}{3}$ **8.** $\frac{1}{13}$
9. 20% **11.** $\frac{13}{25}$ **12.** $\frac{2}{7}$ **13.** $\frac{1}{13}$
14. $\frac{1}{6}$ **15. a.** $\frac{25}{144}$ **b.** $\frac{5}{33}$ **16.** $\frac{1}{4}$,
Independent events

Cumulative Review
Chapters 1–12

1. C **2.** B **3.** B **4.** B **5.** C **6.** A
7. D **8.** D **9.** D **10.** B **11.** A
12. C **13.** B

Credits

CREDITS

725

Photography   **396** Larry Lefever/Grant Heilman Photography   **397T** Peggy &Yoram Kahana/Peter Arnold, Inc.   **397B** Cheryl Fenton*   **398T** Frans Lanting/Minden Pictures   **399** Ross Harrison Koty/Tony Stone Images   **400T** William R. Sallaz/Duomo   **400B** David Parker/SPL/Photo Researchers   **401** Henley & Savage/The Stock Market   **403** Sharon Green/The Stock Market   **404** Dennis Geaney*   **406** GHP Studio*   **407L** Courtesy of Trimble   **407R** Superstock   **409** M. A. Chappell/Animals, Animals   **410** Cathlyn Melloan/Tony Stone Images   **411** Grant Heilman/Grant Heilman Photography   **412T** Scott Camazine/Photo Researchers   **412B** Nigel Cattlin/Photo Researchers   **414** Robert Maier/Earth Scenes   **415T** Stephen Studd/Tony Stone Images   **415B** Courtesy of André Emmerich Gallery, a division of Sothebys   **416** Kindra Clineff/Tony Stone Images   **417** Sander Eric/Liaison International   **419** Tom Bean/DRK Photo   **421** Christophe Lepetit/Liaison International   **422** Francois Gohier/Photo Researchers   **425TL** Marc Chamberlain/Tony Stone Images   **425TCL** Ray Coleman/Photo Researchers   **425TCR** Andrew Syred/Tony Stone Images   **425TR** Christoph Burki/Tony Stone Images   **425BL** Cabisco/Visuals Unlimited   **425BR** Stephen Frisch/Stock, Boston   **426** Ken Karp*   **427** David Hanson/Tony Stone Images   **429T** Runk-Schoenberger/Grant Heilman Photography   **429BL** Ken Karp*   **429BR** Ken Karp*   **430L** ICF/Unika Vaev-USA   **430R** Runk-Schoenberger/Grant Heilman Photography   **431T** Alex S. MacLean/Landslides   **431C** Charles D. Winters/Photo Researchers   **431B** Chris Cheadle/Tony Stone Images   **433L** GHP Studio*   **433R** M. A. Chappell/Animals, Animals   **434L** Dr. Jeremy Burgess/SPL/Photo Researchers   **434CL** Runk-Schoenberger/Grant Heilman Photography   **434CR** Runk-Schoenberger/Grant Heilman Photography   **434R** Cabisco/Visuals Unlimited   **435** Geoffrey Nilsen Photography*

Chapter 9   **440-441(background)** George Dillon/Stock, Boston   **440T** Giraudon/Art Resource, NY   **440BL** Ken Karp*   **440BR** Lewis Bloom/Liaison International   **441T** GHP Studio*   **441B** Stephen Studd/Tony Stone Images   **442T** Charles Guptor/Stock, Boston   **442B** Ron Sherman/Tony Stone Images   **443L** Cheryl Fenton*   **443R** Michael Pole/Westlight   **444** Pat & Tom Leeson/Photo Researchers   **450** Fujifotos/The Image Works   **453** Ken Karp*   **456** Okoniewski/The Image Works   **457** Cosmo Condina/Tony Stone Images   **458** Patricia Case/FPG International   **459** ARCHIV/Photo Researchers   **460T** Jim Wark/Peter Arnold, Inc.   **460B** Thor Bognar/The Stock Market   **461** Superstock   **465** Ken Karp*   **466** Catherine Karnow/Woodfin Camp & Associates   **467** Richard Open/Camerapress/Globe Photos   **469** Michael Collier/Stock, Boston   **470T** Bob Torrez/Tony Stone Images   **470B** Photofest   **471** Western History Collections, University of Oklahoma Libraries   **473L** K. Harrison/The Image Works   **473R** Michael Pole/Westlight   **475** Ron Watts/Westlight   **476** Ed Lallo/Liaison International   **477** Peter Poulides/Tony Stone Images   **478** Culver Pictures   **480T** Frank Siteman/Stock, Boston   **480C** Andy Sacks/Tony Stone Images   **480B** Ken Karp*   **481** Ken Karp*   **482** GHP Studio*   **483** Desmond Burdon/Tony Stone Images   **484L** Dennis Geaney*   **484R** Ken

Karp*   **485** Kevin Morris/Tony Stone Images   **487** GHP Studio*   **488** Cheryl Fenton*   **489** Cheryl Fenton*   **490** John Bradley/Positive Images   **491T** Gary Moon/Tony Stone Images   **491B** Shephard Sherbell/Stock, Boston   **492** Naideau/The Stock Market   **495** Hugh Sitton/Tony Stone Images   **497** Ron Watts/Westlight   **503T** Don Mason/The Stock Market   **503BL** Cheryl Fenton*   **503BR** Ken Karp*

Chapter 10   **504-505(background)** Runk-Schoenberger/Grant Heilman Photography   **504T** The Granger Collection, New York   **504C** David M. Allen/New Pickle Circus   **504B** Michael Dwyer/Stock, Boston   **505T** Courtesy Harvard College Observatory   **505B** Martin Barraud/Tony Stone Images   **506** Jenny Thomas*   **507** Tim Davis/Tony Stone Images   **508L** Digital Art/Tony Stone Images   **508R** Cheryl Fenton*   **509** Blair Seitz/Photo Researchers   **510** Photo Chiasson/Liaison International   **511** Hank Morgan/Photo Researchers   **512T** Camerique/The Picture Cube   **512B** GHP Studio*   **513** Uniphoto Picture Agency   **514** Jose Carrillo/Stock, Boston   **515** Dennis Geaney*   **516** Francois Gohier/Photo Researchers   **517** Alan & Linda Detrick/Photo Researchers   **518** Sepp Dietrich/Tony Stone Images   **519** Bob Daemmrich/Stock, Boston   **520** Joyce Photographics/Photo Researchers   **522** Ken Karp*   **523** John Cancalosi/Stock, Boston   **524** A. B. Dowsett/SPL/Photo Researchers   **525** Alastair Black/Tony Stone Images   **526** Ron Sanford/Tony Stone Images   **529L** Roy Morsch/The Stock Market   **529R** Tim Davis/Tony Stone Images   **531** Peter Fisher/The Stock Market   **531(background)** Stephen Frisch/Stock, Boston   **532L** Alan Levenson/Tony Stone Images   **532R** Runk-Schoenberger/Grant Heilman Photography   **533** Frank Herholdt/Tony Stone Images   **534** David Weintraub/Stock, Boston   **536T** Cosmo Condina/Tony Stone Images   **536B** Superstock   **537** Andy Levin/Photo Researchers   **539** Watson/The Image Works   **540** S. Nielsen/DRK Photo   **542** Peter Vandermark/Stock, Boston   **544** Larry Lefever/Grant Heilman Photography   **545L** Parker/Boon Productions and Dorey Sparre Photography*   **545R** Dennis Geaney*   **547** Robert A. Lubeck/Animals, Animals   **548L** Royal Observatory, Edinburgh/SPL/Photo Researchers   **548C** Andrew Syred/SPL/Photo Researchers   **548R** S. J. Krasemann/Peter Arnold, Inc.   **550** Sanford-Agliolo/The Stock Market   **552** Gregory K. Scott/Photo Researchers   **553** Peter Fisher/The Stock Market   **553(background)** Stephen Frisch/Stock, Boston   **555** Geoffrey Nilsen Photography*

Chapter 11   **560-561(background)** Jerry Jacka Photography   **560L** Henry Groskinsky/Peter Arnold, Inc.   **560TR** ©1996 Cordon Art - Baarn - Holland. All rights reserved   **560BR** Paul J. Sutton/Duomo   **561T** Fred J. Maroon/Photo Researchers   **561B** H. de Marcillac/GLMR/Liaison International   **562T** Ted Horowitz/The Stock Market   **562B** Stock, Boston   **563** Simon Jauncey/Tony Stone Images   **564** Granitsas/The Image Works   **567** James Blank/Bruce Coleman Inc.   **568** A. Autenzio/Explorer   **569** Barry L. Runk/Grant Heilman Photography   **571** Mulvehill/The Image Works   **573** Oliver Benn/Tony Stone Images   **574** Michael Furman/The Stock Market   **575** Ron Schramm   **576** Donald C. Johnson/The

Stock Market   **578T** Jeff Lepore/Photo Researchers   **578B** Jim Corwin/Photo Researchers   **579** David R. Austen/Australia/Stock, Boston   **581** Topham/The Image Works   **582** Frederic Reglain/Liaison International   **583** Peter Menzel/Stock, Boston   **584** M. Grecco/Stock, Boston   **585T** Jay Syverson/Stock, Boston   **585B** Greg Probst/Stock, Boston   **586** Peter Vandermark/Stock, Boston   **587L** Parker/Boon Productions and Dorey Sparre Photography*   **587R** Dennis Geaney*   **589** Michele & Tom Grimm/Tony Stone Images   **591** Simon Jauncey/Tony Stone Images   **592** Howard Bluestein/Photo Researchers   **593** Bill Gillette/Liaison International   **594** Jeff Greenberg/MRP/Photo Researchers   **595** Royal British Columbia Museum   **597L** Dennis Geaney*   **597R** Ken Karp*   **598TL** Ken Karp*   **598TR** Ken Karp*   **598B** The Heard Museum, Phoenix, AZ   **600** Andy Sacks/Tony Stone Images   **602** Lawrence Migdale/Stock, Boston   **603** Farrell Grehan/Photo Researchers   **605** Andy Sacks/Tony Stone Images   **607** Frederick Ayer/Photo Researchers   **608TR** Mark C. Burnett/Stock, Boston   **608BC** Philip & Karen Smith/Tony Stone Images   **608BR** Craig Newbauer/Peter Arnold, Inc.   **609** Christi Carter/Grant Heilman Photography   **610** Will & Deni McIntyre/Photo Researchers   **611** 1996 Cordon Art - Baarn - Holland. All rights reserved.   **611B** Ryan Evans   **612** Russell Abraham Photography   **613** Ed Bock/The Stock Market   **614** Gary Chowanetz/The Stock Market   **615L** Jerry Jacka Photography   **615R** Bill Gillette/Liaison International   **617** Geoffrey Nilsen Photography*   **621T** Paul Chauncey/The Stock Market   **621BL** Ken Karp*   **621BR** Jerry Jacka Photography

Chapter 12   **622-623(background)** Ken Karp*   **622TL** Paul Figura/Liaison International   **622TR** Cheryl Fenton*   **622BL** Chuck Savage/The Stock Market   **622BR** Ken Karp*   **623** Norvia Behling   **624** Liza Loeffler*   **625** Pete Saloutos/The Stock Market   **626L** Bob Daemmrich/The Image Works   **626R** Jenny Thomas*   **627** Hartsfield Atlanta International Airport   **628** Focus of Sports   **629** Ken Karp*   **630T** William R. Sallaz/Duomo   **631L** Ken Karp*   **631R** Amanda Merullo/Stock, Boston   **632T** Steven E. Sutton/Duomo   **632BL** David Madison/Duomo   **632BLC** J.O. Atlanta 96/Liaison International   **632BRC** J.O. Atlanta 96/Liaison International   **632BR** David Madison/Duomo   **633** Gehring/Liaison International   **634** Smith/Stock, Boston   **635T** J.O. Atlanta 96/Liaison International   **635B** Robin Rudd/Unicorn Stock Photos   **636** David Madison/Duomo   **637L** David Madison/Duomo   **637R** Richard Ellis/Sygma   **640L** Ken Karp*   **640R** Parker/Boon Productions and Dorey Sparre Photography*   **641** J.O. Atlanta 96/Liaison International   **642** Ben Van Hook/Duomo   **643** Pete Saloutos/The Stock Market   **645** Ken Karp*   **646L** Gary Williams/Liaison International   **646R** Geoffrey Nilsen Photography*   **647** Peter Beck/The Stock Market   **648** Geoffrey Nilsen Photography*   **649TL** Culver Pictures   **649TR** Culver Pictures   **649B** Jerry Irwin/Photo Researchers   **651** Ken Karp*   **653L** Ken Karp*   **653R** M. B. Duda/Photo Researchers   **654** Gerard Smith/Photo Researchers   **656** Jenny Thomas*   **657L** Katsuyoshi Tanaka/Woodfin Camp & Associates   **657R** Bob Daemmrich/The Image Works   **658** Richard Open/Camera Press/Retna

726

Illustrations

Index

solution, 128, 130, 135–137, 141–143, 145, 147, 150–151, 156–158, 160, 173–176, 178–188, 202–203, 206–212, 238, 251, 290, 304, 378, 480, 486, 496

solution set, 156–158

solving, 125, 128, 130, 133, 135–138, 141–143, 146–154, 156–158, 162, 194, 199, 204, 207, 210, 232, 261, 279, 285, 290, 310, 328, 339, 353–354, 360, 449, 522, 536, 541, 630

standard notation, 102–105, 108–112, 159, 251

step function, 525–527

substituting, 123–126, 128–130, 137–138, 141–142, 174–175, 178–179, 183–185, 187–188, 197, 202, 207, 210, 299, 333, 338

system of linear equations, 202–205, 212

system of linear inequalities, 206–209, 212

term, 532–533, 538, 539–541, 543, 550

trinomial, 533, 535, 539, 554

two-step equation, 150–152

two-variable equation, 178–186, 188, 196–200, 202–205, 210–212, 255, 373

two-variable inequality, 207–210, 212

two-variable relationship, 172–176. *See also* two-variable equation and two-variable inequality

variable, 123–126, 128–130, 133–135, 137–138, 141–143, 146–148, 150–153, 156–158, 162, 172–176, 178–186, 196–200, 202–213, 232, 234–235, 237–238, 243, 255, 311, 328, 426, 532–537

variation, 555

x-axis, 91

x-coordinate, 91

x-intercept, 196

y-axis, 91

y-coordinate, 91

y-intercept, 196

Zero Property of Addition, 67, 141

Alternate angles, 417, 419, 434, 588

Amusement park, 202, 470

Analogy, 232

Angles, 410

acute, 412, 414, 415, 434, 465, 579, 583, 592

alternate exterior, 417, 419, 434

alternate interior, 417, 419, 434, 588

angle bisector, 413–415

complementary, 412–414, 434

congruent, 413, 415–419, 471

corresponding, 417–419, 423, 434, 565–566, 569, 572–573

defined, 410

measuring, 411

obtuse, 412, 414, 415, 434, 465, 614

of polygons, 424–426, 569–583, 588–589

right, 412, 414, 423, 434, 465, 579, 597

of rotation, 594–599

straight, 412, 420, 434, 465

supplementary, 412–415, 418, 434

Angle bisector, 413–415

Angle of rotation, 594

Angle-Side-Angle (ASA), 575

Animal research, 628

Applications. *Real-world applications of mathematics are found throughout this book. A few instances are shown below.*

advertising, 38, 47, 274

agriculture, 395–396, 491

air traffic control, 195

algebra, 246, 328, 333, 354, 359, 367, 399, 400, 406, 415, 426

amusement park, 202, 470

analogy, 232

animal research, 628

archaeology, 324

architecture, 233, 335, 367, 396, 415, 431–432, 594, 613

art, 256, 390, 416, 594–596, 598–599, 602–604, 606–610, 614–615

astronomy, 12, 40, 48, 52, 76, 96, 103–104, 246, 338, 353, 426, 550

astrophysics, 548

aviation, 122–128, 131–136, 138, 224, 250, 284, 399, 415, 520, 644

baking, 153, 177, 378

banking, 62, 68, 78, 305, 308–312, 527, 530

baseball, 14, 30, 629

basketball, 8, 261, 288, 322

biking, 211, 255

biochemistry, 636

biology, 26, 162, 186, 255, 298, 329, 348–349, 359, 516, 550, 641

botany, 334, 351, 609

bowling, 144

bridge building, 565, 567–568, 571, 573–574, 576, 578, 583, 585–586, 591

broadcasting, 460, 633

car dealerships, 626

career, 26, 226, 238, 325, 578

carpentry, 542

cartography, 90–91, 93, 112, 260, 401–406, 408, 499, 578

chance, 130, 225, 278, 527, 635, 642, 647–648, 650, 652, 655, 658, 664–668, 670–671

chemistry, 77, 246, 284, 292, 512

civics, 644

clothing, 629–630

coin collecting, 489

communication, 239, 350

computer, 226, 232, 238, 240, 508, 532

computer programming, 132

conservation, 152, 157–159, 353, 356–357, 361. *See also* recycling

construction, 151, 154, 193–194, 251, 258, 330, 365–367, 374, 378–379, 398, 415, 458, 470, 480, 491, 495, 537, 540, 551, 612, 614

consumer, 4, 9–10, 12–13, 15–16, 19–21, 29, 35, 38, 41, 47, 50, 52, 66, 75, 85–86, 125, 131, 133, 143, 147, 150, 158, 161–162, 170, 184–185, 201, 205, 210, 220, 225, 228–232, 239, 245, 248, 250–251, 264, 272, 274, 278–280, 282, 294–295, 298–306, 308–309, 314–315, 353–354, 356–357, 360, 388, 486, 509, 516–517, 526, 540, 641, 644

cooking, 180, 358, 636

costume design, 459

credit cards, 315

cryptography, 325–326, 332–333, 337, 339, 341–342

dancing, 510

darts, 662

designing, 182

economics, 42, 64, 66, 75–76, 87–88, 120, 153–154, 170, 202, 283, 286, 289, 297, 305, 311–312, 355, 359, 526–527, 544, 550–551

electricity, 143–145, 152–155, 158, 161–162

electronics, 242

energy, 148–149, 159

fabric designing, 610

fine arts, 194, 246, 279, 298, 415, 421, 613

fire fighting, 201

fireworks, 518

fishing, 75

football, 82

fund raising, 514

furniture design, 430

games, 647–648, 650, 653, 655, 658, 664–668, 670–671

genetic engineering, 107, 172

geography, 9, 13, 15, 30, 65, 93, 99, 102, 112, 153, 158, 260, 289, 333, 353–354, 359–360, 372–373, 375–376, 394–395, 401–406, 408, 420, 431, 460, 495, 499, 528

geology, 101, 394, 397, 405, 411, 530, 647

geometry, 94, 99, 112, 124–125, 135, 186, 246, 256, 259, 261–262, 265, 288–289, 292, 334, 339, 367–368, 370, 372–378, 380, 390–392, 394–395, 398–400, 535–536, 546–547, 552

golf, 70, 81

government, 11, 22, 35, 50, 163, 210, 286, 299, 305, 550–551

hang gliding, 203

health, 44, 46, 144, 149, 153, 193, 209, 275–277, 280–281, 284–285, 287, 289, 291, 303, 354, 388

history, 71, 125, 144, 255, 282, 292, 303, 307, 309, 329, 346, 349, 370, 372,

INDEX

U

U.S. customary units, 390, 392, 394
Unit rate, 224, 247–251, 264, 406
Upper quartile, 18–20. *See also* Quartile

V

Variable, 123–124, 128, 137–138, 141–142,
     146–147, 156, 172, 174, 178–179, 186, 206,
     208–209, 213, 235, 243, 328, 532–534, 537
Variation, 555
Venn diagram, 422–423
Verne, Jules, 58
Vertical angles, 418–419, 423, 434
Vertices
     of angles, 410–415
     of cones, 469
     coordinate, 600–601, 603–604, 616
     of polygons, 421–426, 447, 458, 573,
          595–597
     of solid figures, 461, 466
Volleyball, 212
Volume
     of cones, 493–496, 498
     of cubes, 99, 112
     of cylinders, 487, 489–491, 494, 498, 662
     of hemispheres, 534
     of prisms, 476–480, 488–491, 552, 650,
          656, 662
     of pyramids, 493–496, 498
     of spheres, 479, 536

W

Wages. *See* Income
Water, 343, 350
Water testing, 206
Weaving, 416
What Do You Think? 14, 84, 98, 129, 147,
     184, 230, 244, 283, 297, 327, 358, 371, 404,
     429, 453, 484, 515, 545, 587, 597, 640
World Wide Web, 34, 47, 590

X

x-**axis,** 91
x-**coordinate,** 91
x-**intercept,** 196

Y

y-**axis,** 91
y-**coordinate,** 91
y-**intercept,** 196

Z

Zero Property of Addition, 67, 141
Zimmerman, Arthur, 321